ENGLISH LITERATURE

FROM WIDSITH TO THE DEATH OF CHAUCER

A SOURCE BOOK

BY

ALLEN ROGERS BENHAM, A.M., Ph.D.

ASSOCIATE PROFESSOR OF ENGLISH IN THE UNIVERSITY OF WASHINGTON

NEW HAVEN: YALE UNIVERSITY PRESS
LONDON: HUMPHREY MILFORD
OXFORD UNIVERSITY
MDCCCCXVI

THE HENRY WELDON BARNES MEMORIAL
PUBLICATION FUND

The present volume is the fourth work published by the Yale University Press on the Henry Weldon Barnes Memorial Publication Fund. This Foundation was established June 16, 1913, by a gift made to Yale University by William Henry Barnes, Esq., of Philadelphia, in memory of his son, a member of the Class of 1882, Yale College, who died December 3, 1882. While a student at Yale, Henry Weldon Barnes was greatly interested in the study of literature and in the literary activities of the college of his day, contributing articles to some of the undergraduate papers and serving on the editorial board of the Yale Record. It had been his hope and expectation that he might in after-life devote himself to literary work. His untimely death prevented the realization of his hopes, but by the establishment of the Henry Weldon Barnes Memorial Publication Fund his name will nevertheless be forever associated with the cause of scholarship and letters which he planned to serve and which he loved so well.

TO
MY FATHER
AND THE MEMORY OF
MY MOTHER

PREFACE

I

THE title of this venture is to be taken seriously; the
work is a *source-book*, not an *anthology* nor a *text-book;* it
exemplifies and urges in literary history the same methods
that have long been successfully used in constitutional or
political history. The differentia of anthology, text-book,
and source-book merit further consideration.

I take the anthology first; because, since this volume is
a collection of quotations, it may most easily be confused
therewith. But to point out the difference between them is
not difficult. The object of an anthology is to present to
a reader, who perhaps has neither time nor inclination to
examine the whole product, samples of the best literary
product of an epoch or of a nation — best in technique and
in content, appealing to the taste which every cultivated
person aspires to have. The object of a source-book is to
present to a reader, who has perhaps little leisure and meager
library resources at his disposal, such documents from an
age as fundamentally explain the life, ideals, and spirit
thereof. An anthology aims to form taste; a source-book,
to train judgment. The former is a means to appreciation;
the latter, to scholarship.

What is the aim of a text-book in English literary history?
The question can best be answered in a paraphrase of the

words of a current manual; thus: the purpose of this work is threefold; to induce people personally to know and desire the best books, to see that they are the representatives of different ages as well as of different authors, and to appreciate the development of English literature from simplicity to complexity. So far, so good; but the means adopted to attain these worthy ends is characteristic of nearly all the text-books that I have seen: to arrange in chronological order the author's more or less personal opinions of English writers. The chronological order is almost always the sole historical brand on the book.

But chronology is merely the skeleton of history, and, important as a skeleton is, it can hardly serve as the whole body. Other elements must be found in a body and these are but ill-supplied in the ordinary text-book; for in the latter, to drop the figure, the reader gets a second- or third-hand view of the primary facts; he feels no contact with the men and movements that were the original active agents. This contact he does get, however, in the source-book, which "shows the very age and body of the time his form and pressure."

From an anthology, then, my book differs in that it concerns judgment and scholarship rather than taste and appreciation, though these last may be the most precious by-products of the method it exhibits. From a text-book it differs in that it gives a direct rather than an indirect report of its field.

II

We are coming to realize that literary history, like other sorts, is a matter of reports or documents. But in literary history our difficulty has been that we have two sets of documents to deal with; while in political history, for instance, we have but one. Thus, for the age of Chaucer in literary history we have both Chaucer's works and contemporary comment thereon; whereas for the polit-

ical history of the same age we have but the surviving
memorials.

These are classified by historical science as conscious or
unconscious memorials; most weight is given to the former,
and only when they fail are the latter used. Current text-
books, however, have been too prone to describe the unconscious memorials only, and have thus lost their right to
be considered history. I feel that my method is scientifically
sound, because I have quoted generously from the extant
criticism and biography which are the conscious literary
memorials of our Old and Middle English periods.

But literature is not produced in a vacuum; it is a social
institution in a real world, affecting and picturing men who
have real problems and real outlooks which we must see if
we are to draw sound conclusions. Hence, most of the space
in this book is given to the backgrounds, — political, social,
industrial, and cultural, — which largely determine the literary output.

Literature has an instrument, the nature and possibilities
of which must in some degree be sensed, if, again, we are to
draw sound conclusions. Hence, notice is taken here of the
linguistic background, completing the plan.

The material quoted is thus classified in six divisions:
namely, political background, social and industrial background, cultural background, linguistic background, literary
characteristics, and representative authors.

III

To the following authors and publishers I wish to record
my thanks for permission to quote from works written or
published by them: Professor F. M. Anderson of Dart-
mouth College, the version of the *Charter of Winchester* in
*Outlines and Documents of English Constitutional History
during the Middle Ages;* Messrs. Chatto and Windus, passages from the *King's Classics Series;* Messrs. Constable

and Company and Mr. G. G. Coulton, passages from *A Medieval Garner;* Messrs. E. P. Dutton and Company, passages from the *Everyman's Library* and the *Temple Classics;* Messrs. Ginn and Company and Professor E. P. Cheyney, passages from *Readings in English History;* Messrs. Ginn and Company and Professors Cook and Tinker, passages from *Select Translations from Old English Prose;* Messrs. Ginn and Company and Professors Tuell and Hatch, passages from *Selected Readings in English History;* Lieutenant Colonel L. H. Holt, his version of Cynewulf's runic signature from the *Elene;* Messrs. The Macmillan Company, Lord Tennyson's ·translation of the *Battle of Brunanburh,* passages from Mr. G. C. Macaulay's edition of the *Chronicles* of Froissart, from *Bell's English History Source Books*, from Mr. E. F. Henderson's *Select Historical Documents of the Middle Ages*, and from the *Select Documents of English Constitutional History* of Professors Adams and Stephens; the Oxford University Press, passages from several of its publications; Messrs. G. P. Putnam's Sons, passages from Professor Ashley's *Edward III and His Wars* and Mr. A. F. Leach's *Educational Charters and Documents;* Messrs. Charles Scribner's Sons, passages from Dean A. F. West's *Alcuin;* the University of Pennsylvania, passages from the *Pennsylvania Translations and Reprints from the Original Sources of European History.*

It remains to express my thanks to those who have helped me in my work in various ways; in particular, my colleagues in the English department at the University of Washington, Professors Frederick Klaeber, Hardin Craig, and Joseph W. Beach of the University of Minnesota, Albert S. Cook of Yale University, Charles G. Osgood of Princeton University, Felix E. Schelling of the University of Pennsylvania, and John M. Manly of the University of Chicago deserve my gratitude. Professor David Thomson

of the University of Washington did me the great service of
reading all the proofs; I can hardly repay the debt. But,
though many have helped me, I am ultimately responsible
for the contents of this volume, and its failings and peculi-
arities must be charged directly to my account.

SEATTLE, May 5, 1916.   ALLEN R. BENHAM.

CONTENTS AND LIST OF CITATIONS

FROM THE BEGINNINGS TO THE NORMAN CONQUEST

CONTENTS

CONTENTS

CONTENTS

CONTENTS xix

(B) The *Chronicle* on the Salisbury Oath. *Anglo-Saxon Chronicle,*
Entry for the Year 1086. *Tr. cit.* 202
(C) *The Coronation Charter of Henry I.* Tr. in *Pennsylvania Transla-
tions and Reprints from the Original Sources of European History,*
I, 6, pp. 3–5 203
(D) The *Chronicle* on Feudal Anarchy in the Time of King Stephen.
Anglo-Saxon Chronicle. Entries for the Years 1135 and 1137. *Tr.
cit.* 205
(E) *The Reforms of Henry II.*
   (a) William of Newburgh on Henry's General Policy. *History of
English Affairs,* Book II, Chapters 1 and 2. Tr. Joseph Stevenson, *Church Historians of England,* IV, Part 2, pp. 444, 445 . . 209
   (b) *The Assize of Clarendon.* Tr. in *Pennsylvania Translations,* etc.
I, 6, pp. 22–26 212
(F) *Life on a Feudal Manor.*
   (a) Extent of the Manor of Werminton, 1125. Tr. *ibid.,* III, 5, p. 4. 217
   (b) Description of a Thirteenth-century Manor House. Tr. *ibid.,*
p. 30 217
   (c) Extent of the Manor of Bernehorne, 1307. Tr. *ibid.,* p. 7 . . . 218
   (d) Extent of the Manor of Borley. Tr. in Cheyney, *op. cit.,* pp.
212–215 223
   (e) Certificate of Manumission to a Villein. Tr. in *Pennsylvania.
Translations,* etc., III, 5, p. 31 226

2. DOCUMENTS RELATING TO THE GILDS AND TRADE.
(A) *The Gilds.*
   (a) *Ordinances of the Spurriers of London.* Tr. *ibid.,* II, 1, pp. 21–23. 229
   (b) Chaucer's Description of Five Members of a Gild. *Prolog to the
Canterbury Tales,* ll. 361–378. Tr. the Editor from the Text of
Skeat. (Oxford, Clarendon Press, 1894.) 230
   (c) License of Richard II to Establish a Charitable Gild in Birmingham. Toulmin Smith, *English Gilds,* pp. 244, 245. (*Early
English Text Society, Original Series,* XL.) 231
   (d) *Ordinances of the Gild of St. Mary,* Beverly. *Ibid.,* pp. 149, 150. 233
   (e) *Ordinances of the Gild of the Lord's Prayer,* York. *Ibid.,* pp. 137–
140 234
   (f) *The Order of the Pageants of the Play of Corpus Christi at York.*
Tr. in *Pennsylvania Translations,* etc., II, 1, pp. 29–32 237
(B) *Commercial Types and Practices.*
   (a) Chaucer's Description of a Merchant. *Op. cit.,* ll. 270–284.
Tr. Editor from Text *cit.* 241
   (b) The Confession of Avarice from the *Vision of William concerning Piers the Plowman,* B Version, V, ll. 188–303. Tr. Burrell
in *Everyman's Library* Ed. 242
   (c) Gower on the Tricks of Trade. *Mirour de l'Omme* (*Mirror of
Man*), ll. 25, 213–25, 500; 26,077–26, 136. Tr. the Editor from
the Text of Macaulay, *Complete Works of John Gower* (Oxford,
Clarendon Press, 1899–1902), I. 248
(C) *Economic Concepts.*
   (a) Langland (?) on the Genealogy of Money Power. *Op. cit.,* C
Version, III, ll. 116–126. Tr. the Editor from Text *cit.* . . . 255

CONTENTS

xxii

CONTENTS

CONTENTS

CONTENTS

ENGLISH LITERATURE FROM WIDSITH
TO THE DEATH OF CHAUCER

ENGLISH LITERATURE

FROM WIDSITH TO CHAUCER: A SOURCE-BOOK

CHAPTER I

FROM THE BEGINNINGS TO THE NORMAN CONQUEST

I. The Political Background

THOUGH modern scholarship [1] is agreed that the migration to Britain began some time before, the year 449 is the traditional date of the arrival of the Jutes, the earliest of the Teutonic tribes to seek the shores of England. Later came the Angles and Saxons, considerably extending the period of settlement. As we have no record of these events before the middle of the sixth century, it is clear that many particulars, perhaps important particulars, will never be known. The earliest extant accounts are, in chronological order: Gildas, *On the Downfall of Britain*,[2] Bede, *The Ecclesiastical History of the English Nation*,[3] and the *Anglo-Saxon Chronicle* [4] by an unknown compiler. As the Venerable Bede (673–735) is a medieval historian of the best type, I give his account, with which the two others are in substantial agreement.

[1] See Hodgkin, *The History of England from the Earliest Times to the Norman Conquest* (Hunt and Poole, *The Political History of England*, Longmans, Green and Co., 1906 I), pp. 81 *seq.* This gives the latest views of the English conquest of Britain and the latest estimate of the source authorities.

[2] This work is accessible in translation in Giles, *Six Old English Chronicles.* (*Bohn Antiquarian Library*.)

[3] The best edition of Bede's historical works in Latin is the one by Plummer (Oxford, Clarendon Press, 1896). The best edition of the Old English translation of Bede's *Ecclesiastical History* is the one in the *Early English Text Society's Publications* (E. E. T. S.) by Miller, 1890–98.

[4] The best edition is by Plummer (Oxford, Clarendon Press, 1892–99).

In the year of our Lord 449, Martian being made emperor
with Valentinian, and the forty-sixth from Augustus, ruled the
empire seven years. Then the nation of the Angles, or Saxons,
being invited by the aforesaid king,[5] arrived in Britain with three
long ships, and had a place assigned them to reside in by the
same king, in the eastern part of the island, that they might
thus appear to be fighting for their country whilst their real
intentions were to enslave it. Accordingly they engaged with
the enemy,[6] who were come from the north to give battle, and
obtained the victory; which, being known at home in their
own country, as also the fertility of the country, and the cowardice of the Britons, a more considerable fleet was quickly sent
over, bringing a still greater number of men which, being added
to the former, made up an invincible army. The newcomers received of the Britons a place to inhabit, upon condition that
they should wage war against their enemies for the peace and
security of the country, whilst the Britons agreed to furnish
them with pay. Those who came over were of the three most
powerful nations of Germany — Saxons, Angles, and Jutes. From
the Jutes are descended the people of Kent, and of the Isle of
Wight, and those also in the province of the West-Saxons who
are to this day called Jutes, seated opposite to the Isle of Wight.
From the Saxons, that is, the country which is now called Old
Saxony, came the East-Saxons, the South-Saxons, and the West-
Saxons. From the Angles, that is, the country which is called
Anglia, and which is said, from that time, to remain desert to
this day, between the provinces of the Jutes and the Saxons,
are descended the East-Angles, the Midland-Angles, Mercians,
all the race of the Northumbrians, that is, of those nations that
dwell on the north side of the river Humber, and the other nations of the English. The two first commanders are said to have
been Hengist and Horsa. Of whom Horsa, being afterwards
slain in battle by the Britons, was buried in the eastern parts
of Kent, where a monument, bearing his name, is still in existence. They were the sons of Victgilsus, whose father was
Vecta, son of Woden;[7] from whose stock the royal race of many

[5] Vortigern, King of the Britons.   [6] The Picts.
[7] A god, from whose name we get *Wednesday*.

provinces deduce their original. In a short time, swarms of the aforesaid nations came over into the island, and they began to increase so much, that they became terrible to the natives themselves who had invited them. Then, having on a sudden entered into league with the Picts, whom they had by this time repelled by the force of their arms, they began to turn their weapons against their confederates. At first, they obliged them to furnish a greater quantity of provisions; and, seeking an occasion to quarrel, protested, that unless more plentiful supplies were brought them, they would break the confederacy, and ravage all the island; nor were they backward in putting their threats in execution. In short, the fire kindled by the hands of these pagans, proved God's just revenge for the crimes of the people; not unlike that which, being once lighted by the Chaldeans, consumed the walls and city of Jerusalem. For the barbarous conquerors acting here in the same manner, or rather the just Judge ordaining that they should so act, they plundered all the neighbouring cities and country, spread the conflagration from the eastern to the western sea, without any opposition, and covered almost every part of the devoted island. Public as well as private structures were overturned; the priests [8] were everywhere slain before the altars; the prelates and the people, without any respect of persons, were destroyed with fire and sword; nor was there any to bury those who had been thus cruelly slaughtered. Some of the miserable remainder, being taken in the mountains, were butchered in heaps. Others, spent with hunger, came forth and submitted themselves to the enemy for food, being destined to undergo perpetual servitude, if they were not killed even upon the spot. Some, with sorrowful hearts, fled beyond the seas. Others, continuing in their own country, led a miserable life among the woods, rocks, and mountains, with scarcely enough food to support life, and expecting every moment to be their last.

The Teutonic conquest of Britain, however, was not so easy as Bede suggests; British resistance was stubborn and determined,[9] and it was in the midst of these troubled

[8] Britain, before this, had been Christianized; cf. *post*, p. 39.   [9] Cf. *post*, p. 96.

ENGLISH LITERATURE

times that one of the world's great stories found its birth.
This story centers about the hero now known as King
Arthur. Gildas, Bede, and the *Anglo-Saxon Chronicle* make
no mention of him as king, or even as leader. Nennius,
an obscure author of the eighth or ninth century, is the
first to mention his name. English advances in Britain
were brought to a standstill, apparently, for a half century after 500 and it is in this period that Nennius places
Arthur. Nennius [10] tells of Arthur's exploits as follows:

Then it was that the magnanimous Arthur, with all the kings
and military force of Britain, fought against the Saxons. And
though there were many more noble than himself, yet he was
twelve times chosen their commander, and was as often conqueror. The first battle in which he was engaged was at the
mouth of the river Gleni. The second, third, fourth, and fifth,
were on another river, by the Britons called Duglas, in the
region Linuis. The sixth, on the river Bassas. The seventh in
the wood Celidon, which the Britons call Cat Coit Celidon. The
eighth was near Gurnion castle, where Arthur bore the image
of the Holy Virgin, mother of God, upon his shoulders, and
through the power of our Lord Jesus Christ, and the holy Mary,
put the Saxons to flight, and pursued them the whole day with
great slaughter. The ninth was at the City of Legion, which is
called Cair Lion. The tenth was on the banks of the river
Trat Treuroit. The eleventh was on the mountain Breguoin,
which we call Cat Bregion. The twelfth was a most severe contest, when Arthur penetrated to the hill of Badon. In this engagement, nine hundred and forty fell by his hand alone, no one
but the Lord affording him assistance. In all these engagements
the Britons were successful. For no strength can avail against
the will of the Almighty.[11]

[10] Accessible in Giles, *Six Old English Chronicles.*

[11] It is clear that no very important historical inferences can be drawn from
these statements of Nennius. But Arthurian scholarship is agreed that here is the
historical kernel of the story of Arthur. Cf. Maynadier, *The Arthur of the English
Poets* (Houghton, Mifflin & Co., 1907), Chap. 2. Practically all the materials for
a careful study of the earlier forms of the Arthurian story are now available in the

We cannot say to a certainty when the Teutonic conquest of Britain was complete, nor is it germane to our present purpose to investigate the question. But when it was ended, the conquerors in their restless military spirit turned to contests for the mastery among themselves, and these intertribal wars lasted down into the ninth century. So far as the history of English culture is concerned, Northumbria, the Anglian kingdom north of the Humber, as its name indicates, was the first to gain leadership. Northumbrian writers, scribes and monks won an European reputation, but there is no hint of this cultural eminence in the following brief record of Northumbrian supremacy in the entry in the *Anglo-Saxon Chronicle* for the year 617:

This year Ethelfrid king of the North-humbrians was slain by Redwald king of the East-Angles, and Edwin [12] the son of Alla succeeded to the kingdom, and subdued all Britain, the Kentishmen alone excepted. And he drove out the ethelings, sons of Ethelfrid; that is to say, first Eanfrid, Oswald, and Oswy, Oslac, Oswudu, Oslaf, and Offa.

Almost equally brief and barren of suggestion is the following entry in the same compilation for the year 827, though the event there recorded is of immense significance for our literary history, since it is in the West-Saxon dialect that most of our extant Old English literature is written:

This year the moon was eclipsed on the massnight of midwinter. And the same year king Egbert conquered the kingdom of the Mercians, and all that was south of the Humber; and he was the eighth king who was Bretwalda. Ella king of the

Everyman's Library series. The story, as is the case with all the medieval romances extant in earlier and later forms, becomes more and more complex as time goes on. E.g. with the bare narrative of our text compare the more detailed story given in Geoffrey of Monmouth, *History of the Kings of Britain*, Book IX, Chaps. 3 and 4.

[12] The story of Edwin's conversion to Christianity is given *post*, pp. 36–38. His death is referred to *post*, p. 96.

South-Saxons was the first who had thus much dominion; the second was Ceawlin king of the West-Saxons; the third was Ethelbert king of the Kentish-men; the fourth was Redwald king of the East-Angles; the fifth was Edwin king of the North-humbrians; the sixth was Oswald who reigned after him; the seventh was Oswy, Oswald's brother; the eighth was Egbert king of the West-Saxons. And Egbert led an army to Dore against the North-humbrians, and they there offered him obedience and allegiance, and with that they separated.[13]

The last event, or series of events, in the political field, that we need record here is the invasion of the heathen Danes, which began, according to the *Chronicle*, in the year 787. These people, of various Scandinavian origin, had apparently little appreciation of the rather high type of civilization that had been evolved in England; and their career of burning and harrying undid a good deal of slow and painful work. During the reign of Alfred the Great (871–901) the Danes became an integral part of the English nation and in the early eleventh century furnished kings for the English throne. A typical year in their earlier career of devastation, however, is described in the following entry from the *Chronicle* for the year 870:

This year the army [14] rode across Mercia into East-Anglia, and took up their winter quarters at Thetford: and the same winter king Edmund fought against them, and the Danes got the victory, and slew the king, and subdued all the land, and destroyed all the minsters which they came to. The names of their chiefs who slew the king were Hingwar and Hubba. At that same time they came to Medeshamstede, and burned and beat it down, slew abbot and monks, and all that they found there. And that place, which before was full rich, they reduced to nothing. And the same year died archbishop Ceolnoth. Then went Ethelred and Alfred [15] his brother, and took Athel-

[13] On some incidents in one of these intertribal wars, cf. *post*, p. 99.
[14] I.e. the Danish army; the *Chronicle* is very careful to use one word throughout where referring to this army and another when referring to the English forces.
[15] I.e. later Alfred the Great.

red bishop of Wiltshire, and appointed him archbishop of Canterbury, because formerly he had been a monk of the same minster of Canterbury. As soon as he came to Canterbury, and he was stablished in his archibishopric, he then thought how he might expel the clerks who (were) there within, whom archbishop Ceolnoth had (before) placed there for such need . . . as we shall relate. The first year that he was made archbishop there was so great a mortality, that of all the monks whom he found there within, no more than five monks survived. Then for the . . . he (commanded) his chaplains, and also some priests of his vills, that they should help the few monks who there survived to do Christ's service, because he could not so readily find monks who might of themselves do the service; and for this reason he commanded that the priests, the while, until God should give peace in this land, should help the monks. In that same time was this land much distressed by frequent battles, and hence the archbishop could not there effect it, for there was warfare and sorrow all his time over England; and hence the clerks remained with the monks. Nor was there ever a time that monks were not there within, and they ever had lordship over the priests. Again the archbishop Ceolnoth thought, and also said to those who were with him, "As soon as God shall give peace in this land, either these priests shall be monks, or from elsewhere I will place within the minster as many monks as may do the service of themselves: for God knows that I . . ." [16]

II. The Social and Industrial Background

The Roman historian Tacitus gives, in the *Germania*, the first extended account of Teutonic social and industrial life. Though we do not know the sources of his knowledge or his motive in writing this book; though he makes no mention of Angles, Saxons, and Jutes, whom apparently he did not visit; though he wrote at the close of the first century, or early in the second; the *Germania*

---

[16] The manuscript is defective.

must yet be the basis on which our knowledge of early
Germanic life rests, because it is all we have. The statements of Tacitus are borne out in a great number of
cases by the literature extant in the early Teutonic languages. This fact increases our confidence in his work.
The following chapters give the essential features of Tacitus' description.[1]

For myself, I concur in opinion with such as suppose the
people of Germany never to have mingled by inter-marriages
with other nations, but to have remained a people pure, and
independent, and resembling none but themselves. Hence,
amongst such a mighty multitude of men, the same make and
form is found in all, eyes stern and blue, yellow hair, huge bodies,
but vigorous only in the first onset. Of pains and labor they
are not equally patient, nor can they at all endure thirst and
heat. To bear hunger and cold they are hardened by their
climate and soil.

Neither in truth do they abound in iron, as from the fashion
of their weapons may be gathered. Swords they rarely use,[2]
or the larger spear. They carry javelins or, in their own language, *framms*,[3] pointed with a piece of iron short and narrow,
but so sharp and manageable, that with the same weapon they
can fight at a distance or hand to hand, just as need requires.
Nay, the horsemen also are content with a shield and a javelin.
The foot throw likewise weapons missive, each particular is
armed with many, and hurls them a mighty space, all naked
or only wearing a light cassock. In their equipment they
show no ostentation; only that their shields are diversified and
adorned with curious colors.[4] With coats of mail very few are
furnished, and hardly upon any is seen a headpiece or helmet.
Their horses are nowise signal either in fashion or in fleetness;

---

[1] It should be remembered that Tacitus was not in sympathy with the lax
morality of his time in Rome and that he may be idealizing conditions among the
Germans. We should also keep in mind the fact that those features of life in which
Germans most differed from Romans would impress him most deeply.

[2] Swords were named among the Germans and handed down as heirlooms.

[3] This word was adopted into Latin by late Latin writers.

[4] Perhaps the origin of coats of arms.

nor taught to wheel and bound, according to the practice of the Romans: they only move them forward in a line, or turn them right about, with such compactness and equality that no one is ever behind the rest. To one who considers the whole it is manifest, that in their foot their principal strength lies, and therefore they fight intermixed with the horse: for such is their swiftness as to match and suit with the motions and engagements of the cavalry. So that the infantry are elected from amongst the most robust of their youth, and placed in front of the army. The number to be sent is also ascertained, out of every village an hundred, and by this very name they continue to be called at home, those of the hundred band: thus what was at first no more than a number, becomes thenceforth a title and distinction of honor. In arraying their army, they divide the whole into distinct battalions formed sharp in front. To recoil in battle, provided you return again to the attack, passes with them rather for policy than fear. Even when the combat is no more than doubtful, they bear away the bodies of their slain. The most glaring disgrace that can befall them, is to have quitted their shield; nor to one branded with such ignominy is it lawful to join in their sacrifices, or to enter into their assemblies; and many who had escaped in the day of battle, have hanged themselves to put an end to this their infamy.

In the choice of kings they are determined by the splendor of their race, in that of generals by their bravery. Neither is the power of their kings unbounded or arbitrary: and their generals procure obedience not so much by the force of their authority as by that of their example, when they appear enterprising and brave, when they signalise themselves by courage and prowess; and they surpass all in admiration and pre-eminence, if they surpass all at the head of an army. But to none else but the Priests is it allowed to exercise correction, or to inflict bonds or stripes. Nor when the Priests do this, is the same considered as a punishment, or arising from the orders of the general, but from the immediate command of the Deity, Him whom they believe to accompany them in war. They therefore carry with them when going to fight, certain images and figures taken out of their holy groves. What proves the prin-

cipal incentive to their valor is, that it is not at random nor by
the fortuitous conflux of men that their troops and pointed battalions are formed, but by the conjunction of whole families,
and tribes of relations.   Moreover, close to the field of battle
are lodged all the nearest and most interesting pledges of nature.
Hence they hear the doleful howlings of their wives, hence the
cries of their tender infants.   These are to each particular witnesses whom he most reverences and dreads; these yield him the
praise which affects him most.   Their wounds and maims they
carry to their mothers, or to their wives, neither are their
mothers or wives shocked in telling, or in sucking their bleeding
sores.   Nay, to their husbands and sons whilst engaged in battle,
they administer meat and encouragement.

In history we find, that some armies already yielding and
ready to fly, have been by the women restored, through their
inflexible importunity and entreaties, presenting their breasts,
and showing their impending captivity; an evil to the Germans
then by far most dreadful — when it befalls their women.   So
that the spirit of such cities as amongst their hostages are enjoined to send their damsels of quality, is always engaged more
effectually than that of others.   They even believe them endowed with something celestial and the spirit of prophecy.
Neither do they disdain to consult them, nor neglect the re-
sponses which they return.   In the reign of the late Vespasian,
we saw *Veleda* [5] for a long time, and by many nations, esteemed
and adored as a divinity.   In times past they likewise worshipped *Aurinia* [6] and several more, from no complaisance or
effort of flattery, nor as deities of their own creating.

Affairs of smaller moment the chiefs determine: about matters of higher consequence the whole nation deliberates; yet
in such sort, that whatever depends upon the pleasure and decision of the people, is examined and discussed by the chiefs.

[5] Furneaux says this was the name of a prophetess among the Bructeri, one of
the German tribes. See *Germania of Tacitus*, ed. Henry Furneaux (Oxford, Clarendon Press, 1894), p. 54.

[6] Furneaux reads *Albruna* and explains the name as that of one who was skilled
in witchcraft and who interpreted the runes. For the latter, see *post*, pp. 77–82.

Where no accident or emergency intervenes, they assemble upon stated days, either when the moon changes, or is full: since they believe such seasons to be the most fortunate for beginning all transactions. Neither in reckoning of time do they count, like us, the number of days but that of nights.[7] In this style their ordinances are framed, in this style their diets appointed; and with them the night seems to lead and govern the day. From their extensive liberty this evil and default flows, that they meet not at once, nor as men commanded and afraid to disobey; so that often the second day, nay often the third, is consumed through the slowness of the members in assembling. They sit down as they list, promiscuously, like a crowd, and all armed. It is by the Priests that silence is enjoined, and with the power of correction the Priests are then invested. Then the King or Chief is heard, as are others, each according to his precedence in age, or in nobility, or in warlike renown, or in eloquence; and the influence of every speaker proceeds rather from his ability to persuade than from any authority to command. If the proposition displease, they reject it by an inarticulate murmur: if it be pleasing, they brandish their javelins. The most honorable manner of signifying their assent, is to express their applause by the sound of their arms.

In the assembly it is allowed to present accusations, and to prosecute capital offences. Punishments vary according to the quality of the crime. Traitors and deserters they hang upon trees. Cowards, and sluggards, and unnatural prostitutes they smother in mud and bogs under an heap of hurdles. Such diversity in their executions has this view, that in punishing of glaring iniquities, it behoves likewise to display them to sight; but effeminacy and pollution must be buried and concealed. In lighter transgressions too the penalty is measured by the fault, and the delinquents upon conviction are condemned to pay a certain number of horses or cattle. Part of this mulct accrues to the King or to the community, part to him whose wrongs are vindicated, or to his next kindred. In the same

---

[7] Cf. the modern expression *fortnight*.

assemblies are also chosen their chiefs or rulers, such as administer justice in their villages and boroughs. To each of these are assigned an hundred persons chosen from amongst the populace, to accompany and assist him, men who help him at once with their authority and their counsel.

Without being armed they transact nothing, whether of public or private concernment. But it is repugnant to their custom for any man to use arms, before the community has attested his capacity to wield them. Upon such testimonial, either one of the rulers, or his father, or some kinsman dignify the young man in the midst of the assembly, with a shield and javelin.[8] This amongst them is the manly robe, this the first degree of honor conferred upon their youth. Before this they seem no more than part of a private family, but thenceforward part of the Commonweal. The princely dignity they confer even upon striplings, whose race is eminently noble, or whose fathers have done great and signal services to the State. For about the rest, who are more vigorous and long since tried, they crowd to attend: nor is it any shame to be followers, higher or lower, just as he whom they follow judges fit. Mighty too is the emulation amongst these followers, of each to be first in favor with his Prince; mighty also the emulation of the Princes, to excel in the number and valor of followers. This is their principal state, this their chief force, to be at all times surrounded with a huge band of chosen young men,[9] for ornament and glory in peace, for security and defence in war. Nor is it amongst his own people only, but even from the neighboring communities, that any of their Princes reaps so much renown and a name so great, when he surpasses in the number and magnanimity of his followers. For such are courted by Embassies, and distinguished with presents, and by the terror of their fame alone often dissipate wars.

In the day of battle, it is scandalous to the Prince to be surpassed in feats of bravery, scandalous to his followers to fail in matching the bravery of the Princes. But it is infamy during life, and indelible reproach, to return alive from a battle where

[8] Cf. the later ceremony of conferring knighthood.
[9] Cf. the later relation of lords and vassals.

their Prince was slain.[10]   To preserve their Prince, to defend him, and to ascribe to his glory all their own valorous deeds, is the sum and most sacred part of their oath.   The Princes fight for victory; for the Prince his followers fight.   Many of the young nobility, when their own community comes to languish in its vigor by long peace and inactivity, betake themselves through impatience to other States which then prove to be in war.   For, besides that this people cannot brook repose, besides that by perilous adventures they more quickly blazon their fame, they cannot otherwise than by violence and war support their huge train of retainers.   For from the liberality of their Prince, they demand and enjoy that war-horse of theirs, with that victorious javelin dyed in the blood of their enemies.   In the place of pay, they are supplied with a daily table and repasts; though grossly prepared, yet very profuse.   For maintaining such liberality and munificence, a fund is furnished by continual wars and plunder.   Nor could you so easily persuade them to cultivate the ground, or to await the return of the seasons and produce of the year, as to provoke the foe and to risk the wounds and death: since stupid and spiritless they account it, to acquire by their sweat what they can gain by their blood.

Upon any recess from war, they do not much attend the chase. Much more of their time they pass in indolence, resigned to sleep and repasts.   All the most brave, all the most warlike, apply to nothing at all; but to their wives, to the ancient men, and to every the most impotent domestic, trust all the care of their house, and of their lands and possessions.   They themselves loiter.   Such is the amazing diversity of their nature, that in the same men is found so much delight in sloth, with so much enmity to tranquillity and repose.   The communities are wont, of their own accord and man by man, to bestow upon

---

[10] Cf. the conclusion of the Old English *Beowulf*, when Wiglaf reproaches the thanes of Beowulf for deserting and surviving their lord.   See also the entry in the *Chronicle* for the year 755, often called the oldest extant piece of prose narrative in a European vernacular.   It is thought by some to be a prose version of an earlier ballad.   The Old English poem *The Battle of Maldon* also exhibits this notion of the duty of retainers to their lord in the day of battle.   In later times Froissart gives many instances in his *Chronicles of England, France and Spain*.

their Princes a certain number of beasts, or a certain portion of grain; a contribution which passes indeed for a mark of reverence and honor, but serves also to supply their necessities. They chiefly rejoice in the gifts which come from the bordering countries, such as are sent not only by particulars but in the name of the State; curious horses, splendid armor, rich harness, with collars of silver and gold. Now too they have learnt, what we have taught them, to receive money.

That none of the several people in Germany live together in cities, is abundantly known; nay, that amongst them none of their dwellings are suffered to be contiguous. They inhabit apart and distinct, just as a fountain, or a field, or a wood happened to invite them to settle. They raise their villages in opposite rows, but not in our manner with the houses joined one to another. Every man has a vacant space quite round his own, whether for security against accidents from fire, or that they want the art of building. With them in truth, is unknown even the use of mortar and of tiles. In all their structures they employ materials quite gross and unhewn, void of fashion and comeliness. Some parts they besmear with an earth so pure and resplendent, that it resembles painting and colors. They are likewise wont to scoop caves deep in the ground, and over them to lay great heaps of dung. Thither they retire for shelter in the winter, and thither convey their grain: for by such close places they mollify the rigorous and excessive cold. Besides, when at any time their enemy invades them, he can only ravage the open country, but either knows not such recesses as are invisible and subterraneous; or must suffer them to escape him, on this very account that he is uncertain where to find them.

. . . The laws of matrimony are severely observed there; nor in the whole of their manners is there aught more praiseworthy than this: for they are almost the only barbarians contented with one wife, excepting a very few amongst them; men of dignity who marry divers wives, from no wantonness or lubricity, but courted for the luster of their families into many alliances.

To the husband, the wife tenders no dowry; but the husband to the wife. The parents and relatives attend and declare their approbation of the presents, not presents adapted to feminine pomp and delicacy, nor such as serve to deck the new married woman; but oxen and horse accoutered, and a shield, with a javelin and sword. By virtue of these gifts she is espoused. She too on her part brings her husband some arms. This they esteem the highest tie, these the holy mysteries, and matrimonial gods. That the woman may not suppose herself free from the considerations of fortitude and fighting, or exempt from the casualties of war, the very first solemnities of her wedding serve to warn her, that she comes to her husband as a partner in his hazards and fatigues, that she is to suffer alike with him, to adventure alike, during peace or during war. This the oxen joined in the yoke plainly indicate, this the horse ready equipped, this the present of arms. 'Tis thus she must be content to live, thus to resign life. The arms she then receives she must preserve inviolate, and to her sons restore the same, as presents worthy of them, such as their wives may again receive, and still resign to her grandchildren.

They therefore live in a state of chastity well secured; corrupted by no seducing shows and public diversions, by no irritations from banqueting. Of learning and any secret intercourse by letters, they are equally ignorant, men and women. Amongst a people so numerous, adultery is exceedingly rare; a crime instantly punished, and the punishment left to be inflicted by the husband. He, having cut off her hair, expells her from his house naked, in presence of her kindred, and pursues her with stripes throughout the village. For, to a woman who has prostituted her person, no pardon is ever granted. However beautiful she be, however young, however abounding in wealth, a husband she can never find. In truth, nobody turns vices into mirth there, nor is the practice of corrupting and of yielding to corruption, called the custom of the age. Better still do those communities, in which none but virgins marry, and where to a single marriage all their views and inclinations are at once confined. Thus, as they have but one body and one life, they take but one husband, that beyond him they may have no thought, no further wishes, nor love him only as their husband but as their marriage. To restrain generation and the increase of children, is esteemed an abomin-

able sin, as also to kill infants newly born. And more powerful with them are good manners, than with other people are
good laws.

In all their houses the children are reared naked and nasty;
and thus they grow into those limbs, into the bulk, which marvel
we behold. They are all nourished with the milk of their own
mothers, and never surrendered to handmaids and nurses. The
lord you cannot discern from the slave, by any superior delicacy
in rearing. Amongst the same cattle they promiscuously live,
upon the same ground without distinction lie, till at a proper
age the free-born are parted from the rest, and till their bravery
recommend them to notice. Slow and late do the young men
come to the use of women, and thus very long preserve the vigor
of youth. Neither are the virgins hastened to wed. They must
both have the same sprightly youth, the like stature, and marry
when equal and able-bodied. Children are held in the same estimation by their mother's brother as by their father. Some
hold this tie of blood to be most inviolable and binding,[11] and
in receiving of hostages, such pledges are most considered and
claimed, as they who at once possess affections the most unalien-
able, and the most diffuse interest in their family. To every
man, however, his own children are heirs and successors: wills
they do not make; for want of children his next kin inherits;
his own brothers, those of his father, or those of his mother.
To ancient men, the more they abound in descendants, in relatives and kinsfolk, so much the more reverence accrues.

All the enmities of your house, whether of your father or of
your kindred, you must necessarily adopt; as well as all their
friendships. Neither are such enmities unappeasable and permanent; since even for so great a crime as homicide, compensation is made by a fixed number of sheep and cattle,[12] and by
it the whole family is pacified to content. A temper this,
wholesome to the State; because to a free nation, animosities

---

[11] Probably a remnant of the method of tracing descent through the mother,
known as the matriarchate.

[12] Cattle were the medium of exchange; thus the Old English word *feoh* means
both *cow* and *money;* it is our modern word *fee.* Cf. the Latin *pecus* and *pecunia,*
whence *pecuniary.*

and faction are always more menacing and perilous. In social feasts and deeds of hospitality, no nation upon earth was ever more liberal and abounding. To refuse admitting under your roof any man whatsoever, is held wicked and inhuman. Every man receives every comer, and treats him with repasts as large as his ability can possibly furnish. When the whole stock is consumed, he who had treated so hospitably guides and accompanies his guest to a new scene of hospitality; and both proceed to the next house, though neither of them invited. Nor avails it, that they were not; they are there received, with the same frankness and humanity. Between a stranger and an acquaintance, in dispensing the rules and benefits of hospitality, no difference is made. Upon your departure, if you ask anything, it is the custom to grant it; and with the same facility, they ask of you. In gifts they delight, but neither claim merit from what they give, nor own any obligation for what they receive. Their manner of entertaining their guests is familiar and kind.

For their drink, they draw a liquor from barley or other grain; and ferment the same, so as to make it resemble wine. Nay, they who dwell upon the bank of the Rhine deal in wine. Their food is very simple: wild fruit, fresh venison, or coagulated milk. They banish hunger without formality, without curious dressing and curious fare. In extinguishing thirst, they use not equal temperance. If you will but humor their excess in drinking, and supply them with as much as they covet, it will be no less easy to vanquish them by vices than by arms.

Of public diversions they have but one sort, and in all their meetings the same is still exhibited. Young men, such as make it their pastime, fling themselves naked and dance amongst sharp swords and the deadly points of javelins. From habit they acquire their skill, and from their skill a graceful manner; yet from hence draw no gain or hire: though this adventurous gaiety has its reward, namely, that of pleasing the spectators. What is marvellous, playing at dice is one of their most serious employments; and even sober, they are gamesters: nay, so desperately do they venture upon chance of winning or losing, that when their whole substance is played away, they stake their liberty and their persons upon one and the last throw. The loser goes calmly into voluntary bondage. However younger he be, however stronger, he tamely suffers himself to be bound and sold by the winner. Such is their perseverance in an evil course: they themselves call it honor.

Slaves of this class, they exchange away in commerce, to free themselves too from the shame of such a victory. Of their other slaves they make not such use as we do of ours, by distributing amongst them the several offices and employments of the family. Each of them has a dwelling of his own, each a household to govern. His lord uses him like a tenant, and obliges him to pay a quantity of grain, or of cattle, or of cloth. Thus far only the subserviency of the slave extends. All the other duties in a family, not the slaves, but the wives and children discharge. To inflict stripes upon a slave, or to put him in chains, or to doom him to severe labor are things rarely seen. To kill them they sometimes are wont, not through correction or government, but in heat and rage, as they would an enemy, save that no vengeance or penalty follows. The freedmen very little surpass the slaves, rarely are of moment in the house; in the community never, excepting only such nations where arbitrary dominion prevails. For there they bear higher sway than the freeborn, nay, higher than the nobles. In other countries the inferior condition of freedmen is a proof of public liberty.

To the practice of usury and of increasing money by interest, they are strangers; and hence is found a better guard against it, than if it were forbidden. They shift from land to land; and, still appropriating a portion suitable to the number of hands for manuring, anon parcel out the whole amongst particulars according to the condition and quality of each. As the plains are very spacious, the allotments are easily assigned. Every year they change, and cultivate a fresh soil; yet still there is ground to spare. For they strive not to bestow labor proportionable to the fertility and compass of their lands, by planting orchards, by enclosing meadows, by watering gardens. From the earth, corn only is exacted. Hence they quarter not the year into so many seasons. Winter, Spring, and Summer, they understand;

and for each have proper appellations. Of the name and blessings of Autumn, they are equally ignorant.

In conducting their funerals, they show no state or vain-
glory. This only is carefully observed, that with the corpses
of their noted men certain woods are burned. Upon the funeral
pile they accumulate neither apparel nor perfumes. Into the
fire, are always thrown the arms of the dead, and sometimes his
horse. With turf only the sepulcher is raised. The pomp of
tedious and elaborate monuments they contemn, as things grievous to the deceased. Tears and wailings they soon dismiss:
their affliction and woe they long retain. In women, it is reckoned becoming to bewail their loss; in men to remember it.[13]

Doubtless this is a reasonably accurate picture of very
early English life,[14] but migration to insular Britain, by
giving the Teutons a chance to develop the arts of peace,
of which, according to Tacitus, they knew so little, profoundly modified their mode of life. Now one of the main
agencies in this social and industrial transformation was
the monastery. The following section from the *Rule of
St. Benedict*, a document perhaps as influential as any
political constitution ever written, will set forth the monastic attitude toward labor and a typical daily program
of labor and study:

Idleness is the enemy of the soul. And therefore, at fixed
times, the brothers ought to be occupied in manual labor; and
again, at fixed times, in sacred reading. Therefore we believe
that, according to this disposition, both seasons ought to be
arranged; so that, from Easter to the Calends of October,
going out early, from the first until the fourth hour they shall

[13] Cf. *post*, p. 35, the quotation from *Beowulf*. The most useful systematic
commentary upon these selections from Tacitus is Professor Gummere's *Germanic
Origins* (Chas. Scribner's Sons, 1892). Professor George Burton Adams' *Civilization in Europe during the Middle Ages*, Chaps. 2, 4, 5 should also be mentioned
(Chas. Scribner's Sons, 1901).

[14] But see Christabel F. Fiske, *Old English Modifications of Teutonic Racial
Conceptions* in *Studies in Language and Literature in Honor of J. M. Hart* (Henry
Holt & Co., 1910).

do what labor may be necessary. Moreover, from the fourth hour until about the sixth, they shall be free for reading. After the meal of the sixth hour, moreover, rising from table, they shall rest in their beds with all silence; or, perchance, he that wishes to read may so read to himself that he do not disturb another. And the nona (the second meal) shall be gone through with more moderately about the middle of the eighth hour; and again they shall work at what is to be done until Vespers. But, if the exigency or poverty of the place demands that they be occupied by themselves in picking fruits, they shall not be dismayed: for then they are truly monks if they live by the labors of their hands; as did also our fathers and the apostles. Let all things be done with moderation, however, on account of the faint-hearted. From the Calends of October, moreover, until the beginning of Lent they shall be free for reading until the second full hour. At the second hour the tertia (morning service) shall be held, and all shall labor at the task which is enjoined upon them until the ninth. The first signal, moreover, of the ninth hour having been given, they shall each one leave off his work; and be ready when the second signal strikes. Moreover after the refection they shall be free for their readings or for psalms. But in the days of Lent, from dawn until the third full hour, they shall be free for their readings; and, until the tenth full hour, they shall do the labor that is enjoined upon them. In which days of Lent they shall all receive separate books from the library; which they shall read entirely through in order. These books are to be given out on the first day of Lent. Above all there shall certainly be appointed one or two elders, who shall go round the monastery at the hours in which the brothers are engaged in reading, and see to it that no troublesome brother chance to be found who is open to idleness and trifling, and is not intent on his reading; being not only of no use to himself, but also stirring up others. If such a one — may it not happen — be found, he shall be admonished once and a second time. If he do not amend, he shall be subject under the Rule to such punishment that the others may have fear. Nor shall brother join brother at unsuitable hours. Moreover on Sunday all shall engage in reading:

excepting those who are deputed to various duties. But if anyone be so negligent and lazy that he will not or cannot read, some
task shall be imposed upon him which he can do; so that he be
not idle. On feeble or delicate brothers such a labor or art is
to be imposed, that they shall neither be idle, nor shall they be
so oppressed by the violence of labor as to be driven to take
flight. Their weakness is to be taken into consideration by the
abbot.

The economic function of monasteries is suggested by
this additional chapter from the same document:

Artificers, if there are any in the monastery, shall practise
with all humility their special arts, if the abbot permit it. But
if any one of them becomes inflated with pride on account of
knowledge of his art, to the extent that he seems to be conferring
something on the monastery: such a one shall be plucked away
from that art; and he shall not again return to it unless the
abbot perchance again orders him to, he being humiliated. But,
if anything from the works of the artificers is to be sold, they
themselves shall take care through whose hands they (the works)
are to pass, lest they (the intermediaries) presume to commit
some fraud upon the monastery. They shall always remember
Ananias and Sapphira;[15] lest, perchance, the death that they
suffered with regard to the body, these, or all those who have
committed any fraud as to the property of the monastery, may
suffer with regard to the soul. In the prices themselves,
moreover, let not the evil of avarice crop out: but let the
object always be given a little cheaper than it is given by
other and secular persons; so that, in all things, God shall
be glorified.[16]

The following selections are from laws ascribed to
Alfred the Great. But, since law is always and everywhere conservative, they embody much of primitive Teu-

[15] Cf. Acts 5 : 1–5.
[16] For a modern writer's estimate of the economic service of monasteries, see
William Cunningham, *An Essay on Western Civilization in Its Economic Aspects*
(*Medieval and Modern Times*), pp. 35–40 (Cambridge University Press, 1900).

tonic procedure and much of English custom prior to the
time of Alfred.   They, therefore, serve to reveal in its
general outlines the structure of Old English social life
and furnish an accurate index of social conditions.   Inci-
dentally, they show the nature of law in early England.

I, then, Alfred, king, gathered these together, and commanded
many of those to be written which our forefathers held,[17] those
which to me seemed good; and many of those which seemed to
me not good I rejected, by the counsel of my witan,[18] and in
otherwise commanded them to be holden; for I durst not venture to set down in writing much of my own, for it was unknown to me what of it would please those who should come
after us.   But those things which I met with, either of the days
of Ine my kinsman, or of Offa, king of the Mercians, or of
Ethelbert, who first among the English race received baptism,
those which seemed to me the rightest, those I have here gathered together, and rejected the others.

I, then, Alfred, king of the West Saxons, showed these to all
my witan, and they then said that it seemed good to them for
all these to be holden.

At the first we teach that it is most needful that every man
warily keep his oaths and his pledges.   If any one be constrained
to either of these wrongfully, either to treason against his lord
or to any unlawful aid, then it is juster to belie than to fulfil.
But if he pledge himself to that which is lawful to fulfil, and in
that belie himself, let him submissively deliver up his weapon
and his goods to the keeping of his friends, and be in prison forty
days in a king's town: let him there suffer whatever the bishop
may prescribe to him; and let his kinsmen feed him, if himself
he have no food. . . .

If any plot against the king's life, of himself, or by harboring
exiles, or by his men, let him be liable in his life and in all that
he has. . . .

We also ordain to every church that has been hallowed by a
bishop this right of peace, if a man in a feud flee to or reach one,

[17] The conservative and traditionary character of law is well indicated here.
[18] I.e. council of wise men.

that for seven days no one drag him out. . . . He who steals on Sunday or at Christmas or at Easter or on Holy Thursday or on Rogation days, for each of these we will that the fine be twofold, as during the Lenten fast. . . .

If any one fight in the king's hall, or draw his weapon, and he be taken, be it the king's doom, either death or life, as he may be willing to grant him. If he escape, and be taken again, let him pay for himself according to the value of his life. . . .

If a man fight before an archbishop or draw his weapon, let him make amends with one hundred and fifty shillings. If before another bishop or an ealdorman this happen, let him make amends with one hundred shillings.

If any one smite his neighbor with a stone or with his fist, and he nevertheless can go out with a staff; let him get him a leech, and work his work the while that himself may not.

If an ox gore a man or a woman so that they die, let it be stoned, and let not its flesh be eaten. The lord shall not be liable, if the ox were wont to push with its horns for two or three days before, and the lord knew it not; but if he knew it, and he would not shut it in, and it shall then have slain a man or a woman, let it be stoned; and let the lord be slain, or the man be paid for, as the witan decree to be right. If it gore a son or a daughter, let him be subject to the like judgment. But if it gore a servant or slave, let thirty shillings of silver be given to the lord, and let the ox be stoned.

If a man, kinless of paternal relatives, fight, and slay a man, and then if he have maternal relatives, let them pay a third of the price of the slain man's life; his gild-brethren a third part; for a third let him flee. If he have no maternal relatives, let his gild-brethren pay half, for half let him flee.

Injure ye not the widows and the step-children, nor hurt them anywhere: for if ye do otherwise, they will cry unto me, and I will hear them, and I will then slay you with my sword; and I will so do that your wives shall be widows, and your children shall be step-children.

If thou give money in loan to thy fellow who willeth to dwell with thee, urge thou him not as a slave, and oppress him not with the increase.

If a man have only a single garment wherewith to cover himself, or to wear, and he give it (to thee) in pledge; let it be returned before sunset. If thou dost not so, then shall he call unto me, and I will hear him; for I am very merciful.

We also command: that the man who knows his foe to be home-sitting fight not before he demand justice of him. If he have such power that he can beset his foe, and besiege him within, let him keep him within for seven days, and attack him not, if he remain within. And then, after seven days, if he will surrender, and deliver up his weapons, let him be kept safe for thirty days, and let notice of him be given to his kinsmen and his friends. If, however, he flee to a church, then let it be according to the sanctity of the church; as we have before said above. But if he have not sufficient power to besiege him within, let him ride to the ealdorman, and beg aid of him. If he will not aid him, let him ride to the king before he fights. In like manner also, if a man come upon his foe, and he did not before know him to be home-staying; if he be willing to deliver up his weapons, let him be kept for thirty days, and let notice of him be given to his friends; if he will not deliver up his weapons, then he may attack him. If he be willing to surrender, and to deliver up his weapons, and any one after that attack him, let him forgo all claim to the aid of his relatives. We also declare, that with his lord a man may fight without being liable to the charge of homicide, if any one attack the lord: thus may the lord fight for his man. After the same fashion, a man may fight with his blood relative, if a man attack him wrongfully, except against his lord; that we do not allow. . . .

Judge thou evenly: judge thou not one doom to the rich, another to the poor; nor one to thy friend, another to thy foe, judge thou. . . .

If (one's) hearing be impaired (by assault), so that he cannot hear, let sixty shillings be paid as amends. A man's grinder is worth fifteen shillings.

A man's chin bone, if it be cloven, let twelve shillings be paid as compensation.

If a man be wounded on the shoulder so that the joint-oil flow out, let amends be made with thirty shillings.

If the arm be broken above the elbow, there shall be fifteen shillings as compensation.

If the forearm be broken, the compensation is thirty shillings.

If the thumb be struck off, for that the amends shall be thirty shillings.

If the nail be struck off, the compensation shall be five shillings.

If the shooting (i.e. index) finger be struck off, the compensation is fifteen shillings; for its nail, four shillings.

If the middle finger be struck off, the compensation is twelve shillings; and its nail, is two shillings. . . .

If a man's thigh be pierced, let thirty shillings be paid him as compensation; if it be broken, the compensation is likewise thirty shillings.

If the great toe be struck off, let twenty shillings be paid as amends; if it be the second toe, let fifteen shillings be paid. . . .

If a man maim another's hand outwardly, let twenty shillings be paid him as amends, if it can be healed; if it half fly off, then shall the amends be forty shillings.

He who smiteth his father or his mother shall perish by death.

He who stealeth a freeman and selleth him and it be proved against him so that he cannot clear himself, let him perish by death. . . .

If a thief break into a man's house by night and he be there slain, the slayer shall not be guilty of manslaughter. But if he do this after sunrise he shall be guilty of manslaughter, and then he himself shall die, unless he were an unwilling agent. . . .

Swear ye never by heathen gods, nor cry ye unto them for any cause.

An attractive and, at the same time, accurate representation of domestic and industrial life in eleventh-century England is given in a dialog between master and pupil, designed to familiarize boys with Latin. Ælfric, monk and abbot, best extant example of the culture of his day, is the author of this primitive imaginary conversation.

PUPIL. We children beg you, teacher, to teach us how to speak Latin correctly, for we are very ignorant and make mistakes in our speech.

TEACHER. What do you want to talk about?

PUPIL. What do we care what the subject is, provided the language be correct, and the discourse be useful, not idle and base?

TEACHER. Do you desire to be flogged in your learning?

PUPIL. We had rather be flogged for learning's sake than be ignorant; but we know that you are kind and will not inflict blows upon us unless we force you to do so.

TEACHER. I ask an answer to this: What is your work at present?

PUPIL. I am a monk by profession and I sing every day the seven services of the hours with my brethren and am occupied with reading and singing, but nevertheless I should like, between times, to learn Latin.

TEACHER. What do these your comrades know?

PUPIL. Some are plowmen, some shepherds, some oxherds; and some are hunters, some fishermen, some fowlers, some merchants, some shoemakers, some salters, and some bakers.

TEACHER. Plowman, what can you say for yourself? How do you do your work?

PLOWMAN. O, dear master, I work very hard; I go out at daybreak, drive the oxen to the field and yoke them to the plow. Never is winter weather so severe that I dare to remain at home; for I fear my master. But when the oxen are yoked to the plow and the share and coulter fastened on, every day I must plow a full acre or more.

TEACHER. Have you any one to help you?

PLOWMAN. I have a boy who urges on the oxen with a goad. He is now hoarse from cold and shouting.

TEACHER. Do you do anything else in the course of a day?

PLOWMAN. I do a great deal more. I have to fill the bins of the oxen with hay and water them and clean their stalls.

TEACHER. Oh! Oh! that is hard work!

PLOWMAN. The labor is indeed great, because I am not free.

TEACHER. What is your work, shepherd, have you anything to do?

SHEPHERD. Yes indeed, master, I have. In the early morning I drive my sheep to their pasture and stand over them in heat or cold with dogs lest wolves devour them. I lead them back to their folds and milk them twice a day. In addition I move their folds, make cheese and butter and am faithful to my master.

TEACHER. Well, oxherd, what is your work?

OXHERD. O my master, my work is very hard. When the plowman unyokes the oxen, I lead them to pasture and all night I stand over them and watch for thieves. Then in the early morning I turn them over to the plowman after I have fed and watered them.

TEACHER. Is this one of your friends?

OXHERD. Yes, he is.

TEACHER. Can you do anything?

HUNTER. I know one craft.

TEACHER. What is it?

HUNTER. I am a hunter.

TEACHER. Whose?

HUNTER. The king's.

TEACHER. How do you carry on your work?

HUNTER. I weave my nets and put them in a suitable place, and train my dogs to follow the wild beasts until they come unexpectedly to the nets and are entrapped. Then I kill them in the nets.

TEACHER. Can't you hunt without nets?

HUNTER. Yes, I can hunt without them.

TEACHER. How?

HUNTER. I chase wild beasts with swift dogs.

TEACHER. What wild beasts do you catch?

HUNTER. Harts, boars, does, goats and sometimes hares.

TEACHER. Did you go out to-day?

HUNTER. No, because it is Sunday; but I was out yesterday.

TEACHER. What luck did you have?

HUNTER. I got two harts and a boar.

TEACHER. How did you catch them?

HUNTER. The harts I took in a net and the boar I slew.

TEACHER. How did you dare to kill a boar?

HUNTER. The dogs drove him to me, and I, standing opposite to him, slew him suddenly.

TEACHER. You were very brave.

HUNTER. A hunter should not be afraid; for many kinds of wild beasts live in the woods.

TEACHER. What do you do with your game?

HUNTER. I give the king what I take because I am his hunter.

TEACHER. What does he give you?

HUNTER. He clothes me well and feeds me. Occasionally he gives me a horse or a ring that I may pursue my craft more willingly.

TEACHER. What craft do you follow?

FISHERMAN. I am a fisherman.

TEACHER. What do you gain by your craft?

FISHERMAN. Food and clothes and money.

TEACHER. How do you catch your fish?

FISHERMAN. I go out in my boat, throw my net in the river, cast in my hook baited and take in my creel whatever comes to me.

TEACHER. What if they are unclean fish?

FISHERMAN. I throw the unclean ones back and keep the clean for meat.

TEACHER. Where do you sell your fish?

FISHERMAN. In the city.

TEACHER. Who buys them?

FISHERMAN. The citizens; I do not catch as many as I could sell.

TEACHER. What sorts of fish do you catch?

FISHERMAN. Eels and pike, minnows and turbots, trout and lamphreys; in short, whatever swims in running water.

TEACHER. Why don't you fish in the sea?

FISHERMAN. Sometimes I do; but seldom; because a large boat is needed for sea-fishing.

TEACHER. What do you catch in the sea?

FISHERMAN. Herring and salmon, dolphins and sturgeons, oysters and crabs, mussels, periwinkles, cockles, flounders, sole, lobsters and many others.

TEACHER. Wouldn't you like to catch a whale?

FISHERMAN. No.

TEACHER. Why not?

FISHERMAN. Because it is a dangerous thing to catch a whale. It is safer for me to go to the river with my boat than to go with many ships to hunt whales.

TEACHER. Why so?

FISHERMAN. Because I prefer to take a fish that I can kill than one that with a single blow can swallow not only me but my companions also.

TEACHER. Yet, many catch whales without danger and get a good price for them.

FISHERMAN. I know it, but I do not dare; for I am very timid.

TEACHER. What have you to say, fowler? How do you catch the birds?

FOWLER. I entice them in many ways, sometimes with nets, sometimes with nooses, sometimes with lime, sometimes by whistling, sometimes with a hawk and sometimes with traps.

TEACHER. Have you a hawk?

FOWLER. Yes.

TEACHER. Can you tame it?

FOWLER. Yes; what good would it be to me, if I could not tame it?

HUNTER. Give me a hawk.

FOWLER. I will gladly, if you will give me a swift dog. Which hawk do you prefer, the larger or the smaller?

HUNTER. Give me the larger one.

TEACHER. How do you feed your hawks?

FOWLER. They feed themselves and me in the winter and in the spring I let them fly in the woods. In the autumn I take the young birds and tame them.

TEACHER. And why do you let the tame ones go?

FOWLER. Because I don't want to feed them in the summer, since they eat a good deal.

TEACHER. Many people feed those that they have tamed, even through the summer, that they may have them ready again.

FOWLER. Yes, so they do; but I do not take so much trouble for them, because I can get others, not one only, but many more.

TEACHER. What can you say, merchant?

MERCHANT. I say that I am useful to the king and to the magistrates and to the wealthy and to all the people.

TEACHER. How is that?

MERCHANT. I go aboard my ship with my goods and row over parts of the sea, sell my things and buy precious treasures that are not produced in this country. These latter I bring here with great peril from the sea. Sometimes I suffer shipwreck and lose all my wares, hardly escaping with my life.

TEACHER. What do you bring us?

MERCHANT. Purple goods and silk, precious gems and gold, strange raiment and spices, wine and oil, ivory and brass, copper and tin, sulphur and glass, and the like.

TEACHER. Do you sell your goods for the same price for which you bought them?

MERCHANT. No; what profit would I then have from my labor? But I sell them dearer than I bought them, that I may make a profit. Thus I feed myself, my wife and my son.

TEACHER. And you, shoemaker, what do you do that is useful for us?

SHOEMAKER. My craft is a cunning one and very useful to you.

TEACHER. How?

SHOEMAKER. I buy hides and skins and prepare them by my art and make of them various kinds of footwear — slippers, shoes and gaiters; bottles, reins and trappings; flasks and leathern vessels; spurstraps and halters; purses and bags. None of you could pass a winter without the aid of my craft.

TEACHER. Salter, how is your craft useful to us?

SALTER. Who of you would relish his food without the savor of salt? Who could fill either his cellar or his store-room without the aid of my craft? behold, all butter and cheese would you lose, nor would you enjoy even your vegetables, without me.

TEACHER. And what do you say, baker? Does any one need your craft, or could we live without you?

BAKER. Life might be sustained for a while without my craft, but not long nor well. Truly, without my skill, every table would be empty. Without bread all food would cause sickness. I strengthen the heart of man. I am the strength of men and few would like to do without me.

TEACHER. What shall we say of the cook? Do we need his skill for anything?

THE COOK SAYS: If you should send me away from your midst, you would be compelled to eat your vegetables green and your meat uncooked, and you could have no nourishing broth without my skill.

TEACHER. We do not need your skill, nor is it necessary to us; for we ourselves could cook the things which should be cooked and roast the things that should be roasted.

THE COOK SAYS: If you send me away, that is what you will have to do. Nevertheless, without my skill, you cannot eat.

TEACHER. Monk, you who are talking with me, I have persuaded myself that you have good comrades and that they are very necessary. Now, who are these?

PUPIL. I have smiths — a blacksmith, a goldsmith, a silversmith, a coppersmith, a carpenter and many other workers at various trades.

TEACHER. Have you any wise counselor?

PUPIL. I certainly have. How could our community be ruled without a counselor?

TEACHER. What would you say, wise man? Among these crafts which seems to you the greatest?

COUNSELOR. I tell you that among all these occupations the service of God seems to me to hold the first place; for thus it is written in the Gospels: "Seek ye first the kingdom of God and his righteousness and all these things shall be added to you."

TEACHER. And among the worldly crafts which seems to you to be first?

COUNSELOR. Agriculture, because the farmer feeds us all.

THE BLACKSMITH SAYS: Where would the farmer get his plowshare, or mend his coulter when it has lost its point, without my craft? Where would the fisherman get his hook, or the shoemaker his awl, or the tailor his needle, if it were not for my work?

THE COUNSELOR RESPONDS: Verily, you speak the truth; but we prefer to live with the farmer rather than with you; for the farmer gives us food and drink. What you give us in your shop is sparks, noise of hammers and blowing of bellows.

THE CARPENTER SPEAKS: How could you spare my skill in building houses, in the use of various tools, in building ships and in all the things I make?

THE COUNSELOR SAYS: O comrades and good workmen, let us quickly settle these disputes, and let there be peace and harmony among us. Let each one benefit the others with his craft and agree always with the farmer who feeds us and from whom we get fodder for our horses. And this advice I give to all workers, that each one shall follow his own craft diligently, for he who forsakes his craft shall be himself forsaken by his craft. Whoever you are, priest or monk or layman or soldier, exercise yourself in this. Be satisfied with your office; for it is a great disgrace for a man to be unwilling to be what he is, and what it is his duty to be.

TEACHER. Well, children, how have you enjoyed this conversation?

PUPIL. Pretty well, but you speak profoundly and beyond our age. Speak to us according to our intelligence that we may understand what you say.

TEACHER. Here is a simple question for you: why are you so eager to learn?

PUPIL. Because we do not wish to be like stupid animals that do not know anything but grass and water.

TEACHER. And what is your wish?

PUPIL. We wish to be wise.

TEACHER. In what wisdom? Do you wish to be crafty or to assume a thousand shapes, skilful in deceiving, astute in speaking, graceful, speaking good and thinking evil, using soft words, feeding fraud within, like a whited sepulcher, beautiful without, but full of corruption?

PUPIL. We do not wish for this kind of wisdom; for he is not wise who deceives himself with pretenses.

TEACHER. But how would you be wise?

PUPIL. We wish to be simple without hypocrisy, and wise

that we may turn from evil and do good. But you are speaking to us of matters deeper than we are able to understand on account of our years. Speak to us in our own way and not so profoundly.

TEACHER. I will do as you ask. My boy, what did you do to-day?

PUPIL. I did many things. In the night, when I heard the bell, I arose from my bed and went to church. After that we sang of all the saints and morning praise songs, and after that prime and seven psalms with the litany and the first mass. Then we sang terce and did the mass of the day. After this we sang sext and ate and drank and slept. Again we rose and sang nones and now we are before you ready to hear whatever you may say to us.

TEACHER. When will you sing vespers or evensong?

PUPIL. When it is time.

TEACHER. Were you flogged to-day?

PUPIL. No; because I conducted myself carefully.

TEACHER. And what of your companions?

PUPIL. Why do you ask me that? I do not dare to tell you our secrets. Each one knows whether he was flogged.

TEACHER. What do you eat during the day?

PUPIL. As yet I eat meat, for I am a child kept under the rod.

TEACHER. What else do you eat?

PUPIL. Herbs, eggs, fish, cheese, butter, beans and all clean things I eat with great thankfulness.

TEACHER. You are very voracious, because you eat everything that is set before you.

PUPIL. I am not so greedy as to eat all kinds of food at one meal.

TEACHER. Then how?

PUPIL. Sometimes I eat one kind of food at one meal and sometimes another; but always with moderation as it becomes a monk; and not greedily; for I am no glutton.

TEACHER. And what do you drink?

PUPIL. Ale, if I can get it; water, if I have no ale.

TEACHER. Don't you drink wine?

PUPIL. I am not rich enough to buy wine for myself and

wine is not a drink for children or the foolish but for the old and wise.

TEACHER. Where do you sleep?

PUPIL. In the dormitory with the brethren.

TEACHER. Who wakes you for the night songs?

PUPIL. Sometimes I hear the bell and rise; sometimes the master rouses me sternly with the rod.

TEACHER. O good children and winsome pupils, I, your master, exhort you to be obedient to the divine command and keep yourselves pure in all places. Rise immediately at the sound of the church-bell and go into the oratory. Bow humbly before the holy altars, stand meekly and sing in accord. Pray for the erring ones and go out without haste into the cloister or the school.

III. THE CULTURAL BACKGROUND

Our problem here is to try to understand and appreciate the less mechanical phases of Old English life which affected and colored literature; the aims and temper of the people, the foreign influences upon them, their art and learning, the status of poets among them.

1. *Early English Ideals and Temper.* — Tacitus has already suggested at long range what these were, but we need the closer view to be gained from English literature itself. The first illustrative passage chosen is the account, in the earliest Teutonic epic extant, the English *Beowulf*,[1] of the death of the hero. Beowulf has ruled his people for fifty winters after a youth spent in deeds of warlike daring and generous aid to others, truly called chivalric. Feeling his end near, he reviews his life in words which reveal his aims and ideals.[1]

Beowulf discoursed, spoke notwithstanding his wound, his piteous deadly hurt; he was fully conscious that he had lived out his allotted day of earthly joy, that the whole of his destined

[1] On Beowulf as a typical Teutonic hero, see E. Dale, *National Life and Character in the Mirror of Early English Literature*, pp. 23–27 (Cambridge University Press, 1907).

time was measured, (that) death was very near; "Now would I bestow my war-gear on my son, had any heir sprung from my body been given me to come after me. I have guided this people fifty years, nor has there been any folk-king among my neighbors, no not one, who durst attack me in war, grievously oppress me. I awaited on earth my appointed time, guarded well my own, sought no cunning wiles, nor swore many false oaths. Hence, though stricken with deadly wounds, I may rejoice, because the Warden of men cannot lay the murder of kinsmen to my charge when my life parts from my body. Do thou, dear Wiglaf,[2] go quickly to see the treasure beneath the hoary stone, since the dragon[3] lies slain, sleeps sorely wounded, bereft of treasured life. Hasten, that I may look upon the ancient stores of golden wealth, closely examine the bright gems, that I may the more easily thereafter leave my life and the realm which I have long ruled."

The first 2200 lines of the poem *Beowulf* tell the story of Beowulf's adventures in behalf of Hrothgar, king of the Danes, whom Beowulf comes over the sea to help in his efforts to free his land and people of the monster Grendel. On the death of one of Hrothgar's thanes at the hands of Grendel's mother, Beowulf gives the following advice, which may be compared with the words of Tacitus already cited:[4]

Beowulf, son of Ecgtheow, spoke:

"Sorrow not, wise man; to avenge one's friend is better than to mourn much. Each one of us must stay for the end of his life in this world; (therefore) let him who may, do his work of glory before death; this will have been the best course for a hero whose life is done."

No one knows just when the poem *Beowulf* was composed and so the time which elapsed between the date of our first illustration and that of the last must for us be

2 One of Beowulf's most trusted companions.
3 The monster in conflict with which Beowulf got his death-wound.
4 Cf. *ante.*, p. 19.

unmeasured. But in the interim Christianity has been introduced among the English and they are to have the chance of contact with the main stream of world civilization. Later documents will deal more fully with the introduction of Christianity, but here our attention should center on the glimpses we get of traits easily recognized as English to-day; such as, in the story to be quoted, the almost commercial common sense of the priest Coifi, and the reflective sensitiveness of the still pagan nobleman whose unknown name deserves record.

For one's appreciation of the following story, he should know that Bishop Paulinus of York has had one interview with King Edwin of Northumbria regarding the acceptance of Christianity by the latter, and that, using as a means of approach a mystic sign which had been revealed to the king in a vision, the bishop has now come to claim the royal convert.

The king,[5] hearing these words,[6] answered, that he was both willing and bound to receive the faith which he taught; but that he would confer about it with his principal friends and counsellors, to the end that if they also were of his opinion, they might all together be cleansed in Christ the Fountain of Life. Paulinus consenting, the king did as he said; for, holding a council with the wise men, he asked of every one in particular what he thought of the new doctrine, and the new worship that was preached? To which the chief of his own priests, Coifi, immediately answered, "O king, consider what this is which is now preached to us; for I verily declare to you, that the religion which we have hitherto professed has, as far as I can learn, no virtue in it. For none of your people has applied himself more diligently to the worship of our gods than I; and yet there are many who receive greater favors from you, and are more preferred than I, and are more prosperous in all their undertakings. Now if the gods were good for any thing, they would rather forward me, who have

[5] Edwin of Northumbria (585?–633, A.D.)
[6] Cf. Bishop Paulinus of York (died 644 A.D.)

been more careful to serve them. It remains, therefore, that if upon examination you find those new doctrines, which are now preached to us, better and more efficacious, we immediately receive them without any delay."

Another of the king's men, approving of his words and exhortations, presently added: "The present life of man, O king, seems to me, in comparison with that time which is unknown to us, like to the swift flight of a sparrow through the room wherein you sit at supper in winter, with your commanders and ministers, and a good fire in the midst, whilst the storms of rain and snow prevail abroad; the sparrow, I say, flying in at one door, and immediately out at another, whilst he is within, is safe from the wintry storm; but after a short space of fair weather, he immediately vanishes out of sight, into the dark winter from which he emerged. So this life of man appears for a short space, but of what went before, or what is to follow, we are utterly ignorant. If, therefore, this new doctrine contains something more certain, it seems justly to deserve to be followed." The other elders and king's counsellors, by Divine inspiration, spoke to the same effect.

But Coifi added, that he wished more attentively to hear Paulinus discourse concerning the God whom he preached; which he having by the king's command performed, Coifi, hearing his words, cried out, "I have long since been sensible that there was nothing in that which we worshipped; because the more diligently I sought after truth in that worship, the less I found it. But now I freely confess, that such truth evidently appears in this preaching as can confer on us the gifts of life, of salvation, and of eternal happiness. For which reason I advise, O king, that we instantly abjure and set fire to those temples and altars which we have consecrated without reaping any benefit from them." In short, the king publicly gave his licence to Paulinus to preach the Gospel, and renouncing idolatry, declared that he received the faith of Christ: and when he inquired of the high priest who should first profane the altars and temples of their idols, with the enclosures that were about them, he answered, "I; for who can more properly than myself destroy those things which I worshipped through ignorance, for an example to all

others, through the wisdom which has been given me by the true
God?'' Then immediately, in contempt of his former supersti-
tions, he desired the king to furnish him with arms and a stallion; and mounting the same, he set out to destroy the idols;
for it was not lawful before for the high priest either to carry
arms, or to ride on any but a mare. Having, therefore, girt a
sword about him, with a spear in his hand, he mounted the king's
stallion and proceeded to the idols. The multitude, beholding
it, concluded he was distracted; but he lost no time, for as soon
as he drew near the temple he profaned the same, casting into it
the spear which he held; and, rejoicing in the knowledge of the
worship of the true God, he commanded his companions to destroy the temple, with all its enclosures, by fire.[7] This place
where the idols were is still shown, not far from York, to the east-
ward, beyond the river Derwent, and is now called Godmunding-
ham, where the high priest, by the inspiration of the true God,
profaned and destroyed the altars which he had himself consecrated.[8]

2. *Foreign Influences.* — Were we to take in chronological order the foreign influences on the Teutons after their
arrival in Britain, the first to be mentioned would be that
of the Celts who invited them into the island and who
finally gave way before them. But the conclusions of
modern scholarship are that the Celts exercised little if
any immediate influence upon the English.[9] Passing them
by, therefore, the next foreign influence is that of Christianity. This was, as the sequel will show, much more
than a narrowly religious influence. Contact with Christianity in the sixth century of our era meant contact with
the highest and best in civilization. This will be abundantly evident in the documents which follow. Here,

[7] Cf. the advice given by Bishop Daniel of Winchester to St. Boniface in his
labors among the heathen. *English Correspondence of St. Boniface*, pp. 51 *seq.*
(*King's Classics edition*, Chatto and Windus, 1911.)

[8] For a further reference to King Edwin, cf. *post*, p. 99.

[9] Cf. *Cambridge History of English Literature*, I, pp. 305–7 and bibliography to
Chap. XII.

however, our primary interest is in the introduction of Christianity. It was first brought to Britain, apparently, before it became the authorized state religion of the Roman Empire and experienced the fortunes and misfortunes of general Christianity in the pagan world. Our first document will illustrate this pre-German Christianity by picturing the martyrdom of St. Alban. The chronological difficulties in the way of our accepting Bede's statements as he makes them, need not interfere with our getting real information in a general way on religious conditions in pagan Roman Britain.

At that time [10] suffered St. Alban, of whom the priest Fortunatus,[11] in the *Praise of Virgins*, where he makes mention of the blessed martyrs that came to the Lord from all parts of the world, says:

In Britain's isle was holy Alban born.

This Alban, being yet a pagan, at the time when the cruelties of wicked princes were raging against Christians, gave entertainment in his house to a certain clergyman, flying from the persecutors. This man he observed to be engaged in continual prayer and watching day and night; when on a sudden the Divine grace shining on him, he began to imitate the example of faith and piety which was set before him, and being gradually instructed by his wholesome admonitions, he cast off the darkness of idolatry, and became a Christian in all sincerity of heart. The aforesaid clergyman having been some days entertained by him, it came to the ears of the wicked prince, that this holy confessor of Christ, whose time of martyrdom had not yet come, was concealed at Alban's house. Whereupon he sent some soldiers to make a strict search after him. When they came to the martyr's house, St. Alban immediately presented himself to the soldiers, instead of his guest and master, in the habit or long coat which he wore, and was led bound before the judge. It happened that the judge, at the time when Alban was

---

[10] 305 A.D. during the persecutions of Christians under Diocletian.
[11] Cf. *post*, p. 67 and note.

carried before him, was standing at the altar, and offering sacrifice to devils. When he saw Alban, being much enraged that he should thus, of his own accord, put himself into
the hands of the soldiers, and incur such danger in behalf of
his guest, he commanded him to be dragged up to the images of
the devils, before which he stood, saying, "Because you have
chosen to conceal a rebellious and sacrilegious person, rather than
to deliver him up to the soldiers, that his contempt of the gods
might meet with the penalty due to such blasphemy, you shall
undergo all the punishment that was due to him if you abandon
the worship of our religion." But St. Alban, who had voluntarily declared himself a Christian to the persecutors of the faith,
was not at all daunted at the prince's threats, but putting on the
armor of spiritual warfare, publicly declared that he would not
obey the command. Then said the judge, "Of what family or
race are you?" — "What does it concern you," answered Alban,"
"of what stock I am? If you desire to hear the truth of my
religion, be it known to you, that I am now a Christian, and
bound by Christian duties." — "I ask your name;" said the
judge, "tell me it immediately." "I am called Alban by my
parents," replied he; "and I worship and adore the true and
living God, who created all things." Then the judge, inflamed
with anger, said, "If you will enjoy the happiness of eternal life,
do not delay to offer sacrifice to the great gods." Alban rejoined,
"These sacrifices, which by you are offered to devils, neither can
avail the subjects, nor answer the wishes or desires of those that
offer up their supplications to them. On the contrary, whosoever shall offer sacrifice to these images shall receive the everlasting pains of hell for his reward."

The judge, hearing these words, and being much incensed,
ordered this holy confessor of God to be scourged by the executioners, believing he might by stripes shake that constancy of
heart, on which he could not prevail by words. He, being most
cruelly tortured, bore the same patiently, or rather joyfully, for
our Lord's sake. When the judge perceived that he was not to
be overcome by tortures, or withdrawn from the exercise of the
Christian religion, he ordered him to be put to death. Being
led to execution, he came to a river, which, with a most rapid

course, ran between the wall of the town and the arena where he
was to be executed. He there saw a multitude of persons of
both sexes, and of several ages and conditions, who were doubtless assembled by Divine instinct, to attend the blessed confessor and martyr, and had so taken up the bridge on the river,
that he could scarce pass over that evening. In short, almost all
had gone out, so that the judge remained in the city without
attendance. St. Alban, therefore, urged by an ardent and devout
wish to arrive quickly at martyrdom, drew near to the stream,
and on lifting up his eyes to heaven, the channel was immediately
dried up, and he perceived that the water had departed and made
way for him to pass. Among the rest the executioner, who was
to have put him to death, observed this, and moved by Divine
inspiration hastened to meet him at the place of execution, and
casting down the sword which he had carried ready drawn, fell
at his feet, praying that he might rather suffer with the martyr,
whom he was ordered to execute, or, if possible, instead of him.

Whilst he thus from a persecutor was become a companion in
the faith, and the other executioners hesitated to take up the
sword which was lying on the ground, the reverend confessor,
accompanied by the multitude, ascended a hill, about five hundred paces from the place, adorned, or. rather clothed with all
kinds of flowers, having its sides neither perpendicular, nor
even craggy, but sloping down into a most beautiful plain, worthy
from its lovely appearance to be the scene of a martyr's sufferings. On the top of this hill, St. Alban prayed that God would
give him water, and immediately a living spring broke out before
his feet, the course being confined, so that all men perceived that
the river also had been dried up in consequence of the martyr's
presence. Nor was it likely that the martyr, who had left no
water remaining in the river, should want some on the top of the
hill, unless he thought it suitable to the occasion. The river
having performed the holy service, returned to its natural course,
leaving a testimony of its obedience. Here, therefore, the head
of our most courageous martyr was struck off, and here he received the crown of life, which God has promised to those who
love Him.[12] But he who gave the wicked stroke, was not per-

[12] Cf. James 1: 12.

mitted to rejoice over the deceased; for his dropped upon the ground together with the blessed martyr's head.

At the same time was also beheaded the soldier, who before, through the Divine admonition, refused to give the stroke to the holy confessor. Of whom it is apparent, though he was not regenerated by baptism, yet he was cleansed by the washing of his own blood, and rendered worthy to enter the kingdom of heaven. Then the judge, astonished at the novelty of so many heavenly miracles, ordered the persecution to cease immediately, beginning to honor the death of the saints, by which he before thought they might have been diverted from the Christian faith. The blessed Alban suffered death on the twenty-second day of June, near the city of Verulam, which is now by the English nation called Verlamacestir, or Varlingacestir, where afterwards, when peaceable Christian times were restored, a church of wonderful workmanship, and suitable to his martyrdom, was erected. In which place, there ceases not to this day the cure of sick persons, and the frequent workings of wonders.

At the same time suffered Aaron and Julius, citizens of Chester, and many more of both sexes in several places; who, when they had endured sundry torments, and their limbs had been torn after an unheard-of manner, yielded their souls up, to enjoy in the heavenly city a reward for the sufferings which they had passed through.

These untoward conditions did not last long, however, after the time of Alban's martyrdom; for in 312 or 313 Constantine put Christianity on the same basis as other religions in the Empire and the Church doubtless prospered in Britain as did other things Roman. But on the withdrawal of the legions early in the fifth century troublous times came on again and Christian priests were not spared as the pagan Teutons swept in conquest over the island. Britain returned to paganism — this time of a Teutonic type — for about a century and a half and then a process of re-Christianization began. One Gregory, afterwards Pope Gregory I, surnamed the Great, is, according to Bede, responsible for beginning this missionary work among the English. How Gregory became interested in the English is told by Bede as follows:

It is reported, that some merchants, having just arrived at Rome on a certain day, exposed many things for sale in the market place, and abundance of people resorted thither to buy: Gregory [13] himself went with the rest, and among other things, some boys were set to sale, their bodies white, their countenances beautiful, and their hair very fine. Having viewed them, he asked, as is said, from what country or nation they were brought? and was told, from the island of Britain, whose inhabitants were of such personal appearance. He again inquired whether those islanders were Christians, or still involved in the errors of paganism? and was informed that they were pagans. Then fetching a deep sign from the bottom of his heart, "Alas! what pity," said he, "that the author of darkness is possessed of men of such fair countenances; and that being remarkable for such graceful aspects, their minds should be void of inward grace." He therefore again asked, what was the name of that nation? and was answered, that they were called Angles. "Right," said he, "for they have an Angelic face, and it becomes such to be coheirs with the Angels in heaven. What is the name," proceeded he, "of the province from which they are brought?" It was replied, that the natives of that province were called Deiri. "Truly are they *De ira*," said he, "withdrawn from the wrath, and called to the mercy of Christ. How is the king of that province called?" They told him his name was Ella: and he, alluding to the name, said, "Hallelujah, the praise of God the Creator must be sung in those parts."

Then repairing to the bishop of the Roman aposotolical see (for he was not himself then made pope), he entreated him to send some ministers of the word into Britain to the nation of the English, by whom it might be converted to Christ; declaring himself ready to undertake that work, by the assistance of God, if the apostolic pope should think fit to have it so done. Which not being then able to perform, because, though the pope was willing to grant his request, yet the citizens of Rome could not

[13] At this time a deacon in the Church.

be brought to consent that so noble, so renowned, and so learned a man should depart the city; as soon as he was himself made pope, he perfected the long-desired work, sending other preachers, but himself by his prayers and exhortations assisting the preaching, that it might be successful. This account, as we have received it from the ancients, we have thought fit to insert in our *Ecclesiastical History*.

Gregory, now pope, selected Augustine, a Roman priest, as his agent in realizing his long-cherished desire of Christianizing Britain, and sent him to the island with full and wise instructions. How Augustine was received there Bede tells us in the following:

Augustine, thus strengthened by the confirmation of the blessed Father Gregory, returned to the work of the word of God, with the servants of Christ, and arrived in Britain. The powerful Ethelbert was at that time king of Kent; he had extended his dominions as far as the great river Humber, by which the Southern Saxons are divided from the Northern. On the east of Kent is the large Isle of Thanet containing according to the English way of reckoning, six hundred families, divided from the other land by the river Wantsum, which is about three furlongs over, and fordable only in two places, for both ends of it run into the sea. In this island landed the servant of our Lord, Augustine, and his companions, being, as is reported, nearly forty men. They had, by order of the blessed Pope Gregory, taken interpreters of the nation of the Franks, and sending to Ethelbert, signified that they were come from Rome, and brought a joyful message, which most undoubtedly assured to all that took advantage of it everlasting joys in heaven, and a kingdom that would never end, with the living and true God. The king having heard this, ordered them to stay in that island where they had landed, and that they should be furnished with all necessaries till he should consider what to do with them. For he had before heard of the Christian religion, having a Christian wife of the royal family of the Franks, called Bertha; whom he had received from her parents, upon condition that she should be permitted to practise her religion with the Bishop Luidhard, who was sent with her to preserve her faith. Some days after, the king came into the island, and sitting in the open air, ordered Augustine and his companions to be brought into his presence. For he had taken precaution that they should not come to him in any house, lest, according to an ancient superstition, if they practised any magical arts, they might impose upon him, and so get the better of him. But they came furnished with Divine, not with magic virtue, bearing a silver cross for their banner, and the image of our Lord and Saviour painted on a board; and singing the litany, they offered up their prayers to the Lord for the eternal salvation both of themselves and of those to whom they were come. When he had sat down, pursuant to the king's commands, and preached to him and his attendants there present, the word of life, the king answered thus:

"Your words and promises are very fair, but as they are new to us, and of uncertain import, I cannot approve of them so far as to forsake that which I have so long followed with the whole English nation. But because you are come from far into my kingdom, and, as I conceive, are desirous to impart to us those things which you believe to be true, and most beneficial, we will not molest you, but give you favorable entertainment and take care to supply you with your necessary sustenance; nor do we forbid you to preach and gain as many as you can to your religion." [14] Accordingly he permitted them to reside in the city of Canterbury, which was the metropolis of all his dominions, and, pursuant to his promise, besides allowing them sustenance, did not refuse them liberty to preach. It is reported that, as they drew near to the city, after their manner, with the holy cross, and the image of our sovereign Lord and King, Jesus Christ, they, in concert, sung this litany: "We beseech Thee O Lord, in all Thy mercy, that thy anger and wrath be turned away from this city, and from the holy house, because we have sinned. Hallelujah."

As soon as they entered the dwelling-place assigned them, they began to imitate the course of life practised in the primitive

---

[14] This open-mindedness in the king is an early example of the traditional English love for fair play.

church; [15] applying themselves to frequent prayer, watching and fasting; preaching the word of life to as many as they could; despising all worldly things, as not belonging to them; receiving only their necessary food from those they taught; living themselves in all respects conformably to what they prescribed to others, and being always disposed to suffer any adversity, and even to die for that truth which they preached. In short, several believed and were baptized, admiring the simplicity of their innocent life, and the sweetness of their heavenly doctrine. There was on the east side of the city a church dedicated to the honor of St. Martin, built whilst the Romans were still in the island, wherein the queen, who, as has been said before, was a Christian, used to pray. In all this they first began to meet, to sing, to pray, to say mass, to preach, and to baptize, till the king, being converted to the faith, allowed them to preach openly, and build or repair churches in all places.

When he, among the rest, induced by the unspotted life of these holy men, and their delightful promises, which, by many miracles, they proved to be most certain, believed and was baptized, greater numbers began daily to flock together to hear the word, and, forsaking their heathen rites, to associate themselves, by believing, to the unity of the church of Christ. Their conversion the king so far encouraged, as that he compelled none to embrace Christianity, but only showed more affection to the believers, as to his fellow-citizens in the heavenly kingdom. For he had learned from his instructors and leaders to salvation, that the service of Christ ought to be voluntary, not by compulsion. Nor was it long before he gave his teachers a settled residence in his metropolis of Canterbury, with such possessions of different kinds as were necessary for their subsistence.

Meanwhile, Irish missionaries of Christianity had entered the north of England and established churches independent of Rome. While the Roman missionaries were Benedictine monks for the most part, the Irish lived under Rules of Irish origin, such as that of St. Columba. That these Irishmen developed high types of character, learn-

[15] Cf. Acts 4: 32–37.

ing and piety is clear from Bede's account of one of them, Aidan.

From the aforesaid island,[16] and college of monks, was Aidan sent to instruct the English nation in Christ, having received the dignity of a bishop at the time when Segenius, abbot and priest, presided over the monastery; whence, among other instructions for life, he left the clergy a most salutary example of abstinence or continence; it was the highest commendation of his doctrine, with all men, that he taught no otherwise than he and his followers had lived; for he neither sought nor loved any thing of this world, but delighted in distributing immediately among the poor whatsoever was given him by the kings or rich men of the world. He was wont to traverse both town and country on foot, never on horseback, unless compelled by some urgent necessity; and wherever in his way he saw any, either rich or poor, he invited them, if infidels, to embrace the mystery of the faith; or if they were believers, to strengthen them in the faith, and to stir them by words and actions to alms and good works.[17]

His course of life was so different from the slothfulness of our times, that all those who bore him company, whether they were shorn monks or laymen, were employed in meditation, that is, either in reading the Scriptures, or learning psalms. This was the daily employment of himself and all that were with him, wheresoever they went; and if it happened, which was but seldom, that he was invited to eat with the king, he went with one or two clerks, and having taken a small repast, made haste to be gone with them, either to read or write. At that time, many religious men and women, stirred up by his example, adopted the custom of fasting on Wednesdays and Fridays, till the ninth hour, throughout the year, except during the fifty days after Easter. He never gave money to the powerful men of the world, but only meat, if he happened to entertain them; and, on the contrary, whatsoever gifts of money he received from the rich, he either distributed them, as has been said, to the use of the

---

[16] Iona.

[17] This and the later references to Aidan (cf. *post*, pp. 97 *seq.*) remind one of Chaucer's description of the parson in the *Prolog* to the *Canterbury Tales*, ll. 477 *seq.*

poor, or bestowed them in ransoming such as had been wrongfully sold for slaves. Moreover, he afterwards made many of those he had ransomed his disciples, and after having taught and instructed them, advanced them to the order of priesthood.

It is reported, that when King Oswald [18] had asked a bishop of the Scots to administer the word of faith to him and his nation, there was first sent to him another man of more austere disposition, who, meeting with no success, and being unregarded by the English people, returned home, and in an assembly of the elders reported, that he had not been able to do any good to the nation he had been sent to preach to, because they were uncivilized men, and of a stubborn and barbarous disposition. They, as is testified, in a great council seriously debated what was to be done, being desirous that the nation should receive the salvation it demanded, and grieving that they had not received the preacher sent to them. Then said Aidan, who was also present in the council, to the priest then spoken of, "I am of opinion, brother, that you were more severe to your unlearned hearers than you ought to have been, and did not at first, conformably to the apostolic rule, give them the milk of more easy doctrine, till being by degrees nourished with the word of God, they should be capable of greater perfection, and be able to practise God's sublimer precepts." Having heard these words, all present began diligently to weigh what he had said, and presently concluded, that he deserved to be made a bishop, and ought to be sent to instruct the incredulous and unlearned; since he was found to be endued with singular discretion, which is the mother of other virtues, and accordingly being ordained, they sent him to their friend, King Oswald, to preach; and he, as time proved, afterwards appeared to possess all other virtues, as well as the discretion for which he was before remarkable.

These two missionary enterprises, one working north, the other south, were bound eventually to come into collision with each other, especially as the two groups of workers differed in some points of doctrine. At length,

---

[18] Cf. *post*, pp. 95 *seq.*

when both were working in Northumbria,[19] King Oswy
called a conference of the two at the monastery of Abbess
Hild at Whitby. The specific question under discussion
was the proper time for observing Easter. Bede's narrative puts before us the occasion of the conference, the
issues and the course of the argument. The victory of the
Roman party was an important one for English civilization. The date of the conference was 664 A.D.

In the meantime, Bishop Aidan being dead, Finan, who was
ordained and sent by the Scots, succeeded him in the bishopric,
and built a church in the Isle of Lindisfarne, the episcopal see;
nevertheless, after the manner of the Scots, he made it, not of
stone, but of hewn oak, and covered it with reeds; and the same
was afterwards dedicated in honor of St. Peter the Apostle, by
the reverend Archbishop Theodore.[20] Eadbert, also bishop of
that place, took off the thatch, and covered it, both roof and
walls, with plates of lead.
At this time, a great and frequent controversy happened about
the observance of Easter; those that came from Kent or France
affirming, that the Scots kept Easter Sunday contrary to the custom of the universal church. Among them was a most zealous
defender of the true Easter, whose name was Ronan, a Scot
by nation, but instructed in ecclesiastical truth, either in France
or Italy, who, disputing with Finan, convinced many, or at least
induced them to make a more strict inquiry after the truth; yet
he could not prevail upon Finan, but, on the contrary, made him
the more inveterate by reproof, and a professed opposer of the
truth, being of a hot and violent temper. James, formerly the
deacon of the venerable Archbishop Paulinus,[21] as has been said
above, kept the true and Catholic Easter, with all those that he
could persuade to adopt the right way. Queen Eanfleda and her
followers also observed the same as she had seen practised in
Kent, having with her a Kentish priest that followed the Catholic mode, whose name was Romanus. Thus it is said to have

---

[19] Cf. *ante*, p. 5, where reference is made to the political and cultural importance
of Northumbria.

[20] Of Canterbury. Cf. *post*, pp. 57, 62, 109.   [21] Of York.

happened in those times that Easter was twice kept in one year; and that when the king having ended the time of fasting, kept his Easter, the queen and her followers were still fasting, and celebrating Palm Sunday. This difference about the observance of Easter, whilst Aidan lived, was patiently tolerated by all men, as being sensible, that though he could not keep Easter contrary to the custom of those who had sent him, yet he industriously labored to practice all works of faith, piety, and love, according to the custom of all holy men; for which reason he was deservedly beloved by all; even by those who differed in opinion concerning Easter, and was held in veneration, not only by indifferent persons, but even by the bishops, Honorius of Canterbury, and Felix of the East Angles.

But after the death of Finan, who succeeded him, when Colman, who was also sent out of Scotland, came to be bishop, a greater controversy arose about the observance of Easter, and the rules of ecclesiastical life. Whereupon this dispute began naturally to influence the thoughts and hearts of many, who feared, lest having received the name Christians, they might happen to run, or to have run, in vain.[22] This reached the ears of King Oswy and his son Alfrid; for Oswy, having been instructed and baptized by the Scots, and being very perfectly skilled in their language, thought nothing better than what they taught. But Alfrid, having been instructed in Christianity by Wilfrid,[23] a most learned man, who had first gone to Rome to learn the ecclesiastical doctrine, and spent much time at Lyons with Dalfin, archbishop of France, from whom also he had received the ecclesiastical tonsure, rightly thought this man's doctrine ought to be preferred before all the traditions of the Scots. For this reason he had also given him a monastery of forty families, at a place called Rhypum; which place, not long before, he had given to those that followed the system of the Scots for a monastery; but forasmuch as they afterwards, being left to their choice, prepared to quit the place rather than alter their opinion, he gave the place to him, whose life and doctrine were worthy of it.

[22] Cf. Philippians 2: 16.
[23] Of York.

Agilbert, bishop of the West Saxons, above-mentioned, a friend to King Alfrid and to Abbot Wilfrid, had at that time come into the province of the Northumbrians, and was making some stay among them; and at the request of Alfrid, made Wilfrid a priest in his monastery. He had in his company a priest, whose name was Agatho. The controversy being there started, concerning Easter, or the tonsure, or other ecclesiastical affairs, it was agreed that a synod should be held in the monastery of Streaneshalch, which signifies the Bay of the Lighthouse, where the Abbess Hilda,[24] a woman devoted to God, then presided; and that there this controversy should be decided. The kings, both father and son came thither, Bishop Colman with his Scottish clerks, and Agilbert with the priests Agatho and Wilfrid, James and Romanus were on their side; but the Abbess Hilda and her followers were for the Scots, as was also the venerable Bishop Cedd, long before ordained by the Scots, as has been said above, and he was in that council a most careful interpreter for both parties.

King Oswy first observed, that it behoved those who served one God to observe the same rule of life; and as they all expected the same kingdom in heaven, so they ought not to differ in the celebration of the Divine mysteries; but rather to inquire which was the truest tradition, that the same might be followed by all; he then commanded his bishop, Colman, first to declare what the custom was which he observed, and whence it derived its origin. Then Colman said, "The Easter which I keep, I received from my elders, who sent me bishop hither; all our forefathers, men beloved of God, are known to have kept it after the same manner; and that the same may not seem to any contemptible or worthy to be rejected, it is the same which St. John the Evangelist, the disciple beloved of our Lord, with all the churches over which he presided, is recorded to have observed." Having said thus much, and more to the like effect, the king commanded Agilbert to show whence his custom of keeping Easter was derived, or on what authority it was grounded. Agilbert answered, "I desire that my disciple, the priest Wilfrid,

[24] Her life is told in *The Ecclesiastical History*, IV, Chap. 23. She presided over the monastery when Cædmon lived there. Cf. *post*, p. 104.

may speak in my stead; because we both concur with the other followers of the ecclesiastical tradition that are here present, and he can better explain our opinion in the English language, than I can by an interpreter."

Then Wilfrid, being ordered by the king to speak, delivered himself thus: "The Easter which we observe, we saw celebrated by all at Rome, where the blessed apostles, Peter and Paul, lived, taught, suffered, and were buried; we saw the same done in Italy and in France, when we travelled through those countries for pilgrimage and prayer. We found the same practised in Africa, Asia, Egypt, Greece, and all the world, wherever the church of Christ is spread abroad, through several nations and tongues, at one and the same time; except only these and their accomplices in obstinacy, I mean the Picts and the Britons, who foolishly, in these two remote islands of the world, and only in part even of them oppose all the rest of the universe." When he had so said, Colman answered, "It is strange that you will call our labors foolish, wherein we follow the example of so great an apostle, who was thought worthy to lay his head on our Lord's bosom, when all the world knows him to have lived most wisely." Wilfrid replied, "Far be it from us to charge John with folly, for he literally observed the precepts of the Jewish law, whilst the church still Judaized in many points, and the apostles were not able at once to cast off all the observances of the law which had been instituted by God. In which way it is necessary that all who come to the faith should forsake the idols which were invented by devils, that they might not give scandal to the Jews that were among the Gentiles. For this reason it was, that Paul circumcised Timothy, that he offered sacrifice in the temple, that he shaved his head with Aquila and Priscilla at Corinth, for no other advantage than to avoid giving scandal to the Jews. Hence it was that James said, to the same Paul, 'You see, brother, how many thousands of the Jews have believed; and they are all zealous for the law. And yet, at this time, the Gospel spreading throughout the world, it is needless, nay, it is not lawful, for the faithful either to be circumcised, or to offer up to God sacrifices of flesh.' So John, pursuant to the custom of the law, began the celebration of the feast of Easter, on the fourteenth day of the first month, in the evening, not regarding whether the same happened on a Saturday, or any other day. But when Peter preached at Rome, being mindful that our Lord arose from the dead, and gave the world the hopes of resurrection, on the first day after the Sabbath, he understood that Easter ought to be observed, so as always to stay till the rising of the moon on the fourteenth day of the first moon, in the evening, according to the custom and precepts of the law, even as John did. And when that came, if the Lord's day did not fall the next morning after the fourteenth moon, but on the sixteenth, or the seventeenth, or any other moon till the twenty-first, he waited for that, and on the Saturday before, in the evening, began to observe the holy solemnity of Easter. Thus it came to pass, that Easter Sunday was only kept from the fifteenth moon to the twenty-first. Nor does this evangelical and apostolic tradition abolish the law, but rather fulfil it; the command being to keep the passover from the fourteenth moon of the first month in the evening to the twenty-first moon of the same month in the evening; which observance all the successors of St. John in Asia, since his death, and all the church throughout the world, have since followed; and that this is the true Easter, and the only one to be kept by the faithful, was not newly decreed by the council of Nice,[25] but only confirmed afresh; as the Church History informs us.

"Thus it appears, that you, Colman, neither follow the example of John, as you imagine, nor that of Peter, whose traditions you knowingly contradict; and that you agree with neither the law nor the Gospel in the keeping of your Easter. For John, keeping the Paschal time according to the decree of the Mosaic law, had no regard to the first day after the Sabbath, which you do not practice, who celebrate Easter only on the first day after the Sabbath. Peter kept Easter Sunday between the fifteenth and the twenty-first moon, which you do not, but keep Easter Sunday from the fourteenth to the twentieth moon; so that you often begin Easter on the thirteenth moon in the evening, whereof neither the law made any mention, nor did our Lord,

---

[25] The first council of Nice or Nicaea (A.D. 325) where the orthodoxy of Athanasian, as against Arian, theology was settled.

the Author and Giver of the Gospel on that day, but on the fourteenth, either eat the old passover in the evening, or deliver the sacraments of the New Testament, to be celebrated by the church, in memory of his passion. Besides, in your celebration of Easter, you utterly exclude the twenty-first moon, which the law ordered to be principally observed. Thus, as I said before, you agree neither with John nor Peter, nor with the law, nor the Gospel, in the celebration of the greatest festival."

To this Colman rejoined: "Did Anatolius,[26] a holy man, and much commended in church history, act contrary to the law and the Gospel, when he wrote, that Easter was to be celebrated from the fourteenth to the twentieth? Is it to be believed that our most reverent Father Columba [27] and his successors, men beloved by God, who kept Easter after the same manner, thought or acted contrary to the Divine writings? Whereas there were many among them, whose sanctity is testified by heavenly signs and the working of miracles, whose life, customs, and discipline I never cease to follow, not questioning their being saints in heaven."

"It is evident," said Wilfrid, "that Anatolius was a most holy, learned, and commendable man; but what have you to do with him, since you do not observe his decrees? For he, following the rule of truth in his Easter, appointed a revolution of nineteen years, which either you are ignorant of, or if you know it, though it is kept by the whole church of Christ, yet you despise it. He so computed the fourteenth moon in the Easter of our Lord, that according to the custom of the Egyptians, he acknowledged it to be the fifteenth moon in the evening; so in like manner he assigned the twentieth to Easter-Sunday, as believing that to be the twenty-first moon, when the sun had set, which rule and distinction of his it appears you are ignorant of, ·in that you sometimes keep Easter before the full of the moon, that is, on the thirteenth day. Concerning your Father Columba and his followers, whose sanctity you say you imitate, and whose rules and precepts you observe, which have been confirmed by

23 Cf. *post*, p. 113.

27 521–597 A.D., Irish civilizer of Scotland. We have his life by the Abbot Adamnan. The edition by Fowler is the best (Clarendon Press).

signs from heaven, I may answer, that when many, on the day of judgment, shall say to our Lord, 'That in his name they prophesied, and cast out devils, and wrought many wonders,' our Lord will reply, 'That He never knew them.' [28] But far be it from me, that I say so of your fathers, because it is much more just to believe what is good, than what is evil, of persons whom one does not know. Wherefore I do not deny those to have been God's servants, and beloved by Him, who with rustic simplicity, but pious intentions, have themselves loved Him. Nor do I think that such keeping of Easter was very prejudicial to them, as long as none came to show them a more perfect rule; and yet I do believe that they, if any catholic adviser had come among them, would have as readily followed his admonitions, as they are known to have kept those commandments of God, which they had learned and knew.

"But as for you and your companions, you certainly sin, if, having heard the decrees of the Apostolic See, and of the universal church, and that the same is confirmed by holy writ, you refuse to follow them; for, though your fathers were holy, do you think that their small number, in a corner of the remotest island, is to be preferred before the universal church of Christ throughout the world? And if that Columba of yours (and, I may say, ours also, if he was Christ's servant) was a holy man and powerful in miracles, yet could he be preferred before the most blessed prince of the apostles, to whom our Lord said, 'Thou art Peter, and upon this rock I will build my Church, and the gates of hell shall not prevail against it, and to thee I will give the keys of the kingdom of heaven'?" [29]

When Wilfrid had spoken thus, the king said, "Is it true, Colman, that these words were spoken to Peter by our Lord?" He answered, "It is true, O king!" Then says he, "Can you show any such power given to your Columba?" Colman answered, "None." Then added the king, "Do you both agree that these words were principally directed to Peter, and that the keys of heaven were given to him by our Lord?" They both answered, "We do." Then the king concluded, "And I also say unto you, that he is the door-keeper, whom I will not

[28] Cf. Matthew 7: 21–23.   [29] Cf. Matthew 16: 18.

contradict, but will, as far as I know and am able, in all things obey his decrees, lest, when I come to the gates of the kingdom of heaven, there should be none to open them, he being my adversary who is proved to have the keys." [30] The king having said this, all present, both great and small, gave their assent, and renouncing the more imperfect institution, resolved to conform to that which they found to be better.

An earlier discussion has already [31] put before us the economic importance of monasteries and we shall now see their importance for art. We have also observed that the civilizers of Britain were prevailingly monks. The necessity of furnishing their monastic establishments in Britain led to the introduction there of many new trades and artistic objects. The following passage from Bede's *Lives of the Holy Abbots of Wearmouth and Jarrow* will illustrate this point:

Not long after, a merchant-vessel arrived, which enabled him [32] to gratify his wish.[33] At that time, Egbert, king of Kent, had sent out of Britain a man who had been elected to the office of bishop, Wighard by name, who had been adequately taught by the Roman disciples of the blessed Pope Gregory in Kent on every topic of Church discipline: but the king wished him to be ordained bishop at Rome, in order that, having him for bishop of his own nation and language, he might himself, as well as his people, be the more thoroughly master of the words and mysteries of the holy faith, as he would then have these administered, not through an interpreter, but from the hands and by the tongue of a kinsman and fellow-countryman. But Wighard, on coming to Rome, died of a disease, with all his attendants, before he had received the dignity of bishop. Now the Apostolic Father, that the embassy of the faithful might not fail through the death of their ambassadors, called a council, and appointed

---

[30] Cf. the attitude of Coifi toward paganism, *ante*, p. 36.
[31] Cf. *ante*, pp. 19–21.
[32] I.e. Benedict Biscop, master of Bede; cf. *post*, p. 111.
[33] To visit Rome.

one of his Church to send as archbishop into Britain. This was Theodore,[34] a man deep in all secular and ecclesiastical learning, whether Greek or Latin; and to him was given, as a colleague and counsellor, a man equally strenuous and prudent, the abbot Hadrian. Perceiving also that the reverend Benedict would become a man of wisdom, industry, piety, and nobility of mind, he committed to him the newly ordained bishop, with his followers, enjoining him to abandon the travel which he had undertaken for Christ's sake; and with a higher good in view, to return home to his country, and bring into it that teacher of wisdom whom it had so earnestly wished for, and to be to him an interpreter and guide, both on the journey thither, and afterwards, upon his arrival, when he should begin to preach. Benedict did as he was commanded; they came to Kent, and were joyfully received there; Theodore ascended his episcopal throne, and Benedict took upon himself to rule the monastery of the blessed Apostle Peter, of which, afterwards, Hadrian became abbot.

He [35] ruled the monastery for two years; and then sucessfully, as before, accomplished a third voyage from Britain to Rome, and brought back a large number of books on sacred literature, which he had either bought at a price or received as gifts from his friends. On his return he arrived at Vienne, where he took possession of such as he had entrusted his friends to purchase for him. When he had come home, he determined to go to the court of Conwalh, king of the West Saxons, whose friendship and services he had already more than once experienced. But Conwalh died suddenly about this time, and he, therefore, directed his course to his native province. He came to the court of Egfrid, king of Northumberland, and gave an account of all that he had done since in youth he had left his country. He made no secret of his zeal for religion, and showed what ecclesiastical or monastic instructions he had received at Rome and elsewhere. He displayed the holy volumes and relics of Christ's blessed Apostles and martyrs, which he had brought, and found such favor in the eyes of the king, that he forthwith

---

[34] Cf. *ante*, p. 49; *post*, pp. 62, 109.
[35] I.e. Benedict Biscop.

gave him seventy hides of land out of his own estates, and ordered a monastery to be built thereon for the first pastor of his church. This was done, as I said before, at the mouth of the river Were, on the left bank, in the 674th year of our Lord's incarnation, in the second indiction, and the fourth year of Egfrid's reign.

After the interval of a year, Benedict crossed the sea into Gaul, and no sooner asked than he obtained and carried back with him some masons to build him a church in the Roman style, which he had always admired. So much zeal did he show from his love to Saint Peter, in whose honor he was building it, that within a year from the time of laying the foundation, you might have seen the roof on and the solemnity of the mass celebrated therein.

When the work was drawing to completion, he sent messengers to Gaul to fetch makers of glass (more properly artificers), who were at this time unknown in Britain, that they might glaze the windows of his church, with the cloisters and dining-rooms. This was done, and they came, and not only finished the work required, but taught the English nation their handicraft, which was well adapted for enclosing the lanterns of the church, and for the vessels required for various uses. All other things necessary for the service of the church and the altar, the sacred vessels, and the vestments, because they could not be procured in England, he took especial care to buy and bring home from foreign parts.

Some decorations and muniments there were which could not be procured even in Gaul, and these the pious founder determined to fetch from Rome; for which purpose, after he had formed the rule for his monastery, he made his fourth voyage to Rome, and returned loaded with more abundant spiritual merchandise than before. In the first place, he brought back a large quantity of books of all kinds; secondly, a great number of relics of Christ's Apostles and martyrs, all likely to bring a blessing on many an English church; thirdly, he introduced the Roman mode of chanting, singing, and ministering in the church, by obtaining permission from Pope Agatho to take back with him John, the archchanter of the church of St. Peter, and abbot of

.the monastery of St. Martin, to teach the English. This John, when he arrived in England, not only communicated instruction by teaching personally, but left behind him numerous writings, which are still preserved in the library of the same monastery. In the fourth place, Benedict brought with him a thing by no means to be despised, namely, a letter of privilege from Pope Agatho, which he had procured, not only with the consent, but by the request and exhortation of King Egfrid, and by which the monastery was rendered safe and secure for ever from foreign invasion. Fifthly, he brought with him pictures of sacred representations, to adorn the church of St. Peter, which he had built; namely, a likeness of the Virgin Mary and of the twelve Apostles, with which he intended to adorn the central nave, on boarding placed from one wall to the other; also some figures from ecclesiastical history for the south wall, and others from the Revelation of St. John for the north wall; so that every one who entered the church, even if they could not read, wherever they turned their eyes, might have before them the amiable countenance of Christ and his saints, though it were but in a picture, and with watchful minds might revolve on the benefits of our Lord's incarnation, and having before their eyes the perils of the last judgment, might examine their hearts the more strictly on that account.

When Benedict had made this man [36] abbot of St. Peter's and Ceolfrid abbot of St. Paul's, he not long after made his fifth voyage from Britain to Rome, and returned (as usual) with an immense number of proper ecclesiastical relics. There were many sacred books and pictures of the saints, as numerous as before. He also brought with him pictures out of our Lord's history, which he hung round the chapel of Our Lady in the larger monastery: and others to adorn St. Paul's church and monastery, ably describing the connexion of the Old and New Testament; as, for instance, Isaac bearing the wood for his own sacrifice, and Christ carrying the cross on which he was about to suffer, were placed side by side. Again, the serpent raised up by Moses in the desert was illustrated by the Son of Man exalted on the cross. Among other things, he brought two cloaks, all

[36] Easterwine.

of silk, and of incomparable workmanship, for which he received
an estate of three hides on the south bank of the river Were,
near its mouth, from King Alfrid, for he found on his return that
Egfrid had been murdered during his absence.

Christianity is thus seen to have been a constructive
influence in early England; it made for higher culture.
There was, however, a foreign influence brought to bear
on England, which, as we have already seen, was decidedly
destructive; namely, the Danes.[37]   Alcuin (735–804) in
the following letter pleads for national unity and purity
in the presence of the pagan peril:

To the most excellent nation and praiseworthy people and to
the imperial kingdom of the people of Canterbury, the humble
Alcuin sends greeting.

. . . A very great danger threatens this island and the people
dwelling in it.   Behold a thing never before heard of, a pagan
people is becoming accustomed to laying waste our shores with
piratical robbery; and our own people, the Angles, are disagree-
ing [38] among themselves as to kingdoms and kings.   There is
scarcely any one, a thing which I do not say without tears,
found of the ancient lineage of kings, and the more uncertain
the origin the less the bravery.   In like manner throughout all
the churches of Christ teachers of truth have perished; almost
all follow after worldly vanities and hold the regular [39] discipline
in aversion: even their warriors desire avarice rather than justice.   Read Gildas,[40] the wisest Briton, and you will see why the
parents of the Britons lost their kingdom and fatherland; then,
consider yourselves and you will find things almost the same.
Fear for yourselves the statement of the very truth which has
been given in regard to the church, saying, "Every kingdom
divided against itself will not stand." [41]   Behold how great a
division there is between the people and the tribes of the Angles;

---

[37] Cf. *ante*, p. 6.   [38] Cf. *ante*, p. 5.   [39] I. e. monastic.

[40] Cf. *ante*, p. 1.   In the concluding words of the preface to his book Gildas
suggests that his purpose will be to show how the miseries of Britain are due to
her sins.   There are many remarks in the body of the work to the same effect.

[41] Cf. Matthew 12: 25.

and on this account they are failing in their duty to themselves, because they do not preserve among themselves peace and faith. Recall, if it may be done, your bishop, Adelhard,[42] a man wise and venerable; strengthen then the state of your kingdom by his advice, removing the customs displeasing to God; study to do those things which will tend to call upon you his mercy. It is not well that the seat of St. Augustine, our first preacher, should remain vacant; no one else can in any way be ordained in Adelhard's place. It is ruinous to people everywhere not to obey the priests and to drive out from their midst the preachers of safety. Subject yourselves humbly to your bishop, the minister of your safety, that divine grace may follow you in all your works. Believe me, in no other way can you retain God's favor to you; through him you can, I believe, have peace, and hope for eternal safety. Enter into a plan for your prosperity, act manfully, and you will find it well; turn to entreaties, prayers, and fasting, that divine mercy may be gained for you, that it may preserve you in peace and safety, that it may grant to you a safe dwelling in your fatherland and a glorious kingdom in the eternal home. O worthy and venerable brethren, may the right hand of God Omnipotent protect and rule over you, and may it deem you worthy of being exalted in present happiness and eternal bliss.

The following passage, a portion of the sole extant fragment of familiar correspondence in the vernacular of pre-conquest England, puts the attitude of at least one sensitive Englishman before us in a still more intimate way. The letter as we have it is undated, but the indications are that it falls somewhere in the tenth century.

I will also say to you, brother Edward, since you have asked me about this, that you are doing wrong in giving up the English customs which your fathers held, and in hankering after the manners of heathen who hardly allow you to live. You are

[42] Adelhard (his name is spelled Ethelhard in the *Dictionary of National Biography*) was a Mercian consecrated Archbishop of Canterbury in 793. His Kentish subjects were loth to have a Mercian presiding over the see and had expelled him. He is not known as a writer. He died in 805.

making it perfectly clear by your bad habits that you despise
your kin and elders when, in order to annoy them, you dress
after the Danish fashion with neck uncovered and hair straggling down over your eyes. I sha'n't say any more about these
wretched fashions except that books tell us that he shall be excommunicated who follows heathen ways in his life and by that
means dishonors his own people.

3. *Learning in Old England.* — Bede, in an early chapter
of the fourth book of his *Ecclesiastical History*, gives the
following account of the educational activities of Archbishop Theodore of Canterbury and his assistants. Theodore was sent from Rome to carry on the work begun in
England by Augustine, and he left a deep impression on
English learning.

As both of them [43] were well read both in sacred and in secular
literature they gathered a crowd of disciples, and there daily
flowed from them rivers of knowledge to water the hearts of
their hearers; and, together with the books of holy writ, they
also taught them the arts of ecclesiastical poetry, astronomy,
and arithmetic. A testimony of which is, that there are still
living at this day some of their scholars who are as well versed
in the Greek and Latin tongues as in their own, in which they
were born.

Alcuin, in the next century, thus describes in verse the
curriculum of his *alma mater*, the famous school founded at
York by Egbert, one of Bede's pupils. Through this
school, says Mr. Gaskoin, "The old Roman city of Ebo-
racum became the intellectual centre of Christian Europe
north of Italy and Spain, and maintained that position for
nearly half-a-century, till Alcuin left his Northumbrian
home to impart to Frankish pupils at Aachen and at
Tours the learning he had himself amassed under Egbert
and his two successors." [44]

[43] I.e. Archbishop Theodore and Abbot Hadrian, see *ante*, pp. 49, 57; *post*, p. 109.
[44] *Alcuin: His Life and His Work*, p. 33. (C. J. Clay and Sons, 1904).

There the Euboric scholars felt the rule
Of Master Ælbert,[45] teaching in the school.
Their thirsty hearts to gladden well he knew
With doctrine's stream and learning's heavenly dew.
To some he made the grammar understood
And poured on others rhetoric's copious flood.
The rules of jurisprudence these rehearse,
While those recite in high Aonian verse,
Or play Castalia's flutes in cadence sweet
And mount Parnassus in swift lyric feet.
Anon the master turns their gaze on high
To view the travailing sun and moon, the sky
And starry hosts that keep the law of heaven.
The storms at sea, the earthquake's shock, the race
Of men and beasts and flying fowl they trace,[46]
Or to the laws of numbers bend their mind
And search till Easter's annual day they find.
Then, last and best, he opened up to view
The depths of Holy Scripture, Old and New.
Was any youth in studies well approved,
Then him the master cherished, taught and loved,
And thus the double knowledge he conferred
Of liberal studies and the Holy word.

Later on in the same poem, Alcuin catalogs the volumes in the Library at York as follows:

There shalt thou find the volumes that contain
All of the ancient fathers who remain,
With those that glorious Greece transferred to Rome, —
The Hebrews draw from their celestial stream,
And Africa is bright with learning's beam.

[45] Ælbert was the kinsman and eventual successor of Egbert at York.

[46] On the conception of the world current in the days of Alfred the Great, see the first chapter of King Alfred's translation of Orosius (cf. *post*, p. 64 note). This is accessible as *Old South Leaflet* No. 112 (Vol. V., pp. 245–259). Alfred's additions to Orosius' text are there indicated, the text is carefully annotated, and Sir Clements Markham, President of the Royal Geographical Society, comments on King Alfred as a geographer.

Here shines what Jerome,[47] Ambrose,[48] Hilary [49] thought
Or Athanasius [50] and Augustine [51] wrought.
Orosius,[52] Leo,[53] Gregory [54] the Great,
Near Basil [55] and Fulgentius [56] coruscate.

[47] St. Jerome (331–420 A.D.), translator of the Old and New Testaments into Latin. His translation came into common use and is hence known as the Vulgate. He was a pupil of the grammarian Donatus (cf. *infra*) at Rome, became fond of philosophy, and took great pride in his library. Plautus and Cicero were his favorite Latin authors. In 386 he founded a monastery at Bethlehem. His biographical work *De Viris Illustribus* (*On Famous Men*) is the source of much of our information about classical writers. His *Letters* are famous. Jerome was very popular during the Middle Ages. His works are the source from which many quotations found their way into medieval literature.

[48] St. Ambrose (340–397), Christian hymn-writer, who made his songs teach the doctrines of the church.

[49] Hilary was the earliest of the Christian hymn-writers of medieval Europe. He introduced church music from the East. He was born at Poictiers in France late in the third century, became bishop of Poictiers in 353, and died in 368.

[50] St. Athanasius, one of the Greek fathers of the Church (295–373), champion of what turned out to be orthodox Christianity in contrast to the unitarianism of Arius. Athanasius was an orator and controversialist.

[51] St. Augustine (354–430), one of the great theologians. We have his autobiography in his *Confessions*. In 384, he was teaching rhetoric at Milan, and in 387 was converted and baptized. He is the author of many controversial works. His *City of God*, a philosophy of life and the world from the Christian point of view, was finished in 426.

[52] Orosius, who was born in the latter part of the fourth century, was a younger friend and assistant of Augustine. His chief work, *Adversus Paganos Historiarum Libri VII* (*Seven Books of History against the Pagans*), was written to disprove the current statement that the woes of the later Roman Empire were caused by the anger of the pagan gods. Orosius shows that the world had been afflicted by just as terrible calamities before, as after, the introduction of Christianity. His book was the favorite text-book of universal history during the Middle Ages. Alfred translated it into Old English.

[53] Leo I, Pope 440–461. We have his *Letters* and *Sermons*.

[54] Gregory the Great (550–604). The Pope under whose direction Augustine came to England in 597. Gregory wrote several works that were very popular. Among these are his *Cura Pastoralis* (*Pastoral Care*) and his *Dialogs*, translated into English by Alfred the Great or under his direction. Cf. *post*, pp. 123, 129–131.

[55] St. Basil (331–379) was one of the interpreters of Christianity to the Greeks. He was the author of a work on the use of pagan poetry by Christians, which has been translated into modern English by Professor Padelford in *Yale Studies in English, XV*.

[56] Fulgentius (about 480–550) was an African grammarian. He wrote works

Grave Cassiodorus [57] and John Chrysostom [58]
Next Master Bede [59] and learned Aldhelm [60] come,

on mythology, an allegorical interpretation of Virgil and a history, *De Ætatibus Mundi* (*On the Ages of the World*).

[57] Cassiodorous (480–575) was minister of the Ostrogothic dynasty in Italy during the first half of the sixth century. Between 526 and 533 he wrote his *History of the Goths*, now lost. In 537 he brought out his *Variæ* or *Letters*, which are of extreme historical value. He wrote commentaries on the Bible, the *Tripartite History* (a history of the Church), and *Institutiones Divinarum et Humanarum Lectionum* (*Elements of Divine and Human Learning*). The latter, which consists of compendia of the liberal arts, was begun about 543. He composed a treatise on spelling (*De Orthographia*) and a *Chronicon* or *Chronicle*, an abstract of universal history down to 519 A.D. His works were widely known in the Middle Ages.

[58] St. John Chrysostom (344–404) was one of the great preachers of the Church.

[59] Bede, the Englishman so often referred to already. For documents on his life and a list of his works, cf. *post*, pp. 107–117.

[60] Aldhelm (650–709), also an Englishman, Bishop of Sherburne. "Aldhelm," says Bede (*Ecclesiastical History*, Book V., Chap. 18; Giles' tr., p. 267), "when he was only a priest and abbot of the monastery of Malmesbury, by order of a synod of his own nation, wrote a notable book against the error of the Britons, in not celebrating Easter at the proper time, and in doing several other things not consonant to the purity and the peace of the Church; and by the reading of this book he persuaded many of them, who were subject to the West Saxons, to adopt the Catholic celebration of our Lord's resurrection. He likewise wrote a notable book *On Virginity*, which, in imitation of Sedulius (cf. *infra*), he composed double, that is, in hexameter verse and prose. He wrote some other books, as being a man most learned in all respects, for he had a clean style, and was, as I have said, wonderful for ecclesiastical and liberal erudition." William of Malmesbury, the twelfth-century English historian, wrote a life of Aldhelm in which, on the authority of the note-book ascribed to Alfred the Great, he records the familiar story that "Aldhelm had observed with pain that the peasantry were become negligent in their religious duties, and that no sooner was the church service ended than they all hastened to their homes and labors, and could with difficulty be persuaded to attend to the exhortations of the preacher. He watched the occasion, and stationed himself in the character of a minstrel on the bridge over which the people had to pass, and soon collected a crowd of hearers by the beauty of his verse; when he found that he had gained possession of their attention, he gradually introduced among the popular poetry which he was reciting to them, words of a more serious nature, till at length he succeeded in impressing upon their minds a truer feeling of religious devotion; 'whereas, if' . . . 'he had proceeded with severity and excommunication, he would have made no impression whatever upon them.'" (Cf. Wright, *Biographia Britannica Literaria, Anglo-Saxon Period*, p. 215.) We have extant a number of Aldhelm's letters, about one hundred riddles in verse, the treatises *On Virginity*, and various miscellanies. (Cf. *Cambridge History of English Literature*, I., p. 80.)

While Victorinus [61] and Boethius [62] stand
With Pliny [63] and Pompeius [64] close at hand.
Wise Aristotle [65] looks on Tully [66] near,
Sedulius [67] and Juvencus [68] next appear.
There come Albinus,[69] Clement,[70] Prosper [71] too,

[61] Victorinus flourished about 300 A.D. He was a rhetorician, commentator, and translator. Among his translations are certain works on Platonic philosophy. He wrote a treatise on *Meter* in four books. He became a Christian in later life.

[62] Boethius (480–524) was the last of the pagan philosophers. His *De Consolatione Philosophiæ (On the Consolation of Philosophy)* was probably the most popular book on philosophy in the Middle Ages. Alfred the Great translated it into Old English, Chaucer into Middle English, and Queen Elizabeth into the language of her day. Boethius translated and commented on Plato, Aristotle, and Cicero. He wrote works on arithmetic, geometry, and on music which were widely used as text-books.

[63] This is Pliny the Elder, the author, in the first century after Christ, of the *Natural History*, the source of much information during the Middle Ages.

[64] Pompeius Trogus, who lived in the first century before, and the first century after, Christ completed in 9 A.D. the first *Universal History* written in Latin. It has survived to our time in an abridgement.

[65] Aristotle, called by Dante (*Inferno*, IV., 131) "the master of those who know," was probably known at this time in his logical works only, in an abstract by Cassiodorus.

[66] Tully is known more commonly to-day as Cicero (106–43 B.C.). A few only of his speeches and letters could have been known to Alcuin. "He was revered," writes Dr. Sandys (*History of Classical Scholarship*, I., p. 623), "throughout the Middle Ages as the great representative of the liberal art of Rhetoric."

[67] Sedulius (fifth century A.D.) was a hymn-writer and orator. He wrote among other things a *Carmen Paschale (Easter Song)*. He was probably a Scot from Ireland. (March, *Latin Hymns*, p. 248.) Aldhelm, according to Bede, imitated him. (Cf. *supra*.)

[68] Juvencus (about 330 A.D.) was a Christian imitator of Virgil.

[69] The Manuscript here reads *Alcuinas*. Editors generally adopt the reading in the text. Albinus was a learned abbot and friend of Bede. He succeeded Hadrian as abbot at Canterbury in 710. It was he who urged Bede to write his *Ecclesiastical History*. Cf. *post*, p. 109.

[70] This is probably Clement of Alexandria (160–215 A.D.). He was a lecturer at Alexandria. He wrote the *Exhortation*, a learned and systematic attack on paganism, dealing almost entirely with Greek mythology and speculation; *Pædagogus*, a course of instruction resting on reason as well as revelation, partly borrowed from the Greek philosophers; *Miscellanies*, in which he tried to reconcile truth and reason, paganism and Christianity.

[71] Prosper of Aquitaine (403–463 A.D.) was a priest at Marseilles in France. He was a friend of St. Augustine. His literary activity was occupied in historical composition, mostly ecclesiastical.

Paulinus [72] and Arator.[73]   Next we view
Lactantius,[74] Fortunatus.[75]   Ranged in line
Virgilius Maro,[76] Statius,[77] Lucan [78] shine.
Donatus,[79] Priscian,[80] Probus,[81] Procas,[82] start

[72] Paulinus of Nola (353–431) wrote Christian poems showing the influence of Virgil.

[73] Arator (flourished 540 A.D.) is the author of a metrical version of the *Acts of the Apostles*.

[74] Lactantius (flourished 300 A.D.) is often called "the Christian Cicero." He was a teacher of rhetoric at Nicomedia in Bithynia.   He became a Christian later in life and devoted his literary talents to the service of Christianity.   His *Institutes of Divinity* is an exposition of Christian teaching, while his *De Mortibus Persecutorum* (*On the Deaths of the Persecutors*, i.e. The Emperors who persecuted Christians) "had a large effect in fixing the tradition of the later Empire as viewed throughout the Middle Ages." (J. W. Mackail, *Latin Literature*, p. 256.)   His *De Ave Phœnice* (*On the Phœnix*) is undoubtedly the source of the Old English poem of the same title.

[75] Fortunatus (535–600) is the author of an epic on St. Martin of Tours modeled on Virgil and Claudian.

[76] Virgil (70–19 B.C.) was the most popular and best known classical Latin poet of the Middle Ages.   His reputation for learning was such that he became in popular legend a great magician.   Cf. Comparetti, *Vergil in the Middle Ages* (London, Swan, Sonnenschein & Co., 1895).

[77] Statius (40–96 A.D.), Latin epic writer, author of *Thebais* (*Story of Thebes in Greece*); *Achilleis* (*The Life of Achilles*); and of the *Silvæ* (miscellaneous poems).

[78] Lucan (39–65 A.D.) was a Latin epic writer, nephew of Seneca, the philosopher.   Lucan wrote the *Pharsalia*, a poem in ten books, on the civil war between Pompey and Cæsar, in which he takes the side of Pompey.   The poem was very popular during the Middle Ages.

[79] Donatus (flourished 355 A.D.) was the author of a grammar, in shorter and longer form, which was used throughout the Middle Ages.   So well was he known that the word *donet* taken from his name came to mean "grammar." (Cf. *Piers Plowman*, B. Text, V., l. 209.)   Donatus also wrote commentaries on Terence and Virgil.

[80] Priscian is the author of a grammar finished in 526 or 527 A.D.; of a work on numerals, weights and measures; of one on the meters of Terence; and of a volume of rhetorical themes.   The popularity of his grammar is attested by the fact that about a thousand manuscripts of it are extant.   Cf. *post*, p. 134.

[81] Probus (flourished 56–88 A.D.) was the foremost grammarian of the first century after Christ.   He edited Plautus, Terence, Lucretius, Virgil, Horace, and Persius.

[82] According to the *Dictionary of Christian Biography*, one Phocas of Edessa lived not earlier than the eighth century.   He wrote an introduction to the Syriac translation of the works of Dionysius the Areopagite.   I can find no reference to Procas, the name in the text, as a grammarian.

> The roll of masters in grammatic art;
> Eutychius,[83] Servius,[84] Pompey,[85] each extend
> The list, Comminian [86] brings it to an end.
> There shalt thou find, O reader, many more
> Famed for their style, the masters of old lore,
> Whose many volumes singly to rehearse
> Were far too tedious for our present verse.[87]

Alcuin was destined to be of great service to Charlemagne in educational work, but was not entirely satisfied with the educational outlook in his adopted country. He, therefore, writes to the Emperor comparing opportunities in England and France, as follows:

In some measure, however, I,[88] your servant, lack the choicer books of erudition which I had in my own country through the devoted industry of my teacher,[89] and even by my own slighter exertions. I say these things to your Excellency [90] to the end that, if perchance it should please your intent, so desirous of all wisdom, I may be permitted to send over some of our young men to obtain everything we need, and bring back into France the flowers of Britain. In this way not only will York be a garden enclosed, but Tours will have its outflowings of Paradise and its pleasant fruits, so that the south wind may come and blow upon the gardens of the Loire, and the spices thereof may flow out.

As far as my moderate abilities will permit, I will not be slothful in sowing the seeds of wisdom among your servants in these parts, being mindful of the sentence: 'In the morning sow thy

[83] Eutychius (flourished 488 A.D.) was an heretical theologian.

[84] Servius (born about 355 A.D.) "was famous," says Dr. Sandys (*op. cit.*, p. 218) "as a Virgilian commentator, whose work owes much of its value to its wealth of mythological, geographical, and historical learning."

[85] Pompey is a grammarian of uncertain date, used by Servius and Cassiodorus.

[86] Comminian is a Latin grammarian of the latter part of the fourth century.

[87] For a comprehensive account of foreign influence on English, cf. T. G. Tucker, *The Foreign Debt of English Literature* (Geo. Bell and Sons, 1907).

[88] Alcuin.

[89] Cook's note, "Albert, Archbishop of York from 767 to 788."

[90] Charlemagne.

seed, and in the evening withhold not thy hand, for thou knowest not whether shall prosper, either this or that, or whether they
both shall be alike good.' [91]   In the morning, when my studies,
because of my time of life, were flourishing, I sowed in Britain;
now, as my blood grows chill in the evening of my days, I cease
not to sow in France, hoping that both, by the grace of God,
may spring up.[92]

4. *Book-Making in Early England*. — The manufacture
and sale of books have had a great deal to do with the
standardizing of language in modern times.   Our information regarding these matters in the Old English Period is
limited, but we are not left wholly in the dark.   We have
already seen that books were brought from abroad, were
copied in England and gathered into libraries.   Nothing is
more characteristic of the old English civilizers and missionaries than their zeal in the collection of books.   But a fuller
realization of what their enthusiasm meant is had when one
finds out what the mechanical difficulties of book-making
at this epoch were.   These difficulties are made clear in
the document quoted below.   The document consists of
some verses which form *Riddle 27* in the collection of 95
in the Exeter Book, one of the few precious manuscripts
of Old English poetry extant.   These riddles give us many
valuable suggestions on the life of the time and the one
here quoted is among the most important.[93]

A foe deprived me of my life,[94] robbed me of worldly strength,
then dipped me in dampening water; took me thence again and
set me in the sun, where I soon lost the hair with which I had
been covered.   The keen edge of a knife then scraped me, cleansed

[91] Cf. Ecclesiastes 11: 6.

[92] Cf. William of Malmesbury, *Chronicle of the Kings of England*, Giles' tr.,
p. 62 (*Bohn Antiquarian Library*).

[93] The latest information regarding the *Riddles* is in Professor Tupper's edition
in the *Albion Series* (Ginn & Co., 1910).   Cf. also Mr. Wyatt's edition in Heath's
Belles Lettres Series.   Mr. Wyatt takes a different view from Professor Tupper in
many points.

[94] The parchment is speaking.

of all impurities; fingers folded me, and the exultant quill sprinkled me over with useful drops, passed carefully over the brown rim,[95] took up part of the ink, rested again on me, and journied on, leaving a trail of black. A craftsman then bound me in covers of leather, adorned me with gold; so that beauteous, spiral patterns made by artists embellished me. Let now these ornaments, the scarlet dye, and my glorious possessions make widely known the Lord of Hosts, and not the pains of hell. If the children o men will make use of me, they will be the safer and the more successful, the bolder in heart, and the happier in mind, the more prudent in spirit. They will have the more friends, near and dear, true and good, tried and trusty, who will gladly enchance their fame and well-being, surround them with joys and benefits, and hold them fast in bonds of love. Ask what my name is, for the good of men; my name is glorious, of service to mankind, and holy of itself.

5. *The Position of the Poet in the Earliest England.* — In the second chapter of his book *On Germany*, Tacitus remarks that ancient songs are "the only kind of tradition and history that they (the Germans) have"; and in the following chapter he adds, "They have also certain songs, by the intonation of which (*barditus*, as it is called) they excite their courage, while they divine the fortune of the coming battle from the sound itself." Numerous other references [96] indicate that poetry was highly and widely cultivated by the Teutons.

So we are not surprised to find evidence in Old English literature that the scop and gleeman were honored members of society and that the recitation of traditional poems [97] was a favorite form of amusement.

[95] The vessel containing ink.
[96] Professor Gummere, in his *Old English Ballads* (*Athenæum Press Series*, Ginn & Co., 1903), pp. 297–298, has collected the references to the ballads of Europe. Professor Padelford in his *Old English Musical Terms* (*Bonner Beiträge zur Anglistik*, IV.) shows that music of all sorts was highly developed in Old English times.
[97] Cf. William of Malmesbury's references to ballads as historical sources

Three illustrations are cited. The first, from *Widsith*, is of especial importance, since the poem is perhaps our earliest piece of vernacular verse. In the poem a minstrel tells us of his experiences as a traveling entertainer at the courts of several princes.

Widsith unlocked his word-hoard; and then spake
He among men whose travel over earth
Was farthest through the tribes and through the folks;
Treasure to be remembered came to him
Often in hall.

'Thus far I traveled through strange lands, and learnt
Of good and evil in the spacious world;
Parted from home-friends and dear kindred, far
The ways I followed. Therefore I can sing
And tell a tale, recount in the mead-hall
How men of high race gave rich gifts to me.

Thus wandering, they who shape songs for men
Pass over many lands, and tell their need,
And speak their thanks, and ever, south or north,
Meet some one skilled in songs and free in gifts,
Who would be raised among his friends to fame,
And do brave deeds till light and life are gone;
He who thus wrought himself praise, shall have
A settled glory underneath the stars.[98]

(Giles' tr., pp. 138, 148, 315.). Also Wace's references to the truth of the Arthurian legend. Cf. *Arthurian Chronicles*, translated by Eugene Mason, p. 56 (*Everyman's Library* ed.)

[98] The latest work on *Widsith* is the book by Mr. R. W. Chambers, *Widsith, a Study in Old English Heroic Legend*. Mr. Chambers studies all the references in the poem very carefully and makes his book a veritable introduction to Teutonic heroic literature. (Cambridge University Press, 1912.) Professor Gummere, in *The Oldest English Epic* (The Macmillan Co., 1909), has material on *Widsith*. He also deals with *Beowulf, Finnsburg, Waldere, Deor's Lament,* and the *German Hildebrand*. For stories of early Teutonic heroes see also Foulke tr., *History of the Langobards* (Lombards), by Paul the Deacon (*Translations and Reprints from the Original Sources of European History*, University of Pennsylvania, 1907) and Mierow tr., *The Gothic History of Jordanes* (Princeton University Press, 1915).

The second illustration, from *Beowulf*, records an ordinary court entertainment in Heorot, the stately hall built by Hrothgar in which he planned to entertain and care for his thanes. These glimpses of life in the lord's hall have been compared, and properly, to those in the Homeric epics.

Then the mighty spirit [99] whose abode was in darkness, for a time listened in agony to the loud sounds of rejoicing which came each day from the Hall.[100] There was the music of harp, the sweet song of poet. He chanted who knew how to relate from of old the creation of men; recounted how the Almighty wrought the Earth, the beauteous plain, how water encompasses it; how He renowned for his victories, established the sun and moon as lights to lighten the nations, and adorned all the corners of the Earth with boughs and leaves; how he also bestowed life on all the creatures who live and move.

The third illustration, *Deor's Lament*, registers the risks which the scop must have run, since he had to trust to the precarious favor of a prince.

Weland [101] knew anguish; the constant-hearted hero suffered heaviness of heart; he had as his companions sorrow and longing, winter-cold bitterness of spirit; he often experienced woe after Nithhad laid distress on him by cutting his sinew-bands.
He overcame that, so may I this.
Beadohild sorrowed not so much for her brothers' death as she did when she clearly knew that she was with child; she could not think how she might ever endure (her disgrace).

---

[99] I.e. the monster Grendel.   [100] I.e. Heorot, Hrothgar's hall.

[101] The references in the first two strophes are to characters in the legend of Weland. (Cf. Vigfusson and Powell, *Corpus Poeticum Boreale*, I., 168 *seq.*) Weland, according to Teutonic myth, was the first of smiths and held a position analogous to that of Hephæstus or Vulcan in classical myth. Weland and his two brothers entrapped three Swan Maidens and took them as wives. After some years of happiness, the wives, during the absence of their husbands, flew away. Weland, thereupon, was seized by Nithhad, King of the Niars, hamstrung (cf. "cutting his sinew-bands") and compelled to work for him at the forge. Weland took vengeance on Nithhad by killing his sons and violating the virginity of his daughter, Beadohild, referred to in the text as both Beadohild and Mæthilde.

She overcame that, so may I this.

We have heard many things of Maethilde; the love of the Geat [102] was boundless, so that love-sorrow robbed him of sleep.

He overcame that, so may I this.

Theodoric [103] possessed the fortress of the Maerings thirty winters, that was well known to many.

He overcame that, so may I this.

We have heard of the wolfish mind of Eormanric; [104] he ruled the great folk of the Gothic kingdom; that was a grim king! Many a man sat bound with sorrows, with woeful mind, wished enough that there might be an end to this reign.

They overcame that, so may I this.

Sorrowing he sits, deprived of joy; it grows dark in his soul; it seems to him that his share of sorrow is endless. Moreover, he should recollect that throughout the world, the all-knowing Lord makes all things to change: to many a man he shows honor, broad fame; to some, a share of woes.

I will tell of myself that once I was the bard of the Heodenings,[105] dear to my lord — my name was Deor; many winters had I a loyal following and a friendly lord, until now Heorrenda,[106] a man crafty in song, received the land which the protector of heroes gave to me before.

He overcame that, so may I this.

---

[102] I.e. her father Nithhad.

[103] Dietrich of Bern, known to history as Theodoric the Ostrogoth, master of Italy 493–526 A.D., and to legend and saga as one of the great heroes of his race.

[104] Historical King of the Ostrogoths, who, according to Ammianus Marcellinus, committed suicide in 375 A.D. in order to avoid falling into the hands of the Huns.

[105] Descendants of Hedin, seducer of the daughter of Hagen, King of Ireland, personages in the opening part of the great popular German epic of the Middle Ages, *Gudrun*.

[106] To be identified with Horand, famous singer, another character in the *Gudrun*. All of these references serve to show that the Old English had the same stock of legend and saga as their continental brethren. Two articles in *Modern Philology*, IX., one by Professor W. W. Lawrence in No. 1, the other by Professor F. Tupper in No. 2. (July and October, 1911, respectively) will help to clear up the interpretation of *Deor's Lament*. Two convenient handbooks of Teutonic legend and mythology, are the following, both found in the *Temple Encyclopedic Primers Series* published by J. M. Dent & Co.: Jiriczek, *Northern Legends*, tr. by M. Bentinck Smith; and Kaufmann, *Northern Mythology*, tr. by M. Steele Smith.

IV. THE LINGUISTIC BACKGROUND

1. *Bede on the Languages of England.* — We are so accustomed to-day to composition in the vernacular that we seldom stop to think of our real attitude toward our mother tongue. English as a vehicle for the expression of dignified thought has not always enjoyed its present position. Bede's reference, which we quote, betrays no hint that the vernacular has a peculiar status among the possible languages of a community.

This island at present, following the number of the books in which the divine law was written, contains five languages — those of the English, Britons, Scots, Picts and Latins — each examining and confessing one and the same knowledge of the highest truth and of true sublimity.

Scattered references in other writers [1] show that English was considered good enough for everyday purposes but that Latin was the proper language for serious and scholarly works. This is all that can be gathered from our sources as to the attitude of the early English toward their native language.

2. *English and Other Teutonic Languages.* — For somewhat over a century now scholars have been engaged in studying out the connections between English and other European and Asiatic languages. They have concluded that English is no isolated tongue, but that it has relatives in eight, some say nine, groups of languages. These are Sanskrit, Persian, Armenian, Greek, Latin, Albanian, Celtic and Slavic. English itself is included in the group termed the Germanic or Teutonic and finds its nearest relatives there. The versions of the Lord's Prayer in early Teutonic languages quoted below show how similar in some respects these languages are.

[1] E.g. *post*, p. 131.

Gothic (380 A.D.):

Swa nu bidyaith yus: Atta unsar thu in himinam, weihnai
namo thein; quimai thiudinassus theins; wairthai wilya theins
swe in himina yah ana airthai; hlaif unsarana thana sinteinan
gif uns himma daga; yah aflet uns thatei skulans siyaima swaswe
yah weis afletam thaim skulam unsaraim; yah ni briggais uns
in fraistubnyai, ak lauseiuns af thamma ubilin; unte theina ist
thiudangardi, yah mahts, yah wulthus in aiwins. Amen.

Old High German (MS. of the Ninth Century):

Fater unser, thu in himilom bist, giwihit si name thin. queme
richi thin. werde willeo thin, same so in himile endi in erthu.
Broot unseraz emezzigas gib uns hiutu. endi farlaz uns sculdhi
unsero, samo so wir farlazzem scolom unserem. endi ni gileidi
unsih in costunga, auh arlosi unsih fona ubile.

Old Norse (Printed A.D. 1540):

Fathir Vor, sa thu ert a himnum, helgist nafn thitt. Tikl
komi thitt riki. Verthi thinn vili svo a jorthu sem a himni.
Gef oss i dag daglight brauth. Og fyrirlat oss vorar skuldir,
svosem ver fryirlaturm vorum skulunautum. Og inn leith oss
eigi i freistni. Heldr frelsa thu oss af illu: thviatt thitt er rikit,
mattr og dyrth um allthr allda. Amen.

Old English (Late Tenth or Early Eleventh Century):

Eornustlice gebiddath [2] eow thus: Faeder ure thu the eart
on heofonum, si thin nama gehalgod. Tobecume thin rice.
Gewurthe thin willa on eorthan swa swa on heofonum. Urne
gedaeghwamlican hlaf syle us to daeg. And forgyf us urne
gyltas, swa swa we forgyfath urum gyltendum. And ne gelaed
thu us on costunge, ac alys us of yfele. Sothlice.

3. *Specimens of the Old English Dialects with Translations.* — Though the tribes which invaded England all
spoke what they themselves call English, they did not all
speak the same variety of English. We are familiar with
local differences in vocabulary and pronunciation in the

---

[2] In order to make comparison easier I have not used here the character ð
which in Old English represents the *th* sound. Cf. *post*, p. 76.

English spoken to-day and there were the same sorts of differences in early England. Four dialects are usually distinguished, called Northumbrian, Mercian, West-Saxon, and Kentish. The first was the language of the North, the second, that of the Midlands, the third, that of the main portion of Southern England, and the fourth, that of Kent. Specimens will indicate some of the variations among these four dialects. We are fortunate in having the poem known as *Cædmon's Hymn* in two of the dialects, and these versions we quote as our first and fourth specimens. The second is a Mercian version of the *Magnificat*, and the third is the so-called *Codex Aureus Inscription*.

A. Northumbrian.

> Nu scylun hergan hefaenricaes uard,
> metudaes maecti end his modgidanc,
> uerc uuldurfader; sue he uundra gihuaes,
> eci Dryctin, or astelidae.
> He aerist scop aelda barnum
> heben til hrofe, haleg scepen.
> Tha middungeard, moncynnaes uard,
> eci Dryctin, aefter tiadae
> firum foldu, frea allmectig.[3]

B. Mercian.

miclað [4]	sawul	min	dryhten	7 [5] gefaeh	gast
Magnificat	anima	mea	Dominum,	et exultavit	spiritus

min	in	gode	halwyndum	minnum	forðon	gelocade
meus	in	Deo	salutari	meo.	quia	respexit

eaðmodnisse	menenes	his	sehðe	soðlice	of	ðissum
humilitatem	ancillae	suae:	ecce	enim	ex	hoc

eadge	mic	cweoðað	alle	cneorisse	forðon	dyde
beatam	me	dicent	omnes	generationes.	quia	fecit

---

[3] For translation of this and D see *post,* p. 105.

[4] Symbol for *th* sound.

[5] Short-hand sign for *and.*

me	ða miclan	se	maehtig	is	7	halig	noma
mihi	magna	qui	potens	est;	et	sanctum	nomen

his	7	mildheortnis	his	from	cynne	in	cyn
ejus;	et	misericordia	ejus	a	progenie	in	progenie

ondredendum	hine	dyde	maehte	in	earme	his
timentibus	eum.	fecit	potentiam	in	bracchio	suo:

tostregd	oferhogan	on mode	heortan	his	ofdune sette
dispersit	superbos	mente	cordis	sui;	deposuit

maehtge	of	selde	7	upahof	eaðmode	hyngrende
potentes	de	sede;	et	exaltavit	humiles.	esurientes

gefylde	godum	7	weolie	forleort	idelhende	onfoeð
implevit	bonis;	et	divites	dimisit	inanes.	suscipit

	cneht	his	gemyndig	mildheortnisse	his
Israhel	puerum	suum	recordatus	misericordiae	suae

swe	spreocende	wes	to	feadrum	urum	Abram	
sicut	locutus	est	ad	patres		nostros	Abraham,	et

sede	his	oð	in	weoruld
semini	ejus	usque	in	saeculum.[6]

C. Kentish.

Orate pro Ceolheard *presbyteri*, Niclas, 7 Ealhhun, 7 Wulfhelm
Pray for Ceolhard the priest, Niclas, and Ealhhun, and Wulfhelm

aurifex.
the goldsmith.

In nomine Domini nostri Ihesu Christi, ic Aelfred aldermon 7
In the name of our Lord Jesus Christ, I Alfred, a magistrate,

[6] This composition, so far as the English is concerned, is what is known as a gloss; i.e an interlinear translation. We have many of these in Old English and they are of great value in helping us to determine the meanings of words. Read in the modern English Bible, Luke 1: 46–55 for a translation.

Werburg min gefera begetan ðas bec æt hæðnum herge mid
uncre clæne feo ðæt ðonne wæs mid clæne golde. 7 ðæt wit
deodan for
and Werburg my wife reclaimed these books from the heathen
army[7] with our good money; that is with pure gold. And that
we did for

Godes lufan 7 for uncre saule ðearfe, ond for ðon ðe wit noldan
ðæt ðas
God's love and for our souls' need, and because we were unwilling that

halgan beoc lencg in ðære hæðenesse wunaden, 7 nu willað
heo gesellan
these holy books remain longer among the heathen, and now we
are

inn to Cristes circan Gode to lofe 7 to wuldre 7 to
going to give them to the church of Christ for the praise, glory
and

weorfunga, 7 his ðrowunga to ðoncunca, 7 ðæm godcundan
geferscipe to
honor of God, as memorials of His sufferings, and for the enjoyment of

brucenne ðe in Cristes circan dæghwæmlice Godes lof rærað, to
ðæm
the holy company who daily in the church of Christ sing the
praise

gerade ðæt heo mon arede eghwelce monaðe for Aelfred 7
of God, on condition that they pray each month for Alfred and
for

for Werburge 7 for Alhðryðe, heora saulum to ecum lecedome,
ða hwile
Werburg and for Alhthryth, for the everlasting healing of their

---

[7] I.e. the Danish army; cf. *ante*, pp. 6, 60–62.

ðe God gesegen hæbbe ðæt fulwiht æt ðeosse stowe beon mote.
souls, so long as God decrees that baptism may be administered at this

Ec swelce ic Aelfred dux 7 Werburg biddað 7 halsiað on Godes
place. Likewise I Alfred and Werburg beg and entreat in the name of

almaetiges noman 7 on allra his haligra ðæt nænig mon seo to ðon
God almighty and in those of all His saints, that no man be so

gedyrstig ðætte ðas halgan beoc selle oððe aðeode from Cristes circan
bold as to sell these holy books or take them from Christ's church,

ðe hwile ðe fulwiht stondan mote.
so long as baptism is administered here.

Aelfred.   Werburg Alhðryð *eorum filia.*
Alfred.   Werburg.   Alhthryth their daughter.

D. *West Saxon.*

Nu we sculan herian heofonrices Weard,
Metodes mihte and his mongeðanc,
weorc Wuldorfæder; swa he wundra gehwæs,
ece Dryhten, or onstealde.
He ærest gesceop eorðan bearnum
heofon to hrofe, halig Scyppend;
ða middangeard, monncynnes Weard,
ece Dryhten, æfter teode
firum foldan, Frea Ælmihtig.

4. *The Old English Alphabet.* — To-day we use the Latin alphabet with little appreciation that it is an importation, coming in the train of Latin Christianity. The Teutons, however, before the introduction of Christianity, had an

alphabet, known as runic,[8] perhaps a modification of the Greek, and in this character one of the old English men of letters signed his name to four of his poems. We quote his signature from the *Elene* in a passage of autobiographical interest which may be regarded as a supplement to the documents in Section VI.

Old and ready for death by reason of this failing house, I thus have woven a web of words and wondrously have gathered it up; time and again have I pondered and sifted my thought in the prison of the night. I knew not fully the truth concerning the cross until wisdom revealed a broader knowledge through its marvelous power o'er the thought of my heart. I was stained with deeds of evil, fettered in sins, torn by doubts, girt round with bitter needs, until the King of might wondrously granted learning unto me as a comfort for my old age; until he gave unto me his spotless grace, and imbued my heart with it, revealed it as glorious, in time broadened it, set free my body, unlocked my heart, and loosed the power of song, which joyfully and gladly I have used in the world. Not one time alone, but often had I thought upon the tree of glory, before I had the miracle revealed regarding the glorious tree, as in the course of events I found related in books and in writings concerning the sign of victory. Ever until that time was the man buffeted in the surge of sorrow, was he a weakly flaring torch (C)[9] although he had received treasures and appled gold in the mead-hall; wroth in heart (Y), he mourned; a companion to need (N),

---

[8] Cf. *Cambridge History of English Literature*, I., Chap. 2 and bibliography. A. J. Wyatt, in his *Old English Riddles* (D. C. Heath's *Belles Lettres Series*), provides a table of the more common Old English runes and the meanings of their names. The Old English called their alphabet *futhorc*, a word made up of the first six letters of their system, just as the word *alphabet* is made up of the names of the first two letters in the Greek alphabet. The word *rune* means in Old English *secret* or *mystery* as well as *letter of the alphabet*, indicating that to our forefathers there was something mysterious about writing. There was a verb *runian* from the noun *rūn*, and this verb came down into the English of Shakespeare's time as *to round*, meaning *to whisper*, thus carrying on the idea of mystery or secrecy.

[9] The corresponding runic characters in order are: ᚻ, ᛗ, ᛏ, ᛗ, ᛈ, ᚾ, ᚷ, ᚠ. The scholar John M. Kemble, in *Archæologia*, 28: 360–364 (1840), announced his discovery that this combination of runic letters spelled Cynewulf.

he suffered crushing grief and anxious care, although before him his horse (E) measured the miles and proudly ran, decked with gold. Hope (W) is waned, and joy through the course of years; youth is fled, and the pride of old. Once (U) was the splendor of youth (?); now after that allotted time are the days departed, are the pleasures of life dwindled away, as water (L) glideth, or the rushing floods. Wealth (F) is but a loan to each beneath the heavens; the beauties of the field vanish away beneath the clouds, most like unto the wind when it riseth loud before men, roameth amid the clouds, courseth along in wrath, and then on a sudden becometh still, close shut in its narrow prison, crushed by force.

Thus shall all this world pass away, and in like manner devouring flame shall seize upon whoever was born into it, at that time when the Lord himself with a host of angels shall come into judgment. There shall each man hear the doom on all his deeds from the mouth of the judge, and likewise shall pay the penalty for all the foolish words ever spoken by him, and all his overbold thoughts. Then shall the people divide into three parts for the embrace of the flame, every man who hath ever lived throughout the broad earth. Those who have clung fast to the truth shall be highest in the flame, the throng of the blessed, the host of them that yearn for glory, the multitude of the righteous, and thus may they endure and suffer more lightly without distress. He tempers for them all the glare of the flame as shall be most easy for them and most mild. The sinful men, those stained with evil, heroes sad of heart, shall be in the middle place, shrouded with smoke amid the hot surge of fire. The third part, accursed sinful foes, false haters of men, the host of the wicked, shall be in the depth of the surge, bound fast in flame by reason of their former deeds, in the gripe of the glowing coals. Nor shall they come thereafter from the place of punishment to the memory of God, King of glory, but they shall be cast forth, His wrath-stirring foes, from that fierce flame into the depths of hell. Unlike this shall it be with the other two parts: they may look upon the Prince of angels, the God of victories. They shall be refined and freed from their sins, like pure gold that is all cleansed from every alloy, refined and

melted in the surge of the furnace's fire. Thus shall each of
those men be separated and purified from all their guilt, their
deep transgressions, by the fire of the judgment. And thereafter they may enjoy peace and eternal well-being. The Lord
of angels shall be merciful and gracious unto them, inasmuch as
they abhorred each sin, each work of guile, and called upon the
Son of the Creator in their prayers. Wherefore now their forms
shall shine like unto the angels, and they shall enjoy the heritage of the King of glory for ever and ever.[10]   Amen.

V. LITERARY CHARACTERISTICS

1. *The Spirit of Early English Literature.* — It is a difficult matter to choose specific selections to illustrate the
spirit of a body of national literature. But the poems to
be quoted will do much, if read with the writings already
examined in mind, to lead us into sympathetic relations
with the animating motives of Old English literature.

Our first illustration, in the spirited rendering of Tennyson, brings before us that trait of Germanic life which
would occur to many as its leading feature — a devotion
to military pursuits which Tacitus found [1] to be the pre-
dominating business of the German freeman. *The Battle
of Brunanburh* is all the more interesting, since in the original, it is found as the entry for the year 937 in the *Anglo-
Saxon Chronicle* and celebrates the glorious victory won by
Athelstan. "It is a markedly patriotic poem and shows
deep feeling; its brilliant lyrical power, and the national
enthusiasm evident throughout, have made it familiar, in
one form or another, to all lovers of English verse. Great
care was taken with the meter, which is the ancient rhetorical verse." [2]

[10] Cf. C. F. Brown in *Englische Studien*, 40 (1909), pp. 1–29, *Irish-Latin Influence in Cynewulfian Texts.*

[1] Cf. *ante*, pp. 8–19.

[2] See *Cambridge History of English Literature*, I, pp. 151–152; *Political History
of England* (Hunt and Poole), I. (Hodgkin), pp. 334–337.

I

Athelstan [3] King
Lord among Earls,
Bracelet-bestower and
Baron of Barons,
He with his brother,
Edmund [4] Atheling,
Gaining a lifelong
Glory in battle,
Slew with the sword-edge
There by Brunanburh,
Brake the shield-wall,
Hewed the linden-wood,
Hacked the battle-shield,
Sons of Edward [5] with hammered brands.

II

Theirs was a greatness
Got from their grandsires —
Theirs that so often in
Strife with their enemies
Struck for their hoards and their hearths and their homes.

III

Bowed the spoiler,
Bent the Scotsman,
Fell the ship-crews
Doomed to the death.
All the field with blood of the fighters
Flowed, from when first the great
Sun-star of morning-tide,
Lamp of the Lord God,
Lord everlasting,

[3] Athelstan (895–940), grandson of Alfred the Great and King of England, was fighting in this battle against a coalition of Scots and Danes.

[4] Edmund (922?–946), half-brother of Athelstan and his successor as King of England.

[5] Edward, surnamed the Elder (died 924), son of Alfred the Great and his successor as King of England, father of Athelstan and Edmund.

Glode over earth till the glorious creature
Sank to his setting.

IV

There lay many a man
Marred by the javelin,
Men of the Northland
Shot over shield.
There was the Scotsman
Weary of war.

V

We the West-Saxons,
Long as the daylight
Lasted, in companies
Troubled the track of the host that we hated.
Grimly with swords that were sharp from the grindstone,
Fiercely we hacked at the flyers before us.

VI

Mighty the Mercian,
Hard was his hand-play,
Sparing not any of
Those that with Anlaf,[6]
Warriors over the
Weltering waters
Borne in the bark's-bosom,
Drew to this island —
Doomed to the death.

VII

Five young kings put asleep by the sword-stroke,
Seven strong Earls of the army of Anlaf
Fell on the war-field, numberless numbers,
Shipmen and Scotsmen.

[6] There were two Anlafs in the coalition against Athelstan, cousins, both kings
of bands of Danes settled in Ireland.

VIII

Then the Norse leader,[7]
Dire was his need of it,
Few were his following,
Fled to his war-ship;
Fleeted his vessel to sea with the king in it,
Saving his life on the fallow flood.

IX

Also the crafty one,
Constantinus,[8]
Crept to his North again,
Hoar-headed hero!

X

Slender warrant had
He to be proud of
The welcome of war-knives —
He that was reft of his
Folk and his friends that had
Fallen in conflict,
Leaving his son too
Lost in the carnage,
Mangled to morsels,
A youngster in war!

XI

Slender reason had
He to be glad of
The clash of the war-glaive —
Traitor and trickster
And spurner of treaties —
He nor had Anlaf
With armies so broken
A reason for bragging
That they had the better

---

[7] I.e. Anlaf, mentioned above.   [8] King of Scots.

In perils of battle
On places of slaughter —
The struggle of standards,
The rush of the javelins,
The crash of the charges,
The wielding of weapons —
The play that they played with
The children of Edward.

XII

Then with their nailed prows
Parted the Norsemen, a
Blood-reddened relic of
Javelins over
The jarring breaker, the deep-sea billow,
Shaping their way toward Dyflen [9] again,
Shamed in their souls.

XIII

Also the brethren,
King and Atheling,
Each in his glory,
Went to his own in his own West-Saxonland,
Glad of the war.

XIV

Many a carcase they left to be carrion,
Many a livid one, many a sallow-skin —
Left for the white-tailed eagle to tear it, and
Left for the horny-nibbed raven to rend it, and
Gave to the garbaging war-hawk to gorge it, and
That gray beast, the wolf of the weald.

XV

Never had huger
Slaughter of heroes
Slain by the sword-edge —

[9] I.e. Dublin.

Such as old writers
Have writ of in histories —
Hapt in this isle, since
Up from the East hither
Saxon and Angle from
Over the broad billow
Broke into Britain with
Haughty war-workers who
Harried the Welshman, when
Earls that were lured by the
Hunger of glory gat
Hold of the land.[10]

The second illustration is one of the most beautiful of our Old English poems, elegiac in nature, serious and even gloomy in tone. We do not know its date; but it is interesting to compare this product of long-past experience with a poem of comparatively recent origin like Arnold's *Dover Beach* and observe the similarity of mood. English poetry has dealt much with sea-themes and these verses are characteristic. We note the brooding over the power of fate and the spirit of loyalty to one's lord which are common themes of Teutonic poetry.

"Still the lone one and desolate waits for his Maker's ruth —
God's good mercy, albeit so long it tarry, in sooth.
Careworn and sad of heart, on the watery ways must he
Plow with the hand-grasped oar — how long? — the rime-cold sea,

---

[10] Henry of Huntingdon (Forester's tr., *Bohn Antiquarian Library*, p. 169), in his account of the reign of Athelstan, refers to the Battle of Brunanburh and says of the Old English poem: "Of the grandeur of this conflict English writers have expatiated in a sort of poetical description, in which they have employed both *foreign* words and metaphors. I therefore give a faithful version of it, in order that, by translating their recital almost word for word, the majesty of the language may exhibit the majestic achievements and the heroism of the English nation." The italics are mine. Henry lived from 1084 (?) to 1155, and his use of the term *foreign* in relation to Old English indicates that a knowledge of that language was not a part of the equipment of the learned generally in the 12th century. (The quotation is from Huntingdon's *History of the English*, Book V, *anno* 924.)

Tread thy paths of exile, O Fate, who are cruelty."
Thus did a wanderer speak, being heart-full of woe, and all
Thoughts of the cruel slayings, and pleasant comrades' fall:
"Morn by morn I, alone, am fain to utter my woe;
Now is there none of the living to whom I dare to show
Plainly the thought of my heart; in very sooth I know
Excellent is it in man that his breast he straightly bind,
Shut fast his thinkings in silence, whatever he have in his
mind.
The man that is weary in heart, he never can fate withstand;
The man that grieves in his spirit, he finds not the helper's
hand.
Therefore the glory-grasper full heavy of soul may be.
So, far from my fatherland, and mine own good kinsmen free,
I must bind my heart in fetters, for long, ah! long ago,
The earth's cold darkness covered my giver of gold [11] brought
low;
And I, sore stricken and humbled, and winter-saddened, went
Far over the frost-bound waves to seek for the dear content
Of the hall of the giver of rings; [11] but far nor near could I find
Who felt the love of the mead-hall,[12] or who with comforts kind
Would comfort me, the friendless. 'Tis he alone will know
Who knows, being desolate too, how evil a fere is woe;
For him the path of the exile, and not the twisted gold; [13]
For him the frost in his bosom, and not earth-riches [14] old.
"O, well he remembers the hall-men, the treasure bestowed in the
hall;
The feast that his gold-giver [11] made him, the joy at its highth,
at its fall;
He knows who must be forlorn for his dear lord's counsels gone,
Where sleep and sorrow together are binding the lonely one;
When himthinks he clasps and kisses his leader of men, and lays
His hands and head on his knee, as when in the good yore-days,

[11] Kennings for the lord.
[12] Cf. the situation in *Beowulf* where Hrothgar builds his hall Heorot for the care and entertainment of his thanes. The hall of the lord became the center of the social life of the community.
[13] I.e. the ring or bracelet given him by his lord.   [14] I.e. a landed estate.

He sat on the throne of his might, in the strength that wins and
    saves.
But the friendless man awakes, and he sees the yellow waves,
And the sea-birds dip to the sea, and broaden their wings to the
    gale,
And he sees the dreary rime, and the snow commingled with hail.
O, then are the wounds of his heart the sorer much for this,
The grief for the loved and lost made new by the dream of old
    bliss.
His kinsmen's memory comes to him as he lies asleep,
And he greets it with joy, with joy, and the heart in his breast
    doth leap;
But out of his ken the shapes of his warrior-comrades swim
To the land whence seafarers bring no dear old saws for him;
Then fresh grows sorrow and new to him whose bitter part
Is to send o'er the frost-bound waves full often his weary heart.
For this do I look around this world, and cannot see
Wherefore or why my heart should not grow dark in me.
When I think of the lives of the leaders, the clansmen mighty in
    mood;
When I think how sudden and swift they yielded the place where
    they stood.
So droops this mid-earth [15] and falls, and never a man is found
Wise ere a many winters have girt his life around.
Full patient the sage must be, and he that would counsel teach —
Not over-hot in his heart, nor over-swift in his speech;
Nor faint of soul nor secure, nor fain for the fight nor afraid;
Nor ready to boast before he know himself well arrayed.
The proud-souled man must bide when he utters his vaunt, until
He knows of the thoughts of the heart, and whitherward turn
    they will.
The prudent must understand how terror and awe shall be,
When the glory and weal of the world lie waste, as now men see
On our mid-earth, many a where, the wind-swept walls arise,
And the ruined dwellings and void, and the rime that on them
    lies.

[15] In Teutonic mythology earth, the abode of men, was conceived as situated
between the home of the gods and the place of the departed.

The wine-halls crumble, bereft of joy the warriors lie,
The flower of the doughty fallen, the proud ones fair to the eye.
War took off some in death, and one did a strong bird bear
Over the deep; and one — his bones did the gray wolf share;
And one was hid in a cave by a comrade sorrowful-faced.
O, thus the Shaper of men hath laid the earth all waste,
Till the works of the city-dwellers, the works of the giants [16] of
     earth,
Stood empty and lorn of the burst of the mighty revelers'
     mirth.
"Who wisely hath mused on this wallstead, and ponders this
     dark life well,
In his heart he hath often bethought him of slayings many and
     fell,
And these be the words he taketh, the thoughts of his heart to
     tell:
'Where is the horse and the rider? Where is the giver of
     gold?
Where be the seats at the banquet? Where be the hall-joys of
     old?
Alas for the burnished cup, for the byrnied chief to-day !
Alas for the strength of the prince ! for the time hath passed
     away —
Is hid 'neath the shadow of night, as it never had been at all.
Behind the dear and doughty there standeth now a wall,
A wall that is wondrous high, and with wondrous snake-work
     wrought.
The strength of the spears hath fordone the earls and hath made
     them naught,
The weapons greedy of slaughter, and she, the mighty Wyrd; [17]
And the tempests beat on the rocks, and the storm-wind that
     maketh afeard —
The terrible storm that fetters the earth, the winter-bale,

---

[16] We have already seen that according to Tacitus the Teutons did not live in cities. (Cf. *ante*, p. 14.) In fact, they looked on the walls and buildings of cities as miracles, works performed by giants.

[17] I.e. Fate, one of the leading concepts in Teutonic mythology. Cf. the *wierd sisters* in *Macbeth*.

When the shadow of night falls wan, and wild is the rush of the
    hail,
The cruel rush from the north, which maketh men to quail.
Hardship-full is the earth, o'erturned when the stark Wyrds say:
Here is the passing of riches, here friends are passing away;
And men and kinsfolk pass, and nothing and none may stay;
And all this earth-stead here shall be empty and void one
    day'"[18]

    2. Literary Types. — Old English Literature is char-
acterized by its simple literary form and style, its un-
sophisticated versification and rhetoric, and by its restricted
range of types.[19] We have already examined in other connections some of the most abundant sorts of our earliest
writings[20] and thus need add here only such as we have
not touched on.

    The first of these is the homily or sermon, a mode of
expression much used in the Middle Ages for a variety of
purposes. Ælfric, Abbot of Eynsham from 1005 to a date
in the neighborhood of 1020, is the most prolific writer of
homilies in the vernacular whose works have come down to
us. He is the foremost representative of English culture
in the late tenth and early eleventh centuries. His homilies cover a variety of subjects and of them all I have
chosen this fragment, *On the False Gods,* both because of

---

[18] See the essay *Old English Poetry* in Richard's Burton's *Literary Likings*, pp.
175 *seq.* See Apollinaris Sidonius on the Saxon sea-rovers in Hodgkin, *Italy and
Her Invaders*, II, pp. 366, 367. The letter is reprinted in Hodgkin's tr. in Tuell
and Hatch, *Selected Readings in English History*, pp. 9, 10 (Ginn & Co., 1913).
The great mass of extant Old English poetry is religious in subject-matter, but no
essential difference in spirit is to be observed between these religious poems and
the two secular ones quoted. Hence, I have not thought it necessary to include
here any passages from the religious poems.

[19] This statement is true, of course, only in relation to the complexity of the
later periods.

[20] E.g. passages from history on pp. 2–7, 36–38, 39–56, etc.; laws on pp. 22–25;
a dialog on pp. 26–34; letters on pp. 60, 61, 68; narrative verse on pp. 34, 35, 63–
68, 69, 71, 72; lyrics on pp. 72–73, 83–91; a form of bequest on pp. 77–79.

its intrinsic merit and because of the light it throws on the culture of the day.[21]

Beloved brethren, divine Scripture teaches us the worship of one true God, in these words, "There is one Lord, one faith, one baptism, one God and Father of all, who is above all, and through all, and in you all. Of Him are all things, and through Him are all things, and in Him are all things; to whom be glory forever. Amen."[22]

The Almighty Father begat a Son of Himself, without intercourse of woman, and by the Son He made all creatures, both seen and unseen. The Son is just as old as the Father, for the Father was always without beginning, and the Son was always begotten of Him without beginning, as mighty as the Father. The Holy Ghost is not begotten but is the Will and the Love of the Father and the Son, of them both alike; and by the Holy Ghost are quickened all creatures that the Father created by His Son, who is His Wisdom. The Holy Trinity is one Almighty God, ever without beginning and end. They are three in name — Father, Son, and Holy Ghost — but they are not three Gods; these three are one Almighty God, inseparable, for in these three there is one nature, one intelligence, and one energy in all things, and it is better for us to believe truly in the Holy Trinity, and to confess it, than to wonder too much about it.

This Trinity created the bright angels, and then Adam and Eve as human beings, giving them dominion over earthly creatures. And they might have lived forever, without death, if they had never broken that one commandment of God. Adam then dwelt in happiness, free from care, and no creature could harm him so long as he kept the heavenly behest. No fire hurt him, though he stepped into it, nor could water drown the man, even if he suddenly ran into the waves. Neither could any wild beast injure him. No more could hunger, nor thirst, grievous cold, nor extreme heat, nor sickness afflict Adam in the world, so long as he kept that little commandment with faith. But

---

[21] Material to be introduced in the next section will show what the range of Old English literature is; e.g. Alfred's and Ælfric's prefaces. Cf. *Cambridge History of English Literature*, I, Chap. VII, and bibliography for a treatment of the Old English homilists.   [22] Ephesians 4: 5.

when he had sinned and broken God's behest, he lost happiness, and lived in toil, so that lice and fleas boldly bit him whom formerly not even the serpent had dared to touch. Then he had to beware of water and of fire, and to be on the watch lest harm befall him, and to provide food for himself by his own toil. Moreover, the natural gifts with which God had endowed him he had to guard with great care in order to keep them. Even so the good do still, they who with toil keep themselves from sins.

The sun also, and likewise the moon, were deprived of their fair light after Adam's guilt, though not of their own deserts. The sun had been seven times brighter before man sinned, while the moon had the light which the sun now gives us. Nevertheless, after the Day of Judgment they shall again have their full light with which they were created. And the moon shall not grow old, but shall shine undiminished, even as the sun does now.

With much effort men may bring it to pass that they dwell with God in eternal happiness after the Day of Judgment, forever without death, if in their deeds they now obey His commandments. But those who deny God shall be plunged into hell, into everlasting punishments and endless torments.

Now we do not read in Scripture that men set up idolatry during any of the time before Noah's flood, and not until the giants made the wonderful tower after Noah's flood, and God gave them as many tongues as there were workmen. Then they separated and went into distant lands, and mankind increased. Then they were taught by the old devil who had formerly deceived Adam, and they wickedly fashioned gods for themselves, forsaking the Creator who had made them men. And they con-s'dered it the part of wisdom to worship as gods the sun and the moon, because of their resplendent light, and offered them gifts, neglecting their Creator. Some men also said of the bright stars that they were gods, and willingly worshipped them. Some believed in fire, for its quick burning, some also in water, and worshipped these as gods; while others believed in the earth, since it nourishes all things. But they might have discerned, if they had had the sense, that there is one God who created all things for men's use, through His great goodness. Creatures do just as their Creator taught them, and can do nothing but the will of the Lord, for there is no Creator save the one true God. And we worship Him with firm faith, saying with our lips, and in all sincerity of mind, that He alone is God who created all things. Yet the heathen would not be satisfied with so few gods, but began to worship as gods various giants, and men who, though they lived shamefully, were powerful in worldly affairs, and terrible in their lives.

There was a man living in the island Crete, whose name was Saturn, so violent and cruel that he devoured his sons when they were born, in an unfatherly manner making their flesh food for himself. Yet he left one alive, though he had previously devoured the brothers. This one was called Jove, malignant and mighty. He drove his father out of the aforesaid island, and would have slain him had he approached. This Jove was so licentious that he married his sister, who was named Juno, a very great goddess. Their daughters were Minerva and Venus, both of whom the father foully debauched; and many of his kinswomen he also infamously defiled. These wicked men were the greatest gods that the heathen worshipped and converted into gods. The son, however, was more worshipped in their foul idolatry than was the father. This Jove was the most venerable of all the gods whom the heathen in their error had; among certain nations he was called Thor, most beloved of the Danish people. His son was named Mars, who continually made dissensions, and stirred up calumnies and misery. The heathen worshipped him as a great god; and as often as they marched out, or decided to fight, they offered their sacrifices in advance to this god, believing that he could aid them greatly in battle, since he loved battle.

There was a man named Mercury while he lived, very crafty and deceitful in deeds, loving thefts and falsehood. The heathen made him a powerful god, offering him gifts at the meeting of the ways, and bringing him sacrifices on the high hills. This god was honored among all the heathen; in Danish he is called Odin.

A certain woman was named Venus, the daughter of Jove, so vile in lust that her father and also her brother had her as a harlot, as did also some others; yet the heathen honor her as a great goddess, as the daughter of their god. Many other gods, and also goddesses, were devised in various ways, and held in great honor throughout the whole world, to the ruin of mankind; but these, notwithstanding their shameful lives, must be reckoned the principal ones. The artful devil who lurks about men led the heathen into the great error of taking for gods foul men who loved sins that please the devil, and brought it to pass that their worshippers also loved their filthiness, and were estranged from Almighty God, who loathes sin and loves purity.

They also appointed a day for the sun and the moon and for the other gods, giving to each his day — Sunday to the sun, Monday to the moon; the third day they devoted to Mars, their battle-god, that he might aid them. The fourth day they gave, for their own advantage, to the aforesaid Mercury, their great god. The fifth day they solemnly consecrated to Jove, the greatest god. The sixth day they appointed for the shameless goddess called Venus — Frigg in Danish. To the ancient Saturn, father of the gods, they gave their own profit, the seventh day, the last of all, though he was the oldest.

Wishing to pay the gods still more honor they bestowed on them stars, as if they had dominion over them — the seven heavenly bodies, the sun and the moon, and the five others which always move toward the east, against the firmament, but which the heaven always turns back. Yet the stars shone in the heavens at the beginning of the world, before the wicked gods were born, or chosen as divinities.

The second literary type chosen for illustration here is the saint's life, a peculiarly medieval form.[23] And from all the Old English lives of saints, I have selected Ælfric's *Life of Saint and King Oswald* because of its national interest.

After Augustine came to England, there was a noble king called Oswald in the land of the Northumbrians, who believed

[23] Cf. Chaucer, *Troilus and Criseyde*, Book II, ll. 117–118, where Cressida, presumably a Trojan, speaks of reading saints' lives.

greatly in God. He went in his youth from his friends and
kindred by sea to Scotland,[24] and was there forthwith baptized,
together with his companions who had traveled with him. About
that time Edwin his uncle, king of the Northumbrians, who believed in Christ,[25] was slain by the British king named Cadwalla,
and (also) two of his successors within two years; and this
Cadwalla slew and shamefully ill-treated the Northumbrian
people after their lord's fall, until Oswald the blessed extinguished
his wickedness.[26] Oswald came to him and fought boldly against
him with a little army, but his faith strengthened him, and
Christ helped him to the slaughter of his enemies. Then Oswald
raised a cross quickly to the honor of God before he came to
battle, and cried to his companions, "Let us fall down before
the cross, and pray the Almighty that He will save us against
the proud enemy who desires to kill us. God Himself knoweth
well that we fight justly against this cruel king, to deliver our
people." Then they all fell down in prayer with Oswald, and
afterward on the next morning went to the fight, and there won
the victory, even as the almighty ruler granted them for Oswald's faith, and subdued their enemies the proud Cadwalla,
with his great host, who thought that no army could withstand
him. The same cross which Oswald had there erected, afterward stood there for worship. And many infirm men were
healed, and also cattle through the same cross, as Bede hath
related to us.

A certain man fell on ice and broke his arm, and lay in bed
very severely afflicted, until some one fetched to him, from the
aforesaid cross, some part of the moss with which it was overgrown, and the sick man was forthwith healed in sleep in the
same night, through Oswald's merits. The place is called Heaven-
field in English, near the long wall which the Romans built,
where Oswald overcame the cruel king. And afterward there
was reared a very famous church to the honor of God who liveth

[24] I.e. Ireland.

[25] Skeat's note refers to Bede, *Ecclesiastical History of the English Nation*, III, 2.
Cf. *ante*, pp. 6, 36–38.

[26] This sentence will illustrate the statement on p. 3, *ante*, about the slowness of
the English conquest of Britain.

for ever. Well then ! Oswald began to enquire concerning the
will of God as soon as he obtained sovereignty, and desired to
convert his people to the faith and to the living God. Then he
sent to Scotland where the faith was then, and prayed the chief
men that they would grant his requests, and send him some
teacher who might allure his people to God, and this was granted
to him. Then they sent straightway to the blessed king a certain venerable bishop, named Aidan.[27] He was a very famous
man in the monastic way of life, and he had cast away all
worldly cares from his heart, desiring nothing but God's will.
Whatever came to him of the king's gifts, or (of those) of rich
men, that he quickly distributed to the poor and needy with
benevolent mind. Lo then ! Oswald the king rejoiced at his
coming, and honorably received him as a benefit to his people,
that their faith might be turned again to God from the apostasy
to which they had been turned. It befell then that this believing king explained to his counsellors in their own language the
bishop's preaching with glad mind, and was his interpreter, because he knew Irish well, and bishop Aidan could not as yet
turn his speech into the Northumbrian dialect [28] quickly enough.
The bishop then went preaching faith and baptism throughout
all Northumbria and converted the people to God's faith, and
he ever set them a good example by (his) works, and himself so
lived as he taught others. He loved self-restraint and holy
reading, and zealously drew on young men with knowledge, so
that all his companions, who went with him, had to learn the
Psalms or some reading, whithersoever they went, preaching to
the people. He would seldom ride, but traveled on his feet, and
lived as a monk among the laity with much discretion and true
virtues. King Oswald became very charitable and humble in manners, and in all things bountiful, and they reared churches every-
·where in his kingdom, and monastic foundations with great zeal.
    It happened upon a certain occasion that they sat together,
Oswald and Aidan, on the holy Easter Day; then they bare
to the king the royal meats on a silver dish. And anon there
came in one of the king's thegns who had charge of his alms,
and said that many poor men were sitting in the streets, come

[27] Cf. *ante*, p. 47.   [28] Cf. *ante*, p. 76.

from all quarters to the king's alms-giving. Then the king immediately sent to the poor the silver dish, victuals and all, and bade the men cut the dish in pieces and give it to the poor, to each of them his portion, and they then did so. Then the noble bishop Aidan took the king's right hand with much joy, and cried out with faith, thus saying to him: "May this blessed right hand never rot in corruption." And it happened to him even as Aidan had prayed for him, that his right hand is sound until this day. Then Oswald's kingdom became greatly enlarged, so that four peoples received him as their lord, Picts, Britons, Scots and Angles, even as the Almighty God united them for the purpose, because of Oswald's merits, who ever honored Him. He completed in York the noble minster which his kinsman Edwin had before begun, and labored for the heavenly kingdom with continual prayers, much more than he cared how he might preserve the transitory dignities in the world, which he little loved. He would very often pray after matins, and stand in the church apart in prayer from the time of sun-rise with great fervor; and wheresoever he was he ever worshipped God with the palms of his hands uplifted heavenward.

At that same time also a certain bishop [29] came from the city of Rome, called Birinus, to the king of the West Saxons, called Cynegils, who was yet a heathen, as was all the land of the West Saxons. Birinus indeed came from Rome by desire of the Pope, who was then in Rome, and promised that he would execute God's will and preach to the heathen the Savior's name and the true faith in far lands. Then he came to Wessex, which was as yet heathen, and converted to God the king Cynegils and all his people to the faith with him. Then it happened that the faithful Oswald, the king of the Northumbrians, had come to Cynegils, and took him to baptism, fain of his conversion. Then the kings, Cynegils and Oswald, gave to the holy Birinus the city of Dorchester for a bishop's see and he dwelt therein, exalting the praise of God, and guiding the people in the faith by his teaching for a long time, until he happily departed to Christ; and his body was buried in the same city, until afterwards bishop

[29] Skeat's note refers to Bede, *op. cit.*, III, 7.

Hedda carried his bones to Winchester, and with honor deposited them in the old Minster, where men honor them yet.

Now Oswald the king held his kingdom [30] gloriously as for the world, and with great faith, and in all his deeds honored his Lord, until he was slain in the defence [31] of his people in the ninth year that he had obtained the rule, when he himself was thirty-eight years old. It happened because Penda, king of the Mercians, made war upon him, he who had formerly assisted Cadwalla at the slaying of his kinsman king Edwin; and this Penda knew nothing of Christ, and all the Mercian people were unbaptized as yet. They both came to battle at Maserfield, and engaged together until the Christians fell, and the heathen approached the holy Oswald. Then he saw approach his life's ending, and he prayed for his people who died falling, and commended their souls and himself to God, and thus cried in his fall, "God have mercy on our souls." Then the heathen king commanded to strike off his head and his right arm, and to set them up as a mark (trophy). Then after the slaying of Oswald his brother Oswy [32] succeeded to the kingdom of Northumbria, and rode with an army to where his brother's head was fastened on a stake, and took his head and his right hand, and with reverence brought them to Lindisfarne church.

There was fulfilled, as we said before, that his right hand continueth whole with the flesh, without any corruption, as the bishop had said. The arm was laid reverently in a shrine wrought of silver-work in Saint Peter's Minster within the town of Bamborough, by the sea-strand, and lieth there as sound as when it was cut off. His brother's daughter afterward became Queen of Mercia, and asked for his bones and brought them to Lindsey, to Bardney Minster, which she greatly loved. But the monks would not, by reason of human error, receive the Saint, but they pitched a tent over the holy bones that were within the hearse. Behold then God showed that he

[30] Skeat's note refers to Bede, *op. cit.*, III, 9.

[31] These statements that follow will illustrate the remarks on p. 5, *ante*, regarding the intertribal wars of the English.

[32] This is the same Oswy who called the conference at Whitby in 664. Cf. *ante*, pp. 49–56.

was a holy saint so that a heavenly light, being extended over
the tent, stood up to heaven like a lofty sunbeam all night long,
and the people beheld it throughout all the province, greatly
wondering. Then the monks were much affrighted, and prayed
then in the morning that they might reverently receive the
Saint, him whom they had before refused. Then they washed
the holy bones, and bare them reverently to a shrine in the
church, and laid them up. And there were healed through his
holy merits many infirm men of various diseases. The water
with which they had washed the bones within the church had
been poured out as it were in a corner, and the earth afterward
that had received the water became a remedy to many. By
means of that dust devils were put to flight from men who before
were afflicted with madness. So also from the spot where he
fell slain in the battle men took of the earth for diseased men,
and put it in water for the sick to taste, and they were healed
through the holy man.

A certain wayfaring man rode towards the field, when his
horse became sick, and soon fell down there rolling all over the
earth, most like a mad creature. While it was thus rolling about
the extensive field, it came at length where king Oswald fell in
the flight, as we have said before; and it rose up as soon as it
touched the place, whole in all its limbs, and the master rejoiced
thereat; the rider then went forward on his way whither he had
intended. Then there was a maiden lying in paralysis, long
afflicted; he began to relate what had happened to him during
the ride and they carried the maiden to the aforesaid place.
Then she fell asleep, and soon afterwards awoke, sound in all
her limbs from the terrible disease; she covered up her head
and blithely journied home, going on foot as she had never done
before.

Again afterward, a certain horseman bound on an errand was
passing by the same place, and bound up in a cloth some of the
holy dust from the precious place, and carried it forward with
him to where he was hastening. He met with some merry guests
at the house; he hung the dust on a high post, and sat with the
revellers rejoicing together. There was a great fire made in the
midst of the guests, and the sparks wound towards the roof

quickly, until the house suddenly became all on fire, and the revellers fled frightened away. The house was entirely consumed except the one post whereon the holy dust was hung. The post alone remained whole, together with the dust, and they greatly wondered at the holy man's merits, that the fire could not consume the mould. And many men afterward sought the place, fetching thence their cure, and (some) for each of their friends.

His fame spread widely throughout those lands,[33] and also to Ireland, and also southward to Frankland (Germany), even as a certain mass-priest told concerning one man. The priest related that there was in Ireland a learned man who took little heed of his doctrine, and he cared little about his soul's needs, or his Creator's commands, but passed his life in foolish works until he became sick, and was brought (near) to his end. Then he called the priest who afterwards made it known thus, and said to him forthwith with sorrowful voice, "Now must I die a wretched death, and go to hell for wicked deeds; now would I make amends, if I might remain and turn to God and to good ways, and change all my life to God's will; and I know that I am not worthy of the respite, except some saint intercede for me to the Savior Christ. Now it is told us that a certain holy king is in your country, named Oswald; now if thou hast anything (as a) relic of the saint, give it me, I pray thee." Then the priest said to him, "I have (a piece) of the stake on which his head stood, and if thou wilt believe, thou shalt become whole." So the priest had pity on the man, and scraped (shaved) into holy water some of the sacred tree and gave to the diseased man to drink, and he soon recovered, and afterward lived long in the world, and turned to God with all his heart, and with holy works; and whithersoever he came he made known these wonders. Therefore no man ought to nullify that which he of his own will promiseth to Almighty God when he is sick, lest he should lose himself, if he deny that to God.

Now saith the holy Bede who indited this book,[34] it is no wonder that the holy king should heal sickness, now that he liveth in heaven, because he desired to help, when he was here

---

[33] Skeat's note refers to Bede, *op. cit.*, III, 13.
[34] Evidently Bede's *Ecclesiastical History* is meant.

on earth, the poor and weak, and to give them sustenance. Now hath he honor with Almighty God in the eternal world for his goodness. Afterward the holy Cuthbert,[35] when he was yet a boy, saw how the angels of God carried the soul of Aidan, the holy bishop, joyfully to Heaven, to the eternal glory which he had merited on earth. The holy Oswald's bones were afterwards brought after many years into Mercia to Gloucester, and God there often showed many wonders through the holy man. For this be glory to the Almighty God, who reigneth in eternity for ever and ever. Amen.

As the modern drama originated in the services of the church, we shall close this part of our study by citing a translation of the Winchester trope of 973, which gives us an exact account of this primitive religious play.

While the third lesson is being read, let four brothers put on their robes; and let one in his alb enter as if for some other duty, go up to the sepulcher without making any demonstration, and, holding a palm in his hand sit down there quietly. And, while the third responsory is being performed, let the remaining three brothers, all in their copes, carrying in their hands thuribles with incense in them, come slowly before the sepulcher as those who are looking for something would come. These things are done in imitation of the angel sitting at the tomb, and of the women coming with spices to anoint the body of Jesus.

When the brother sitting near the tomb sees the three, walking around, and as it were looking for something, approach him, let him begin to chant sweetly in a moderately loud voice:

"Whom seek ye in the sepulcher, O worshippers of Christ?" And when this has been intoned to the end, let the three respond in unison:

"Jesus of Nazareth, O dweller in the sky."

And let the former say to them;

"He is not here; He is risen as He said: Go, announce His resurrection from the dead."

---

[35] Saintly Bishop of Lindisfarne (d. 687), whose life was written by Bede; see Bede's statement, *post*, p. 113.

At this word of command, let the three turn, saying to the chorus:

"Alleluia, the Lord is risen."

Then, let the brother sitting there, as if to call them back, repeat the antiphone:

"Come, see the place where the Lord lay: alleluia: alleluia !"

While he is saying this, let him stand up, draw a curtain, and show them that the cross has disappeared from the place, and that only the linen cloths in which the cross had been wrapped are there. And when they understand these facts, let them set down their thuribles which they had carried into the sepulcher, let them take up the cloths, and spread them out before the congregation: and, as if to show that the Lord was risen and not wrapped in them, let them sing this antiphone:

"The Lord is risen from the tomb,
He who hung upon the tree for us."

And let them put the clothes upon the altar. At the end of the antiphone let the prior, rejoicing in the triumph of our King, in that He had conquered death and risen, begin the hymn:

"We praise Thee, O God,"

As this begins, the bells are all rung together; after this, let the priest say the verse thus far:

"In Thy resurrection, O Christ";

and let him then begin matins, saying:

"Lord, haste Thee to my help."

VI. REPRESENTATIVE AUTHORS

The larger share of medieval literature in the whole of Western Europe is anonymous. Literary fame, apparently, did not appeal so strongly to the poet as to make him wish to be known for his fruits. Consequently we have little medieval literary biography. In England, however, several names of authors have come down to us with what may be regarded as authentic lists of their works.

Cædmon is generally regarded as the earliest English

man of letters for whom we have even the suggestion of a biography.   This is recorded by Bede in his *Ecclesiastical History of the English People*, IV, Chap. 24, quoted below. Modern scholarship holds that the Old English poems whose names correspond to the titles of Cædmon's poems mentioned toward the close of this chapter cannot, for linguistic reasons, be ascribed to Cædmon.   He may have written parts of them, but in their present form they cannot be his.[1]

There was in the monastery of this abbess [2] a certain brother especially distinguished by the grace of God, since he was wont to make poems breathing of piety and religion.   Whatever he learned of sacred Scripture by the mouth of interpreters, he in a little time gave forth in poetical language composed with the greatest sweetness and depth of feeling, in English, his native tongue; and the effect of his poems was ever and anon to incite the souls of many to despise the world and long for the heavenly life.   Not but that there were others after him among the people of the Angles who sought to compose religious poetry; but none there was who could equal him, for he did not learn the art of song from men nor through the means of any man; rather did he receive it as a free gift from God.   Hence it came to pass that he never was able to compose poetry of a frivolous or idle sort; none but such as pertains to religion suited a tongue so religious as his.   Living always the life of a layman until well advanced in years, he had never learned the least thing about poetry.   In fact, so little did he understand of it that when at a feast it would be ruled that every one present should, for the entertainment of the others, sing in turn, he would, as soon as he saw the harp coming anywhere near him, jump up from the table in the midst of the banqueting, leave the place, and make the best of his way home.

This he had done at a certain time, and leaving the house where the feast was in progress, had gone out to the stable where

---

[1] See *Cambridge History of English Literature*, I, for chapters on Old English literature and the latest bibliographies.   The latter are not always exhaustive.

[2] Hild, superior of the monastery at Whitby, whose life is narrated in the chapter preceding the account of Cædmon.

the care of the cattle had been assigned to him for that night. There, when it was time to go to sleep, he had lain down for that purpose. But while he slept some one stood by him in a dream, greeted him, called him by name, and said, "Cædmon, sing me something." To this he replied, "I know not how to sing, and that is the very reason why I left the feast and came here, because I could not sing." But the one who was talking with him answered, "No matter, you are to sing for me." "Well, then," said he, "What is it that I must sing?" "Sing," said the other, "the beginning of created things." At this reply he immediately began to sing verses in praise of God the Creator, verses that he had never heard, and whose meaning is as follows: "Now should we praise the Keeper of the heavenly kingdom, the might of the Creator and His counsel, the works of the Father of glory; how He, though God eternal, became the Author of all marvels. He, the almighty Guardian of mankind, first created for the sons of men heaven as a roof, and afterwards the earth." [3] This is the meaning, but not the precise order, of the words which he sang in his sleep; for no songs, however well they may be composed, can be rendered from one language into another without loss of grace and dignity. When he rose from sleep, he remembered all that he had sung while in that state and shortly after added, in the same strain, many more words of a hymn befitting the majesty of God.

In the morning he went to the steward who was set over him, and showed him what gift he had acquired. Being led to the abbess, he was bidden to make known his dream and repeat his poem to the many learned men who were present, that they all might give their judgment concerning the thing which he related, and whence it was; and they were unanimously of the opinion that heavenly grace had been bestowed upon him by the Lord. They then set about expounding to him a piece of sacred history or teaching, bidding him, if he could, to turn it into the rhythm of poetry. This he undertook to do, and departed. In the morning he returned and delivered the passage assigned to him, converted into an excellent poem. The abbess,

[3] See two versions of this poem, one in the West Saxon dialect and one in the Northumbrian, *ante*, pp. 76, 79.

honoring the grace of God as displayed in the man, shortly afterward instructed him to forsake the condition of a layman and take upon himself the vows of a monk. She thereupon received him into the monastery with his whole family, and made him one of the company of the brethren, commanding that he should be taught the whole course and succession of Biblical history. He, in turn, calling to mind what he was able to learn by the hearing of the ear, and, as it were, like a clean animal, chewing upon it as a cud, transformed it all into most agreeable poetry; and, by echoing it back in a more harmonious form, made his teachers in turn listen to him. Thus he rehearsed the creation of the world, the origin of man, and all the story of Genesis; the departure of Israel from Egypt and their entry into the promised land, together with many other histories from Holy Writ; the incarnation of our Lord, His passion, resurrection, and ascension into heaven; the coming of the Holy Ghost and the teaching of the apostles; moreover he made many poems about the terror of the future judgment, the awfulness of the pains of hell, and the joy of the heavenly kingdom, besides a great number about the mercies and judgments of God. In all these he exerted himself to allure men from the love of wickedness, and to impel them to the love and practice of righteous living; for he was a very devout man, humbly submissive to the monastic rule, but full of consuming zeal against those who were disposed to act otherwise.

Hence it came to pass that he ended his life with a fair death. For when the hour of his departure drew nigh, he was afflicted for the space of a fortnight with a bodily weakness which seemed to prepare the way; yet it was so far from severe that he was able during the whole of that time to walk about and converse. Near at hand there was a cottage, to which those who were sick and appeared nigh unto death were usually taken. At the approach of evening on the same night when he was to leave the world, he desired his attendant to make ready a place there for him to take his rest. The attendant did so, though he could not help wondering at the request, since he did not seem in the least like a person about to die. When he was placed in the infirmary, he was somehow full of good humor, and kept talking

and joking with those who had already been brought there.
Some time after midnight he asked whether they had the eucharist at hand. "What do you need of the eucharist?" they
answered, "you aren't going to die yet, for you are just as full
of fun in talking with us as if nothing were the matter with
you." "Never mind," said he, "bring me the eucharist." Taking it in his hand, he asked, "Are you all at peace with me, and
free from any grudge or ill-will?" "Yes," they all responded,
"we are perfectly at peace with you, and cherish no grievance
whatever." "But are you," said they, "entirely at peace with
us?" "Yes, my dear children," he answered without hesitation,
"I am at peace with all the servants of God." And thus saying,
he made ready for his entrance into the other life by partaking
of the heavenly journey-bread. Not long after he inquired,
"How near is it to the hour when the brethren are wakened for
lauds?" "But a little while," was the reply. "Well then," said
he, "let us wait for that hour," and, making over himself the
sign of the cross, he laid his head on the pillow, and falling into
a light slumber ended his life in silence. And so it came to pass
that, as he had served the Lord in simplicity and purity of mind
and with serene attachment and loyalty, so by a serene death
he left the world, and went to look upon His face. And meet
in truth it was that the tongue which had indited so many helpful words in praise of the Creator, should frame its very last
words in His praise, while in the act of signing himself with the
cross, and of commending his spirit into His hands. And that
he foresaw his death is apparent from what has here been related.[4]

Bede (672–735), the authority to whom we have so often
referred, is a medieval scholar of the best type. His text-
books on various subjects were used all over Western
Europe. "We ask with earnest desire," says St. Boniface
in a letter to Egbert of York, "that to bring joy into our
sorrow as you have done before, you should take care to
send us a tiny gleam from that candle of the Church, which

[4] Verse composition was among the regular accomplishments of the English
scholars of this time. Cf. *The English Correspondence of St. Boniface*, ed. *cit.*, pp.
40, 100.

the Holy Spirit lit within the limits of your province; that
is that you should deign to send across some part of the
commentaries which Bede, that saintly priest and investigator of the Holy Scriptures, composed, especially, if it
be possible, his *Homilies* and his *Proverbs of Solomon*, for
they will be very convenient and useful to us in our preaching. We have heard that he wrote commentaries on these
subjects." [5] Dante places Bede in the Heaven of the Sun
along with other great scholars.[6] We quote three documents regarding the life and work of Bede. The first,
the *Preface* to the *Ecclesiastical History*, gives us his attitude toward his work and his method of research.

I formerly, at your [7] request, most readily transmitted to you
the *Ecclesiastical History of the English Nation*, which I had newly
published, for you to read, and give it your approbation; and
I now send it again to be transcribed, and more fully considered
at your leisure. And I cannot but commend the sincerity and
zeal, with which you not only diligently give ear to hear the
words of the Holy Scripture, but also industriously take care to
become acquainted with the actions and sayings of former men
of renown, expecially of our own nation. For if history relates
good things of good men, the attentive hearer is excited to imitate that which is good; or if it mentions evil things of wicked
persons, nevertheless the religious and pious hearer or reader,
shunning that which is hurtful and perverse, is the more earnestly
excited to perform those things which he knows to be good, and
worthy of God. Of which you also being deeply sensible, are
desirous that the said history should be more fully made familiar
to yourself, and to those over whom the Divine Authority has
appointed you governor, from your great regard to their general
welfare. But to the end that I may remove all occasion of
doubting what I have written, both from yourself and other
readers or hearers of this history, I will take care briefly to
intimate from what authors I chiefly learned the same.

[5] *Ibid.*, p. 136. See T. Wright, *Biographia Britannica Literaria* (1842), I, for a
collection of all the materials of literary biography for the Old English period.
[6] Cf. *Paradiso*, X.   [7] Ceolwulf, King of Northumbria (d. 764).

My principal authority and aid in this work was the learned
and reverend Abbot Albinus;[8] who, educated in the Church of
Canterbury by those venerable and learned men, Archbishop
Theodore[9] of blessed memory, and the Abbot Hadrian,[10] transmitted to me by Nothelm,[11] the pious priest of the Church of
London, either in writing, or by word of mouth of the same
Nothelm, all that he thought worthy of memory, that had been
done in the province of Kent, or the adjacent parts, by the disciples of the blessed Pope Gregory,[12] as he had learned the same
either from written records, or the traditions of his ancestors.
The same Nothelm, afterwards going to Rome, having, with
leave of the present Pope Gregory,[13] searched into the archives
of the holy Roman Church, found there some epistles of the
blessed Pope Gregory, and other popes; and returning home,
by the advice of the aforesaid most reverend father Albinus,
brought them to me, to be inserted in my history. Thus, from
the beginning of this volume to the time when the English nation received the faith of Christ, have we collected the writings

[8] Abbot of St. Peter's, Canterbury (d. 732). Cf. *ante*, p. 66.

[9] Of Canterbury, cf. *ante*, pp. 49, 57, 62. Theodore was a native of Tarsus in
Cilicia and born about 602. He studied at Athens and was a well-known monastic
scholar on his arrival in Rome in 668. He arrived in Canterbury in May, 669,
where he effected great reforms, ecclesiastical and educational. Though a very
religious man, his piety was not of a sort to attract monastic historians for no
miracles are ascribed to him. He died on Sept. 19, 690. The chief source of our
knowledge of his life is Bede, *The Ecclesiastical History*, etc. See the *Dictionary of
National Biography* for a full modern account.

[10] Cf. *ante*, p. 57, Abbot of St. Peter's, Canterbury. There is no article on him
in either the *Dictionary of National Biography*, Smith and Wace, *Dictionary of
Christian Biography*, or *The Encyclopædia Britannica*. From the biographies of
Archbishop Theodore, however, we learn that Adrian or Hadrian, an African by
birth, was the person originally selected by Pope Vitalian as Archbishop of Canterbury to succeed Wighard, who had died in Rome before consecration. Adrian
declined the office, but followed Theodore to England, where he became the Archbishop's chief helper and Abbot of St. Peter's.

[11] Died 739; tenth Archbishop of Canterbury. See the article in the *Dictionary
of National Biography*.

[12] Gregory the Great (*circa* 540–*circa* 604), christianizer of England. Cf. *ante*,
pp. 42–46; 64.

[13] Gregory II, d. Feb. 731. Before consecration as pope, Gregory had been
papal librarian (Plummer).

of our predecessors, and from them gathered matter for our history; but from that time till the present, what was transacted in the Church of Canterbury, by the disciples of St. Gregory or their successors, and under what kings the same happened, has been conveyed to us by Nothelm through the industry of the aforesaid Abbot Albinus. They also partly informed me by what bishops and under what kings the provinces of the East and West Saxons, as also of the East Angles, and of the Northumbrians, received the faith of Christ. In short I was chiefly encouraged to undertake this work by the persuasions of the same Albinus. In like manner, Daniel,[14] the most reverend Bishop of the West Saxons, who is still living, communicated to me in writing some things relating to the ecclesiastical history of that province, and the next adjoining to it of the South Saxons, as also of the Isle of Wight. But how, by the pious ministry of Cedd [15] and Ceadda,[16] the province of the Mercians was brought to the faith of Christ, which they knew not before, and how that of the East Saxons recovered the same, after having expelled it, and how those fathers lived and died, we learned from the brethren of the monastery, which was built by them, and is called Lastingham. What ecclesiastical transactions took place in the province of the East Angles, was partly made known to us from the writings and traditions of our ancestors, and partly by relation of the most reverend Abbot Esius.[17] What was done towards promoting the faith, and what was the sacerdotal succession in the province of Lindsey, we had either from the letters of the most reverend prelate Cunebert,[18] or by word of mouth from other persons of good credit. But what was done in the Church throughout the province of the Northumbrians, from the time when they received the faith of Christ till this present, I received not from any particular author; but by the faithful testimony of innumerable witnesses, who might

[14] Died 745; Bishop of Winchester 705–744. See the article in the *Dictionary of National Biography*. The writer of the article calls Daniel one of the "most learned, energetic and influential bishops" of the Old English Church.

[15] Cf. Bede, *Ecclesiastical History*, Book III, Chaps. 21–23, 25; Book IV, Chap. 1.   [16] *Ibid.*

[17] This is the sole reference in history to this person.

[18] I can find nothing about him.

know or remember the same; besides what I had of my own knowledge. Wherein it is to be observed that what I have written concerning our most holy father, Bishop Cuthbert,[19] either in this volume, or in my treatise on his life and actions, I partly took, and faithfully copied from what I found written of him by the brethren of the Church of Lindisfarne; but at the same time took care to add such things as I could myself have knowledge of by the faithful testimony of such as knew him. And I humbly entreat the reader, that if he shall in this that we have written find anything not delivered according to the truth, he will not impute the same to me, who, as the true rule of history requires, have labored sincerely to commit to writing such things as I could gather from common report, for the instruction of posterity.

Moreover, I beseech all men who shall hear or read this history of our nation, that for my manifold infirmities both of mind and body, they will offer up frequent supplications to the throne of Grace. And I further pray, that in recompense for the labor wherewith I have recorded in the several countries and cities those events which were most worthy of note, and most grateful to the ears of their inhabitants, I may for my reward have the benefit of their pious prayers.

The second document regarding Bede is the conclusion to the *Ecclesiastical History*, in which we find an account of his life and a list of his works.

Thus much of the *Ecclesiastical History of Britain*, and more especially of the English nation, as far as I could learn either from the writings of the ancients, or the tradition of our ancestors, or of my own knowledge, has, with the help of God, been digested by me Bede, the servant of God, and priest of the monastery of the blessed apostles, Peter and Paul, which is at Wearmouth and Jarrow; who being born in the territory of that same monastery, was given, at seven years of age, to be educated by the most reverend Abbot Benedict,[20] and afterward

[19] Died 687; Bishop of Lindisfarne. See article in the *Dictionary of National Biography*. Bede wrote two lives of him. See *post*, p. 113; *ante*, p. 102.
[20] I.e. Benedict Biscop; cf. *ante*, pp. 56–60.

by Ceolfrid; and spending all the remaining time of my life in that monastery, I wholly applied myself to the study of Scripture, and amidst the observance of regular discipline, and the daily care of singing in the church, I always took delight in learning, teaching, and writing. In the nineteenth year of my age, I received deacon's orders; in the thirtieth, those of the priesthood, both of them by the ministry of the most reverend Bishop John, and by order of the Abbot Ceolfrid. From which time, till the fifty-ninth year of my age, I have made it my business, for the use of me and mine, to compile out of the works of the venerable Fathers, and to interpret and explain according to their meaning these following pieces:

On the Beginning of *Genesis*, to the Nativity of Isaac and the Reprobation of Ismael, three books.

On the Tabernacle and its Vessels, and of the Priestly Vestments, three books.

On the first Part of *Samuel*, to the Death of Saul, four books.

Of the Building of the Temple, of allegorical exposition, like the rest, two books.

Item, on the *Book of Kings*, thirty questions.

On Solomon's *Proverbs*, three books.

On the *Canticles*, seven books.

On *Isaiah*, *Daniel*, the twelve Prophets, and Part of *Jeremiah*, Distinctions of Chapters, collected out of St. Jerome's [21] Treatise.

On *Esdras* and *Nehemiah*, three books.

On the *Song of Habacuc*, one book.

On the Book of the blessed Father Tobias, one Book of Allegorical Exposition concerning Christ and the Church.

Also, Chapters of Readings on Moses's *Pentateuch, Joshua*, and *Judges*.

On the *Books of Kings* and *Chronicles*.

On the Book of the blessed Father Job.

On the Parables, *Ecclesiastes*, and *Canticles*.

On the Prophets *Isaiah, Esdras* and *Nehemiah*.

On the *Gospel of Mark*, four books.

On the *Gospel of Luke*, six books.

Of Homilies on the Gospel, two books.

[21] Cf. *ante*, p. 64.

On the Apostle, I have carefully transcribed in order all that I have found in St. Augustine's [22] Works.

On the *Acts of the Apostles*, two books.

On the seven Catholic Epistles, a book on each.

On the *Revelation of St. John*, three books.

Also, Chapters of Readings on all the *New Testament*, except the Gospel.

Also a book of Epistles to different Persons, of which one is of the Six ages of the world; one of the Mansions of the Children of Israel; one on the Words of Isaiah, "And they shall be shut up in one prison, and after many days shall they be visited;" one of the Reason of the Bissestile, or Leap-Year, and of the Equinox, according to Anatolius.[23]

Also, of the Histories of Saints. I translated the *Book of the Life and Passion of St. Felix Confessor*, from Paulinus's [24] Work in metre, into prose.

The Book of the Life and Passion of St. Anastasius, which was ill translated from the Greek, and worse amended by some unskilful person, I have corrected as to the sense.

I have written the *Life of the Holy Father Cuthbert*,[25] who was both monk and prelate, first in heroic verse, and then in prose.

The History of the Abbots of this Monastery,[26] in which I rejoice to serve the Divine Goodness, viz., Benedict, Ceolfrid, and Huetbert, in two books.

The Ecclesiastical History of our Island and Nation in five books.

The Martyrology of the Birth-days of the Holy Martyrs, in which I have carefully endeavoured to set down all that I could find, and not only on what day, but also by what sort of combat, or under what judge they overcame the world.

---

[22] Cf. *ante, ibid.*

[23] Bishop of Laodicea in Syria Prima, 269. Famed for his acquaintance with the liberal arts. His book on the Easter question was especially famous. See Smith & Wace, *op. cit.*

[24] 353–431 A.D., Bishop of Nola, author of fifty-one extant letters, thirty-six poems and a *Panegyric* on Theodosius. Several of his poems relate to Felix. See the articles on Felix and Paulinus in Smith & Wace, *op. cit.*

[25] Cf. *ante*, pp. 102, 111.

[26] Cf. the excerpt, *ante*, pp. 56–60.

A Book of Hymns in several sorts of metre, or rhyme.

A Book of Epigrams in heroic or elegiac verse.

Of the Nature of Things, and *Of the Times*,[27] one book each.

Also, *Of the Times*, one larger book.

A Book of Orthography digested in alphabetical order.

Also a *Book of the Art of Poetry*, and to it I have added another little *Book of Tropes and Figures;* that is, of the Figures and Manners of Speaking in which the Holy Scriptures are written.

And now, I beseech Thee, good Jesus, that to whom thou hast graciously granted sweetly to partake of the words of Thy wisdom and knowledge, Thou wilt also vouchsafe that he may some time or other come to Thee, the fountain of all wisdom, and always appear before Thy face, who livest and reignest world without end. Amen!

> Here Ends, By God's Help,
> The Fifth Book
> *Of The Ecclesiastical History*
> *Of The English Nation.*[28]

Our third document regarding Bede is the beautiful letter which Cuthbert, one of Bede's pupils, wrote concerning his master's death.

> Cuthbert, his fellow learner, to his beloved co-lector Cuthwin, health forever in God.

I was very glad to receive the little gift which you sent me and I read with pleasure your scholarly and devout letter in which — and this was what I especially wanted — I learned that masses are being celebrated and holy prayers offered diligently by you in behalf of our father and master Bede, dear to God. For this reason more from love of him than confidence

---

[27] The accepted treatise on astronomy in early England in Bede's time and subsequently. Ælfric translated it into Old English. The extant treatise, published in Old English with a modern translation in Wright's *Popular Treatises on Science Written during the Middle Ages*, has been the subject of controversy as to its authorship. Cf. White, *Ælfric: A New Study of His Life and Writings*, Index and appendix III.

[28] Bede's complete works in Latin are to be found in Migne, *Patrologia Latina*, Vols. 90–95, Paris, 1844, and in the edition of J. A. Giles, 5 vols., London, 1843–44.

in my own ability, it is a (sacred) pleasure (to me) to report in a few words, how he passed from this life, especially since I know that you have wished and desired this.

He had been ill and particularly had been troubled with asthma, but yet had felt scarcely any pain. This was for about two weeks before Easter. He was cheerful and happy, giving thanks to Almighty God every day and night, or rather every hour up to the day of our Lord's Ascension, that is May 26 (735). He daily gave lessons to us his pupils and busied himself the remaining time each day in singing psalms, as far as he could. He was even anxious to pass the whole night joyously in prayer and thanksgiving to God, except when a short nap interfered. Even then, however, waking up, he meditated on the customary scriptural songs and with hands uplifted did not forget to return thanks to God. I am free to confess that I never saw or heard of any one else so zealous in giving thanks to the living God.

O truly blessed man! he frequently repeated the remark of St. Paul the apostle when he said, "It is a fearful thing to fall into the hands of the living God," [29] and many other passages of Holy Scripture, and thus warned us to rouse ourselves from the sleep of the spirit by thinking of our final hour. And he talked to us in our own language — for he was learned in our songs — speaking as follows of the terrible separation of soul and body: "In the presence of his necessary departure, no one is wiser than he need be. Before he go hence, let him consider what good or ill he has done and how he is to be judged after death." He would sing antiphons for our consolation and his own, one of which is: "O King of Glory, Lord of Hosts, who didst in triumph rise above all heavens, forsake us not as orphans, but send down upon us the promise of the Father, the Spirit of Truth. Alleluia." When, however, he reached the petition "do not forsake us orphans" he burst into tears and wept much. And after the hour he took up again what he had begun. This was his daily practice: and we, indeed, hearing, grieved with him and wept. Now we read, now wept; nay we read in tears.

[29] Cf. Hebrews 10: 31.

In such exalted pleasure we passed the period from Easter to Pentecost. And he was very happy and gave thanks to God, because he was thought fit for such infirmity. And he often said: "God scourgeth every son whom he receiveth;" [30] and repeated the remark of Ambrose: [31] "I have not so lived as to be ashamed to live among you; nor do I fear to die, because we have a gracious Lord."

At this time of which I am speaking, he seemed anxious to finish two tasks which I should mention in addition to the lessons which we daily received from him and to the singing of psalms. These were the translation into our tongue for the use of the holy church the Gospel of St. John from the beginning to the passage reading "But what are these among so many?" [32] and the rendering into English of certain excerpts from the books of Bishop Isidore; [33] for he said: "I do not want my boys to read a falsehood, and labor in vain in this matter after my death." When, however, the Tuesday before our Lord's Ascension came, his asthma grew worse and a slight swelling of his feet appeared. But he taught and dictated in good spirits all that day and would often say, among other things: "Be quick in your learning, because I don't know how long I may hold out or whether my Creator will shortly take me hence." Yet we thought that he was scarcely conscious of his (real) condition. He passed the night thus, awake, in thanksgiving. As the dawn of Wednesday came on, he bade us write diligently what we had started; and we did so up to nine o'clock in the morning. Then we walked in procession with the relics of the saints, as the custom of that day demanded.

But there was one of us with him who said to him: "There is still unfinished one chapter of the book you have been dictating. But it seems hard to ask you further questions." "It is easy," he replied, "take your pen, see that it is in good shape and write fast." At three o'clock in the afternoon, Bede said to me: "I have some things of value in my chest, such as pepper,

[30] Cf. Hebrews 12: 6.   [31] Cf. *ante*, p. 64.   [32] Cf. John 6: 9.

[33] Bishop of Seville 600–636. Author of the famous *Etymologies* or *Origins*, an early medieval encyclopedia in twenty books, source of the information of a great number of medieval scholars. See the exhaustive article in Smith and Wace, *op. cit.*

handkerchiefs and incense. Run quickly and bring the priests of the monastery to me that I too may distribute the little gifts which God has given me." I did it in fear and trembling, and when they came he spoke to them one and all, entreating them and beseeching them to say masses and offer prayers for him diligently; to which they gladly agreed. For they all wept and were grieved, especially because of the fact that he had said that they should see his face no more in this world. But they rejoiced that he said: "It is time, if it seem best to my Creator, that I, freed from the flesh, go to Him who, when I was not, formed me from nothing. I have lived long, and the devoted Judge has planned my life well for me. The time of my release is at hand, for my spirit desires to see Christ my King in His beauty." Speaking thus and saying many other things useful for our instruction, he passed his last day in joy even unto vespers.

Then the boy called Wilbert, mentioned before, said: "Dear master, there is still one sentence not translated." He replied: "'Tis well; write." And after a little, the boy said: "Now it is all translated." And he: "'Tis well; it is finished; you have spoken the truth. Take my head in your hands, because I want very much to sit facing my holy place where I used to pray, that I may sit and call upon my Father." And thus upon the floor of his small cell, singing "Glory to Father, Son and Holy Spirit," he breathed his last. And we must be sure that because he labored devotedly here to the praise of God, angels bore his spirit to the joys of heaven which he had longed for.

All who heard of or saw the death of our father Bede aid that they had never seen any one else end his life in such devotion and calm. As you have heard, he sang, as long as there was breath in his body, the Gloria and other songs to the praise of God, and with uplifted hands did not cease to return thanks to God. You should know that many other things could be told and written of him, but that my crude language makes my account brief; yet I purpose, with the help of God, to write more fully of him later the things which I have seen and heard.

Cædmon and Bede were natives of northern England.[34]
Most of the Old English literature extant, however, is in
the language of southern or Saxon England. Modern
scholars, therefore, say that the standard language of pre-
conquest England was West Saxon. It is generally conceded that the man who is responsible for the literary
eminence of Wessex is Alfred the Great. Four documents
illustrating the life and works of Alfred are cited here.
The first is a selection from our earliest biography of an
English layman, Asser's *Life of Alfred*. Asser's book has
been the object of much skepticism, but the learned world
at present seems to agree with Mr. Stevenson that it is
both authentic and authoritative.[35]

In the year of our Lord's incarnation 849, was born Alfred,
king of the Anglo-Saxons, at the royal village of Wanating, in
Berkshire, which country has its name from the wood of Berroc,
where the box-tree grows most abundantly. His genealogy is
traced in the following order: King Alfred was the son of King
Ethelwulf, who was the son of Egbert, who was the son of El-
mund, who was the son of Eafa, who was the son of Eoppa, who
was the son of Ingild. Ingild, and Ina, the famous king of the
West-Saxons, were two brothers. Ina went to Rome, and there
ending this life honourably, entered the heavenly kingdom, to
reign there for ever with Christ. Ingild and Ina were the sons

[34] The birthplace of Cynewulf, of whose life all that we know in his own words
has been given *ante*, p. 80, has been the subject of much controversy. See the
Introduction to the *Crist*, ed. A. S. Cook (Ginn & Co., *Albion Series*, 1900) and
Charles W. Kennedy, *The Poems of Cynewulf* (E. P. Dutton & Co., 1910). The
latter is a complete translation of all of Cynewulf's signed poems and those attributed to him.

[35] Cf. *Asser's Life of King Alfred, together with the Annals of Saint Neots errone-
ously ascribed to Asser*, edited, with Introduction and Commentary, by William
Henry Stevenson (Oxford, Clarendon Press, 1904). Mr. Stevenson's, of course, is
an edition of the Latin text. This has been translated by Professor A. S. Cook,
Asser's Life of King Alfred (Ginn & Co., 1906). The most complete modern sum-
mary of Alfred's life and accomplishments is Charles Plummer, *The Life and
Times of Alfred the Great; Being the Ford Lectures for 1901* (Oxford, Clarendon
Press, 1902). All the histories of England have more or less material on Alfred.

of Cœnred, who was the son of Ceolwald, who was the son of
Cudam, who was the son of Cuthwin, who was the son of Ceawlin, who was the son of Cynric, who was the son of Creoda, who
was the son of Cerdic, who was the son of Elesa, who was the
son of Gewis, from whom the Britons name all that nation
Gegwis, who was the son of Brond, who was the son of Beldeg,
who was the son of Woden, who was the son of Frithowald, who
was the son of Frealaf, who was the son of Frithuwulf, who was
the son of Finn of Godwulf, who was the son of Geat, which
Geat the pagans long worshipped as a god. Sedulius[36] makes
mention of him in his metrical Paschal poem, as follows:

> When gentile poets with their fictions vain,
> In tragic language and bombastic strain,
> To their god Geat, comic deity,
> Loud praises sing, etc.

Geat was the son of Tætwa, who was the son of Beaw, who
was the son of Sceldi, who was the son of Heremod, who was
the son of Itermon, who was the son of Hathra, who was the
son of Guala, who was the son of Bedwig, who was the son of
Shem, who was the son of Noah, who was the son of Lamech,
who was the son of Methusalem, who was the son of Enoch,
who was the son of Malaleel, who was the son of Cainian, who
was the son of Enos, who was the son of Seth, who was the son
of Adam.

In the same year,[37] king Ethelwulf sent his son Alfred, above-
named, to Rome, with an honourable escort both of nobles and
commoners. Pope Leo (the fourth) at that time presided over
the apostolic see, and he anointed for king the aforesaid Alfred,
and adopted him as his spiritual son.

He was loved by his father and mother, and even by all the
people, above all his brothers, and was educated altogether at
the court of the king. As he advanced through the years of
infancy and youth, his form appeared more comely than that
of his brothers; in look, in speech, and in manners he was more
graceful than they. His noble nature implanted in him from
his cradle a love of wisdom above all things; but, with shame

---

[36] Cf. *ante*, p. 66 and note.   [37] 853.

be it spoken, by the unworthy neglect of his parents and nurses, he remained illiterate even till he was twelve years old or more; but he listened with serious attention to the Saxon poems which he often heard recited, and easily retained them in his docile memory. He was a zealous practiser of hunting in all its branches, and hunted with great assiduity and success; for skill and good fortune in this art, as in all others, are among the gifts of God, as we also have often witnessed.

On a certain day, therefore, his mother was showing him and his brothers a Saxon book of poetry, which she held in her hand, and said, "Whichever of you shall the soonest learn this volume shall have it for his own." Stimulated by these words, or rather by the Divine inspiration, and allured by the beautifully illuminated letter at the beginning of the volume, he spoke before all his brothers, who, though his seniors in age, were not so in grace, and answered, "Will you really give that book to one of us, that is to say, to him who can first understand and repeat it to you?" At this his mother smiled with satisfaction, and confirmed what she had before said. Upon which the boy took the book out of her hand, and went to his master to read it, and in due time brought it to his mother and recited it.

After this he learned the daily course, that is, the celebration of the hours, and afterwards certain psalms, and several prayers, contained in a certain book which he kept day and night in his bosom, as we ourselves have seen, and carried about with him to assist his prayers, amid all the bustle and business of this present life. But, sad to say, he could not gratify his most ardent wish to learn the liberal arts, because, as he said, there were no good readers at that time in all the kingdom of the West Saxons.[38]

This he confessed, with many lamentations and sighs, to have been one of his greatest difficulties and impediments in this life, namely, that when he was young and had the capacity for learning, he could not find teachers; but, when he was more advanced in life, he was harassed by so many diseases unknown to all the physicians of this island, as well as by internal and external anxieties of sovereignty, and by continual invasions of the pagans,

[38] Cf. *post*, Alfred's *Preface* to Gregory's *Cura Pastoralis*, pp. 129–131.

and had his teachers and writers also so much disturbed, that
there was no time for reading. But yet among the impediments
of this present life, from infancy up to the present time, and,
as I believe, even until his death, he continued to feel the same
insatiable desire of knowledge, and still aspires after it.[39]

The sons and daughters, whom he had by his wife . . . were
Ethelfled the eldest, after whom came Edward, then Ethelgiva,
then Ethelswitha, and Ethelwerd, besides those who died in
their infancy, one of whom was Edmund. Ethelfled, when she
arrived at a marriageable age, was united to Ethered, earl of
Mercia; Ethelgiva was dedicated to God, and submitted to the
rules of a monastic life. Ethelwerd the youngest, by the divine
counsels and the admirable prudence of the king, was consigned
to the schools of learning, where, with the children of almost all
the nobility of the country, and many also who were not noble,
he prospered under the diligent care of his teachers. Books in
both languages, namely, Latin and Saxon, were read in the school.
They also learned to write; so that before they were of an age
to practise manly arts, namely, hunting and such pursuits as
befit noblemen, they became studious and clever in the liberal
arts. Edward and Ethelswitha were bred up in the king's court
and received great attention from their attendants and nurses;
nay, they continue to this day, with the love of all about them,
and showing affability, and even gentleness towards all, both
natives and foreigners, and in complete subjection to their
father; nor, among their other studies which appertain to this
life and are fit for noble youths, are they suffered to pass their
time idly and unprofitably without learning the liberal arts; for
they have carefully learned the Psalms and Saxon books, especially the Saxon poems, and are continually in the habit of
making use of books.

In the meantime, the king, during the frequent wars and other
trammels of this present life, the invasion of the pagans, and his
own daily infirmities of body, continued to carry on the government, and to exercise hunting in all its branches; to teach his

[39] The chapters omitted here deal with the wars of Alfred's father and brothers
against the Danes, their several deaths, his own accession to the throne, marriage
and early fortunes in war.

workers in gold and artificers of all kinds, his falconers, hawkers and dog-keepers; to build houses, majestic and good, beyond all the precedents of his ancestors, by his new mechanical inventions; to recite the Saxon books, and especially to learn by heart the Saxon poems, and to make others learn them; and he alone never desisted from studying, most diligently, to the best of his ability; he attended the mass and other daily services of religion; he was frequent in psalm-singing and prayer, at the hours both of the day and the night. He also went to the churches, as we have already said, in the night-time to pray, secretly, and unknown to his courtiers; he bestowed alms and largesses on both natives and foreigners of all countries; he was affable and pleasant to all, and curiously eager to investigate things unknown. Many Franks, Frisians, Gauls, pagans, Britons, Scots, and Armoricans, noble and ignoble, submitted voluntarily to his dominion; and all of them, according to their nation and deserving, were ruled, loved, honored, and enriched with money and power. Moreover, the king was in the habit of hearing the divine scriptures read by his own countrymen, or, if by any chance it so happened, in company with foreigners, and he attended to it with sedulity and solicitude. His bishops, too, and all ecclesiastics, his earls and nobles, ministers and friends, were loved by him with wonderful affection, and their sons, who were bred up in the royal household, were no less dear to him than his own; he had them instructed in all kinds of good morals, and among other things, never ceased to teach them letters night and day; but as if he had no consolation in all these things, and suffered no other annoyance either from within or without, yet he was harassed by daily and nightly affliction, that he complained to God, and to all who were admitted to his familiar love, that Almighty God had made him ignorant of divine wisdom, and of the liberal arts; in this emulating the pious, the wise, and wealthy Solomon, king of the Hebrews, who at first, despising all present glory and riches, asked wisdom of God and found both, namely, wisdom and worldly glory; as it is written, "Seek first the kingdom of God and his righteousness, and all these things shall be added unto you." [40]

[40] Cf. Matt. 6: 33.

But God, who is always the inspector of the thoughts of the mind within, and the instigator of all good intentions, and a most plentiful aider, that good desires may be formed, — for he would not instigate a man to good intentions, unless he also amply supplied that which the man justly and properly wishes to have, — instigated the king's mind within; as is written, "I will hearken what the Lord God will say concerning me." [41] He would avail himself of every opportunity to procure coadjutors in his good designs, to aid him in his strivings after wisdom, that he might attain to what he aimed at; and, like a prudent bird, which rising in summer with the early morning from her beloved nest, steers her rapid flight through the uncertain tracks of ether, and descends on the manifold and varied flowers of grasses, herbs, and shrubs, essaying that which pleases most, that she may bear it to her home, so did he direct his eyes afar, and seek without, that which he had not within, namely, in his own kingdom.

But God at that time, as some consolation to the king's benevolence, yielding to his complaint, sent certain lights to illuminate him, namely, Werefrith, bishop of the church of Worcester, a man well versed in divine scripture, who, by the king's command, first turned the books of the *Dialogs* [42] of Pope Gregory and Peter, his disciple, from Latin into Saxon, and sometimes putting sense for sense, interpreted them with clearness and elegance. After him was Plegmund, a Mercian by birth, archbishop of the church of Canterbury, a venerable man, and endowed with wisdom; Ethelstan also, and Werewulf, his priests and chaplains, Mercians by birth, and erudite. These four had been invited out of Mercia by king Alfred, who exalted them with many honors and powers in the kingdom of the West-Saxons, besides the privileges which archbishop Plegmund and bishop Werefrith enjoyed in Mercia. By their teaching and wisdom the king's desires increased unceasingly, and were gratified. Night and day, whenever he had leisure, he commanded such men as these to read books to him; for he never suffered himself to be

[41] Cf. Psalms 85: 8.
[42] This work as thus translated is still extant, ed. Hecht in Grein, *Bibliothek der Angelsächsischen Prosa* (*Library of Anglo-Saxon Prose*), V.

without one of them, wherefore he possessed a knowledge of every book, though of himself he could not yet understand anything of books, for he had not yet learned to read any thing.

But the king's commendable avarice could not be gratified even in this; wherefore he sent messengers beyond the sea to Gaul, to procure teachers, and he invited from thence Grimbald, priest and monk, a venerable man, and good singer, adorned with every kind of ecclesiastical discipline and good morals, and most learned in all kinds of literary science and skilled in many other arts. By the teaching of these men the king's mind was much enlarged, and he enriched and honored them with much influence.

In these times, I [43] also came into Saxony out of the furthest coasts of Western Britain; and when I had proposed to go to him through many intervening provinces, I arrived in the country of the Saxons, who live on the right hand, which in Saxon is called Sussex, under the guidance of some of that nation; and there I first saw him in the royal vill, which is called Dene. He received me with kindness, and among other familiar conversation, he asked me eagerly to devote myself to his service and become his friend, to leave everything which I possessed on the left, or western bank of the Severn, and he promised he would give more than an equivalent for it in his own dominions. I replied that I could not incautiously and rashly promise such things; for it seemed to me unjust, that I should leave those sacred places in which I had been bred, educated and crowned, and at last ordained, for the sake of any earthly honor and power, unless by compulsion. Upon this, he said, "If you cannot accede to this, at least, let me have your service in part: spend six months of the year with me here, and the other six in Britain." [44] To this, I replied, "I could not even promise that easily or hastily without the advice of my friends." At length, however, when I perceived that he was anxious for my services, though I knew not why, I promised him that if my life was spared, I would return to him after six months, with such a reply as should be agreeable to him as well as advantageous to

[43] I.e. Asser, the author of the biography. (Died 909?)
[44] I.e. Wales; cf. *ante*, p. 118.

me and mine. With this answer he was satisfied, and when I had given him a pledge to return at the appointed time, on the fourth day we left him and returned on horseback towards our own country.

After our departure, a violent fever seized me in the city of Winchester, where I lay for twelve months and one week, night and day, without hope of recovery. At the appointed time, therefore, I could not fulfil my promise of visiting him, and he sent messengers to hasten my journey, and to inquire the cause of my delay. As I was unable to ride to him, I sent a second messenger to tell him the cause of my delay, and assure him that, if I recovered from my infirmity, I would fulfil what I had promised. My complaint left me, and by the advice and consent of all my friends, for the benefit of that holy place, and of all who dwelt therein, I did as I had promised to the king, and devoted myself to his service, on the condition that I should remain with him six months in every year, either continuously, if I could spend six months with him at once, or alternately, three months in Britain and three in Saxony.[45] For my friends hoped that they should sustain less tribulation and harm from king Hemeid, who often plundered that monastery and the parish of St. Deguus, and sometimes expelled the prelates, as they expelled archibishop Novis, my relation, and myself; if in any manner I could secure the notice and friendship of the king.

In the same year [46] also Alfred, king of the Anglo-Saxons, so often before mentioned, by divine inspiration, began, on one and the same day, to read and to interpret; but that I may explain this more fully to those who are ignorant, I will relate the cause of this long delay in the beginning.

On a certain day we were both of us sitting in the king's chamber talking on all kinds of subjects, as usual, and it happened that I read to him a quotation out of a certain book. He heard it attentively with both his ears, and addressed me with a thoughtful mind, showing me at the same moment a book which he carried in his bosom, wherein the daily courses and psalms, and prayers which he had read in his youth, were written, and he commanded me to write the same quotation in that book.

[45] I.e. the part of the island of Britain under English rule.   [46] 887.

Hearing this, and perceiving his ingenuous benevolence, and devout desire of studying the words of divine wisdom, I gave, though in secret, boundless thanks to Almighty God, who had implanted such a love of wisdom in the king's heart. But I could not find any empty space in that book wherein to write the quotation, for it was already full of various matters; wherefore I made a little delay, principally that I might stir up the bright intellect of the king to a higher acquaintance with the divine testimonies. Upon his urging me to make haste and write it quickly, I said to him, "Are you willing that I should write that quotation on some leaf apart? For it is not certain whether we shall not find one or more other such extracts which will please you; and if that should so happen we shall be glad that we have kept them apart." "Your plan is good," said he, and I gladly made haste to get ready a sheet, in the beginning of which I wrote what he bade me; and on the same day, I wrote therein, as I had anticipated, no less than three other quotations which pleased him; and from that time we daily talked together, and found out other quotations which pleased him, so that the sheet became full, and deservedly so; according as it is written, "The just man builds upon a moderate foundation, and by degrees passes to greater things." Thus, like a most productive bee, he flew here and there, asking questions, as he went, until he had eagerly and unceasingly collected many various flowers of divine Scriptures, with which he thickly stored the cells of his mind.

Now when that first quotation was copied, he was eager at once to read, and to interpret in Saxon, and then to teach others; even as we read of that happy robber, who recognized his Lord, aye, the Lord of all men, as he was hanging on the blessed cross, and, saluting him with his bodily eyes only, because elsewhere he was all pierced with nails, cried, "Lord, remember me when thou comest into thy kingdom!" [47] for it was only at the end of his life that he began to learn the rudiments of the Christian faith. But the king, inspired by God, began to study the rudiments of divine Scripture on the sacred solemnity of St. Martin (Nov. 11), and he continued to learn the flowers collected by

[47] Luke 23: 42.

certain masters, and to reduce them into the form of one book as he was then able, although mixed one with another, until it became almost as large as a psalter. This book he called his Enchiridion or Manual, because he carefully kept it at hand day and night, and found, as he told me, no small consolation therein.

After long reflection on these things,[48] he at length, by a useful and shrewd invention, commanded his chaplains to supply wax in a sufficient quantity, and he caused it to be weighed in such a manner that when there was so much of it in the scales, as would equal the weight of seventy-two pence, he caused the chaplains to make six candles thereof, each of equal length, so that each candle might have twelve divisions marked longitudinally upon it. By this plan, therefore, those six candles burned for twenty-four hours, a night and day, without fail, before the sacred relics of many of God's elect, which always accompanied him wherever he went; but sometimes when they would not continue burning a whole day and night, till the same hour that they were lighted the preceding evening, from the violence of the wind, which blew day and night without intermission through the doors and windows of the churches, and fissures of the divisions, the plankings, or the wall, or the thin canvas of the tents, they then unavoidably burned out and finished their course before the appointed time; the king therefore considered by what means he might shut out the wind, and so by a useful and cunning invention, he ordered a lantern to be beautifully constructed of wood and white ox-horn, which, when skilfully planed till it is thin, is no less transparent than a vessel of glass. This lantern therefore, was wonderfully made of wood and horn, as we before said, and by night a candle was put into it, which shone as brightly without as within, and was not extinguished by the wind; for the opening of the lantern was also closed up, according to the king's command, by a door made of horn.

By this contrivance, then, six candles, lighted in succession, lasted four and twenty hours, neither more nor less, and, when these were extinguished others were lighted.

He strove also, in his own judgments, for the benefit of both the noble and the ignoble, who often perversely quarrelled at

[48] On some method of telling time at night.

the meetings of his earls and officers, so that hardly one of them
admitted the justice of what had been decided by the earls and
prefects, and in consequence of this pertinacious and obstinate
dissension, all desired to have the judgment of the king, and
both sides sought at once to gratify their desire.   But if any
one was conscious of injustice on his side in the suit, though by
law and agreement he was compelled, however reluctant, to go
before the king, yet with his own good will he never would consent to go.   For he knew, that in the king's presence no part of
his wrong would be hidden;   and no wonder, for the king was
a most acute investigator in passing sentence, as he was in all
other things.   He inquired into almost all the judgments which
were given in his own absence, throughout all his dominion,
whether they were just or unjust.   If he perceived there was iniquity in those judgments, he summoned the judges, either
through his own agency, or through others of his faithful servants, and asked them mildly, why they had judged so unjustly;
whether through ignorance or malevolence;   i.e., whether for the
love or fear of any one, or hatred of others;   or also for the desire
of money.   At length, if the judges acknowledged they had
given judgment because they knew no better, he discreetly and
moderately reproved their inexperience and folly in such terms
as these: "I wonder truly at your insolence, that, whereas by
God's favor and mine, you have occupied the rank and office
of the wise, you have neglected the studies and labors of the
wise.   Either, therefore, at once give up the discharge of the
temporal duties which you hold, or endeavor more zealously to
study the lessons of wisdom.   Such are my commands."   At
these words the earls and prefects would tremble and endeavor
to turn all their thoughts to the study of justice, so that, wonderful to say, almost all his earls, prefects, and officers, though unlearned from their cradles, were sedulously bent upon acquiring
learning, choosing rather laboriously to acquire the knowledge
of a new discipline than to resign their functions;   but if any
one of them from old age or slowness of talent was unable to
make progress in liberal studies, he commanded his son, if he
had one, or one of his kinsmen, or, if there was no other person
to be had, his own freedman or servant, whom he had some time

before advanced to the office of reading, to recite Saxon books before him night and day, whenever he had any leisure, and they lamented with deep sighs, in their inmost hearts, that in their youth they had never attended to such studies; and they blessed the young men of our days, who happily could be instructed in the liberal arts, whilst they execrated their own lot, that they had not learned these things in their youth, and now, when they are old, though wishing to learn them, they are unable.

Alfred's literary work was mostly in the form of translation from the Latin. For several of his translations, however, he wrote prefaces of his own composition and these are among the most interesting pieces of Old English prose that we have. Two of these prefaces are quoted here. Alfred, introducing to Bishop Wærfrith of Worcester his translation of Pope Gregory's *Cura Pastoralis*, writes as follows of his educational plans for England: [49]

King Alfred bids greet Bishop Werfrith with his words lovingly and with friendship; and I let it be known to thee that it has very often come into my mind what wise men there formerly were throughout England, both of sacred and secular orders; and what happy times there were then throughout England; and how the kings who had power over the nation in those days obeyed God and His ministers; how they preserved peace, morality, and order at home, and at the same time enlarged their territory abroad; and how they prospered both with war and with wisdom; and also how zealous the sacred orders were both in teaching and learning, and in all the services they owed to God; and how foreigners came to this land in search of wisdom and instruction, and how we should now have to get them from abroad if we were to have them. So general was its decay in England that there were very few on this side of the Humber who could understand their rituals in English, or translate a letter from Latin into English; and I believe that there were not many beyond the Humber. There were so few of them that

[49] The document will also illustrate intellectual conditions in late ninth century England.

I cannot remember a single one south of the Thames when I came to the throne. Thanks be to Almighty God that we have any teachers among us now. And therefore I command thee to do as I believe thou art willing, to disengage thyself from worldly matters as often as thou canst, that thou mayest apply the wisdom which God has given thee wherever thou canst. Consider what punishments would come upon us on account of this world, if we neither loved it (wisdom) ourselves nor suffered other men to obtain it; we should love the name only of Christian, and very few the virtues. When I considered all this, I remembered also that I saw, before it had been all ravaged and burned, how the churches throughout the whole of England stood filled with treasures and books; and there was also a great multitude of God's servants, but they had very little knowledge of the books, for they could not understand anything of them, because they were not written in their own language. As if they had said: "Our forefathers, who formerly held these places, loved wisdom and through it they obtained wealth and bequeathed it to us. In this we can still see their tracks, but we cannot follow them, and therefore we have lost both the wealth and the wisdom, because we would not incline our hearts after their example." When I remembered all this, I wondered extremely that the good and wise men who were formerly all over England, and had perfectly learned all the books, had not wished to translate them into their own language. But again I soon answered myself and said: "They did not think that men would ever be so careless, and that learning would so decay; through that desire they abstained from it, since they wished that the wisdom in this land might increase with our knowledge of languages." Then I remembered how the law was first known in Hebrew, and again, when the Greeks had learned it, they translated the whole of it into their own language, and all other books besides. And again the Romans, when they had learned them, translated the whole of them by learned interpreters into their own language. And also all other Christian nations translated a part of them into their own language. Therefore it seems better to me, if you think so, for us also to translate some books which are most needful for all men to know into the lan-

guage which we can all understand, and for you to do as we
very easily can if we have tranquillity enough,[50] that is, that all
the youth now in England of free men, who are rich enough to
be able to devote themselves to it, be set to learn as long as
they are not fit for any other occupation, until they are able to
read English writing well; and let those be afterwards taught
more in the Latin language who are to continue in learning, and
be promoted to a higher rank. When I remembered how the
knowledge of Latin had formerly decayed throughout England,
and yet many could read English writing, I began, among other
various and manifold troubles of this kingdom, to translate into
English the book which is called in Latin *Pastoralis*, and in
English *Shepherd's Book*, sometimes word by word, and sometimes according to the sense, as I had learned it from Plegmund
my archbishop, and Asser my bishop, and Grimbald my mass-
priest, and John my mass-priest. And when I had learned it
as I could best understand it, and as I could most clearly interpret it, I translated it into English; and I will send a copy to
every bishopric in my kingdom; and in each there is a book-
mark worth fifty mancuses. And I command in God's name
that no man take the book-mark from the book, or the book
from the monastery. It is uncertain how long there may be such
learned bishops as now, thanks be to God, there are nearly
everywhere; therefore I wish them always to remain in their
places unless the bishop wish to take them with him, or they
be lent out anywhere, or any one be making a copy from them.

The popularity and influence of Boethius' *On the Consolation of Philosophy* has already been referred to.[51] From
Alfred's translation of this book we quote the preface and
concluding prayer, for the light they throw on Alfred's
character. In his *Preface* Alfred says:

Alfred, King, was translator of this book, and turned it from
book-latin into English, as it now is done. Sometimes he set
word for word, sometimes translated according to the general

[50] Cf. *ante*, p. 120, Asser's *Life of Alfred*, Chap. 76; *post*, p. 131, preface to his
translation of Boethius, *On the Consolation of Philosophy*.
[51] Cf. *ante*, p. 66 and note.

sense, as he the most plainly and most clearly could render it
(hindered as he was) by the various and manifold worldly occupations which often busied him both in mind and in body. The
occupations are to us very difficult to be numbered, which in his
days came upon the kingdoms which he had undertaken, yet,
when he had learned this book, and turned it from Latin into
the English language, he afterwards composed it in verse, as it
now is done. And he now prays and in God's name implores
every one of those whom it lists to read this book, that he would
pray for him, and not blame him if he more rightly understood
it than he could. For every man must, according to the measure
of his understanding and according to his leisure, speak that
which he speaks, and do that which he does.

Alfred in his concluding prayer writes as follows:

O Lord God Almighty, creator and governor of all creatures,
I beseech thee by thy great mercy, and by the sign of the holy
cross, and by the virginity of the blessed Mary, and by the obedience of the blessed Michael, and by the love of all thy saints
and their merits; that thou wouldest direct me better than my
conduct toward thee would warrant; and direct me to thy will,
and to my soul's need, better than I myself know; and make
steadfast my mind to thy will and to my soul's need; and remove from me foul lust and all unrighteousness; and defend me
against my enemies, visible and invisible; and teach me to do
thy will; that I may inwardly love thee above all things, with
pure mind and with pure body; for thou art my creator and my
redeemer, my help, my comfort, my trust and my hope. To thee
be praise and glory now and forever, world without end. Amen.[52]

Of Ælfric,[53] who has already been described as the best

[52] On Alfred as a character in English literature, see J. Loring Arnold, *King
Alfred in English Poetry*. Add George H. McKnight, *Alfred the Great in Popular
Tradition* in *Studies in Language and Literature in Honor of J. M. Hart* (Henry
Holt & Co., 1910) and G. K. Chesterton, *Varied Types*, pp. 199–206.

[53] The latest summary of our knowledge of Ælfric's life will be found in the
Encyclopædia Britannica, ed. 11. The most extensive review of the materials is
in Caroline L. White, *Ælfric: a New Study of His Life and Writings*, 1898. (*Yale
Studies in English*, 2.) All of Ælfric's prefaces are there collected and a bibliography in chronological order shows the history of Ælfric research.

representative of the culture of his time,[54] we have no contemporary biography. In fact, it was not until the Reformation,[55] when his theological views in opposition to transubstantiation became important to the reformers, that biographical notice of him began to be taken. But the theories concerning his identity have been conflicting and Mr. Hunt concludes, "All that can certainly be known about Ælfric must be gleaned from his writings."[56] The conclusions of modern scholarship are that he was born about 955 and died after 1020. His education was the typical monastic training of his day and his calling that of a monk, first at Winchester, then at Cernel and, finally, at Eynsham, where he became abbot.

For light on his personality, his prefaces are our best source, and of these I quote three; namely, that to the second volume of his *Homilies*,[57] which indicates the sources of his inspiration and his method as a writer; that to his *Latin Grammar*, which reveals his interest in learning and education, his desire to be useful to his generation and his modesty; and that to his paraphrase of Genesis, which exhibits his sense of literary responsibility.

I, Ælfric a monk, have translated this book from Latin books into the English tongue, for those men to read who do not know Latin. I have taken it from the holy gospels, and have treated it according to the expositions of the illustrious doctors whose names I wrote in the former book, in the Latin preface.[58] I have

[54] Cf. *ante*, p. 25.

[55] Miss White (*op. cit.*, p. 199) cites Bale, *Illustrium Maioris Britanniæ Scriptorum . . .*, etc., Ipswich, 1558, as the earliest biographical notice of Ælfric. But Mr. Lane-Poole and Miss Bateson in their 1902 (Clarendon Press) edition of Bale, *Index Britanniæ Scriptorum*, say (note, p. vii) that the *Illustrium Maioris Britanniæ Scriptorum Summarium* was published at Ipswich in 1548. A second edition entitled *Illustrium Maioris Britanniæ Catalogus* was published at Basle in two parts, dated Sept. 1557 and Feb. 1559 respectively.

[56] In the *Dictionary of National Biography*, article *Ælfric*.

[57] An example of these has already been given; cf. *ante*, pp. 91–95.

[58] Ælfric mentions St. Augustine of Hippo, St. Jerome, Bede, Gregory the Great, Smaragdus and Haymo as the sources of his material in the *Homilies*. For

disposed in two books the narratives which I have translated,
thinking it would be less tedious to hear if one book should be
read in the course of one year, and the other the year following. In each of these books there are forty discourses, without
the preface: but they are not all taken from the gospels, many
of them being collected from the lives or the passions of God's
saints — but only of those whom the English nation honors with
feast-days. Before each discourse I have put the title in Latin,
but any one who wishes may change the order of the chapters
after the preface.

The *Preface* to the *Grammar* is as follows:

I, Ælfric, planned to translate this little book of grammar
into the English language from the Latin (of Priscian),[59] after
I rendered the two books of eighty narratives;[60] because grammar is the key which unlocks the meaning of books, and I
thought that this book might help boys at the beginning of
learning, until they came to greater scholarship. It behooves
every man, who has any valuable skill, to make it useful to
other men, and invest the talent which God has invested in him,
in other men, lest God's money lie idle and he be called an unprofitable servant, be bound and cast into outer darkness, as
the holy Gospel saith. It befits young men to learn wisdom,
and old men to teach their juniors, because through learning is
the faith established. And every man who is learned, is blessed,
and the intelligence of him who will neither learn nor teach, if
he can, will grow dull to holy learning, and he will gradually
depart from God. Whence are wise teachers to come among
God's people, if they do not learn in youth, and how can the
faith advance, if learning and teaching are exhausted? God's
servants and "minstermen" need, therefore, to be warned, lest
holy learning in our day cool and disappear, as has been the
case in England for a few years now, so that no English priest

information about the first four, cf. *ante*, pp. 64, 65. Smaragdus was Abbot of
St. Mihiel in the diocese of Verdun and fl. 810. He was biblical commentator,
homilist and hagiographer. Haymo (*circa* 778–853) was an Anglo-Saxon ecclesiastic who became Bishop of Halberstadt in 840.

[59] I carried this reference over from the Latin Preface.
[60] Evidently the *Homilies.*

knew how to compose or think out a letter in Latin, until Archbishop Dunstan [61] and Bishop Æthelwold [62] revived learning in the monasteries. I, therefore, do not assert that this book will take one very far in learning, but it will be, nevertheless, a beginning in each language,[63] if any one cares to use it.

I beg now in God's name that, if any one wishes to copy this book, he follow this archtype carefully; because I have not the power (to prevent mistakes) if some one come to grief through false interpreters. (It is true) it will then be their risk, not mine. The copyist who makes mistakes does a great deal of harm, if he is unwilling (to try) to correct his errors.

The *Preface* to the paraphrase of *Genesis* runs thus:

(Here) begins the Preface to the English Translation of Genesis.

Ælfric the monk humbly greets Æthelwærd the magistrate. You requested me, dear sir, to translate from Latin into English the Book of Genesis; but when I was loth to grant your request, you said that I need not translate further in the book than the account of Isaac, the son of Abraham; because some one else had already prepared you a version from that point to the end of the book. Now it seems to me, dear sir, that the task is very dangerous for me or any one else to undertake, for I am afraid that if some unthinking person reads the book or hears it read, he will imagine that he may live now under the new dispensation just as the patriarchs lived before the old law was given,

[61] Archbishop of Canterbury 959–979. He was a very influential statesman of the time; Ælfric overestimates his ecclesiastical importance. Cf. Stubbs, *Memorials of St. Dunstan* (*Rolls Series*, 1874), which contains the early lives of Dunstan and his letters. The *Anglo-Saxon Chronicle* also gives information regarding him.

[62] (908?–984) Bishop of Winchester. We have his life by Ælfric. He was the real leader in the English religious revival of the 10th century. Cf. the Middle English poem on St. Dunstan in Mätzner, *Alt-Englische Sprach-Proben*, I, 1, pp. 170–176, translated into Modern English verse in Weston, *Chief Middle English Poets*, pp. 37–41 (Houghton, Mifflin & Co., 1914). For a modern historian's view of Dunstan, see John Richard Green, *The Conquest of England*, pp. 269–275, 281–283, 286, 287, 304–309.

[63] Latin and English (?).

or as they lived under the law of Moses. I once knew that a certain priest, who was my master at the time, had a copy of the Book of Genesis and a smattering of Latin. He remarked with regard to the patriarch Jacob that he had four wives, two sisters and their respective maid-servants. His statement was correct, but he did not know, nor did I at the time, what a difference there is between the old dispensation and the new. In the beginning of things in this world, the brother married his sister, and sometimes a father had children by his own daughter, and polygamy was practised that people might increase in numbers, and one could not marry unless he wedded his own relatives. But if any one were to live now as men lived before Moses or under his dispensation, that person would not only not be a Christian, but he would also not be fit for a Christian to eat with. The untutored priests, if they understand a modicum of Latin, immediately imagine themselves great scholars, but they do not yet appreciate the spiritual sense of what they read, nor do they see how the old law was a symbol of what was coming, or how the new covenant after the coming of Christ was the fulfilment of the old ordinances, which the old covenant foreshadowed as coming in Christ and His elect. They often ask, also, with regard to St. Paul why they may not marry as the apostle Peter did. But they refuse to reflect that St. Peter lived according to the law of Moses up to the time when Christ was manifested in the flesh and began to preach His Holy Gospel, and chose Peter as His first companion. Then Peter immediately abandoned his wife, as did the other apostles who were married. All left both wives and property and followed the new law of purity which Christ by His teachings established. Priests are ordained as teachers for the ignorant. Now it behooved them to be able to understand the old dispensation as well as what Christ Himself and His apostles taught in the new, that they might instruct the people effectively in the faith of God, and be wise guides to good works.

We say that this book has a deep spiritual meaning, but we write down nothing but the simple words. So it will appear to the uninstructed that its whole meaning is included in the plain text; but this is far from being the case. This book is

called Genesis, that is the Book of Beginnings, for it is the first
of books and tells of creation; but it says nothing of the creation of angels. It begins thus: "In the beginning God created
the heavens and earth." . . . It is a fact that God almighty did
create in the beginning whatever creatures He wished to create.
But, nevertheless, spiritually, Christ is the Beginning, as He
Himself said to the Jews: "I who speak to you am the Beginning." [64]   Through this Beginning God the Father wrought
heaven and earth, because He made all creatures through the
Son [65] who was born the Wisdom of a wise Father. Again an
early verse of this book ends thus: "The Spirit of God moved
upon the face of the waters." . . . God's Spirit is the Holy
Spirit through whom the Father gave life to all creatures that
He made through the Son, and the Holy Spirit moves in the
hearts of men and gives us forgiveness of sins, first by water in
baptism, and then through penitence; and if any one rejects
the forgiveness that the Holy Spirit offers, his sin is unpardon-
able forever. Again, the Holy Trinity is implied in this book,
that is in the word which God spake, saying: "Let US make
man in OUR image." In that He said, "Let US make," is the
Trinity implied; while in that He said, "In OUR image," is
the true Unity implied. He did not use the plural, saying, "In
OUR images;" but He used the singular, saying, "In OUR
image." Again, there came three angels to Abraham and he
conversed with them as if they were one. (Ælfric means that
this incident symbolizes the Trinity.) How did the blood of
Abel cry out to God if the misdeeds of a person do not accuse
him before God without words? From these few illustrations
you can see how deep the book is in its spiritual meaning, even
though it is a short book. To continue, Joseph, who was sold
into Egypt and saved his kinsfolk from the great famine, is a
symbol of Christ, who was sold to Death for our sake and saved
us from the everlasting famine of Hell torment. That great
tabernacle which Moses made with wonderful skill in the wilderness, as God Himself instructed him, foreshadowed God's invitation which He Himself offered through His apostles with many

[64] Cf. Revelation 1: 8; 21: 6; 22: 13.
[65] Cf. John 1: 3.

graces and winning words. To adorn the tabernacle the people brought gold and silver and precious stones and diverse (other) gifts; some also brought goats'-hair, as God had commanded. The gold betokened our faith and hope which we should offer to God; the silver God's words and the holy lessons which we should learn from God's works; the precious stones symbolized the manifold blessings which we have received from the hand of God through human agency; the goats'-hair the keen repentance which men should feel for their sins. The Israelites also offered many kinds of animals to God within the tabernacle and this act symbolizes many things. Thus it was decreed that the tail should be entire on any animal offered in sacrifice because God wishes that we always do well to the end of our lives. Thus is the tail offered in our works.

The Book of Genesis is thus very concisely written and yet very profound in spiritual meaning. Besides, it is arranged just as God Himself dictated it to Moses and so we dare write no more in English than the Latin has, nor change the arrangement, save so far as may be necessary since English and Latin do not have the same idioms. Whoever translates from Latin into English, or uses a Latin text as the basis for English teaching, must write so that the meaning is plain in English. Otherwise, the result is very misleading for the reader who knows no Latin. It should also be remembered that some heretics desired to cast aside the old law, and others wished to keep the old and discard the new, as the Jews do; but Christ and His apostles taught us both to keep the old spiritually and observe the new truly in our deeds. God gave us two eyes and two ears, two nostrils and two lips, two hands and two feet, and He wished also to have two covenants established on this earth, the old and the new, because He does as seems best to Him, has no counsellor, nor can any one say to Him, "Why dost Thou thus?" We should adjust our wills to His laws and not try to change his decrees according to our desires. My final word is that after this I shall never dare nor desire to translate another book from Latin into English; and I beg of you, dear sir, not to ask me to, lest I be disobedient, if I refuse, or untruthful, if I accede to your wish. God be gracious to you forever.

I request now, in the name of God, that, if any one wishes to copy this book, he make a careful copy of this text, because I have no power to prevent the publication of a false text if one should be spread abroad by lying copyists. A bungler can do much harm if he is unwilling to correct his mistakes.[66]

[66] This document exhibits the medieval fondness for and inclination to allegorical interpretation. Cf. the statements of Bede regarding some of his books; e.g. those on p. 112, *ante*.

CHAPTER II

I. THE POLITICAL BACKGROUND

"It is the judgment of most scholars that the Norman Conquest had a more profound influence upon English history than any other single event." [1] We are, therefore, justified in citing here two of the rather numerous accounts [2] of this event or series of events. The first is the entry for the year 1066 in the Worcester version or manuscript of the anonymous *Anglo-Saxon Chronicle*, already quoted in the first chapter.[3] From this narrative, evidently by an Englishman, we get the bare facts of the Norman invasion with a minimum of interpretation. The writer is clearly a man inclined to a religious view of history.

In this year King Harold came from York to Westminster, at that Easter which was after the mid-winter in which the King [4] died; and Easter was then on the day sixteenth before

[1] A. B. White, *The Making of the English Constitution*, p. 73 (G. P. Putnam's Sons, 1908).

[2] Chronicles are abundant in England 1066–1400 and nearly every chronicler felt called upon to embody in his own work as much material from all available sources as he could find. This makes our accounts numerous, though, obviously, not of equal value. Three accounts, in addition to our citations, are easily accessible in Cheyney, *Readings in English History*, pp. 95–110; those, namely, of Wace, *Roman de Rou* (*Romance of Rollo*), pp. 117–120, 127, 128; of William of Poitou in *Scriptores Normannorum Historiæ* (*Writers of the History of the Normans*), pp. 201 *seq.;* and of *Symeonis Monachi Historia Regum* (*Simeon the Monk's History of the Kings*), Rolls Series, lxxv, part 2, p. 188.

[3] Cf. *ante*, pp. 5, 6, 7, 83.

[4] I.e. Edward the Confessor, King 1042–1066. "The Norman Conquest of England, from a literary point of view, did not begin on the autumn day that saw Harold's levies defeated by Norman archers on the slopes of Senlac. It began with

the Kalends of May.[5] Then was, over all England, such a token
seen in the heavens, as no man ever before saw. Some men
said it was cometa the star, which some call the haired star;
and it appeared first on the eve Litania Major, the eighth before
the Kalends of May,[6] and so shone all the seven nights. And
soon after came in Tosty [7] the earl from beyond sea into the
Isle of Wight, with so great a fleet as he might procure; and
there they yielded him as well money as food. And King Harold,
his brother, gathered so great a ship-force, and also a land-force,
as no king had before done; because it was made known to him
that William the Bastard [8] would come hither and win the land;
all as it afterwards happened. And the while, came Tosty the
earl into Humber with sixty ships; and Edwin [9] the earl came
with a land-force and drove him out. And the boatmen forsook
him; and he went to Scotland with twelve vessels. And there
met him Harold King of Norway with three hundred ships; and
Tosty submitted to him and became his man. And they both
went into Humber, until they came to York; and there fought
against them Edwin the earl [10] and Morcar the earl,[10] his brother:
but the Northmen had the victory. Then was it made known
to Harold King of the English that this had thus happened:
and the battle was the vigil of St. Matthew.[11] Then came Harold our King unawares on the Northmen and met with them
beyond York, at Stamford-bridge, with a great army of English
people; and there during the day was a very severe fight on

the years which, from his early youth onwards, Edward the Confessor, the grandson of a Norman duke, had spent in exile in Normandy; and with his intimacy
with 'foreigners' and its inevitable consequences." A. R. Waller in *Cambridge
History of English Literature*, i, p. 165.

[5] I.e. April 16.   [6] I.e. April 24.

[7] Son of Godwin Earl of Wessex and brother of King Harold II, Tostig had
been appointed Earl of Northumbria in 1055 by Edward the Confessor, passing
over Waltheof, son of Earl Siward, the legitimate claimant of the earldom. But
about ten years later the Northumbrians rose in revolt against Tostig and threw
off his rule, choosing in his stead Morcar or Morcere, brother of Edwin, Earl of
Mercia.

[8] William the Conqueror.   [9] See previous note.

[10] See previous note (9): Edwin and his brother Morcar were opponents of the
house of Godwin.

[11] I.e. Sept. 21.

both sides.   There was slain Harold the Fairhaired [12] and Tosty
the earl; and the Northmen who were there remaining were put
to flight; and the English from behind hotly smote them, until
they came, some to their ships, some were drowned, and some
also burned; and thus in divers ways they perished, so that
there were few left; and the English had possession of the place
of carnage.   The King then gave his protection to Olave, son
of the King of the Norwegians and to their bishop and to the
Earl of Orkney and to all those who were left in the ships: and
then they went up to our King and swore oaths that they ever
would observe peace and friendship towards this land; and the
King let them go home with twenty-four ships.   These two general battles were fought within five days.   Then came William
Earl of Normandy into Pevensey [13] on the eve of St. Michael's-
mass; [14] and soon after they were on their way, they constructed
a castle at Hasting's-port.   This was then made known to King
Harold and he then gathered a great force and came to meet
him at the estuary of Appledore; [15] and William came against
him unawares, before his people were set in order.   But the King,
nevertheless, strenuously fought against him with those men
who would follow him; and there was a great slaughter made on
either hand.   There was slain King Harold and Leofwin the
earl,[16] his brother, and Girth the earl,[17] his brother, and many
good men; and the Frenchmen had possession of the place of
carnage, all as God granted them for the people's sins.   Archbishop Aldred [18] and the townsmen of London would then have
child Edgar [19] for king, all as was his true natural right: and
Edwin and Morcar vowed to him that they would fight together
with him.   But in that degree that it ought ever to have been

[12] This was not Harald I, Haarfagr or Fairhaired, King of Norway from about
860 to about 930, but Harald III, Haardraacle or Hard-ruler (1015–1066), King
of Norway, 1046–1066.   [13] In Sussex

[14] September 28.   [15] In Kent.

[16] Earl of East Anglia, fourth son of Godwin Earl of Wessex.

[17] Fifth son of Godwin Earl of Wessex, governor of Kent in 1049, probably
under his father's direction. According to Hunt in the *Dictionary of National
Biography* (article *Leofwine*) L. was never an earl.   [18] Of York.

[19] Grandson of Edmund Ironside, who was displaced as King of England by
Cnut in 1016, and grand-nephew of Edward the Confessor.   Edgar died in 1120.

forwarder, so was it ever from day to day later and worse; so that at the end all passed away. This fight was done on the day of Calixtus the Pope.[20] And William the earl went afterwards again to Hastings, and there awaited to see whether the people would submit to him. But when he understood that they would not come to him, he went upwards with all his army which was left to him, and that which afterwards had come from over sea to him; and he plundered all that part which he overran, until he came to Berkhampstead.[21] And there came to meet him Archbishop Aldred, child Edgar, Edwin the earl, Morcar the earl, and all the chief men of London; and (they) then submitted for need (to William) after the most harm had been done: and it was very unwise that they had not done so before; since God would not better it, for our sins: and they delivered hostages and swore oaths to him; and he vowed to them that he would be a loving lord to them: and nevertheless, during this, they (the Normans?) plundered all that they overran. Then, on midwinter's-day,[22] Archbishop Aldred consecrated him King at Westminster; and he gave a pledge upon Christ's book and also swore, before he would set the crown upon his head, that he would govern the nation as well as any king before him had at the best done, if they would be faithful to him. Nevertheless, he laid a tribute on the people, very heavy; and then went, during Lent, over sea to Normandy, and took with him Archbishop Stigand [23] and Aylnoth [24] Abbot of Glastonbury and child Edgar, Edwin the earl, Morcar the earl, Waltheof the earl and many other good men of England. And Bishop Odo [25] and William [26] the earl remained here behind and they built castles wide throughout the country and distressed the poor, and ever after it grew greatly in evil. May the end be when God will !

[20] October 14.   [21] In Hertford.   [22] Christmas Day.

[23] Of Canterbury. Stigand was an Englishman who displaced Robert of Jumieges as Archbishop of Canterbury. In the appointment, "the pope, however, was not consulted, and his decision that the proceeding was unlawful gave William a second pretext for his later invasion of England." Cross, *A History of England and Greater Britain*, p. 57 (The Macmillan Co., 1914).

[24] Not in the *Dictionary of National Biography*.

[25] Bishop of Bayeux, half-brother of William the Conqueror, later appointed Earl of Kent.   [26] William FitzOsbert, created Earl of Hereford.

Alongside of this story of the Battle of Hastings put the following, the product of a later generation and the source of many accounts in current text-books. Its author, William of Malmesbury (*circa* 1080–*circa* 1143), has, since the days of Milton,[27] been recognized as the best of twelfth-century historians. He prided himself not so much on giving the facts as on interpreting them correctly and fully.

King Edward declining into years, as he had no children himself, and saw the sons of Godwin growing in power, despatched messengers to the king of Hungary to send over Edward, the son of his brother Edmund, with all his family, intending, as he declared, that either he or his sons, should succeed to the hereditary kingdom of England, and that his own want of issue should be supplied by that of his kindred. Edward came in consequence but died almost immediately at St. Paul's in London; he was neither valiant nor a man of abilities. He left three surviving children; that is to say, Edgar [28] who, after the death of Harold, was by some elected king; and who, after many revolutions of fortune, is now living wholly retired in the country, in extreme old age; Christina, who grew old at Romsey in the habit of a nun; Margaret, whom Malcolm King of the Scots espoused. Blessed with a numerous offspring, her sons were Edgar and Alexander, who reigned in Scotland after their father in due succession: for the eldest, Edward, had fallen in battle with his father: the youngest, David, noted for his meekness and discretion, is at present King of Scotland. Her daughters were Matilda, whom in our time King Henry [29] has married, and Maria, whom Eustace the younger, Count of Boulogne, espoused. The King, in consequence of the death of his relative, losing his first hope of support, gave the succession to William Earl of Normandy. He was well worthy of such a gift, being a young man of superior mind, who had raised himself to the highest eminence by his unwearied exertion: moreover, he was his nearest relative by blood, as he was the son of Robert, the son of Richard

[27] *History of England*, Book iv, Mitford's ed., v, p. 172.
[28] I.e. the child Edgar of the preceeding passage.
[29] I.e. Henry I, youngest son of William the Conqueror.

the second, whom we have repeatedly mentioned as the brother
of Emma,[30] Edward's mother. Some affirm that Harold himself
was sent into Normandy by the King for this purpose: others,
who knew Harold's more secret intentions, say that he being
driven thither against his will, by the violence of the wind, imagined this device in order to extricate himself. This, as it appears
nearest the truth, I shall relate. Harold, being at his country
seat of Boseham, went for recreation on board a fishing vessel,
and, for the purpose of prolonging his sport, put out to sea;
when, a sudden tempest arising, he was driven with his companions on the coast of Ponthieu. The people of that district,
as was their native custom, immediately assembled from all
quarters; and Harold's company, unarmed and few in number,
were, as it easily might be, quickly overpowered by an armed
multitude and bound hand and foot. Harold, craftily meditating a remedy for this mischance, sent a person whom he had
allured by very great promises, to William, to say that he had
been sent into Normandy by the King for the purpose of expressly confirming in person the message which had been imperfectly delivered by people of less authority; but that he was
detained in fetters by Guy Count of Ponthieu and could not
execute his embassy: that it was the barbarous and inveterate
custom of the country, that such as had escaped destruction at
sea, should meet with perils on shore: that it well became a
man of his dignity not to let this pass unpunished; that to suffer
those to be laden with chains who appealed to his protection
detracted somewhat from his own greatness: and that if his captivity must be terminated by money, he would gladly give it to
Earl William, but not to the contemptible Guy. By these means
Harold was liberated at William's command and conducted to
Normandy by Guy in person. The Earl entertained him with
much respect both in banqueting and in vesture according to
the custom of his country and, the better to learn his disposition
and at the same time to try his courage, took him with him in

[30] Emma had married (1) Ethelred the Unready, King of England 979–1016,
father of Edward the Confessor; (2) Cnute, King of England 1016–1035. The
son of Cnute and Emma was Hardicnute, King of England 1040–1042. One source
of our knowledge of this period is a work called *Encomium Emmæ* (*Praise of Emma*).

an expedition he at that time led against Brittany.   There,
Harold, well proved both in ability and courage, won the heart
of the Norman; and, still more to ingratiate himself, he of his
own accord, confirmed to him by oath the castle of Dover, which
was under his jurisdiction, and the Kingdom of England after
the death of Edward. Wherefore, he was honored both by having his daughter, then a child, betrothed to him, and by the
confirmation of his ample patrimony [31] and was received into
the strictest intimacy. Not long after his return home, the King
was crowned at London on Christmas-day and, being there
seized with a disorder of which he was sensible he should die,
he commanded the church of Westminster to be dedicated on
Innocents'-day.[32] Thus, full of years and of glory, he surrendered
his pure spirit to heaven, and was buried on the day of the
Epiphany [33] in the said church, which he first in England, had
erected after that kind of style which now almost all attempt to
rival at enormous expense. The race of the West Saxons which
had reigned in Britain five hundred and seventy-one years from
the time of Cerdic, and two hundred and sixty-one from Egbert,
in him ceased altogether to rule.   For, while the grief for the
King's death was yet fresh, Harold, on the very day of the
Epiphany, seized the diadem and extorted from the nobles their
consent; though the English say that it was granted him by the
King: but I conceive it alleged, more through regard to Harold,
than through sound judgment, that Edward should transfer his
inheritance to a man of whose power he had always been jealous.
Still, not to conceal the truth, Harold would have governed the
kingdom with prudence and with courage, in the character he
had assumed, had he undertaken it lawfully. Indeed, during
Edward's lifetime, he had quelled by his valor, whatever wars
were excited against him; wishing to signalize himself with his
countrymen and looking forward with anxious hope to the crown.
He first vanquished Griffin King of the Welsh, as I have before
related, in battle; and, afterwards, when he was again making
formidable efforts to recover his power, deprived him of his
head; appointing as his successors two of his own adherents,

[31] Harold had succeeded his father Godwin as Earl of Wessex in 1053.
[32] I.e. December 28, 1065.   [33] I.e. January 6, 1066.

that is, the brothers of Griffin, Blegant and Rivallo, who had
obtained his favor by their submission. The same year Tosty
arrived on the Humber from Flanders with a fleet of sixty ships
and infested with piratical depredations those parts which were
adjacent to the mouth of the river; but, being quickly driven
from the province by the joint force of the brothers Edwin and
Morcar, he set sail towards Scotland; where, meeting with Harold
Harfager King of Norway then meditating an attack on England
with three hundred ships, he put himself under his command.
Both then with united forces, laid waste the country beyond the
Humber; and falling on the brothers, reposing after their recent
victory and suspecting no attack of the kind, they first routed
and then shut them up in York. Harold, on hearing this, proceeded thither with all his forces, and, each nation making every
possible exertion, a bloody encounter followed: but the English
obtained the advantage and put the Norwegians to flight. Yet,
however reluctantly posterity may believe it, one single Norwegian for a long time delayed the triumph of so many and such
great men. For, standing on the entrance of the bridge which is
called Standford Bridge, after having killed several of our party,
he prevented the whole from passing over. Being invited to surrender, with the assurance that a man of such courage should
experience the amplest clemency from the English, he derided
those who entreated him; and immediately reproached the set
of cowards who were unable to resist an individual. No one
approaching nearer, as they thought it unadvisable to come to
close quarters with a man who had desperately rejected every
means of safety, one of the King's followers aimed an iron javelin at him from a distance and transfixed him as he was boast-
fully flourishing about and too incautious from his security, so
that he yielded the victory to the English. The army immediately passing over without opposition, destroyed the dispersed
and flying Norwegians. King Harfager and Tosty were slain;
the King's son with all his ships was kindly sent back to his
own country. Harold, elated by his successful enterprise, vouchsafed no part of the spoil to his soldiers. Wherefore, many, as
they found opportunity, stealing away, deserted the King, as he
was proceeding to the battle of Hastings. For with the excep-

tion of his stipendiary and mercenary soldiers, he had very few of the people with him; on which account, circumvented by a stratagem of William's, he was routed with the army he headed, after possessing the kingdom nine months and some days. The effect of war in this affair was trifling; it was brought about by the secret and wonderful counsel of God; since the Angles never again in any general battle, made a struggle for liberty, as if the whole strength of England had fallen with Harold, who certainly might and ought to pay the penalty of his perfidy, even though it were at the hands of the most unwarlike people. Nor in saying this, do I at all derogate from the valor of the Normans, to whom I am strongly bound, both by my descent and for the privileges that I enjoy. Still those persons appear to me to err who augment the numbers of the English and underrate their courage; who, while they design to extol the Normans, load them with ignominy. A mighty commendation indeed! that a very warlike nation should conquer a set of people who were obstructed by their multitude and fearful through cowardice! On the contrary, they were few in number and brave in the extreme; and, sacrificing every regard to their bodies, poured forth their spirit for their country. But as these matters await a more detailed narrative, I shall now put a period to my second book, that I may return to my composition, and my readers to the perusal of it, with fresh ardor. . . .

When King Edward had yielded to fate, England, fluctuating with doubtful favor, was uncertain to which ruler she should commit herself: to Harold, William or Edgar: for the King had recommended him also to the nobility, as nearest to the sovereignty in point of birth; concealing his better judgment from the tenderness of his disposition. Wherefore, as I have said above, the English were distracted in their choice, although all of them openly wished well to Harold. He, indeed, once dignified with the diadem, thought nothing of the covenant between himself and William: he said that he was absolved from his oath because his daughter, to whom he had been betrothed, had died before she was marriageable. For this man, though possessed of numberless good qualities, is reported to have been careless about abstaining from perfidy, so that he could by any device, elude the reasonings of men on this matter. Moreover, supposing that the threats of William could never be put into execution, because he was occupied in wars with neighboring princes, he had, with his subjects, given full indulgence to security. For indeed, had he not heard that the King of Norway was approaching, he would neither have condescended to collect troops, nor to array them. William, in the meantime, began mildly to address him by messengers; to expostulate on the broken covenant; to mingle threats with entreaties; and to warn him that, ere a year had expired, he would claim his due by the sword, and that he would come to that place where Harold supposed he had firmer footing than himself. Harold again rejoined what I have related concerning the nuptials of his daughter and added that he had been precipitate on the subject of the kingdom in having confirmed to him by oath another's right without the universal consent and edict of the general meeting and of the people: again that a rash oath ought to be broken; for if the oath or vow which a maiden under her father's roof made concerning her person without the knowledge of her parents was adjudged invalid, how much more must that oath be which he had made concerning the whole kingdom when under the King's authority, compelled by the necessity of the time and without the knowledge of the nation. Besides, it was an unjust request, to ask him to resign a government which he had assumed by the universal kindness of his fellow subjects and which would neither be agreeable to the people nor safe for the military.

In this way, confounded either by true or by plausible arguments, the messengers returned without success. The earl, however, made every necessary preparation for war during the whole of that year; retained his own soldiers with increased pay and invited those of others; ordered his ranks and battalions in such wise that the soldiers should be tall and stout; that the commanders and standard-bearers, in addition to their military science, should be looked up to for their wisdom and age; insomuch that each of them, whether seen in the field or elsewhere, might be taken for a prince, rather than a leader. The bishops and abbots of those days vied so much in religion, and the nobility in princely liberality, that it is wonderful, within a period of sixty years, how either order should have become so unfruitful in goodness, as to take up a confederate war [34] against justice: the former, through desire of ecclesiastical promotion, embracing wrong in preference to right and equity; and the latter, casting off shame, and seeking every occasion for begging money as for their daily pay. But at that time the prudence of William, seconded by the providence of God, already anticipated the invasion of England; and, that no rashness might stain his just cause, he sent to the pope, formerly Anselm Bishop of Lucca, who had assumed the name of Alexander,[35] alleging the justice of the war which he meditated with all the eloquence he was master of. Harold omitted to do this, either because he was proud by nature or else distrusted his cause; or because he feared that his messengers would be obstructed by William and his partisans, who beset every port. The pope, duly examining the pretensions of both parties, delivered a standard to William as an auspicious presage of the kingdom: on receiving which, he summoned an assembly of his nobles, at Lillebourne, for the purpose of ascertaining their sentiments on this attempt. And when he had confirmed by splendid promises all who approved his design he appointed them to prepare shipping, in proportion to the extent of their posses-sions. Thus they departed at that time; and in the month of August reassembled in a body at St. Vallery,[36] for so that port is called by its new name. Collecting, therefore, ships from every quarter, they awaited the propitious gale which was to carry them to their destination. When this delayed blowing for several days, the common soldiers, as is generally the case, began to mutter in their tents, "The man must be mad who wishes to subjugate a foreign country; that God opposed him who withheld the wind; that his father purposed a similar attempt and was in like manner frustrated; that it was the fate of that family to aspire to things beyond their reach and find God for their adversary." In consequence of these things, which were enough to enervate the force of the brave, being publicly noised abroad, the duke held a council with his chiefs and ordered the body of St. Vallery to be brought forth and to be exposed to the

[34] A reference to the disorders of the reign of Stephen; cf. *post*, pp. 206–209.
[35] Alexander II.   [36] In Picardy.

open air for the purpose of imploring a wind. No delay now interposed but the wished-for gale filled their sails. A joyful clamor then arising summoned every one to the ships. The earl himself first launching from the continent awaited the rest at anchor nearly in mid-channel. All then assembled round the crimson sail of the admiral's ship; and having first dined they arrived after a favorable passage at Hastings. As he disembarked he slipped down but turned the accident to his advantage; a soldier who stood near calling out to him, "You hold England, my lord, its future king." He then restrained his whole army from plundering; warning them that they should now abstain from what must hereafter be their own; and for fifteen successive days he remained so perfectly quiet that he seemed to think of nothing less than of war.

In the meantime Harold returned from the battle with the Norwegians; happy in his own estimation at having conquered; but not so in mine, as he had secured the victory by parricide.[37] When the news of the Normans' arrival reached him, reeking as he was from battle, he proceeded to Hastings though accompanied by very few forces. No doubt the fates urged him on, as he neither summoned his troops nor, had he been willing to do so, would he have found many ready to obey his call; so hostile were all to him, as I have before observed, from his having appropriated the northern spoils to himself. He sent out some persons, however, to reconnoiter the number and strength of the enemy: these, being taken within the camp, William ordered to be led amongst the tents, and, after feasting them plentifully, to be sent back uninjured to their lord. On their return Harold inquired what news they brought: when, after relating in full the noble confidence of the general, they gravely added that almost all his army had the appearance of priests, as they had the whole face, with both lips, shaven. For the English leave the upper lip unshorn, suffering the hair continually to increase; which Julius Cæsar [38] in his treatise on the Gallic War affirms to have been a national custom with the ancient inhabitants of Britain. The King smiled at the simplicity of the relators, ob-

[37] Fratricide rather; he had helped kill his brother Tostig.
[38] Book iv, chapter 14. (Giles' note.)

serving with a pleasant laugh that they were not priests but soldiers, strong in arms and invincible in spirit. His brother Girth, a youth on the verge of manhood and of a knowledge and valor surpassing his years, caught up his words, "Since," said he, "you extol so much the valor of the Norman, I think it ill-advised for you, who are his inferior in strength and desert, to contend with him. Nor can you deny being bound to him by oath, either willingly or by compulsion. Wherefore, you will act wisely, if, yourself withdrawing from this pressing emergency, you allow us to try the issue of a battle. We, who are free from all obligation, shall justly draw the sword in defence of our country. It is to be apprehended that, if you engage, you will be subjected either to flight or to death, whereas, if we only fight, your cause will be safe at all events: for you will be able to rally the fugitives and to avenge the dead."

His unbridled rashness yielded no placid ear to the words of his adviser, thinking it base and a reproach to his past life to turn his back on danger of any kind; and with similar impudence, or, to speak more favorably, imprudence, he drove away a monk, the messenger of William, not deigning him even a complacent look; imprecating only that God would decide between him and the earl. He was the bearer of three propositions; either that Harold should relinquish the kingdom, according to his agreement, or hold it of William, or decide the matter by single combat in the sight of both armies. For William claimed the kingdom on the ground that King Edward by the advice of Stigand the Archbishop and of the earls Siward and Godwin had granted it to him and had sent the son and nephew of Godwin to Normandy as sureties of the grant. If Harold should deny this, he would abide by the judgment of the pope or by battle, on all which propositions the messenger being frustrated by the single answer I have related, returned and communicated to his party fresh spirit for the conflict.

The courageous leaders mutually prepared for battle, each according to his national custom. The English, as we have heard, passed the night without sleep in drinking and singing and, in the morning, proceeded without delay towards the enemy; all were on foot, armed with battle-axes, and covering themselves

in front by the junction of their shields they formed an impene-
trable body, which would have secured their safety that day, had
not the Normans by a feigned flight induced them to open their
ranks which till that time according to their custom were closely
compacted. The King himself on foot stood with his brother
near the standard, in order that, while all shared equal danger,
none might think of retreating. This standard William sent
after the victory to the pope; it was sumptuously embroidered
with gold and precious stones, in the form of a man fighting.

On the other side the Normans passed the whole night in confessing their sins and received the sacrament in the morning.
Their infantry with bows and arrows formed the vanguard, while
their cavalry, divided into wings, were thrown back. The earl,
with a serene countenance declaring aloud that God would favor
his as being the righteous side, called for his arms; and presently
when through the hurry of his attendants he had put on his
hauberk the hind part before, he corrected the mistake with a
laugh: saying, "My dukedom shall be turned into a kingdom."
Then beginning the song of Roland,[39] that the warlike example
of that man might stimulate the soldiers, and calling on God
for assistance, they began the battle on both sides. They fought
with ardor, neither giving ground, for a great part of the day.
Finding this, William gave a signal to his party that by a feigned
flight they should retreat. Through this device the close body
of the English, opening for the purpose of cutting down the
straggling enemy, brought upon itself swift destruction; for the
Normans, facing about, attacked them thus disordered, and compelled them to fly. In this manner, deceived by a stratagem,

[39] This is the name of the national epic of early France, corresponding roughly
to the Old English *Beowulf*. Whether the song started at Hastings was any part
of the extant Song of Roland cannot be stated, but Malmesbury's words indicate,
at least, that the story of Roland was popular. Wace (cf. *post*, p. 559), in his *Brut*,
ii, 11, l. 8035 *seq.*, says that the minstrel who started the song at Hastings was named
Taillefer. The most popular edition of the extant *Chanson de Roland* (*Song of Roland*) is by Leon Gautier, with text, translation (into modern French), introduction,
notes, variant readings and glossary. This edition was first published at Tours in
1872 and has been often reissued. The Old French has been rendered into modern
English prose by Isabel Butler (*Riverside Literature Series*, Houghton Mifflin Co.,
1904).

they met an honorable death in avenging their country; nor
indeed were they at all backward in avenging themselves, as,
by frequently making a stand, they slaughtered their pursuers
in heaps: for, getting possession of an eminence, they drove
down the Normans when roused with indignation and anxiously
striving to gain the higher ground, into the valley beneath,
where, easily hurling their javelins and rolling down stones on
them as they stood below, they destroyed them to a man. Besides, by a short passage, with which they were acquainted,
avoiding a deep ditch, they trod under foot such a multitude of
their enemies in that place that they made the hollow level with
the plain by the heaps of carcasses. This vicissitude of first one
party conquering and then the other prevailed as long as the
life of Harold continued; but when he fell from having his brain
pierced with an arrow, the flight of the English ceased not until
night. The valor of both leaders was here eminently conspicuous.

Harold, not content with the mere duty of a general in exhorting others, diligently entered into every soldier-like office; often
he would strike the enemy when coming to close quarters, so that
none could approach him with impunity; for immediately the
same blow levelled both horse and rider. Wherefore, as I have
related, receiving the fatal arrow from a distance, he yielded to
death. One of the soldiers with a sword gashed his thigh, as he
lay prostrate; for which shameful and cowardly action he was
branded with ignomy by William and dismissed the service.

William too was equally ready by his voice and by his presence to be the first to rush forward, to attack the thickest of
the foe. Thus everywhere raging, everywhere furious, he lost
three choice horses which were that day pierced under him. The
dauntless spirit and vigor of the intrepid general, however, still
persisted though often called back by the kind remonstrance of
his body-guard: he still persisted, I say, till approaching night
crowned him with complete victory. And no doubt, the hand
of God so protected him that the enemy should draw no blood
from his person, though they aimed so many javelins at him.

This was a fatal day to England, a melancholy havoc of our
dear country, through its change of masters. For it had long
since adopted the manners of the Angles which had varied

greatly according to the times; for in the first years of their
arrival they were barbarians in their look and manners, warlike in their usages, heathen in their rites; but, after embracing
the faith of Christ, by degrees and in the process of time, from
the peace they enjoyed, regarding arms in a secondary light
only, they gave their whole attention to religion. I say nothing
of the poor, the meanness of whose fortune often restrains them
from overstepping the bounds of justice: I omit men of ecclesiastical rank whom sometimes respect for their profession and
sometimes the fear of shame, suffer not to deviate from the
truth: I speak of princes who from the greatness of their power
might have full liberty to indulge in pleasure; some of whom,
in their own country and others at Rome, changing their habit,
obtained a heavenly kingdom and a saintly intercourse. Many
during their whole lives in outward appearance only embraced
the present world in order that they might exhaust their treasures on the poor, or divide them amongst monasteries. What
shall I say of the multitudes of bishops, hermits and abbots?
Does not the whole island blaze with such numerous relics of
its natives that you can scarcely pass a village of any consequence
but you hear the name of some saint, besides the numbers of
whom all notices have perished through the want of records?
Nevertheless, in process of time, the desire for literature and
religion decayed for several years before the arrival of the Normans. The clergy, contented with a very slight degree of learning, could scarcely stammer out the words of the sacraments;
and a person who understood grammar [40] was an object of wonder and astonishment. The monks mocked the rule of their
order by fine vestments and the use of every kind of food. The
nobility, given up to luxury and wantonness, did not go to
church in the morning after the manner of Christians, but merely
in a careless manner heard matins and masses from a hurrying
priest in their chambers amid the blandishments of their wives.
The commonalty, left unprotected, became a prey to the most
powerful who amassed fortunes by either seizing on their property or by selling their persons into foreign countries; although
it is an innate quality of this people to be more inclined to

[40] I.e. Latin.

revelling than to the accumulation of wealth. There was one custom, repugnant to nature, which they adopted; namely, to sell their female servants, when pregnant by them and after they had satisfied their lust, either to public prostitution, or foreign slavery. Drinking in parties was a universal practice, in which occupation they passed entire nights as well as days. They consumed their whole substance in mean and despicable houses; unlike the Normans and French who, in noble and splendid mansions, lived in frugality. The vices attendant on drunkenness which enervate the mind followed; hence it arose that engaging William more with rashness and precipitate fury than military skill they doomed themselves and their country to slavery by one, and that an easy, victory. "For nothing is less effective than rashness and what begins in violence quickly ceases or is repelled." In fine, the English at that time wore short garments reaching to the mid-knee; they had their hair cropped; their beards shaven; their arms laden with golden bracelets; their skin adorned with tattooed designs. They were accustomed to eat till they became surfeited and to drink till they were sick. These latter habits they imparted to their conquerors; as to the rest they adopted their manners. I would not, however, have these bad propensities universally ascribed to the English. I know that many of the clergy at that day trod the path of sanctity by a blameless life; I know that many of the laity, of all ranks and conditions, in this nation were well-pleasing to God. Be injustice far from this account; the accusation does not involve the whole indiscriminately. "But, as in peace, the mercy of God often cherishes the bad and the good together; so, equally, does His severity sometimes include them both in captivity."

Moreover, the Normans, that I may speak of them also, were at that time and are even now, proudly apparelled, delicate in their food but not excessive. They are a race inured to war and can hardly live without it; fierce in rushing against the enemy, and where strength fails of success ready to use stratagem or to corrupt by bribery. As I have said, they live in large houses with economy, envy their equals, wish to excel their superiors and plunder their subjects, though they defend them from others; they are faithful to their lords, though a slight offence renders them perfidious. They weigh treachery by its chance of success and change their sentiments for money. They are, however, the kindest of nations and they esteem strangers worthy of equal honor with themselves. They also intermarry with their vassals. They revived by their coming the observances of religion which were everywhere grown lifeless in England. You might see churches rise in every village and monasteries in the towns and cities, built after a style unknown before; you might behold the country flourishing with renovated rites; so that each wealthy man accounted that day lost to him which he had neglected to signalize by some magnificent action. But, having enlarged sufficiently on these points, let us pursue the transactions of William.[41]

In less than a century after the Conquest, fresh continental contact and influence were thrust upon England when Henry of Anjou, great-grandson of William the Conqueror, came to the English throne. The vigor of his

[41] In addition to the written sources of information on the Norman Conquest of England, we have the famous Bayeux Tapestry. "It is a pictorial story of the events from the time Harold was blown across the Channel in 1065, to his death. It is embroidered on a strip of canvas nineteen inches wide and two hundred and thirty-one feet long. It was probably designed for the Bayeux Cathedral, where it is still preserved." Cross, *op cit.*, p. 60. It was made under the orders of Odo, half-brother of the Conqueror. The latest detailed political history of this period is Adams, *Political History of England, 1066–1216.* (Vol. ii in Hunt and Poole, *Political History of England,* Longmans, Green and Co., 1905.) Norman ascendancy in England was not established by the single victory at Hastings; William was occupied for several years in "putting down risings and overcoming resistance to the extension of his authority." Cross, *op. cit.,* p. 77. It was at this time that the hero Hereward was active. He is mentioned by Florence of Worcester, *Chronicle,* tr. Forester, p. 177 (*Bohn Antiquarian Library,* 1854) as "a man of great bravery." He is given a good deal of attention in Ingulph's *Chronicle of the Abbey of Croyland,* tr. Riley (*Bohn Antiquarian Library,* 1854), pp. 135–143, Index. This, Professor Freeman holds, may embody genuine Croyland tradition. (*Dictionary of National Biography,* article *Ingulph.*) See also *Anglo-Saxon Chronicle,* entries for 1070 and 1071. Charles Kingsley in *Hereward the Wake* (1866) has made an interesting story of his life, real and fictitious. Other literary works treating the period of the Conquest are Bulwer Lytton, *Harold: the Last of the Saxons* (1848) and Tennyson, *Harold* (1876).

policies, primarily intended to strengthen the royal powers,
and the long life of the dynasty established by him,[42] make
it worth while to become acquainted with him.   He is
thus described by Peter of Blois (*circa* 1135–*circa* 1205),
secretary to Richard and Baldwin, successive archbishops
of Canterbury.

What you[43] have urgently asked me, — to send you a true
account of the appearance and habits of the lord king of England,
is indeed beyond my power.   For that task even the genius of a
Virgil would seem insufficient.   But what I know I will tell without
malice or slander.

Of David it is written in praise of his beauty,[44] that he was of
a ruddy complexion, and you know that the lord king was somewhat ruddy until venerable old age[45] and the coming of gray
hair changed him a little.   He is of medium height, so that
among short men he appears tall and not insignificant among
taller ones.   His head is round in shape, as if it were the seat
of great wisdom and the special sanctuary of noble counsel.   In
size it harmonizes well with his neck and the proportions of his
whole body.   His eyes are round, and when he is in a peaceable
mood, dove-like and quiet; but when he is angry and his spirit
is disturbed, they seem to flash fire and are like lightning.   He
is not bald, but his hair is kept close-cut.   His face is lion-like
and quadrangular in shape.   His nose is prominent, in keeping
with the symmetry of his whole body; his highly-arched feet,
limbs suited for horsemanship, broad chest and brawny arms
proclaim him a man strong, active and daring. . . . His hands
by their coarseness show the indifference of the man, for he
neglects them absolutely and never puts on a glove except when
he is hawking.   Every day, all day long, he is standing on his
feet, whether at mass, in council, or engaged in other public
business, and although his limbs are terribly bruised and dis-
colored from the effects of hard riding, he never sits down unless

[42] The Plantagenets reigned in England 1154–1399.
[43] The letter is addressed to William Archbishop of Palermo, Sicily.
[44] Cf. 1 Samuel 16: 12.
[45] Henry II was born in 1133 and this letter was written in 1177.

he is on horseback or is eating. In one day, if business demands it, he accomplishes four or five days' journeys, and so by his rapid and unexpected movements he often forestalls and defeats the plans of his enemies. He wears straight boots, a plain hat and easy dress. An ardent lover of field sports, he is no sooner through with a battle than he is exercising with hawk and hound. He would find his heavy weight a burden did he not overcome his tendency to corpulence by fasting and exercise. He is still able to mount a horse and ride with all the lightness of youth, and he tires out the strongest men by his travels nearly every day. For he does not, like other kings, stay quiet in his palace, but, rushing through the provinces, he inquires into the deeds of all men, judging especially those whom he has appointed to be judges over others.

No one is more shrewd in counsel, more ready in speech, more fearless in danger, in prosperity more prudent, in adversity more steadfast. The man whom he has once loved he always loves, but he will rarely admit to familiarity one whom he has once found disagreeable. Unless he is in council or at his books he always has in his hands a bow, a sword, spears and arrows. For whenever he can take a respite from cares and anxieties he occupies himself with private reading, or in the midst of a group of clergymen, endeavors to solve some knotty problem. Your king [46] knows literature well, but ours is much better versed in it.[47] For I know the attainments of each of them in the knowledge of books. You know that the lord king of Sicily was my pupil for a year, and after he had learned from you the elements of versification and literary art, by my industry and care he gained the benefit of fuller knowledge. But, as soon as I left the kingdom, throwing aside his books, he gave himself up to the idleness of the palace. But as for the lord king of England, his

[46] William II, King of Sicily.

[47] Henry II, was a great patron of literary men and scholars; cf. Stubbs, *Seventeen Lectures on the Study of Mediæval and Modern History*, Lectures vi and vii. *Learning and Literature at the Court of Henry II.* Henry's wife, Eleanor of Aquitaine, was the friend and patroness of many Provençal troubadours. Another description of Henry from the works of Giraldus Cambrensis (*Rolls Series*, xxi, Part 5, pp. 302–306, accessible in Cheyney, *op. cit.*, pp. 137–139) agrees in the main with this of Peter of Blois, but emphasizes the secular character of Henry's reign.

daily leisure is habitually devoted to the discussion of questions. None more than our king is honorable in speech, restrained in eating, moderate in drinking, none is more noble at home; hence, his name is spread out like sweet ointment and the whole church of the saints celebrates his alms. Our king is of a peaceful disposition, victorious in war, glorious in peace, and above all the desirable things in the world he zealously looks out for the peace of his people. Whatever he thinks or says or does is for the peace of his people. That his people may have peace he constantly undergoes troublesome and grievous toil. With a view to the peace of his people he calls councils, makes treaties, forms alliances, humbles the proud, threatens war, strikes terror to rulers. For the peace of his people he uses that enormous wealth which he gives, receives, collects and spends. No one is more skilful or lavish than he in building walls, defenses, fortifications, moats, places of enclosure for game and fish, and in building palaces.

His father, a very powerful and noble count,[48] made great additions to his territory, but he, by the strength of his own hand adding to his father's possessions the duchies of Normandy, Aquitaine and Brittany, the kingdoms of England, Scotland,[49] Ireland and Wales, has beyond measure surpassed his noble father's claims to greatness. No one is more gentle to the afflicted, more kind to the poor, more oppressive to the proud: for he has always made it a study like a god to put down the insolent, to raise the oppressed, and to the arrogance of pride to oppose continual and grievous persecutions. But although, after the custom of the kingdom, he takes a very powerful and important part in making appointments, yet he has always kept his hands clean and free from all venality. I will not describe, but will merely touch in passing, those other gifts, both of mind

[48] Geoffrey of Anjou (1113–1151) married in 1129 Matilda, daughter of Henry I of England, and widow of Henry V, Holy Roman Emperor. He ruled Anjou for approximately 20 years, most of which was spent in wars with the Angevin barons and for the conquest of Normandy, which was in the hands of Robert Curthose, eldest son of William the Conqueror, or of his family.

[49] Peter grows rather enthusiastic here; Scotland and Wales were not a part of Henry's domain and but a portion of Ireland was included therein.

and body, with which nature has endowed him far above other men; for I confess my incompetence, and indeed I should consider Cicero or Virgil unequal to so great a task.[50] . . .

This other letter throws additional light on the disposition of the King:

Peter of Blois, Archdeacon of Bath, to Roger the deacon, greeting and good counsel:

No teacher is more trustworthy or more efficient than he who has tested by experience the theory that he teaches. Not long since I was sent to the King on business connected with the church of Canterbury.[51] As usual I went into his presence cheerfully, but reading and understanding from his face the vexation of his spirit, I immediately closed my lips and held my tongue, fearful lest I should increase his irritation, for to me his face was a faithful interpreter of his mind. So I postponed my business until a more favorable hour and a more serene countenance should prosper it. For he who approaches an angry prince on business is like unto one who spreads his nets in a storm. He who offers himself to the tempest without waiting for smoother water quickly destroys both himself and his nets. I know that your mission to the King is a disagreeable one, therefore it behooves you to carry yourself all the more cautiously.

[50] This document is part of letter dccc. in vol. vii of *Materials for the History of Archbishop Thomas Becket* (*Rolls Series*, 1875–1885, ed. Robertson and Sheppard). The earlier part of the letter exhorts Archbishop William to show kindness to pilgrims and thanks him for certain gifts. The latter part of the letter asserts that Henry II is guiltless of the death of Becket, tells of the king's visit to the martyr's tomb, his victory over the Scots and his suppression of the rebellion of his sons.

[51] As stated in the next section (*post*, p. 162) some of the most important of Henry's political activities involved the position of the church. The document in which his position regarding the relation of church and state is set forth in its most extreme form is the famous *Constitutions of Clarendon* (1164). The Latin text of this is in Stubbs, *Select Charters*, 8th ed., pp. 137 *seq.* (Oxford, Clarendon Press, 1895). It will be found translated into English in Adams and Stephens, *Select Documents of English Constitutional History* (New York, The Macmillan Co., 1901), pp. 11–14; in Cheyney, *op. cit.*, pp. 148–150; and in Lee, *Source Book of English History* (New York, Henry Holt and Co., 1900), pp. 133–136. *The Constitutions of Clarendon* should not be confused with *The Assize of Clarendon* (1166) to be quoted *post*, pp. 212–216.

For even pleasant news may be irritating at an inopportune time and some times disagreeable matter may be so presented as to give pleasure. Do not hurry to bring your business before the King until the way is prepared by me or some one else who knows his habits. For he is a lamb when his mind is at ease, but a lion or more fierce than a lion when he is aroused. It is no joke to incur the anger of one in whose hands are honor and disgrace, heirship and exile, life and death. Witness Solomon: [52] the anger of a king is the messenger of death.[53]

The most spectacular events of Henry's reign are undoubtedly those that center around his efforts to subordinate the church to the royal power. The contest between church and state in post-Conquest England was not a new problem of Henry's reign; for Anselm and William Rufus had had their difficulties: but the struggle was at its most acute stage at this time and led to results which were soon incorporated in popular tradition.[54] Thomas a Becket,

[52] Proverbs 16: 14.

[53] Peter of Blois became Archdeacon of Bath soon after 1173.

[54] Becket was canonized by Pope Alexander III in 1173. His tomb soon became the favorite English resort of religious pilgrims. Chaucer's *Canterbury Tales* are told on a pilgrimage to this shrine. Of the seven-volume *Materials for the History of Thomas Becket*, the first contains the *Life and Passion of St. Thomas by William, the Monk of Canterbury* (written about 1172), the greater part of which consists of stories of the miracles wrought at the tomb of the martyr. The second volume contains *The Passion of St. Thomas of Canterbury* and *The Miracles of St. Thomas of Canterbury* by Benedict of Peterborough, the *Life of St. Thomas, Archbishop of Canterbury and Martyr* by John of Salisbury (cf. *post*, pp. 559–563) and Alan of Tewkesbury and the *Life of St. Thomas, Archbishop of Canterbury and Martyr* by Edward Grim, from which we quote, *post*, pp. 163–166. The third volume has the lives by William Fitzstephen (died 1190?), from which we quote the introduction, known as *The Description of London* (cf. *post*, pp. 309–320) and Herbert of Bosham (flourished 1162–1186). The fourth volume has two anonymous lives, the extracts from the chronicles bearing on the history of Becket and the life commonly called *Quadrilogus*, i.e, composed from four sources. The fifth, sixth and seventh volumes contain letters pertaining to the career of Becket. The amount of material available on Becket is thus evidently abundant. These materials are all in Latin. Becket soon became the subject of vernacular literature as well, as the poem on his life and death attests. [(Cf. Mätzner, *Alt-Englische Sprach-Proben* (*Specimens of the Old English Language*), i, pp. 176–193, translated into modern English verse

moreover, Henry's opponent in the strife, was the latter's best friend and had been appointed archbishop because Henry thought he would certainly take the King's side on the subjects at issue. Henry's disappointment and vexation finally became so aggravated at Becket's successful championship [55] of the church that he was led to make his famous angry outcry, "My subjects are sluggards, men of no spirit; they keep no faith with their lord, they allow me to be made the laughing-stock of a low-born clerk." The result was that four knights at once started for Canterbury, followed the monks into the Cathedral, and murdered the Archbishop in the transept on December 29, 1170. Edward Grim, an attendant of Becket's, with him at the time, thus describes the incidents of the murder.

When the monks entered the church the four knights followed immediately behind with rapid strides. With them was a certain subdeacon, armed with malice, like their own, Hugh, fitly surnamed for his wickedness, Mauclerc, who showed no reverence for God or the saints, as the result showed. When the holy archbishop entered the church the monks stopped vespers which they had begun and ran to him, glorifying God that they saw their father who they had heard was dead, alive and safe. They hastened, by bolting the doors of the church, to protect their shepherd from the slaughter. But the champion, turning to them, ordered the church doors to be thrown open, saying, "It is not meet to make a fortress of the house of prayer, the

in Weston, *The Chief Middle English Poets*, pp. 41–56 (Boston, Houghton Mifflin, 1914)]. See also H. Snowden Ward, *The Canterbury Pilgrimages* (Lippincott, 1905), Stanley, *Historical Memorials of Canterbury*, now available in *Everyman's Library*, Tennyson, *Becket* (1884), which gives a wonderfully accurate and vivid account of the career of Becket.

[55] The last cause of contention between King and Archbishop was the coronation of Henry's eldest son, often in contemporary documents termed Henry III, as his successor. This was the prerogative of the Archbishop of Canterbury, but Henry had the ceremony performed, in Becket's absence on the Continent, by the Archbishop of York. Becket, thereupon, excommunicated and suspended many of the King's followers.

church of Christ: though it be not shut up it is able to protect
its own; and we shall triumph over the enemy rather in suffering
than in fighting, for we came to suffer, not to resist." And
straightway they entered the house of peace and reconciliation
with swords sacrilegiously drawn, causing horror to the beholders
by their very looks and the clanging of their arms.

All who were present were in tumult and fright, for those who
had been singing vespers now ran hither to the dreadful spectacle.

Inspired by fury the knights called out, "Where is Thomas
Becket, traitor to the king and realm?" As he answered not,
they cried out the more furiously, "Where is the archbishop?"
At this, intrepid and fearless (as it is written, "The just, like
a bold lion, shall be without fear"),[56] he descended from the
stair where he had been dragged by the monks in fear of the
knights, and in a clear voice answered, "I am here, no traitor
to the king, but a priest. Why do ye seek me?" And whereas
he had already said that he feared them not, he added, "So I
am ready to suffer in His name, who redeemed me by His blood;
be it far from me to flee from your swords or to depart from
justice." Having thus said, he turned to the right, under a
pillar, having on the one side the altar of the Blessed Mother
of God and ever Virgin Mary, on the other that of St. Benedict the Confessor, by whose example and prayers, having crucified the world with its lusts, he bore all that the murderers
could do, with such constancy of soul as if he had been no longer
in the flesh.

The murderers followed him. "Absolve," they cried, "and
restore to communion those whom you have excommunicated,
and restore their powers to those whom you have suspended."
He answered, "There has been no satisfaction, and I will not
absolve them." "Then you shall die," they cried, "and receive what you deserve." "I am ready," he replied, "to die for
my Lord, that in my blood the church may obtain liberty and
peace. But in the name of Almighty God I forbid you to hurt
my people, whether clerk or lay." Thus piously and thoughtfully did the noble martyr provide that no one near him should
be hurt or the innocent be brought to death, whereby his glory

[56] Cf. Proverbs 28: 1.

should be dimmed as he hastened to Christ. Thus did it become the martyr knight to follow in the foot-steps of his Captain and Saviour who, when the wicked sought Him, said, "If ye seek me, let these go their way." [57]

Then they laid sacrilegious hands on him, pulling and dragging him that they might kill him outside the church, or carry him away a prisoner, as they afterwards confessed. But when he would not be forced away from the pillar, one of them pressed on him and clung to him more closely. Him he pushed off, calling him, "pander," and saying, "Touch me not, Reginald; you owe me fealty and subjection; you and your accomplices act like madmen." The knight, fired with terrible rage at this rebuke, waved his sword over the sacred head. "No faith," he cried, "nor subjection do I owe you against my fealty to my lord the king." Then the unconquered martyr, seeing the hour at hand which should put an end to this miserable life, and give him straightway the crown of immortality promised by the Lord, inclined his head as one who prays, and, joining his hands, lifted them up and commended his cause and that of the church to God, to St. Mary and to the blessed martyr Denys.[58] Scarce had he said the words when the wicked knight, fearing lest the archbishop should be rescued by the people and escape alive, leapt upon him suddenly and wounded this lamb who was sacrificed to God, on the head, cutting off the top of the crown which the sacred unction of the chrism had dedicated to God; and by the same blow he wounded the arm of him who tells this. For he, when the others, both monks and clerks, fled, stuck close to the sainted archbishop and held him in his arms till the arm he interposed was almost severed.

Behold the simplicity of the dove, the wisdom of the serpent,[59] in the martyr who opposed his body to those who struck, that he might preserve his head, that is, his soul and the church, unharmed; nor would he use any forethought against those who destroyed the body whereby he might escape. O worthy shepherd, who gave himself so boldly to the wolves that his flock

[57] Cf. John 18: 8.
[58] Converter and patron Saint of Gaul, supposed to have been martyred in the Valerian persecution. [59] Cf. Matthew 10: 16.

might not be torn. Because he had rejected the world, the
world in wishing to crush him unknowingly exalted him. Then
he received a second blow on the head, but still stood firm. At
the third blow, he fell on his knees and elbows, offering himself
a living victim, and saying in a low voice, "For the name of
Jesus and the protection of the church I am ready to embrace
death." Then the third knight inflicted a terrible wound as he
lay, by which the sword was broken against the pavement, and
the crown, which was large, was separated from the head; so
that the blood white with the brain, and the brain red with
blood, dyed the surface of the virgin mother church with the life
and death of the confessor and martyr in the colors of the lily
and the rose.

The fourth [60] knight prevented any from interfering, so that
the others might freely perpetrate the murder. In order that a
fifth blow might not be wanting to the martyr who was in other
things like Christ, the fifth (no knight, but that clerk who had
entered with the knights) put his foot on the neck of the holy
priest and precious martyr, and, horrible to say, scattered his
brains and blood over the pavement, calling out to the others,
"Let us away, knights; he will rise no more." [61]

The efforts of Henry II to strengthen the royal power,
seconded by the policy of the ministers of his successor,
Richard I, succeeded so well that England in the latter
years of the twelfth century seemed well started as an
absolute monarchy. Two causes, however, intervened to
change the trend of events. One was the arbitrary and
capricious use of his power by King John, the worst of the
Angevins; the second, the discovery by the barons, under
the leadership of Archbishop Stephen Langton of Canter-

[60] The four knights were Reginald de Fitzurse, Hugh de Moreville, William
Tracy and Richard de Brut.

[61] Henry was on the Continent when Becket was murdered, and when the news
was brought to him, he expressed his grief, was deeply repentant, paid a humiliating
visit to the tomb of the martyr, and sought absolution from the pope. But it should
be remembered that, though the terms, so to speak, of the struggle between Becket
and Henry were religious, its underlying importance — the enhancing of the royal
power by subordinating that of the church — is political.

bury,[62] that the relation between king and barons was a contractual one, and that the violation of the contract by one party nullified its application to the other. Roger of Wendover, a contemporary chronicler, in the following passage tells how the barons acted on this knowledge and compelled the king to grant them Magna Charta, called by the Earl of Chatham the first element in the "Bible of the English Constitution." [63]

Of the demand made by the barons of England for their rights.

A.D. 1215; which was the seventeenth year of the reign of King John; he held his court at Winchester at Christmas for one day, after which he hurried to London, and took up his abode at the New Temple, and at that place the . . . nobles came to him in gay military array, and demanded the confirmation of the liberties and laws of King Edward,[64] with other liberties granted to them and to the kingdom and church of England, as were contained in the charter and . . . laws of Henry I; [65] they also asserted that, at the time of his absolution [66] at Winchester, he had promised to restore those laws and ancient liberties and was bound by his own oath to observe them. The King, hearing the bold tongue of the barons in this demand, much feared an attack from them, as he saw that their demands were a matter of importance and difficulty, and he therefore asked a truce till the end of Easter, that he might, after due deliberation, be able to satisfy them as well as maintain the dignity of his crown. After much discussion on both sides the King at length, although unwillingly, procured the Archbishop of Canterbury, the Bishop of Ely and William Marshal as his sureties, that on the day agreed on, he would in all reason satisfy them all, on which the nobles returned to

[62] Cf. Kate Norgate, *John Lackland*, pp. 211–234 (The Macmillan Co., 1902), where the writer makes it clear that it was the discovery of the *Charter of Henry I* that showed the barons a way out of the difficulty with John.

[63] Cf. Goodrich, *Select British Eloquence*, p. 112.

[64] I.e. the Confessor.   [65] Cf. *post*, pp. 203 *seq.*

[66] John had been excommunicated by Pope Innocent III in 1209, had submitted and been absolved by Archbishop Langton in 1213.

their homes. The King, however, wishing to take precautions against the future, caused all the nobles throughout England to swear fealty to him alone against all men, and to renew their homage to him; and, the better to take care of himself, he, on the day of St. Mary's Purification,[67] assumed the cross of our Lord,[68] being induced to this more by fear than by devotion. . . .

Of the principal persons who compelled the King to grant the laws and liberties

In Easter week of this same year, the . . . nobles assembled at Stamford, with horses and arms; for they had now induced almost all the nobility of the whole kingdom to join them, and constituted a very large army; for in their army were computed to be two thousand knights, besides horse soldiers, attendants and foot soldiers who were variously equipped. . . .[69]

All of these being united by oath, were supported by the concurrence of Stephen Archbishop of Canterbury who was at their head. The King at this time was awaiting the arrival of his nobles at Oxford. On the Monday next after the octaves of Easter,[70] the said barons assembled in the town of Brackley: and when the King learned of this, he sent the Archbishop of Canterbury and William Marshal Earl of Pembroke with some other prudent men to them to inquire what the laws and liberties were which they demanded. The barons then delivered to the messengers a paper containing in a great measure the laws and ancient customs of the kingdom, and declared that, unless the King immediately granted them and confirmed them under his own seal, they would by taking possession of his fortresses force him to give them sufficient satisfaction as to their previously presented demands. The Archbishop with his fellow messengers then carried the paper to the King, and read to him the heads of the paper one by one throughout. The King when he heard the purport of these heads derisively said with the greatest indignation, "Why, amongst these unjust demands, did not the barons ask for my kingdom also? Their demands are vain and

[67] February 2.   [68] I.e. vowed he would go on Crusade.
[69] Names of "chief promoters of this pestilence" follow.
[70] I.e. the second Monday after Easter.

visionary and are unsupported by any plea of reason whatsoever."
And at length he angrily declared with an oath that he would
never grant them such liberties as would render him their slave.
The principal of these laws and liberties, which the nobles required to be confirmed to them, are partly described above in
the charter of King Henry and partly are extracted from the
old laws of King Edward, as the following history will show in
due time.

The Castle of Northampton besieged by the barons

As the Archbishop and William Marshal could not by any
persuasions induce the King to agree to the demands, they returned by the King's order to the barons and duly reported all
that they had heard from the King to them; and when the
nobles heard what John said, they appointed Robert Fitz-
Walter commander of their soldiers, giving him the title of
"Marshal of the army of God and the holy church," and then,
one and all flying to arms, they directed their forces toward
Northampton. On their arrival there they at once laid siege
to the castle, but after having stayed there for fifteen days and
having gained little or no advantage, they determined to move
their camp; for having come without petrariæ [71] and other
engines of war, they, without accomplishing their purpose, proceeded in confusion to the castle of Bedford. At that siege the
standard-bearer of Robert Fitz-Walter, amongst other slain, was
pierced through the head with an arrow from a cross-bow and
died, to the grief of many.

How the city of London was given up to the barons

When the army of the barons arrived at Bedford, they were
received with all respect by William de Beauchamp. There also
came to them there messengers from the city of London, secretly telling them, if they wished to get into that city, to come
there immediately. The barons, inspirited by this agreeable
message, at once moved their camp and arrived at Ware; after
this they marched the whole night and arrived early in the

[71] Machines for throwing stones.

morning at the city of London, and, finding the gates open, they on the 24th of May, which was the Sunday next before our Lord's Ascension, entered the city without any tumult whilst the inhabitants were performing divine service, for the rich citizens were favorable to the barons and the poor were afraid to murmur against them. The barons having thus got into the city, placed their own guards in charge of each of the gates and then arranged all matters in the city at will. They then took security from the citizens and sent letters throughout England to those earls, barons and knights who appeared to be still faithful to the King, though they only pretended to be so, and advised them with threats, as they regarded the safety of all their property and possessions, to abandon the King who was perjured and who warred against his barons, and together with them to stand firm and fight against the King for their rights and for peace; and that, if they refused to do this, they, the barons, would make war against them all, as against open enemies, and would destroy their castles, burn their houses and other buildings, and destroy their warrens, parks and orchards.[72] . . . The greatest part of these, on receiving the message of the barons, set out to London and joined them, abandoning the King entirely. The pleas of the exchequer and of the sheriffs' courts ceased throughout England, because there was no one to make a valuation for the King, or to obey him in anything.

The conference between the King and the barons

King John, when he saw that he was deserted by almost all, so that out of his regal superabundance of followers he scarcely retained seven knights, was much alarmed lest these barons should attack his castles and reduce them without difficulty, as they would find no obstacle to their so doing; and he deceitfully pretended to make peace for a time with the . . . barons, and sent William Marshal Earl of Pembroke with other trustworthy messengers to them and told them that, for the sake of peace and for the exaltation and honor of the kingdom, he would willingly grant them the laws and liberties they required; he

[72] Names of those to whom the message was sent follow.

also sent word to the barons by the same messengers to appoint a fitting day and place to meet and carry all these matters into effect. The King's messengers then came in all haste to London, and without deceit reported to the barons all that had been deceitfully imposed upon them; they in their great joy appointed the fifteenth of June for the King to meet them, at a field lying between Staines and Windsor. Accordingly, at the time and place agreed on, the King and nobles came to the appointed conference, and when each party had stationed themselves apart from the other, they began a long discussion about terms of peace and the aforesaid liberties. There were present on behalf of the King the archbishops, Stephen of Canterbury and H. of Dublin, the bishops W. of London, P. of Winchester, H. of Lincoln, J. of Bath, Walter of Worcester, W. of Coventry and Benedict of Rochester; master Pandulph familiar of our lord the pope, and brother Almeric the master of the knights-templars in England; the nobles, William Marshal Earl of Pembroke, the Earl of Salisbury, Earl Warrene, the Earl of Arundel, Alan de Galway, W. Fitz-Gerald, Peter Fitz-Herbert, Alan Basset, Matthew Fitz-Herbert, Thomas Basset, Hugh de Neville, Hubert de Burgh seneschal of Poictou, Robert de Ropley, John Marshall and Philip d'Aubeny. Those who were on behalf of the barons it is not necessary to enumerate, since the whole nobility of England were now assembled together in numbers not to be computed. At length, after various points on both sides had been discussed, King John, seeing that he was inferior in strength to the barons, without raising any difficulties, granted the laws and liberties listed below, and confirmed them by his charters. . . . [73]

"To insure the inforcement of the terms of the charter a committee of twenty-four barons and the Lord Mayor of London were appointed who were authorized to levy war on the King until any transgression of which he might be guilty should have been amended. This machinery for securing its observance was the weakest thing about it,

[73] Magna Charta follows. See the text as it appears in the various source books of English history.

for there could be no peaceful progress under any such
arrangement. It was soon given up, and before the century had passed we find a body in the making to whom, in
due course of time, the maintenance of its great principles
was intrusted." [74] This body has gradually developed into
what we now call parliament, elements of which had been
in existence for some time. Thus, Tacitus [75] records that
the members of the various Teutonic tribes conferred and
voted regarding the course of action to be taken by the
tribe; Alfred the Great promulgated [76] his laws with the
sanction of the wise men; representative juries elected in
the several counties undertook various sorts of royal business from the time of Henry II and furnished the typical
procedure for the election of representatives to parliament.[77]

The year 1295 is marked by the assembling of what has
long been known as "the Model Parliament." It was "not
the 'product' of grand purposeful building for the future," [78] but of anxiety about the immediate problems of
1295. Edward I, "needed money as never before, and he
used the means to obtain it which the experience of the
past thirty years and his instincts as a practical statesman suggested. He needed the help of all classes and, as far
as conditions allowed, he took them all into his confidence.
It can hardly be thought that the representative elements
were really asked to give their consent to taxation, but
their good will could be gained and consultation with them
facilitated assessment and collection. There was no grand
theorizing. . . ." [79]

Specimen writs of summons to the three estates show us

[74] Cross, op. cit., p. 144. The word parliament means talking or conference and
is used a great deal in literature 1100–1400 in this sense. We must not import into
the medieval use of the word our modern conceptions of parliament as an institution.   [75] Cf. ante, pp. 10–12.   [76] Ibid., pp. 22–25.
[77] The origin and early history of parliament are carefully treated in White, op.
cit., pp. 298–401.   [78] Ibid., p. 298.   [79] Cf. White, op. cit., p. 329.

how the matter of a national representative assembly was presented in 1295 and outline the business of the assembly when called.

(a) Summons of a Bishop to Parliament, 1295

The King to the venerable father in Christ Robert, by the same grace archbishop of Canterbury, primate of all England, greeting. As a most just law, established by the careful providence of sacred princes, exhorts and decrees that what affects all, by all should be approved, so also, very evidently should common danger be met by means provided in common. You know sufficiently well, and it is now, as we believe, divulged through all regions of the world, how the king of France fraudulently and craftily deprives us of our land of Gascony, by withholding it unjustly from us. Now, however, not satisfied with the before-mentioned fraud and injustice, having gathered together for the conquest of our kingdom a very great fleet, and an abounding multitude of warriors, with which he has made a hostile attack on our kingdom and the inhabitants of the same kingdom, he now proposes to destroy the English language altogether from the earth, if his power should correspond to the detestable propostion of the contemplated injustice, which God forbid. Because, therefore, darts seen beforehand do less injury, and your interest especially, as that of the rest of the citizens of the same realm, is concerned in this affair, we command you, strictly enjoining you in the fidelity and love in which you are bound to us, that on the Lord's day next after the feast of St. Martin, in the approaching winter, you be present in person at Westminster; citing beforehand the dean and chapter of your church, the archdeacons and all the clergy of your diocese, causing the same dean and archdeacons in their own persons, and the said chapter by one suitable proctor, and the said clergy by two, to be present along with you, having full and sufficient power from the same chapter and clergy, to consider, ordain and provide, along with us and with the rest of the prelates and principal men and other inhabitants of our kingdom, how the dangers and threatened evils of this kind are to be met. Witness the king at Wangham, the thirtieth day of September.

(b) Summons of a Baron to Parliament, 1295

The king to his beloved and faithful relative, Edmund, Earl of Cornwall, greeting. Because we wish to have a consultation and meeting with you and with the rest of the principal men of our kingdom, as to provision for remedies against the dangers which in these days are threatening our whole kingdom, we command you, strictly enjoining you in the fidelity and love in which you are bound to us, that on the Lord's day next after the feast of St. Martin's, in the approaching winter, you be present in person at Westminster, for considering, ordaining and doing along with us and with the prelates, and the rest of the principal men and other inhabitants of our kingdom, as may be necessary for meeting dangers of this kind.

Witness the king at Canterbury, the first of October.

(c) Summons of Representatives of Shires and Towns to Parliament, 1295

The king to the sheriff of Northamptonshire. Since we intend to have a consultation and meeting with the earls, barons and other principal men of our kingdom with regard to providing remedies against the dangers which are in these days threatening the same kingdom, and on that account have commanded them to be with us on the Lord's day next after the feast of St. Martin, in the approaching winter, at Westminster, to consider, ordain, and do as may be necessary for the avoidance of these dangers, we strictly require you to cause two knights from the aforesaid county, two citizens from each city in the same county, and two burgesses from each borough, of those who are especially discreet and capable of laboring, to be elected without delay, and to cause them to come to us at the aforesaid time and place.

Moreover, the said knights are to have full and sufficient power for themselves and for the community of the aforesaid county, and the said citizens and burgesses for themselves and the communities of the aforesaid cities and boroughs separately, then and there for doing what shall then be ordained according to the common counsel in the premises, so that the aforesaid business shall not remain unfinished in any way for defect of this power. And you shall have there the names of the knights, citizens and burgesses and this writ.

Witness the king at Canterbury, on the third day of October.

A phrase in the third sentence of the first writ suggests a cause on which much English treasure and life were spent in the concluding century of our period. The kings of France and England, close territorial rivals on the Continent, each trying to unify and increase his lands, many times made it their chief business to check each other's movements. Hence, there is much anti-French sentiment in fourteenth-century English literature and we must take account of the fact here.

But, before we turn to this subject, there is another which we must take notice of, also a matter of foreign policy and one that loomed large in English feeling and imagination. This is the relation of England and Scotland. From about 1290 until 1707, when England and Scotland were united, there was more or less friction [80] between the two countries. In all this long history of strife, no event made so deep a popular impression as the disastrous defeat of English arms by the Scotch at Bannockburn in 1314. Geoffrey le Baker of Swinbrooke, a contemporary chronicler, thus describes a famous incident in the battle.

On that night you might have seen the English host deep in their cups, wassailing and toasting immoderately; on the other hand the Scots silently kept their vigil fasting, their every thought centered in their desire for their country's freedom; [81] and this desire, though ungrounded, was vehement and equal to all risks. On the morrow the Scots seized the most advan-

[80] There is little doubt that the almost constant border strife between England and Scotland, making the Scotch marches a region of perpetual adventure, is the explanation of the fact that so many of the English and Scottish popular ballads are located there. In the field of the poetry of art, cf. Blind Harry's *Wallace* and Barbour's *Bruce*.

[81] Cf. Malmesbury's contrast of English and Normans, *ante*, pp. 152–153.

tageous position, and dug pits three feet deep and as wide across, stretching along the whole line, from the right wing to the left. These they covered over with a light framework of twigs and osiers, that is to say, with hurdles; and then over the top they strewed turf and grass, so that men could cross them on foot with care, but the weight of cavalry could not be supported. In accordance with their royal leader's command none of the Scots were mounted, and their army, drawn up in the usual divisions, was posted in solid formation at no great distance from this pit, which had been warily, not to say craftily, set between themselves and the English. On the other side, as the English army advanced from the west, the rising sun flashed upon their golden shields and polished helms. Their vanguard consisted of light horse and heavy cavalry, all unconscious of the Scots' pit, with its cunningly contrived light covering; in the second division were men-at-arms and archers held in reserve to give chase to the enemy; in the third was the King,[82] with the bishops and other churchmen, and among them the brave knight, Hugh Spenser. The cavalry of the vanguard advanced against the enemy and fell headlong, as their horses stumbled into the ditch, with their forefeet caught in the broken hurdles; and when these fell through, the enemy came up and slew them, giving quarter only to the rich, for ransom.

Froissart, the brilliant French chronicler from whom so much of our knowledge of the spirit of the fourteenth century comes, in the following words tells us further of the military methods of the Scots in a fashion which closely approaches the language of balladry.

The winter and lent [83] passed in perfect peace, but at Easter, Robert, King of Scotland, sent a message of defiance to King Edward, informing him of his intention to enter England and devastate the country by fire. Upon this, Sir John de Hainault [84] was sent for, who, true to the interest of the young King

[82] I.e. Edward II.
[83] I.e. spring. This account is of Scotch-English operations in 1328, just after the coronation of Edward III.
[84] A close friend of Edward III and later his uncle by marriage.

and his mother, soon arrived with a considerable band of followers at the city of York, and joined the English on their march to meet the enemy.

The Scots are a bold, hardy race, and much inured to war. When they invaded England, they were all usually on horseback, except the camp-followers; they brought no carriages, neither did they encumber themselves with any provision. Under the flap of his saddle each man had a broad plate of metal; and behind his saddle a little bag of oatmeal, and baked upon the plates; for the most part, however, they ate the half-sodden flesh of the cattle they captured, and drank water. In this manner, then, under the command of the Earl of Moray and Sir James Douglas, they made their present invasion, destroying and burning wherever they went. As soon, however, as the English King came in sight of the smoke of the fires which the Scots were making, an alarm was sounded, and everyone ordered to prepare for combat; but there were so many marshes between the two armies that the English could not come up with the enemy; they lay, therefore, that night in a wood, upon the banks of a small river, and the King lodged in a monastery hard by. The next day, it was determined, as the Scots seemed to avoid battle, and to be sheering off to their own country, to hasten their march, and to endeavor to intercept them as they repassed the Tyne. At the sound of the trumpet all the English were to be ready; each man taking with him but one loaf of bread slung at his back after the fashion of a hunter, so that their march might not be retarded.

As it had been ordered, so it was executed; the English started at daybreak, but, with all their exertion, did not reach the Tyne till vespers, when, to their great mortification, after waiting some time, they discovered that the Scots had gained the river, and passed over before them.

Their scanty store of provisions being now exhausted, the English suffered greatly from hunger, and it rained so incessantly that the horses, as well as the men, were almost worn out. However, they were still bent upon encountering the Scots, and the King offered a large reward to any one who should inform him where they were to be found. They had now been several days seeking for information, when, about three o'clock one afternoon, a squire came galloping up to the King, and reported that he had seen the enemy — that they were but a short distance from them, and quite as eager for battle as themselves. Edward upon this put his army in array, continued marching, and soon came in sight of the Scots, who were drawn up in three battalions, on the slope of a mountain, at the foot of which ran a rapid river, full of large stones and rocks, and very difficult to cross. When the English lords perceived the disposition of the enemy, they sent heralds, offering to fight them in the plain; but the Scots would consent to no arrangement, and having kept the English in suspense for some days, at last retired. During all this time there were frequent skirmishes, and many lives lost on both sides; and though there was no general engagement between the two armies, the Scots were driven back into their own country, and both parties quite tired out. Edward, on his way home, halted his weary forces at Durham, where he paid homage to the church and bishopric, and gave largesses to the citizens. Sir John and his company, heartily thanked and rewarded for their services, were escorted by twelve knights and two-hundred men-at-arms to Dover, whence they embarked for Hainault.

It is thus evident that the Scots were an unsatisfactory enemy so long as they were so ably led and employed such tactics. But King Robert Bruce died of leprosy in April, 1328, leaving his son David, a child of seven, his heir; the King's death, coupled with the determination of the English to wipe out the disgrace of Bannockburn, at length brought about the desired result, and on July 19, 1333, Edward defeated the Scots at Halidon Hill. Lawrence Minot, whose few extant patriotic poems are all we know of him, celebrates this victory in stirring verse. So keen is his sense of the relation of Bannockburn and Halidon Hill, that he names his poem after the first battle but devotes his attention to exultation over the second and its results. We quote a translation into modern verse.

(Now to tell you I will turn
  Of the battle of Bannockburn.)
Scots out of Berwick and Aberdeen,
At the Burn of the Bannock were ye too keen.
There ye slew many guiltless, as now ye have seen.
And now has King Edward wreaked vengeance, I ween.
It is avenged, I wot, well worth the while,
Wreaked upon the Scots, for they are full of guile.

Where are ye Scots from St. John's town?
The boast of your banners is all beaten down.
When ye fell to your boasting King Edward was boun
To kindle your care and crack your crown.
He has cracked your crown, well worth the while!
Shame o'ertake the Scots, for they are full of guile.

Scots out of Sterling stern were and stout:
Of God and good men no fear they had nor doubt;
Now have the robbers themselves turned about;
But King Edward at last has rifled their rout.
He has rifled their rout, well worth the while;
For the Scots are as fond of gauds as of guile.
Poor roughfoot rivling, now wakens thy care!
Bag-bearing boaster, thy dwelling is bare!
False wretch and forsworn where now wilt thou fare?
Go, get thee to Bruges and bide thy time there!
There, wretch, shalt thou pine and weary the while;
Thy dwelling in Dundee is gone through thy guile.

The Scot goes to Bruges, and beats the streets.
Threats to the English he alway repeats.
Loud makes he his moan to all whom he greets;
Few mind his laments, well worth the while;
He mingles his threats with wiles and with guile.

But for many who threaten and speak now full ill
'Twere better, sometimes, they should be stone-still.
The brash Scot with his threats has wind only to spill;
For Edward, our King, will at last have his will.
He had his will at Berwick, well worth the while;
Scots gave him the keys, but look out for their guile.

In alarm at the success of Edward, the Scots sent King
David to France and secured the aid of King Philip VI,[85]
who determined to take the offensive against the English.
Thus was begun the Hundred Years' War between England and France when Edward in October, 1337, proclaimed himself king of France. The basis on which he
did this is set forth by Froissart as follows:

Now sheweth the history that . . . Philip le Beau, king of
France, had three sons and a fair daughter named Isabel, married into England to King Edward the second; and these three
sons, the eldest named Louis, who was king of Navarre in his
father's days and was called King Louis Hutin; the second had
to name Philip the Great or the Long, and the third was called
Charles; and all three were kings of France after their father's
decease by right succession each after other, without having
any issue male of their bodies lawfully begotten. So that after
the death of Charles, last king of the three, the twelve peers
and all the barons of France would not give the realm to Isabel,
the sister, who was Queen of England, because they said and
maintained, and yet do, that the realm of France is so noble
that it ought not to go to a woman,[86] and so consequently not
to Isabel, nor to the king of England, her eldest son. For they
determined the son of the woman to have no right nor succession by his mother, since they declared the mother to have no
right; so that by these reasons the twelve peers and barons of
France by their common accord did give the realm of France
to the lord, Philip of Valois, nephew sometime to Philip le Beau,
king of France, and so put out the queen of England and her
son, who was as the next heir male, as son to the sister to Charles,
the last king of France. Thus went the realm of France out of the
right lineage, as it seemed to many folk, whereby great wars have

[85] France and Scotland had made an alliance in 1295 "by which Scotch manners
and customs were profoundly influenced by the French" (Cross, *op. cit.*, p. 170)
and the consequences of which were "most significant for England's foreign and
domestic history." (*Ibid.*, p. 169.) It is these complications which are referred to
in the writs of summons to the Model Parliament of 1295. (Cf. *ante*, pp. 173, 175.)

[86] The principle known as the Salic Law.

moved and fallen, and great destructions of people and countries in the realm of France and other places, as ye may
hereafter see. This is the very foundation of this history, to
recount the great enterprises and great feats of arms that have
fortuned and fallen. Sith the time of the good Charlemagne,
king of France, there never fell so great adventures. . . .

Of these "great enterprises and great feats of arms"
none is more important than the battle of Crécy, August
26, 1346, thus narrated by Froissart:

The Englishmen, who were in three battles,[87] lying on the
ground to rest them, as soon as they saw the Frenchmen approach, rose upon their feet fair and easily without any haste
and arranged their battles. In the first which was the prince's [88]
battle, the archers stood in the manner of a herse,[89] and the men
of arms in the bottom of the battle. The earl of Northhampton and
the earl of Arundel, with the second battle, were on a wing in good
order, ready to comfort the prince's battle, if need were.

The lords and knights of France came not to the assembly in
good order, for some came before and some came after in such
evil order that one of them did trouble another. When the
French king saw the Englishmen his blood changed, and he said
to his marshals, "Make the Genoways [90] go on before and begin
the battle in the name of God and St. Denis." [91] There were
of the Genoways crossbows about fifteen thousand, but they
were so weary of going afoot that day a six leagues armed with
their crossbows, that they said to their constables, "We be not
well ordered to fight this day, for we be not in case to do any
feats of arms: we have more need of rest." These words came
to the earl of Alençon, who said, "A man is well at ease to be
charged with such a set of rascals, to be faint and fail now at
most need." Also the same season there fell a great rain and
lightning with terrible thunder, and before the rain there came
flying over both battles a great number of crows for fear of the

[87] I.e. divisions.
[88] Edward the Black Prince, eldest son of Edward III, made his debut as a
warrior in this battle.   [89] I.e. a harrow.   [90] I.e. Genoese.
[91] I.e. Patron saint of France, as St. George of England.

tempest coming. Then anon the air began to wax clear, and
the sun to shine fair and bright, the which was right in the
Frenchmen's eyen [92] and on the Englishmen's backs. When the
Genoways were assembled together and began to approach, they
uttered very great cries to abash the Englishmen, but they
stood still and stirred not for all that; then the Genoways
again a second time made a great and a fell cry, and stept forward a little, and the Englishmen removed not one foot; thirdly
again they cried out and then they shot fiercely with their crossbows. Then the English archers stept forth one pace and let
fly their arrows, so wholly and so thick that it seemed snow.
When the Genoways felt the arrows piercing through heads,
arms and breasts, many of them did cast down their crossbows
and did cut their strings and returned discomfited. When the
French king saw them fly away, he said, "Slay these rascals,
for they shall let [93] and trouble us without reason." Then you
should have seen the men of arms dash in among them and kill
a great number of them; and ever still the Englishmen shot
whereas they saw the thickest press; the sharp arrows ran into
the men of arms and into their horses, and many fell, horses
and men, among the Genoways, and when they were down they
could not rise again; the press was so thick that one overthrew
another. And also among the Englishmen there were certain
rascals that went afoot with great knives, and they went in
among the men of arms and slew and murdered many as they
lay on the ground, both earls, knights and squires, whereof the
king of England was after displeased, for he had rather they
had been taken prisoners.

The valiant king of Bohemia, called Charles of Luxembourg,
for all that he was nigh blind, when he understood the order of
battle, he said to them about him, "Where is the lord Charles,
my son?" His men said, "Sir, we cannot tell; we think he be
fighting." Then he said, "Sirs, ye be my men, my companions
in this journey.[94] I require you to bring me so far forward that
I may strike one stroke with my sword." They said they would
do his commandment, and to the intent that they should not
lose him in the press, they all tied the reins of their bridles each

---

[92] I.e. eyes.   [93] I.e. hinder.   [94] I.e. "day's work."

to the other and set the king before to accomplish his desire, and so they went on their enemies. The lord Charles of Bohemia, his son, who wrote himself king of Almaine [95] and bare the arms, he came in good order to the battle; but when he saw that the matter went awry on their party, he departed, I cannot tell you which way. The king, his father, was so far forward that he strake a stroke with his sword, yea, and more than four and fought valiantly, and so did his company; and they adventured themselves so forward that they were all there slain, and the next day they were found in the place about the king, and all their horses tied each to the other. . . .

In the morning, the day of the battle, certain Frenchmen and Almains [96] perforce opened the archers of the prince's battle and came out and fought with the men of arms, hand to hand. Then the second battle of the Englishmen came to succour the prince's battle, the which was time, for they had as then much ado; and they with the prince sent a messenger to the king who was on a little windmill hill. Then the knight said to the king, "Sir, the earl of Warwick, and the earl of Oxford, Sir Raynold Cobham, and other, such as be about the prince, your son, are fiercely fought withal and are sorely handled; wherefore they desire that you and your battle [97] will come and aid them; for if the Frenchmen increase, as they doubt they will, your son and they shall have much ado." Then the king said, "Is my son dead or hurt on the earth felled?" "No, sir," quoth the knight, "but he is hardly matched; wherefore he hath need of your aid." "Well," said the king, "return to him and to them that sent you hither, and say to them that they send no more to me for any adventure that falleth, as long as my son is alive; and also say to them that they suffer him this day to win his spurs; for if God be pleased, I will this journey [98] be his and the honor thereof, and to them that be about him." Then the knight returned again to them and shewed the king's words, the which greatly encouraged them, and repoined [99] that they had sent to the king as they did.

[95] I.e. Germany.   [96] I.e. Germans.
[97] The king was evidently in command of the third division of the English.
[98] I.e. "day's work."   [99] I.e. felt sorry.

In the evening the French king, who had left about him no more than threescore persons, one and another, whereof sir John of Hainault was one, who had remounted once the king, for his horse was slain with an arrow, then he said to the king, "Sir, depart hence, for it is time; lose not yourself wilfully; if ye have loss at this time, ye shall recover it again another season." And so he took the king's horse by the bridle and led him away in a manner perforce. Then the king rode until he came to the castle of Broye. The gate was closed, because it was by that time dark; then the king called the captain, who came to the walls and said, "Who is it that calleth there this time of night?" Then the king said, "Open your gate quickly, for this is the fortune of France." The captain knew then it was the king, and opened the gate and let down the bridge. Then the king entered, and he had with him but five barons, sir John of Hainault, sir Charles of Montmorency, the lord of Beaujeu, the lord d'Aubigny and the lord of Montsault. The king would not tarry there, but drank and departed thence about midnight, and so rode by such guides as knew the country till he came in the morning to Amiens, and there he rested.

This Saturday the Englishmen never departed from their battles for chasing of any man, but kept still their field, and ever defended themselves against all such as came to assail them. This battle ended about evensong time.

Crécy and Poictiers (Sept. 19, 1356), "those withering overthrows for the chivalry of France,"[100] with the intervening siege and capture of Calais (Sept. 2, 1346–Aug. 3, 1347), mark the height of English success in the war with France. Economic difficulties at home, coupled with the failing health of the Black Prince, the generalship of Bertrand du Guesclin, Constable of France, and the sur-

---

[100] The phrase is De Quincey's; cf. his *Joan of Arc*, Professor Turk's *Athenæum Press* ed., p. 265. Cf, "The . . . consequences (of Crecy) were momentous; the very foundations of medieval society were shaken when the flower of French mailed knighthood had to yield to yeomen archers and Welsh and Irish serfs armed with knives and spears. It was a mortal blow at the old system of warfare and the social and political structure built upon it." Cross, *op. cit.*, p. 196.

prising [101] statesmanship of the unmilitary Charles V, caused the tide to turn, and the long reign of Edward III ended gloomily [102] in 1377. His eldest son had died the preceding year, leaving a son, Richard surnamed of Bordeaux, a boy of ten, who now succeeded his grandfather as Richard II. But the problems left over from the preceding reign, the solution of which grew increasingly difficult during the minority and irresponsible rule of the young king, finally led to his deposition, the second in his family in a century, in 1399. For some reason, contemporary chronicle accounts of the events culminating in this deposition are scanty and unsatisfactory. We shall depend on the allegorical story in the following poem which gives, better than any other material, a sense of the complex situation in 1399. The poem now known as *Richard the Redeless* (i.e. *Richard Lackwisdom*) [103] was ascribed by the late Professor Skeat to the author of the *Vision of William concerning Piers the Plowman*.

. . . As I passed to my prayers where priests were at mass
In a blessed old borough that Bristol [104] is called,

[101] Cf. the remark of Edward III quoted, from I know not what source, in Cross, *op. cit.*, p. 204, "'There never was a king who had less to do with arms, yet there was never a king who gave me so much to do.'"

[102] Cf. the statement in *Brut* (*Early English Text Society* ed., *Original Series*, cxxxvi, p. 334), quoted in Vickers, *England in the Later Middle Ages* (G. P. Putnam's Sons, 1914), p. 243, "For as in the beginning all things were joyful and pleasing to him and to all the people, and in middle life he surpassed all men in high joy and worship and blessedness, so, when he drew into age, degenerating through lust and other sins, gradually all those blessed and joyful things, good fortune and prosperity, decreased and fell away, and unfortunate things and unprofitable harms, with many ills, began to spring up, and, what is worse, continued long after." (I have translated the passage.)

[103] But see Manly in the *Cambridge History of English Literature*, ii, pp. 41, 42.

[104] "In this same year (1398) King Richard went into Ireland the second time, that is to say in the end of the same year. And in the beginning of the twenty-third year of his reign (i.e. 1399) Harry Duke of Lancaster, who had been exiled, came back to England; and he landed in the north country at a place men call Ravenspur. And with him the Archbishop of Canterbury, sir Thomas of Arundel, that was exiled the same time. And anon there came to him Harry Earl of Northum-

In the temple of Trinity in midst of the town,
Whose title is Christ Church, down among commons,
Sudden there surged up seldom known things,
Quite wondrous to wise men, as well they might be,
Forerunners of fears and doubts following after.
So sore were the sayings of both the two sides,[105]
Of Richard who ruled so rich and so noble,
· When he warred in the west against the wild Irish,
That .Henry had entered upon the east coast
Whom all the land loved in length and in breadth,
And rose with him rapid to right all his wrongs,[106]

berland and sir Harry Percy and many other lords who had been left here in England. And the aforesaid Harry Duke of Lancaster from thence anon with all his host went toward Bristol, where he found sir William Scrope, treasurer of England, sir John Bushy and sir John Green who were all three condemned there and beheaded. And anon afterward in the same year many Londoners went to Westminster, imagining that they would find King Richard there. . . . And sir William Bagot, knight, was taken in Ireland near Dublin, and brought to London and put in Newgate prison, and at length released because of his clever defense." Tr. the Editor from *Chronicles of London,* ed. C. L. Kingsford, p. 19 (Oxford, Clarendon Press, 1905). The poem begins abruptly; the writer evidently wishes to represent himself as in the midst of things and thus locates himself at Bristol.

[105] I.e. the country was receiving contradictory reports of what was going on.

[106] In a contemporary French poem *Traison et Mort du Roy Richart* (*The Betrayal and Death of King Richard*), whose author is very sympathetic to the cause of Richard, the Earl of Northumberland is represented as sent by Henry to treat with the King regarding the import of Henry's return to England. Northumberland, on being asked what Henry desires, replies to the King, "My dear sire, . . . my lord of Lancaster has sent me to tell you what he most wishes for in this world is to have peace and a good understanding with you, and greatly repents, with all his heart, of the displeasure he hath caused you now and at other times, and asks nothing of you in this living world, save that you would consider him as your cousin and friend, and that you would please only to let him have his land, and that he may be Seneschal of England as his father and his predecessors have been, and that all other things of bygone time may be put in oblivion between you two. . . ." (Translated in Locke, *War and Misrule,* being a source book of English history 1307–1399 in *Bell's English History Source Books,* 1913.) On the death of John of Gaunt, father of Henry of Lancaster, Richard, according to Froissart, confiscated the family lands and deprived Henry of his hereditary office. It was because of this that he returned to England. (Cf. Froissart, *op. et ed. cit.,* p. 462). As regards the exile of Henry compare the following from *Chronicles of London* already cited, p. 18 " . . . About St. Bartholomew's tide in the twenty-first year (1397) of King Richard, at Coventry before him the Duke of Hereford (later our Harry Duke of Lancaster)

For he would reward them for the work after.
These jarring tales troubled me, for they were true,
And worried my wit with vexatious regard;
For it passed all my power of perception and thought,
How such wonderful works would come to an end.
But in sooth when they gathered, some sought to repent,[107]
As in Christendom's circle conceivable is,
(Saying) 'twere sad royal reason reformed not at all
The mischief and misrule that men had endured.

I pitied his passion who Prince was of Wales,
And also our crowned king till Christ send another;
And, though I were little like lord to his liege,[108]
My whole heart was his while he healthily ruled.
As I utterly knew not how things would turn out,
Whether God would soon give him the grace to amend,
To again be our guide or grant it another,
This made me to muse much and oftimes consider
To pen him a parchment to pray him be better,
And move him his mind from misrule to betake,
To praise loud the Prince who paradise made,
To fill him with faith all fortune above,
And not pine in impatience 'gainst Providence' will,
But meekly to suffer whatso were him sent.
And if it might like him to look o'er my leaves,
That made are to mend him for all his misdeeds,
And keep him in comfort in Christ and naught else,
I'd be glad that his spirit might spring for my speech,
But glum if it grieved him, by God that me bought.

and the Duke of Norfolk should have fought within lists. But anon after they had
taken their positions, the King took the contest into his own hands; and so they
fought not. And there in the same place they were both exiled. That is to say,
Harry Duke of Hereford for ten years, and Thomas Duke of Norfolk for an hundred years." (Tr. the Editor as are all the other passages quoted from this document). Cf. the representation of this in Shakespeare, *Richard II*, Act I, scenes
1 and 3.

[107] I.e. some of those who had joined Henry changed their minds and went over
to Richard.

[108] I.e. the writer is so insignificant that his opinion made little difference one
way or the other.

After this exposition of the occasion of his poem and his purpose in writing it, the author goes on to explain at some length that he disclaims any proud purpose and begs that his work be accepted in the spirit in which it was written. He adds that he has the young especially in mind in order to save them from the ill results of will-fulness. This completes the introduction to the poem. The first section or *passus* opens as follows with the author's view of the causes of Richard's fall:

Now, Richard the Redeless, have ruth on yourself,
Who lawless have led both your life and your people;
For through wiles and by wrong and waste in your time
You have lightly been lifted from what you thought lief,
And through willfulest works your will has been changed,
And bereft have you been of both riot and rest.
Your cares were renewed through your own cursed council,
And crazed has your crown been for covetousness.[109]
The love of money is the root of all evils.[110]
Of allegiance now learn a lesson or two,
Its source of security, staple supply —

[109] *The Chronicles of London*, already cited, devote 28 pages to an account of the deposition of Richard and statement of the charges against him. Of these latter there are 33 and of these 8 deal with money matters. The following (p. 30) is the most striking of the list: "also, whereas the king of England may honestly and sufficiently live off the profits and revenues of his realm and the patrimony belonging to the Crown, without oppressing his people while the realm is not charged with the cost and expense of war, Richard, being, so to speak, all his time in truce between the realm of England and his adversary (i.e. France), hath given, granted and done away to diverse persons very unworthy, the most part of what belongs to the Crown. And furthermore (he) hath put so many charges of grants and taxes on his subjects and lieges, and that almost every year, that overmuch and exces-sively he has oppressed his people to the great hindering and impairing of his realm by poverty. And the same goods that have been so raised have not been spent for the profit or worship of the realm, but for the commendation of his own name and pomp and vain glory, dispersing the same goods unprofitably. And yet the greatest sums of money are owing in the realm for victuals and expenses of his household, though he has had more riches than any of his progenitors that any man can reckon or have in mind."

[110] This line is a translation of the Vulgate reading of 1 Tim. 6: 10.

Not dread nor din nor deeming untrue,
Not creation of coin for commerce in guile,
Not pillage of people your princes to please;
Not wanton caprice against wisdom's will;
Not taxation of towns without any war
By robbers who rioters ruthless were aye;
Not appraising by poleax that pitiless falls,
Nor debts from your dicing, demur as you may;
Not letting of law down by pampering love.[111]
    If this, for a dull noll, be darkly drawn up,
Much need is there not to muse thereupon;
For mad as I am and little mind have,
I could it portray in a very few words;
For loveless allegiance availeth but little.

Later on, after speaking of the happy auspices under which Richard had become king, the writer recurs to his fall as follows:

    What became of this crown would a clerk [112] here might tell;
But as well as I can I propose to declare,
And name I no names but those that were nighest:
Very privately plucked they your great power away,
And quite royally rode they throughout all your realm;
From tillers, like tyrants, they took what they pleased,
And paid them with pate-blows when pennies were few.
For none of your people durst plain of their wrongs
For dread of your dukes and of double their woe.
Men might as well hunt for a hare with a taper
As hope for amends for all their misdeeds,

[111] Thirteen of the charges against Richard in *The Chronicles of London* account deal with his abuse of the legal system of England, one of which (p. 28) goes as follows: "Also, notwithstanding that the King at his coronation swore that in all his judgments he should do and ordain to be done even and righteous justice and righteousness in mercy and truth by all his power and might; nevertheless he without any sort of mercy with great vigor ordained upon great pain that no manner of man should speak or pray him for any sort of grace or mercy for Harry Duke of Lancaster. In which thing the same king against all bonds of charity broke his aforesaid oath which he had made."

[112] I.e. a more learned man than the present writer.

Or a plea against pensioners publish at all.[113]
For blinded with friendship were you for all these;
There was no single person to punish the wrongs,
And this maddened your men, as needs it must do:
They wist not for woe to whom to complain.
For, as it was said, in earlier days,
"Where the grooms and good freemen are all alike great,
'Tis sad for the dwellings and dwellers therein." [114]
They led you with love who law feared to meet
In judging your dukes' deeds, so dark were they then.
    Thus cracked was your crown, to be newly recast,
Through parting with power to paramours base.

Later on in the third *passus* of his poem the writer
touches more specifically on judicial abuses as the cause
of the King's ruin, as follows:

But still there's a foul fault that often I find:
They (i.e. royal agents) pry after presents before pleas are drawn,
And abate all the bills of those that bring none (i.e. no pres-
    ents);
And whoso is grouchy or groans at their grants (i.e. the con-
    clusion of his case)
May lose his life lightly and no less a pledge.[115]
Thus mightiest lords do lower the law,
Who more than all others misdoers maintain.

[113] Charge 5 in *The Chronicles of London* (p. 27) asserts: At the same time the king raised a great company of evil doers in Chester "of whom some went alway with the King through the realm, and cruelly slew many lieges of the realm as well within the King's house as without; and some they beat, wounded, maimed and robbed, and took up victuals without payment and ravished wives and other women. And although great pleas and complaints were made, spoken and declared in the King's hearing, he, nevertheless, took no heed, nor arranged to ordain any remedy or help for the trouble. But he let them alone and favored them in their evil deeds, trusting in them more than in all the other lieges of his realm. Wherefore all the true subjects of this realm grew very active amongst themselves and engendered great cause and matter of indignation amongst them."

[114] A saying, according to Skeat, attributed to Bede.

[115] Charge 21 in *The Chronicles of London* (p. 33) states that the King, in order to raise money, encouraged various people to spy on the nobles and clergy and bring in accusations of treason against them.

For maintenance (i.e. abetting evil doers) aye — much more is
the pity ! —
Hath many more men at meat and at meals
Than ever a Christianlike king that you knew;
For, as Reason and Right rehearsed to me once,
These men are the ones who make the most woe.
For chiders of Chester [116] were chose many days
To be counsel for cases that came before court,
And pleaded Pie-Poudre [117] for all sorts of plaints.
They cared for no coifs that court-lawyers use,
But made many motions that man never thought (of before),
And falsehood they feigned till they drew out a fine,
And knew none of the cases commonly called.
No other sign had they to show up the law
But a pallet [118] of leather their heads to protect
And cover them up in lieu of a cap.
They conjured up quarrels the people to quench,
And pleaded with polaxes, sword points and pikes;
As doom was declared they drew out their blades,
And lightly they lent men the lore of long bats.[119]
They lacked all the virtues a lawyer should have,
For, before the case opened, they called out the end,
Without hope of appeal 'less one hated his life.
And if one complained to the prince, guard of peace,
Regarding these mischievous mongers of wrong,
He was easy arrested, ungraciously seized,
And mummed on the mouth [120] and menaced with death.
They laid on your lieges, King, many a lash,
Nor dreaded a deal the doom of the law.
None dared in the realm to rebuke them when wrong,
No judge, nor yet justice, that judgment would give
For aught that they took, or trespassing deed.

[116] Cf. note 113 on p. 190, *ante*.
[117] Skeat notes, "i.e. in the court of Pie-Poudre; the summary court formerly held at fairs, and so called from the dusty feet (*pieds poudreux*) of those present."
[118] Skeat says in his note "a leathern head-piece."
[119] Skeat paraphrases, "And gave men the free experience of their long staves."
[120] I.e. slapped on the mouth and told to keep "mum."

The author further dilates on the troublous condition
of England, couching his thoughts in allegorical terms
drawn from the current natural history, now become fabulous, of which writers were so fond even to the time of
Lyly and Shakespeare.[121] Our poet thus applies the habits
of the hart and the partridge respectively to the state of
the country:

> I refer to the Hart [122] that in height of his time —
> When pasture thus pricks him and his proper age —
> When he's hobbled on earth an hundred of years,
> So he's feeble in flesh, in fell and in bones,
> His custom's to come and catch, if he can,
> Such adders as harm all other clean beasts.
> Through bushes [123] and brakes this beast in his way,
> Goes seeking and searching for adders, the shrews,
> That steal to our homesteads to sting us to death.
> And when it has happened the Hart catches one,
> He puts him to pain as one would treat prey
> And feeds on the venom a long time on end.
> This is clearly his nature — not to grieve colts.[124]

[121] Cf. *As you Like It*, II, i, ll. 12–17:

> Sweet are the uses of adversity,
> Which like the toad, ugly and venomous,
> Wears yet a precious jewel in his head;
>   And this our life exempt from public haunt,
> Finds tongues in trees, books in the running brooks,
> Sermons in stones, and good in everything.

[122] Skeat's note reads, "The story of the hart, in the old Bestiaries, is that,
when he grows old, he seeks out an adder and swallows it; but, the adder's poison
causing him to burn, he rushes to the water and drinks plentifully, so rendering
the venom harmless; after which he sheds his horns, and renews his strength."
The point of the use of the hart here is that the white hart was the favorite badge
of Richard II. His retainers had it on their liveries. Cf. the translation of the
story of the hart in the Bestiary in Weston, *Chief Middle English Poets* (Houghton
Mifflin Co., 1914), p. 328.

[123] The reference to the bushes here seems to be a pun on the name of Sir John
Bushy, one of the best known cronies of Richard; cf. the note on p. 185, *ante*.

[124] On this and the other animals mentioned here, cf. Skeat's note, "The *horse*
is Richard Fitz-alan, Earl of Arundel, beheaded on Tower-hill A.D. 1397; the *colt*,

Nor harass good horses, harnessed and tamed,
Nor strive with the Swan, though he should attack,[125]
Nor bait the fell Bear, nor bind him up either,
Nor wistfully woo his willingest kin,[126]
Nor list him to look at allies when they bleed;
This is all against Nature, as clerks have declared:
   On account of ingratitude, the free man is recalled to slavery,
as in the prick of conscience and in civil law.[127]
And, therefore, our hart his health has quite missed,
And could not pass even the point of his prime.
Now construe this who can — I no more can say.[128]
   Now I'll fare to the fowl which I mentioned before.
Of all the billed birds that build on the ground
My pleasure's to praise the partridge's [129] way,
That in season of summer when sitting is near,
And each fowl with his fere doth follow his kind,
This bird by a bank doth build up her nest,

his son Thomas, who fled to join Henry, and was one of the small company who
landed with him at Ravenspur; the *swan*, Thomas, Duke of Gloucester, Richard's
uncle, so treacherously murdered by his orders at Calais, about the same time that
Arundel was beheaded; and the *bear*, Thomas Beauchamp, Earl of Warwick, seized
with Arundel by Richard's orders, and banished by him for life to the Isle of Man,
though afterwards released by Henry. They were named from their badges, the
white horse being that of Arundel, the *swan* that of Gloucester, which he had adopted
from his father Edward III, who sometimes used it; and the *black bear* that of the
Earl of Warwick." Five of the charges against Richard in the *Chronicles of London*
account of his deposition, cited before, have to do with his treatment of the Duke of
Gloucester, the Earl of Arundel and the Earl of Warwick. Thus, the fourth charge
states that the King put to death the first two and doomed the last and the Lord
Cobham to perpetual imprisonment, though they all had royal charters of pardon.

   [125] I.e. not even though Gloucester should take the initiative against the Crown.
   [26] Cf. the quotation from *Traison et Mort du Roy Richart* on p. 186, *ante*, and from
Froissart, *ed. cit.*, p. 468, where Richard requests an interview with Henry of Lancaster.
   [127] This is the translation of a sentence in Latin inserted into the English text;
is the expression "prick of conscience" a reference to the Middle English work of
that name?
   [128] The general meaning seems to be that, whereas the noble hart recoups himself by hunting adders (i.e. the "undesirable citizens" of the country), Richard
has oppressed and killed off the most noteworthy people in the community and has
thus failed to make his way.
   [129] This account of the partridge, too, is derived from the Bestiary. Cf. Wright,
Popular Treatises on Science Written during the Middle Ages (London, 1841), p. 108.

And heaps up her eggs and heats them all well.
And, when the dam's done what belongs to the deed,
And hopes all to hatch ere harvest begin,
Then comes on a coward who wears a gray coat,
As nice in her noll as if she'd made the nest,
Another proud partridge, approaches the place,
And privily hides there until the dam pass;
Then seizes the seat with all her soft plumes,
And sits on the eggs that the other has laid.
She covers them well till the young come to life,
And fosters and feeds them till feathers appear,
And coats given by Nature compass them round.
But as soon as they stiffen so they can step,
Then comes up and cries their own cunning dam,
And they know well her note at the very first noise,
And leave quite the lurker that erstwhile them led —
For their stomachs too seldom the substitute filled,
And their limbs were too lean, for with hunger they'd lived.
Now, daily they cheerily dine with their dam
And she fosters them forth until they can fly.
    "What may this all mean, man?" well may you me ask,
"For it's darkly endited, for dull brain too hard;
Wherefore I wish now it might be your will
To tell what is proved by the partridge's case."
Ah! go to, Hick Heavy-head, hard is your noll
To catch any cunning if craftily said!
Did you not hear what I spoke but just now —
The Eagle [130] had entered his own in the East
And cried and called out for his own kind of birds
Annoyed in his nest and nourished full ill
And worried to death by a leader all wrong?
But these needy nestlings the note having heard
Of the great Eagle, good angel of all,
Broke from the bushes [131] and briars that tore them,

----

[130] The Eagle is Henry of Lancaster, who apparently had taken over this badge, one of the numerous insignia of his grandfather, Edward III (Skeat's note).
[131] The reference to the bushes is again a pun on the name of Sir John Bushy. Cf. *ante*, p. 185.

And, bent upon reaching him, burnished their bills
And followed him fiercely to fight out his wrongs;
They with their bills babbled how beaten they'd been,
And troubled with twigs for twenty-two [132] years.
Thus, left they the leader who led them awry,
And missed not a thing but taxed up their corn,[133]
And gathered their groats with guile as I trow.
They followed their father with faith strong and free;
Because he would feed them and foster them further,
And bring them from bondage to which they'd been broke.
Then sighed all the swimmers (i.e. the friends of Gloucester)
     because the Swan [134] failed,
And followed this Falcon (i.e. the Eagle) throughout fields and
     towns,
With many fair fowls, though many were faint
And heavy for hurt which had come to the Horse.
Yet they fluttered all forth as fast as they could,
To have from the Eagle some help from their harm;
For he headed them all and was highest of heart
In keeping the crown as the chronicle [135] tells.
He cheered up the Bear and broke off his bonds,
And left him at large, to leap where he would.
And then all the bear-cubs (i.e. Warwick's friends) burst out
     at once,
As fain as the fowl that flies in the sky,
That brought to his own and unbound was the boss.[136]

[132] I.e. for the term of Richard's reign.

[133] I.e. Richard's tax-gatherers were very careful to list all one's property for assessment and even took all of a farmer's crops as taxes.

[134] See the note on the meanings of these animal names, *ante*, p. 192.

[135] Just what chronicle is meant there is no means of knowing, but it is interesting that in *The Chronicles of London* (*ed. cit.*, p. 43), after the account of the deposition of Richard, there is inserted Henry's challenge of the crown, as follows: "In the name of the Father, Son and Holy Ghost, I, Harry of Lancaster, claim the realm of England and the crown with all the members and appurtenances. As I that am descended by direct line of the blood, coming from the good King Harry III. And through that right, that God of His grace hath sent to me, with help of my kin and of my friends to recover it. The which realm was on the point of being undone for lack of governance and good law."

[136] The very word of the text.

They gathered to-gether in a great rout,
To help out the heirs [137] who long had been wronged.
Out on the green [138] they cackled their grief
For friends that had fallen through foul schemes of crime.
They mourned for the murder of manfullest knights,
Sternly withstanding many a storm;
They 'monished the Marshal [139] for his misdeeds,
Who ill-knew his craft when he covered the Horse.
And aye as they followed this Falcon about
At each moving foot for vengeance they cried
On all that assented to that evil deed.

The poem concludes with the following vivid narrative,
which furnishes a kind of composite picture of the last
parliaments of Richard's reign. The poem ends abruptly
and is unfinished, as its beginning is missing.

For where now was Christian king you ever knew
That held such an household, measured by half,
As Richard in England's realm others "misruled."
So that not all his fines for faults or fee-farms,
Nor forfeitures many that fell in his day,
Nor nonages [137] numberless ever renewed,
Like March [140] and like Mowbray and manifold more,

[137] According to feudal law (cf. *post*, p. 203) the suzerain had a right to a certain
fine, much like a modern inheritance tax, when the heir succeeded to his property.
According to *The Chronicles of London* (*ed. cit.*, p. 28), the sixth charge against Richard was that his assessment of fines and ransoms was excessive and could not be
depended upon; i.e. after an offender or suitor had paid his fine, he was just as
likely as not to be called on to pay it again.

[138] This reference to the green, again, is doubtless a pun on the name of Sir Henry
Green, one of Richard's friends.

[139] Skeat's note, "The Earl-marshal was Thomas De Mowbray, Duke of Norfolk, son-in-law to the Earl of Arundel. The latter was executed by Richard's
orders; and, as Froissart tells us, the Earl-marshal actually bandaged his father-in-
law's eyes at the execution. . . . This is why the poet says Mowbray knew his
craft ill; for the office of a Marshal (lit. servant of the horse) is to attend to the
wants of a horse, not to bandage its eyes."

[140] Cf. "At the death of the vassal, the possession of his holding reverted to the
over lord as a result of the latter's abiding proprietorship; when the heir of the deceased vassal took possession of the land, the payment of the relief was an acknowl-

Nor all cases in courts the king could control,
Nor selling that soaks up silver right fast,
Nor profits of lands in the princely domain,
When accounts were cast up, with the custom of wills,
Could reach far enough, even adding his rents,
To pay the poor people purveyance's [141] cost,
Without praying Parliament for poundage [142] beside,
And fifteenths and tenths, [143]
And custom of cloth for sale at the fairs? [144]
Yet if credit had come not in at the last,
Though the curse of the commons has cleaved to it aye,

edgement of this fact. When the heir was a minor, the lord was his guardian during minority and received more or less of the land's income during that time." White, *op. cit.*, p. 106, note. The Earls of March were descendants in the female line of Lionel Duke of Clarence, third son of Edward III, and rightful heirs to the throne after Richard II. Roger Earl of March died in 1398 and was succeeded by his son Edmund, a minor. The Mowbrays were Earls of Nottingham and, later, Dukes of Norfolk; "John de Mowbray and Thomas de Mowbray both succeeded to the title while in their minority in this reign." (Skeat's note.)

[141] Purveyance was provision for the subsistence of the King and his train during a royal progress through the country; cf. note on p. 190, *ante*.

[142] A tax on merchandise, assessed by weight.

[143] "So-called because, originally and usually, they consisted of a tenth of the revenues or chattels of burgesses and a fifteenth from the landholders of shires." Cross, *op. cit.*, p. 210, note.

[144] Cf. "Outside the local markets and the towns, trading centered in the great annual fairs. The most famous of these were at Stourbridge and Winchester. The Stourbridge fair controlled the trade of the eastern counties and the Baltic Sea. Every trade and nationality was represented. It was under the control of the corporation of Cambridge, it was opened annually on 18 September, when temporary booths were set up, and it continued for three weeks. More important still was the Winchester fair under the control of the Bishop of Winchester. Lying between Southampton and London it was the great mart for the southeast. It opened every year on the eve of St. Giles (31 August) and lasted for sixteen days. During the session of the fair all trade was suspended in the neighborhood and weights and measures were carefully scrutinized. The fairs had a special law administered in the Pie Powder Court, so-called from the French *Pieds poudrés* (dusty feet; cf. *ante*, p. 191) in reference to the traveling merchants and others who came under its jurisdiction. In return for privileges and protection the merchants paid heavy toll to the lord who controlled the fair, and curious cases are on record of those who tried to evade their obligations by digging their way in under the palisades. Other fairs were held at Boston, St. Ives, Oxford, and Stamford." *Ibid.*, p. 163.

They'd been drawn to the devil because of their debts.
And when riot and revelry'd used up the rent,
And nothing was left except the bare bags,[145]
Then fell they to force to fill them again
And feignéd some folly that never them failed,
And cast out their coils in council at even
To parliament privily for their own profit.

The writs went out secretly sealed up with wax,
For peers and for prelates who then should appear;
And riders they sent out to neighboring shires
To choose [146] them such knights as would cheerfully come
To sit for the shire in seats with the great.
And, when the day came for the deed to be done,
The sovereigns assembled and knights of the shire.
And, first, as their form is, they start to declare
The cause of their coming and then the King's will.

Comely a clerk then commenced to call out,
And the points he pronounced to all present there,
And a motion for money was mainly the thing,
For glossing the great [147] lest grief should arise.

[145] Doubtless a punning reference to Sir William Bagot, a third of Richard's notorious friends; cf. *ante*, p. 185.

[146] The nineteenth charge against King Richard in *The Chronicles of London* account of his deposition (*ed. cit.*, p. 32) runs as follows: "Also, whereas by old statute and custom of his realm in the convocation and summoning of every parliament, the people of the realm in every shire were wont, and still should be free, to choose the knights of the shire for the Parliament, and to show their griefs and suggest remedies for them as it seemed to them best for their success. The King now, (however), to the intent that he might the more freely have his foolish desire performed, sends out ofttimes his commands to divers sheriffs, that they should choose certain persons whom he names himself, to come to his Parliament, and no others. And these knights, thus being favorable, the King can bring round to his purpose and desire to consent to him, either by menaces and threats, or else by gifts; and thereby make ordinances that should turn to the great prejudice of the realm and very expensive to the people; and especially, that of granting to the same King the wool subsidy (i.e. the returns from the tariff on wool shipped out of England, which was ordinarily granted from Parliament to Parliament and thus offered a means of controlling the royal conduct) for the term of his life and other subsidies for certain years, to the great oppressing of his people."

[147] I.e. Parliament was asked to provide money to gloss over the offenses of the great, on the plea that, if they did not, worse things would happen to England.

And when he had told the tale to the end,
They decided to meet on the morrow ere meat,
These knights of the towns, to consider the same
With citizens sent from the shires to their sire,
To review all the bills and grant the requests.
　　But yet, as a manner of making men blind,[148]
Some argued against the right to assess;
And said, "We are servants and salaries get,
And are sent by the shires their griefs to show forth,
And parley for profit to them, not to pass
And grant of their gold for the good of the great
In a very wrong way unless there were war;
And if we are false to our friends back at home,
We'll be but ill worthy of winning our pay."
　　Then sat some like ciphers in numerous seats
That number a place but nothing avail; [149]
°And some had but supped with Simon at eve,[150]
And showed for the shire but lost all the show; [151]
And some others were tattlers and went to the King
And soon made him foes of his earlier friends [152]
Who believed in the best and "unblameworthy" were
By King or by council or even by commons,
If one could keep count of the meaning of things.
Some slumbered and slept and said almost *nil;*

[148] I.e. as a "bluff" or "blind."

[149] I.e. zero has a place in the list of figures, but there's "nothing in it."

[150] Skeat says, "I have no doubt that 'to sup with Simon' means here to sup with ecclesiastics, to share in the revels which some churchmen indulged in. Simon means Simon Peter, and is used elsewhere . . . as a general name for the clergy." . . .

[151] I.e. they were in their seats but knew nothing of what was going on.

[152] Charge 25 against Richard in *The Chronicles of London* account (*ed. cit.*, p. 34) of his deposition reads as follows: "Also, the same King is wont of custom to be so variable and feigning in his words and writing, and also contrary to himself, and especially in writing to the Pope and to other kings and lords outside the realm, and also within to other subjects of his, that almost there was no believing man might have notice of his condition, or might trust him. But he was held so untrue and unstable that it turned not only to the slander of his own person, but also to that of all the realm, and especially among strange nations of all the world having knowledge thereof."

Some mumbled and murmured, nor knew what they meant;
And some had been hired (i.e. bribed) and so held their peace.
And no further would fare for fear of their boss;
And some were so sullen and sad (i.e. heavy) in their wits
That ere they could come to the close they were clogged
And could not construe the conclusion at all, —
No baron on bench nor burgess could either —
So blind and so bald and bare-faced was the reason.
And some were so fierce at the very first go,[153]
They shot out a spinnaker, crowded all sail
Before the wind freshly to make a good flight.
Then the lords lay in lee with ballast and cargo
And bore up the barge whose master they blamed,
That he knew not the course belonged to the craft,
And warnéd him wisely from fair-weather side.
But the mast in the midst at the end of a month
Bent nigh to bursting and brought them to land;
For, had they not steered well and struck all their sails,
And abated their bounty before the blast came,
They all had gone backward over the board.
     And some were encumbered with counsel before,
And wist well enough just how it would end,
If of the assembly some did not repent.
Some followed majorities whate'er they meant;
And some went so far but no farther would go.
Some parleyed as pertly as they approved,
And called more for coin the King owed to them
Than for comfort to commons who made up the cost;
They were promised some post if they'd give their support,
To be served quite securely by the same silver.
And some dreaded dukes and Do-well [154] foresook.

---

[153] A rather good picture of those who, like Chaucer's man-of-law were busy, but seemed busier than they were, and of those who are always ready to give advice from a safe distance.   [154] I.e. righteous conduct.

II. The Social and Industrial Background

From the poem just examined, it is clear that the fall of the Plantagenets was due largely to inability to comprehend and cope with changing economic conditions, which will now be more fully illustrated. We shall return on our track and trace with some care the economic and industrial history of England 1066–1400.

Of all the social institutions introduced into England by the Normans in 1066, none is so important and so far-reaching as the feudal system, which is best described as a device for the control at once of land-holding and military service, two matters of primary interest to a new government. It has already been pointed out that some elements of this system are to be found in Germanic life as far back as the time of Tacitus.[1] But, perhaps because of its geographical isolation, the system did not arrive at a very high stage of development in pre-Conquest England, and to the Normans must be given the credit of so improving and fostering the plant, that they may almost be said to have introduced it. Our first illustration of its life in England is the following general statement of the reciprocal duties of lords and vassals, a statement, to be sure, in laws ascribed to Henry I, but doubtless true of conditions in the time of his father, the Conqueror:

If one's lord is attacked, any vassal may without punishment come to his assistance, and should obey him in every legitimate way, except in treachery, theft, murder, and in short in things like these which are allowable to no one and are infamous in law.[2]

[1] Cf. *ante*, pp. 9, 12, 13, 14. The best recent treatment of feudalism in England is Mary Bateson, *Mediæval England* (*Stories of the Nations Series*, G. P. Putnam's Sons, second impression, 1905). The entire volume is devoted to a study of the industrial and social phases of feudalism, whose history is divided into Norman Feudalism 1066–1154, the Lawyer's Feudalism 1154–1250, and Decadent Feudalism 1250–1350.

[2] This paragraph and the next are from section lxxxii of the *Laws of Henry I*, and the full title of the section is *Of Various Sorts of Feuds in Order*.

Likewise, the lord ought equally at fitting times to help his vassal with counsel and aid, and in every possible way, without (risk of) forfeiture.

Every lord may summon his vassal, that they may come to terms in his (i.e. the lord's) court; and (even) if the vassal lives on an out-of-the-way manor of the fief, he will go to the court, if his lord summons him. If his liege hold several fiefs, the man of the one is not legally to be compelled to attend the court of another, unless the case (involved) is under the jurisdiction of the second to which he has been summoned.[3]

If the vassal hold of several lords and belong to different fiefs, he owes more (duty) to him, and his residence will be under the jurisdiction of him, whose liegeman he is, however much he hold of others.

Every vassal owes fidelity to his lord touching the latter's life, bodily members, earthly honor and keeping of his counsel, in every honorable and advantageous way, saving only his faith in God and fidelity to his earthly king. Theft, however, and treachery and murder and whatever is contrary to (the law of) God and the Catholic faith, are to be demanded of or performed by no one; but the faith should be kept with all lords, except that more fidelity is due to the earlier and to him who is the liege (in each case). And, if any vassal seek another lord for himself, he should be free to do so.

William I, however, was not content with the somewhat loosely articulated form of feudalism brought from Normandy; but in 1086, according to the entry in the *Anglo-Saxon Chronicle* for that year, he brought it about that every landholder of any importance in England took an oath of direct allegiance to the King. The *Chronicle* entry reads as follows:

This year the King wore his crown and held his court at Winchester at Easter, and he so journeyed forward that he was at Westminster during Pentecost, and there he dubbed his son

---

[3] This paragraph and the two following are from section lv of the *Laws of Henry I*, whose full title is *Of the Privilege of a Lord over His Vassal*.

Henry [4] a knight.   And afterwards he travelled about, so that he came to Salisbury at Lammas; [5] and his witan, and all the land-holders of substance in England, whose vassals soever they were, repaired to him there, and they all submitted to him, and became his men, and swore oaths of allegiance, that they would be faithful to him against all others.

Specific information regarding important feudal occasions and duties is afforded by the *Coronation Charter of Henry I.* as follows:

In the year of the incarnation of the Lord, 1101, Henry, son of King William, after the death of his brother William, by the grace of God, king of the English, to all faithful, greeting:

1. Know that by the mercy of God, and by the common counsel of the barons of the whole kingdom of England, I have been crowned king of the same kingdom; and because the kingdom has been oppressed by unjust exactions, I, from regard to God, and from the love which I have toward you, in the first place make the holy church of God free, so that I will neither sell nor place at rent, nor, when archbishop, or bishop, or abbot is dead, will I take anything from the domain of the church, or from its men, until a successor is installed into it.   And all the evil customs by which the realm of England was unjustly oppressed will I take away, which evil customs I partly set down here.

2. If any one of my barons, or earls, or others who hold from me shall have died, his heir shall not redeem his land, as he did in the time of my brother, but shall relieve it by a just and legitimate relief.   Similarly also the men of my barons shall relieve their lands from their lords by a just and legitimate relief.

3. And if any one of the barons or other men of mine wishes to give his daughter in marriage, or his sister or niece or relation, he must speak with me about it, but I will neither take anything from him for this permission, nor forbid him to give

[4] Later King Henry I.

[5] 1 August (Old Calendar), 12 August (New Calendar).   The word *Lammas* is the Old English Hlafmaesse, "loafmass" or wheat harvest.

her in marriage, unless he should wish to join her to my enemy. And if when a baron or other man of mine is dead a daughter remains as his heir, I will give her in marriage according to the judgment of my barons, along with her land. And if when a man is dead his wife remains and is without children, she shall have her dowry and right of marriage, and I will not give her to a husband except according to her will.

4. And if a wife has survived with children, she shall have her dowry and right of marriage, so long as she shall have kept her body legitimately, and I will not give her in marriage, except according to her will. And the guardian of the land and children shall be either the wife or another one of the relatives as shall seem to be most just. And I require that my barons should deal similarly with the sons and daughters or wives of their men.

5. The common tax on money [6] which used to be taken through the cities and counties, which was not taken in the time of King Edward, I now forbid altogether henceforth to be taken. If any one shall have been seized, whether a moneyer or any other, with false money, strict justice shall be done for it.

6. All fines and all debts which were owed to my brother, I remit, except my rightful rents, and except those payments which had been agreed upon for the inheritances of others or for those things which more justly affected others. And if any one for his own inheritance has stipulated anything, this I remit, and all reliefs which had been agreed upon for rightful inheritances.

7. And if any one of my barons or men shall become feeble, however he himself shall give or arrange to give his money, I grant that it shall be so given. Moreover, if he himself, prevented by arms, or by weakness, shall not have bestowed his money, or arranged to bestow it, his wife or his children or his parents, and his legitimate men shall divide it for his soul, as to them shall seem best.

8. If any of my barons or men shall have committed an offence he shall not give security to the extent of forfeiture of his money, as he did in the time of my father, or of my brother, but accord-

[6] *Monetagium*, which is here translated "tax on money," was a payment made to the king or other lord, periodically, on condition that he would not change the standard of value during a given period. It was customary in Normandy.— Ducange.

ing to the measure of the offence so shall he pay, as he would have paid from the time of my father backward, in the time of my other predecessors; so that if he shall have been convicted of treachery or of crime, he shall pay as is just.

9. All murders, moreover, before that day in which I was crowned king, I pardon; and those which shall be done henceforth shall be punished justly according to the law of King Edward.

10. The forests, by the common agreement of my barons, I have retained in my own hand, as my father held them.

11. To those knights who hold their land by the cuirass, I yield of my own gift the lands of their demesne ploughs free from all payments and from all labor, so that as they have thus been favored by such a great alleviation, so they may readily provide themselves with horses and arms for my service and for the defence of the kingdom.

12. A firm peace in my whole kingdom I establish and require to be kept from henceforth.

13. The law of King Edward I give to you again with those changes with which my father changed it by the counsel of his barons.

14. If any one has taken anything from my possessions since the death of King William, my brother, or from the possessions of any one, let the whole be immediately returned without alteration, and if any one shall have retained anything thence, he upon whom it is found will pay it heavily to me. Witnesses Maurice, bishop of London, and Gundulf, bishop, and William, bishop-elect, and Henry, earl, and Simon, earl, and Walter Giffard, and Robert de Montfort, and Roger Bigod, and Henry de Port, at London, when I was crowned.

"Feudalism," says Meredith, "is not an objectionable thing if you can be sure of the lord." [7] Unfortunately, however, the personal element in the system was so large that its operation was always uncertain. At least, Englishmen in the time of King Stephen (1135–1154) found it so, for their representative gives in the entries in the *Anglo-*

[7] Cf. *The Egoist*, p. 94 (*Pocket Revised* ed., Charles Scribner's Sons).

Saxon Chronicle for the years 1135 and 1137 the following account of feudal anarchy in the reign of that king:

This year, at Lammas, King Henry [8] went over sea: and on the second day, as he lay asleep in the ship, the day was darkened universally and the sun became as if it were a moon three nights old with the stars shining round it at mid-day. Men greatly marvelled and great fear fell on them and they said that some great event should follow thereafter — and so it was, for the same year the King died in Normandy on the day after the feast of St. Andrew. Soon did this land fall into trouble, for every man greatly began to rob his neighbor as he might. Then King Henry's sons and his friends took his body and brought it to England and buried it at Reading. He was a good man and great was the awe of him; no man durst ill-treat another in his time: he made peace for men and deer. Whoso bare his burden of gold and silver, no man durst say to him aught but good. In the meantime his nephew Stephen de Blois had arrived in England and he came to London and the inhabitants received him and sent for the Archbishop, William Corboil, who consecrated him King on midwinter day. In this King's time was all discord and evil-doing and robbery; for the powerful men who had kept aloof, soon rose up against him; the first was Baldwin de Redvers, and he held Exeter against the King, and Stephen besieged him, and afterwards Baldwin made terms with him. Then the others took their castles and held them against the King, and David King of Scotland betook him to Wessington (Derbyshire), but notwithstanding his array, messengers passed between them, and they came together and made an agreement, though it availed little. . . .

This year [9] King Stephen went over sea to Normandy and he was received there because it was expected that he would be altogether like his uncle and because he had gotten possession of his treasure, but this he distributed and scattered foolishly. King Henry had gathered together much gold and silver, yet did he no good for his soul's sake with the same. When King Stephen came to England, he held an assembly at Oxford; and there he seized Roger Bishop of Salisbury and Alexander Bishop

[8] I.e. Henry I.   [9] I.e. 1137.

of Lincoln and Roger the chancellor, his nephew, and he kept them all in prison till they gave up their castles. When the traitors perceived that he was a mild man and a soft and a good, and that he did not enforce justice, they did all wonder. They had done homage to him, and sworn oaths, but they had no faith; all became forsworn and broke their allegiance, for every rich man built his castles and defended them against him, and they filled the land full of castles. They greatly oppressed the wretched people by making them work at these castles, and when the castles were finished they filled them with devils and evil men. Then they took those whom they suspected to have any goods, by night and by day, seizing both men and women, and they put them in prison for their gold and silver and tortured them with pains unspeakable, for never were any martyrs tormented as these were. They hung some up by their feet, and smoked them with foul smoke; some by their thumbs, or by the head, and they hung burning things on their feet. They put a knotted string about their heads and twisted it till it went into the brain. They put them into dungeons wherein were adders and snakes and toads and thus wore them out. Some they put into a crucet-house, that is, into a chest that was short and narrow, and not deep, and they put sharp stones in it and crushed the man therein so that they broke all his limbs. There were hateful and grim things called Sachenteges in many of the castles which two or three men had enough to do to carry. The Sachentege was made thus: it was fastened to a beam, having a sharp iron to go round a man's throat and neck, so that he might no ways sit nor lie nor sleep but that he must bear all the iron. Many thousands they exhausted with hunger. I cannot and I may not tell of all the wounds and all the tortures that they inflicted upon the wretched men of this land; and this state of things lasted the nineteen years that Stephen was king, and ever grew worse and worse. They were continually levying an exaction from the towns, which they called Tenserie, and when the miserable inhabitants had no more to give, then plundered they and burnt all the towns, so that well you might walk a whole day's journey nor ever would you find a man seated in a town or its lands tilled.

Then was corn dear and flesh and cheese and butter, for there was none in the land — wretched men starved — some lived on alms who had formerly been rich; some fled the country — never was there more misery and never did heathen act worse than these. At length they spared neither church nor churchyard but they took all that was valuable therein, and then burned the church and all together. Neither did they spare the lands of bishops nor those of abbots nor those of priests; but they robbed the monks and the clergy, and every man plundered his neighbor as much as he could. If two or three men came riding to a town, all the township fled before them and thought that they were robbers. The bishops and the clergy were ever cursing them, but this to them was nothing, for they were all accursed and forsworn and reprobate. The earth bore no corn, you might as well have tilled the sea, for the land was all ruined by such deeds and it was openly said that Christ and his saints slept. These things, and more than we can say, did we suffer during nineteen years because of our sins. Through all this evil time the Abbot Martin [10] held his abbacy for twenty years and a half and eight days, with many difficulties and he provided the monks and guests with all necessaries, and kept up much alms in the house; and withal he worked upon the church, and annexed thereto lands and rents, and enriched it greatly, and furnished it with robes: and he brought the monks into the new monastery on St. Peter's day [11] with much pomp. This was in the year 1140 of our Lord's incarnation, the twenty-third year after the fire. And he went to Rome and was well received there by Pope Eugenius, from whom he obtained sundry privileges, to wit, one for all the abbey lands and another for the lands that adjoin the monastery, and had he lived longer, he meant to do as much for the treasurer's house. And he regained certain lands that powerful men possessed by force; he won Cotingham and Easton from William Malduit who held Rockingham castle, and from Hugh of Walteville he won Hirtlingbery and Stanwick and sixty shillings yearly out of Oldwinkle. And he increased the number of monks and

[10] I.e. of Peterborough, where this MS. of the *Chronicle* was written.
[11] I.e. June 29.

planted a vineyard and did many good works and improved the town; and he was a good monk and a good man and, therefore, God and good men loved him. Now will we relate some part of what befell in King Stephen's time. In his reign the Jews of Norwich bought a Christian child before Easter and tortured him with all the torments wherewith our Lord was tortured, and they crucified him on Good Friday for the love of the Lord, and afterwards buried him. They believed that this would be kept secret, but our Lord made manifest that he was a holy martyr, and the monks took him and buried him honorably in the monastery, and he performed manifold and wonderful miracles through the power of our Lord, and he is called St. William.[12]

Henry II, a person whose vigor and energy have already been described for us,[13] set about correcting these abuses. His reform policy is thus outlined by William of New-burgh, a great historian of the twelfth century:

In the eleven hundred and fifty-fourth year from the delivery of the Virgin, Henry, grandson of Henry the elder, by his daughter the late empress, having arrived in England from Normandy, after the demise of King Stephen, received his hereditary kingdom; and, being greeted by all and consecrated king with the holy unction,[14] was hailed throughout England by crowds, exclaiming, "Long live the King." The people, having experienced the misery of the late reign, whence so many evils had originated, now anticipated better things of their new sovereign, more especially as prudence and resolution and a strict regard to justice were apparent in him;[15] and at his outset he bore the appearance of a great prince. Moreover, he issued an

[12] On the medieval attitude toward the Jews, cf. *post*, pp. 277; 407; 462–465.

[13] Cf. *ante*, pp. 158–162.

[14] He was crowned at Westminster on Sunday 19th December. (Stevenson's note.)

[15] Evidently this was a common reaction; the writer of the entry for the year 1154 in the Peterborough MS. of the *Anglo-Saxon Chronicle* pens the following striking sentence, "When the King (Stephen) died, the Earl (Henry, still Earl or Count of Anjou) was beyond sea, and no man durst do other than good for very dread of him." *Tr. cit.* This 1154 entry is the last in the *Chronicle* and is by many taken to mark the end of the Old English period of our language and literature.

edict, that such foreigners as had flocked to England under
King Stephen for the sake of booty, as well as military service
— and especially the Flemings of whom a vast number at that
time burthened the kingdom, should return to their own country by an appointed day, to stay beyond which would be attended with certain danger. Terrified at this edict, they glided
away in a moment, as quickly as a phantom vanishes; while
numbers wondered at their instantaneous disappearance. He
next commanded the newly-erected castles, which were not in
being in the days of his grandfather, to be demolished, with the
exception of a few advantageously situated, which he wished to
retain for himself or his partisans, for the defence of the kingdom. He then paid serious attention to public regulations and
was anxiously vigilant that the vigor of the law which in King
Stephen's time had appeared lifeless and forgotten, should be
revived. He appointed officers of law and justice throughout
his realm for the purpose of restraining the audacity of offenders, and administering redress to complainants according to the
merits of the case; while he himself either enjoyed his pleasure
or bestowed his royal care on more important avocations. As
often, however, as any of the judges acted remissly or improp-
erly and he was assailed by the complaints of the people, the
King applied the remedy of his royal revision and properly
corrected their negligence or excess. Such being the outset of
the new sovereign, the peaceably disposed congratulated and
commended, while the lawless muttered and were terrified. The
ravening wolves fled or were changed to sheep; or if not totally
changed, yet they dwelt harmlessly amid the flock, through fear
of the law. Swords were beaten into plowshares and spears into
pruning hooks; none learned war any more,[16] but all enjoyed
the leisure of that long-wished-for tranquillity now kindly accorded them by God, or were intent on their several employments. . . .

The King, reflecting that the royal revenues which, in the
time of his grandfather, had been very ample, were greatly reduced, because through the indolence of King Stephen, they
had, for the most part, passed away to numerous other masters,

[16] Cf. Isaiah 2: 4.

commanded them to be restored entire by the usurper, of whatsoever degree, and brought back to their former jurisdiction and
condition. Such as had hitherto become proprietors in royal
towns and villages produced for their defence the charters which
they had either extorted from King Stephen, or earned by their
services: but these could avail them nothing, as the grants of
an usurper could not be permitted to operate against the claims
of a lawful prince. Highly indignant at first thereat, but afterwards terrified and dispirited, they resigned — though reluctantly, yet entirely — everything they had usurped and held
for a considerable time as if by legal title. Whilst all throughout each county of the kingdom submitted to the royal pleasure
. . . the King proceeded beyond the Humber and summoned
William Earl of Albermarle,[17] who in the times of Stephen had
been more truly a king there than his master, to surrender in
this respect as well as the others, to the weight of his authority.
Hesitating a long while and boiling with indignation, he at last,
though sorely hurt, submitted to his power and very reluctantly
resigned whatever of the royal domains he had possessed for
many years, more especially that celebrated and noble castle of
Scarborough. . . .

Phrases like "strict regard to justice," "serious attention to public regulations," or "vigor of the law" in the
preceding document open long vistas into the field of
Henry's activities, which may be comprehensively described as a return to the work of his grandfather, Henry
I, in establishing feudalism on a sound legal basis. "Trained
in the law," says Miss Bateson, "a lover of the subtleties
of law, canon and civil, he and his staff of learned clerks
made it their business to smooth away those ragged edges
which the first Norman kings had left in the fitting of
Norman on to the English law. In the process many and
great changes were made, changes calculated to strengthen
the central [18] as against the feudal power. A lawyer king

[17] He had been created Earl of Yorkshire by King Stephen and had possessed
the larger portion of that country. See Dugdale, *Baronage*, I, 62. (Stevenson.)
[18] Cf. *ante*, p. 158.

found further a grand opportunity before him to display his learning and his strength when he engaged in one of the longest and most exciting rounds in the periodic wrestling match between church and state."[19] One of Henry's devices for improving the legal system of England and the administration of justice was the *Assize of Clarendon*, promulgated in 1166, just a century after the battle of Hastings. In a modern English translation of the twelfth-century Latin, it reads as follows:

Here begins the Assize of Clarendon, made by King Henry II, with the assent of the archbishops, bishops, abbots, earls and barons of all England.

§ 1. In the first place, the aforesaid King Henry, with the consent of all his barons, for the preservation of the peace and the keeping of justice, has enacted that inquiry should be made through the several counties and through the several hundreds, by twelve of the most legal men of the hundred and by four of the most legal men of each manor, upon their oath that they will tell the truth, whether there is in their hundred or in their manor, any man who has been accused or publicly suspected of himself being a robber, or murderer, or thief, or of being a receiver of robbers, or murderers, or thieves, since the lord king has been king. And let the justices make this inquiry before themselves, and the sheriffs before themselves.

§ 2. And let any one who has been found by the oath of the aforesaid to have been accused or publicly suspected of having been a robber, or murderer, or thief, or a receiver of them, since the lord king has been king, be arrested and go to the ordeal of water and let him swear that he has not been a robber, or murderer, or thief, or receiver of them since the lord king has been king, to the value of five shillings, so far as he knows.

§ 3. And if the lord of the man who has been arrested or his steward or his men shall have claimed him, with a pledge, within the third day after he has been seized, let him be given up and his chattels until he himself makes his law.

19 *Op. cit.* p. 141. Cf. *ante*, p. 161.

§ 4. And when a robber, or murderer, or thief, or receiver of them shall have been seized through the above-mentioned oath, if the justices are not to come very soon into that county where they have been arrested, let the sheriffs send word to the nearest justice by some intelligent man that they have arrested such men, and the justices will send back word to the sheriffs where they wish that these should be brought before them; and the sheriffs shall bring them before the justices; and along with these they shall bring from the hundred and the manor where they have been arrested, two legal men to carry the record of the county and of the hundred as to why they were seized, and there before the justice let them make their law.

§ 5. And in the case of those who have been arrested through the aforesaid oath of this assize, no one shall have court, or judgment, or chattels, except the lord king in his court before his justices, and the lord king shall have all their chattels. In the case of those, however, who have been arrested, otherwise than through this oath, let it be as it has been accustomed and ought to be.

§ 6. And the sheriffs who have arrested them shall bring such before the justice without any other summons than they have from him. And when robbers, or murderers, or thieves, or receivers of them, who have been arrested through the oath or otherwise, are handed over to the sheriffs they also must receive them immediately without delay.

§ 7. And in the several counties where there are no jails, let such be made in a borough or in some castle of the king, from the money of the king and from his forest, if one shall be near, or from some other neighboring forest, on the view of the servants of the king; in order that in them the sheriffs may be able to detain those who have been seized by the officials who are accustomed to do this or by their servants.

§ 8. And the lord king, moreover, wills that all should come to the county courts to make this oath, so that no one shall remain behind because of any franchise which he has or court or jurisdiction which he has, but that they should come to the making of this oath.

§ 9. And there is to be no one within a castle or without a

castle or even in the honor of Wallingford, who may forbid the sheriffs to enter into his court or his land for seeing to the frankpledges and that all are under pledges; and let them be sent before the sheriffs under a free pledge.

§ 10. And in cities and boroughs, let no one have men or receive them in his house or in his land or his soc, whom he does not take in hand that he will produce before the justice if they shall be required, or else let them be under a frankpledge.

§ 11. And let there be none within a city or borough or within a castle or without, or even in the honor of Wallingford, who shall forbid the sheriffs to enter into his land or his jurisdiction to arrest those who have been charged or publicly suspected of being robbers or murderers or thieves or receivers of them, or outlaws, or persons charged concerning the forest; but he requires that they should aid them to capture these.

§ 12. And if any one is captured who has in his possession the fruits of robbery or theft, if he is of bad reputation and has an evil testimony from the public, and has not a warrant, let him not have law. And if he shall not have been accused on account of the possession which he has, let him go to the water.

§ 13. And if any one shall have acknowledged robbery or murder or theft or the reception of them in the presence of legal men or of the hundred, and afterwards shall wish to deny it, he shall not have law.

§ 14. The lord king wills, moreover, that those who make their law and shall be absolved by the law, if they are of very bad testimony, and publicly and disgracefully spoken ill of by the testimony of many and legal men, shall abjure the lands of the king, so that within eight days they shall go over the sea, unless the wind shall have detained them; and with the first wind which they shall have afterward they shall go over the sea, and they shall not afterward return into England, except on the permission of the lord king; and then let them be outlawed if they return, and if they return they shall be seized as outlaws.

§ 15. And the lord king forbids any vagabond, that is a wandering or an unknown man, to be sheltered anywhere except in a borough, and even there he shall be sheltered only one night, unless he shall be sick there, or his horse, so that he is able to show an evident excuse.

§ 16. And if he shall have been there more than one night, let him be arrested and held until his lord shall come to give securities for him, or until he himself shall have secured pledges; and let him likewise be arrested who has sheltered him.

§ 17. And if any sheriff shall have sent word to any other sheriff that men have fled from his county into another county, on account of robbery or murder or theft, or the reception of them, or for outlawry or for a charge concerning the forest of the king, let him arrest them. And even if he knows of himself or through others that such men have fled into his county, let him arrest them and hold them until he shall have secured pledges from them.

§ 18. And let all sheriffs cause a list to be made of all fugitives who have fled from their counties; and let them do this in the presence of their county courts, and they will carry the written names of these before the justices when they come first before these, so that they may be sought through all England, and their chattels may be seized for the use of the king.

§ 19. And the lord king wills that, from the time when the sheriffs have received the summons of the justices in eyre to appear before them with their county courts, they shall gather together their county courts and make inquiry for all who have recently come into their counties since this assize; and that they should send them away with pledges that they will be before the justices, or else keep them in custody until the justices come to them, and then they shall have them before the justices.

§ 20. The lord king, moreover, prohibits monks and canons and all religious houses from receiving any one of the lesser people as a monk or canon or brother, until it is known of what reputation he is, unless he shall be sick unto death.

§ 21. The lord king, moreover, forbids any one in all England to receive in his land or his jurisdiction or in a house under him any one of the sect of those renegades who have been excommunicated and branded at Oxford. And if any one shall have received them, he will be at the mercy of the lord king, and the house in which they have been shall be carried outside the

village and burned. And each sheriff will take this oath that
he will hold this, and will make all his servants swear this,
and the stewards of the barons, and all knights and free tenants
of the counties.

§ 22. And the lord king wills that this assize shall be held in
his kingdom so long as it shall please him.

The feudal documents so far quoted have illustrated
mainly the governmental and legal aspects of a great social
system. Materials will now be adduced to do a like service for the life of those who lived under the system;
namely, English manorial documents. "The manor,"
says Professor Cheyney, "was the most fundamental institution of medieval society. In the use of the term as
a territorial expression, equivalent to villa, vill, or township, a manor was a stretch of country occupied by a
rural population, grouped in a single village, or perhaps
in several hamlets, surrounded by agricultural lands. Part
of the land of the manor, known as the desmesne, was
cultivated by the lord of the manor through a bailiff or
other officers; the remainder was used by tenants, free
and serf, who cultivated their scattered holdings and, in
the form of compulsory services, performed most of the
labor on the demesne lands. The manor, in this sense,
was the agricultural unit of the country, and had its own
internal organization based upon the form of distribution
of the land, the method of its cultivation, and the reciprocal relations of the demesne and the rest of the land.
The greater part of England was divided into such manors,
either contiguous or separated by unused stretches of
moor, fen, or forest." [20]

[20] *Pennsylvania Translations and Reprints from the Original Sources of European
History*, iii, 5, p. 1. Valuable and interesting comment on these documents will
be found in chapter 2 (*Village Life Six Hundred Years Ago*) of Jessopp, *The Coming
of the Friars and Other Historic Essays* (G. P. Putnam's Sons, 1908). This essay
is largely reprinted in Tuell and Hatch, *Selected Readings in English History* (Ginn
and Co., 1913).

The manorial system naturally developed greatly in complexity during our period. Our first document is a survey or "extent" of a manor belonging to Peterborough Abbey about 1125. The record is comparatively simple.

In Werminton are 7 hides at the taxation of the king. And of this land 20 full villeins and 29 half-villeins hold 34 virgates and a half; and for these the full villeins work 3 days a week through the year; and the half tenants as much as corresponds to their tenancies. And all these men have 16 plows, and they plow 68 acres and a half, and besides this they do 3 boonworks with their plows, and they ought to bring from the woods 34 wagon loads of wood. And all these men pay 4£. 11s. 4d. And to the love feast of St. Peter 10 rams and 400 loaves and 40 platters and 34 hens and 260 eggs. And there are 8 socmen who have 6 plows. In the demesne of the court are 4 plows of 32 oxen, and 9 cows and 5 calves, and 1 riding horse and 129 sheep and 61 swine and 1 draught-horse and 1 colt. And there is 1 mill with 1 virgate of land and 6 acres which pays 60s. and 500 eels. And Ascelin the clerk holds the church, with 2 virgates of land from the altar of St. Peter of Borough. Robert, son of Richard, has 2 virgates and a half. In this vill 100 sheep can be placed.

The following description of a manor house at Chingford, Essex, in 1265 will bring before us both the general possibilities of a manorial dwelling and the arrangement of manorial grounds. The manor house was the residence of the lord of the manor or his representative, the official center of the community.

He [21] received also a sufficient and handsome hall well ceiled with oak. On the western side is a suitable bed, on the ground, a stone chimney, a wardrobe and a certain other small chamber; at the eastern end is a pantry and a buttery. Between the hall and the chapel is a side-room. There is a decent chapel covered with tiles, a portable altar, and a small cross. In the hall are four tables on trestles. There are likewise a good kitchen well

[21] I.e. the heir to the property.

covered with tiles, with a furnace and ovens, one large, the other small, for cakes, two tables, and alongside the kitchen a small house for baking. Also a new granary covered with oak shingles, and a building in which the dairy is contained, though it is divided. Likewise a chamber suited for clergymen and a necessary chamber. Also a hen-house. These are within the inner gate.

Likewise outside of that gate are an old house for the servants, a good stable, long and divided, and to the east of the principal building, beyond the smaller stable, a solar for the use of the servants. Also a building in which is contained a bed; also two barns, one for wheat and one for oats. These buildings are enclosed with a moat, a wall, and a hedge. Also beyond the middle gate is a good barn, and a stable for cows and another for oxen, these old and ruinous. Also beyond the outer gate is a pigstye.

Two more village surveys or "extents" follow, one, dated 1307, for the manor of Bernehorne; another, dated 1308, for the manor of Borley. The first is quoted because of the detailed way in which the various feudal services, due from the many tenants, are indicated in it. The Borley extent is cited because it states the right of common, of mill, and of court and because it gives apparently careful expression to common notions of feudal duties, as, for example, in the last paragraph. Both documents indicate the kind of accounts kept on a feudal estate. It is rather amusing in the first or Bernehorne survey to find several times the statement that a given service is of no gain to the lord, coupled with insistence that the service must, nevertheless, be performed.

Extent of the manor of Bernehorne, made on Wednesday next after the feast of St. Gregory the Pope, in the thirty-fifth year of the reign of King Edward, in the presence of Brother Thomas, keeper of Marley, John de la More, and Adam de Thruhlegh, clerks, on the oath of William de Gocecoumbe, Walter le Parker, Richard le Knyst, Richard the son of the latter, Andrew of Estone,

Stephen Morsprich, Thomas Brembel, William de Swynham, John Pollard, Roger le Glide, John Syward and John de Lillingewist, who say etc., that there are there all the following things:

The jurors say that the principal messuage and its garden with the herbage and curtilage are worth yearly 6s. 8d.; and the dovecote is worth yearly 5s.; and the windmill is worth yearly 20s.

And there are there 12 acres of thick undergrowth whence the pannage and herbage are worth yearly 2s.

And there are there 42 acres of maritime [22] land in a certain place called Scotsmarsh, each acre of which is worth yearly 12d., the sum being 42s.

And there are there 7 acres and 1 rood of maritime land in a certain place called Aldithewisse; and 47 acres and 3 roods of maritime land in a certain place called Flittermarsh, each acre of which is worth yearly 12d., the sum being 55s.

And there are there 22 acres of maritime land in two places called Pundfold and Longrech; and 7 acres of maritime land in a certain place called Wyssh, and 8 acres and 3 roods of maritime land in a certain place called Upcroft marsh, and 3 acres and a half of maritime land in a certain place called Redewysshe; and each acre is worth yearly 12d., the sum being 41s. 3d. [23]

. . . .

The total of the acres of woods is 12 acres. The total of the acres of arable land is 444 acres and 3 roods, of which 147 acres 4 roods are maritime land, 101 acres marshy land, and 180 acres waste ground.

The total of the acres of meadow is 13 acres 1 rood.

The total of the whole preceding extent 18£. 10s. 4d.

John Pollard holds a half acre in Aldithewisse and owes 18d. at the four terms, and owes from it relief and heriot.

John Suthinton holds a house and 40 acres of land and owes 3s. 6d. at Easter and Michaelmas. [24]

[22] Apparently land which was close to the salt marsh but yet capable of being cultivated, since agricultural services of the villein tenants are mentioned subsequently. Bernehorne is in Sussex, quite near the sea. (The notes on this document are Prof. Cheyney's.)

[23] Various numbers of acres of land situated in different places and at values from 3d. to 18d. per acre a year are here named.   [24] I.e. Sept. 29.

William of Swynhamme holds 1 acre of meadow in the thicket of Swynhamme and owes 1d. at the feast of Michaelmas.

Ralph of Leybourne holds a cottage and 1 acre of land in Pinden and owes 3s. at Easter and Michaelmas, and attendance at the court in the manor every three weeks, relief and heriot.

Richard Knyst of Swynhamme holds two acres and a half of land and owes yearly 4s.

William at Knelle holds 2 acres of land in Aldithewisse and owes yearly 4s.

Roger le Glede holds a cottage and 3 roods of land and owes 2s. 6d. at Easter and Michaelmas.

Alexander Hamound holds a little piece of land near Aldithe-wisse and owes 1 goose, of the value of 2d.

The sum of the whole rent of the free tenants, with the value of the goose, is 18s. 9d.

They say moreover that John of Cayworth holds a house and 30 acres of land, and owes yearly 2s. at Easter and Michaelmas; and he owes a cock and two hens at Christmas, of the value of 4d.

And he ought to harrow for 2 days at the Lenten sowing with one man and his own horse and his own harrow, the value of the work being 4d.; and he is to receive from the lord on each day 3 meals, of the value of 5d., and then the lord will be at a loss of 1d. Thus his harrowing is of no value to the service of the lord.

And he ought to carry the manure of the lord for 2 days with 1 cart, with his own 2 oxen, the value of the work being 8d.; and he is to receive from the lord each day 3 meals of the price as above. And thus the service is worth 3d. clear.

And he shall find 1 man for 2 days for mowing the meadow of the lord, who can mow, by estimation 1 acre and a half, the value of the mowing of an acre being 6d.; the sum is therefore 9d.; and he is to receive each day 3 meals of the value given above; and thus that mowing is worth 4d clear.

And he ought to gather and carry that same hay which he has cut, the price of the work being 3d.

And he shall have from the lord 2 meals for 1 man, of the value of 1½d. Thus the work will be worth 1½d. clear.

And he ought to carry the hay of the lord for 1 day with a cart and 3 animals of his own, the price of the work being 6d. And he shall have from the lord 3 meals of the value of 2½d. And thus the work is worth 3½d. clear.

And he ought to carry in autumn beans or oats for 2 days with a cart and 3 animals of his own, the value of the work being 12d. And he shall receive from the lord each day 3 meals of the value given above; and thus the work is worth 7d. clear.

And he ought to carry wood from the woods of the lord as far as the manor [25] for two days in summer with a cart and 3 animals of his own, the value of the work being 9d. And he shall receive from the lord each day 3 meals of the price given above; and thus the work is worth 4d. clear.

And he ought to find 1 man for 2 days to cut heath, the value of the work being 4d., and he shall have 3 meals each day of the value given above; and thus the lord will lose, if he receives the service, 3d. Thus that mowing is worth nothing to the service of the lord.

And he ought to carry the heath which he has cut, the value of the work being 5d. And he shall receive from the lord 3 meals at the price of 2½d. And thus the work will be worth 2½d. clear.

And he ought to carry to Battle [26] twice in the summer season, each time half a load of grain, the value of the service being 4d. And he shall receive in the manor each time 1 meal of the value of 2d. And thus the work is worth 2d. clear.

The total of the rents, with the value of the hens, is 2s. 4d.

The total of the value of the works is 2s. 3½d.; owed from the said John yearly.

William of Cayworth holds a house and 30 acres of land and owes at Easter and Michaelmas 2s. rent. And he shall do all customs just as the foresaid John of Cayworth.

William atte Grene holds a house and 30 acres of land and owes in all things just as the said John.

Alan atte Felde holds a house and 16 acres of land (for which

---

[25] I.e. the manor-house.

[26] The manor of Bernehorne was a holding of Battle Abbey, the foundation of William the Conqueror after the battle of Hastings.

the sergeant pays to the court of Bixley 2s.),[27] and he owes at Easter and Michaelmas 4s., attendance at the manor court, relief and heriot.

John Lyllingwyst holds a house and 4 acres of land and owes at the two terms 2s., attendance at the manor court, relief and heriot.

The same John holds 1 acre of land in the fields of Hoo and owes at the two periods 2s., attendance, relief and heriot.

Reginald atte Denne holds a house and 18 acres of land and owes at the said periods 18d., attendance, relief and heriot.

Robert of Northehou holds 3 acres of land at Saltcote and owes at the said periods attendance, relief and heriot.

Total of the rents of the villeins, with the value of the hens, 20s.

Total of all the works of these three villeins, 6s. 10½d.

And it is to be noted that none of the above named villeins can give their daughters in marriage nor cause their sons to be tonsured,[28] nor can they cut down timber growing on the lands they hold, without license of the bailiff or sergeant of the lord, and then for building purposes and not otherwise. And after the death of any one of the foresaid villeins the lord shall have as a heriot his best animal, if he had any; if however he have no living beast the lord shall have no heriot, as they say. The sons or daughters of the foresaid villeins shall give for entrance into the holding after the death of their predecessors as much as they give of rent per year.

Silvester the priest holds 1 acre of meadow adjacent to his house, and owes yearly 3s.

Total of the rent of tenants for life, 3*s*.

Petronilla atte Holme holds a cottage and a piece of land and owes at Easter and Michaelmas . . .; attendance, relief and heriot.

---

[27] Bixley was a neighboring manor, held by the Bishop of Chichester, having certain claims over some of the land in the manor of Bernehorne.

[28] That is to let them enter the clergy. This was not only a common prohibition according to the custom of many manors but was enacted in statute law. "Sons of rustics ought not to be ordained without the assent of the lord on whose land they are known to have been born." Constitutions of Clarendon, c. 16 (A.D. 1164).

Walter Herying holds a cottage and a piece of land and owes at Easter and Michaelmas 18d., attendance, relief and heriot.

Isabella Mariner holds a cottage and owes at the feast of St. Michael 12d., attendance, relief and heriot.[29]

. . . .

Total of the rents of the said cotters, with the value of the hens, 34s. 6d. .

And it is to be noted that all the said cotters shall do as regards giving their daughters in marriage, having their sons tonsured, cutting down timber, paying heriot, and giving fines for entrance just as John of Cayworth and the rest of the villeins formerly mentioned.

Note, fines [30] and penalties, with heriots and reliefs, are worth yearly 5s.

The survey of Borley is as follows:

Extent of the manor of Borley made there on Tuesday next after the feast of St. Matthew the Apostle, A.D. 1308, in the first year of the reign of King Edward, son of King Edward, in the persence of John le Doo, steward, by the hands of William of Folesham, clerk, on the oath of Philip, the reeve of Borley, Henry Lambert, Dennis Rolf, Richard at Mere, Walter Johan and Robert Ernald, tenants of the lord in the said vill of Borley. These all, having been sworn, declare that there is one mansion well and suitably built; that it is sufficient for the products of the manor, and that it contains in itself, within the site of the manor, four acres, by estimation. The grass there is worth yearly, by estimation, 2s.; and the pasturage there is worth yearly 12d., sometimes more and sometimes less, according to its value. And the fruit garden there is worth yearly, in apples and grapes, perhaps 5s. and sometimes more. Total, 8s.

[29] Eleven other cotters are named holding cottages and amounts of land varying from a rood to three and a half acres and giving payments up to three shillings, and the other services.

[30] A "fine" was a payment made to the lord by any one who acquired land in the manor in any other way than by inheritance, in which case the payment was relief. The usual word for a penalty was not "fine" but "amerciament"; or it was recorded that a person was "in mercy."

And it is to be known that the lord is the true patron of the church of Borley, and the said church is worth yearly, according to assessment, in grains, in offerings, in dues and in other small tithes £10.

And there is one water mill in the manor, and it is worth yearly on lease 60s. And the fish pond in the mill dam, with the catch of eels from the .race, is worth yearly, by estimation, 12d. Total, 61s.

There is there a wood called le Hoo, which contains 10 acres, and the underbrush from it is worth yearly, without waste, 5s.; and the grass from it is worth yearly 5s.; and the feeding of swine there is worth yearly 12d. And there is there a certain other wood called Chalvecroft, which contains, with the ditches, 5 acres. And the herbage there is worth yearly 2s. 6d.; and the underbrush there is worth yearly 3s.; and the feeding of swine there is worth yearly 6d. Total value, 17s.

There are there, of arable land in demesne, in different fields 300 acres of land, by the smaller hundred. And it is worth yearly, on lease, £15, at the price of 12d. per acre. Total acreage, 300. Total value, £15.

And it is to be known that the perch of land in that manor contains 16½ feet, in measuring land. And each acre can be sown suitably with 2½ bushels of wheat, with 2½ bushels of rye, with 2½ bushels of peas, with 3 bushels of oats, and this sown broadcast, and with 4 bushels of barley, even measure. And each plow should be joined with 4 oxen and 4 draught horses. And a plow is commonly able to plow an acre of land in a day, and sometimes more.

There are likewise of mowing meadow in various places 29 acres and 1 rood. This is worth yearly £7 6s. 3d., at 5s. an acre. Total acreage, 29A., 1R. Total of pence, £7 6s. 3d.

There are likewise of enclosed pasture 28 acres, and this is worth yearly 42s. at 18d. per acre. Of this 16 acres are assigned to the dairy for the cows, and 12 for the oxen and young bullocks. Total, 42s.

It is to be known that the lord may have in the common pasture of Borley, along with the use of the fresh meadows and of the demesnes of the lord, in the open time, 100 sheep, by the greater hundred. And their pasture, per head, is worth 2s. yearly, and not more, on account of the allowance of food to the shepherd. Total, 20s.

There is there likewise a certain court of free tenants of the lord and of the customary tenants, meeting every three weeks. And the fines and perquisites thence, along with the view of frankpledge, are worth 20s. a year. . . .

There are, moreover of the services of the aforesaid customary tenants $22\frac{1}{2}$ tasks, of which each task requires plowing upon the land of the lord at different seasons. And a task at the convenience of the lord at all plantings is worth $10\frac{1}{2}d$. Total, 19s. $8\frac{1}{4}d$.

There are, moreover, of the autumn works of the aforesaid customary tenants from the first of August to the feast of St. Michael, 424 days' work, the price of each day's work being 2d. Total, 41s. 2d.

The sum of the total value, according to the extent, is £43 19s. $\frac{3}{4}d$.

Likewise from Reginald Crummelond 10s. yearly, discovered after the extent was made up, as above. From which should be subtracted 7d. rent owed to Lady Felicia of Sender, yearly, for a certain meadow called Baselymede, near Radbridge. There remains £43 18s. $5\frac{3}{4}d$., plus 10s. as above.

And it is to be known that the lord prior of Christ Church of Canterbury has his liberty in the vill of Borley; and he has jurisdiction over thieves caught on the manor and tenants of the manor taken outside the manor with stolen goods in their hands or on their backs. And the judicial gallows of this franchise stand and ought to stand at Radbridge. And now let us inquire concerning the pillory and tumbrel. It is reported by the jury that it ought to stand beyond the outer gates toward the west, next to the pigstye of the lord.

And it is to be remembered that as often as it is necessary for the reeve and four men to be present before the justices in eyre or anywhere else, that is to say, at the jail delivery of our lord the King, or wheresoever it may be, the lord ought to find two men at his expense before the same justices; and the villagers of Borley will find three men at their expense; and this according to custom from a time to which, as it is said, memory does not extend.

And it is to be known that when any customary tenant of the land in the manor dies, the lord will have as a heriot the best beast of that tenant found at the time of his death. And if he have not a beast, he shall give to the lord for a heriot 2s. 6d. And the heir shall make a fine to the lord for the tenement which was his father's, if it shall seem to be expedient to him; if not, he shall have nothing. Nevertheless, to the wife of the deceased tenant shall be saved the whole of the tenement which was her husband's on the day he died, to be held of the lord as her free bench till the end of her life, if she shall remain without a husband, and on performing the services due and customary thence to the lord. If, however, through the license of the lord, she shall have married, the heirs of the aforesaid deceased shall enter upon the aforesaid tenement by the license of the lord, and shall give one half of the said tenement to the widow of the deceased as dowry.

Our final entry in this section is a thirteenth century certificate of manumission, issued to a villein when his lord had made up his mind to free him. The certificate illustrates both the procedure of manumission, the condition of the villein before he attained freedom and the privileges to which he was admitted when free.

To all the faithful of Christ to whom the present writing shall come, Richard by the divine permission abbot of Peterborough and the convent of the same place, eternal greeting in the Lord. Let all know that we have manumitted and liberated from all yoke of servitude William, the son of Richard of Wythington whom previously we have held as our born bondman, with his whole progeny and all his chattels, so that neither we nor our successors shall be able to require or exact any right or claim in the said William, his progeny, or his chattels. But the same William with his whole progeny and all his chattels will remain free and quit and without disturbance, exaction, or any claim on the part of us or our successors by reason of any servitude, forever. We will moreover and concede that he and his heirs shall hold the messuages, land, rents and meadows in Wythington which his ancestors held from us and our predecessors, by giving and performing the fine which is called merchet for giving his daughter in marriage and tallage from year to year according to our will — that he shall have and hold these for the future from us and our successors freely, quietly, peacefully, and hereditarily, by paying thence to us and our successors yearly 40s. sterling, at the four terms of the year, namely; at St. John the Baptist's day, 10s., at Michaelmas, 10s., at Christmas, 10s., and at Easter, 10s., for all service, exaction, custom, and secular demand: saving to us nevertheless attendance at our court of Castre every three weeks, wardship and relief, and outside service of our lord the king, when they shall happen. And if it shall happen that the said William or his heirs shall die at any time without an heir, the said messuage, land, rents, and meadows with their appurtenances shall return fully and completely to us and our successors. Nor will it be allowed to the said William or his heirs the said messuage, land, rents, meadows, or any part of them to give, sell, alienate, mortgage, or in any way encumber by which the said messuage, land, rents, and meadows should not return to us and our successors in the form declared above. But if this should occur later their deed shall be declared null and what is thus alienated shall come to us and our successors. In testimony of which duplicate seals are appended to this writing, formed as a chirograph, for the sake of greater security. These being witnesses, etc. Given at Borough, for the love of lord Robert of good memory, once abbot, our predecessor and maternal uncle of the said William, and at the instance of the good man brother Hugh of Mutton, relative of the said abbot Robert; A.D. 1278, on the eve of Pentecost.

Manufacture and trade, nearly unknown to the Germans described by Tacitus,[31] gradually grew in importance and

[31] Cf. *ante*, pp. 8–19. Among the numerous treatises on English industrial history at this time may be mentioned: Traill, *Social England*, ii, Chapters 5, 6 (Cassell & Co., 2d ed., 1895); Ashley, *English Economic History*, ii (Longmans, Green & Co., 1894); Cheyney, *Social and Industrial History of England*, Chapters 1–5 (The Macmillan Co., 1901); Cunningham, *Growth of English Industry and Commerce*, i

complexity in our period and came by degrees into the
control of gilds, organizations which undoubtedly originated in voluntary associations for the attainment of some
common object, but settled into rigidly governed bodies.
The gild merchant of a community was a combination of
its mercantile forces for the complete control of trade, and
in many cases became identical with the municipal or
borough corporation. The craft gilds were organizations
not unlike modern trade unions, for the control of labor,
price and output in a given occupation, and, sometimes,
as in the case of London, came to perform important
municipal functions. These highly developed forms of
gild organization, however, did not drive out the earlier
type of voluntary clubs, for the latter give every evidence
of continuing vigor, making gild life in the later thirteenth
century and throughout the fourteenth very complex. The
craft gilds undoubtedly set up the standard for early
university organization in England, where the first scholastic foundations are practically gilds of masters and of
students respectively. Gilds of various sorts became important enough, in their own eyes at least, to seek and
secure charters of privileges, as did cities and towns.
It is clear that gilds would be most easily organized and
most numerous in urban communities and, hence, we are
safe in describing the gild as the typical organizing force
in medieval city life, as feudalism was in corresponding
rural life.

Our first document referring to the gilds is the *Ordinances
of the Spurriers of London*, a craft gild. This set of by-laws
will show us what a typical craft gild tried to do and what
it conceived it had a right to expect of its members.

(Cambridge University Press, 3d. ed., 1903). See also Bland, Brown and Tawney,
English Economic History: Select Documents, ed. 2. (Geo. Bell and Sons, 1915),
White and Notestein, *Source Problems in English History*, pp. 109–157, *An Aspect
of the Agricultural Labor Problem in the Fourteenth Century* (Harper and Bros.,
1915.)

Be it remembered, that on Tuesday, the morrow of St. Peter's Chains, in the nineteenth year of the reign of King Edward III, the articles underwritten were read before John Hammond, mayor, Roger de Depham, recorder, and the other aldermen; and seeing that the same were deemed befitting, they were accepted and enrolled in these words.

In the first place, — that no one of the trade of spurriers shall work longer than from the beginning of the day until curfew rung out at the Church of St. Sepulchre, without Newgate; by reason that no man can work so neatly by night as by day. And many persons of the said trade, who compass how to practice deception in their work, desire to work by night rather than by day; and then they introduce false iron, and iron that has been cracked, for tin, and also they put gilt on false copper, and cracked. And further, — many of the said trade are wandering about all day, without working at all at their trade; and then, when they have become drunk and frantic, they take to their work, to the annoyance of the sick, and all their neighborhood, as well by reason of the broils that arise between them and the strange folks who are dwelling among them. And then they blow up their fires so vigorously, that their forges begin all at once to blaze to the great peril of themselves and of all the neighborhood around. And then, too, all the neighbors are much in dread of the sparks, which so vigorously issue forth in all directions from the mouths of the chimneys in their forges. By reason thereof it seems unto them that working by night should be put an end to, in order such false work and such perils to avoid: and therefore the mayor and the aldermen do will, by the assent of the good folks of the said trade, and for the common profit, that from henceforth such time for working, and such false work made in the trade, shall be forbidden. And if any person shall be found in the said trade to do the contrary hereof, let him be amerced, the first time in 40d., one-half thereof to go to the use of the Chamber of the Guildhall of London, and the other half to the use of the said trade; the second time, in half a mark, and the third time in 10s., to the use of the same Chamber and trade; and the fourth time, let him forswear the trade forever.

Also that no one of the said trade shall hang his spurs out on Sundays, or any other days that are double feasts; but only a sign indicating his business: and such spurs as they shall so sell, they are to show and sell within their shops, without exposing them without, or opening the doors or windows of their shops, on the pain aforesaid.

Also, that no one of the said trade shall keep a house or shop to carry on his business, unless he is free of the city; and that no one shall cause to be sold, or exposed for sale, any manner of old spurs for new ones, or shall garnish them or change them for new ones.

Also, that no one of the said trade shall take an apprentice for a less term than seven years, and such apprentice shall be enrolled according to the usages of the said city.

Also, that if any one of the said trade, who is not a freeman, shall take an apprentice for a term of years, he shall be amerced as aforesaid.

Also, that no one of the said trade shall receive the apprentice, serving-man or journeymen of another in the same trade, during the term agreed upon between his master and him; on the pain aforesaid.

Also, that no alien of another country, or foreigner of this country, shall follow or use the said trade, unless he is enfranchised before the mayor, aldermen and chamberlain; and that by witness and surety of the good folks of the said trade, who will undertake for him as to his loyalty and his good behavior.

Also, that no one of the said trade shall work on Saturdays, after None has been rung out in the City; and not from that hour until the Monday morning following.

Chaucer has described in the *Prolog* to the *Canterbury Tales* five members of a gild which was not, however, a craft gild, but must have been more or less of a social club made up of the members of various craft organizations. His words also tell us somewhat of the social privileges of the members of the gilds.

A haberdasher and a carpenter, a weaver, a dyer and an upholsterer were with us [32] also, clothed in the same livery, that

[32] I.e. on the pilgrimage to Canterbury.

of a solemn and great fraternity. Their gear had been freshly and newly adorned; their table knives were in sheaths capped not with brass but with silver, wrought full clean and well, and their pouches also were in good shape. Each of them seemed, indeed, to be a fair burgess, (worthy) of sitting in a gild-hall on a dais. Each one on account of his wisdom was capable of being an alderman. They had rent enough and other property, and their wives would likewise agree (to let them be aldermen). Otherwise the wives would be much to blame. For it is very pleasant to be called "madame," to go to festivals at the head of the procession and to have one's mantle royally borne.

The document which follows is a royal license, given by Richard II in 1392 after due investigation, for the foundation of a charitable gild whose membership was to include the whole population of the town of Birmingham, if they cared to join.

The King to all, etc., Greeting. Know ye, that whereas on the 25th October in the sixth year of our reign, by our letters patent, we granted license to Thomas Sheldone, now dead, John Coleshulle, John Goldsmythe, and William atte Slowe, Burgesses of Bermyngeham, enabling them to give and assign certain lands, tenements, and rents, with their appurtenances, in Bermyngeham and Egebaston, not held of us in chief, and worth twenty marks a year, to two chaplains, for the celebration of divine service in the church of St. Martin of Bermyngeham, to the honor of God, the blessed Mary his mother, the Holy Cross, St. Thomas the Martyr,[33] and St. Katherine; to be held by the said chaplains and their successors for ever; as in those letters patent is more fully set forth: — Now, in consideration of our said letters patent, which have never, as is said, taken effect, and which the Bailiffs and Commonalty (of Bermyngeham) have sent back into our Chancery to be cancelled, and upon the prayer of the Bailiffs and Commonalty themselves, and for fifty pounds which they have paid to us, we do, for us and our heirs, so far as in us lies, grant and give license to the said Bailiffs

[33] I.e. Thomas a Becket.

and Commonalty, that they may make and found, in honor of
the Holy Cross, a Gild and brotherhood of brethren and sisteren
among themselves in that town, to which shall belong as well
the men and women of the town of Bermyngeham as men and
women well disposed in other towns and in the neighborhood;
and that they may make and ordain a Master and Wardens
of the Gild and brotherhood, who shall have rule and governance over the same; and may make and found a chantry, for
the celebration by chaplains of divine service in the church of
St. Martin of Bermyngeham; and may do and find other works
of charity, for our welfare and that of the Queen, and for the
brethren and sisteren of the said Gild and brotherhood, and
for all good-doers to them, and for their souls' sake and those
of all Christians, according as the ordering and will of the said
Bailiffs and Commonalty shall appoint in that behalf.   And
further, we grant and give license, for us and our heirs, to the
said John Coleshulle, John Goldsmythe, and William atte Slowe,
that they may give and assign to the said Master and Wardens
eighteen messuages, three tofts, six acres of land, and forty
shillings of rent, with the appurtenances, in the said towns of
Bermyngeham and Egebaston, which are not held of us, to have
and to hold to them and their successors, Masters and Wardens
of the said Gild and brotherhood, to enable them to find there
for ever chaplains to celebrate divine service, and to do other
works of charity for ever, as aforesaid, according to their ordering and will.   And we grant our special license to the same
Master and Wardens that they may take the messuages, land,
and rents aforesaid, with the appurtenances, from the afore-
named John, John, and William, and hold them, to themselves
and their successors, finding thereout chaplains to celebrate
divine service in the church aforesaid, and doing other works of
charity, for ever, according to their own ordering and will as is
before said; the statute against putting lands in mortmain notwithstanding; desiring that neither the aforesaid John, John,
and William, nor their heirs, nor the said Master and Wardens
nor their successors, shall, by reason of that statute, be charged,
troubled, or in any way made to suffer, either by us or our heirs,
or by any Justices, Escheators, Sheriffs, or other Bailiffs or

Ministers whomsoever, of us or our heirs: Saving however, to the chief lords of the fee, the services due and accustomed. Witness, etc.   Given at Moulton, on the 7th day of (August).

The next two documents, *Ordinances of the Gilds of St. Mary and of The Lord's Prayer* respectively, are particularly interesting and significant for our purposes, because these gilds were founded for the express object of performing pageants or plays. The first, that of St. Mary, was to have charge of an annual festal procession in honor of the Virgin Mary at Beverly, though it had charitable duties as well. The relation of these pageants to plays is well known. The other gild, that of The Lord's Prayer, similarly, was founded at York to perform a play on the Paternoster (Lord's Prayer) which play was probably not, as the name might suggest, like a morality play with personification of the several petitions, but a saints' play in which various saints were seen struggling with the seven deadly sins, the respective opposites of the seven petitions in the Prayer.[34]

(a) This gild was founded, by persons named in the return, on January 25th, A.D. 1355.

There shall be an alderman and two stewards of the gild, who shall manage its affairs according to what the brethren and sisteren shall have agreed. The brethren and sisteren shall each pay, on entry, towards the expenses of the gild, five shillings, and one pound of wax, or more. Every year, on the feast of the Purification of the Blessed Mary,[35] all the brethren and sisteren shall meet together in a fit and appointed place, away from the church: and there, one of the gild shall be clad in comely fashion as a queen, like to the glorious Virgin Mary, having what may seem a son in her arms: and two others shall be clad like Joseph and Simeon; and two shall go as angels, carrying a candle-bearer on which shall be twenty-four thick

[34] I owe this information to Professor Hardin Craig of the University of Minnesota.   [35] I.e. February 2.

wax lights. With these and other great lights borne before
them and with much music and gladness, the pageant Virgin
with her son, and Joseph and Simeon, shall go in procession to
the church. And all the sisteren of the gild shall follow the
Virgin: and afterwards all the brethren: and each of them
shall carry a wax light weighing half a pound. And they shall go
two and two, slowly pacing to the church: and when they shall
have got there, the pageant Virgin shall offer her son to Simeon
at the high altar: and all the sisteren and brethren shall offer
their wax lights, together with a penny each. All this having
been solemnly done, they shall go home again with gladness.
And any brother or sister who does not come, unless cause for
staying away be shown, shall pay half a pound of wax to the
gild. On the same day, after dinner, the brethren and sisteren
shall meet together, and shall eat bread and cheese and drink
ale, rejoicing in the Lord, in the praise of the glorious Virgin
Mary: and they shall then and there choose, with the assent of
the elder part of the brethren and sisteren of the gild, an alderman and stewards for the next year, who shall at once undertake
the affairs of the gild. Prayers and offerings shall be given for
the dead. The alderman and stewards of the gild shall visit
those brethren and sisteren who are poor, ailing or weak and
who have not enough of their own to live upon: and they shall
give to these as they think right out of the gild stock, as has
been agreed: namely, to each one so being poor, ailing or weak,
eightpence, sixpence or at least fourpence, every week, to help
their needs. And if any of those poor brethren dies, or any
other of the gild who is not well off, he shall be buried at the
cost of the gild and have all becoming services.

(b) As to the beginning of the said gild, be it known that,
once on a time, a play, setting forth the goodness of the Lord's
Prayer, was played in the city of York: in which play all manner
of vices and sins were held up to scorn, and the virtues were
held up to praise. This play met with so much favor that many
said, "Would that this play could be kept up in this city, for
the health of souls and for the comfort of the citizens and neighbors." Hence, the keeping up of that play in times to come,
for the health and amendment of the souls as well of the up-

holders as of the hearers of it, became the whole and sole cause of the beginning and fellowship of the brethren of this brotherhood. And so, the main charge of the gild is, to keep up this play, to the glory of God, the maker of the said prayer, and for the holding up of sins and vices to scorn. And because those who remain in their sins are unable to call God their Father, therefore, the brethren of the gild are, first of all, bound to shun company and businesses that are unworthy, and to keep themselves to good and worthy businesses. And they are bound to pray for the brethren and sisteren of the gild, both alive and dead, that the living shall be able so to keep the gild that they may deserve to win God's fatherhood, and that the dead may have their torments lightened. Also, they are bound to come to the burial services of the dead brethren and sisteren of the gild. And if any one does not leave enough to meet the cost of such services, the rest of the brethren shall bear the cost. And if any brother dies and is buried away from this city, the brethren shall hold services for him within the city of York. Also, it is forbidden that any brother of the gild shall, in the belief that he will have help from his brethren, be forward in getting into law suit or quarrel, or in upholding any wrongful cause whatever, upon pain of losing all help and friendship, or any relief from the gild. And because vain is the gathering of the faithful unless some work of kindliness is done, therefore, the brethren have made this ordinance: That if haply it befall that any of the brethren be robbed, or his goods or chattels perchance be burned, or he be imprisoned for any wrongful cause, or be brought to want through any visitation of God, the other brethren shall for kindness' sake, help him according to his need, under the guidance of the wardens of the gild, so that he may not haply perish through lack of help. Also, they are bound to find one candle-bearer, with seven lights, in token of the seven supplications in the Lord's Prayer: which candle-bearer shall hang in the cathedral church of York, and be lighted on Sundays and feast days, to the glory and honor of God Almighty, the Maker of that Prayer, of St. Peter the glorious confessor, of St. William and of all saints. Also, they are bound to make, and as often as need be, to renew, a table showing the whole meaning and use

of the Lord's Prayer, and to keep this hanging against a pillar
in the said cathedral church near to the aforesaid candle-bearer.
Also, they are bound, as often as the said play of the Lords'
Prayer is played in the city of York, to ride with the players
thereof through the chief streets of the city of York: and, the
more becomingly to mark themselves while thus riding, they
must all be clad in one suit.   And to ensure good order during
the said play, some of the brethren are bound to ride or to walk
with the players until the play is wholly ended.   And once in
a year a feast shall be held, and fresh wardens shall be chosen
by the gild, and a true account shall be given to the newly
chosen wardens of all that has been done on behalf of the gild
during the last year.   Also, it is ordained that no one shall be
let come into this gild, until after he shall have been questioned
by the wardens of the gild as to whether he has bent his will to
live rightly, and so to deal towards the gild and its affairs that
he may be at one with the wardens.   And, because the founders
of the said gild well knew that they themselves might not be
wise enough to make, at once, all needful ordinances, therefore,
at the end of the *Ordinances* then made, they added this clause:
"Whensoever, and as often soever, as it may perchance happen
that we or our successors, wardens and brethren of this gild,
may become wiser than we now are, none of us nor our successors shall be deemed a rebel, or as standing out against our
wishes or against those of any of our successors, if haply we put
forth, or there shall be put forth at any time hereafter, any new
ordinance that will be for the greater glory of God or the welfare of this gild."   Under which saving clause other wardens of
the gild have since added, that a chaplain shall, once a year,
celebrate divine service before the gild, for the good of the
brethren and sisteren of the gild, alive and dead, and for that
of the good-doers to the gild.   Moreover, the brethren are wont
to meet together at the end of every six weeks, and to put up
special prayers for the welfare of our lord the King and for the
good governance of the kingdom of England and for all the
brethren and sisteren of this gild, present and absent, alive and
dead, and for all the benefactors of the gild or to the gild brethren: and also, once in a year, to have a general service for the

dead brethren and sisteren. There do not belong to the gild any rents of land, nor any tenements, nor any goods save only the properties needed in the playing of the before-named play: which properties are of little or no worth for any other purpose than the said play. And the gild has one wooden chest in which the said properties are kept.

(It is added that), as the seals of the wardens of the gild will be unknown to many, they have asked that the seal of the Vicar-General of the Archbishop of York shall be put to this return: which has accordingly been done, in witness of the truth of the return, on the 21st January, 1388 (9).

The last entry in this section devoted to the gilds is the *Order of the Pageants of the Play of Corpus Christi at York*. The list was made up in 1415, a little after the end of our period, but it doubtless represents conditions in the last decade of the fourteenth century as well as in the opening years of the fifteenth. Note the cooperation of town authorities with the gilds in the production of the play.

The Order of the Pageants of the Play of Corpus Christi, in the time of the mayoralty of William Alne, in the third year of the reign of Henry V, anno (year) 1415, compiled by Roger Burton, town clerk, —

Tanners. — God the Father Omnipotent creating and forming the heavens, the angels and archangels, Lucifer and the angels who fell with him into the pit.

Plasterers. — God the Father in his substance creating the earth and all things which are therein, in the space of five days.

Cardmakers. — God the Father forming Adam from the mud of the earth, and making Eve from Adam's rib, and inspiring them with the breath of life.

Fullers. — God forbidding Adam and Eve to eat of the tree of life.

Coopers. — Adam and Eve and the tree between them, the serpent deceiving them with apples; God speaking to them and cursing the serpent, and an angel with a sword driving them out of Paradise.

Armorers. — Adam and Eve, an angel with a spade and distaff appointing them their labor.

Glovers. — Abel and Cain sacrificing victims.

Shipwrights. — God warning Noah to make an ark out of planed wood.

Fishmongers and Mariners. — Noah in the ark with his wife, three sons of Noah with their wives, with various animals.

Parchment-makers and Book-binders. — Abraham sacrificing his son Isaac on the altar.

Hosiers. — Moses lifting up the serpent in the wilderness, King Pharaoh, eight Jews looking on and wondering.

Spicers. — A doctor declaring the sayings of the prophets concerning the future birth of Christ. Mary, the angel saluting her; Mary saluting Elizabeth.

Pewterers and Founders. — Mary, Joseph wishing to send her away, the angel telling them to go over to Bethlehem.

Tilers. — Mary, Joseph, a nurse, the child born and lying in a manger between an ox and an ass, and an angel speaking to the shepherds, and to the players in the next pageant.

Chandlers. — Shepherds speaking to one another, the star in the East, an angel announcing to the shepherds their great joy in the child which has been born.

Goldsmiths, Goldbeaters and Moneyers. — Three kings coming from the East, Herod questioning them about the child Jesus, and the son of Herod and two counsellors and a herald. Mary with the child and the star above, and three kings offering gifts.

(Formerly) The House of St. Leonard, (now) Masons. — Mary, with the boy, Joseph, Anna, the nurse, with the young doves. Simeon receiving the boy into his arms, and the two sons of Simeon.

Marshalls. — Mary with the boy and Joseph fleeing into Egypt, at the bidding of the angel.

Girdlers, Nailers, and Sawyers. — Herod ordering the male children to be slain, four soldiers with lances, two counsellors of the king, and four women weeping for the death of their sons.

Spurriers and Lorimers. — Doctors, the boy Jesus sitting in the temple in the midst of them, asking them questions and replying to them, four Jews, Mary and Joseph seeking him, and finding him in the temple.

Barbers. — Jesus, John the Baptist baptizing him, and two angels attending.

Vinters. — Jesus, Mary, bridegroom with the bride, ruler of the feast with his slaves, with six vessels of water in which the water is turned into wine.

Smiths. — Jesus on a pinnacle of the temple, and the devil tempting him with stones, and two angels attending, etc.

Curriers. — Peter, James, and John; Jesus ascending into a mountain and transfiguring himself before them. Moses and Elias appearing, and the voice of one speaking in a cloud.

Ironmongers. — Jesus, and Simon the leper asking Jesus to eat with him; two disciples, Mary Magdalene bathing Jesus' feet with her tears and drying them with her hair.

Plumbers and Patternmakers. — Jesus, two apostles, the woman taken in adultery, four Jews accusing her.

Pouchmakers, Bottlers, and Capmakers. — Lazarus in the sepulchre, Mary Magdalene and Martha, and two Jews wondering.

Spinners and Vestmakers. — Jesus on an ass with its colt, twelve apostles following Jesus, six rich and six poor, eight boys with branches of palm, singing Blessed, etc., and Zaccheus climbing into a sycamore tree.

Cutlers, Bladesmiths, Shearers, Scalers, Bucklermakers, and Horners. — Pilate, Caiaphas, two soldiers, three Jews, Judas selling Jesus.

Bakers. — The passover lamb, the Supper of the Lord, twelve apostles, Jesus girded with a towel, washing their feet, institution of the sacrament of the body of Christ in the new law, communion of the apostles.

Cordwainers. — Pilate, Caiaphas, Annas, fourteen armed soldiers, Malchus, Peter, James, John, Jesus, and Judas kissing and betraying him.

Bowyers and Fletchers. — Jesus, Annas, Caiaphas, and four Jews beating and scourging Jesus. Peter, the woman accusing Peter, and Malchus.

Tapestrymakers and Couchers. — Jesus, Pilate, Annas, Caiaphas, two counsellors and four Jews accusing Jesus.

Littesters. — Herod, two counsellors, four soldiers, Jesus, and three Jews.

Cooks and Watercarriers. — Pilate, Annas, Caiaphas, two Jews,, and Judas bringing back to them the thirty pieces of silver.

Tilemakers, Millers, Furriers, Hayresters, Bowlers. — Jesus, Pilate, Caiaphas, Annas, six soldiers holding spears with banners, and four others leading Jesus away from Herod, asking to have Barabbas released and Jesus crucified, and likewise binding and scourging him, and placing the crown of thorns upon his head; three soldiers casting lots for the clothing of Jesus.

Shearmen. — Jesus, stained with blood, bearing the cross to Calvary. Simon of Cyrene, the Jews compelling him to carry the cross; Mary the mother of Jesus; John the apostle then announcing the condemnation and passage of her son to Calvary. Veronica wiping the blood and sweat from the face of Jesus with a veil on which is imprinted the face of Jesus, and other women mourning for Jesus.

Pinmakers, Latenmakers, and Painters. — The cross, Jesus stretched upon it on the ground; four Jews scourging Him and binding Him with ropes, and afterwards lifting the cross, and the body of Jesus nailed to the cross on Mount Calvary.

Butchers and Poultry Dealers. — The cross, two thieves crucified, Jesus hanging on the cross between them, Mary the mother of Jesus, John, Mary, James, and Salome. A soldier with a lance, a servant with a sponge, Pilate, Annas, Caiaphas, the centurion, Joseph of Arimathea and Nicodemus placing Him in the sepulchre.

Saddlers, Glaziers and Joiners. — Jesus conquering hell; twelve spirits, six good, and six evil.

Carpenters. — Jesus rising from the sepulchre, four armed soldiers, and the three Marys mourning. Pilate, Caiaphas, and Annas. A young man seated at the sepulchre clothed in white, speaking to the women.

Winedrawers. — Jesus, Mary Magdalene with aromatic spices.

Brokers and Woolpackers. — Jesus, Luke, and Cleophas in the guise of travelers.

Scriveners, Illuminators, Pardoners and Dubbers. — Jesus, Peter, John, James, Philip, and the other apostles with parts of a

. baked fish, and a honey-comb; and Thomas the apostle touching the wounds of Jesus.

Tailors. — Mary, John the evangelist, the eleven apostles,
two angels, Jesus ascending before them, and four angels carrying
a cloud.

Potters. — Mary, two angels, eleven apostles, and the Holy
Spirit descending upon them, and four Jews wondering.

Drapers. — Jesus, Mary, Gabriel with two angels, two virgins
and three Jews of Mary's acquaintance, eight apostles, and two
devils.

Linen-weavers. — Four apostles carrying the bier of Mary, and
Fergus hanging above the bier, with two other Jews and an angel.

Woolen-weavers. — Mary ascending with a throng of angels,
eight apostles, and the apostle Thomas preaching in the desert.

Innkeepers. — Mary, Jesus crowning her, with a throng of
angels singing.

Mercers. — Jesus, Mary, the twelve apostles, four angels with
trumpets, and four with a crown, a lance, and two whips, four
good spirits, and four evil spirits, and six devils.

The growing importance of commercial life in the period
1066–1400 has already been referred to,[36] and this importance is shown by the appearance, at least sporadically,
of characters from mercantile life in current literature.
But, as against the ideal of business ethics set up in the
Ordinances of the Gild of Spurriers,[37] just cited, these de-
scriptions of commercial types and practices nearly all
deal with the shady side of business life. The correct
inference from this is probably not that all merchants and
bankers in the Middle Ages were uniformly dishonest, but
that normal routine procedure was too prosaic to attract
the attention of the literary man or poet. Our first passage is Chaucer's description of a Merchant, from the
Prolog to the *Canterbury Tales.*

There was a Merchant with a forked beard, clad in motley
and sitting high (awkwardly) on his horse. He wore a Flemish

---

[36] Cf. *ante,* p. 227.　　　　　[37] *Ibid.,* p. 229.

beaver hat; his boots were neatly tied. He spoke very solemnly and his conversation always bore on his gainful bargains. He wanted the sea policed at any cost between Middleburg and Orewell.[38] He well knew how to make a profit by his exchange of crowns in the different money-markets of Europe. This worthy man laid out his wit well; no one knew that he was in debt, so dignified was he in his governance with his bargains and his agreements for borrowing money. Forsooth he was altogether a very worthy man, but, to tell the truth, I don't know what his name was.

In the poem known as *The Vision of William concerning Piers the Plowman*, long ascribed to William Langland,[39] we have curiously realistic pictures of many features of fourteenth-century life. In one section of the poem there is a series of confessions of the seven deadly sins, the longest of which, very interestingly, is by Covetousness and includes a good account of sharp retail practices which sounds very modern. Covetousness has had a long business experience in various trades, and, like Chaucer's Merchant, has been both tradesman and banker. We need to keep in mind the fact that, in the Middle Ages, all legal trade was retail.

> Then came Covetise, him cannot I describe,
> So hungry and hollow Sir Harvey's self he looked:
> Beetle-browed, babber-lipped, with his bleared eyes,
> And, like a leather purse, his cheeks lolled down
> Below his chin and shivered with age.
> A hood upon his head, and a lousy hat on top,
> A tawny cloak upon him, twelve winters old,
> All torn and rotten and full of creeping lice;

---

[38] The wool trade was one of the staple English trades at this time; the wool was shipped extensively from Orewell, near Harwich, to Middleburg, in the Low Countries; hence, this merchant wishes this trade route kept free of pirates, which were quite common.

[39] The best reference on the present state of scholarly opinion on the "Piers Plowman" question is *The Cambridge History of English Literature*, ii, Chapter 1 and *Bibliography*.

But, if a louse could leap away, she had not been there,
So threadbare was the cloth of it.
"I have been covetous," quoth this caitiff, "I do acknowledge it,
Once I served Sim At-stile, and was his 'prentice bound,
First I learned to lie, a page or two of lies,
Then to weigh false was my second lesson,
To Winchester and Weyhill I went to the fair
With all kinds of merchandise as my master bade,
But had not the grace of Guile gone with me and my goods,
They had been unsold seven years, God's my witness.
Then I passed to the drapers, to learn my other lessons,
To draw the edges out that the flannel might seem longer.
Among the rich striped cloths I learned another lesson,
Threaded them with pack-needles, fastened them together,
Put them in a press, pinned them down therein,
Till ten yards or twelve made out — thirteen.

My wife was a weaver, woolen cloths she made,
She spake to her spinners   to spin it soft,
But the pound-weight she
    paid by   weighed a quarter more
Than my own balance did,   when I weighed fair.
I used to buy her barley,   she brewed it to sell,
Penny ale and thick ale,   she mixed it together,
For laborers and poor folk. It lay by itself;
The best ale in my bower,   or in my bedchamber;
Any man that boozed of that never bought other,
Fourpence a gallon,   and no good measure either
When it was served in cups. In that wife was cunning;
Rose of the Small Shop   was her true name,
She had been a huckster   these eleven winters.

"But now I swear, so may I
    thrive,   this cheating I will stop,
Nevermore will I weigh false,   nor cheat in selling,
But I will wend me to Wal-
    singham,   and my wife with me,
And pray to Bromholm cross, to save me from my sins."

"Didst ever repent?   didst never restitution make?"

"Yes, once I was in an inn,   with a heap of travellers,
I rose when they were sleeping,   and rifled their packs."

"That was no restitution,   that was a robber's theft;
Thou hadst deserved hanging   more than all thy cheating
for that   else."
"I thought rifling *was* restitu-
tion," says he,   "I never learned my book;
I know no French i'faith,   only from far Norfolk."

"Didst ever use usury,   in all thy lifetime?"

"Nay saving in my youth,   with Lombards and Jews,
I weighed a pence with a
weight,   I pared the heaviest,
And lent money on pledge,   the pledge was worth more than
the loan.

I wrote me out agreements;   if the borrower failed his day,
I gat me more wealth   than through merciful lending.

"I have lent to lords and ladies, and myself redeemed the pledge;
I lent to folks that were will-
ing to lose   a bit from every coin.
I had bankers' letters   and took my coin to Rome,
I counted it right here,   but there it was less."

"Didst ever lend to lords   in return for their protection?"
"Ay, I have lent to lords;   they never loved me after;
I have made many a knight   into mercer and draper,
They gave me colors to wear,   thus were my 'prentices,
Never a pair of gloves   did they pay me for the same."

"Hast thou pitied the poor,   who sometimes must needs borrow?"

"Ay, as much pity   as pedlars have on cats,
Would kill them and they
catch them,   for the sake of their skins."
"Art thou free among thy neigh-
bors   with thy meat and drink?"

"I am held as courteous as a dog is in a kitchen;
That is the name I have among them."
"God grant thee never his grace through all thy life,
Save thou repent thee soon and use well thy goods.
God grant thy sons after thee no joy of that thou winnest,
And thine executors no profit in that thou leavest them;
That which was won by wrong shall be spent by the wicked,
For neither Pope nor Pardoner hath ever power
To pardon thee thy sins, save thou make reparation."

THE SIN IS NOT REMITTED SAVE RESTITUTION BE MADE.

"Ay, I have won my goods with false word and wit,
I have gathered what I have with glosing and with guile;
I mixed my merchandise, I made a fine array,
But the best was outside the shop and the worst inside —
There was wit in that.
And if my neighbor had man or beast better at all than mine,
I tried many a trick to get for mine own,
And, save I got it otherwise, at the last I stole it;
I shook his purse out or I picked his locks.

"If I went to the plough, I pinched of his half-acre,
A foot or a furrow of my neighbor's land,
If I reaped I would reach over, or bade them that reaped for me
Seize with their sickles what I never sowed.
In holy days at church, when I heard mass,
I had no will to weep my sins;
Nay I mourned my loss of goods, and not my body's guilt.
When I did deadly sin, I feared it not so much,
As when I lent and thought it lost when payment was delayed.
If I sent my servant to Bruges or Prussia land,
To do traffic with money and to make exchange,
No man could comfort me, nor mass nor matins,

Nor penance done,
nor paternoster prayed;
My mind was on my goods,
not on God's grace."

WHERE YOUR TREASURE IS THERE SHALL YOUR HEART BE ALSO. [40]

"In sooth," Repentance said,
Were I a Friar, in good faith,
I would take no money of
thine,
Nor mend our church with
gold of thine,
By my soul's health I would
not
For the best book in our
House,
If I knew thee to be what thou
sayest

"I have pity on thy life,
for all the gold in earth,

nor robe me in goods of thine,
nor take a dinner's cost from
thee;

a penny pittance of thee
though the leaves were burnt
gold;

I would sooner starve."

BETTER DIE THAN LIVE ILL.

"I counsel any faithful friar
I would liever, by our Lord,
Than have food and finding

never to sit at board of thine
live upon watercress
from a false man's fortune.

WHEN THOU EATEST RICH FOOD THOU ART ANOTHER'S SLAVE;
FEED ON THINE OWN LOAF AND BE FREE.

"Thou art unnatural;
Make reparation,
All that take of thy goods,
Are bound at the High Judge-
ment
The priest that taketh tithe
of thee,
Shall share thy purgatory
Never workman in this world
Look in the Psalter:

I cannot pardon thee.
and reckon with them all.
God is my witness,

to help thee to restore.

if he know thee what thou art,
and help to pay thy debt.
shall thrive on thy winnings;

FOR LO THOU DESIREDST TRUTH. [41]

"Then thou shall know fully   what usury doth mean,
And what the priest's penance is who is proud of thine offerings;

[40] Matt. 6: 21.   [41] Psalm 51: 6.

For a harlot of her body hire may more boldly pay church
tithe
And shall sooner come to heaven than an arrant usurer like thee,
God be my witness."

Then that shrew waxed despairing, and would have hanged
himself,
Had not Repentance comforted him thus:
"Have mercy in thy thoughts, and in thy prayers pray for it,
For God's mercy is more than all His other works,
And all this world's wickedness, that man can work or think,
Is no more to the mercy of God than is a spark in Thames.
Thou hast not good enough in thee to buy thee a wastel cake,
Saving by penitence, or work of thy two hands.
The goods thou hast gotten began in falsehood,
And long as thou livest on thou payest not but borrowest them
more;
And if thou know not to whom to make thy reparation,
Take thy money to the Bishop, bid him use it for thy soul;
He shall answer for thee at the High Judgment day,
For thee — and many more."

The "moral Gower," [42] too, the contemporary of Chaucer
and of the author or authors of *The Vision of William
concerning Piers the Plowman*, has something to say about
the evils of trade in his day. Gower, in fact, speaks his
mind on the subject in many places in his writings; of
all his remarks I have selected the following passages from
his French poem *Mirour de l'omme*, usually known by its
Latin title *Speculum Meditantis* (the French title means
The Mirror of Man, the Latin, *The Looking-glass of One
Thinking*). This poem was long supposed to be lost, but
was identified as still extant by its latest editor in 1895.
The poem as a whole is a comprehensive commentary in
about 30,000 lines on the author's times. The poet speaks
thus of commercial matters:

[42] Cf. Chaucer, *Troilus and Criseyde*, Book V, l. 1856.

Everybody knows that of our bounden duty we should preach to the vicious for their amendment, (though) we should not flatter the virtuous by commenting on their virtue, for to blame the evil is to praise the good; and for this reason if I tell fools the truth about their folly, no wise man need be at all angry at what I say; for Reliability alongside of Trickery is rendered more praiseworthy by the appearance of its opposite.

The good are good, the bad are bad; wherefore if I preach to the dishonest, it ought not to be a matter of any consequence to those who are honest; for each according to his works should have his praise or his blame. To tell the truth, the merchant who sets his thoughts on deceit and he who puts in every-day in honest toil are not of the same quality; both, to be sure, are working for gain, but they are not at all alike.

Of one sort of merchant at the present day people speak very commonly; Trick is his name, full of guile, and if you seek from the East to the very extremest West, there is no city nor beautiful town where Trick does not gather his harvest. Trick in Bordeaux, at Seville and at Paris buys and sells; Trick has his ships and his troops of servants, and of noble riches Trick has ten times more than other people.

Trick at Florence and at Venice has his depositary and the freedom of the town, as well as at Bruges and at Ghent; in his care, too, is put the noble city on the Thames which Brutus [43] founded long ago; but Trick is now about to throw it into confusion by fleecing his neighbors of their goods; for he cares not under what guise he acts, whether it be before or behind;

[43] This legend of the origin of things British as due to the efforts of one Brutus, from whose name by a sort of umlaut *Britain* is derived, was first given currency by Geoffrey of Monmouth in his *Historia Regum Britanniae* (*History of the Kings of Britain*), of whom more later. (Cf. *post*, pp. 544–550; 556–558). In order, apparently, to give prestige to the legendary lore of romantic Britain, of which his book was to be so full, Geoffrey represents Brutus, a grandson of Æneas, as coming to the island since called Britain and starting a civilization there which was to rival the ancient in its glory. Brutus founded London, which is frequently styled in medieval writers New Troy. See Geoffrey of Monmouth, *op. cit.*, Book I, Chaps. 3–18. The best modern English translation of Geoffrey's *History* is that of Dr. Sebastian Evans in the *Temple Classics* edition or *Everyman's Library*. There is also a translation by Giles in *Six Old English Chronicles*. (*Bohn Library*.)

he goes about seeking his own good and despises the common profit.

Sometimes Trick is a grocer, but he is not very trustworthy in the matter of buying by one weight, and on the other hand of selling by a lighter weight than he bought by before, so that by deceit he keeps the surplus and his customer the deficit (in measure or weight): but what does he care, for Trick has so set his heart on money that he always looks out for a sharp bargain?

Trick also with his trickery oftentimes as a mercer deceives, but in a very different way, for he is full of cunning, of wiles and of cranks, to make fools of other people, so that he may get possession of their silver. He speaks so politely and makes himself orally such good company. But in thought he is subtley looking out for your money, behind the mask of courtesy.

This sort of bird [44] is never speechless, and so he is more clamorous than a sparrowhawk: when he sees people whom he doesn't know, he approaches and draws near, with calls and cries, saying: "Come right in without delay! Beds, kerchiefs, ostrich feathers, sandals, silks and goods from oversea: come in, I'll show you everything, for if you'll buy, you need go no further; here is the best stock on the street."

But look out for one thing: if once you enter his premises, be very wise in your buying, for Trick never gives himself away: by his covert guile he will give you chalk for cheese. You would think from what he says that that wild nettle is a precious rose, so polite is his appearance; but if you wish to be safe, do not rest with his paper.

Again, Trick is a draper and then he knows how to catch the people who are buying cloth. He will swear in God's name, if you'll buy, that he is giving you a good bargain and just measure; but I assure you it will be a case of chance (whether you get what you should), if he once gets your money: for, whatever he says or swears, his game is always quite different from looking after your rights.

For they tell us, and I believe it, that that which loves darkness,[45] hates and avoids the light: hence, when I see the draper

[44] Literally, "that which is drawn out of this cage."   [45] Cf. John 3: 20.

in his house, it seems to me he has no clear conscience: for dark is the window where he does business with you, so that you can hardly tell green from blue: he is also shady in his manner, for no one can trust his first word as to price.

At a double price darkly with an oath, he puts up his cloth for sale and thus beguiles you with the more subtlety, for he makes you believe that he is doing you a favor, when he has thus contrived: for he will say that he has quoted you this price in order to have your friendship, and has gained nothing by your custom; whereas, the measure and the bargain will tell you it is quite otherwise.

Thus, Trick in his draper's business is intent upon a double deceit. He is deceitful in his business when he is selling woolens: for here Trick is in his element — in cities he is received, in the country he is known, he goes about picking up bargains, he has his brokers retained, he turns things upside down and makes the first last.[46]

Trick's attitude is quite worldly, for he completely overlooks the good of others and seeks always his own advancement: but he is especially subtle when he controls the wool staple,[47] for he is then dealing in and speaking of his own good at close range (though no one suspects it); whatever comes into his neighborhood there, he gets a goodly share of ill-gotten gain therefrom; but his conscience will never rest easy unless God absolve him.

O wool, noble dame, you are the goddess of merchants, to serve you they are all ready; you make some mount to the heights of riches and fortune and you cause others to fall to ruin; the staple, in whatever neighborhood located, is not without fraud and crooked dealing which wound the human con-

[46] Matthew 19: 30.

[47] "By the close of the thirteenth century England had come to be the great wool-producing country of Europe, with her chief market among the Flemish weavers. Accordingly, various attempts were made to fix the towns or staples where the wool should be sold. Sometimes they were in England, sometimes in the Low Countries, while, for a short period in the reign, trade was free and the staple towns were done away with altogether. In 1362 the staple was removed to Calais, where it remained, except for short intervals, till the town passed back to the French in 1558." Cross, *op. cit.*, p. 212.

science. O wool, Christians as well as pagans and Saracens seek to have you and confess to you.

O wool, we ought not to keep silent about your doings in strange lands; for the merchants of all countries, in times of peace, in times of war, are coming to look for you because of their great love; for whoever else has his enemies, you are never without good friends, who have given themselves to your service for your profit: you are cherished throughout the world, the law of which you are guardian can do great things because of you.

Over all the world you are taken, by land and sea, but you are directed to the richest people: you are a native of England, but that you are ill-managed, people say in divers tongues; for Trick, who has a great deal of money, has been made regent of your staple, and has his own way in strange countries, looks out for his own advantage and injures the rest of us.

O beautiful, O white, O delightful one, the love of you stings and binds so that the hearts who make merchandise of you are not able to disengage themselves from you; thus they start many a scheme and lay many a trap in order to catch you: and then they make you cross the sea, as the one who is properly the queen of their navy, and in order to get you people to come enviously and covetously to bargain for you.

Exchange, usury and desire for gain, O wool, under your guidance come and take service in the very court; and Trick there makes provision for them (i.e. the king and his ministers); he makes them acquainted with Avarice,[48] and in order to make a profit, he has them retain brokers. But if any one desires to keep free of fraud, Trick at once gets ahead of him, and thus I have seen several cease to practise the ancient usages of loyalty in order to keep up the wool trade.

But let him gain who will, one in our country could in my opinion wonder a great deal at the Lombards,[49] who are aliens

[48] Cf. *ante*, p. 198, where Parliament is charged with granting illegally the wool subsidy to Richard II for life.

[49] I.e. Italians, from whom Lombard St. in London was named, who, with the Jews, carried on, often under royal protection, the business of banking, frowned on by the Church. On one of these Italian banking firms that failed in 1345, see *post*, pp. 261–262.

and yet will assert the right to stay in our country just as freely and acceptably as if they had been born and brought up among us; in order to beguile us they appear to be our friends, and under that cloak they have set their hearts on robbing us of our silver and our gold.

These Lombards give us a bad bargain, they exchange their straw for our grain, for two goods they do us four ills, they bring to us their fustian, and in their falsity drain us of our fine nobles[50] of royal gold and of our sterling coins of pure metal; this is one of the principal causes why our land is so ill-off; but if people would take my advice, may God help me, such fellows would not be so near us.

But they, for their part, are so skillful in playing the game of brokerage and business, that by deceit and flattery they bring around to their will the government of our country with which they are more familiar than are others: hence, it is common report that they spy on our councils, whence great perils often come to us, and any one who to-day has his eyes open will see the plain folly of it.

Look there at some Lombards coming up like fellows poorly dressed but by their deceit and talent for conspiracy before they have gone a step they dress themselves more nobly than the burgesses of our city; and if they feel the need of power or of friendship, they know how to get it by fraud and subtlety, for their cause is advanced whether we like it or not.

There is no reason I can see, nay rather, we ought to cry shame on such lords as, in order to get gifts by chicanery, are willing to give credence or faith to such gentry as lie in wait to ruin us for their own gain: but it is a great pity that our gov-

---

[50] "Edward III . . . made several important innovations: he not only issued a gold coinage, but also larger silver coins, viz., groats (fourpence) and half groats (twopence); his second coin was the Noble. . . . This beautiful work of art was current for six shillings and eightpence. On the obverse the king standing in the ship, is supposed to refer to the victory over the French fleet off Sluys in 1340." Bartholomew, *A Literary Historical Atlas of Europe*, pp. 104, 105. (*Everyman's Library*, 1910.) The volume contains a very good series of plates of English coins, as well as excellent maps of Europe in general, plans of important battle-fields and maps of literary localities, such as the English Lake Country, the Burns country, and many others.

ernment, which ought to administer the law in our behalf, has thrown our merchants into slavery and secretly enfranchised aliens to rob us.

But covetousness has conquered all, for he who gives will have friends and can bring his plans to a (successful) issue, it is the custom in my country: but one who pays attention to my advice will be able to see on all sides, both at home and abroad, that trickery in business is always with us; and further (he will perceive) that the people who live by their trades are all trained in one school.

The writer goes on at some length to speak of other trades, such as druggists, goldsmiths, furriers, bakers and butchers, but concludes the passage I wish to include with this rather brisk account of the means of trickery in the liquor business:

If you are ever going to know Trick, you will know him by his piment, his claree and his new ypocras. With these he fattens his purse, when city dames, who before visiting the minster or the market come tripping in the morning to the tavern. But then Trick is well paid, for each one will try wine provided it is anything but vinegar.

And then will Trick make them understand that, if they will just wait, they may have vernage, Greek wine and Malvesie. To cozen them into spending more money, he will name them wines of several sorts — of Crete, Ribole and Roumania, he will describe wines of Provence and Monterosso, he will say that he has in his cellar Riviera and Muscatel for sale,— but he hasn't a third of all these; rather he says so as a novelty that he may induce them to drink.

From one cask, forsooth, he will draw them ten different wines, when once he has them seated in their chairs; and so he says to them, "O my dear ladies, make good cheer, drink just as you please, for we have sufficient leisure." Then Trick has his heart's desire, when he has such chamberers who know how to deceive their husbands; for it is all one to him if they are thieves, so long as he makes his profit.

Better than any master of the black art, Trick knows all the art of wine selling, its tricks and wiles; he will counterfeit with his craft Rhein wine with vintage of France; truly, such as never grew anywhere save on the banks of the Thames he will brisk up and disguise and say it's Rhenish in the pitcher, so knowingly does he devise. There is no man so wide-awake that Trick does not trap him in the end.

If Trick is a wicked one in wine, he is still worse, by common report, in beer: I say this not for the French, but for the English who daily at the ale-house drink: but especially for the poorer sort who have neither a head nor a tail [51] of their own unless it come from their labor, and who all make a great clamor that the keeper of the ale-house is not reliable.[52]

Every system of economic and industrial practice is accompanied, as it were, by some sort of system of economic thought, including explanations, justifications and rules of action. Thus the system of slave labor in ancient Greece is postulated by Plato and Aristotle. And in the Middle Ages, while economics, in any modern sense of that term, was far from being thought of as a science separate from ethics or jurisprudence, there are a good many statements of concepts which are recognizable as economic. One of these has already been cited in the note on page 188, *ante*, where, in one of the charges against Richard II, the implication is left with the reader that in medieval public economy the theory was that the king was expected to live off the revenues of the estates belonging to the crown

[51] Literally, "cross or pile," i.e. the face or the reverse of a coin.

[52] I got the suggestion of including here these passages from Gower from G. G. Coulton, *A Medieval Garner*, pp. 575–578 (Constable and Co., Ltd., 1910), a book which Professor John M. Manly called to my attention. But though I have had Mr. Coulton's translation by me, I have both made my own and included more than he. Mr. Coulton in his prefatory note says that the second passage translated consists of ll. 18, 421, *seq.*, whereas it is ll. 26, 077–26, 136. The subject-matter of Gower's diatribe is similar to that in a sermon of Berthold of Regensburg, the popular German preacher of the thirteenth century. The sermon is translated in Coulton, *op. cit.*, pp. 348–354. Cf. Herbert Spencer, *The Morals of Trade* in *Essays: Moral, Political and Æsthetic*, 1864.

without recourse to taxation.[53]   This is an outgrowth of the feudal conception of land-holding and is a leading doctrine in the economic thought of the time.

Two other important medieval economic concepts are included here: the genealogy of money-power and the doctrine of usury.   The passage setting forth the first is taken from *The Vision of William concerning Piers the Plowman*, from which quotation has already been made.[54] In the earlier sections of this poem one of the most promi-nent characters is Lady Meed, who, in the allegory, is usually interpreted to be Bribery on the one hand or Reward on the other.   It seems, however, that, on account of her conduct in the poem, she should be explained as Money-power.   It is represented that the color of Meed, so to speak, will depend upon her alliances (and this is the reason she is personated as a woman); that is, if she is married to Conscience, as the king suggests, all will be well, but if she is wedded to Falsehood, as is proposed by Flattery and Liar, two other characters in the allegory, all will be ill.   The latter marriage, however, is about to take place when certain protests regarding it come in and the case is brought before the king himself for trial.   In the course of the latter the following statement of the genealogy of Meed is made:

Then Theology [55] flared up when he heard this tale, and said to sir Simony,[56] "Now may you have sorrow because you have arranged such a wedding as may anger Truth.   And woe to your council before this marriage be consummated!   For Meed is a woman whose mother was Amends; though Falsehood were her father and Fickle-Tongue her sire, yet Amends was her mother by the testimony of good witnesses.   Without the con-

---

[53] Cf. Haney, *History of Economic Thought*, p. 79 (Macmillan Co., 1911).
[54] Cf. *ante*, pp. 242–247.
[55] I.e. Canon Law; the Church had judicial control of marriage.
[56] A clerical friend of Meed.

sent of her mother Amends, Meed may not be wedded, for
Truth promised her (the mother) faithfully to espouse one of her
daughters, and the agreement has God's blessing provided there
is no guile, and you have given her (Meed) as Guile directed,
God give you sorrow!"

Amends, the mother of Meed, should be explained as the
poet's characterization of the medieval doctrine of "just
price"; that is, "every commodity had some one true
value which was objective and absolute, and was to be
determined in the last analysis by the common estimation
of the cost of production." [57]   Now, Amends means "exact
compensation for" and as such corresponds clearly with
the medieval idea that in a business transaction no profit
should be made on either side: each should give an exact
equivalent to the other. Thus, Thomas Aquinas says,
". . . if either the price exceeds the value, or conversely,
the value exceeds the price of the thing, the balance of
justice is destroyed." [58]   Aquinas was the great philosophic
authority in the late thirteenth and the fourteenth centuries. But Amends was married to Falsehood, though an
earlier line states that Meed was illegitimate,[59] and the
issue of the union was Meed. This exactly accords with
the doctrine of the church fathers, copied by most medieval
writers, that Money-power is evil by nature. "This was
based on a theological distinction between human nature
as it existed on its first creation, and then as it became
in the state to which it was reduced after the fall of Adam.
Created in original justice, as the phrase ran, the powers
of man's soul were in perfect harmony. His sensitive nature, i.e. his passions, were in subjection to his will, his
will to his reason, his reason to God. Had man continued
in this state of innocence, government, slavery, and private property would never have been required." [60]

[57] Haney, *op. cit.*, p. 76.   [58] *Ibid.*, p. 77.   [59] Cf. Text, Passus III, l. 24.
[60] Bede Jarrett, *Mediæval Socialism*, p. 9. (T. C. and E. C. Jack, *The People's*

The protest of Canon Law, that Meed and her fiancé Falsehood are within the forbidden degrees of relationship, is successful and the marriage does not take place. But the fact that Meed is tried before the king himself is interesting as suggesting another economic idea of the time; Meed is the ward of the king — this is the only basis on which she is brought before the king for trial; for in feudal law the vassal was subject to his lord's court. The royal guardianship of Meed, however, bears out the theory that she is Money-power in general, since royal care of the money of the country is a cardinal doctrine in medieval economic thought.[61]

The medieval theory of usury fits in well with the concept of money-power just expounded. The first passages to be submitted are from the *Ayenbite of Inwyt* (*Remorse of Conscience*) of Dan Michel, which he tells [62] us he finished in 1340. The work is "a translation of a popular French treatise, the *Somme des Vices et des Vertus* (or *Sum of Vices and Virtues*, known also as *Li Livres roiaux des Vices et des Vertus* or *The Royal Books of Vices and Virtues* and *Somme le Roi* or *Sum the King*) compiled, in 1279, by frère Lorens, a dominican, at the request of Philip the Bold, son and successor of Louis IX. This, in its turn, was borrowed from other writers, and was composed of various homilies, on the ten commandments, the creed, the seven deadly sins, the knowledge of good and evil, the seven petitions of the Paternoster, the seven gifts of the Holy Ghost, the seven cardinal virtues and confession, many of which exist in manuscripts anterior to the time of frère Lorens.

"The treatment of these subjects, especially in the section on the seven deadly sins, is allegorical. The sins are first compared with the seven heads of the beast which

---

Books, London, 1913). This gives a theoretic basis for the diatribes against trade, already quoted.   [61] Cf. Haney, *op. cit.*, p. 79.   [62] See *post.*, p. 503.

St. John saw in the Apocalypse; then, by a change of
metaphor, pride becomes the root of all the rest, and each
of them is represented as bringing forth various boughs.
Thus, the boughs of pride are untruth, despite, presumption, ambition, idle bliss, hypocrisy and wicked dread;
while from untruth spring three twigs, foulhood, foolishness and apostasy. This elaborate classification into
divisions and subdivisions is characteristic of the whole
work, and becomes not a little tiresome; on the other
hand, the very frequent recourse to metaphor which accompanies it serves to drive the lesson home. Idle bliss
is the great wind that throweth down the great towers,
and the high steeples, and the great beeches in the woods,
by which are signified men in high places; the boaster is
the cuckoo who singeth always of himself.

"Sometimes these comparisons are drawn from the natural history of the day, the bestiaries, or, as Dan Michel
calls them, the 'bokes of kende' (books of nature). Thus,
flatterers are like to nickers (sea-fairies), which have the
bodies of women and the tails of fishes, and sing so sweetly
that they make the sailors fall asleep, and afterwards swallow them; or like the adder called 'serayn,' which runs
more quickly than a horse, and whose venom is so deadly
that no medicine can cure its sting. Other illustrations
are borrowed from Seneca, from Æsop, Boethius, St.
Augustine, St. Gregory, St. Bernard, St. Jerome and St.
Anselm." [63]

Using the complex system of division referred to, the
author makes Usury the first root of Avarice and then
discusses the different sorts of Usury. Later he makes
Chaffering the eighth bough of Avarice.

There are seven kinds of usury. The first is lending that
lendeth silver for other things, where over and above the capi-

[63] *Cambridge History of English Literature*, I, pp. 395, 396.

tal sum the lender taketh the profits either in pence, or in horses, or in corn, or in wine, or in fruits of the ground that he taketh in mortgage, without reckoning these profits as part-payment. And what is worse, he will reckon twice, or even thrice in the year in order to raise the rate of usury, and yet he hath gifts as well for each term; and he maketh often of the usury a principal debt. These are usuries evil and foul. The courteous lender is he that lendeth without always making bargains for profit, either in pence, or in horses, or in cups of gold, or in silver, or in robes, or in tuns of wine, or in fat swine, or in services of horses or carts, or providings for himself or his children, or in any other things that he takes by reason of the loan. This is the first manner of usury, that is, lending wickedly. The second manner of usury is in those that do not themselves lend, but that which their fathers or the fathers of their wives or their elders have received in pledge and they inherit, by usury they retain and will not yield it up. The third manner of usury is in them that have shame to lend with their own hand, but they lend their pence through their servants or other men. These are the master money-lenders. Of such sin great men are not quit, who hold and sustain Jews and usurers that lend and destroy the country; and the great men take the rewards and the great gifts, and oftentimes the ransom money of the goods of the poor. The fourth manner is in those that lend with other men's silver that they buy at small cost in order to lend at a greater. These are the little usurers that teach so much foul craft. The fifth manner is in bargaining when men sell a thing, whatsoever it is, for more than it is worth at the time. And what is worse, is wickedly selling at that time when they see their wares are most needed; then they sell the thing for twice the dearer, or thrice as much as the thing is worth. Such folk do much evil. For their bargaining destroyeth and maketh beggars of knights and nobles that follow tournaments. And they take their lands and their heritage in pledge and mortgage, from which they never acquit them. Others sin in buying things, as corn, or wine, or other things, for less than half the pence that it is worth, and then they sell them again for twice as much, or thrice the dearer. Others buy things when they are least worth and of great cheapness, as corn sold in harvest time, or wine, or bargains, in order to sell them again whenever they are most dear. And they wish for a dear time in order to sell the dearer. Others buy corn in the blade and vines in the flower, when they are of fair-shewing and good forwardness, that they may have, whatever befal, their wealth safe. The sixth manner is when they give their pence to merchants in such wise that they are fellows in winning but not in losing. . . . The seventh manner is in those that lend their poor neighbors, in their needs, a little silver, or corn, or do them a little courtesy. And when they see them poor and needy, then they make with them a bargain to do their work, and for the pence they have before given to the poor man or the corn they have lent him, they have three pennyworth of work for one penny.

The eighth bough of Avarice is chaffering, wherein one sinneth in many ways, for worldly winning; and, namely, in seven manners. The first is to sell the things as dear as one may, and to buy as good cheap as one may. The next is lying, swearing, and forswearing, the higher to sell their wares. The third manner is by weights and measures, and that may be in three ways. The first when one hath divers weights or divers measures, and buyeth by the greatest weights or the greatest measures and selleth by the least. The other manner is when one hath rightful weights and rightful measures to sell untruly, as do the taverners that fill the measure with scum. The third manner is when those that sell by weight contrive that the thing that they weigh showeth more heavy. The fourth manner to sin in chaffering is to sell to time. Of this we have spoken above. The fifth manner is to sell otherwise than one hath showed before; as doth these scriveners that showeth good letter at beginning and after do badly. The sixth is to hide the truth about the thing that one will sell, as do the dealers of horses. The seventh is to contrive that the thing one selleth maketh for to show better than it is; as do the sellers of cloth that choose dim places wherein to sell their cloth. In many other manners one may sin in chafferings, but long thing it were to say.[64]

[64] On this medieval antipathy to usury cf. Tacitus' reference to the absence of the practice among the early Germans; *ante*, p. 18.

Our last passage deals with a specific instance where the evil practice of usury is censured. Giovanni Villanni (1275–1348), a merchant and politician of Florence, his native city, wrote a historical work which he calls *Historie Fiorentine (Florentine History)* or *Cronica Universale (Universal Chronicle)*, and which begins with Biblical times and comes down to the year 1348. There is no better authority for the intellectual and economic life of Florence in the first forty-eight years of the fourteenth century, which Villani observed at first hand. In one of the later chapters of his work he thus records the failure of a well-known Italian banking house. The causes of the failure, he says, in quite the medieval fashion, are avarice and usury.

In the year 1345 in the month of January failed the company of the Bardi, who had been the greatest merchants in Italy. And the reason was that they, like the Peruzzi, had lent their money and that invested with them to king Edward of England and to the king of Sicily; and that the Bardi found they had owing to them from the king of England, what with capital and interest and gifts promised by him, 900,000 florins of gold, and on account of his war with the king of France he was unable to pay; and from the king of Sicily 100,000 florins of gold. And to the Peruzzi were owing from the king of England 600,000 florins of gold, and from the king of Sicily 100,000 florins of gold, and a debt of 350,000 florins of gold, so they must stop payment to citizens and foreigners, to whom the Bardi alone owed more than 550,000 florins of gold. Whereby many other smaller companies and individuals whose money was in the hands of the Bardi or Peruzzi or others who had failed, were ruined and so became bankrupt. By this failure of the Bardi, Peruzzi, Acciajuoli, and Bonaccorsi — of the company of Uzzano Perandoli, and many other small companies and individual craftsmen, owing to the burdens on the state and the disordered loans to lords, of which I have made mention (though not of all, which were too long to tell), came greater ruin and discomfiture to our city of Florence than any our state had received, if the reader well considered the damage caused by such a loss of treasure and money lost by our citizens, and lent from avarice to lords. O cursed and greedy usury, full of the vice of avarice reigning in our blind and mad citizens of Florence, who from covetousness to gain from great lords put their wealth and that of others in their power and lordship to lose, and ruin our republic; for there remained no substance of money in our citizens, except in a few craftsmen and lenders who with their usury consumed and gained for themselves the scattered poverty of our citizens and subjects. But not without cause come to states and citizens the secret judgments of God, to punish the sins which have been committed, as Christ with his own mouth said in the gospel "Ye shall die in your sin." The Bardi agreed to give up to their creditors their possessions, which they estimated would come to 9 shillings and 3 pence in the pound, but at a fair price did not come to six shillings in the pound.

Medieval life was corporate in character; that is, men thought of themselves not as individuals but as members of groups; this is why excommunication, boycott and outlawry were so terrible to the medieval man — they excluded him from his group and cut him off from all the emoluments, prerogatives and privileges of his group. The fact of the corporate character of medieval life also accounts for the sumptuary legislation [65] of the Middle Ages, the attempt minutely to regulate the equipment and expenditure of various social ranks and classes. Two phases of this "corporation" have already been illustrated, the feudal system of landholding and military service and the gild system of commerce and trade respectively. There is a third phase left, the religious orders of monks and friars.

In the first chapter two passages from *The Rule of St. Benedict* were quoted [66] to illustrate the economic function

[65] Cf. the English statute of 1363, designed to regulate wearing apparel, quoted in Locke, *War and Misrule*, pp. 56–59 (*Bell's English History Source Books*, 1913).
[66] Cf. *ante*, pp. 19–21.

of monasteries, but here are to be included documents which will show how complex the monastic system had grown and how in some ways it had degenerated. As a background for these, however, a description of the monastic ideal in general will be used and for this purpose a selection from the *Dialogus Miraculorum* (*Dialog of Miracles*) by Cæsarius of Heisterbach has been chosen. Cæsarius, to be sure, was a German, but the ideal set forth in his book was European in its scope, applying to England as well as to Germany. Cæsarius was educated in Cologne, became Prior and Teacher of the Novices at the Cistercian monastery of Heisterbach, and between 1220 and 1235 wrote his *Dialog*, a book intended for the guidance and instruction of the novices in the monastery, some biographies and treatises on chronology [67] and a book of Homilies. The persons in the *Dialog* are a Monk and a Novice.

In the Monastery of St. Chrysanthius (in the Eiffel) there dwelt a schoolmaster named Ulrich, a Frenchman by birth, of great prudence and learning. The revenues of his office were so small that he could not avoid falling into debt. One of the brethren at the Præmonstratensian Monastery of Steinfeld, perceiving that he was a man of great learning, oft-times persuaded him to enter his monastery by grace of conversion. At last this Ulrich, by divine inspiration, answered thus: "I owe a little money; pay that, and I will come to you." When the Provost of the aforesaid monastery heard this, he gladly paid the money, and Ulrich forthwith took the habit. Not long afterwards, he was elected Provost of that house: (for there were as yet no Abbots in the Præmonstratensian order). Considering then that, with this office, he had undertaken the keeping not of flocks and lands but of men's souls, he busied himself with the uprooting of vices rather than with the amassing of money, knowing that covetousness is the root of all evil.[68]

[67] The reader has doubtless noticed that medieval records of all sorts reckon time by the Church calendar of holidays and saints' days. This fact accounts for the great number of treatises on chronology written in the Middle Ages.
[68] Cf. 1 Tim. 6: 10.

Now he had a lay brother so skilful and circumspect in the management of worldly things, so careful and exact, that everything passed through his hands, and he was almost the only one who provided the monastery farms with all that they needed, both ploughs and cattle and money. He was all in all, disposing everything, neglecting nothing, adding field to field and joining vineyard to vineyard. The Provost, marking this, and, reading in the Scriptures that nothing was more wicked than avarice called the lay-brother to him one day, and said: "Dost thou know, my bearded [69] fellow, wherefore I am come into this Order?" (Now he was uncunning in the German tongue; and therefore to the lay-brethren all his speech seemed crooked and distorted.) The lay-brother answered: "I know not, my Lord." "Then I will tell thee: for I am come hither to weep in this spot for my sins. Wherefore art thou come hither?" The other made answer: "My Lord, for the same cause." "If then," said the Provost, "thou art come to bewail thy sins, thou shouldest have kept the fashion of a penitent: assiduous in church, in watchings, in fastings: constant in prayer to God for thy sins. For it is no part of penitence to do as thou dost — to disinherit thy neighbors and (in the words [70] of the prophet Habacuc) to load thyself with thick clay. Whereunto the lay-brother answered: "Lord, those possessions which I get are continuous with the fields and vineyards of our convent." "Well," said the Provost, "when these are bought, thou must needs buy those also which border thereon. Knowest thou what Isaiah saith? 'Woe unto you that join house to house and lay field to field even to the end of the place: shall you alone dwell in the midst of the earth?' [71] For thou settest no bounds to thy covetousness. When thou shalt have gotten all the land of this province, thou shalt cross the Rhine at a stride: then shalt thou go on even to the mountains; nor even so shalt thou rest until thou be come to the sea. There at last, methinks, shalt thou halt,

---

[69] "The lay-brethren, unlike the monks, let their beards grow." (Mr. Coulton's note.)

[70] The only words of this tenor to be found in Habacuc are in the second chapter and sixth verse; the modern Revised version does not mention clay.

[71] Cf. Isaiah 5: 8.

for the sea is broad and spacious, and thy stride is short. Abide therefore within thy cloister, haunt thy church, that thou mayest bewail thy sins night and day. Wait awhile, and thou shalt have enough earth beneath thee and above thee and within; for dust thou art and into dust thou shalt return." [72] Some of the elder brethren, hearing this, said: "Lord, lord, if this lay-brother be removed, our house will go to rack and ruin." Whereunto he answered: "Better the house should perish, than the soul:" and paid no heed to their prayers. *Novice.* He was a true shepherd, knowing that the sheep committed to him had been redeemed not with corruptible things as gold and silver, but with the precious blood of Christ, as of a lamb unspotted and undefiled.[73] *Monk.* This appeared plainly enough in his words and actions. For in the days when Rheinhold was made Archbishop of Cologne, and found the revenues of the see mortgaged and the farms desolate, he was persuaded to borrow from the different Cistercian houses in his diocese faithful and prudent lay-brethren who might watch over the farms and reform the revenues by their industry. When therefore he had accepted this counsel, and had collected certain lay-brethren both of the hill and of the plain, he was persuaded to take this aforesaid lay-brother also. Wherefore he sent an honorable ambassador, who, after greeting the Provost from the Archbishop, added: "My lord hath a small boon to ask of you which ye should not deny him." "Nay," answered the Provost, "it is my Lord's part not to ask me, but to command." Then said the other: "The Archbishop beseeches you to lend him such and such a lay-brother for such and such uses." Whereunto the Provost answered with all due humility, constancy and gentleness: "I have two hundred sheep at such a Grange, so and so many in such and such others; oxen have I likewise and horses; let my Lord take then of whatsoever he will; but a lay-brother committed to my soul he shall never have for such uses, since it is not for sheep and oxen that I am to render account at the judgment-day before the Supreme Shepherd, but for souls that have been committed to my care." He left also another proof of his liberality, a somewhat profitable example against monastic avarice. One day, before that

[72] Cf. Genesis 3: 19.   [73] Cf. 1 Peter 1: 18, 19.

aforesaid lay-brother was removed from his office, the Provost came to one of his granges; wherein, seeing a comely foal, he enquired of the same brother whose it was or whence it came. To whom the brother answered: "Such and such a man, our good and faithful friend, left it to us at his death." "By pure devotion," asked the Provost, "or by legal compulsion?" "It came through his death," answered the other, "for his wife, since he was one of our serfs, offered it as a heriot." [74] Then the Provost shook his head and piously answered: "Because he was a good man and our faithful friend, therefore hast thou despoiled his wife? Render therefore her horse to this forlorn woman; for it is robbery to seize or detain other men's goods, since the horse was not thine before (the man's death)."

The same Provost, being a man of prudence, was unwilling to take the younger brethren with him when he went abroad on the business of the monastery; for he knew that this was inexpedient for them, by reason of the devil's temptations. Now it befel on a day that he took with him one of the youths; and as they were together, talking of I know not what, they met a comely maiden. The Provost, of set purpose, reined in his steed and saluted her most ceremoniously; she in her turn stood still and bowed her head to return his salute. When, therefore, they had gone a little further, the Provost (willing to tempt the youth) said: "Methinks that was a most comely maiden." "Believe me, my Lord," replied the youth, "she was most comely in mine eyes also." Whereupon the Provost answered: "She hath only this blemish, namely, that she hath but one eye!" "In truth, my Lord," replied the youth, "she hath both her eyes; for I looked somewhat narrowly into her face." Then was the Provost moved to wrath, and said: "I too will look narrowly into thy back! Thou shouldest have been too simple to know whether she were male or female." When therefore he was come back to the monastery, he said to the elder monks: "Ye, my Lords, sometimes blame me that I take not the younger brethren abroad with me." Then he expounded this whole case, and chastised the youth sternly with words and stripes. This same Provost was so learned that (as it was told me by an elder

---

[74] For the matter of the heriot see *ante*, p. 222.

monk of that house) he preached a sermon in the Chapter-General of Citeaux one day when he came thither for the business of his Order.

Novice. It oftentimes happens that great men wrest from their subjects money or possessions to which they have little right, and build therefrom Houses of religion. May the Religious knowingly accept such alms as these? *Monk.* Whatsoever gnaweth the conscience, defileth the conscience. Yet know that such things are sometimes done by God's just judgment, as thou mayest learn by the following example. A certain great and noble man, willing to build on his lands a House of our Order, and finding a spot suitable for a monastery, drove out its inhabitants partly by bribes, partly by threats. But the Abbot who was to send monks to that place, fearing divine displeasure if the poor were thus deprived of their possessions, prayed to God that He might vouchsafe to reveal His will in that case. Then was that just man not suffered to dwell long in anxious suspense concerning this matter: for one day, as he was in prayer, he heard a voice saying unto him in the words of the Psalmist: "Thou, my God, hast given an inheritance to them that fear Thy name." [75] Rising therefore from his knees, he forthwith understood, how it was God's will that undevout men should be cast forth from these lands, and that men who feared and praised God should be settled there: as we read that the Lord gave to the children of Israel the lands of the Canaanites and other unclean nations. Yet these must not be construed into a precedent; for all covetousness and injustice should be abhorred by the Religious. *Novice.* Yea, and scandal should all the more be avoided in such matters, because secular folk are unwilling to have Religious for their neighbors.

This is a high unworldly ideal; probably it unfortunately remained mostly an ideal, for a monastery was a great corporation with many problems to solve and obligations to meet. The abbot was supposed both to maintain a high standard of religious life in his house and to perform in an efficient manner many of the functions of the manager

[75] The concordance gives no such verse.

of a modern business concern. It is true that he had his
assistants, but the responsibility came back in the ultimate
to the abbot; and if he did not always perform all his
functions in an equally satisfactory way, his delinquencies
must be debited to the account of human nature. We are
fortunate in the possession of a monastic chronicle, *The
Chronicle of Jocelin of Brakelond*,[76] which gives us a very
intimate sense of the quality of life in the Abbey of St.
Edmundsbury in the latter part of the twelfth century,
and from which we shall quote. It is not a romantic
picture that is there set before us, but a realistic one, giving us plenty of detail of the homely routine of the great
establishment. The monks are everyday, flesh-and-blood
Englishmen, daily companions of the author Jocelin, of
whom we know nothing save what he himself tells us in
his book. He was a monk, had likely been brought up
and educated in the monastery, and shows himself a person
of some learning, since he quotes Virgil, Horace and Ovid.
His *Preface* is as follows: *

I have undertaken to write of those things which I have seen
and heard, and which have occurred in the church of Saint Edmund, from the year in which the Flemings [77] were taken without the town, in which year I also assumed the religious habit,
and in which Prior Hugh was deposed and Robert made Prior
in his room. And I have related the evil as a warning, and the
good for an example.[78]

[76] This is the chronicle which Carlyle used as the basis of his picture of the
past in *Past and Present*. The original chronicle is in Latin and was first republished
in modern times by the Camden Society in 1840; it also finds place in Thomas
Arnold, *Memorials of St. Edmund's Abbey*, I, pp. 209–336. It was first translated
into modern English by Tomlins as *Monastic and Social Life in the Twelfth Century,
as Exemplified in the Chronicle of Jocelin of Brakelond* in 1844.

* This and the other passages from Jocelin's *Chronicle* which follow are
quoted by permission of Messrs. Chatto and Windus from their edition in the
King's Classics Series.

[77] The allusion is to the battle of Fornham, November, 1173.

[78] Perhaps the best treatment of English monastic life in general is Gasquet,

We gather from the opening chapter that the business of the monastery was rather run down when Jocelin's story begins:

In those days Abbot Hugh grew old, and his eyes were dim. He was a good and kindly man, a godfearing and pious monk, but in temporal matters he was unskilful and improvident. He relied too much on his own intimates and believed too readily in them, rather trusting to a stranger's advice than using his own judgment. It is true that discipline and the service of God, and all that pertained to the rule, flourished greatly within the cloister, but without the walls all things were mismanaged. For every man, seeing that he served a simple and ageing lord, did not that which was right, but that which was pleasing in his own eyes. The townships and all the hundreds of the abbot were given to farm; the woods were destroyed, and the houses on the manors were on the verge of ruin; from day to day all things grew worse. The abbot's sole resource and means of relief was in borrowing money, that so it might at least be possible to maintain the dignity of his house. For eight years before his death, there was never an Easter or Michaelmas which did not see at least one or two hundred pounds added to the debt. The bonds were ever renewed, and the growing interest was converted into principal.

This disease spread from the head to the members, from the ruler to his subjects. So it came to pass that if any official had a seal of his own, he also bound himself in debt as he listed, both to Jews and Christians. Silken caps, and golden vessels, and the other ornaments of the church, were often placed in pledge without the assent of the monastery. I have seen a bond made to William FitzIsabel for a thousand and two score pounds, but know not the why nor wherefore. And I have seen another bond to Isaac, son of Rabbi Joce, for four hundred pounds, but know not wherefore it was made. I have seen also a third bond to Benedict, the Jew of Norwich, for eight hundred and fourscore pounds, and this was the origin and cause of that debt.

English Monastic Life, The Antiquary's Books, 4th ed. (London, Methuen & Co., 1910).

Our buttery was destroyed, and the sacristan William received it to restore whether he would or no. He secretly borrowed forty marks at interest from Benedict the Jew, and made him a bond, sealed with a certain seal which was wont to hang at the shrine of St. Edmund. With this the gilds and brotherhoods used to be sealed; afterwards, but in no great haste, it was destroyed by order of the monastery. Now when that debt increased to one hundred pounds, the Jew came, bearing letters of the lord king concerning the sacristan's debt, and then at last that which had been hidden from the abbot and the monks appeared. So the abbot in anger would have deposed the sacristan, alleging a privilege of the lord pope that enabled him to remove William his sacristan when he would. However, there came one to the abbot, who pleaded for the sacristan, and so won over the abbot that he suffered a bond to be made to Benedict the Jew for four hundred pounds, payable at the end of four years, that is, a bond for the hundred pounds to which the interest had increased, and for another hundred pounds which the same Jew had lent to the sacristan for the use of the abbot. And in full chapter the sacristan obtained that all this debt should be paid, and a bond was made and sealed with the seal of the monastery. For the abbot pretended that the debt was no concern of his, and did not affix his seal. However, at the end of the four years there was nothing wherewith the debt might be discharged, and a new bond was made for eight hundred and fourscore pounds, which was to be repaid at stated times, every year fourscore pounds.

And the same Jew had many other bonds for smaller debts, and one bond which was for fourteen years, so that the sum of the debt owing to that Jew was a thousand and two hundred pounds, over and above the amount by which usury had increased it.

Then came the almoner of the lord king and told the lord abbot that many rumors concerning these great debts had come to the king. And when counsel had been taken with the prior and a few others, the almoner was brought into the chapter. Then, when we were seated and were silent, the abbot said: "Behold the almoner of the king, our lord and friend and yours, who, moved by love of God and Saint Edmund, has shown to us that the lord king has heard some evil report of us and you, and that the affairs of the church are ill-managed within and without the walls. And therefore I will, and command you upon your vow of obedience, that you say and make known openly how our affairs stand." So the prior arose, and speaking as it were one for all, said that the church was in good order, and that the rule was well and strictly kept within, and matters outside the walls carefully and discreetly managed; and that though we, like others round us, were slightly involved in debt, there was no debt which might give us cause for anxiety. When he heard this, the almoner said that he rejoiced greatly to hear this witness of the monastery, by which he meant these words of the prior. And the prior, and Master Geoffrey of Coutances, answered in these same words on another occasion, when they spoke in defence of the abbot at the time when Archibishop Richard, by virtue of his legatine power, came into our chapter, in the days before we possessed that exemption which we now enjoy.

Now I was then in my novitiate, and on a convenient occasion talked of these things to my master, who was teaching me the Rule, and in whose care I was placed; he was Master Samson, who was afterwards abbot. "What is this," I said, "that I hear? And why do you keep silence when you see and hear such things — you, who are a cloistered monk, and desire not offices, and fear God rather than man?" But he answered and said, "My son, the newly burnt child feareth the fire, and so is it with me and with many another. Prior Hugh has been lately deposed and sent into exile; Dennis, and Hugo, and Roger de Hingham have but lately returned to the house from exile. I was in like manner imprisoned, and afterwards was sent to Acre, for that we spoke to the common good of our church against the will of the abbot. This is the hour of darkness; this is the hour in the which flatterers triumph and are believed; their might is increased, nor can we prevail against them. These things must be endured for a while; the Lord see and judge!"

At length Abbot Hugh fell from his horse and was killed and Jocelin tells us how the monastery was taken over by the officers of the king, just as would be the case with any other feudal barony:

When Abbot Hugh had been laid to rest, it was decreed in the chapter that one should tell the death of the abbot to Ranulf de Glanvill,[79] Justiciar of England. Master Samson and Master Robert Ruffus hastened across the sea, bearing this same news to the lord King, and obtained from him letters directing that the possessions and revenues of the monastery, which were distinct from those of the abbot, should remain entirely in the hands of the prior and of the monastery, and that the rest of the abbey's property should be in the hands of the King. The wardship of the abbey was given to Robert de Cokefield and to Robert de Flamvill the seneschal, who at once placed under surety and pledges those of the servants and relatives of the abbot to whom the abbot had given anything after he fell ill, or who had taken anything from the property of the abbot. And they also treated the chaplain of the abbot in the same way, for whom the prior became surety. And entering our vestry, they made a double inventory of all the ornaments of the church.

Meanwhile the monks in a very human way gossip over the qualifications of the possible successors of Abbot Hugh:

The abbacy being vacant, we often, as was right, made supplication unto the Lord and to the blessed martyr Edmund that they would give us and our church a fit pastor. Three times in each week, after leaving the chapter, did we prostrate ourselves in the choir and sing seven penitential psalms. And there were some who would not have been so earnest in their prayers if they

---

[79] Chief justiciar of England and reputed author of *Tractatus de legibus et consuetudinibus regni Angliæ* (*Tractate on the Laws and Customs of the Kingdom of England*), first printed in 1554. After rising through various grades of public office, he became the right-hand man of Henry II, and during the latter's repeated absences from England was practically viceroy. On Henry's death in 1189, Glanville was removed from office by Richard I, heavily fined and imprisoned. On his release he took the cross and died at the siege of Acre in 1190. His book noted above is a practical treatise on the forms of procedure in the king's Court and "as the source of our knowledge of the *curia regis*, and for the information it affords regarding ancient customs and laws, it is of great value to the student of English history." (*Enclyclopædia Britannica*, ed. 11, article *Glanvill*).

had known who was to become abbot. As to the choice of an abbot, if the king should grant us free election, there was much difference of opinion, some of it openly expressed, some of it privately; and every man had his own ideas.

One said of a certain brother, "He, that brother, is a good monk, a likely person. He knows much of the rule and of the customs of the church. It is true that he is not so profoundly wise as are some others, but he is quite capable of being abbot. Abbot Ording was illiterate, and yet he was a good abbot and ruled this house wisely; and one reads in the fable that the frogs did better to elect a log to be their king than a serpent, who hissed venomously, and when he had hissed, devoured his subjects." Another answered, "How could this thing be? How could one who does not know letters preach in the chapter, or to the people on feast days? How could one who does not know the scriptures have the knowledge of binding and loosing? For the rule of souls is the art of arts, the highest form of knowledge. God forbid that a dumb idol be set up in the church of Saint Edmund, where many men are to be found who are learned and industrious."

Again, one said of another, "That brother is a literate man, eloquent and prudent, and strict in his observance of the rule. He loves the monastery greatly, and has suffered many ills for the good of the church. He is worthy to be made abbot." Another answered, "From good clerks deliver us, oh Lord ! That it may please Thee to preserve us from the cheats of Norfolk; we beseech Thee to hear us !"

And again, one said of one, "That brother is a good husbandman; this is proved by the state of his office, and from the posts in which he has served well, and from the buildings and repairs which he has effected. He is well able to work and to defend the house, and he is something of a scholar, though too much learning has not made him mad. He is worthy of the abbacy." Another answered, "God forbid that a man who can neither read nor sing, nor celebrate the holy office, a man who is dishonest and unjust, and who evil intreats the poor men, should be made abbot."

Again, one said of another, "That brother is a kindly man,

friendly and amiable, peaceful and calm, generous and liberal, a
learned and eloquent man, and proper enough in face and gait.
He is beloved of many within and without the walls, and such
an one might become abbot to the great honour of the church,
if God wills." Another answered, "It is no credit, but rather a
disgrace, in a man to be too particular as to what he eats and
drinks, to think it a virtue to sleep much, to know well how
to spend and to know little how to gain, to snore while others
keep vigil, to wish ever to have abundance, and not to trouble
when debts daily increase, or when money spent brings no return; to be one who hates anxiety and toil, caring nothing while
one day passes and another dawns; to be one who loves and
cherishes flatterers and liars; to be one man in word and another
in deed. From such a prelate the Lord defend us."

And again, one said of his friend, "That man is almost wiser
than all of us, and that both in secular and in ecclesiastical
matters. He is a man skilled in counsel, strict in the rule,
learned and eloquent, and noble in stature; such a prelate would
become our church." Another answered, "That would be true,
if he were a man of good and approved repute. But his character has been questioned, perhaps falsely, perhaps rightly. And
though the man is wise, humble in the chapter, devoted to the
singing of psalms, strict in his conduct in the cloister while he
is a cloistered monk, this is only from force of habit. For if
he have authority in any office, he is too scornful, holding monks
of no account, and being on familiar terms with secular men,
and if he be angry, he will scarce say a word willingly to any
brother, even in answer to a question."

I heard in truth another brother abused by some because he
had an impediment in his speech, and it was said of him that
he had pastry or draff in his mouth when he should have spoken.
And I myself, as I was then young, understood as a child, spake
as a child; and I said that I would not consent that any one
should be made abbot unless he knew something of dialectic,
and knew how to distinguish the true from the false. One, moreover, who was wise in his own eyes, said, "May Almighty God
give us a foolish and stupid pastor, that he may be driven to use
our help." And I heard, forsooth, that one man who was indus-

trious, learned, and pre-eminent for his high birth, was abused by some of the older men because he was a novice. The novices said of their elders that they were invalid old men, and little capable of ruling an abbey. And so many men said many things, and every man was fully persuaded in his own mind.

At length, after an election formula which delighted Carlyle in its simplicity, Samson the subsacristan was chosen Abbot. He had been recognized for some time as a man of power, though he was a silent fellow. Abbot Hugh had tried to flatter him [80] and had said to his intimates that Samson was the only man he had found whom he had not been able to bend to his own will. He was zealous for learning [81] and had great religious sensibility, for when he heard of the capture of Jerusalem by the Saracens, "he began to wear undergarments made of horse hair, and a horse-hair shirt, and gave up the use of flesh and meat."[82] "He was an eloquent man, speaking both French and Latin, but rather careful of the good sense of that which he had to say than of the style of his words. He could read books written in English very well, and was wont to preach to the people in English, but in the dialect of Norfolk, where he was born and bred." [83] He was a careful manager [84] and very patriotic, since he gave more than his share for the ransom of King Richard I.[85] The beginning of his rule in the monastery is thus described by Jocelin:

In those days I was prior's chaplain, and within four months was made chaplain to the abbot. And I noted many things and committed them to memory. So, on the morrow of his feast, the abbot assembled the prior and some few others together, as if to seek advice from others, but he himself knew what he would do.

He said that a new seal must be made and adorned with a mitred effigy of himself, though his predecessors had not had

---

[80] Jane's translation in the *King's Classics Series*, pp. 9, 10.   [81] *Ibid.*, p. 57.
[82] *Ibid.*, p. 63.   [83] *Ibid.*, p. 64.   [84] *Ibid.*, pp. 66–67.   [85] *Ibid.*, p. 85.

such a seal. For a time, however, he used the seal of our prior, writing at the end of all letters that he did so for the time being because he had no seal of his own. And afterwards he ordered his household, and transferred various officials to other offices, saying that he proposed to maintain twenty-six horses in his court, and many times he declared that "a child must first crawl, and afterwards he may stand upright and walk." And he laid this especial command upon his servants, that they should take care that he might not be laid open to the charge of not providing enough food and drink, but that they should assiduously provide for the maintenance of the hospitality of the house.

In these matters, and in all the things which he did and determined, he trusted fully in the help of God and his own good sense, holding it to be shameful to rely upon the counsel of another, and thinking he was sufficient unto himself. The monks marvelled and the knights were angered; they blamed his pride, and often defamed him at the court of the king, saying that he would not act in accordance with the advice of his freemen. He himself put away from his privy council all the great men of the abbey, both lay and literate, men without whose advice and assistance it seemed impossible that the abbey could be ruled. For this reason Ranulf de Glanvill, justiciar of England, was at first offended with him, and was less well-disposed towards him than was expedient, until he knew well from definite proofs that the abbot acted providently and prudently, both in domestic and in external affairs.

Samson's talents for government were not suffered to remain long in the obscurity of the monastery; he soon got into public office, as Jocelin tells us in the following chapter:

Seven months had not yet passed since his election, and, behold! letters of the lord pope were sent to him appointing him a judge for hearing causes. In the performance of this work he was rude and inexperienced, though he was skilled in the liberal arts and in the holy scriptures, as being a literate man, brought up in the schools and a ruler of scholars, and renowned and well proved in his own work. He therefore associated with himself two clerks who were learned in the law and joined them with him, using their advice in church matters, while he spent his leisure in studying the decrees and decretal letters. And the result was that in a little while he was regarded as a discreet judge, by reason of the books which he had read and the causes which he had tried, and as one who proceeded in the cases which he tried according to the form of law. And for this cause one said, "Cursed be the court of this abbot, where neither gold nor silver profit me to confound my enemy!"

In course of time, he became somewhat skilled in temporal matters, being guided by his commonsense, for his mind was so subtle that all men wondered, and Osbert FitzHerbert, the under-sheriff, used to say, "This abbot is given to disputation; if he goes on as he has begun, he will blind us all, however many we be." But the abbot, being approved in these matters, was made a justice in eyre, though he kept himself from error and wandering. But "envy seeks out the highest." His men complained to him in the court of St. Edmund, since he would not give judgment hastily or believe every spirit, but proceeded in a judicial manner, knowing that the merits of the cases of suitors are made clear by discussion. It was said that he would not do justice to any complainant, unless money were given or promised; and because his aspect was acute and penetrating, and his face, like Cato's, rarely smiling, it was said that his mind lent rather to severity than to mercy. Moreover, when he took fines for any crime, it was said that judgment rejoiced against mercy, for in the opinion of many, when it came to a matter of taking money he rarely remitted that which he might lawfully take.

So his wisdom increased, as well as his care in managing affairs, and in improving his state, and in spending honorably.

Some of the abbey's financial difficulties were conceived as due to the Jews, and Samson finally secured royal permission to drive them from the neighborhood.

The recovery of the manor of Mildenhall for one thousand one hundred silver marks, and the expulsion of the Jews from the town of St. Edmund's, and the foundation of a new hospital at Babwell, were signs of great virtue.

The lord abbot sought letters from the king that the Jews might be expelled from the town of St. Edmund's, asserting that whatever is in the town of the blessed Edmund, or within the district subject to the jurisdiction of the monastery, belongs of right to the Saint, and that consequently the Jews ought either to be the men of St. Edmund, or else be driven from the town. Leave, therefore, was given to him to eject them, provided that they should have all their chattels, as well as the value of their houses and lands. And when they were sent forth, and under armed force were conducted to various towns, the abbot ordered that in every church and before every altar those should be solemnly excommunicated who should henceforth receive Jews or entertain them as guests in the town of St. Edmund's. This provision was afterwards modified by the justices of the king, to the effect that if Jews should come to the great pleas of the abbot in order to exact debts due to them from their debtors, then for this reason they might be entertained for two days and two nights in the town, and depart in peace on the third day.

Samson was a stout defender of the monastery's rights, even against archbishops and kings.

In a manor of the monks of Canterbury, which is called Eleigh, and which is in the hundred of the abbot, there chanced to be a murder. But the archbishop's men would not allow the murderers to take their trial in the court of St. Edmund. Then the abbot made complaint to king Henry, and said that archbishop Baldwin was claiming the liberties of our church for himself, on the ground of a new charter which the king had given to the church of Canterbury after the death of the blessed Thomas.

Then the king answered that he had never given a charter to the prejudice of our church, and that he did not wish to take from the blessed Edmund anything which he had formerly possessed. On hearing this, the abbot said to his intimate advisers: "It is wiser counsel that the archbishop should make complaint of me than that I should make complaint of the archbishop. I wish to place myself in possession of this liberty, and then I will defend myself with the help of St. Edmund, in whose right our charters bear witness that this liberty is."

Accordingly, unexpectedly, and very early in the morning, with the help of Robert de Cokefield, about eighty armed men were sent to the town of Eleigh, and took those three murderers by surprise and brought them bound to St. Edmund's, and cast them into the dungeon of the prison. And when the archbishop made complaint of this, Ranulf Glanvill, the justiciar, commanded that those men should be bound by surety and pledges to stand their trial in the court wherein they ought to stand it; and the abbot was summoned to come to the court of the king and to make reply concerning the violence and injury which he was said to have done to the archbishop. And the abbot many times presented himself at the court, without attempting to make excuse.

At last, at the beginning of the fasting time, they stood before the king in the chapter-house of Canterbury, and the charters of the two churches were read publicly. And the lord king answered, "These charters are of equal age, and come from the same king Edward. I know not what to say, save that the charters are contradictory." To this the abbot replied, "Whatever may be said about the charters, we are seised of the liberty, and have been in the past, and on this point I will submit to the verdict of the two counties, Norfolk and Suffolk, which will allow this."

Archbishop Baldwin, however, having first taken counsel with his men, said that the men of Norfolk and Suffolk loved St. Edmund greatly, and that a large part of those counties was under the rule of the abbot, and therefore he would not abide by their arbitration. But the king was angry and offended at that, and rising up, left the place, saying, "He that is able to receive it, let him receive it." And thus the matter was postponed, and is still undecided.

But I saw that some of the men of the monks of Canterbury were wounded to the death by the rustics of the township of Midling, which is situated in the hundred of St. Edmund, and as they knew that the prosecutor is bound to go to the court of the defendant, they preferred to be silent and to hide the matter, rather than complain of it to the abbot or his officers, since they were in nowise willing to come and plead in the court of St. Edmund.

After these things the men of Eleigh set up a certain measure for the doing of justice in cases where bread and corn had been measured with false measures, and the abbot made complaint of this to the lord bishop of Ely, who was at that time justiciar and chancellor. But he would not hear the abbot, because he was alleged to be scenting the archbishopric, which was then vacant. When, however, he had come among us, and was received as legate, before he departed, he made prayer at the shrine of the holy martyr. And the abbot, seizing the opportunity, said in the hearing of all who were present, "My lord bishop, the liberty, which the monks of Canterbury claim, is the right of St. Edmund, whose body is here, and as you will not assist me to protect the liberty of his church, I put a complaint between you and him. Henceforth he may secure his right." The chancellor did not condescend to make any answer, and within a year was forced to leave England, and suffered divine vengeance.

But when the same chancellor had returned from Germany and had landed at Ipswich, and spent the night at Hitcham, a report came to the abbot that the chancellor wished to pass through St. Edmund's, and to hear mass with us on the morrow. Therefore the abbot forbade the celebration of the divine offices while the chancellor was present in the church, for he said that he had heard in London that the bishop of London had pronounced the chancellor excommunicate, in the presence of six bishops, especially for the violence which he had done to the archbishop of York, at Dover, and that the said chancellor, while excommunicate, had departed from England.

Accordingly, when the chancellor came among us on the morrow, he found no one to chant mass for him, either clerk or monk. But the priest, indeed, who stood at the first mass and at the canon of the mass, and the other priests by the altars, ceased, and stood with unmoved lips, until a messenger came and said that he had left the church. The chancellor took no notice openly, but he did many ills to the abbot, until, by the mediation of friends, they both returned to the kiss of peace.

In the matter, too, of the commercial rights of the monastery Samson showed himself true to his namesake.

The merchants of London wished to be quit from toll at the fair of St. Edmund's. Many, however, though unwillingly and under compulsion, paid it, and on this account many tumults and a great disturbance occurred between the citizens of London in their court. Wherefore, having held a meeting about the matter, they sent word to abbot Samson that they ought to be quit of toll throughout all England, under the authority of the charter which they held from king Henry the Second.

To this the abbot answered that, were it needful, he could easily bring the king to warrant him that he had never made them a charter in prejudice of our church, or to the injury of the liberties of St. Edmund, to whom the holy Edward had granted and confirmed toll and theam and all regalian rights before the conquest of England. And he added that king Henry had given to the Londoners quittance from toll throughout his own demesnes, where he had the right to give it; for in the city of St. Edmund's he could not give it, for it was not his to give.

When the Londoners heard this, they decreed with common assent that none of them should come to the fair of St. Edmund's and for two years they did absent themselves, whence our fair suffered great loss, and the offerings in our sacristy were greatly diminished. Eventually, when the bishop of London and many others had mediated, an agreement was reached between them and us whereby they should come to the fair, and some of them should pay toll, but this should be at once returned to them, that by such a device the privilege of both parties might be maintained.

But as time went on, when the abbot had come to an agreement with his knights, and as it were, rested in peace, lo ! again, "The Philistines be upon thee, Samson !"[86] For the Londoners, with one voice, threatened to level with the earth the stone houses, which the abbot had built in the same year, or to take distress a hundredfold from the men of St. Edmund, if the abbot

[86] Cf. Judges 16: 4–22.

did not at once make reparation to them for the wrong which
they had suffered from the bailiffs of the town of St. Edmund's.
For they had taken fifteen pence from the carts of the citizens
of London, which were coming from Yarmouth and carrying her-
rings, and which passed through our town. And the citizens of
London said that they had been quit of toll in every market,
and always and in every place, throughout all England, from
the time when the city of Rome was first founded, at which
time the city of London was also founded. They said that they
ought to have this privilege throughout all England, both on the
ground that their city was a privileged city, which had been
the metropolis and capital of the kingdom, and on the score of
the antiquity of the city.

The abbot, however, asked for a truce on this dispute for a
reasonable time, until the return of the king to England, that
he might consult with him on this matter; and taking the advice
of men skilled in the law, he handed back to the complainants
those fifteen pence as a pledge, without prejudice to the question of the right of either party.

In the tenth year of the abbacy of abbot Samson, by common
counsel of our chapter, we made complaint to the abbot in his
court and said that the receipts from all the goods of the towns
and boroughs of England were increased, and had grown to the
advantage of the possessors and the greater profit of their lords,
save in the case of this town, which had been wont to pay forty
pounds and had never had its dues increased. And we said that
the burghers of the city were responsible for this, since they held
so many and such large stands in the market-place, shops and
sheds and stalls, without the assent of the monastery, and at the
sole gift of the bailiffs of the town, who were annual holders
of their offices, and as it were servants of the sacristan, being
removable at his good pleasure.

But when the burghers were summoned, they answered that
they were under the jurisdiction of the king, and that they ought
not to make reply, contrary to the liberty of the towns and their
charters, concerning that which they had held and their fathers
well and in peace, for one year and a day without dispute. And
they said that it was the old custom that the bailiffs should,

without consulting the monastery, give to them places for shops and sheds in the market-place, in return for some annual payment to the bailiwick. But we disputed this, and wished the abbot to dispossess them of such things as they held without having any warrant for them.

Then the abbot came to our council, as if he had been one of ourselves, and privately informed us that he wished, so far as he could, to do right to us; but that he had to proceed in a judicial manner, and that he could not, without the judgment of the court, dispossess his free men of their lands and revenues, which they had, whether rightly or wrongly, held for many years. He added that if he were to do this, he would be liable to punishment at the discretion of the king and at the assizes of the kingdom.

The burghers, therefore, took counsel and offered the monastery a revenue of a hundred shillings for the sake of peace, and that they might hold that which they held as they had been accustomed. But we would not grant this, preferring to postpone the matter, and perchance hoping that in the time of another abbot, either we might recover all, or change the place of the fair; and so the matter for many years advanced no further.

The management of the cellar had always been a difficulty in the abbey, and, after trying various other expedients, Samson decided to undertake it himself, with what results is shown in the following:

In the year of grace one thousand one hundred and ninety-seven, certain changes and alterations were made in our church, which may not be passed over in silence. When our cellarer did not find his ancient revenues sufficient, abbot Samson ordered that fifty pounds should be given him in annual increase from Mildenhall by the hand of the prior. This was not to be paid at one time, but in instalments every month, that in each month there might be something to spend, and that the whole might not be used up in one part of the year; and so it was done for one year.

But the cellarer and his assistants complained of this, and he said that if he had had that money in his hands, he would have provided for himself and gathered stock for himself. Then the abbot, against his will indeed, granted that request. And when the beginning of August came, the cellarer had already spent the whole amount, and moreover owed twenty-six pounds, and was bound to pay a debt of fifty pounds before Michaelmas.

And when the abbot heard this, he was wroth, and spoke thus in the chapter, "I have often threatened that I would take our cellar into my own hands owing to your incompetence and extravagance, since you bind yourselves with great debt. I placed my clerk with your cellarer as a witness, that the office might be managed with greater care. But there is no clerk or monk who dares tell me the cause of the debt. It is said, indeed, that the too elaborate feasts in the prior's house, which occur with the assent of the prior and of the cellarer, and the superfluous expense in the guest-house owing to the carelessness of the guest-master, are the cause of it. You see," he went on, "the great debt which is pressing on us; tell me your opinion as to the way in which the matter should be remedied."

Many of the cloistered monks, hearing this, and, as it were, laughing to themselves, were pleased with what was said, and said privately that what the abbot said was true. The prior cast the blame on the cellarer, and the cellarer on the guest-master, and the guest-master made excuse for himself. We, of course, knew the true reason, but were silent from fear. On the morrow the abbot came and again said to the monastery, "Give me your advice as to how your cellar may be more thoughtfully and better managed." And there was no one who would answer a word, save one who said that there was no waste at all in the refectory whence any debt or burden could arise. And on the third day the abbot said the same words, and one answered, "The advice ought to come from you, as from our head."

Then the abbot said, "Since you will not give advice, and cannot rule your house for yourselves, the control of the monastery falls upon me as your father and chief guardian. I receive," he went on, "into my own hand your cellar and the charge of

the guests, and the task of getting supplies within and without."
And with these words, he deposed the cellarer and guest-master,
and replaced them with two monks, with the titles of sub-cellarer
and guest-master, and associated with them a clerk of his table,
master G., without whose assent nothing was to be done in the
matter of food and drink, or in expenditure or in receipts. The
former buyers were removed from the work of buying in the
market, and food was to be purchased by a clerk of the abbot,
and our deficits were to be made good from the abbot's treasury.
Guests who ought to be received were received, and those who
ought to be honored were honored. Officials and cloistered
monks alike took their meals in the refectory, and on all sides
superfluous expenses were cut down.

But some of the cloistered monks said among themselves,
"There were seven, yes, seven, who devoured our goods, and if
one had spoken of their devouring, he would have been regarded
as one guilty of high treason." Another said, as he stretched
forth his hands to heaven, "Blessed be God, who hath given such
a desire to the abbot, that he should correct so great faults."
And many said that it was well done.

Others said that it was not well done, thinking so great a
reformation derogatory to the honor of the house, and calling
the discretion of the abbot the ravening of a wolf; and in truth
they called to mind old dreams, to the effect that he who should
become abbot would raven as a wolf.

The knights were astonished, the people marvelled, at these
things which had been done, and one of the common sort said,
"It is a strange thing that the monks, being so many and learned
men, should allow their affairs and revenues to be confused and
mingled with the affairs of the abbot, when they had always
been wont to be separated and parted asunder. It is strange
that they do not guard themselves against the danger which will
come after the death of the abbot, if the lord king should find
things in this state."

A certain man again said that the abbot was the only one
who was skilled in external affairs, and that he ought to rule all,
who knew how to rule all. And one there was who said, "If
there were but one wise monk in so great a monastery, who

might know how to rule the house, the abbot would not have done such things." And so we became a scorn and derision to those who were round about us.

About this time it happened that the anniversary of abbot Robert was to be celebrated in the chapter, and it was decreed that a Placebo and a Dirige should be sung more solemnly than was wont, that is, with ringing of the great bells, as on the anniversaries of abbots Ording and Hugh. The cause of this was the noble deed of the said abbot Robert, who separated our goods and revenues from those of the abbot. But this solemnity was due to the counsel of some that so the heart of the lord abbot might be moved to do well. One there was, however, who thought that this was to be done to the shame of the abbot, who was accused of wishing to confound and intermingle his affairs and revenues and ours, in that he had taken our cellar into his own hand.

Then when the abbot heard the unusual ringing of bells, and knew well and considered that this was contrary to custom, he wisely hid the cause of the action and sang mass solemnly. But on the following Michaelmas, since he wished to silence the murmurs of some men in part, he appointed him who had been sub-cellarer to the post of cellarer, and ordered another to be nominated as sub-cellarer, though the same clerk remained with them and procured all needful things as before. But when that clerk passed the bounds of moderation, saying, "I am Bu," — whereby he meant that the cellarer had passed the bounds of temperance in drinking, — and when, without consulting the abbot, he held the court of the cellarer and took sureties and pledges, and received the revenues for the year and spent them with his own hand, he was publicly called chief cellarer by the people.

And when the clerk often wandered through the court, and many poor and rich debtors followed him as if he had been master and chief agent, as well as claimants of divers sorts and on divers matters, perchance one of our officials stood in the court. He saw this, and wept for shame and confusion, thinking that this was a shame to our church, and thinking of the danger which would result, and thinking that a clerk was preferred to a monk to the prejudice of the whole monastery. Accordingly he, whoever he was, procured by means of another, that this should be fitly and moderately pointed out to the lord abbot, and it came to pass that it was brought to the abbot's knowledge how arrogant the clerk was, and what he did to the shame and wrong of all; and that he was the cause of great disturbance and discord in the monastery. But when the abbot heard this, he at once ordered word to be sent to the cellarer and to the said clerk, and commanded that the cellarer should henceforth regard himself as cellarer in the receipts of money, and in holding pleas, and in all other matters, saving this only, that the said clerk should assist him, not on an equality, but as a witness and adviser.[87]

Thus the story runs on, adding detail to detail of our knowledge of monastic life. We see King John on a visit to the monastery and learn of his niggardliness, we hear of various new disputes between various officers; but, as Jessopp says,[88] these serve to vary the monotony of routine. We are furnished a list of the knights of the abbey and their duties and learn of the death and election of a prior. The *Chronicle* comes to no particular conclusion and ends before the death of Samson leaving "the monastery at peace with all men." But the monastic system decayed, and when we get down to these portraits of monastic figures by Chaucer, we see little in them to connect them with either an exalted religious life or a strenuous business life in the community.

There was also a nun, a prioress,[89] who was very simple and coy in her smiling; her greatest oath was but by St. Loy.[90] She was called Madame Eglantine. She performed divine service very well, intoned in her nose in seemly fashion, and she

[87] Cf. Augustus Jessopp, *Daily Life in a Medieval Monastery* in *The Coming of the Friars* (G. P. Putnam's Sons, 15th impression, 1908).

[88] *The Coming of the Friars*, p. 139.

[89] I.e. among the pilgrims to Canterbury.

[90] Patron saint of goldsmiths who refused to swear an oath; to say, therefore, that the Prioress' greatest oath was by St. Loy is to say that she swore not at all.

spoke French properly after the school of Stratford-on-the-Bowe,
for Parisian French was unknown to her. She was well-bred at
meals and let no morsel fall from her lips nor did she wet her
fingers much in the sauce. She could carry a morsel well and
see to it that no drop fell upon her breast. She had set her
heart on having good manners. She wiped her upper lip so
clean that not a bit of grease was seen in her cup after she had
taken a drink. She reached after her food politely and really
was good company and very pleasant and amiable in bearing,
took pains to imitate courtly behavior, to be stately in carriage
and held worthy of reverence. And, to speak of her sensibili-
ties, she was so loving and piteous that she would weep if she
saw a mouse if it were caught in a trap or bleeding. She had
some little dogs that she fed on roast meat and fine bread and
would weep bitterly if one of them died, or even if you hit
one smartly with a stick; all with her was sensibility and tenderness. Her hood was very neatly fastened; her nose straight;
her eyes gray as glass; her mouth small, soft and red. She had
a wonderful forehead, it was almost a span high, I believe; and,
to be accurate, she was not undergrown. Her cloak was very
chic, as I was aware. She had a set of coral beads on her arm,
varied with green ones at intervals, and on this string of beads
hung a very fine brooch of gold on which was first engraved a
capital A and then the legend, *Amor vincit omnia* (Love conquers all).

There was a monk, a splendid candidate for athletic honors,
a bold rider who loved hunting; a manly man, capable of being
an abbot. He had many a fancy horse in his stable; and, when
he rode, you could hear his bridle jingling in the whistling wind
as clear and as loud as does the bell of the chapel of this lord's
monastery. The Rule of St. Maur or of St. Benedict, because
they were old and somewhat strict, he disregarded. He was
inclined to pooh-pooh old things and take his stand with the
moderns. He didn't care a plucked hen for the text that says
that hunters are not holy men, nor for the idea that a monk
out of his cloister is like a fish out of water. He held such
things not worth an oyster, and I was rather disposed to agree
with him. Why should he study and make himself mad with

always poring over a book in the cloister or doing manual labor, as St. Augustine bade? How is the world to be served? Let Augustine follow such courses if he likes them. Therefore, this monk was a hunter in earnest; he had some greyhounds, swift as birds in flight; his whole heart was set on riding and hunting rabbits — he spared no expense. I noticed that his sleeves were trimmed at the wrist with fur and that the finest to be had; and that to fasten his hood under his chin he had a very curious pin made of gold — a lover's knot formed the larger end of it. His head was bald and shone like glass, his face, also, shone as if it had been oiled. He was a lord fat and in a flourishing physical condition; his eyes, deepset and rolling in his head, gleamed like the fires under a furnace; his boots were supple and his horse well cared for. Now certainly he was a fine specimen of a prelate — he was not pale like a tormented ghost. Of all roasts he liked best a fat swan. His riding horse was as brown as a berry.

The restlessness and skepticism largely engendered in Europe by the Crusades roused many good souls to a feeling that a great revival of gospel Christianity was needed.[91] Two of these, Dominic, a Spaniard, and Giovanni Bernardone, an Italian better known as Francis of Assisi, founded new religious fraternities or brotherhoods since called orders of friars (from Latin *frater*, brother), Dominicans or Black Friars and Franciscans or Gray Friars, named from the respective colors of their clothing. These friars were not to remain in solitude, devoted to self-cultivation like monks, but were bound to go out among the people preaching and offering practical assistance of all kinds. Francis, soon canonized, insisted that his companions should work in absolute poverty, depending on alms for subsistence. This principle was likewise later adopted by St. Dominic. On the whole the Franciscan order has left us better records of its activities and was the more characteristic of the whole movement, and our first two documents relate to

[91] Cf. the title essay in Jessopp, *op. cit.*

it. The first consists of the more important provisions in the *Rule of St. Francis*, the constitution of his order.

(After a long prolog.) I. In the name of God: here begins the *Rule of the Friars Minor*,[92] the first chapter.

The rule for the life of the friars minor is this, to observe and keep the holy gospel of our Lord Jesus Christ by living in obedience without property and in chastity. Brother Francis promises obedience and reverence to the lord Pope Honorius and to his lawful successors and to the Church of Rome. All other brothers are bound to obey Brother Francis[93] and his successors.

II. Of Those Who Are to Be Admitted to This Life and How They May Be Admitted.

If any who desire to take up this life come to our brethren, let the latter send them to the provincial ministers,[94] to whom only is granted license to receive brothers. The ministers shall diligently examine the candidates in the Christian faith and the sacraments of the Church. The ministers shall carefully examine and if the applicants steadfastly believe in them (i.e. the faith and the sacraments referred to) and will truly and faithfully grant and confess them, and (agree) steadfastly to keep them to the end of their lives: and if they are not married: . . . let the ministers say to them the words of the holy gospel, namely that they go and sell all their goods, and themselves try to distribute the proceeds to the poor:[95] but if they cannot do the latter, their good intention is sufficient. And the brethren shall

[92] St. Francis with characteristic humility dubbed his followers "brothers of lower rank than all others," hence friars minor or minorites. The materials for our knowledge of the life and character of St. Francis are practically all included in the *Temple Classics* and *Everyman's Library;* these include *The Little Flowers; The Mirror of Perfection*, the *Life* by Bonaventura, and other *Lives*. The standard work of modern scholarship on St. Francis is the *Life* by Paul Sabatier. It has been translated from the original French into English. (Charles Scribner's Sons, 1912.) [93] St. Francis always called himself Brother Francis.

[94] Europe, for purposes of organization, was divided into sections called provinces and over each of these was set a sort of superintendent called a provincial minister. Notice that the titles of even the superior officers in the order mean service; *minister* is from the identical Latin word meaning *servant*, cf. Matt. 20: 25–28.   [95] Cf. Matt. 19: 21.

see to it that they do not meddle with nor busy themselves with their temporal good nor with the procuring thereof, in order that instead they may freely do whatsoever God suggests or inspires in their minds. Nevertheless, if advice be demanded or asked of them in this matter, the ministers have permission to send them (i.e. the persons asking the advice) to God-fearing persons, by whose counsel their goods may be distributed and given to the poor.

Then after this (examination and giving up their property) the ministers shall give the initiates the clothing of probation, that is to say, two coats without hoods, a cord, a femoral and a shirt. Unless it be thought expedient by the said ministers that the time of probation be lengthened or shortened in special cases, when the year of probation is finished and ended, the probationers may be received to obedience and profession.

And in no wise may it be lawful for them to forsake this religious order, after and according to the commandment of the Pope, for, as the holy gospel says, no man putting his hand to the plow and looking back is fit for the kingdom of heaven.[96]

And those who have made their profession and promised obedience shall have one coat with a hood and another without . . . and such as have need or are constrained by necessity may wear shoes. And all the brethren must be clothed in simple and cheap garments. And they may patch and mend them with pieces of sack-cloth or with other pieces, with the blessing of God. And I warn the brethren not to despise nor judge [97] such men as they see clothed in delicate and soft raiment, or with colored and costly array, or using delicious meats and drinks, but I charge each one rather to judge and despise himself.

III. How the Brethren Should Behave Themselves when They Travel.

I counsel and also warn and exhort my brethren in our Lord Jesus Christ that they brawl not, nor strive in their words of communication nor judge and condemn other men; but that they be meek, peaceable, soft,[98] gentle and courteous, speaking honestly and answering every man as they should and ought.

[96] Cf. Luke 9: 62.   [97] Cf. Matt. 7: 1.   [98] Cf. Proverbs 15: 1.

And they shall not ride unless they be constrained by evident necessity or else by sickness. Into what house or place soever they enter they shall first say, "Peace be unto this house." [99] And, according to the holy gospel, they may eat of all such food as is set before them.

IV. That the Brethren May not Receive Any Coin or Money.

I command steadfastly and strictly all the brethren that in no wise they receive any sort of coin or money, either directly in person or through any sort of intermediary. Nevertheless, for the needs of sick brothers, and for the clothing of the brethren, through spiritual friends, the ministers only and custodians and wardens shall have diligent care and charge according to the places, to the times and seasons, and to cold countries and regions, as it shall seem to them expedient according to their necessity and need. Saving this always, that, as I said before, they may not receive any sort of coin or money.

V. How the Brethren Shall Busy and Occupy Themselves in Bodily Labor.

The brethren to whom God hath given grace and strength to labor shall truly and devoutly work in such wise that Idleness,[100] the enemy of the soul, being excluded and put away, they quench not the inward fervor and spirit of holy prayer and devotion to which all transitory and temporal things ought to yield and give place. As for pay for their labor they may receive for themselves and their brethren those things that are needful and necessary for their bodies except coin or money. (Let them receive their pay) in a lowly and meek spirit, as pertains to the servants of God and the true followers of most perfect and holy poverty.

VI. How the Brethren May not in any wise Burden Themselves with Any Kind of Property.

The brethren shall have no property, either in houses or lands, or rents or any sort of thing, but shall be like pilgrims and

---

[99] Cf. Luke 10: 1–16.
[100] Cf. *ante*, p. 19, the first quotation from the *Rule of St. Benedict*.

strangers [101] in this world, in poverty and meekness, serving Almighty God. They shall boldly,[102] faithfully, surely and meekly go for alms. Nor shall they, nor ought they to be ashamed, for our Lord made Himself poor in this world.[103]

VII. Of Penance to Be Enjoined on the Brethren that Fall into Sin.

VIII. Of the Election of the Minister General of This Fraternity and of the Chapter at Whitsuntide. (Pentecost, fifty days after Easter.)

IX. Of the Preachers.

The brethren shall not preach in the diocese of any bishop who forbids them to do so. And none of the brethren shall be so bold as to preach to the people unless he has been examined, approved by the minister general of this brotherhood and admitted by him to the office of preaching. I warn also and require and exhort the same brethren that in their preaching their words and speech be select and chaste to the profit and edification of the people, showing to them vices and virtues, pain and joy in few words; because our Lord's sermons on earth were but brief.

X. Of the Admonition and Correction of the Brethren.

XI. That the Brethren Are Forbidden to Enter Nunneries.

XII. Of Those that Desire to Go among the Saracens or Other Unbelievers.

Whosoever of the brethren by divine inspiration wishes to go among the Saracens or other infidels, shall seek permission of their provincial ministers and the latter shall not grant it except to such as they think to be serious and able and sufficient to be sent. These things by obedience I enjoin on the ministers that they ask and request one of the cardinals of the Pope and of the Holy Church of Rome to be governor, defender and corrector of this brotherhood, that we always being subject and abject under the feet of Holy Church, being stable and steadfast in the catholic and Christian faith, may truly keep

[101] Cf. Hebrews 11: 13.   [102] Cf. Matt. 7: 7.   [103] Cf. 2 Cor. 8 : 9.

poverty and meekness and the holy gospel of our Lord Jesus Christ, which we have steadfastly and strictly vowed and promised to do.

Conclusion.

And, therefore, in no way shall it be lawful for any man to violate or oppose this charter or writing of our confirmation, or to go contrary to it, or to move against it by boldness and presumption or by rash audacity in any way, for whosoever is so hardy as to presume or undertake to do such a thing shall know and understand that he thereby will fall into the great wrath of God and of His blessed apostles Peter and Paul.

Given at the Lateran, November 26, in the eighth year of our pontificate (1224).

(A long note on chapter 5 follows.)

Thomas of Eccleston, a writer of whom we know only what he tells us in his book, *Liber de Adventu Minorum in Angliam* (*Account of the Arrival of the Minorites in England*), but who seems to be a careful investigator of Franciscan history and was a contemporary of King Henry III of England (king 1216–1272), describes in the following paragraphs how the doctrines of St. Francis were brought to England. It is to be noted that, according to this account, the Dominicans had already established themselves in London and at Oxford when the Franciscans arrived.

In the year of our Lord 1224, in the time of the lord Pope Honorius, and in the same year in which the *Rule of the Blessed Francis* was confirmed by him, in the eighth year of the reign of King Henry, son of John, on the third day after the Feast of the Nativity of the Blessed Virgin,[104] which fell that year on a Sunday, the Minorite Brethren first landed in England at Dover; there were four clerks and five laymen. The following were the clerks: first, Brother Agnellus of Pisa, a deacon of about thirty years old, who had been appointed by the Blessed Fran-

[104] Sept 11. (The Feast of the Nativity of the Virgin is on Sept. 8.)

cis in the last general chapter, Provincial Minister in England.
. . . The second was Brother Richard of Ingworth, an Englishman, a priest and preacher somewhat more advanced in years,
who was the first to preach to the people beyond the mountains.[105] . . . The third was Brother Richard of Devon, also an
Englishman, a young acolyte, who left us divers examples of
longsuffering and obedience. . . . The fourth was Brother William Ashby, a youthful Englishman, still a novice wearing the
garb of probation.

The laymen were these: First, Brother Henry of Ceruise, a
Lombard, who, on account of his sanctity and great discretion,
was made warden of London, and who, when his period of labor
in England was completed, after the numbers of the brethren had
been increased, returned to his own country. The second was
Brother Laurence, from Beauvais, who was engaged at the beginning in uncompleted work, according to the injunctions of
the *Rule*; afterwards he journeyed to the Blessed Francis, whom
he was favored to see frequently, and by whose conversation
he was comforted; finally, the holy Father freely gave him his
robe, and with a most pleasant benediction sent him back joyful
to England. . . . The third was Brother W. of Florence, who
returned to France, soon after the reception of the brethren (in
England). The fourth was Melioratus; the fifth, Brother Jaco-
bus Ultramontanus, still a novice in the garb of probation.

These nine, who had been brought across for charity to England and freely supplied with necessaries by the monks of Fé-
camp, came to Canterbury and abode at the priory of the Holy
Trinity for two days; then four of them, to wit, Brother Richard
of Ingworth, Brother Richard of Devon, Brother Henry and
Brother Melioratus, proceeded to London. The five others went
to the Hospital of Poor Priests, where they remained until they
had prepared a place of residence for themselves; soon after, a
small room within the school was given to them, where they
remained from day to day, shut up almost constantly. When
the scholars returned home in the evening, the brethren entered
the house where the scholars had been seated, made themselves
a fire, and sat near it; sometimes, when they wished to drink,

[105] I.e. north of the Alps.

they placed on a fire a pot with the dregs of beer, and put a dish in the pot, and drank in turn, speaking each some words of pious instruction; and as he bears witness who shared in their real simplicity, and was a participator in their holy poverty, their drink was often so thick that, when the pots came to be heated, they poured in water, and so drank with pleasure.

The four brethren, of whom I have spoken above, when they came to London, betook themselves to the Friars Preachers (i.e. the Dominicans), by whom they were kindly received, and with whom they remained for two weeks, eating and drinking what was set before them, like intimate friends. Afterwards they hired a house in the village of Cornhill, where they constructed cells, stuffing the interstices between the cells with grass. They remained until the following summer in their early simplicity, without a chantry, because they had as yet no privilege to erect altars and celebrate divine service in their house. Just before the Feast of All Saints,[106] and before Brother Agnellus had come to London, Brother Richard of Ingworth and Brother Richard of Devon came to Oxford, and there also were most kindly received by the Preaching Friars in whose refectory they ate and in whose dormitory they slept for eight days. Afterwards they hired for themselves a house in the parish of St. Ebba and there remained without a chantry until the following summer. There the Blessed Jesus sowed a grain of mustard-seed which afterwards became the greatest among herbs.[107] From that place Brother Richard of Ingworth and Brother Richard of Devon set out to Northampton where they took up their abode in the hospital. And afterwards they hired for themselves a house in the parish of St. Egidius, where the first warden was Brother Peter of Spain who wore an iron corslet next his body and furnished many other examples of perfection. The first warden of Oxford was Brother William Ashby, hitherto a novice; he was now given the dress of the Order. The first warden of Cambridge was Brother Thomas of Spain; of Lincoln, Brother Henry Misericorde, a layman. The lord John Travers first received the brethren at Cornhill, and gave them a house; a certain layman from Lombardy was appointed warden, who first taught letters

[106] Nov. 1.   [107] Cf. Matt. 13: 31, 32.

by night in the church of the Blessed Peter at Cornhill, and afterwards became Vicar of England, while Brother Agnellus went to the general chapter. In the vicarate he had as his associate Brother Richard of Ingworth; in the end, being unable to endure such heights of prosperity and being weakened by so many orders, he became insane and apostatized from the Order. It is worthy of note that in the second year of the administration of Brother Peter, fifth Minister of England, that is to say, in the thirty-second year after the arrival of the brethren in England, the number of brethren living in the province of England, in forty-nine places, amounted to twelve hundred forty-two.

The movement flourished, got to itself learning, and produced great scholars. Englishmen of European scholastic reputation like Alexander Hales, Roger Bacon,[108] and Duns Scotus were Franciscans; continentals like Albertus Magnus and Thomas Aquinas, the official theologians of the Church, were Dominicans. In less than fifty years after the Minorites landed at Dover, a member of the Order had become Archbishop of Canterbury and Bonaventura, General of the Order, had declined the Archbishopric of York. "In 1281 Jerome of Ascoli, Bonaventura's successor as General, was elected Pope, assuming the name of Nicholas IV." [109]

But for some reason the movement lost the purity of its early ideals, the orders fell into decay, and within a century of the election of Nicholas IV, we find an English poem like the following, purporting to be written by a novice in one of the orders, full of severe censure of the everyday life of the friars.

No priest, monk, canon nor any man of religion is so fervent in his devotion as is this holy friar. For some devote themselves to chivalry, some to rioting and ribaldry; but friars devote themselves to great study and to long prayers; whoso keeps

[108] Cf. *post*, pp. 391–401.   [109] Cf. Jessopp, *op. cit.*, p. 45.

their whole *Rule* both in word and deed will certainly, I am sure, reap heaven's bliss as his reward.

Men can see by their faces that they are men of severe penance and also that their living is thin and weak. I have lived now forty years and fatter men in the kidneys I never saw than these friars in countries where they wander about. Without meat they become so emaciated and penance so subdues them that each must ride on horseback when they must pack up and leave town.

Alas ! that it ever should be so that such clerks as they should walk from town to town to seek their living. By God who won all this world, he who organized this order methinks must have been a very simple sort of man. For they have naught to live by, they wander here and there and deal in divers merchandise just as if they were pedlars.

They deal in purses, pins and knives, in girdles and gloves for girls and women; but always the husband comes off ill where friars are numerous. For when the goodman is from home and the friar comes to his dame, he spares neither for sin nor shame to do his will. If they got no help from housewives when husbands are not in, the welfare of the friars would be bad and they would brew so thin !

Some friars carry rich furs about for greater dames and stout to trim their clothes on the outside with, after they are finished. For some vaire,[110] for others gryse,[110] for some cloth and others silk, and also many sorts of spice they carry in their bags. Whatever pleases the women the friars have at hand; but the husband who must foot the bill gets but small return.

Tricks they know and many a scheme; for one can with a pound of soap get him a kirtle and a cape and something else to boot. Why should I swear an oath? There is no pedlar that carries a pack can sell his wares half so dear as that friar can. For if he gives a woman a knife that cost but two-pence, he will have pay worth ten knives, I know before he goes.

Let every man that lives here, if he have wife or fair daughter, allow no friar to shrive them in public or in private. Though women seem steadfast in heart, they can make their hearts

---

[110] Various kinds of fine furs for which we have no modern equivalent names.

changeable with fair behest and fable and fulfill their desires. Beware always of the limitor [111] and of his fellow as well, for if they play their tricks in your house, it will probably turn out ill for you.

.   .   .   .

They say that they (the friars) destroy sin, but they (really) maintain people most therein; for if a man had slain all his kin, let him go to a friar for absolution, and for less than a pair of shoes he will wash the murderer clean and declare that the sin he has committed will never harm his soul. It seems in sooth that men say of them in many different lands that the cursed caitiff Cain founded these orders.

Now see in truth whether it be so: the name Carmelite [112] begins with C, Augustinian [112] begins with A, Jacobin with I and Minorite with M; thus Caim [113] started these four orders and filled the world with error and hypocrisy. All the wickedness that men can recount dwells among them; there is no room for other. souls in hell, there is such a crowd of friars.

They travel eagerly and busily, to humiliate the secular clergy; [114] they slander them and thus do wrong. Whoso lives many years will see that it will happen to the friars as it did to the Templars [115] who lived among us so long. For they did

[111] A friar licensed to beg in a certain district and limited to that district.

[112] Augustinians and Carmelites were less important orders of friars founded after the greater two.

[113] The preferred spelling of the name in the Middle Ages.

[114] Secular clergy or secular priests, so-called to distinguish them from regular clergy or those living under monastic or other rules, were priests living out in the world (Latin *sœculum*) among the people; they were also called possessioners because they were in possession of the parish churches and incomes.

[115] The Knights Templars or Poor Knights of Christ and of the Temple of Solomon were one of the three great military orders (the other two were the Teutonic Knights and the Knights of St. John or Knights Hospitallers) founded in the twelfth century. Its object was to protect pilgrims after the first Crusade. The Order became widespread, popular and wealthy, its history is that of the Crusades. The Order was suppressed in France, where it originated, on charges of heresy and immorality, after several knights had been tortured and after a trial which lasted for two years, on May 6, 1312. The real motive for the suppression was that the Order had become so great that Philip IV (the Fair) of France felt that in the interest of centralizing authority in his realm, he would have to get rid of it.

not regard religion but lived as they pleased, but they were brought down and destroyed through the ordinance of the king.

The friars are doing dreadful things that can never come to good ending; the friar will go on for eight or nine years or perhaps ten or eleven.[116]   But when his time has fully passed he then has no scruple about stealing six or seven marks from any body.   These friars, so wily and so gay, have arranged such anniversary masses that no possessioners [114] can keep up with them.

It fell to them to live entirely by begging on alms gathered from place to place and for all that helped them they were to pray and sing (masses).   But now this land is raked so clean that secular priests [114] can scarcely get positions on account of these friars.   That is a wonderful thing and a quaint custom ordained among them that friars are become annual priests and in that way sell their songs.

Very wisely they can preach and talk; but they do nothing but talk.   I was a friar for a long time and therefore know whereof I speak.   But when I saw that their lying didn't agree with their preaching, I cast off my friar's clothing and straightway went my way.   Other leave took I none when I went but I sent them all to the devil, both prior and convent.

Though I am out of the order I am no apostate; I lacked one month of twelve and nine odd days or ten (of completing my novitiate).   I made ready to leave; before the day came to take the final vow I went my way throughout the town in sight of many men.   Lord God, who with such dreadful pains didst redeem mankind, let no man after me have the desire to be a friar.[117]

[116] The friars' organizations, along with other religious corporations, were done away with in England in the time of Henry VIII.

[117] It would almost seem that Chaucer had this poem before him when he composed his description of the friar in the *Prolog to the Canterbury Tales*. Cf. ll. 208–271.   He uses many of the same expressions as occur in this poem. Cf. Skeat's notes to Chaucer's account of the friar.   Chaucer, in fact, has little that is serious to say of any of the regular clergy, i.e. those living under rules.   But he makes up for this in his portrait of the country priest.   Cf. *Prolog to the Canterbury Tales*, ll. 479–530.   The picture there given reminds one of the character of Dr. Primrose in the *Vicar of Wakefield*, or of Cowper's model preacher in the *Task*, Book III, ll. 395–413.

The Teutonic heirs of the Roman Empire, who, in their earlier years, according to Tacitus,[118] had shunned cities, began about the tenth century, in England at least, to build towns or boroughs and by 1300 or 1400 had come to regard them as very important. The name borough (Old English *burh*), the characteristic medieval name for towns in England, meant originally a fortified place, and, as applied to towns, probably goes back to the time when Edward the Elder (king 900–924), in his efforts to reconquer the Danelagh, fortified high places and assigned chiefs as their guardians. About the high place was an open space "inclosed by a ditch, re-enforced by a rampart of earth protected by a wooden palisade. Often people coming to these strongholds for protection engaged in trade and other industries." [119] These traders and artisans, desiring the protection of the fortification and the chief and, later, eager for more freedom and scope for their own action, are the organizers of the gilds of which we have treated,[120] and the leaders in demanding from nobles and kings charters in which their exact rights and duties as burgesses should be set forth. It is from town charters that some of our most valuable information regarding town life is derived. These charters are very numerous; for, though but eighty English towns are named in *Doomsday Book*, the Norman Conquest, by stimulating foreign trade and keeping up a connection with the Continent, gave a great impetus to city life; and England built many towns. But these charters are also very much alike, and hence one or two samples will illustrate the whole mass.[121]

---

[118] Cf. *ante*, p. 14.   [119] Cross, *op. cit.*, p. 47.   [120] Cf. *ante*, p. 228 *seq.*

[121] That must have been a kind of charter which Leofric, at the plea of Godiva, granted to Coventry. The story, as told in Sir William Dugdale's *Antiquities of Warwickshire* (1656), is as follows: "The Countess Godiva, bearing an extraordinary affection to this place (Coventry), often and earnestly besought her husband that, for the love of God and the blessed Virgin, he would free it from that grievous servitude whereunto it was subject; but he, rebuking her for importuning him in a

Before quoting the charters, however, we should notice another sort of interesting municipal document, namely, the statement of town custom. For this purpose the *Customs of Chester* and *Newcastle-upon-Tyne*, the former from *Doomsday Book*, have been selected.

(*a*) The city of Chester, in the time of King Edward, paid tax as being of fifty hides;[122] three and a half hides of which were outside of the city. That is, one and a half hides were beyond the bridge, and two hides in Newton and Redcliff, and in the bishop's borough; these paid tax with the city.

In the time of King Edward, there were in the city 431 houses paying tax. And besides these the bishop had 56 tax-paying houses. Then the city paid ten and a half marks [123] of silver; two parts belonged to the king and the third to the earl. And the following laws existed there:

When peace had been granted by the hand of the king, or by his letter or through his bailiff, if any one broke it, the king had 100 shillings for it. But if the same peace of the king, at his order had been granted by the earl, if it was broken, of the 100 shillings which were given therefor, the earl had the third penny.

manner so inconsistent with his profit, commanded that she should thenceforward forbear to move thereon; yet she, out of her womanish pertinacity, continued to solicit him, insomuch that he told her if she would ride on horseback naked from one end of the town to the other, in sight of all the people, he would grant her request. Whereunto she replied, 'But will ye give me leave to do so?' And he replying, 'Yes,' the noble lady, upon an appointed day, got on horseback naked, with her hair loose, so that it covered all her body but her legs; and thus performing her journey, she returned with joy to her husband, who thereupon granted to the inhabitants a charter of freedom. . . . In memory whereof the picture of him and his lady was set up in a south window of Trinity Church in this city about Richard II's time, his right hand holding a charter with these words written thereon:

'I, Luriche, for love of thee,
doe make Coventry Tol-free.'"

The Works of Tennyson with Notes by the Author, edited by Hallam, Lord Tennyson (The Macmillan Co., 1913), pp. 901, 902. Cf. Tennyson's *Godiva* and Landor's *Leofric and Godiva*. Leofric died in 1057.

[122] A hide was a unit of taxation or of measurement, equalling in the latter case approximately 120 acres. It is here evidently the former.

[123] The mark of silver was equal to 13*s*. 4*d*.; of gold, £6.

If, however, the same peace was infringed when granted by the reeve of the king or the officer of the earl, it was compounded for by forty shillings, and the third penny belonged to the earl.

If any free man of the king broke the peace which had been granted and killed a man in his house, all his land and money came to the king, and he himself became an outlaw. The earl had the same concerning his man making this forfeiture. No one, however, except the king, was able to grant peace again to an outlaw.

He who shed blood between Monday morning and the ninth hour of Saturday compounded for it with ten shillings. From the ninth hour of Saturday to Monday morning bloodshed was compounded for with twenty shillings. Similarly any one paid twenty shillings who did this in the twelve days after Christmas, on the day of the Purification of the Blessed Mary, on the first day of Easter, the first day of Pentecost, Ascension Day, on the Assumption or Nativity of the Blessed Mary and on the day of All Saints.

He who killed a man on these holy days compounded for it with £4; but on other days with forty shillings. Similarly he who committed burglary or assault, on those feast days or on Sunday £4. On other days forty shillings.

Any one setting prisoners free [124] in the city gave ten shillings. But if the reeve of the king or of the earl committed this offence he compounded for it with twenty shillings.

He who committed theft or robbery or exercised violence upon a woman in a house compounded for each of these with forty shillings.

If a widow had illegitimate intercourse with any one she compounded for it with twenty shillings; a girl, however, with ten shillings for a similar cause.

He who in the city seized upon the land of another and was not able to prove it to be his, was fined forty shillings. Similarly also he who made a claim upon it, if he was not able to prove it to be his.

He who wished to make relief of his own land or that of his relative gave ten shillings.

[124] The word *hangewitham*, thus translated, has also been considered to mean the offence of hanging a person without warrant of law. — Ducange.

If he was not able or did not wish to do this the reeve took his land into the hand of the king.

He who did not pay the tax at the period at which he owed it compounded for it with ten shillings.

If fire burned the city, he from whose house it started compounded for it with three oras[125] of pennies, and gave to his next neighbor two shillings. Of all these forfeitures two parts belonged to the king and the third to the earl.

If without the license of the king ships came to the port of the city or departed from the port, from each man who was on the ships the king and the earl had forty shillings. If against the peace of the king and after his prohibition the ship approached, as well it as the men, with all things which were upon it, did the king and the earl have.

If, however, with the peace and license of the king it had come, those who were in it sold what they had in peace; but when it went away, four pence from each lading did the king and the earl have. If to those having martens' skins the reeve of the king gave orders that to no one should they sell until they had first brought them and shown them to him, he who did not observe this compounded for it by paying forty shillings.

A man or a woman making false measure in the city, and being arrested, compounded for it with four shillings. Similarly a person making bad ale, was either placed in the ducking stool or gave four shillings to the reeve. This forfeiture the officer of the king and of the earl received in the city, in whosesoever land it had been, either of the bishop or of another man. Similarly also, if any one held the toll back beyond three nights, he compounded for it with forty shillings.

In the time of King Edward there were in this city seven moneyers,[126] who gave seven pounds to the king and the earl, besides the ferm,[127] when the money was turned over.

[125] An ora is a number of pennies, varying in different times and places, here possibly sixteen or twenty.
[126] The moneyers were men who had the contract for coining money, paying a fee for the privilege of reserving to themselves the seigniorage.
[127] A ferm was a fixed amount paid as a lump sum in place of a number of smaller or more irregular payments.

There were at that time twelve judges of the city, and these were from the men of the king, and of the bishop, and of the earl; if any one of these remained away from the hundred court on the day in which it sat, without a clear excuse, he compounded for it with ten shillings, between the king and the earl.

For repairing the city wall and the bridge the reeve summoned one man to come from each hide of the county. If the man of any one did not come his lord compounded for it to the king and the earl with forty shillings. This forfeiture was in addition to the ferm.

This city paid at that time of ferm £45 and three bundles of marten's skins. The third part belonged to the earl, and two to the king.

When Earl Hugh received it, it was worth only £30, for it was much wasted. There were 205 fewer houses than there had been in the time of King Edward. Now there are just as many there as he found.

Murdret held this city from the earl for £70 and one mark of gold. He had at ferm for £50 and one mark of gold all the pleas of the earl in the county and in the hundreds, with the exception of Inglefeld.

The land on which the temple of St. Peter stands, which Robert of Rodelend claimed for demesne land, as the county has proved, never pertained to the manor, outside the city, but pertains to the borough; and it has always been in the custom of the king and the earl, like that of other burgesses.

(b) These are the laws and customs which the burgesses of Newcastle-upon-Tyne had in the time of Henry, king of England, and ought to have:

Burgesses may make seizure for debt from those dwelling outside, within their market place and without, and within their house and without, and within their borough and without, without the license of the reeve, unless courts are held in the borough, and unless they are in the army or on guard at a castle.

From a burgess a burgess is not allowed to make seizure for debt without the license of the reeve.

If a burgess has agreed upon anything in the borough with

those dwelling outside, the debtor, if he acknowledges it, must pay the debt himself, or he must grant right in the borough.

Suits which arise in the borough are to be held and finished there, except those which belong to the king's crown.

If any burgess is summoned on any prosecution, he shall not plead outside of the borough except for want of a court. Nor must he respond without day and term, unless he shall have first fallen into an absurd defense; except with regard to things which pertain to the crown.

If a ship has put in at Tynemouth and wishes to depart, it is allowed to the burgesses to buy whatever they wish.

If a suit arises between a burgess and a merchant, it shall be settled before the third tide.

Whatever merchandise a vessel has brought by sea ought to be carried to land, except salt and brine, which ought to be sold on the ship.

If anyone has held land in burgage for a year and a day justly and without prosecution, he need not make defense against a claimant, unless the claimant has been outside the realm of England, or in the case where he is a boy having no power to speak.

If a burgess has a son in his house, at his table, the son shall have the same liberty as his father.

If a villain comes to stay in a borough, and there for a year and a day stays as a burgess in the borough, let him remain altogether, unless it has been said beforehand by himself or by his lord that he is to remain for a certain time.

If any burgess makes an accusation concerning any matter, he cannot wage battle against a burgess, but let the burgess defend himself by law, unless it is concerning treason, when he ought to defend himself by battle. Nor can a burgess wage battle against a villain, unless he has first departed from his burgage.

No merchant, unless he is a burgess, may buy any wool, hides, or other merchandise, outside of the town, nor inside of the borough except from burgesses.

If forfeiture happens to a burgess, he shall give six *oras* to the reeve.

In the borough there is no merchant, nor heriot, nor blood fine, nor *stengesdint*.

Each burgess may have his oven and hand-mill if he wishes, saving the king's right to the oven.

If a woman is in transgression concerning bread or concerning ale, no one ought to intermeddle except the reeve. If she shall have transgressed a second time, let her be whipped for her transgression. If for a third time she shall have transgressed, let justice be done upon her.

No one except a burgess may buy clothes for dyeing, nor make, nor shear them.

A burgess may give his land, or sell it, and go whither he wishes, freely and quietly, unless he is engaged in a suit.

The charters selected are those of Lincoln, granted by Henry II, and of Winchester, granted by his son Richard I, which follow:

(a) Henry, by the grace of God, king of England, duke of Normandy and Aquitaine, count of Anjou, to the bishop of Lincoln, justiciars, sheriffs, barons, officers and all his faithful, French and English, of Lincoln, greeting. Know that I have conceded to my citizens of Lincoln all their liberties and customs and laws, which they had in the time of Edward and William and Henry, kings of England; and their gild merchant of the men of the city and of other merchants of the county, just as they had it in the time of our aforesaid predecessors, kings of England, best and most freely. And all men who dwell within the four divisions of the city and attend the market are to be at the gilds and customs and assizes of the city as they have been best in the time of Edward, William and Henry, kings of England. I grant to them moreover, that if anyone shall buy any land within the city, of the burgage of Lincoln, and shall have held it for a year and a day without any claim, and he who has bought it is able to show that the claimant has been in the land of England within the year and has not claimed it, for the future as before he shall hold it well and in peace, and without any prosecution. I confirm also to them, that if anyone shall have remained in the city of Lincoln for a year and a day without claim on the part of any claimant, and has given the customs, and is able to show by the laws and customs of the city that the claimant has been in existence in the land of England and has not made a claim against him, for the future as in the past he shall remain in peace, in my city of Lincoln, as my citizen. Witnesses, E., bishop of Lisieux; Thomas, chancellor; H., constable; Henry of Essex, constable. At Nottingham.

(*b*) Richard, by the Grace of God, King of England, Duke of Normandy, etc., to the archbishops, bishops, abbots, earls, barons, justices, sheriffs, ministers, and all bailiffs, and his faithful subjects of his whole land, greeting. Know ye, that we have granted to our citizens of Winchester, of the gild merchant, that none of them shall be impleaded outside the walls of the city of Winchester in any plea, except pleas of outside tenures, moneyers and our ministers being excepted. We have granted also to them that none of them engage in the duel, and that for pleas pertaining to our crown they may proceed according to the ancient custom of the city. These things also we have granted to them, that the citizens of Winchester, of the gild merchant, be quit of duty, custom and bridge toll, in the market and outside, and through the sea ports of our whole land this side of the sea and beyond; and that no one be amerced save according to the ancient law of the city, as it prevailed in the time of our ancestors; and that they shall hold justly all their lands and tenures and pledges and dues. And, in the case of their lands and tenures, which are in another city, their rights shall be maintained according to the custom of the city; and for all dues adjustable at Winchester and for the pledges made there, they shall hold pleas at Winchester. And if anyone in our whole land takes duty or custom from the men of Winchester, of the gild merchant, after he has failed of right, the sheriff of Southampton or the reeve of Winchester shall take a pledge for his appearance at Winchester. Moreover, for the benefit of the city, we have granted to them, that they shall be quit of exactions and levies, except a levy made by our sheriff or other officer.

These said customs we grant to them, and all other liberties and franchises which they had in the time of our ancestors; and if any unjust customs have been levied in war, they shall cease; and whoever seeks the city of Winchester with his merchandise, from whatever place, whether a foreigner or other, shall come, stay and return in our peace, rendering right customs, and no one shall disturb him, on account of this, our charter. Therefore, we wish and firmly decree that they and their heirs have by inheritance and hold all the aforesaid, of us and our heirs. Witness, Walter, Archbishop of Rouen; Roger of Bath, Henry of Coventry, bishops; Bertram of Verdun, John Marshall, William Marshall. Given by the hand of John of Alencon, archdeacon of Lisieu, our vice-chancellor, at Nunancurte, on the fourteenth day of March, in the first year of our reign.

London is naturally the most interesting of all English cities, and we are fortunate in possessing a very spirited and detailed account of London life in the late twelfth century, which will be quoted entire. This *Description of London* was written by William Fitzstephen, a devoted follower of Thomas a Becket, as an introduction to his *Life* of his master.[128]

Of the Situation of the Same (London).

Amongst the noble and celebrated cities of the world, that of London, the capital of the kingdom of England, is one of the most renowned, possessing above all others abundant wealth, extensive commerce, great grandeur and magnificence. It is happy in the salubrity of its climate, in the profession of the Christian religion, in the strength of its fortresses, the nature of its situation, the honor of its citizens and the chastity of its matrons; in its sports, too, it is most pleasant, and in the production of illustrious men most fortunate. All which things I wish separately to consider.

Of the Mildness of the Climate.

There then

"Men's minds are soft'ned by a temp'rate clime,"

not so, however, that they are addicted to licentiousness, but so that they are not savage and brutal, but rather kind and generous.

[128] I.e. Thomas a Becket.

Of the Religion.

There is in St. Paul's church an episcopal see: it was formerly metropolitan, and, it is thought, will be again, should the citizens return to the island: unless perhaps the archiepiscopal title of St. Thomas,[129] and his bodily presence there, should always retain that dignity at Canterbury where it now is. But as St. Thomas has ennobled both these cities, London by his birth, and Canterbury by his death, each of them, with respect to the saint, has as much to allege against the other, and with justice too. As regards divine worship, there are also in London and in the suburbs thirteen larger conventual churches, besides one hundred and thirty-six lesser parochial ones.

Of the Strength of the City.

On the east stands the Palatine tower, a fortress of great size and strength, the court and walls of which are erected upon a very deep foundation, the mortar used in the building being tempered with the blood of beasts. On the west are two castles strongly fortified; the wall of the city is high and thick, with seven double gates, having on the north side towers placed at proper intervals. London formerly had walls and towers in like manner on the south, but that most excellent river the Thames, which abounds with fish and in which the tide ebbs and flows, runs on that side and has in a long space of time washed down, undermined and subverted the walls in that part. On the west also, higher up the bank of the river, the royal palace rears its head, an incomparable structure, furnished with a breastwork and bastions, situated in a populous suburb, at a distance of two miles from the city.

Of the Gardens.

Adjoining to the houses on all sides lie the gardens of those citizens that dwell in the suburbs, which are well furnished with trees, spacious and beautiful.

Of the Pasture and Tillage Lands.

On the north side too are fields for pasture and a delightful plain of meadow land, interspersed with flowing streams, on which stand mills, whose clack is very pleasing to the ear. Close by lies an immense forest, in which are densely wooded thickets,

[129] Cf. *ante*, p. 163.

the coverts of game, stags, fallow-deer, boars and wild bulls. The tillage lands of the city are not barren gravelly soils, but like the fertile plains of Asia which produce abundant crops and fill the barns of their cultivators with

"Ceres' plenteous sheaf."

Of the Springs.

There are round London, on the northern side, in the suburbs, excellent springs; the water of which is sweet, clear and salubrious,

"'Mid glistening pebles gliding playfully:"

amongst which Holywell, Clerkenwell and St. Clement's well are of most note and most frequently visited, as well by the scholars from the schools as by the youth of the city when they go out to take the air in the summer evenings. The city is delightful indeed when it has a good governor.

Of the Honor of the Citizens.

This city is ennobled by her men, graced by her arms and peopled by a multitude of inhabitants; so that in the wars under King Stephen [130] there went out to muster, of armed horsemen, esteemed fit for war, twenty thousand, and of infantry sixty thousand. The citizens of London are respected and noted above all other citizens for the elegance of their manners, dress, table and discourse.

Of the Matrons.

The matrons of the city are perfect Sabines.[131]

Of the Schools.

The three principal churches possess, by privilege and ancient dignity, celebrated schools; yet often, by the favor of some person of note or of some learned men eminently distinguished for their philosophy, other schools are permitted upon sufferance. On festival days the masters assemble their pupils at those churches where the feast of the patron saint is solemnized; and there the scholars dispute, some in a demonstrative way, and other logically; some again recite enthymemes, while others use the more perfect syllogism. Some, to show their abilities,

[130] Cf. *ante*, pp. 205–209.
[131] Reference to the Sabine women of Roman history.

engage in such disputation as is practised among persons contending for victory alone; others dispute upon a truth, which is the grace of perfection. The sophisters, who argue upon feigned topics, are deemed clever according to their fluency of speech and command of language. Others endeavor to impose by false conclusions. Sometimes certain orators in their rhetorical harangues employ all the powers of persuasion, taking care to observe the precepts of the art and to omit nothing apposite to the subject. The boys of the different schools wrangle with each other in verse and contend about the principles of grammar or the rules of the perfect and future tenses. There are some who in epigrams, rimes and verses use that trivial raillery so much practised among the ancients, freely attacking their companions with Fescennine [132] license, but suppressing the names, discharging their scoffs and sarcasms against them, touching with Socratic wit the failings of their school fellows or perhaps of greater personages, or biting them more keenly with a Theonine [133] tooth. The audience,

> "well disposed to laugh,
> With curling nose double the quivering peals."

Of the Manner in which the Affairs of the City Are Disposed.

The artizans of the several crafts, the vendors of the various commodities and the laborers of every kind have each their separate station which they take every morning. There is also in London, on the bank of the river, among the wine-shops which are kept in ships and cellars, a public eating-house: there every day, according to the season, may be found viands of all kinds, roast, fried and boiled, fish large and small, coarser meat for the poor, and more delicate for the rich, such as venison, fowls and small birds. If friends, wearied with their journey, should unexpectedly come to a citizen's house, and, being hungry, should not like to wait till fresh meat be bought and cooked:

> "The canisters with bread are heap'd on high;
> The attendants water for their hands supply."

---

[132] Fescennium was a town of Etruria and "From this town the Romans are said to have derived the Fescennine songs bandied about at harvest festivals; these were usually of a coarse and boisterous character." (Smith, *Smaller Classical Dictionary.*) [133] Could this be a misprint for "Leonine"?

Meanwhile, some run to the river side and there every thing that they could wish for is instantly procured. However great the number of soldiers or strangers that enter or leave the city at any hour of the day or night, they may turn in there if they please and refresh themselves according to their inclination; so that the former have no occasion to fast too long, or the latter to leave the city without dining. Those who wish to indulge themselves would not desire a sturgeon or the bird of Africa [134] or the goodwit of Ionia, when the delicacies that are to be found there are set before them. This indeed is the public cookery and is very convenient to the city and a distinguishing mark of civilization. Hence we read in Plato's Gorgias, "Juxta medicinam esse coquorum officium, simulantium et adulationem quartæ particulæ civilitatis." [135] There is without one of the gates, immediately in the suburb, a certain smooth field in name and in reality. There every Friday, unless it be one of the more solemn festivals, is a noted show of well-bred horses exposed for sale. The earls, barons and knights, who are at the time resident in the city, as well as most of the citizens, flock thither either to look on or to buy. It is pleasant to see the nags with their sleek and shining coats, smoothly ambling along, raising and setting down alternately, as it were their feet on either side: in one part are horses better adapted to esquires; these, whose pace is rougher but yet expeditious, lift up and set down, as it were, the two opposite fore and hind feet together; [136] in another the young blood colts, not yet accustomed to the bridle,

---

[134] A species of goose.

[135] This must be a quotation from some garbled medieval Latin translation of the *Gorgias*. Translated literally into modern English, it reads, "The art of cookery, of those who pretend to flatter the fourth part of the state, is next to medicine." In the *Gorgias* Socrates is discussing rhetoric with Gorgias, Polus, and Callicles. He maintains that rhetoric, usually called the art of persuasion, is really no art at all, but bears the same relation to the right and wrong of argument as the art of costuming bears to gymnastic art, or sophistry to legislation, or cookery to medicine. Fitzstephen either had a bad translation or he has misunderstood his text, for, whereas he would put cookery next to medicine, Socrates contrasts them as sham and true art respectively. See Jowett's translation of the *Gorgias* in his *Dialogs of Plato*, iii, pp. 49–51 (New York, Charles Scribner's Sons, 1911).

[136] I.e. the horses were pacers.

"Which upright walk on pasterns firm and straight,
    Their motions easy, prancing in their gait,"

in a third are the horses for burden, strong and stout-limbed;
and in a fourth, the more valuable chargers of an elegant shape
and noble height, with nimbly moving ears, erect necks and
plump haunches. In the movements of these the purchasers
observe first their easy pace and then their gallop, which is
when the fore-feet are raised from the ground and set down
together, and the hind ones in like manner, alternately. When
a race is to be run by such horses as these and perhaps by
others, which in like manner, according to their breed, are
strong for carriage and vigorous for the course, the people raise
a shout and order the common horses to be withdrawn to another
part of the field. The jockeys, who are boys expert in the management of horses, which they regulate by means of curb-bridles,
sometimes by threes and sometimes by twos, according as the
match is made, prepare themselves for the contest. Their chief
aim is to prevent a competitor getting before them. The horses,
too, after their manner, are eager for the race; their limbs
tremble, and, impatient of delay, they cannot stand still; upon
the signal being given, they stretch out their limbs, hurry over
the course and are borne along with unremitting speed. The
riders, inspired with the love of praise and the hope of victory,
clap spurs to their flying horses, lashing them with their whips
and inciting them by their shouts. You would think with
Heraclitus [137] that all things were in motion, and that Zeno's [138]
opinion was altogether erroneous, when he said that there was
no such thing as motion and that it was impossible to reach the
goal. In another quarter, apart from the rest, stand the goods
of the peasants, implements of husbandry, swine with their long
sides, cows with distended udders,

"Oxen of bulk immense, and woolly flocks."

[137] Heraclitus was a Greek philosopher who flourished at Ephesus about 500 B.C.
His writings had the reputation of being very obscure. According to him fire was
the underlying motive power of the universe. He held, as our text states, that all
things were in constant flux.

[138] This is Zeno the Eleatic philosopher, so called from the town of Elea in Southern Italy, where he flourished about 488 (?) B.C. He argued for the unreality of

There too stand the mares fitted for the plow, the dray and the
cart, of which some are big with foal, others have their frolic-
some colts running close by their sides.   To this city from every
nation under heaven merchants bring their commodities by sea,

> "Arabia's gold, Sabæa's [139] spice and incense,
> Scythia's keen weapons, and the oil of palms
> From Babylon's rich soil, Nile's precious gems,
> Norway's warm peltries, Russia's costly sables,
> Sera's [140] rich vestures and the wines of Gaul,
> Hither are sent."

According to the evidence of chroniclers London is more
ancient than Rome: for, as both derive their origin from the
same Trojan ancestors, this was founded by Brutus before that
by Romulus and Remus.[141]   Hence it is that, even to this day,
both cities use the same ancient laws and ordinances.   This,
like Rome, is divided into wards; it has annual sheriffs instead
of consuls; it has an order of senators and inferior magistrates
and also sewers and aqueducts in its streets; each class of suits,
whether of the deliberative, demonstrative or judicial kind has
its appropriate place and proper court; on stated days it has
its assemblies.   I think that there is no city in which more approved customs are observed, in attending churches, honoring
God's ordinances, keeping festivals, giving alms, receiving strangers, confirming espousals, contracting marriages, celebrating
weddings, preparing entertainments, welcoming guests and also
in the arrangement of the funeral ceremonies and the burial of
the dead.   The only inconveniences of London are the immoder-
ate drinking of foolish persons and the frequent fires.   Moreover, almost all the bishops, abbots and great men of England
are in a manner citizens and freemen of London; as they have
magnificent houses there to which they resort, spending large
sums of money, whenever they are summoned thither to councils
and assemblies by the king or their metropolitan, or are compelled to go there by their own business.

motion and space. He should not be confused with the other Zeno of the 4th
and 3d centuries B.C., the founder of Stoicism.

[139] I.e. Arabia.   [140] I.e. China.   [141] Cf. *ante*, p. 248.

Of the Sports.

Let us now proceed to the sports of the city; since it is expedient that a city be not only an object of utility and importance but also a source of pleasure and diversion. Hence even in the seals of the chief pontiffs, up to the time of Pope Leo,[142] there was engraved on one side of the Bull the figure of St. Peter as a fisherman, and above him a key stretched out to him, as it were, from heaven by the hand of God, and around him this verse,

"For me thou left'st thy ship, receive the key."

On the obverse side was represented a city, with this inscription, GOLDEN ROME. It was also said in praise of Augustus Cæsar and the city of Rome,

"All night it rains, the shows return with day,
Cæsar, thou bear'st with Jove alternate sway."

London, instead of theatrical shows and scenic entertainments, has dramatic performances of a more sacred kind, either representations of the miracles which holy confessors have wrought, or of the passions and sufferings in which the constancy of martyrs was signally displayed.[143] Moreover, to begin with the sports of the boys, for we have all been boys, annually on the day which is called Shrovetide,[144] the boys of the respective schools bring each a fighting cock to their master and the whole of that forenoon is spent by the boys in seeing their cocks fight in the school-room. After dinner all of the young men of the city go out into the fields to play at the well-known game of foot-ball. The scholars belonging to the several schools have each their ball; and the city tradesmen, according to their respective crafts, have theirs. The more aged men, the fathers of the players and the wealthy citizens come on horseback to see the contests of the young men, with whom after their manner, they participate, their natural heat seeming to be aroused by the sight of so much agility and by their participation in the amusements of unrestrained youth. Every Sunday in Lent,

---

[142] I have been unable to find which Pope Leo is meant.
[143] A clear reference to religious plays.
[144] The Tuesday before Ash-Wednesday, the first day of Lent.

after dinner, a company of young men enter the fields, mounted on warlike horses —

> "On coursers always foremost in the race";

of which

> "Each steed's well-trained to gallop in a ring."

The lay-sons of the citizens rush out of the gates in crowds, equipped with lances and shields, the younger sort with pikes from which the iron heads have been taken off, and there they get up sham fights and exercise themselves in military combat. When the king happens to be near the city, most of the courtiers attend and the young men who form the households of the earls and barons and have not yet attained the honor of knighthood, resort thither for the purpose of trying their skill. The hope of victory animates every one. The spirited horses neigh, their limbs tremble, they champ their bits, and, impatient of delay, cannot endure standing still. When at length

> "The charger's hoof seizes upon the course,"

the young riders having been divided into companies, some pursue those that go before without being able to overtake them, whilst others throw their companions out of their course and gallop beyond them. In the Easter holidays they play at a game resembling a naval engagement. A target is firmly fastened to the trunk of a tree which is fixed in the middle of the river, and in the prow of a boat driven along by oars and the current stands a young man who is to strike the target with his lance; if, in hitting it, he break his lance and keep his position unmoved, he gains his point and attains his desire: but if his lance be not shivered by the blow, he is tumbled into the river, and his boat passes by driven along by its own motion. Two boats, however, are placed there, one on each side of the target, and in them a number of young men to take up the striker, when he first emerges from the stream or when

> "A second time he rises from the wave."

On the bridge and in balconies on the banks of the river stand the spectators

> "well disposed to laugh."

During the holidays in summer the young men exercise themselves in the sports of leaping, archery, wrestling, stone-throwing,
slinging javelins beyond a mark and also fighting with bucklers.
Cytherea leads the dance of the maidens who merrily trip along
the ground beneath the uprisen moon. On almost every holiday
in winter, before dinner, foaming boars and huge-tusked hogs,
intended for bacon, fight for their lives, or fat bulls or immense
boars are baited with dogs. When that great marsh which
washes the walls of the city on the northside is frozen over, the
young men go out in crowds to divert themselves upon the ice.
Some, having increased their velocity by a run, placing their
feet apart and turning their bodies sideways, slide a great way:
others make a seat of large pieces of ice like mill-stones and a
great number of them running before and holding each other by
the hand, draw one of their number who is seated on the ice:
if at any time they slip in moving so swiftly all fall down headlong together. Others are more expert in their sports upon the
ice; for fitting to and binding under their feet the shinbones of
some animal, and taking in their hands poles shod with iron,
which at times they strike against the ice, they are carried along
with as great rapidity as a bird flying or a bolt discharged from
a cross-bow. Sometimes two of the skaters having placed themselves a great distance apart by mutual agreement, come together from opposite sides; they meet, raise their poles and
strike each other; either one or both of them fall, not without
some bodily hurt: even after their fall they are carried along
to a great distance from each other by the velocity of the motion; and whatever part of their heads comes in contact with
the ice is laid bare to the very skull. Very frequently the leg
or arm of the falling party, if he chance to light upon either of
them, is broken. But youth is an age eager for glory and desirous of victory, and so young men engage in counterfeit battles,
that they may conduct themselves more valiantly in real ones.
Most of the citizens amuse themselves in sporting with merlins,
hawks and other birds of a like kind and also with dogs that
hunt in the woods. The citizens have the right of hunting in
Middlesex, Hertfordshire, all the Chilterns and Kent as far as
the river Cray. The Londoners, then called Trinovantes, re-

pulsed Caius Julius Cæsar, a man who delighted to mark his
path with blood. Whence Lucan says,

"Britain he sought, but turn'd his back dismay'd." [145]

The city of London has produced some men who have subdued
many kingdoms and even the Roman empire; and very many
others whose virtue has exalted them to the skies, as was promised to Brutus [146] by the oracle of Apollo:

"Brutus, there lies beyond the Gallic bounds
An island which the western sea surrounds:

. . . .

To reach this happy shore thy sails employ:
There fate decrees to raise a second Troy,
And found an empire in thy royal line
Which time shall ne'er destroy, nor bounds confine."

Since the planting of the Christian religion there, London has
given birth to the noble emperor Constantine [147] who gave the
city of Rome and all the insignia of the empire to God and St.
Peter and Pope Sylvester,[148] whose stirrup he held, and chose
rather to be called defender of the holy Roman church than
emperor: and that the peace of our lord the Pope might not, by
reason of his presence be disturbed he withdrew from the city
which he had bestowed upon our lord the Pope and built for
himself the city of Byzantium. London also in modern times

[145] Cf. Lucan, *Pharsalia*, Book ii, l. 572.   [146] Cf. *ante*, pp. 248, 315.

[147] A mistake of Fitzstephen's enthusiasm or ignorance.

[148] A reference to the famous donation of Constantine embodied in a document
known as *Constitutum Constantini* (*The Decree of Constantine*). This was possibly
published about 754 A.D., but, according to the article on the Donation in the *New
International Enclyclopedia*, was never used before the thirteenth century to vindicate papal claims to temporal power. It is difficult to tell here whether Fitzstephen refers to the *Constitutum* or simply to the tradition of the gift. If to the
former, his reference would antedate the *Enclyclopedia's*. The pontificate of Sylvester I, the Sylvester referred to in the text, extended from 314–335. Laurentius
Valla (*circa* 1406–1457), the eminent Italian Renaissance scholar, proved in 1439
that the Constitutum was a forgery in his book *De Falso Credita et Ementita Constantini Donatione Declamatio* (*Speech concerning the Falsely Credited and Forged
Donation of Constantine*). A translation of the *Constitutum* is to be found in Henderson, *Select Historical Documents of the Middle Ages*, pp. 319–329 (George Bell
and Sons, 1892).

has produced illustrious and august princes, the empress Matilda,[149] King Henry III [150] and St. Thomas,[151] the archbishop and glorious martyr of Christ than whom no man was more guileless or more devoted to all good men throughout the whole Roman world.

"The city is delightful indeed," remarks Fitzstephen of London, "when it has a good governor." [152] Unfortunately, good governors were not always the lot of London, as we see from the following document, which is interesting on two accounts; one, that it is the first petition in the English language presented to Parliament; the other, that it records an account of London municipal politics in the later fourteenth century. It is preserved in a MS. in the Public Record Office, London, and bears date, 1386.

To the most noble and worthy lords, most righteous and wise advisors to our liege lord the King, make complaint, if you please, the folk of the Mercers' Company of London as citizens of the same, of many subtle wrongs as well as open oppressions done them for a long time past. One of which was that, whereas the election of a mayor is made by the freemen of the city with the good and peaceable advice of the wisest and truest men, every year freely — notwithstanding this freedom or franchise, by force, Nicholas Brembre [153] with his followers nominated himself, the next year after John Northampton, as is well known, and with violence and by main strength, was chosen mayor, to the destruction of the rights of many, contrary to the peace aforementioned. For in the same year, the aforesaid Nicholas, unnecessarily, against the peace, made divers armed attacks by day as well as by night and destroyed the King's true lieges, some by open slaughter, some by false imprisonments; and some fled the city for fear, as it is openly known.

And, further, to maintain these wrongs and many others, the next year after, the same Nicholas, against the aforesaid

---

[149] Daughter of Henry I of England.   [150] Eldest son of Henry II.
[151] Thomas a Becket.   [152] Cf. *ante*, p. 311.
[153] See the article on him in the *Dictionary of National Biography*.

freedom and true summons, made open proclamation that no
man should come to vote for mayor but those who were summoned; and all that were summoned were of his persuasion and
party. And on the night next following he had a great quantity
of arms and armor carried to the gild-hall, with which both
aliens and citizens were armed in the morning contrary to his
own proclamation, which was to the effect that no one should
be armed; and certain ambuscades were laid, so that, when the
freemen of the city came to vote for mayor, armed men broke
out upon them, crying, "Slay, slay," and followed them. And
so the people for fear fled to their houses and other places of
hiding, as if they were in a land at war and afraid of being
killed *en masse.*

And from that time to this the office of mayor has been held
as if by conquest or force, and so have many other offices, so
that any man, known to be discontented, complaining at or
expressing himself in opposition to any of these wrongs, or accused by the statement of any one at all, even if the charge
were ever so false, was impeached, if Nicholas willed it, anon was
imprisoned, and, though it were on the false testimony of the
lowest officer that it pleased him to maintain, was held untrue
to our King; for, if any one accused an officer suborned by
Nicholas, of wrong or anything else, he pledged Nicholas against
his accuser and Nicholas, though unworthy as he himself admitted, represented the King. Also, if any man because of
service or for any other permissible reason approached a lord,
to whom Nicholas was afraid his evil courses might become
known, he was at once accused of being false to the interests of
the city and so to the King.

And if a general complaint were made against his treachery,
as by us of the Mercers' Company or any other craft, or if any
general method of withstanding him were broached, or, — as
time out of mind has been the custom, — people would club
together, however lawful or profitable it might be for us, we
were at once accused of disturbing the peace and many of us
are still under false indictments. And we are openly slandered,
considered false and traitors to our King; for this same Nicholas
said before the mayor, aldermen and our craft gathered in a place

of record, that twenty or thirty of us should be hanged and
drawn, which charge, may it please your worships, should be
proved or disproved before a fair judge, that the truth may be
known; for truth amongst us is either the prerogative of a few,
or else for many a day none of us may show himself; and not
only has it (the truth) been obscured and hidden by man now,
but also aforetime, the most profitable points of true governance
of the city, gathered together after protracted labor of discreet
and wise men, without the advice of true men — in order that
these points might not be known nor kept in force — in the
time of mayor Nicholas Exton were completely destroyed by fire.

And so far have these false ways gone that often he, Nicholas
Brembre, has said, in support of his falsehood, our liege lord's
will was such as it never was, we submit. He said also, when
he had slandered us, that those who would admit that they
had been false to the King, the King would pardon, cherish and
be kind to: and if any of us all, who with God's help have been
and shall be found true, was so bold as to offer to prove himself
true, he was at once ordered to prison, as well by the mayor
now in office as by his predecessor, Nicholas Brembre.

Also, we have often been commanded, by our loyalty, to do
unnecessary and illegal acts and also by the same token kept
from things necessary and lawful, as was shown when a company of good women, in a case where men were helpless, went
barefoot to our liege lord to seek grace of him for true men as
they supposed; for then were such proclamations made that no
man or woman should approach our liege lord to ask grace, and
overmany other commandments also, before and since, by the
suggestion and information of such as would not their treachery
were known to our liege lord. And, lords, by your leave, our
liege lord's commandment, to simple and unassuming men, is
a great thing to be used so familiarly without need; for they,
unwise in using it, may easily sin against it.

Therefore, gracious lords, may it please you to take heed in
what manner and when our liege lord's power has been misused
by the aforesaid Nicholas and his followers, for since these
wrongs aforesaid seem the accidental or common outward
branches, it is clear the root of them is a rotten substance or

stock within, namely, the aforesaid briar or bramble (*Brembre*, a variant spelling of *bramble*), who practices wrong against the city and others, if it please you, as may be shown and well-known by an impartial judge and mayor of our city; the which with your rightful lordships' foremost remedy granted, as God's law and reason will, namely, that no man should be judge in his own cause, wrongs will be more openly known and truth appear at the door. Otherwise among us, we cannot know in what manner it will appear without more trouble, since the governance of the city stands, as has been said before, and will stand while victuallers [154] are allowed to assume such state; the which governance, formerly hidden from many, now shows itself openly whether it has been a cause or beginning of division in the city and afterward in the kingdom, or not.

Wherefore, for greatest need, we meekly petition you, most worthy, righteous and wise lords and council to our liege lord the King, graciously to correct all the wrongs aforesaid, and that it please your lordships to be gracious mediators between us and our liege lord the King, that such wrongs may be known to him, and that we may show ourselves and then be held as true to him as we are and ought to be. Also, we beseech your gracious lordships that if any of us, individually or collectively, are impeached before our liege lord or his worthy council by connivance of others, or approach to the King, as by Brembre or his abettors by false witness, because it stood otherwise among us than as now proved it has stood, or by any other wrong suggestion by which our liege lord has been unlawfully informed, that then your worships may be such that we may come in answer to excuse ourselves; for we know well, at least most of us do and we hope all do, that all such wrongs have been unwitting on our part, or else entirely against our will.

And, righteous lords, as one of the greatest remedies, among others, to withstand many of the aforesaid troubles among us, we pray with meekness for this especially, that the statute ordained and made by Parliament, held at Westminster in the sixth year of our King now reigning, may be enforced and executed here in London as elsewhere in the realm; to wit:

[154] Brembre was a victualler by trade.

. . . It is ordained and ordered that neither in the city of London nor in any other city, borough, manor or sea-port, throughout the entire aforesaid realm, shall any victualler have judicial jurisdiction over another person, nor exercise it, nor enjoy it in any manner, except on manors where another person cannot be found according to this statute unless the same judge for the time in which he is in office leave off and abstain from his victualling, on pain of losing his goods, etc.

England in the fourteenth century may be said to have become conscious of the labor problem. This is indicated by the fact that a series of royal ordinances, culminating in a statute in 1357, tried unsuccessfully to deal with the matter by legislation. Realization of the labor difficulty was aided by the appearance in England about 1348 of the Black Death, a form of the bubonic plague, which carried off about one-third of the population of the country. Henry Knighton, a contemporary chronicler, thus comments on the Black Death and couples it with an account of labor conditions: [155]

Then the grievous plague penetrated the seacoasts from Southampton and came to Bristol and there almost the whole strength of the town died, struck as it were by sudden death; for there were few who kept their beds more than three days or two days or half a day: and after this the fell death broke forth on every side with the course of the sun. There died at Leicester in the small parish of St. Leonard more than 380, in the parish of Holy Cross more than 400, in the parish of St. Margaret of Leicester more than 700, and so in each parish a great number. Then the Bishop of Lincoln sent through the whole bishopric and gave general power to all and every priest, both regular and secular, to hear confessions and absolve with full and entire episcopal authority except in matters of debt, in which case the dying man, if he could, should pay the debt while he lived, or others should fulfil that duty from his property after

[155] Cf. F. A. Gasquet, *The Great Pestilence* (*A.D. 1348–9*), (Simpkin, Marshall, Hamilton, Kent and Co., Ltd., 1893).

his death. Likewise the pope granted full remission of sins to whoever was absolved in peril of death and granted that this power should last until next Easter, and everyone could choose a confessor at his will. In the same year there was a great plague of sheep everywhere in the realm, so that in one place there died in pasturage more than 5000 sheep and so rotted that neither beast nor bird would touch them. And there were small prices for everything an account of the fear of death. For there were very few who cared about riches or anything else. For a man could have a horse which before was worth 40*s*. for 6*s*. 8*d*., a fat ox for 4*s*., a cow for 12*d*., a heifer for 6*d*., a fat wether for 4*d*., a sheep for 3*d*., a lamb for 2*d*., a big pig for 5*d*., a stone of wool for 9*d*. Sheep and cattle went wandering over fields and through crops and there was no one to go and drive or gather them, so that the number cannot be reckoned which perished in the ditches in every district for lack of herdsmen; for there was such a lack of servants that no one knew what he ought to do. In the following autumn no one could get a reaper for less than 8*d*. with his food, a mower for less than 12*d*. with his food. Wherefore, many crops perished in the fields for want of someone to gather them: but in the pestilence year, as is above said of other things, there was such abundance of all kinds of corn that no one much troubled about it. The Scots, hearing of the cruel pestilence of the English, believed it had come to them from the avenging hand of God, and — as it was commonly reported in England — took for their oath when they wanted to swear, "By the foul death of England." But when the Scots, believing the English were under the shadow of the dread vengeance of God, came together in the forest of Selkirk with purpose to invade the whole realm of England, the fell mortality came upon them, and the sudden and awful cruelty of death winnowed them, so that about 5000 died in a short time. Then the rest, some feeble, some strong, determined to return home, but the English followed and overtook them and killed many of them.

Master Thomas of Bradwardine [156] was consecrated by the

---

[156] Chaucer refers to him in his *Nun's Priest's Tale*, l. 422, as a great theological authority.

pope archbishop of Canterbury, and when he returned to England he came to London, but within two days was dead. He was famous beyond all other clerks in the whole of Christendom, especially in theology, but likewise in the more liberal sciences. At the same time priests were in such poverty everywhere that many churches were widowed and lacking the divine offices, masses, matins, vespers, sacraments and other rites. A man could scarcely get a chaplain under 10 pounds or 10 marks to minister to a church. And when a man could get a chaplain for 5 or 4 or even for 2 marks with his food when there was an abundance of priests before the pestilence, there was scarcely any one now who was willing to accept a vicarage for 20 pounds or 20 marks; but within a short time a very great multitude of those whose wives had died in the pestilence flocked into orders, of whom many were illiterate and little more than laymen, except so far as they knew how to read although they could not understand.

Meanwhile, the King sent proclamation into all the counties that reapers and other laborers should not take more than they had been accustomed to take, under the penalty appointed by statute. But the laborers were so lifted up and so obstinate that they would not listen to the King's command, but if any one wished to have them, he had to give them what they wanted, and either lose his fruit and crops or satisfy the lofty and covetous wishes of the workmen. And when it was known to the King that they had not observed his command and had given greater wages to the laborers, he levied heavy fines upon abbots, priors, knights, lesser and greater, and other great folk and small folk of the realm, of some 100s., of some 40s., of some 20s., from each according to what he could give. He took from each carucate [157] of the realm 20s. and, notwithstanding this, a fifteenth. And afterwards the King had many laborers arrested and sent them to prison; many withdrew themselves and went into the forests and woods; and those who were taken were heavily fined. Their ringleaders were made to swear that they would not take daily wages beyond the ancient custom, and they were freed from prison. And in like manner was done with the other

[157] I.e. 100 acres.

craftsmen in the burroughs and villages. . . . After the aforesaid pestilence, many buildings, great and small, fell into ruins
in every city, borough and village for lack of inhabitants, likewise, many villages and hamlets became desolate, not a home
being left in them, all having died who dwelt there; and it was
probable that many such villages would never be inhabited again.
In the winter following there was such a want of servants in
work of all kinds, that one would scarcely believe that in times
past there had been such a lack. . . . And so all necessaries became so much dearer that what in times past had been worth
1d. was then worth 4d. or 5d.

Magnates and lesser lords of the realm who had tenants made
abatements of the rent in order that the tenants should not go
away on account of the want of servants and the general dearness: some, half the rent; some more, some less, some for two
years, some for three, some for one year, according as they could
agree with them. Likewise, those who received of their tenants
day-work throughout the year, as is the practice with villeins,
had to give them more leisure, and remit such works, and either
entirely to free them, or give them an easier tenure at a small
rent, so that homes should not be everywhere irrecoverably
ruined, and the land everywhere remain entirely uncultivated.

Knighton speaks of labor ordinances and describes their
general tenure; the following proclamation addressed to the
sheriff of Kent gives us in more detail the provisions of
practically all the labor laws of the time, clearly outlines
the problem, and states the penalties for violation.

The king to the sheriff of Kent, greeting. Because a great
part of the people, and especially of workmen and servants,
have lately died in the pestilence, many seeing the necessities of
masters and great scarcity of servants, will not serve unless they
may receive excessive wages, and others preferring to beg in idleness rather than by labor to get their living; we, considering the
grievous incommodities which of the lack especially of plough-
men and such laborers may hereafter come, have upon deliberation and treaty with the prelates and the nobles and learned
men assisting us, with their unanimous counsel ordained:

328 ENGLISH LITERATURE

That every man and woman of our realm of England, of what condition he be, free or bond, able in body, and within the age of sixty years, not living in merchandize, nor exercising any craft, nor having of his own whereof he may live, nor land of his own about whose tillage he may occupy himself, and not serving any other; if he be required to serve in suitable service, his estate considered, he shall be bound to serve him which shall so require him; and take only the wages, livery, meed, or salary which were accustomed to be given in the places where he oweth to serve, the twentieth year of our reign of England, or five or six other common years next before. Provided always, that the lords be preferred before others in their bondmen or their land tenants, so in their service to be retained; so that, nevertheless, the said lords shall retain no more than be necessary for them. And if any such man or woman being so required to serve will not do the same, and that be proved by two true men before the sheriff, bailiff, lord, or constable of the town where the same shall happen to be done, he shall immediately be taken by them or any of them, and committed to the next gaol, there to remain under strait keeping, till he find surety to serve in the form aforesaid.

If any reaper, mower, other workman or servant, of what estate or condition he be, retained in any man's service, do depart from the said service without reasonable cause or license, before the term agreed, he shall have pain of imprisonment; and no one, under the same penalty, shall presume to receive or retain such a one in his service.

No one, moreover, shall pay or promise to pay to any one more wages, liveries, meed, or salary than was accustomed, as is before said; nor shall any one in any other manner demand or receive them, upon pain of doubling of that which shall have been so paid, promised, required or received, to him who thereof shall feel himself aggrieved; and if none such will sue, then the same shall be applied to any of the people that will sue; and such suit shall be in the court of the lord of the place where such case shall happen.

And if lords of towns or manors presume in any point to come against this present ordinance, either by them or by their

servants, then suit shall be made against them in the form aforesaid, in the counties, wapentakes, and trithings, or such other
courts of ours, for the penalty of treble that so paid or promised
by them or their servants. And if any before this present ordinance hath covenanted with any so to serve for more wages, he
shall not be bound, by reason of the said covenant, to pay more
than at another time was wont to be paid to such a person; nor
under the same penalty, shall presume to pay more.

Item. Saddlers, skinners, white tawyers, cordwainers, tailors,
smiths, carpenters, masons, tilers, shipwrights, carters, and all
other artificers and workmen, shall not take for their labor and
workmanship above the same that was wont to be paid to such
persons the said twentieth year, and other common years next
preceding, as before is said, in the place where they shall happen
to work; and if any man take more he shall be committed to
the next gaol, in manner as before is said.

Item. That butchers, fishmongers, hostelers, brewers, bakers,
poulterers, and all other sellers of all manner of victuals, shall
be bound to sell the same victuals for a reasonable price, having
respect to the price that such victuals be sold at in the places
adjoining, so that the same sellers have moderate gains, and not
excessive, reasonably to be required according to the distance
of the place from which the said victuals be carried; and if any
sell such victuals in any other manner, and thereof be convicted,
in the manner and form aforesaid, he shall pay the double of
the same that he so received to the party injured, or in default
of him, to any other that will sue in this behalf. And the mayors
and bailiffs of cities, boroughs, merchant towns, and others, and
of the ports and maritime places, shall have power to inquire of
all and singular, which shall in any thing offend against this,
and to levy the said penalty to the use of them at whose suit
such offenders shall be convicted. And in case the same mayors
and bailiffs be negligent in doing execution of the premises, and
thereof be convicted before our justices, by us to be assigned,
then the same mayors and bailiffs shall be compelled by the
same justices to pay the treble of the thing so sold to the party
injured, or in default of him, to any other that will sue; and
nevertheless they shall be grievously punished on our part.

And because many strong beggars, as long as they may live by begging, do refuse to labor, giving themselves to idleness and vice, and sometimes to theft and other abominations; none upon the said pain of imprisonment, shall, under the color of pity or alms, give anything to such, who are able to labor, or presume to favor them in their idleness, so that thereby they may be compelled to labor for their necessary living.

It would appear that this law was drastic enough to meet the situation, but that it did not is clear from the fact that nearly the same statute was re-enacted thirteen times in the century following 1349. Labor troubles continued and combined with other things to produce several protests against the medieval system in the latter years of the fourteenth century. Perhaps the most violent and practical of these was the Peasants' Revolt of 1381. The following account of some episodes in this revolt from the pen of Froissart makes it very vivid. In these chapters the writer largely abandons "the glowing, rich and powerful" [158] style of his usual "feudal painting" [158] and gives us a rapid account of events. His lack of sympathy with the laborers, just what is to be expected from Froissart, the friend of aristocrats and kings, is evident. [159]

While these conferences [160] were going forward, there happened in England great commotions among the lower ranks of the people, by which England was near ruined without resource. Never was a country in such jeopardy as this was at that period,

[158] Cf. Scott, *Walpole* in *The Lives of the Novelists*, p. 192. Ed. Saintsbury in *Everyman's Library*.

[159] Some would include in these protests passages from the *Vision of William concerning Piers the Plowman*. But, while the author or authors of this work are critical of the abuses that have found their way into the medieval system, it is quite clear that he or they had no thoroughgoing dissatisfaction with the system in itself. Langland, if we may still use that name, was a prophet in the Old Testament sense; that is, he desired that the medieval system might be restored in its pristine purity rather than that any other be put in its place. On the prophets see Wallis, *The Sociological Study of the Bible* (The University of Chicago Press, 1912).   [160] The negotiations with the Scots, mentioned *post*, p. 338.

and all through the too great comfort of the commonalty. Rebellion was stirred up, as it was formerly done in France by the Jacques Bons-hommes,[161] who did much evil, and sore troubled the kingdom of France. It is marvellous from what a trifle this pestilence raged in England. In order that it may serve as an example to mankind, I will speak of all that was done, from the information I had at the time on the subject.

It is customary in England, as well as in several other countries, for the nobility to have great privileges over the commonalty, whom they keep in bondage; that is to say, they are bound by law and custom to plough the lands of gentlemen, to harvest the grain, to carry it home to the barn, to thrash and winnow it: they are also bound to harvest the hay and carry it home. All these services they are obliged to perform for their lords, and many more in England than in other countries. The prelates and gentlemen are thus served. In the counties of Kent, Essex, Sussex, and Bedford, these services are more oppressive than in all the rest of the kingdom.

The evil-disposed in these districts began to rise, saying they were too severely oppressed; that at the beginning of the world there were no slaves, and that no one ought to be treated as such, unless he had committed treason against his lord, as Lucifer had done against God; but they had done no such thing, for they were neither angels nor spirits, but men formed after the same likeness with their lords, who treated them as beasts. This they would not longer bear, but had determined to be free, and if they labored or did any other works for their lords, they would be paid for it.

A crazy priest in the county of Kent, called John Ball, who, for his absurd preaching, had been thrice confined in the prison of the archbishop of Canterbury, was greatly instrumental in inflaming them with those ideas. He was accustomed, every Sunday after mass, as the people were coming out of the church, to preach to them in the market-place and assemble a crowd around him; to whom he would say: "My good friends, things cannot go on well in England, nor ever will, until everything

---

[161] A contemptuous name given by French nobles to French peasants who after the battle of Poitiers (1356) rose in revolt against their lords, but were put down.

shall be in common; when there shall neither be vassal nor lord, and all distinctions levelled; when the lords shall be no more masters than ourselves. How ill have they used us! and for what reason do they thus hold us in bondage? Are we not all descended from the same parents, Adam and Eve? and what can they show, or what reasons give, why they should be more the masters than ourselves? except, perhaps, in making us labor and work, for them to spend. They are clothed in velvets and rich stuffs, ornamented with ermine and other furs, while we are forced to wear poor cloth. They have wines, spices, and fine bread, when we have only rye and the refuse of the straw; and, if we drink, it must be water. They have handsome seats and manors, when we must brave the wind and rain in our labors in the field; but it is from our labor that they have wherewith to support their pomp. We are called slaves; and, if we do not perform our services, we are beaten, and we have not any sovereign to whom we can complain, or who wishes to hear us and do us justice. Let us go to the king, who is young, and remonstrate with him on our servitude, telling him we must have it otherwise, or that we shall find a remedy for it ourselves. If we wait on him in a body, all those who come under the appellation of slaves, or are held in bondage, will follow us, in the hopes of being free. When the king shall see us, we shall obtain a favorable answer, or we must then seek ourselves to amend our condition."

With such words as these did John Ball harangue the people, at his village every Sunday after mass, for which he was much beloved by them. Some who wished no good declared it was very true, and murmuring to each other, as they were going to the fields, on the road from one village to another, or at their different houses said, "John Ball preaches such and such things, and he speaks truth."

The archbishop of Canterbury, on being informed of this, had John Ball arrested, and imprisoned for two or three months by way of punishment; but it would have been better if he had been confined during his life, or had been put to death, than to have been suffered thus to act. The archbishop set him at liberty, for he could not for conscience' sake have put him to death. The moment John Ball was out of prison, he returned to his former errors. Numbers in the city of London having heard of his preaching, being envious of the rich men and nobility, began to say among themselves that the kingdom was too badly governed, and the nobility had seized on all the gold and silver coin. These wicked Londoners, therefore, began to assemble and to rebel: they sent to tell those in the adjoining counties they might come boldly to London, and bring their companions with them, for they would find the town open to them, and the commonalty in the same way of thinking; that they would press the king so much there should no longer be a slave in England.

These promises stirred up those in the counties of Kent, Essex, Sussex, and Bedford, and the adjoining country, so that they marched towards London; and, when they arrived near, they were upwards of sixty thousand. They had a leader called Wat Tyler, and with him were Jack Straw and John Ball: these three were their commanders, but the principal was Wat Tyler. This Wat had been a tiler of houses, a bad man, and a great enemy to the nobility. When these wicked people first began to rise, all London, except their friends, were very much frightened. The mayor and rich citizens assembled in council, on hearing they were coming to London, and debated whether they should shut the gates and refuse to admit them; but, having well considered, they determined not to do so, as they should run a risk of having the suburbs burnt.

The gates were therefore thrown open, when they entered in troops of one or two hundred, by twenties or thirties, according to the populousness of the towns they came from; and as they came into London they lodged themselves. But it is a truth, that full two-thirds of these people knew not what they wanted, nor what they sought for: they followed one another like sheep, or like to the shepherds of old, who said they were going to conquer the Holy Land, and afterwards accomplished nothing. In such manner did these poor fellows and vassals come to London from distances of a hundred and sixty leagues, but the greater part from those counties I have mentioned, and on their arrival they demanded to see the king. The gentlemen of the country, the knights and squires, began to be alarmed when they saw the people thus rise; and, if they were frightened, they had sufficient reason, for less causes create fear. They began to collect together as well as they could.

The same day that these wicked men of Kent were on their road towards London, the princess of Wales,[162] mother to the king,[163] was returning from a pilgrimage to Canterbury. She ran great risks from them; for these scoundrels attacked her car, and caused much confusion, which greatly frightened the good lady, lest they should do some violence to her or to her ladies. God, however, preserved her from this, and she came in one day from Canterbury to London, without venturing to make any stop by the way. Her son Richard [163] was this day in the Tower of London: thither the princess came, and found the king attended by the earl of Salisbury, the archbishop of Canterbury, sir Robert de Namur, the lord de Gommegines and several more, who had kept near his person from suspicions of his subjects who were thus assembling without knowing what they wanted. This rebellion was well known to be in agitation in the king's palace before it broke out and the country people had left their homes; to which the king applied no remedy, to the great astonishment of every one. In order that gentlemen and others may take example, and correct wicked rebels, I will most amply detail how this business was conducted.

On Monday preceding the feast of the Holy Sacrament,[164] in the year 1381, did these people sally forth from their homes to come to London to remonstrate with the king, that all might be made free, for they would not there should be any slaves in England. At Canterbury they met John Ball (who thought he should find there the Archbishop, but he was at London), Wat Tyler, and Jack Straw. On their entrance into Canterbury they were much feasted by every one, for the inhabitants were of their way of thinking; and, having held a council, they resolved to march to London, and also to send emissaries across the Thames to Essex, Suffolk, Bedford, and other counties, to press the people to march to London on that side, and thus, as it were, to surround it, which the king would not be able to prevent. It was their intention that all the different parties should be

[162] Widow of the Black Prince.   [163] Richard II.
[164] I am unable to find out what day this was.

collected together on the feast of the holy Sacrament, or on the following day.

Those who had come to Canterbury entered the church of St. Thomas, and did much damage: they pillaged the apartments of the archbishop, saying, as they were carrying off different articles: "This chancellor of England has had this piece of furniture very cheap: he must now give us an account of the revenues of England, and of the large sums he has levied since the coronation of the King." After they had defrauded the abbey of St. Vincent, they set off in the morning, and all the populace of Canterbury with them, taking the road towards Rochester. They collected the people from the villages to the right and left, and marched along like a tempest, destroying every house of an attorney or king's proctor, or that belonged to the archbishop, sparing none.

On their arrival at Rochester they were much feasted, for the people were awaiting for them, being of their party. They advanced to the castle, and seizing a knight called sir John de Newton, who was constable of it and captain of the town, they told him that he must accompany them as their commander-in-chief, and do whatever they should wish. The knight endeavored to excuse himself, and offered good reasons for it, if they had been listened to; but they said to him, "Sir John, if you will not act as we shall order, you are a dead man." The knight, seeing this outrageous mob ready to kill him, complied with their request, and very unwillingly put himself at their head. They had acted in a similar manner in the other counties of England, in Essex, Suffolk, Cambridge, Bedford, Stafford, Warwick, and Lincoln, where they forced great lords and knights, such as the lord Manley, a great baron, sir Stephen Hales, and sir Thomas Cossington, to lead and march with them. Now, observe how fortunately matters turned out, for had they succeeded in their intentions they would have destroyed the whole nobility of England: after this success, the people of other nations would have rebelled, taking example from those of Ghent and Flanders, who were in actual rebellion against their lord.[165]   In this same

[165] Philip van Artevelde was at this time leading the burghers of Flanders against their Count Louis. The revolt was crushed with the aid of Philip the Bold of Burgundy, son-in-law of Louis.

year the Parisians acted a similar part, arming themselves with leaden maces.[166] They were upwards of twenty thousand, as I shall relate when I come to that part of my history; but I will first go on with this rebellion in England.

When those who had lodged at Rochester had done all they wanted, they departed, and, crossing the river, came to Dartford, but always following their plan of destroying the houses of lawyers or proctors on the right and left of their road. In their way they cut off several men's heads, and continued their march to Blackheath, where they fixed their quarters: they said they were armed for the king and commons of England. When the citizens of London found they were quartered so near them, they closed the gates of London Bridge: guards were placed there by orders of sir William Walworth, mayor of London, and several rich citizens who were not of their party; but there were in the city more than thirty thousand who favored them.

Those who were at Blackheath had information of this; they sent, therefore, their knight to speak with the king, and to tell him that what they were doing was for his service, for the kingdom had been for several years wretchedly governed to the great dishonor of the realm and to the oppression of the lower ranks of the people, by his uncles,[167] by the clergy, and in particular by the archbishop of Canterbury, his chancellor, from whom they would have an account of his ministry. The knight dared not say nor do anything to the contrary, but, advancing to the Thames opposite the Tower, he took boat and crossed over. While the king and those with him in the Tower were in great suspense, and anxious to receive some intelligence, the knight came on shore: way was made for him, and he was conducted to the king, who was in an apartment with the princess his mother. There were also with the king his two maternal brothers, the earl of Kent and sir John Holland, the earls of Salisbury, Warwick, Suffolk, the archbishop of Canterbury, the great prior of the Templars in England, sir Robert de Namur, the lord de Vertain, the lord de Gommegines, sir Henry de

[166] A renewal about this time of the movement referred to on p. 331.
[167] Notably by Thomas, Duke of Gloucester, and John of Gaunt, Duke of Lancaster.

Sausselles, the mayor of London, and several of the principal citizens.

Sir John Newton, who was well known to them all, for he was one of the king's officers, cast himself on his knees and said: "My much redoubted lord, do not be displeased with me for the message I am about to deliver to you; for, my dear lord, through force I am come hither." "By no means, sir John; tell us what you are charged with: we hold you excused." "My very redoubted lord, the commons of your realm send me to you to entreat you would come and speak with them on Blackheath. They wish to have no one but yourself; and you need not fear for your person, for they will not do you the least harm: they always have respected and will respect you as their king; but they will tell you many things, which they say it is necessary you should hear; with which, however, they have not empowered me to acquaint you. But, dear lord, have the goodness to give me such an answer as may satisfy them, and that they may be convinced I have really been in your presence; for they have my children as hostages for my return, whom they will assuredly put to death if I do not go back."

The king replied, "You shall speedily have an answer." Upon this he called a council to consider what was to be done. The king was advised to say that if on Thursday they would come down to the river Thames, he would without fail speak with them. Sir John Newton, on receiving this answer, was well satisfied therewith, and, taking leave of the king and barons, departed: having entered his boat, he recrossed the Thames and returned to Blackheath, where he had left upwards of sixty thousand men. He told them from the king, that if they would send on the morrow morning their leaders to the Thames, the king would come and hear what they had to say. This answer gave great pleasure, and they were contented with it: they passed the night as well as they could; but you must know that one-fourth of them fasted for want of provision, as they had not brought any with them, at which they were much vexed, as may be supposed.

At this time the earl of Buckingham [168] was in Wales, where

[168] Constable of England and therefore an important man in this emergency.

he possessed great estates in right of his wife, who was daughter of the earl of Hereford and Northampton; but the common report about London was that he favored these people: some assured it for a truth, as having seen him among them, because there was one Thomas very much resembling him from the county of Cambridge. As for the English barons who were at Plymouth making preparations for their voyage, they had heard of this rebellion, and that the people were rising in all parts of the kingdom. Fearful lest their voyage should be prevented, or that the populace, as they had done at Southampton, Winchelsea, and Arundel, should attack them, they heaved their anchors, and with some difficulty left the harbor, for the wind was against them, and put to sea, when they cast anchor to wait for a wind.

The duke of Lancaster [169] was on the borders, between la Morlane, Roxburgh, and Melrose, holding conferences with the Scots: he had also received intelligence of this rebellion, and the danger his person was in, for he well knew he was unpopular with the common people of England. Notwithstanding this, he managed his treaty very prudently with the Scots commissioners, the earl of Douglas, the earl of Moray, the earl of Sutherland, the earl of Mar, and Thomas de Vesey. The Scotsmen who were conducting the treaty on the part of the king and the country knew also of the rebellion in England, and how the populace were rising everywhere against the nobility. They said that England was shaken and in great danger of being ruined, for which in their treaties they bore the harder on the duke of Lancaster and his council.

We will now return to the commonalty of England, and say how they continued in their rebellion.

On Corpus Christi [170] day king Richard heard mass in the tower of London, with all his lords, and afterwards entered his barge, attended by the earls of Salisbury, Warwick, and Suffolk, with other knights. He rowed down the Thames towards Rotherhithe, a manor belonging to the crown, where were upwards of ten thousand men, who had come from Blackheath to see the king and to speak to him: when they perceived his barge ap-

[169] John of Gaunt, the King's uncle.   [170] Thursday, June 13.

proach, they set up such shouts and cries as if all the devils in hell had been in their company. They had their knight, sir John Newton, with them; for, in case the king had not come and they found he had made a jest of them, they would, as they had threatened, have cut him to pieces.

When the king and his lords saw this crowd of people, and the wildness of their manner, there was not one among them so bold and determined but felt alarmed: the king was advised by his barons not to land, but to have his barge rowed up and down the river. "What do ye wish for?" demanded the king; "I am come hither to hear what you have to say." Those near him cried out with one voice: "We wish thee to land, when we will remonstrate with thee, and tell thee more at our ease what our wants are." The earl of Salisbury then replied for the king, and said: "Gentlemen, you are not properly dressed, nor in a fit condition for the king to talk with you."

Nothing more was said; for the king was desired to return to the Tower of London from whence he had set out. When the people saw they could obtain nothing more, they were inflamed with passion, and went back to Blackheath, where the main body was, to relate the answer they had received, and how the king was returned to the Tower. They all then cried out, "Let us march instantly to London." They immediately set off, and, in their road thither, they destroyed the houses of lawyers, courtiers, and monasteries. Advancing into the suburbs of London, which were very handsome and extensive, they pulled down many fine houses: in particular, they demolished the prison of the king called the Marshalsea, and set at liberty all those confined within it. They did much damage to the suburbs, and menaced the Londoners at the entrance of the bridge for having shut the gates of it, saying they would set fire to the suburbs, take the city by storm, and afterwards burn and destroy it.

With respect to the common people of London, numbers were of their opinions, and, on assembling together, said: "Why will you refuse admittance to these honest men? They are our friends, and what they are doing is for our good." It was then found necessary to open the gates, when crowds rushed in, and

ran to those shops which seemed well stored with provision: if
they sought for meat or drink it was placed before them, and
nothing refused, but all manner of good cheer offered, in hopes
of appeasing them.

Their leaders, John Ball, Jack Straw, and Wat Tyler, then
marched through London, attended by more than twenty thousand men, to the palace of the Savoy, which is a handsome building on the road to Westminster, situated on the banks of the
Thames, belonging to the duke of Lancaster; they immediately
killed the porters, pressed into the house, and set it on fire. Not
content with committing this outrage, they went to the house
of the knights-hospitalers of Rhodes, dedicated to St. John of
Mount Carmel, which they burnt, together with their hospital
and church. They afterwards paraded the streets, and killed
every Fleming they could find, whether in house, church, or hospital; not one escaped death. They broke open several houses
of the Lombards, taking whatever money they could lay their
hands on, none daring to oppose them. They murdered a rich
citizen called Richard Lyon, to whom Wat Tyler had been formerly servant in France; but, having once beaten this varlet, he
had not forgotten it, and, having carried his men to his house,
ordered his head to be cut off, placed upon a pike, and carried
through the streets of London. Thus did these wicked people
act like madmen; and, on this Thursday, they did much mischief to the city of London.

Towards evening they fixed their quarters in a square called
St. Catherine's, before the Tower, declaring they would not depart thence until they should obtain from the king everything
they wanted, and have all their desires satisfied; and the chancellor of England made to account with them, and show how
the great sums which had been raised were expended; menacing, that if he did not render such an account as was agreeable
to them, it would be the worse for him. Considering the various
ills they had done to foreigners, they lodged themselves before
the Tower. You may easily suppose what a miserable situation the king was in, and those with him; for at times these
rebellious fellows hooted as loud as if the devils were in them.

About evening a council was held in the presence of the king,

the barons who were in the Tower with him, sir William Walworth the mayor, and some of the principal citizens, when it
was proposed to arm themselves, and during the night to fall
upon these wretches, who were in the streets and amounted to
sixty thousand, while they were asleep and drunk, for then they
might be killed like flies, and not one in twenty among them
had arms. The citizens were very capable of doing this, for
they had secretly received into their houses their friends and
servants, properly prepared to act. Sir Robert Knolles remained
in his house, guarding his property, with more than six score
companions completely armed, who would have instantly sallied
forth. Sir Perducas d'Albreth was also in London at that
period, and would have been of great service; so that they could
have mustered upwards of eight thousand men, well armed. But
nothing was done; for they were too much afraid of the commonalty of London; and the advisers of the king, the earl of
Salisbury and others, said to him: "Sir, if you can appease them
by fair words, it will be so much better, and good humoredly
grant them what they ask; for, should we begin what we cannot
go through, we shall never be able to recover it: it will be all
over with us and our heirs, and England will be a desert."
This counsel was followed, and the mayor ordered to make no
movement. He obeyed, as in reason he ought. In the city of
London, with the mayor, there are twelve sheriffs, of whom
nine were for the king and three for these wicked people, as it
was afterwards discovered, for which they then paid dearly.

On Friday morning those lodged in the square before St.
Catherine's, near the Tower, began to make themselves ready;
they shouted much, and said that if the king would not come
out to them, they would attack the Tower, storm it, and slay all
in it. The king was alarmed at these menaces, and resolved to
speak with them; he therefore sent orders for them to retire to
a handsome meadow at Mile-end, where, in the summer time,
people go to amuse themselves, and that there the king would
grant them their demands. Proclamation was made in the King's
name for all those who wished to speak with him to go to the
above-mentioned place, where he would not fail to meet them.

The commonalty of the different villages began to march

thither; but all did not go, nor had they the same objects in view, for the greater part only wished for the riches and destruction of the nobles, and the plunder of London. This was the principal cause of their rebellion, as they very clearly showed; for when the gates of the Tower were thrown open, and the king, attended by his two brothers, the earls of Salisbury, of Warwick, of Suffolk, sir Robert de Namur, the lords de Vertain and de Gommegines, with several others, had passed through them, Wat Tyler, Jack Straw, and John Ball, with upwards of four hundred, rushed in by force, and, running from chamber to chamber, found the archbishop of Canterbury, whose name was Simon, a valiant and wise man, and chancellor of England, who had just celebrated mass before the king: he was seized by these rascals, and beheaded. The prior of St. John's suffered the same fate, and likewise a Franciscan friar, a doctor of physic, who was attached to the duke of Lancaster, out of spite to his master, and also a serjeant-at-arms of the name of John Laige. They fixed these four heads on long pikes, and had them carried before them through the streets of London: when they had sufficiently played with them, they placed them on London Bridge, as if they had been traitors to their king and country.

These scoundrels entered the apartment of the princess, and cut her bed, which so much terrified her that she fainted, and in this condition was by her servants and ladies carried to the river-side, when she was put into a covered boat, and conveyed to the house called the Wardrobe, where she continued that day and night like to a woman half dead, until she was comforted by the king her son, as you shall presently hear.

When the king was on his way to the place called Mile-end, without London, his two brothers, the earl of Kent and sir John Holland, stole off and galloped from his company, as did also the lord de Gommegines, not daring to show themselves to the populace at Mile-end for fear of their lives.

On the king's arrival, attended by the barons, he found upwards of sixty thousand men assembled from different villages and counties of England: he instantly advanced into the midst of them, saying in a pleasant manner, "My good people, I am your king and your lord: what is it you want? and what do you wish to say to me?" Those who heard him answered, "We wish thou wouldst make us free forever, us, our heirs and our lands, and that we should no longer be called slaves, nor held in bondage." The king replied, "I grant your wish: now, therefore, return to your homes and the places from whence you came, leaving behind two or three men from each village, to whom I will order letters to be given sealed with my seal, which they shall carry back with every demand you have made fully granted: and, in order that you may be the more satisfied, I will direct that my banners shall be sent to every stewardship, castlewick, and corporation." These words greatly appeased the novices and well-meaning ones who were there, and knew not what they wanted, saying, "It is well said: we do not wish for more." The people were thus quieted, and began to return towards London.

The king added a few words, which pleased them much: "You, my good people of Kent, shall have one of my banners; and you also of Essex, Sussex, Bedford, Suffolk, Cambridge, Stafford, and Lincoln, shall each of you have one; and I pardon you all for what you have hitherto done; but you must follow my banners, and now return home on the terms I have mentioned." They unanimously replied they would. Thus did this great assembly break up, and set out for London. The king instantly employed upwards of thirty secretaries, who drew up the letters as fast as they could; and, having sealed and delivered them to these people, they departed, and returned to their own counties.

The principal mischief remained behind: I mean Wat Tyler, Jack Straw, and John Ball, who declared that though the people were satisfied, they would not thus depart; and they had more than thirty thousand who were of their mind. They continued in the city, without any wish to have their letters, or the king's seal; but did all they could to throw the town into such confusion that the lords and rich citizens might be murdered, and their houses pillaged and destroyed. The Londoners suspected this, and kept themselves at home, with their friends and servants, well armed and prepared, every one according to his abilities.

When the people had been appeased at Mile-end Green, and were setting off for their different towns as speedily as they could receive the king's letters, king Richard went to the Wardrobe, where the princess was in the greatest fear: he comforted her, as he was very able to do, and passed there the night.

I must relate an adventure which happened to these clowns before Norwich, and to their leader, called William Lister, who was from the county of Stafford. On the same day these wicked people burnt the palace of the Savoy, the church and house of St. John, the hospital of the Templars, pulled down the prison of Newgate, and set at liberty all the prisoners, there were collected numerous bodies from Lincolnshire, Norfolk, and Suffolk, who proceeded on their march towards London, according to the orders they had received, under the direction of Lister.

In their road they stopped near Norwich, and forced every one to join them, so that none of the commonalty remained behind. The reason why they stopped near Norwich was, that the governor of the town was a knight called sir Robert Salle; he was not by birth a gentleman, but, having acquired great renown for his ability and courage, king Edward [171] had created him a knight: he was the handsomest and strongest man in England. Lister and his companions took it into their heads they would make this knight their commander, and carry him with them, in order to be the more feared. They sent orders to him to come out into the fields to speak with them, or they would attack and burn the city. The knight, considering it was much better for him to go to them than they should commit such outrages, mounted his horse, and went out of the town alone, to hear what they had to say. When they perceived him coming, they showed him every mark of respect, and courteously entreated him to dismount, and talk with them. He did dismount, and committed a great folly; for, when he had so done, having surrounded him, they at first conversed in a friendly way, saying,"Robert, you are a knight, and a man of great weight in this country, renowned for your valor; yet, notwithstanding all this, we know who you are: you are not a gentleman, but the son of a poor mason, just such as ourselves. Do you come with us, as our commander, and we will make so great a lord of you that one quarter of England shall be under your command."

[171] King Edward III.

The knight, on hearing them thus speak, was exceedingly angry; he would never have consented to such a proposal; and, eyeing them with inflamed looks, answered, "Begone, wicked scoundrels and false traitors as you are: would you have me desert my natural lord for such a company of knaves as you? I would much rather you were all hanged, for that must be your end." On saying this, he attempted to mount his horse; but, his foot slipping from the stirrup, his horse took fright. They then shouted out, and cried, "Put him to death." When he heard this, he let his horse go; and, drawing a handsome Bordeaux sword, he began to skirmish, and soon cleared the crowd from about him, that it was a pleasure to see. Some attempted to close with him; but with each stroke he gave, he cut off heads, arms, feet, or legs. There were none so bold but were afraid; and sir Robert performed that day marvellous feats of arms. These wretches were upwards of forty thousand; they shot and flung at him such things, that had he been clothed in steel instead of being unarmed, he must have been overpowered: However, he killed twelve of them, besides many whom he wounded. At last he was overthrown, when they cut off his legs and arms, and rent his body in piecemeal. Thus ended sir Robert Salle, which was a great pity; and when knights and squires in England heard of it, they were much enraged.

On the Saturday morning the king left the Wardrobe, and went to Westminster, where he and all the lords heard mass in the abbey. In this church there is a statue of our Lady [172] in a small chapel that has many virtues and performs great miracles, in which the kings of England have much faith. The king, having paid his devotions and made his offerings to this shrine, mounted his horse about nine o'clock, as did the barons who were with him. They rode along the causeway to return to London; but, when they had gone a little way, he turned to a road on the left to go from London.

This day all the rabble were again assembled, under the conduct of Wat Tyler, Jack Straw, and John Ball, to parley at a place called Smithfield, where, every Friday, the horse-market is kept. They amounted to upwards of twenty thousand, all

[172] The Virgin Mary.

of the same sort. Many more were in the city, breakfasting and drinking Rhenish and Malmsey Madeira wines, in taverns and at the houses of the Lombards, without paying for anything; and happy was he who could give them good cheer. Those who were collected in Smithfield had the king's banners, which had been given to them the preceding evening; and these reprobates wanted to pillage the city this same day, their leaders saying "That hitherto they had done nothing. The pardons which the king has granted will not be of much use to us; but, if we be of the same mind, we shall pillage this large, rich, and powerful town of London, before those from Essex, Suffolk, Cambridge, Bedford, Warwick, Reading, Lancashire, Arundel, Guildford, Coventry, Lynne, Lincoln, York, and Durham shall arrive; for they are on the road, and we know for certain that Vaquier and Lister will conduct them hither. If we now plunder the city of the wealth that is in it, we shall have been beforehand, and shall not repent of so doing; but if we wait for their arrival, they will wrest it from us." To this opinion all had agreed, when the king appeared in sight, attended by sixty horse. He was not thinking of them, but intended to have continued his ride without coming into London: however, when he came before the abbey of St. Bartholomew, which is in Smithfield, and saw the crowd of people, he stopped, and said he would not proceed until he knew what they wanted; and, if they were troubled he would appease them.

The lords who accompanied him stopped also, as was but right, since the king had stopped; when Wat Tyler, seeing the king, said to his men, "Here is the king: I will go and speak with him: do not you stir from hence until I give you a signal." He made a motion with his hand, and added, "When you shall see me make this sign, then step forward, and kill every one except the king; but hurt him not, for he is young, and we can do what we please with him; for, by carrying him with us through England, we shall be lords of it without any opposition." There was a doublet-maker of London, called John Ticle, who had brought sixty doublets, with which some of the clowns had dressed themselves; and on his asking who was to pay, for he must have for them thirty good marks, Tyler replied, "Make thyself easy, man; thou shalt be well paid this day: look to me for it: thou hast sufficient security for them." On saying this, he spurred the horse on which he rode, and, leaving his men, galloped up to the king, and came so near that his horse's head touched the crupper of that of the king. The first words he said, when he addressed the king, were, "King, dost thou see all those men there?" "Yes," replied the king; "why dost thou ask?" "Because they are all under my command, and have sworn by their faith and loyalty to do whatever I shall order." "Very well," said the king; "I have no objections to it." Tyler, who was only desirous of a riot, answered, "And thinkest thou, king, that those people and as many more who are in the city, also under my command, ought to depart without having had thy letters? Oh no, we will carry them with us." "Why," replied the king, "so it has been ordered, and they will be delivered out one after the other: but, friend, return to thy companions, and tell them to depart from London: be peaceable and careful of yourselves, for it is our determination that you shall all of you have your letters by villages and towns, as it has been agreed on."

As the king finished speaking, Wat Tyler, casting his eyes around him, spied a squire attached to the king's person bearing his sword. Tyler mortally hated this squire; formerly they had had words together, when the squire ill-treated him. "What, art thou there?" cried Tyler: "give me thy dagger." "I will not," said the squire: "why should I give it thee?" The king, turning to him, said, "Give it him, give it him;" which he did, though much against his will. When Tyler took it, he began to play with it and turn it about in his hand, and, again addressing the squire, said, "Give me that sword." "I will not," replied the squire; "for it is the king's sword, and thou art not worthy to bear it, who art but a mechanic; and, if only thou and I were together, thou wouldst not have dared to say what thou hast for as large a heap of gold as this church." "By my troth," answered Tyler, "I will not eat this day before I have thy head." At these words, the mayor of London, with about twelve more, rode forward, armed under their robes, and, pushing through the crowd, saw Tyler's manner of behaving: upon which he said, "Scoundrel, how dare you thus behave in the presence of the king, and utter such words? It is too impudent for such as thou." The king then began to be enraged and said to the mayor, "Lay hands on him."

Whilst the king was giving this order, Tyler had addressed the mayor, saying, "Hey, in God's name, what I have said, does it concern thee? what dost thou mean?" "Truly," replied the mayor, who found himself supported by the king, "does it become such a stinking rascal as thou art to use such speech in the presence of the king, my natural lord? I will not live a day, if thou pay not for it." Upon this, he drew a kind of scimitar he wore, and struck Tyler such a blow on the head as felled him to his horse's feet. When he was down, he was surrounded on all sides, so that his men could not see him; and one of the king's squires, called John Standwich, immediately leaped from his horse, and, drawing a handsome sword which he bore, thrust it into his belly, and thus killed him.

His men, advancing, saw their leader dead, when they cried out, "They have killed our captain: let us march to them, and slay the whole." On these words, they drew up in a sort of battle-array, each man having his bent bow before him. The king certainly hazarded much by this action, but it turned out fortunate; for when Tyler was on the ground, he left his attendants, ordering not one to follow him. He rode up to these rebellious fellows, who were advancing to revenge their leader's death, and said to them, "Gentlemen, what are you about? you shall have no other captain but me: I am your king: remain peaceable." When the greater part of them heard these words, they were quite ashamed, and those inclined to peace began to slip away. The riotous ones kept their ground, and showed symptoms of mischief, and as if they were resolved to do something.

The king returned to his lords, and asked them what should next be done. He was advised to make for the fields; for the mayor said "that to retreat or fly would be of no avail. It is proper we should act thus, for I reckon that we shall very soon receive assistance from London, that is, from our good friends who are prepared and armed, with all their servants in their houses." While things remained in this state, several ran to

London, and cried out, "They are killing the king! they are killing the king and our mayor." Upon this alarm, every man of the king's party sallied out towards Smithfield, and to the fields whither the king had retreated; and there were instantly collected from seven to eight thousand men in arms.

Among the first, came sir Robert Knolles and sir Perducas d'Albreth, well attended; and several of the aldermen, with upwards of six hundred men-at-arms, and a powerful man of the city called Nicholas Bramber, the king's draper, bringing with him a large force, who, as they came up, ranged themselves in order, on foot, on each side of him. The rebels were drawn up opposite them: they had the king's banners, and showed as if they intended to maintain their ground by offering combat. The king created three knights: sir William Walworth, mayor of London, sir John Standwich, and sir Nicholas Bramber. The lords began to converse among themselves, saying, "What shall we do? We see our enemies, who would willingly have murdered us if they had gained the upper hand." Sir Robert Knolles advised immediately to fall on them and slay them; but the king would not consent, saying, "I will not have you act thus: you shall go and demand from them my banners: we shall see how they will behave when you make this demand; for I will have them by fair or foul means." "It is a good thought," replied the earl of Salisbury.

The new knights were therefore sent, who, on approaching, made signs for them not to shoot, as they wished to speak with them. When they had come near enough to be heard, they said, "Now attend; the king orders you to send back his banners, and we hope he will have mercy on you." The banners were directly given up, and brought to the king. It was then ordered, under pain of death, that all those who had obtained the king's letters should deliver them up. Some did so; but not all. The king, on receiving them, had them torn in their presence. You must know that from the instant when the king's banners were surrendered, these fellows kept no order; but the greater part, throwing their bows to the ground, took to their heels and returned to London.

Sir Robert Knolles was in a violent rage that they were not

attacked, and the whole of them slain; but the king would not consent to it, saying, he would have ample revenge on them, which in truth he afterwards had.

Thus did these people disperse, and run away on all sides. The king, the lords, and the army returned in good array to London, to their great joy. The king immediately took the road to the Wardrobe, to visit the princess his mother, who had remained there two days and two nights under the greatest fears, as indeed she had cause. On seeing the king her son, she was mightily rejoiced, and said, "Ha, ha, fair son, what pain and anguish have I not suffered for you this day!" "Certainly, madam," replied the king, "I am well assured of that; but now rejoice and thank God, for it behoves us to praise him, as I have this day regained my inheritance, and the kingdom of England, which I had lost."

The king remained the whole day with his mother. The lords retired to their own houses. A proclamation was made through all the streets, that every person who was not an inhabitant of London, and who had not resided there for a whole year, should instantly depart; for that, if there were any found of a contrary description on Sunday morning at sunrise, they would be arrested as traitors to the king, and have their heads cut off. After this proclamation had been heard, no one dared to infringe it; but all departed instantly to their homes, quite discomfited. John Ball and Jack Straw were found hidden in an old ruin, thinking to steal away; but this they could not do, for they were betrayed by their own men. The king and the lords were well pleased with their seizure: their heads were cut off, as was that of Tyler, and fixed on London bridge, in the place of those gallant men whom they beheaded on the Thursday. The news of this was sent through the neighboring counties, that those might hear of it who were on their way to London, according to the orders these rebels had sent to them: upon which they instantly returned to their homes, without daring to advance further.[173]

---

[173] For the historical study of this episode in English history, cf. the following: Powell, *The Rising in East Anglia in 1381* (Cambridge University Press, 1896); Kriehn, *Studies in the Sources of the Social Revolt of 1381* (*American Historical Review*, VII, pp. 254–285; 458–484); Oman, *The Great Revolt of 1381* (Oxford,

Our final entry in this section devoted to the social and industrial background of this period in English literary history is also a protest, though a more or less humorous one. It is the poem, *The London Lyckpenny*, long ascribed, on the sole testimony of the sixteenth-century antiquarian John Stowe, to John Lydgate. But this external evidence is very late and "of internal evidence, there is not a shred to render Lydgate's authorship probable."[174] The poem, then, is anonymous, but we can still enjoy its humorous complaint.

> To London once my steppes I bent,
>> Where trouth in no wyse should be faynt.
> To Westmynster-ward I forthwith went,
>> To a man of law to make complaynt:
> I sayd, "For Marys love, that holy saynt,
>> Pyty the poore that wold proceede (i.e. go to law) !"
> But for lack of mony I cold not spede.
>
> And as I thrust the prese amonge,
>> By froward chance my hood was gone;
> Yet for all that I stayed not longe,
>> Tyll to the Kynges Bench I was come:
> Before the judge I kneled anon,
>> And prayed hym for Gods sake to take heede;
> But for lack of mony I myght not speede.

Clarendon Press, 1906). A considerable body of literature has been inspired by this revolt. Chaucer, to be sure, mentions it but once (cf. *The Nun's Priest's Tale, Canterbury Tales*, B, ll. 4584, 4585), but a large part of the *Vox Clamantis* (*Voice of One Crying*) by Gower is devoted to it. There are accounts in other chroniclers. (For Knighton's account see Cheyney, *Readings in English History*, pp. 261–265; for Adam of Usk's, Locke, *War and Misrule 1307–1399*, pp. 71–73). Then there is an Elizabethan play of 1587, *Jack Straw*, to be found in *Dodsley's Old Plays* (1744). Next comes Southey's play, *Wat Tyler* (1794). The most famous writing inspired by the rebellion is probably *The Dream of John Ball*, by William Morris (1888); the latest is the novel, *Long Will*, by Florence Converse (1903), which connects Langland with the revolt.

[174] Cf. E. P. Hammond in *Anglia*, XX, pp. 404–420. The quotation in the text is from p. 409.

Beneth hem sat clarkes, a great rout,
   Which fast dyd wryte by one assent:
There stoode up one and cryed about,
   "Rychard, Robert and John of Kent!"
I wyst not well what this man ment,
   He cryed so thycke there in dede;
But he that lackt mony myght not spede.

Unto the Common Place (Pleas) I yode (went) thoo (then),
   Where sat one with a sylken hoode;
I dyd hym reverence, for I ought to do so,
   And told my case as well as I coode,
How my goodes were defrauded me by falshood:
   I gat not a mum of his mouth for my meed,
   And for lack of mony I myght not spede.

Unto the Rolles I gat me from thence,
   Before the clarkes of the Chancerye,
Where many I found earnyng of pence;
   But none at all once regarded mee.
I gave them my playnt uppon my knee:
   They lycked it well, when they had it reade;
   But, lackyng mony, I could not be sped.

In Westmynster Hall I found out one
   Which went in a long gown of raye (a striped cloth):
I crowched and kneled before him anon;
   For Maryes love, of help I hym praye.
"I wot not what thou meanest," gan he say;
   To get me thence he dyd me bede (bid):
For lack of mony I cold not speed.

Within this hall nether rich nor yett poore
   Would do for me ought, although I shold dye.
Which seing, I gat me out of the doore,
   Where Flemynges began on me for to cry,
   "Master, what will you copen (cheapen) or by?
   Fyne felt hattes, or spectacles to reede?
Lay down your sylver, and here you may speede."

Then to Westmynster Gate I presently went,
  When the sonne was at hyghe pryme.
Cookes to me they tooke good entente,
  And proferred me bread with ale and wyne,
Rybbes of befe both fat and ful fyne;
  A fayre cloth they gan for to sprede:
But, wantyng mony, I myght not then speede.

Then unto London I dyd me hye;
  Of all the land it beareth the pryse.
"Hot pescodes!" one began to crye;
  "Strabery (strawberries) rype!" and "cherryes in the ryse
    (on the branch)!"
One bad me come near and by some spyce;
  Peper and saffrone (saffron) they gan me bede (offer):
But for lack of mony I myght not speed.

Then to the Chepe (Eastcheap) I gan me drawne,
  Where much people I saw for to stand.
One ofred me velvet, sylke and lawne;
  An other he taketh me by the hande:
"Here is Parys thred, the fynest in the land."
  I never was used to such thynges in dede,
And, wantyng mony, I myght not speed.

Then went I forth by London stone,
  Thoroughout all Canwyke streete:
Drapers mutch cloth me offred anone.
  Then met I one cryed, "Hot shepes feet!"
One cryde, "Makerell!" "Ryshes (rushes) grene!" another gan
    greete;
  On bad me by a hood to cover my head.
But for want of mony I myght not be sped.

Then I hyed me into Est Chepe:
  One cryes, "Rybbes of befe!" and many a pye;
Pewter pottes they clattered on a heap:
  There was harpe, pype and mynstralsye;
"Yea, by Cock!" "Nay, by Cock!" some began crye;

Some songe of Jenken and Julyan for there mede.
But for lack of mony I myght not spede.

Then into Cornhyll anon I yode,
  Where was mutch stolen gere among:
I saw where honge myne owne hoode,
  That I had lost amonge the thronge;
To by my own hood I thought it wronge;
  I knew it as well as I dyd my crede;
But for lack of mony I could not spede.

The taverner tooke me by the sleve;
  "Sir," sayth he, "wyll you our wyne assay?"
I answered, "That can not mutch me greve;
  A peny can do no more then it may."
I drank a pynt and for it dyd paye;
  Yet sore a-hungerd from thence I yede (went),
And, wantyng mony, I cold not spede.

Then hyed I me to Belyngsgate (Billingsgate),
  And one cryed, "Hoo! go we hence!"
I prayed a barge-man, for Gods sake,
  That he would spare me my expence.
"Thou scapst not here," quod he, "under two pence;
  I lyst not yet bestow my almes dede."
Thus, lackyng mony, I could not speede.

Then I convayed me into Kent,
  For of the law I would meddle no more;
Because no man to me tooke entent,
  I dyght me to do as I dyd before.
Now Jesus, that in Bethlem was bore,
  Save London, and send trew lawyers there made!
For who-so wantes mony with them shall not spede!

III. THE CULTURAL BACKGROUND

1. *Ideals of the Period.* — The official clerical philosophy
of the Middle Ages included a doctrine which was so strong
an influence on medieval culture that it deserves treatment

by itself.   This is the doctrine or ideal of asceticism; i.e. the belief that this life in itself is inherently bad; that delight in the world as we perceive it by the senses is an ill-omen for the life of the spirit; and that mortification "of the four great natural passions — joy, hope, fear and grief,"[1] is the way of salvation.   Asceticism, says Professor Ross, "is the resource of a rising contemplative class in getting the upper hand of rude, violent men. . . . The volume and persistence of the world's asceticism cannot be understood until we take note of it as instrument of social control."[2]

The typical medieval writer is the ecclesiastic; his literary talent finds expression in homily, saint's life, vision, allegory or religious play; and all of these inculcate directly the philosophy of asceticism.   This we must understand in order to appreciate this large body of medieval literature.

On the other hand, lay-literature in the Middle Ages, small in bulk at first but growing larger as the course of the world proceeds, is critical of the ascetic spirit.   But again, the latter must be before us or we cannot see the point of the criticism, which may take the form of subtle satire.

The document selected to illustrate this ascetic ideal is the *Debate between the Body and the Soul.*   The poem, too, is typical of a large body of didactic verse presenting doctrine in the form of discussion; and, further, it is interesting because it is a vision poem, that peculiar product of the medieval mind.

The poem was evidently popular since it is found in six MSS.   The only difficulty in our including it here is its length — in the original it consists of 61 stanzas of 8 lines each.   But this obstacle has been overcome by presenting a partial synopsis with direct quotation of the more impressive stanzas.

In the opening stanza we are introduced to a vision of the

[1] Cf. Robinson, *Readings in European History*, I, p. 88 (Ginn and Co., 1904).
[2] *Social Control*, pp. 310, 311 (The Macmillan Co., 1901).

death of a knight who had led a gay life. His soul, about
to leave his body, addresses the latter, so foul and black,
and wishes to know what has become of all the pleasures
in which the body was wont to indulge:

> "Where now are all thy rich and costly weeds,
> Thy sumpter horses and thy silken bed,
> Thy pacing palfreys, and the other steeds
> That thou hast often with thy right hand led;
> Thy swift-winged falcons that were wont to scream,
> And all the baying hounds that thou hast fed?
> God grants but little to thee, it would seem,
> Now all thy former friends have from thee fled." [3]

At the conclusion of this list of pleasures, which includes
several stanzas, the body admits that it did indulge in
them, but asserts that everything was done at the instance
of the soul. The body says:

> "I served thy pleasure ever, night and day,
> At darkening even and at dewy morn;
> E'en as a child thou guidedst me at play,
> Yea, from the very day when thou wert born.
> Thou, who couldst judge of good and evil deeds,
> Shouldst have known how to count the bitter cost
> Of acts like mine, and where such folly leads;
> Blame, then, thyself, if now thou shalt be lost." [4]

The soul's reply, one of the best passages in the whole
poem, is quoted in full:

> The spirit answered, "Body, be thou still;
> And of thy fierce words have a care;
> Think not to chide and mock me at thy will
> That swollen like a bottle liest there.
> Think not, O wretch, though thou art soon to fill
> With thy foul flesh a dark and narrow grave,
> That, after all the deeds thou didst of ill,
> Thou yet so easily thyself shalt save.

[3] Stanza 4.   [4] Stanza 8.

" Think not to get sweet peace, thus stained with sin,
There where thou liest, mouldering in the clay;
Though thou shalt be decayed without, within,
And wafted by the idle wind away,
Still shalt thou rise complete from out the sod
Again to meet me at the judgment day,
And come before the dooming bar of God,
Where we the penalty of sin must pay.

"Thou wert assigned to me to teach me good,
But when thou thought'st to do some evil deed,
I could not hold thee back, strive as I would;
I had to follow thee, instead of lead.
Thee I withstood as firmly as I could,
But bit in teeth, like a rebellious steed,
Thou wouldst not cleave to innocence or good,
Thou followedst sin and wrong with shameful speed.

"I wished to show thee what was fair, what bad;
Tell thee of Christ and of His church on earth;
But thou, in thy career, so wild and mad,
Receiv'dst my teaching but with mocking mirth.
Although with fervor I might preach and pray,
Thy wicked mind and heart were not inspired;
But still rejected good from day to day,
And did whatever evil they desired.

"I bade thee think upon thy poor soul's needs,
Matins and masses, vesper, evensong;
But thou wert fain to do first other deeds,
And at my warning words laughed loud and long;
By field and stream, swift as an arrow speeds,
Didst hasten to the Court to do men wrong;
But for the sake of pride or other meeds
Little of right thou didst among the throng.

"Who is a greater traitor to his lord,
Or who can less contrive to do his will,
Than one he trusts in every act and word
Through every day and hour to serve him still?

And while thou wert so prosperous and great,
And while I searched and sought with all my might
Thy rest and peace, thou strov'dst to seal my fate,
And plunge me ever into hell's dark night.

"Now may the wild beasts roam the fields at will,
Or lie in peace beneath the branch and leaf;
And birds fly freely over mead and hill;
For thy false heart may cause them no more grief:
Thy lips are dumb, thy ears no sound can hear,
Thy eyes are blinded by the hand of death,
Thou liest loathsome, grinning on thy bier,
From thy foul form there comes an evil breath.

"No lovely lady, whom in days of old
Thou didst caress and woo with glances sweet,
Would lie beside thee where thou liest cold,
Though all the wide world's wealth were at her feet.
Thou art unlovely, fearsome now to see;
Those icy lips tempt not for kisses meet;
Thou hast no friend who would not wildly flee,
·If he should meet thee strolling on the street." [5]

The body again answers that his whole conduct was
suggested by the soul. But the latter reminds the body
that their constant association was not voluntary, at least
on his part:

"Of the same woman were we born and bred,
O body, both together, without doubt;
Together were we fostered fair and fed,
Till thou didst learn to speak and run about.
And softly thee with tenderest love I led,
To cause thee woe I never did incline,
To lose thy service was my constant dread —
I knew no other body would be mine." [6]

[5] Stanzas 9–16 inclusive.   [6] Stanza 22.

"Thy flesh and blood seemed very fair to me:
I wished to see thee thrive while thou didst live;
For all my love was truly placed on thee,
And peace and rest I ever sought to give.
But thou didst grow so stubborn and unkind,
So weak in works, so blind to what was best,
I tried no longer to oppose thy mind;
Although I ever lived within thy breast.

"So for our ruin thou didst everything
Of malice, envy, gluttony and pride,
That was displeasing unto heaven's King
And ever in His anger didst abide.
So evermore thou hadst thy sinful way
And none of thy foul pleasures wouldst thou leave;
Full dearly now I for thy sins must pay —
Ah, well-a-day, too sorely must I grieve.

"Of what would surely come to thee and me
A faithful warning oft to thee I gave;
But as an idle tale it seemed to thee,
That thou couldst fall into the silent grave.
Thou didst all evil things the world thee bade,
And took each pleasure which thy flesh did crave;
I suffered thee, and was myself as mad —
Thou the wild master; I, thy wretched knave." [7]

The body in its turn asserts that all knowledge of right
or wrong comes from the soul and again places the responsibility for his conduct on the soul:

"Think'st thou, O spirit, a reward to gain
By saying falsely that thou wert my thrall?
Or to escape from punishment and pain
By lying words and groans and tears withal?
In all my life long never did I aught,
Or stole or robbed or sinned in any way,

[7] Stanzas 24–26 inclusive.

But that from thee first came the wicked thought:
He who has earned the punishment must pay.

"How could I know what act was wrong, what right,
What I should take or what I should forgo,
Except the things thou placedest in my sight,
Because I deemed that wisdom thou didst know?
When evil were the deeds thou taughtest me,
And then to me thou didst begin to moan,
Thy way being evil, as I then could see,
I strove another time to have mine own.

"But hadst thou then, as Christ deserved of thee,
My flesh subdued with hunger, thirst and cold,
Remembering naught of good was known to me,
When in my wickedness I grew so bold,
All I had undertaken in my youth
That had I followed still when I was old;
Thou letst me ever wander north and south
And have my will and my own false way hold.

"Thou never shouldst, for any life or land,
Nor any other worldly joy to win,
Have suffered me to turn to either hand,
To any act that led to shame or sin.
But thee I found so easy to control,
Of so small wit, so swayed by every wind
As is a waving wand, O wretched soul —
No reason to cease sinning could I find.

"Thou knew'st that every man is prone to sin;
From the beginning it was always so;
And strives the pleasures of the world to win,
And serves the fiend that is our deadly foe.
So, when I turned to sin, like all my kind,
Thou shouldst have kept me from these evils all:
But when the blind attempt to lead the blind,
Into the ditch they both are sure to fall." [8]

[8] Stanzas 27-31 inclusive. For the reference in the last two lines cf. Matt.
15: 14.

The soul admits that he felt his responsibility for the care of the body, but concludes that both body and spirit have been beguiled by the world, the flesh and the devil:

"The false, foul fiend of hell, that enviously
Has ever looked upon all humankind,
Was alway as a spy to thee and me
When I a good thought put into thy mind.
The world and flesh he had for company,
That many a soul before deceivéd had;
These three, who knew the foolishness of thee,
Beguiled thee, wretched one, and made thee mad." [9]

This draws from the body a bitter lament over his misspent life. Among other things the body bewails the fact that he was fated to be a human body. Why could he not have been a brute and so have avoided all these troublesome moral problems? The soul, however, breaks in to remark that nothing can now shield them from the consequences of their sin; the hell-hounds are at hand:

"Should all the men who still retain their lives,
And all the dark robed priests who masses sing,
And all the gracious maidens and good wives
And widows weep for us and their hands wring —
If five times every one who is alive,
And five times over every earthly thing
Should plead, since we our own selves did not shrive —
Us unto heaven's bliss they could not bring.

"Body, I may no longer with thee dwell;
Nor stand beside thee here to speak with thee;
For now I hear the hell-hounds' piercing yell;
And fiends more than a man did ere this see
Are coming now to drag me down to hell:
And from them I can never hope to flee;
But with thy skin and blood, remember well,
At doomsday shalt thou be again with me." [10]

[9] Stanza 33.   [10] Stanzas 44, 45.

A vivid description of the torture of the body follows:

They [11] said that rich and costly weeds to wear
Was on the earth the thing he [12] loved the best;
Therefore, a devil's cloak was there,
All burning hot, and on him it was pressed.
With hot clasps was it fastened, close and tight,
Clinging with torture to his back and breast.
A helmet on his head by no means light
They placed and then led forth a horse all dressed.

A bridle was brought forth to place on it;
A cursed devil as a colt then seemed,
Horridly grinning, flames his red eyes lit,
Upon his head and throat the bright fire gleamed.
A saddle in the middle of the side,
Full of sharp spurs, all glowing red and hot,
Whereon the wretched spirit was to ride —
A fearful seat and rough it was, I wot.

Upon the saddle was he slung,
Where he should suffer ever more and more,
A thousand devils then his death song sung,
Pursued him here and there and beat him sore;
With hot spears, then, he through and through was stung:
All torn and bruised he was from head to feet,
At every step forth glowing sparks were flung,
As from a brand that burns with fervent heat.

When he a while had ridden on that road,
From off the saddle where he had been placed
He was cast down to earth as is a toad,
And hell-hounds fierce and cruel then him chased.
They tore great pieces from him on the way
As shrieking madly he was hellward led;
A man might mark by bloody drops that day
Where the wild fiends and that poor soul did tread.

[11] I.e. the torturing fiends.   [12] I.e. the guilty body.

In cruel sport they bade him blow his horn,
Cry on his hounds Bauston and Bevis too;
As in the days of yore, at early morn
Out hunting he was ever wont to do.
A hundred howling devils in a row
Beat him with cords, and shouted curses bold,
Until they reached that dark pool, loathed and low,
Where hell is, as I often have been told.

And when they had to that dark dwelling won,
The fiends cast into air so wild a yell,
The solid earth it opened up anon,
And smoke and vapor from it up did swell;
Odor of pitch and brimstone forth did go;
For five miles round men might perceive it well —
Lord, he would be a man in fearful woe
Who must endure a tenth of such a smell.[13]

The poem concludes with the futile plea of the soul for
mercy, the casting of the body into hell, and the dreamer's
reflections on the experience, exhorting men to repent while
yet there is time.

Interweaving with this ascetic ideal and yet contrasting
with it was chivalry, which can best be described as a
system of social life and manners, the cultural reflection
of the feudal system.   Chivalry has its roots [14] in the Teu-

---

[13] Stanzas 50–56 inclusive. For a satire on the ascetic ideal see the beast epic
of *Reynard the Fox.* Mr. Jacobs' adaptation in *Burt's Home Library* gives a very
good version of the numerous tales. The *Introduction* is also a valuable account
of the sources and relations of the various stories.

[14] Cf. e.g. *ante,* p. 12, the Teutonic ceremony for initiating the youth into the
tribe. The English before the Norman Conquest may even have made some progress in systematizing the conferring of knighthood. Cf. the following record in
Ingulph, *Chronicle of the Abbey of Croyland,* ". . . It was the custom of the English,
that he who was about to be lawfully consecrated a knight should, the evening before the day of his consecration, with contrition and compunction, make confession
of all his sins, before some bishop, abbot, monk or priest, and should, after being
absolved, pass the night in a church, giving himself up to prayer, devotion and
mortification. On the following day he was to hear mass and to make offering of

tonic military spirit and this, consecrated by the church, blossomed in the knightly ideals of courtesy, individual accomplishments, and morality. Much of the literature of our period aims directly or covertly to teach the principles of chivalry, as for example this French story of *Sir Hugh of Tabarie.*

In the years when Saladin was King, there lived a Prince in Galilee, who was named Sir Hugh of Tabarie. On a day he was with other Christian men who gave battle to the Turks, and, since it pleased God to cast his chivalry behind him, Sir Hugh was taken prisoner, and many another stout knight with him. When dusk closed down on the field, the Prince was led before Saladin, who, calling him straightway to mind, rejoiced greatly and cried, "Ah, Sir Hugh, now are you taken." "Sire," answered the brave knight, "the greater grief is mine." "By my faith, Hugh, every reason have you for grief, since you must either

a sword upon the altar, and, after the gospel, the priest was to bless the sword and, with a blessing, lay it upon the neck of the knight; on which, after having communicated at the same mass in the sacred mysteries of Christ, he became a lawful knight. The Normans held in abomination this mode of consecrating a knight, and did not consider such a person to be a lawful knight, but a mere tardy trooper, and a degenerate plebeian." Riley's translation in *Bohn's Antiquarian Library,* 1854 (George Bell and Sons). Too much importance must not be assigned to this notice on account of the doubtful character of the *Chronicle* from which it is quoted. But Miss Dodd in her *Early English Social History from the Chronicles* (London, George Bell and Sons, Ltd., 1913), quotes it as of some value on p. 134. Chaucer draws three pictures of chivalric personages, the knight, the squire and the yeoman. Cf. *Prolog to the Canterbury Tales,* ll. 42–117. His *Knight's Tale* is a good example of the romance of chivalry, drawing its material from the "matter of antiquity" (cf. *post,* p. 518). The best general treatment of chivalry in English is Francis Warre Cornish, *Chivalry* in the *Social England Series* (The Macmillan Co., 1901). The most extensive work published is by Alwin Schultz, *Das Höfische Leben* (*The Courtly Life*) (Leipzig, S. Hirzel, 1889). For chivalry in its bearing on English literature consult W. H. Schofield, *Chivalry in English Literature: Chaucer, Malory, Spenser, Shakespeare* (*Harvard Studies in Comparative Literature,* II, the Harvard University Press, 1912). On the courtly person and his counterpart, the villein, cf. S. L. Galpin, *Cortois and Villain in French and Provençal Poetry,* 1200–1400, pp. 95, 96 (Yale Dissertation on the subject published by the author and printed by Ryder's Printing House, New Haven). See also C. S. Baldwin, *An Introduction to English Medieval Literature* (Longmans, Green and Co., 1914), *chivalry* and *courtly love* in the *Index.*

pay your ransom or die." "Sire, I am more fain to pay ransom than to die, if by any means I may find the price you require of me." "Is that truly so?" said the King. "Sire," said Sir Hugh, "in the fewest words, what is the sum you demand of me?" "I ask of you," replied the King, "one hundred thousand besants." [15] "Sire, such a sum is too great a ransom for a man of my lands to pay." "Hugh," said the king, "you are so good a knight, and so hardy, that there is none who hears of your prison and this ransom, but will gladly send of his riches for your ease." "Sire," said he, "since thus it must be, I promise to pay the sum you require, but what time do you grant me to find so mighty a ransom?" "Hugh," said the King, "I accord you the grace of one year. If within the year you count me out the tale of these besants, I will take it gladly; but if you fail to gain it then must you return to your prison and I will hold you more willingly still." "Sire, I pledge my word and my faith. Now deliver me such a safe conduct that I may return in safety to my own land."

"Hugh, before you part I have a privy word to speak to you." "Sire, with all my heart, and where?" "In this tent, close by." When they had entered into the pavilion, the Emperor Saladin sought to know in what fashion a man was made knight of the Christian chivalry, and required of him that he should show it to his eyes. "Sire, whom then should I dub knight?" "Myself," answered the King. "God forbid that I should be so false as to confer so high a gift and so fair a lordship even upon the body of so mighty a prince as you." "But wherefore?" said the King. "For reason, sire, that your body is but an empty vessel." "Empty of what, Sir Hugh?" "Sire, of Christianity and of baptism." "Hugh," said he, "think not hardly of me because of this. You are in my hand, and if you do the thing that I require of you, what man is there to blame you greatly when you return to your own realm? I seek this grace of you,

---

[15] The coin referred to here is probably the gold bezant, more properly called solidus, issued by the emperors at Constantinople in the Middle Ages, worth in present American money $2.43. There was also a silver coin of the same issue, called the white bezant, worth 70 cents. The word *bezant* comes from the name of the city Byzantium, so called before Constantine made it over into Constantinople.

rather than of another, because you are the stoutest and the most perfect knight that ever I may meet." "Sire," said he, "I will show you what you seek to know, for were it but the will of God that you were a christened man, our chivalry would bear in you its fairest flower." [16] "Hugh," said he, "that may not be."

Whereupon Sir Hugh made ready all things necessary for the making of a knight; and having trimmed the hair and beard of the King in seemly fashion, he caused him to enter within the bath and inquired, ' Sire, do you understand the meaning of this water?" "Hugh, of this I know nothing." "Sire, as the little child comes forth from the waters of baptism clean of sin, so should you issue from this bath washed pure of all stain and villainy." "By the law of the Prophet, Sir Hugh, it is a fair beginning." Then Sir Hugh brought the Sultan before an untouched bed, and having laid him therein, he said, "Sire, this bed is the promise of that long rest in paradise which you gain by the toils of chivalry." So when the King had lain softly therein for a little space, Sir Hugh caused him to stand upon his feet, and having clothed him in a fair white vesture of linen and silk, said, "Sire, this spotless stole you first put on is but the symbol of a body held and guarded clean." Afterwards he set upon the King a gown of scarlet silk and said, "Sire, this vermeil robe keeps ever in your mind the blood a knight must shed in the service of his God and the defence of Holy Church." Then taking the King's feet in his hands, he drew thereon shoes of brown leather, saying, "Sire, these brown shoes with which you are shod, signify the color of the earth from which you came, and to which you must return; for whatever degree God permits you to attain, remember, O mortal man, that you are but dust." Then Sir Hugh raised the Sultan to his feet and girt him with a white baldric, saying, "Sire, this white cincture I belt about your loins is the type of that chastity with which you must be girded withal. For he who would be worthy of such dignity as this must ever keep his body pure as any maid." After this was brought to Sir Hugh a pair of golden spurs and these he did upon the shoes with which the sultan was shod, saying, "Sire, so swiftly as the destrier plunges in the fray at the prick of these

[16] Cf. Saladin as Scott pictures him in *The Talisman*.

spurs, so swiftly, so joyously, should you fight as a soldier of
God for the defence of Holy Church." Then at the last Hugh
took a sword, and holding it before the King, said, "Sire, know
you the three lessons of this glaive?" "What lessons are these?"
"Courage, justice and loyalty. The cross at the hilt of his
sword gives courage to the bearer, for when the brave knight
girds his sword upon him he neither can, nor should, fear the
strong adversary himself. Again, sire, the two sharp edges of
the blade teach loyalty and justice, for the office of chivalry is
this, to sustain the weak against the strong, the poor before
the rich, uprightly and loyally." The King listened to all these
words very heedfully and at the end inquired if there was nothing more that went to the making of a knight. "Sire, there is
one thing else but that I dare not do." "What thing is this?"
"It is the acolade." "Grant me now the acolade and tell me
the meaning thereof." "Sire, the acolade is a blow upon the
neck [17] given with a sword, and the significance thereof is that
the newly made knight may always bear in mind the lord who
did him that great courtesy. But such a stroke will I not deal
to you, for it is not seemly, since I am here your prisoner."

That night Saladin, the mighty Sultan, feasted in his chamber with the fifty greatest lords of his realm, emirs, governors
and admirals, and Sir Hugh of Tabarie sat on a cushion at his
feet. At the close of the banquet Sir Hugh rose up before the
King and said, "Sire, grant me grace. I may not forget that
you bade me to seek out all fair and honorable lords, since there
is none who would not gladly come to my help in this matter
of my ransom. But, fair Sir King, in all the world shall I never
find a lord so wise, so hardy and so courteous as yourself. Since
you have taught me this lesson, it is but just and right that I
should pray you to be the first to grant me aid herein."

Then Saladin laughed loudly out of a merry heart and said,
"Pray God that the end be as sweet as the beginning. Truly,
Sir Hugh, I will not have it on my conscience that you miss
your ransom because of any meanness of mine, and, therefore,
without guile, for my part I will give you fifty thousand besants."

[17] Cf. the possibly Old English custom recorded in the extract from Ingulph's
Chronicle, ante, p. 364.

Then the great Sultan rose from his throne, and taking Prince Hugh with him, came to each of the lords in turn, emir, governor and admiral, and prayed of him aid in the business of this ransom. So all the lords gave largely out of a good heart in such measure that Sir Hugh presently acquitted himself of his ransom and returned to his own realm from among the paynim.

The pomp and circumstance of chivalry are well illustrated in the following passage from *Gawain and the Green Knight* which the late Gaston Paris, the great French authority on medieval literature, called the pearl of English medieval romance. At the opening of the story, while Arthur is celebrating New Year's Day at Camelot, a gigantic Green Knight, riding a green horse, enters and offers to allow any of King Arthur's knights to strike him with his ax a blow on the neck, provided the respondent will allow the challenger to return the compliment the following year. At first all are dumfounded, but at length Gawain, the pattern knight, screws up his courage to undertake the enterprise. After the proper preparations have been made, Gawain cuts off the Green Knight's head and it rolls about the floor. But the giant unconcernedly picks it up by the hair, gets back on his horse, and rides off, reminding Gawain of his promise to meet him at the Green Chapel the next year. Our passage tells how, after his time of respite is over, Gawain prepares to redeem his promise.[18]

> Yule is now o'erpast and the year is gone.
> Each season has succeeded in due turn;
> For after Christmas time comes crabbed Lent,
> Demanding fish for flesh and simpler cheer.
> Then the world's weather with the winter strives,
> The cold withdraws itself, the clouds uplift,

---

[18] Cf. a complete verse translation of Gawain and the Green Knight in Weston, *Romance, Vision and Satire* (Houghton Mifflin Co., 1912). The same translator before had published a partial prose rendering of the story as Vol. I of the series *Arthurian Romances Unrepresented in Malory* (David Nutt, 1900).

And softly falls the rain in showers warm
On the fair plains on which the flowers appear.
The meadows and the groves are clad in green,
Birds busk themselves to build and blithely sing
For solace of soft summer that ensues:
Upon the banks the bonny blossoms bloom,
Both rich and rank, and noble notes enough
Are heard in fairest woods from dawn to dark.

After the summer season with soft winds,
When Zephyr breathes his soul on seeds and herbs,
Full joyous is the growth that waxes there,
When the dark dew drips from the drooping leaves
Beneath the blissful blush of the bright sun.
And then comes harvest, hardening the grain,
And warning it to wax for winter ripe.
With drought he drives the dust into the air
On high and wafts it widely over face of fields.
The wroth wind of the welkin with the sun
Angrily wrestles and the leaves drop down
From ageing trees and light upon the ground:
And gray are all the groves that were so green
But yesterday, and ripe is all the fruit
That then was flower; so goes the gliding year
Into its many yesterdays, and so
The winter comes again, and the world needs
No sage to tell us this.

          Now when the morn
Of Michaelmas [19] was come, with warning sad
Of winter near, full oft thought Gawain
Of that dread journey which he soon must take.

Yet till All-Hallows' [20] Day he lingered there
With Arthur, who, on that same day, made feast
For that brave hero's sake, with revelry,
And all the richness of the Table Round —
The courteous knights and comely ladies there

[19] Sept. 29.   [20] Nov. 1.

Were all in sorrow for that well loved knight;
And, though they spoke no word to tell their grief,
Still many there were joyless for his lot.
After the meat, with mourning Gawain turned
Unto his king and uncle and then spoke
About his riding and his words were these,
"Now, liege lord of my life, your leave I crave,
You know my plight and, therefore, I am bound
To say no more. In honor am I pledged
To set forth on the morrow on my search
For that Green Knight as God may give me light."

Then came together all the noblest knights,
Ywain and Eric and full many more,
Sir Dodinel le Sauvage, the great duke
Of Clarence, Launcelot and Lionel,
Lucan, the Good, Sir Bors, Sir Bedivere,
Both mighty men, and heroes many too,
With Mador de la Porte. These courtiers all
Got round the King, with heavy hearts,
To give their counsel unto Sir Gawain.
Much grief and weeping was there in the hall
That such a gallant knight should wend his way
On such an errand, seeking for a blow
So deadly, and should deal no other stroke
With his good sword. But he made good cheer
And said, "Why shrink? What yet remains
To do for a brave man but prove his fate,
However dire and fearsome it may be?"

He dwelt there all that day, but the next morn
He rose up early, asking for his arms,
Which then were brought and in this knightly wise:
First a rich carpet on the floor was laid —
How gaily on it glittered the gold gear
As the knight stepped thereon and grasped the steel!
Clad was he in a doublet of rich silk
With a close hood, well made and lined throughout
With soft, warm fur. Steel shoes upon his feet

They set and wrapped his limbs in shining greaves
With knee caps polished bright and fastened firm
About his knees with knots of gleaming gold.
His thighs were cased in cuisses of strong steel,
Fast closed with leather thongs. They gave him then
The shield of polished steel rings, firmly sewn
Upon fair stuff; and burnished braces strong
Upon his arms, with elbow pieces stout,
They tightly lashed, and gave him too the gloves
Of steel to shield his hands, and other gear
That should protect him in his hour of need.
And over all they cast a rich surcoat;
And fastened on his heels the golden spurs;
And by a silken girdle to this hero's side
They bound a sword full sure.

                      When he was garbed
In harness thus, his armor was right rich,
For the least loop or latchet of that mail
Burned with bright gold. Accoutered as he was,
He harkened to the mass and offering made
At high church altar. Then to king
And nobles of the court and ladies fair
He came and farewell bade them courteously,
Who kissed him and commended him to Christ.
Then Gringalet his steed, with saddle girt
That glistened bright with many a gilded fringe,
Stood ready for the venture, decked anew.
The bridle barred with buttons of clear gold,
The covertures and trappings of that steed,
The crupper and the long and flowing skirts
Accorded with the saddle, for they shone
And glittered, like the rising sun's bright rays,
With rich red gold.

                  His helmet then he took
And raised it hastily and on his head
He set it high and hasped it fast behind.
All strongly was it made and lined throughout.

Over the ventail was a kerchief light,
Broidered and bound about with finest gems
On a broad silken ribbon, and gay birds,
And many a turtle and true lover's knot
Were also broidered there, entwined so thick,
It seemed that many maidens must have wrought
Quite seven winters long to finish it.
But the fair circlet that his helmet crowned
Was wealthier still of price, adorned as 'twas
With a device of diamonds, large and pure.

Then showed they him the shield of splendid red,
Whereon the pentangle enamelled was
In golden hue. And why the noble prince
Bore this device, I fain would tell,
Although I thus must tarry in my tale.
It is a sign which Solomon once set,
Betokening truth, by title that it had;
Because it is a figure with five points,
Each line of which another overlaps,
And hath nowhere beginning nor an end,
Being an endless knot in English speech.
Hence, it was suited well unto this knight
And his clear arms, for faithful in five-fold
Was good Gawain, and pure as gold was he,
Void of all ill and well endowed
With virtues all: and so this mark
He bore upon his shield and outer coat,
As truest hero and as gentlest knight.

Faultless in his five senses was he first;
And his five fingers never played him false;
And all his trust was in the five great wounds
That Christ felt on the cross, as told in Creed.
And when in battle he was sore beset
He wist well that he drew his conquering strength
From the five joys which Heaven's Queen
Had of Her Child. For this cause did he bear
An image of Our Lady, wrought out well,

On one half of his shield, that when he looked
On Her sweet face he should not lack for aid.
And the fifth five that my fair hero used
I find were frankness and good fellowship
Above all else; and purity of soul,
And courtesy, that never failed or swerved,
And sweet compassion, that surpasseth all.
In these five virtues was he wrapped and clothed,
And all these, five-fold, were linked each with each,
So that they had no end; and they were fixed
Upon five points that ne'er were known to want —
Nor were they joined or sundered anywhere,
Nor could ye a beginning find or end.
Therefore, upon his shield was shaped that knot,
All painted with keen gold on ground of red,
Which is the pure pentangle, as they know
Who learning have. So Gawain was prepared
And took his lance in hand and bade good-bye
Unto them all — he feared forevermore.[21]

A concrete expression of the spirit of chivalry is to be
seen in the supposed founding by Edward III in 1344 of
the Order of the Garter, modeled on the knighthood of
King Arthur. The event is thus described in the *Continuation of the Chronicles* by Adam of Murimuth, a contemporary.

In the year 1344, the king, Edward III, ordered a great
tournament to be held on the nineteenth day of January in the
place of his birth, that is, in the castle of Windsor; and this

[21] The story ends as follows: "As the next New Year drew nigh, Gawain, riding
wild ways afar in his search, was received and nobly entertained at Christmastide
in a castle whose lord promised to escort him betimes to the Green Chapel hard by.
Meantime showing as a guest the noblest and most scrupulous courtesy, Gawain
was three times tempted by his host's lady in vain. Then standing by the Green
Chapel to receive the return stroke, he was but grazed; for the Green Knight, re-
vealing himself as the lord of the castle and the deviser of the temptations, declared
himself satisfied that Gawain was indeed worthy." Baldwin, *op. cit.*, p. 155.

he caused to be publicly proclaimed a sufficiently long time beforehand as well in foreign parts as in England. He invited to this by his own letters all the ladies of the south of England and the wives of all the citizens of London. There assembled in the said castle on Sunday, the twentieth of January, earls, barons, knights and very many ladies. There the king provided the customary banquet so that the great hall was filled with the ladies, not a single man being present excepting only two knights who had come from France for this occasion. At this banquet there were present two queens, nine countesses, wives of the barons, knights and citizens, who could not easily be counted, and who had been placed by the king himself in their seats according to rank.

The Prince of Wales, the duke of Cornwall, the earls, barons and knights ate together with the people in a tent and other places where food supplies and all other necessaries had been prepared freely for all without murmur; and in the evening there was dancing. For the three following days the king with nineteen other knights kept a jousting against all who came from without; and the same lord, not on account of royal favor but because of great skill which he showed and because of the good fortune which he had, for three days gained the palm among those at home. A foreign lord, knight of Stapleton, gained the victory on the first day, on the second Philip Despenser, on the third John Blount. On the Thursday following the tournament of the sons, the lord king gave a banquet at which he founded the order of the Round Table, and under a certain form belonging to the said Round Table he received the oaths of certain earls, barons and knights whom he wished to belong to this said Round Table; and he fixed the day for holding the Round Table for the next day of Pentecost following, giving to all present the right of returning home with their badges of honor. Afterwards he ordered a very fine building to be erected there, in which the said Round Table could meet at the designated time. For the erection of this building he brought in stonecutters, carpenters and other workmen, ordering wood as well as stone to be procured, sparing neither labor nor expense.

The chivalric spirit also found expression in the Crusades, that series of expeditions lasting from 1096 to 1272, which purposed to protect the Holy Sepulcher from the Turks and secure it as a permanent shrine for Christendom. This purpose the Crusades failed to achieve, but, in lieu of gaining their primary object, served as a great cultural stimulus to the European mind by bringing it into touch with an alien civilization of apparently high attracting power.   Undoubtedly the most picturesque figure among English crusaders is Richard the Lion-Hearted, patron of knights and troubadours, himself a knight and troubadour.   Richard soon became a romantic figure and, though the prosaic facts of his life were known, had ascribed to him a legendary genealogy and career which put him on a par with King Horn, Havelock, King Arthur and Guy of Warwick.   William of Malmesbury thus describes the enthusiasm aroused by the first Crusade, an enthusiasm typical of that aroused by all the others.[22]

In the year of the incarnation 1095, pope Urban the second, who then filled the papal throne, passing the Alps, came into

[22] On the Crusades in general consult the medieval histories and Archer and Kingsford, *The Crusades: the Story of the Latin Kingdom of Jerusalem* (*The Story of the Nations Series*, G. P. Putnam's Sons, 1895).   Villehardouin and De Joinville, *Chronicles of the Crusades* is a number in *Everyman's Library*.   On literary material from the Crusades, see Vaublanc translation in Munroe and Sellery, *Medieval Civilization*, enlarged ed., pp. 269–277 (The Century Co., 1910).   See also Chaucer, *The Squire's Tale* in *The Canterbury Tales* with Skeat's notes.   Martha Pike Conant in the *Introduction* to her *Oriental Tale in England in the Eighteenth Century* (Columbia University Studies in Comparative Literature; Columbia University Press, 1908), has a few remarks about oriental influences in the Middle Ages.   On Richard as a crusader, see Archer, *The Crusade of Richard I* (*English History Told by Contemporaries*, G. P. Putnam's Sons, 1886).   On Richard as a troubadour, see J. F. Rowbotham, *Troubadours and Courts of Love*, chap. v, pp. 60–73 (*The Social England Series*; The Macmillan Co., 1905).   On Richard as a hero of romance, see Weston, *The Chief Middle English Poets*, pp. 123–132 and notes (Houghton Mifflin Co., 1914).   The Crusades left one indelible mark on European romance — the villains of many romances are Saracens.   This trait comes down at least as far as Spenser.

France. The ostensible cause of his journey was that, being driven from Rome by the violence of Guibert,[23] he might prevail on the churches on this side of the mountains to acknowledge him. His more secret intention was not so well known; this was, by Bohemond's [24] advice, to excite almost the whole of Europe to undertake an expedition into Asia; that in such a general commotion of all countries, auxiliaries might easily be engaged by whose means both Urban might obtain Rome; and Bohemond, Illyria and Macedonia. . . . Still, nevertheless, whatever might be the cause of Urban's mission, it turned out of great and singular advantage to the Christian world. A council, therefore, was assembled at Clermont which is the most noted city of Auvergne. . . . A clear and forcible discourse, such as should come from a priest, was addressed to the people on the subject of an expedition of Christians against Turks.[25] . . . The bulk of the auditors were extremely excited and attested their sentiments by a shout, pleased with the speech and inclined to the pilgrimage. And immediately in the presence of the Council some of the nobility, falling down at the knees of the pope, consecrated themselves and their property to the service of God. Among these was Aimar, the very powerful bishop of Puy, who afterwards ruled the army by his prudence and augmented it through his eloquence. In the month of November, then, in which the council was held, each departed to his home: and the report of this good resolution soon becoming general, it gently wafted a cheering gale over the minds of

---

[23] I.e. Guibert of Ravenna (*circa* 1030–1100), antipope under the title Clement III from June 25, 1080 to his death in September 1100. Urban II, of course, did not recognize him as pope, and hence our story calls him by his personal, not his papal, name. Guibert maintained himself at Rome from 1084 until he was driven out by the crusaders in 1097.

[24] I.e. Bohemond I (*circa* 1058–1111), Prince of Otranto and later of Antioch, a Norman, son of Robert Guiscard, Duke of Calabria and Apulia. Bohemond was a trusted adviser of Urban II and the real leader of the first Crusade. For the various accounts of the capture of Jerusalem by Bohemond and his colleagues in 1099, see Duncalf and Krey, *Parallel Source Problems in Medieval History* (*Harper's Parallel Source Problems*, Harper and Brothers, 1912), pp. 95–133. Bohemond had a strenuous life in his struggles against the Turks and the Eastern Emperor.

[25] The sermon of Urban follows.

Christians: which being universally diffused, there was no nation so remote, no people so retired, as not to contribute its portion. This ardent love not only inspired the continental provinces but even all who had heard the name of Christ whether in the most distant lands or savage countries. The Welshman left his hunting; the Scot his fellowship with lice; the Dane his drinking party; the Norwegian his raw fish. Lands were deserted of their husbandmen; houses of their inhabitants; even whole cities migrated. There was no regard to relationship, affection to their country was held in little esteem, God alone was placed before their eyes. Whatever was stored in granaries or hoarded in chambers, to answer the hopes of the avaricious husbandman, or the covetousness of the miser, all was deserted, they hungered after Jerusalem alone. Joy attended those who went while grief oppressed those who remained. But why do I say remained? You might see the husband departing with his wife, indeed, with all his family; you would smile to see the whole household loaded on a wagon, about to proceed on their way. The road was too narrow for the traffic, the path too confined for the travelers, so thickly were they thronged with endless multitudes. The number surpassed all human imagination, though the itinerants were estimated at six millions. Doubtless, never did so many nations unite in one opinion; never did so immense a population subject their unruly passions to one, and almost to no, direction. For the strangest wonder to behold was, that such a countless multitude marched gradually through various Christian countries without plundering, though there was none to restrain them. Mutual regard blazed forth in all, so that if any one found in his possession what he knew did not belong to him, he exposed it everywhere for several days to be claimed; and the desire of the finder was suspended till perchance the wants of the loser might be repaired.

As a specific instance of interest in the first Crusade a little nearer England, notice the following account by Florence of Worcester of how Robert, Duke of Normandy, eldest son of William the Conqueror, mortgaged his duchy in order to follow the suggestion of Pope Urban. The King

William mentioned in the text is William II, Rufus, second
son of William I the Conqueror.

After this, Robert, Earl of Normandy, proposing to join the
Crusade to Jerusalem, sent envoys to England, and requested
his brother King William that, peace being restored between
them, he would lend him ten thousand silver marks, receiving
Normandy in pledge. The King, wishing to grant his request,
called on the English lords to assist him with money, each according to his means, as speedily as possible. Therefore, the
bishops, abbots and abbesses broke up the gold and silver ornaments of their churches and the earls, barons and viscounts
robbed their knights and villeins, and brought to the King a
large sum of money. With this he crossed the sea in the month
of September, made peace with his brother, advanced him six
thousand six hundred and sixty-six pounds, and received from
him Normandy as security for its repayment.

Just one incident in the crusading career of Richard I
may be cited here as a sample passage from his life. This
is the account from the *Itinerary of Richard I*, by Richard
of the Holy Trinity, of the King's prowess at the siege of
Joppa in 1192. The writer describes himself in his *Prolog*
as an eye-witness of the events he records and excuses the
want of literary finish in his book on the plea that he composed on the spot and did not have time to revise. Modern
critics are disposed to accept his statements as correct.
Joppa at the time in question was in Christian hands, but
Saladin, hearing that Richard was absent from the town,
determined to besiege it. The Christians sent a message
of distress to Richard, who responded by at once sending
on his main force by land, while he with a smaller body
of warriors came up to Joppa by sea. The incident then
developed thus:

The Turks, discovering the arrival of the King's fleet, sallied
down to the seaside with sword and shield and sent forth showers
of arrows: the shore was so thronged with their numbers that

there was hardly a foot of ground to spare. Neither did they confine themselves to acting on the defensive, for they shot their arrows at the crews of the ships, and their cavalry spurred their horses into the sea to prevent the King's men from landing. The King, gathering his ships together, consulted with his officers what was the best step to take. "Shall we," said he, "push on against this rabble multitude who occupy the shore, or shall we value our lives more than those of the poor fellows who are exposed to destruction for want of our assistance?" Some of them replied that further attempts were useless, for it was by no means certain that any one remained alive to be saved, and how could they land in the face of so large a multitude? Richard looked around thoughtfully, and at that time saw a priest plunge into the water and swim toward the royal galley. When he was received on board, he addressed the King with palpitating heart and spirits almost failing him. "Most noble King, the remnant of our people, waiting for your arrival are exposed like sheep to be slain, unless divine grace bring you to the rescue." "Are any of them still alive, then?" asked Richard, "and if so, where are they?" "Some of them are still alive," said the priest, "and hemmed in and at the last extremity in front of yonder tower." "Please God, then," replied the King, "by whose guidance we have come, we will die with our brave brothers in arms, and a curse light on him who hesitates." The word was forthwith given, the galleys were pushed to land, the king dashed forward into the waves with his thighs unprotected by armor, and up to his middle in the water; he soon gained firm footing on the dry strand: behind him followed Geoffrey du Bois and Peter de Pratelles, and in the rear came all the others rushing through the surf. The Turks stood to defend the shore which was covered with their numerous troops. Richard, with an arbalest which he held in his hand, drove them back right and left; his companions pressed upon the recoiling enemy whose courage quailed when they saw it was the King, and they no longer dared to meet him. He brandished his fierce sword, which allowed them no time to resist, but they yielded before his fiery blows, and were driven in confusion with blood and havoc by the King's men until the shore was entirely cleared of them. They brought then together beams, poles and wood, from the old ships and galleys, to make a barricade; and the King placed there some knights, servants and arbalesters to keep guard and to dislodge the Turks, who, seeing that they could no longer oppose our troops, dispersed themselves on the shore with cries and yells in one general flight. The King then, by a winding stair, which he had remarked in the house of the Templars, was the first to enter the town, where he found more than three thousand Turks turning over everything in the houses and carrying away spoil. The brave King had no sooner entered the city, than he caused his banners to be set up on an eminence, that they might be seen by the Christians in the tower, who, taking courage at the sight, rushed forth in arms from the tower to meet the King, and at the report thereof the Turks were thrown into confusion. Richard, meanwhile, with brandished sword, still pursued and slaughtered the enemy, who were thus enclosed between the two bodies of Christians and filled the streets with their dead. Why need I say more? All were slain except such as took to flight in time; and thus those who had before been victorious were now defeated and received condign punishment, while the King still continued the rout, showing no mercy to the enemies of Christ's Cross, whom God had given into his hands; for there never was a man on earth who so abominated cowardice as he.

The same writer thus characterizes Richard:

His generosity and his virtuous endowments the Ruler of the World should have given to the ancient times, for in this period of the world, as it waxes old, such feelings rarely exhibit themselves, and, when they do, they are objects of wonder and astonishment. He had the valor of Hector, the magnanimity of Achilles, and was equal to Alexander and not inferior to Roland in bravery; nay, he outshone many illustrious characters of our own times. The liberality of a Titus was his, and, what is so rarely found in a soldier, he was gifted with the eloquence of Nestor and the prudence of Ulysses; and he showed himself preeminent in the conclusion and transaction of business, as one whose knowledge was not without active good-will to aid it,

nor his good-will wanting in knowledge. Who, if Richard were
accused of presumption, would not readily excuse him, knowing
him for a man who never knew defeat, impatient of an injury,
and impelled irresistibly to vindicate his rights, though all he
did was characterized by innate nobleness of mind. Success made
him better fitted for action, Fortune ever favors the brave and,
though she works her pleasure on whom she will, Richard was
never to be overwhelmed with adversity. He was tall of stature, graceful of figure, his hair between red and auburn, his
limbs were straight and flexible, his arms rather long and not
to be matched for wielding the sword or for striking with it,
his long legs suited the rest of his frame, while his appearance
was commanding and his manners and habits suitable; and he
gained the greatest celebrity not more from his high birth than
from the virtues that adorned him. But why need we take much
labor in extolling the fame of so great a man? He needs no
superfluous commendation, for he has a sufficient meed of praise
which is the sure companion of great actions. He was far
superior to all others both in moral goodness and in strength
and memorable for prowess in fight; and his mighty deeds outshone the most brilliant description we could give of them.
Happy in truth might he have been deemed, had he been without rivals who envied his glorious actions, and whose only cause
of enmity was his magnificence and his being the searcher after
virtue rather than the slave of vice.[26]

2. *Foreign Influence.* — A simple but comprehensive
title in this chapter for the above topic might be the single
word *French.* Beginning as far back as the reign of Edward the Confessor, who was brought up in Normandy,
and coming down in successive waves almost to the days
of Chaucer, French was the dominant foreign force in
English culture. After the Normans came Henry II with
his Angevins, bringing with them in Queen Eleanor a

[26] The list of great men to whom Richard is here compared comprises most of
the names of the heroes most admired in the Middle Ages; the only serious omission is that of Judas Maccabæus. We have already referred to Abbot Samson's
devotion to Richard; cf. *ante,* p. 275.

382   ENGLISH LITERATURE

representative of the civilization of Provence, the home of
the troubadours, a land quite different in history and tradition from Northern France, the home of the Normans.
And Henry II, it should be remembered, controlled more
territory on the Continent than did his liege, the King of
France. And the Angevins were followed by other French
men and fashions soon to be dominant in England.[27]

But French influence in this age means more than the
mere influence of France. It involves a whole congeries
of cultural forces gathered in Gaul from the entire continent of Europe, Asia Minor and Africa. It is said that
St. Francis owes his name Francisco to his knowledge of
French affairs and language [28] and Dante records Parisian
habit in at least one regard.[29] In fact, the connection of
France with the wide world seems electric; no sooner was
an idea broached or a movement started anywhere than
the news was flashed to Paris and the idea or the movement became prominent there. And England, from her
close connection with France, was especially susceptible
to all these things. The Crusades, the friars, the new
orders of knighthood, the most recent developments in
philosophy and theology and Arthurian romance all came
to England from France.

But, to recur to French influence in the narrower sense,
notice this account of his education among some autobiographical remarks by Giraldus Cambrensis (1146–1220?),
a story repeated in the lives of many prominent men of
his and later days. Giraldus, or Gerald de Barri, a Welshman, was one of the most prominent men at the literary
court of Henry II and the author of the *Topography of
Ireland*, a *History of the Conquest of Ireland*, an *Itinerary*

---

[27] French prisoners of the Hundred Years' War contributed their share to English culture; among them was King John II of France, captured with his young
son at Poitiers in 1356 and a prisoner in England 1357–60.
[28] Cf. Jessopp, *op. cit.*, p. 10.   [29] Cf. *Purgatorio*, XI, 81.

through Wales, a *Description of Wales* and the *Gemma Ecclesiastica (Churchly Jewel),* a manual of instruction for Welsh priests. Gerald frequently refers to his own life in his works, as in this extract from the first of the four works just mentioned, and one of his many affectations is to speak of himself in the third person, as he does here: [30]

Giraldus was born in the southern part of Wales near the seacoast of Dyved, not far from the principal town of Pembroke, the castle of Mainarpir. He sprang from freeborn parents; for his mother was Angarath, daughter of Nesta, the noble daughter of Rhys, chieftain of South Wales, and a son of Theodore. She married a most excellent man, William de Barri, and from this marriage Giraldus was born. He was the youngest of four brothers. When the three others were busy in their childish pleasures, building in the sand and gravel now camps, now towns, now palaces, he, in his own fashion, alone in his play, devoted his entire energy to the construction of churches or monasteries. After his father, watching him, had considered this with admiration, influenced as if by inspiration, he determined with prophetic soul that this son must devote himself to literature and the liberal arts. . . .

[30] For studies of French influence at this time in England, see Tucker, *op. cit.;* Rowbotham, *op. cit.;* the *Cambridge History of English Literature,* I, chap. viii and bibliography; W. H. Schofield, *English Literature from the Conquest to Chaucer* (The Macmillan Co., 1906), the *Introduction* and chaps. 2, 3, 4. Mr. Schofield introduces many quotations into his text, but unfortunately he doesn't give us the exact source of his material. Thus on pp. 12 and 13 he quotes testimony to the pre-eminence of Paris from Chrestien de Troyes, Bartholomæus Anglicus and Richard of Bury, but gives no clue to the location of the passages in the respective works. His treatment of this subject, however, is brilliant. See also Baldwin, *op. cit.,* Index, and Traill, *Social England,* I, pp. 344–356 (Cassell and Co., 1894–1898). Many references to the importance of French will be found later in this section and in sections iv, v, and vi, *post,* cf. pp. 418, 559–562 and the Index. It is rather suggestive, in this matter of French influence, that the songs of the birds near the end of Chaucer's *Parlement of Foules* and of the laborers at the end of the *Prolog* to the *Vision of William concerning Piers the Plowman* are alike French. (Cf. Chaucer, *Parlement of Foules,* ll. 673–679; *Vision,* etc., *Prolog,* A text l. 103, B text l. 224, C text l. 228.) One of these poems, Chaucer's, is courtly, celebrating the marriage of Richard II and Anne of Bohemia; the other is plebeian.

In the process of time a desire for higher study and progress led him (i.e. Giraldus) to cross over three times to France. For three periods of several years he studied the liberal arts in Paris, and at length, equaling the greatest teachers, excellently taught the trivium [31] and obtained especial praise for his rhetorical ability. He was thoroughly devoted to his studies, showing no levity or jesting in deed or in spirit, so much so that when the doctors of arts wished to give an example of the good scholar, they mentioned Giraldus above all others. So, as he was worthy to give an example of all scholarly excellence and preeminence in early childhood, since his good deeds continued, he could do so in youth as well. . . .

After arrangements had been completed, Giraldus, since he believed nothing finished as long as anything higher remained, looking not back but ever striving towards the future, ascended step by step without cessation. Since the treasures of books were greater abroad, he determined to cross over to France for higher and more mature study, and in Paris to apply himself diligently anew to his choicer studies. He was to erect on the foundation of arts and letters the walls of canon law and to finish the sacred roof of theology above. Thus a building of triple structure connected by the firmest of joints would be strong in lasting qualities. When for many years he had applied his studious mind to civil law, then at length had turned it to more sacred heights, he obtained so great influence in cases of canon law, which by established custom were discussed on Sundays, that on the day on which it was known that such questions were to be debated, so great a throng of almost all of the doctors with their scholars came forth for the pleasure of hearing him, that scarcely was there a house large enough to hold the audience. For so much did he aid the reasonings of canon law by his rhetorical skill, so much did he adorn the cause, as well by his figures of speech and brilliant style as by depth of thought, and so well did he adapt the sayings of philosophers and authors,

[31] I.e. the more elementary group of medieval studies comprising grammar (i.e. Latin), rhetoric, and logic; the second group of four studies — music, arithmetic geometry, and astronomy — made up the quadrivium. Trivium and quadrivium together made up the list of the seven liberal arts.

with wondrous aptness fitting them in proper places, that just as the more learned and adept agreed with him, so much the more eagerly and attentively they applied their minds and thoughts to listen and commit to memory. . . .

Let us now return to our own affairs and likewise to the continuation of the narrative. Giraldus, after a long period of study determined to return to his father land. He waited for his messengers to bring him money until long after the date set for their return. Meanwhile his creditors, to whom he was greatly in debt, kept pressing him impatiently and rudely from day to day. Grieving, anxious and almost desperate he went to the chapel of St. Thomas of Canterbury [32] and St. Germain d'Auxerre founded and dedicated by the archbishop of Rheims, brother of King Louis. To this chapel, founded in honor of that saint [32] at the time of his martyrdom, Giraldus fled for refuge, with his friends, to beg and implore the aid of the martyr, [32] knowing indeed, as the philosopher ˙ Philo [33] says, that when human aid fails we must hasten to the divine. When the mass had been piously heard and an offering presented, a reward for his piety was divinely given, for he received in the same hour his messenger with joy and prosperity. It was indeed a wonderful interposition of God, who gains in His own way from human affairs His holy results, and although He knows that His gifts are given purely from love, nevertheless wishes them to be gained, as it were, by prayers and deeds.

3. *Learning in the Period.* — "When we try to picture to ourselves," says Symonds, "the intellectual and moral state of Europe in the Middle Ages, some fixed and almost stereotyped ideas immediately suggest themselves. We think of the nations immersed in a gross mental lethargy; passively witnessing the gradual extinction of arts and sciences which Greece and Rome had splendidly inaugurated; allowing libraries and monuments of antique civilization to crumble into dust; while they trembled under a

[32] I.e. Thomas a Becket.
[33] A Jewish-Hellenistic philosopher born at Alexandria about 25 A.D. While in ritual a strict Jew, in interpretation of Scripture he was allegorical and theosophic.

dull and brooding terror of coming judgment, shrank from natural enjoyment as from deadly sin, or yielded themselves with brutal eagerness to the satisfaction of vulgar appetites." [34] Symonds goes on to show that this view of medieval Europe, so long held, is erroneous and that the Middle Age was an epoch of great zeal for intellectual endeavor and learning, a conclusion that is now generally accepted. In fact, we can say that Europe at this time was in one of its most active periods, but that if the results of her research were not always commensurate with her effort, it was because of lack of materials and tools to work with, as Roger Bacon complains. [35]

One of the most enthusiastic scholars and thinkers of the epoch was Abelard, worthy of "renown by virtue of his extraordinary intellectual power and bold honesty of scientific attitude." [36] In the first letter in the first volume of Cousin's edition of his works, Abelard reviews his "calamities," describes his own eager pursuit of knowledge, the jealousy of less keen fellow-students and teachers, and his retirement to a solitary place in order to devote himself to his own studies and thoughts. But he was to be disappointed, for thither followed him a great company of disciples, and in his account of their conduct we have a striking testimony to their zeal. [37]

---

[34] *Wine, Women, and Song*, p. 1 (*King's Classics* ed.; Chatto and Windus, 1907).
[35] Cf. *post*, p. 391.   [36] Schofield, *op. cit.*, p. 52.
[37] The most thorough and comprehensive study of medieval culture is H. Osborn Taylor, *The Medieval Mind: a History of the Development of Thought and Emotion in the Middle Ages*, 2 vols. (The Macmillan Co., 1911). Mr. Taylor had come to this study after two other important books on the history of culture; viz. *Ancient Ideals*, 2 vols. (Published for the Columbia University Press by The Macmillan Co., 1900) and *The Classical Heritage of the Middle Ages* (*Columbia University Studies in Literature:* the Columbia University Press, 1903; 2d ed). The Macmillan Co. announces (March, 1915) another work, doubtless of the same high quality, to be entitled *Deliverance: the Freeing of the Spirit in the Ancient World.* On English Learning in our period, cf. Traill, *op. cit.*, I, pp. 332–343; 429–440; II, pp. 61–74; Schofield, *op. cit.*, chap. 2; the *Cambridge History of English Literature,*

I, therefore,[38] withdrew to a solitary spot that I knew of in the country of Troyes. Here I received the gift of some land whereon, with the assent of the bishop of that diocese, I first built a little oratory of reeds and straw which I dedicated to the name of the Holy Trinity. Here I lived in hiding with a certain clerk for my companion and could with truth chant that psalm to the Lord, "Lo, I have gone far off flying away; and I abode in the wilderness." [39] When the scholars heard this, they began to flock together from all parts, leaving their cities and towns and coming to live in my wilderness. Here, instead of spacious houses, they built themselves little tabernacles; for delicate food they ate naught but herbs of the field and rough country bread; for soft couches they gathered together straw and stubble, nor had they any tables save clods of earth. They seemed in very truth to imitate those ancient philosophers of whom Jerome [40] thus wrote in his second book against Jovinian, "Through the senses, as through windows, vices creep into the soul. . . . Impelled by such reasons, many philosophers have left the press of cities and suburban gardens, where the fields are pleasantly watered and the trees thick with foliage; where birds chirp and living pools mirror the sky; where the brook babbles on its way and many other things entice men's ears or eyes; lest through the luxury and abundance of plenty a soul's strength be turned to weakness and its modesty violated. For indeed it is unprofitable to gaze frequently on that whereby thou mayest one day be caught, and to accustom thyself to such things as thou shalt afterwards scarce be able to lack. For the Pythagoreans also, avoiding such frequented spots were wont to dwell in the wilderness and the desert." Moreover, Plato himself, though he was

I, chap. ix; I, chap. xv and bibliographies. On Abelard, cf. Joseph McCabe, *Abelard* (G. P. Putnam's Sons, 1901); Gabriel Compayre, *Abelard and the Origin and Early History of Universities* (*Great Educators Series*; Charles Scribner's Sons, 1893). *The Letters of Abelard to Eloise* are accessible in an English version partly translation, partly paraphrase, in the *Temple Classics Series* (E. P. Dutton and Co.). In Robinson, *op. cit.*, I, pp. 446–452, further passages from the letter quoted in the text are translated, as well as the *Introduction* and sample questions from Abelard's *Sic et Non* (*Yes and No*).

[38] I.e. because of his scholastic troubles with his former colleagues.

[39] Cf. Psalm ?   [40] Cf. *ante*, p. 64.

a rich man whose costly couch Diogenes [41] once trod under his
muddy feet, chose the Academy, a villa far from the city and
not only solitary but pestilent also, as the fittest spot for the
entire study of philosophy, that the assaults of lust might be
broken by the anxiety and frequent pressure of sickness and
that his disciples might feel no other delights save in those
things that he had taught them. Such is also the life which the
sons of the prophets are said to have led who clung around
Elisha,[42] and of whom, as of the monks of those days, this same
Jerome writeth in his letter to the monk Rusticus, saying among
other things, "The sons of the prophets, who, as we read in the
Old Testament, were monks, built themselves little lodges hard
by the river Jordan, and, leaving towns with their multitudes,
lived upon coarse meal and wild herbs." Such then were my
disciples who, building their little huts there beside the river
Arduzon, seemed rather hermits than scholars. Yet, the greater
was the press of pupils flocking thither, and the harder the life
which they suffered to hear my teaching, the more glorious did
my rivals think this to me and the more ignominious to themselves. For, after having done all that they could against me,
they grieved now that all things should work together to me for
good;[43] wherefore, to quote my Jerome again, "though I had
withdrawn far from cities, market-places, quarrels and crowds,
yet even so, as Quintilian [44] saith, envy found me in my hiding

[41] Diogenes the famous Cynic, a contemporary of Plato and Alexander the Great,
who lived in a tub and made himself notorious by despising riches and inveighing
against luxury. Most of our knowledge of him comes from Diogenes Laertius
(*circa* 118 A.D.–217), Φιλοσόφων Βίοι (*Lives of the Philosophers*). The latter does
not record the story to which our text alludes, but does tell the following, which
is somewhat like it: "On one occasion Plato had invited some friends who had
come to him from Dionysius to a banquet, and Diogenes trampled on his carpets,
and said, 'Thus I trample on the empty pride of Plato'; and Plato made him
answer, 'How much arrogance are you displaying, O Diogenes! when you think
that you are not arrogant at all.' But, as others tell the story, Diogenes said
'Thus I trample on the pride of Plato'; and that Plato rejoined, 'With quite as
much pride yourself, O Diogenes.'" Tr. Yonge, *The Lives and Opinions of Eminent
Philosophers*, p. 226 (*Bohn's Library*, 1905 ed.; George Bell and Sons).
[42] Cf. 2 Kings 2; 9: 1.   [43] Cf. Romans 8: 28.
[44] Quintilian (*circa* 35 A.D.–*circa* 97), Roman rhetorician and teacher of elocu-
tion, whose *De Institutione Oratoria Libri* XII (*Twelve Books on the Education of*

place." For these fellows, complaining within themselves and groaning with envy, said, "Behold, the whole world hath gone after him; [45] we have profited naught in persecuting him; nay, we have added rather to his renown. We have sought to extinguish his name and have kindled it the more. Lo, these scholars have all necessaries at hand in their towns; yet, contemning the delights of the city, they flock together to the penury of this wilderness, and are miserable by their own choice." Yet it was then my intolerable poverty more than anything else that drove me to become a master in the schools; for I could not dig, and to beg I was ashamed; wherefore, falling back upon the art which I knew, I was compelled to employ my tongue instead of the labor of my hands. My scholars, of their own accord, provided me with all necessaries not only in food and raiment but in tilling of the fields and defraying the cost of buildings, so that no household care might withdraw me from my studies. Seeing then that my oratory could no longer hold even a small portion of them, they must needs extend it, building it more solidly with stones and wood. Though formerly it had been established and hallowed in the name of the Holy Trinity, yet because I had there found a refuge in mine exile and some small share of the grace of God's consolation had been breathed into my despair, therefore in memory of that loving kindness I called it the Paraclete.

The same enthusiasm is reflected in a poem found in the collection of medieval student songs known as *Carmina Burana* and thus translated by Symonds:

> I, a wandering scholar lad,
>   Born for toil and sadness,
> Oftentimes am driven by
>   Poverty to madness.
>
> Literature and knowledge
>   Fain would still be earning

the Orator) was a standard text-book on rhetoric and criticism for centuries. The tenth book opens with a condensed survey of Greek and Latin Literature whence many medieval writers drew their knowledge of the names and characteristics of classical authors. [45] Cf. John 12: 19.

Were it not that want of pelf
  Makes me cease from learning.

These torn clothes that cover me
  Are too thin and rotten;
Oft I have to suffer cold,
  By the warmth forgotten.

Scarce I can attend at church,
  Sing God's praises duly;
Mass and vespers both I miss,
  Though I love them truly.

Oh, thou pride of N——,
  By thy worth I pray thee
Give the suppliant help in need,
  Heaven will sure repay thee.

Take a mind unto thee now
  Like unto St. Martin; [46]
Clothe the pilgrim's nakedness,
  Wish him well at parting.

So may God translate your soul
  Into peace eternal,
And the bliss of saints be yours
  In His realm supernal. [47] *

[46] Martin, son of a Roman military tribune, was born about 316 A.D. He retired to religious solitude late in life, whence he was drawn to become bishop of Tours in 374. He was stationed at Amiens during the severe winter of 332 and, noticing a man shivering with the cold, took his own coat from his shoulders and cut it in two with his sword, giving half to the shiverer and keeping half for himself.

[47] Chaucer's Oxford clerk (cf. *Prolog to the Canterbury Tales*, ll. 285–310) was perhaps a scholar of this sort. But see the article of H. S. V. Jones in the *Publications of the Modern Language Association of America*, XX, no. 1 (March 1912), in which the writer, in opposition to most of the commentators, takes the view that Chaucer's clerk was not a mendicant. He had the same enthusiasm for learning, however.

* By permission of Messrs. Chatto and Windus from their edition in the *King's Classics Series.*

The author of *Piers the Plowman's Creed* (dated by Skeat about 1394) thinks that this zeal for book-learning has gone so far as to be a nuisance and a menace. He says:

Now-a-days every shoemaker's son must be sent to school and every beggar's brat study his books, come to be a writer, dwell with a lord or falsely be a friar, and serve the fiend. So that, instead of the beggar's brat we shall have a bishop who will sit close to the peers of the land. And the sons of lords will bow low to these rascals and knights will crouch and scrape to them. And their fathers were shoemakers, soiled with grease, and their teeth jagged as a saw from working with leather! Alas, that the lords of the land believe in such wretches and trust such vagabonds on account of their mild words. They (i.e. the lords) should make the sons of their own brothers or others of gentle blood, bishops. It would seem better so rather than to foster traitors and allow false friars to become fat and flourishing and cumber their flesh. These climbing knaves were fitter to wash dishes rather than to have the chief seats at table and be served with silver. They ought to fill their stomachs from a great bowl of beans and bacon rather than eat roast partridges, plover or peacocks.

Roger Bacon (1214–1292) was the greatest scholar of his day, equally remarkable as scientist, linguist, man of letters and philosopher. He entered, much to his regret later, the Franciscan order, the superiors of which viewed his studies with suspicion and did all they could to make him unproductive. It finally required a special command of Pope Clement IV to enable him to write his principal books. Bacon, however, was not satisfied with a 'mere reproduction of current learning; he insisted on advancing. In the following extracts from his works he complains of various obstacles in the way of productive scholarship in his time:

If the saints made mistakes in their translations, much more do these men, who have little or no title to sanctity at all. So, though we have numerous translations of all the sciences by Gerard of Cremona,[48] Michael Scot,[49] Alfred the Englishman,[50] Herman the German [50] and William Fleming,[50] there is such utter falsity in all their writings that none can sufficiently wonder at it. For a translation to be true, it is necessary that the translator know the language from which he is translating, the language into which he translates and the science he wishes to work in. But who is he? and I will praise him, for he has done marvellous things. Certainly none of the above-named had any true knowledge of the tongues or of the sciences, as is clear, not from their translations only, but from their condition of life. All were alive in my time; some in their youth, contemporaries of Gerard of Cremona who was somewhat more advanced in years among them. Herman the German, who was very intimate with Gerard, is still alive and a bishop. When I questioned him about certain books of logic which he had to translate from the Arabic, he roundly told me that he knew nothing of logic and therefore did not care to render them; and certainly, if he was unacquainted with logic, he could know nothing of other sciences as he ought. Nor did he understand Arabic, as he confessed, because he was rather an assistant in the translations than the real translator. For he kept Saracens about him in Spain who had the principal hand in his versions. In the same way, Michael the Scot claimed the merit of numerous

[48] *Circa* 1114–1187 A.D.; medieval translator of Ptolemy's *Astronomy*. Gerard studied in the Moslem school at Toledo. He translated sixty-six other scientific works.

[49] *Circa* 1175–*circa* 1234. He was probably a Scotchman (see Bacon's next reference to him below, where he is called *Michael the Scot*). Educated at Oxford, Paris, and Bologna, Michael spent most of his later life at the court of the Emperor Frederick II in Sicily. He came back to Oxford about 1230 with translations of and commentaries on Aristotle. He wrote the *Physiognomiæ Magistri Michaelis Scoti* (*Master Michael Scot on Physiognomy*) and *Mensa Philosophica* (often translated as *The Philosopher's Banquet*). His life in Sicily gave him an opportunity to translate the Arabic commentaries on Aristotle. He wrote on astronomy and alchemy and later came to be known as a magician. Cf. Scott, *The Lay of the Last Minstrel*, the action of which centers about the traditional grave of Michael Scot at Melrose Abbey.

[50] The names of these three are not to be found in modern works of reference.

paraphrases. But it is certain that Andrew, a Jew, labored at them more than he did. And even Michael, as Herman reported, did not understand either the sciences or the tongues. And so of the rest; especially the notorious William Fleming who is now in such reputation. Whereas it is well known to the literati at Paris that he is ignorant of the sciences in the original Greek, to which he makes such pretensions; and therefore, he translates incorrectly and corrupts the philosophy of the Latins. For Boethius [51] alone was well acquainted with the languages and their interpretation. My Lord Robert (Grosseteste) [52] by reason of his long life and the wonderful methods he employed, knew the sciences better than any other man; for though he did not understand Greek or Hebrew, he had many assistants. But all the rest were ignorant of the tongues and the sciences, and above all this William Fleming who has no satisfactory knowledge of either and yet has undertaken to revise all our translations and give us new ones. But I have seen his books and I know that they are faulty and that they should be avoided. For as at this time the enemies of the Christians, the Jews, the Arabs and the Greeks, have the sciences in their own tongues, they will not allow the Christians the use of perfect MSS., but they destroy and corrupt them, particularly when they see incompetent people, who have no acquaintance with the tongues and the sciences, presuming to make translations. . . .

---

[51] Cf. *ante*, p. 66.

[52] *Circa* 1175–1253 A.D., statesman, theologian, writer, Bishop of Lincoln. He was born of humble parentage, educated at Oxford, and became proficient in law, medicine, and natural science. He taught at Oxford, where he became chancellor. He was the first rector of a school established at Oxford about 1224 by the Franciscan friars, whom he gladly welcomed on their arrival in England. He was chosen Bishop of Lincoln in 1235 and showed himself an ecclesiastical reformer of a severe type, for which reason he had a hard time in putting his ideas into practice. He was independent in his attitude toward papal encroachments in England in his time. He wrote in French *Chasteau d'Amour* (*The Castle of Love*), an allegorical work whose popularity is shown by the fact that it was several times translated into English. (See an extract translated in Shackford, *Legends and Satires from Medieval Literature*, pp. 95–97; Ginn and Co., 1913.) His *Epistolæ* (*Letters*) have been ed. for the *Rolls Series* (XXV, 1861), by H. R. Luard. See the story of his attitude toward minstrelsy, *post*, p. 450.

The scientific books of Aristotle,[53] of Avicenna,[54] of Seneca,[55] of Cicero [56] and other ancients cannot be had except at great cost; their principal works have not been translated into Latin, and copies of others are not to be found in ordinary libraries or elsewhere. The admirable work of Cicero *De Republica* [56] is not to be discovered anywhere, so far as I can hear, although I have made anxious inquiry for it in different parts of the world and by various messengers. And so of many other works of which I sent extracts to your Beatitude.[57] I could never find the works of Seneca until after the time when I received your commands,[58] although I made diligent search for them for twenty years and more. And so it is with many more useful books of this noble science (ethics). . . .

And so, all who know anything at all disregard the false translations of Aristotle, and seek such remedy as they can. This is a truth which men lost in learning will not consider; but they seek consolation for their ignorance like brutes. If I had control over the books of Aristotle (as we have them now), I would have them all burned; for to study them is but lost time and a source of error and multiplication of ignorance beyond all human power to calculate. And, seeing that the labors of

[53] Cf. *ante*, p. 66. Other remarks of Bacon about Aristotle follow in our extracts and show his ascendency in medieval thought.

[54] I.e. Abn Ali al Hossein Ibn Sina (980–*circa* 1037 A.D). It is from the sound of the last two words in his name that the common designation of him comes. He was an Arabian physician and philosopher whose great work was a system of medicine based on Arabic translation of Greek works. He was to a large extent a disciple of Aristotle in philosophy. On medieval medicine and literature, see P. A. Robin, *The Old Physiology in English Literature* (E. P. Dutton and Co., 1911). On medical learning, see Chaucer's description of the Doctor of Physic, *Prolog to the Canterbury Tales*, ll. 411–444 and Skeat's notes.

[55] *Circa* B.C. 4–A.D. 65. He was born at Cordova in Spain, but came to Rome at an early age, where he studied eloquence and the Stoic philosophy. He became tutor to Nero and later one of his ministers and for some time exercised a good influence over the Emperor. But Nero became jealous of him and Seneca committed suicide at his orders. He is the author of many ethical works and the reputed writer of several tragedies which have had a marked influence on modern plays.

[56] Cf. *ante*, p. 66; the *De Republica*, probably modeled on the *Republic* of Plato, is still lost, except for fragments.

[57] I.e. Pope Clement IV, to whom Bacon addressed his works.

[58] It was about 1265 that the Pope directed Bacon to put his works into shape.

THE CULTURAL BACKGROUND

Aristotle are the foundation of all science, no one can tell how much the Latins waste now because they have accepted evil translations of the Philosopher; wherefore, there is no full remedy anywhere. Any one who would glory in the knowledge of Aristotle ought to learn it in its original and native tongue but now there is uniform falsity of rendering as well in philosophy as in theology. For all the translators (of the Bible) before St. Jerome [59] erred cruelly, as he himself says over and over again. . . . We have few profitable books of philosophy in Latin, for Aristotle wrote a thousand volumes, as we read in his *Life*, whereof we possess only three of any importance; his *Logic*, his *Natural History* and his *Metaphysics*. . . . But the vulgar herd of students, with their leaders, have nothing to rouse them to any worthy effort, wherefore they feebly dote over these false versions, wasting their time and their money. For outward appearance alone possesses them; nor do they care what they know but only what they may seem to know in the eyes of the senseless multitude.

So likewise numberless matters of God's wisdom are still wanting. For many books of Holy Writ are not translated; for example two books of the Maccabees [60] which I know exist in the Greek, and many other books of many prophets which are cited in the Books of Kings and Chronicles. Moreover, Josephus [61] in his *Antiquities* is utterly false as to the course of time without which nothing can be known of the history of the sacred text; wherefore, unless the translation is revised, he is worthless

[59] Cf. *ante*, p. 66.

[60] I.e. two books of Hebrew history treating the period later than that covered in the present biblical canon. These, like other books in the Hebrew Bible, were translated into Greek in the *Septuagint* version between 286 and 284 B.C.

[61] A Jew known nowadays by his Latin name only. He was born of royal and sacerdotal parentage about 37 A.D. and was well educated in both Hebrew and Greek literature. At the outbreak of the war between the Romans and the Jews about 65 A.D. he was Roman governor of Galilee. He was present in the army of Titus at the siege and fall of Jerusalem in 70. Thereafter he lived at Rome till about 100 A.D. and devoted himself to literary studies. His extant genuine works are: a *History of the Jewish War* (in Greek) in 7 books, twenty books of Jewish *Antiquities*, being a history of the Jews from the earliest times to the death of Nero, an *Apology for the Jews against Apion* and an *Autobiography*. He is a very valuable authority for Jewish History.

and sacred history will perish. Besides, the Latins lack innumerable books of the Hebrew and Greek expositors; such as, Origen,[62] Basil,[63] Gregory Nazianzen,[64] Damascenus,[65] Dionysius,[66] Chrysostom [67] and other noble doctors, in Hebrew as well as in Greek. Therefore, the church slumbers, for in this matter she does naught nor has done for these seventy years past, except that the Lord Robert (Grosseteste) [68] of holy memory, Bishop of Lincoln, translated into Latin from the books of St. Dionysius [69] and Damascenus and a few other consecrated teachers. Wonderful is the negligence of the church; for there has been no supreme pontiff since the days of Pope Damasus,[70] nor any inferior cleric who has been solicitous for the church through translations save only the above mentioned glorious bishop. . . .

(A) root of the difficulty (of accurate scholarship) is that we ought to have excellent mathematicians who should not only know what exists, original or translated, in connection with the sciences, but be able to make additions to them, a thing which is easy for good mathematicians to do. For there are only two perfect mathematicians, Master John of London [70] and Master Peter de Maharn-Curia,[70] a Picard. There are two other good ones, Master Campanus de Novaria [70] and Master Nicholas,[70] the teacher of Aumary de Montfort.[71] For without mathe-

[62] *Circa* 185 A.D.–*circa* 254. He was an Alexandrian by birth and education and a great exponent of the ascetic ideal of life; well known in his time and later as a great teacher and expositor of Christian doctrine, the most weighty theologian that the church had produced up to his time. He is sometimes called the father of the allegorical method of interpreting Scripture. His system of theology Περί Ἀρχων (*De Principiis, On Fundamentals*) develops the theology of the fourth gospel.

[63] Cf. *ante*, p. 64.

[64] *Circa* 329–390 A.D. Saint and Bishop of Constantinople. He was well educated in the Greek philosophical schools of his day. He is one of the Greek fathers of the church, chiefly famous as a theologian and a defender of orthodox Athanasian doctrine as against the heresy of Arius. His theological teaching is best embodied in his five *Theological Orations*. We also have some works of his denouncing the Emperor Julian, the Apostate, many letters and some poems, mostly autobiographical. [65] (?)

[66] Dionysius the Areopagite, the reputed author of a work on the *Celestial Hierarchies*, first noticed in the sixth century.

[67] Cf. *ante*, p. 65.   [68] Cf. *ante*, p. 393.   [69] Pope from 366 to 384.

[70] These names I can't find in modern reference books.

[71] The son of the celebrated Simon de Montfort; see *post*, pp. 472–480.

matics nothing worth knowing in philosophy can be attained. . . . And, therefore, it is indispensable that good mathematicians be had and they are scarce. Nor can any one obtain their services, especially the best of them, except it be the Pope or some great prince. . . . For he would hardly condescend to live with any one who wished to be the lord of his own studies and prosecute philosophical investigations at his pleasure.

And besides this expense (of subsidizing mathematicians), other great expenses would have to be incurred. Without mathematical instruments no science can be mastered; and these are not to be found among the Latins and could not be made for two or three hundred pounds. And besides, better tables are absolutely necessary, for although the certifying of the tables is done by instruments, yet this cannot be accomplished without a large number of instruments; and they are hard to use and hard to keep because of (the danger of) rusting, and they cannot be moved from place to place without risk of breaking them; and a man cannot have everywhere and on all occasions new instruments which he ought to have, unless he have certified tables. These tables are called *Almanac* or *Tallignum* in which, once for all, the motions of the heavens are certified from the beginning to the end of the world without daily labor; so that a man can find everything in the heavens every day, as we find in the calendar the feast-days of the saints; and then every day we could consider in the heavens the causes of all things which change on the earth, and seek similar positions (of the heavens) in times past, and discover similar effects. And likewise of the future. And so everything might be known. These tables would be worth a king's ransom and, therefore, could not be made without vast expense. And I have often attempted the composition of such tables, but could not finish them through lack of funds and the folly of those whom I had to employ. For, first of all, it would be necessary that ten or twelve boys should be instructed in the ordinary canons and astronomical tables; and when they knew how to work them, then for a year they ought to (try to) discover the motions of each planet singly for every day and every hour, according to all the variations of their motions and other changes in the heavens.

Then there are other instruments and tables of practical geometry and practical arithmetic and music which are of great utility and indispensably required. But more than any of these it would be requisite to obtain men who have a good knowledge of optics (perspectivam scientiam) and its instruments. For this is the science of true vision and by vision we know all things. For a blind man knows nothing of the world; sight reveals to us the differentia of things, as Aristotle says and we know by experience. This science certifies mathematics and all other things, because astronomical instruments do not work except by vision, in accordance with the laws of that science. Nor is it wonderful if all things are known by mathematics, and yet all things by this science (optics), because, as I have said before, the sciences are intimately connected, although each has its proper and peculiar province. . . . But this science has not hitherto been read at Paris nor among the Latins (i.e. in Italy); (nor any where else) except twice at Oxford in England; and there are not three persons acquainted with its power. Wherefore, he who pretends to be an authority, of whom I have spoken before, knows nothing of the importance of optics, as appears from his books, for he has never written one on this science, which he would have done had he known it, nor in his other writings has he said anything about it. . . . They are but few who know these things as in the case of mathematics, and are not to be had except at a high price; and costly likewise are the instruments of this science which are very difficult to make and more expensive than those necessary for mathematics. . . .

I say this because I am sorry for this ignorance and that of the generality; for without these they can know nothing. No author among the ancient masters or the moderns has written about them; but I have labored at them for ten years, as far as I could find time, and I have examined them narrowly as well as I could, reducing them to writing since the time when I received your mandate. . . .

(Another) important thing which is a cause of error in the pursuit of wisdom at present is this: that for forty years past certain men have arisen . . . who have made themselves into masters and doctors of theology and philosophy, though they themselves have never learned anything of any account; nor will they nor can they learn by reason of their position, and I will take care to show by argument . . . within the compass of the following pages why I think so. And, though I grieve for and pity these as much as I can, yet truth prevails over all and, therefore, I will here expound at least some of the things which are publicly done and are known to all men, though few turn their hearts to regard either this or other profitable considerations by reason of the cause of error which I here set forth, whereby almost all men are basely blinded. These are boys who are inexperienced in the knowledge of themselves and of the world and of the learned languages, Greek and Hebrew, which, I will prove later on, are necessary to study; they are ignorant also of all parts of the world's philosophy and wisdom when they so presumptuously enter upon the study of theology, which requires all human wisdom, as the saints teach and as all wise men know. For, if truth is anywhere, here it is found; here, if anywhere is falsehood condemned, as Augustine [72] says in his book *Of Christian Doctrine*. These are boys of the two . . . orders,[73] like Albert [74] and Thomas [75] and others, who, as in

[72] Cf. *ante*, p. 64.

[73] I.e. the Franciscan and Dominican orders of friars, as the sequel shows.

[74] I.e. Albertus Magnus or Albert of Cologne (1206?–1280). He was of noble German family and educated at Padua, where he studied Aristotle. He entered the Dominican order in 1221 or 1223. He studied theology under Dominican rule at Bologna and elsewhere and then was lecturer at Cologne, whence he went to Paris, took his doctor's degree and taught. He was canonized in 1622. He, along with Thomas Aquinas, to be mentioned in our next note, endeavored to bring Christian theology into harmony with Aristotle. He had of Aristotle only a Latin translation of an Arabic translation of the Greek. His works in the Paris edition by Borgnet, 1890, fill 36 volumes. He was the most learned and the most widely read theologian of his time. His philosophical works, which are mostly condensations of and commentaries on Aristotle, are arranged on the Aristotelian scheme. His nickname was Doctor Universalis (Universal Doctor). In theology his principal works are a three-volume commentary on *The Sentences of Peter Lombard* (cf. *post*, p. 433) and a two-volume *Summa Theologiæ* (*Digest of Theology*).

[75] I.e. Thomas Aquinas or Thomas of Aquino (*circa* 1226–1274), known by the nicknames of *Doctor Communis, Doctor Angelicus, Princeps Scholasticorum, Doctor Ecclesiæ* (*General Encyclopedia, Angelic Doctor, Chief of the Scholastics, Doctor of the Church*). He was of noble Italian family, educated at the Benedictine monastery

many cases, enter those orders when they are twenty years old or less. This is the common course, from the English Sea to the borders of Christendom, and especially outside . . . France; so that in Acquitaine, Provence, Spain, Italy, Germany, Hungary, Dacia and everywhere boys are promiscuously received into the orders from their tenth to their twentieth year; boys too young to be able to know anything worth knowing, even though they were not already possessed with the afore-mentioned causes of human error; wherefore, at their entrance into the orders, they have no knowledge of any value for theology. Many thousands become friars who cannot read their Psalter or their Donat; [76] yet, immediately after their admission, they are set to study theology. And from the beginning of the orders, especially from the time when learning began to flourish in them, the first students were like the later ones (i.e. this has always been the custom among the friars). And they have given themselves to this study of theology which needs the whole of human wisdom. Wherefore, they must of necessity fail to reap any great profit, especially seeing that they have not taken lessons from others in philosophy since their entrance, and, most of all, because they have presumed in those orders to enquire into philosophy by themselves and without teachers, so that they are become masters in theology and in philosophy before being disciples. Wherefore, infinite error reigns among them, although for certain reasons this is not apparent by the devil's instigation and by God's permission. One cause of this (failure of the lack of learning among the friars to impress the public) is that the orders have the outward show of sanctity; wherefore it is plausible to the world that men in so holy a state would not

of Monte Cassino and the University of Naples. He entered the Dominican order in 1243. He studied at Paris and in 1245 at Cologne under Albertus Magnus. He taught at Paris, later in Rome, Bologna, Pisa and elsewhere in Italy. His chief theological works are a commentary on *The Four Books of Sentences of Peter Lombard*, a *Summa Theologiæ*, *Quæstiones Disputatæ et Quodlibetales* (*Disputed and General Questions*), *Opuscula Theologica* (*Minor Theological Works*). He has become the official theologian of the Catholic Church; his works were edited in 1882 with the especial sanction of Pope Leo XIII.

[76] I.e. their Latin grammar; for a note on Donatus, from whose name the word *donat* comes, cf. *ante*, p. 67.

presume to have such qualities as they could not prove that they had.[77] . . .

Compilation was an art much practised in the Middle Ages; many encyclopedias were made. A medieval writer in his *Prolog* to his translation of one of these, the *De Proprietatibus Rerum* (*On the Properties of Things*), by Bartholomæus Anglicus (Bartholomew the Englishman) tells us the purpose of his work. Bartholomew was an English scholar of the thirteenth century; he studied and taught theology at Paris, and entered the Franciscan order about 1230. His book was a common source of information on natural history and was translated into French in 1372, into English in 1398 and into Spanish and Dutch in the fifteenth century. It has often been reprinted. Our translator says of the arrangement and aim of the book:

True it is that after the noble and expert doctrine of wise and well-learned philosophers, left and remaining with us in writing, we know that the properties of things follow and ensue their substance. Herefore it is that after the order and distinction of substances, the order and distinction of the properties of things shall be and ensue. Of the which things this work of all the books ensuing, by grace, help and assistance of Almighty God, is compiled and made. Marvel not, ye witty and eloquent readers, that I, thin of wit and void of cunning, have translated this book from Latin into our vulgar language, as a thing profitable to me and peradventure to many other, which understand not Latin, nor have the knowledge of the properties of things, which things be approved by the books of great and cunning clerks and by the experience of most witty and noble

---

[77] Bacon himself, like Michael Scot, became in the popular imagination a great magician; cf. the Elizabethan play, *Friar Bacon and Friar Bungay*, by Robert Greene. For comment and illustrative material, the best edition of this play is that of Ward, *Marlowe's Dr. Faustus and Greene's Friar Bacon and Friar Bungay*, 4th ed. (Oxford, Clarendon Press, 1901). Perhaps a more accurate text of the play is that in Neilson, *The Chief Elizabethan Dramatists* (Houghton Mifflin Co., 1911). The play can also be had in the *Temple Dramatists Series* (E. P. Dutton and Co.).

philosophers. All these properties be full necessary and of great
value to them that will be desirous to understand the obscuri-
ties or darkness of holy scriptures: which be given to us under
figures, under parables and semblance, or likelihoods of things
natural and artificial. Saint Denys,[78] that great philosopher
and solemn clerk, in his book named *The Heavenly Hierarchies
of Angels*, testifieth and witnesseth the same, saying in this
manner: Whatsoever any man will conject, feign, imagine, suppose or say: it is a thing impossible that the light of the heavenly
divine clearness, covered and closed in the deity, or in the god-
head, should shine upon us, if it were not by the diversities of
holy covertures. Also it is not possible, that our wit or intend-
ment might ascend unto the contemplation of the heavenly
hierarchies immaterial, if our wit be not led to the consideration
of the greatness or magnitude of the most excellent beauteous
clarity, divine and invisible. Reciteth this also the blessed
apostle Paul [79] in his epistles, saying that by these things visible,
which be made and be visible, man may see and know by his inward sight intellectual, the divine, celestial and godly things,
which be invisible to this our natural sight. Devout doctors
of theology or divinity, for this consideration prudently and
wisely read and use natural philosophy and moral, and poets
in their fictions and feigned informations, unto this fine and end,
so that by the likelihood or similitude of things visible our wit
or our understanding spiritually, by clear and crafty utterance
of words, may be so well ordered and uttered: that these things
corporeal may be coupled with things spiritual, and that these
things visible may be conjoined with things invisible. Excited
by these causes to the edifying of the people contained in our
Christian faith of Almighty Jesus, whose majesty divine is
incomprehensible: and of whom to speak it becometh no man,
but with great excellent worship and honor and with an inward
dreadful fear. Loth to offend, I purpose to say somewhat under
the correction of excellent learned doctors and wise men, what
every creature reasonable ought to believe in this our blessed
Christian faith.*

[78] I.e. Dionysius the Areopagite; cf. *ante*, p. 396.   [79] Cf. Romans 1: 20.

* By permission of Messrs. Chatto and Windus from their Edition in the *King's Classics Series.*

So much for science; [80] as for literary scholarship, Chaucer in some lines from his poem, *The Hous(e) of Fame*, has left us his view of the great poets and literary men of the past. *The Hous(e) of Fame*, an allegorical-dream ✳ poem, is interesting, according to Dr. Root,[81] because in it Chaucer has embodied a very noble philosophy of life and because he has revealed himself in it more fully than in any of his other longer poems. The poem is in three books, in the first of which Chaucer tells how in a dream he found himself in the glass Temple of Venus, the walls of which were painted over with the story of Æneas. There are also reminders of other love stories of the past, but the poet is not satisfied with the Temple, even though it is so beautiful, and leaves, whereupon he finds himself alone on a vast sandy desert. His interpreter is an eagle, who in the second book gives an account of Chaucer's past life and, taking him up into the sky, shows him a panoramic view of the kingdoms of earth and heaven. In the third book we are shown the dwelling place of the goddess of fame on a mountain of ice on which the names of the famous are written. The sides of the mountain are so slippery that it is very hard to climb it and the melting of the ice easily makes the names disappear. In the building on the top of the mountain is a great hall and in this Chaucer finds some pillars on which are inscribed names of some likely to be remembered longer than others. Of these he speaks as follows:

These of whom I am about to speak, I saw standing there, without doubt: upon an iron [82] pillar strong that was completely covered with tiger's blood, was that inhabitant of Toulouse known

[80] Cf. Steele, *Mediæval Lore* (*King's Classics Series;* J. W. Luce and Co.) for generous extracts from the most interesting parts of the work of Bartholomæus Anglicus.

[81] Cf. *The Poetry of Chaucer* (Houghton Mifflin Co., 1906), chap. vii.

[82] These, because they all wrote war poetry, are represented on iron pillars; iron was the metal of Mars.

as Statius,[83] who carried the fame of Thebes upon his shoulders and also that of the cruel Achilles. And by him stood . . . upon a wonderfully high iron pillar the great Homer,[84] and with him were Dares [85] and Dictys,[86] Lollius,[87] Guido della Colonna [88] and the English Geoffry.[89] And each of these, to my great joy, was engaged in maintaining the reputation of Troy. Its fame was so great that it was no easy task to look after it. But yet I could see that there was a little envy in their midst; one said,[90] for instance, that Homer wrote lies in his poetic feigning, that he was too favorable to the Greeks in his representation of the Trojan War, and that, hence, what he wrote was fabulous.

Then I saw standing on a pillar of tinned iron that Latin poet Virgil [91] who has long sustained the fame of Æneas.

And next him on a copper pillar Ovid,[92] the clerk of Venus, who has sown broadcast the fame of the great god of love. And he was still working at his task here when I saw him on a pillar as high as I could follow with my eyes. And, therefore, this

[83] Statius, a Latin poet who died about 96 A.D. He wrote the *Thebaid*, an account of the history and wars of Thebes in Greece, and the *Achilleid*, a story of the life and exploits of Achilles. Statius was a native of Naples, but there was a medieval tradition that he was a native of Toulouse in southern France; Dante, for example, whom Chaucer is following here, says (*Purgatorio*, xxi, 89) that Statius was a Toulousan. Statius was much read in the Middle Ages; he was the conductor of Dante through part of purgatory.

[84] Homer, the author of the *Iliad* and the *Odyssey*, was a mere name to medieval Europe unable to read Greek.

[85] Dares was the name affixed to a late Latin work which professed to correct the errors of Homer in regard to the Trojan War. Dares was supposed to give the Phrygian or Trojan side of the story.

[86] Dictys, likewise, was the name given another late Latin work written to correct Homer. Dictys was represented as a Cretan, an eyewitness of the struggle.

[87] The identity of Lollius has not been satisfactorily settled.

[88] An Italian writer whose *Historia Trojana* (*Trojan History*) was finished in 1287.

[89] I.e. Geoffrey of Monmouth, cf. *ante*, p. 248 and *post*, pp. 545–549; 557, 558.

[90] Guido was one of those who said this. (See Skeat's notes throughout here.)

[91] "'Homer's iron is admirably represented as having been by Virgil covered over with tin': note in Bell's Chaucer." — Skeat's note.

[92] Ovid is here taken as the representative love poet; he was a contemporary of Virgil and is the most immoral of the classical poets, curiously popular in the Middle Ages.

hall of which I am writing, grew a thousand feet higher, longer and broader than it was before — this I am sure of.

Then I saw on a pillar of iron of a very hard sort the great poet Lucan.[93] And on his shoulders he was bearing, as high as I could see, the fame of Julius and Pompey. And by him stood all those clerks who write of the mighty works of Rome, so that if I were to enumerate them all, I should have to tarry all too long. And next him on a pillar of sulphur, raging as if he were mad, was Claudian [94] . . . who has borne up the fame of hell, of Pluto and of Proserpine who is the queen of that dark place.[95]

In the Middle Ages, as in other periods in the history of Western Europe, learned men were gathered in schools of various sorts and gave themselves to the training of their successors. In the past too much has been made of the differences between medieval and modern conditions of education, for the probabilities are that medieval men were much like ourselves. At least, the educational process in the fourteenth century began with much the same human material as to-day, if we can put any faith in the following description of himself as a schoolboy by Lydgate (?1370–?1451) in his poem *The Testament of Dan John Lydgate.*

During the time of this green season — I mean the period of my immaturity running from childhood to my fifteenth year — by experience, as was clear, (I) was garish, strange in my actions, disposed to many unbraided passions.

(I was) void of reason, given to willfulness, froward to vir-

[93] Cf. *ante,* p. 67.

[94] Claudius Claudianus, a fourth-century Latin poet, wrote a work called *De Raptu Proserpinæ (On the Stealing of Proserpine),* which is here referred to.

[95] For the suggestion to include this passage in my text I am indebted to Professor Charles G. Osgood of Princeton University. The most exhaustive account of the learning of Chaucer, and an account that throws a good deal of light on all medieval learning, is that of Professor Lounsbury in his *Studies in Chaucer,* chapter v. A much condensed account of a medieval author's reading is that in Baldwin, *op. cit.,* pp. 191–196. Cf. Dante's view of the great men of letters of the past and of the heroes and heroines of mythology in *Inferno,* IV, ll. 80–144.

tue, not mindful of thrift, loath to learn, not fond of concentration save on play or mirth, not inclined to read or spell, following all the appetites belonging to childhood, easily excited, wild and seldom sad, weeping for nothing and soon after laughing.

(I was) ready at slight provocation to strive with a play-mate, as my feelings were my only guide; sometimes I stood in awe of the rod — my only fear was a thrashing; "creeping like snail unwillingly to school"; [96] losing time; like a young unbridled colt, making my friends spend their goods for nothing.

I was wont to come late to school, to attend not for the sake of learning but to keep up appearances, ready to quarrel with my companions, all my pleasure was found in practical jokes. And when I was rebuked for this, my scheme was to make up a lie and muse upon it in order to excuse myself when I did wrong.

I had no respect for my betters, and gave no heed to my sovereigns at all, grew obstinate in disobedience, ran into gardens where I stole apples, spared neither hedge nor wall in gathering fruit, was more ready to pluck grapes off other men's vines than to say matins.

My heart was set on making fun of others and playing tricks on them, contriving evil schemes against them, on cavorting and making faces like a monkey. When I did wrong I could accuse others. I employed all my senses foolishly, was readier to count cherry stones than to go to church or listen to the sacristy bell.

I hated to get up and still more to go to bed, was ready for dinner without washing my hands. My Paternoster (the Lord's Prayer) or Creed I threw to the dogs — this was my way. I was shaken with every wind like a wanton reed, and, when scolded by my friends and told to mend my faults, turned a deaf ear and didn't care to listen to them.

Chaucer, in the story which the prioress tells in the *Canterbury Tales*, describes the education afforded by the primary schools of the period.

[96] *As You Like It*, ii, vii, ll. 146, 147.

There was in Asia, in a great city, among Christians, a Jewish quarter [97] protected by a lord of that country for the sake of foul usury and filthy lucre, hateful to Christ and His following; and through its streets men could ride or walk, for it was free and open on each side.

Down at the further end of this part of the city there was a Christian school in which there were many children of Christian blood who were learning . . . year by year such things as people usually learn in that sort of school, namely, to sing and to read, as small children do in their childhood.

Among these children was a widow's son, a little student, seven years old, who went to school every day and also, whenever he saw the image of Christ's mother, was in the habit of kneeling down and saying his *Hail, Mary*, as he went along. . . .

This little child, as he sat studying his primer, heard the hymn *Alma Redemptoris* (*Dear Mother of Our Lord*) sung, as children were learning to sing from the *Antiphonal*, and he drew as near as he dared and listened to the words and notes until he knew the first stanza by rote.

He didn't at all understand the Latin, for he was young and of tender years; but one day he begged one of his companions to explain the song to him in his mother-tongue, or tell him why the hymn was used. He made this plea often, kneeling down on his little bare knees.

His mate, who was somewhat older, answered him in this way, "This song, I have heard, was written about our Blessed Lady free, to greet her and also to ask her to be our help and succor when we die. I can't tell you any more about this matter; I have learned to sing the song, but I don't know much grammar (Latin)."

After learning to read and sing, boys went on to the study of grammar (Latin) as a prerequisite to any further studies. The Latin authors commonly read were Virgil, Ovid, and the prose writers of the later Roman empire.

---

[97] Chaucer thus transfers the European attitude toward the Jews to the Orient. On the English attitude toward the Jews at this time, cf. *ante*, pp. 209, 277 and *post*, pp. 462–465.

Exercises in composition in prose and verse evidently accompanied this reading. The pagan character of this regimen drew the following spirited protest from the reforming Bishop Grandisson of Exeter in 1357:

John etc., to his beloved sons in Christ, all the archdeacons in our cathedral church of Exeter and their Officials, health etc.

Not without frequent wonder and a feeling of pity have we personally experienced, and daily experience, among the masters or teachers of boys and of the unlearned of our diocese, that they, while instructing them in grammar, observe a form and order of teaching which are preposterous and useless, indeed superstitious and more like heathens than Christians, in that as soon as their scholars have learnt to read or say even very imperfectly the Lord's Prayer, with the Hail Mary and the Creed, also Matins and the Hours of the Blessed Virgin, and the like, which are necessary for faith and the safety of their souls, though they do not know how to construe or understand any of the things before-mentioned, or to decline or parse any of the words in them, they make them pass on prematurely to learn other school books of poetry or in metre. And so it happens that when they are grown up they do not understand what they say or read every day; moreover, which is even more damnable, through want of understanding they do not know the catholic faith.

Desiring, therefore, by all the ways and means possible, to root out so dreadful and stupid an abuse which has become too usual in our diocese, we commission and command you to order and enjoin on all masters or teachers of boys, presiding over Grammar Schools within the boundaries of your archdeaconry, by our authority, as by virtue of these presents we strictly order and enjoin, that they shall not make the boys whom they receive to learn grammar only to read or learn Latin, as hitherto, but leaving everything else make them construe and understand the Lord's Prayer and Ave Mary (Hail, Mary), the Creed, Matins and Hours of the Blessed Virgin, and decline the words there and parse them before they let them go on to other books. Informing them that we do not intend to mark any boys with

a clerical character unless they have by this means been found
to have become proficient.

Dated at our manor of Chudleigh 13 February, 1356–7, and
the thirtieth year of our consecration.

After spending some time in the grammar school, the
student naturally passed on to the university, where, after
courses in the seven liberal arts — grammar, logic, rhetoric (the *trivium*, the program of the undergraduate), arithmetic, geometry, music and astronomy (the *quadrivium*)
— and the three philosophies — natural, moral and meta-
physical, a thirteenth-century addition to the university
course — he might proceed to the study of law, medicine
and theology.

The unfortunate rival claims of Oxford and Cambridge
to priority of foundation and the obstinate determination
to substantiate these claims by documents, even forged
ones, have vitiated nearly all the early accounts of university origins in England. So we cannot present any
trustworthy contemporary narrative of the beginnings of
English university life, but must piece together an account
from casual references [98] in contemporary literature. In
the later thirteenth century, however, we get a considerable number of rather extended notices of these things from
which satisfactory inferences as to historical facts can be
drawn. From the following *Rules of Oxford*, for example,
we learn a good deal about conditions there. These *Rules*
were compiled about 1292.

Each book of the house, now or hereafter to be given out,
shall be taken only after a large deposit has been left, in order
that the one having it may the more fear to lose it; and let a
duplicate receipt be made, of which one part shall be kept in
the common custody, and the other be taken by the scholar

[98] These references are collected in Leach, *Educational Charters and Documents
598–1909*, pp. 100–109 (Cambridge University Press — in the United States, G. P.
Putnam's Sons, 1911).

having the book; and let no book be given outside of the college without a still better bond, and with consent of all the scholars. . . .

No one shall interfere with the regular arrangement of the household either in the choice of dinners or in the occupation of the rooms of the house, but each scholar shall give diligent assistance; and especially they shall not exceed an expense of twelve pence a week each from the common treasury, except in the three principal weeks, unless a special dispensation has been given by the university. . . .

All the scholars of the house shall often speak Latin, in order that they may obtain an easier and more ready and more decorous manner of speaking in disputations and in other proper circumstances.

Let them all live honorably, like clerics, as becomes saints, not fighting, nor using tales or scurrilous language, nor singing love songs, nor telling tales of love adventures or such as lead to evil thoughts; nor ridiculing any one or stirring him to anger, nor shouting so that students may be interfered with in their study or rest.

Masters of the liberal arts willingly perform varied and heavy labors in lecturing and discussing, for the profit and advantage of their pupils, but on account of stinginess, which has grown up in these modern days more than formerly, they are not sufficiently rewarded by them for these labors, as is befitting and as was formerly done; therefore, it is made a rule, that each student under the faculty of arts attending in the hall at the usual weekly exercises shall pay, for either the old or new logic,[99] at least twelve pence for the whole year, dividing it in proper proportions for the separate terms.

Those who shall regularly hear lectures on books on physics must pay eighteen pence for hearing these books for a year.

It is made a rule that masters of the grammar schools shall be required to dispute on grammar on Thursdays.

[99] The old logic was the realistic logic developed in the earlier Middle Ages on the basis of very poor and meager translations of Aristotle; the new logic was the nominalistic logic developed by Abelard. Cf. Hastings Rashdall, *The Universities of Europe in the Middle Ages* (Oxford at the Clarendon Press, 1895), *Index*.

Since it has been made law from old time, that masters holding schools of grammar should, on their oath, give attention to
the positive knowledge of their pupils; yet some, looking for
gain and profit and forgetful of their own salvation, treating that
statute with contempt, have presumed to give what they call
"cursory lectures," to the evident injury of their students; the
chancellor, wishing to look out for the profit of the . . . students, and especially the younger ones, as he is bound to do,
has suspended such attendance, which is not only frivolous but
injurious to the advancement of the said younger pupils, and
has made a law, that whosoever shall in future wish to conduct
schools of grammar shall desist from cursory lectures of this kind,
upon pain of being deprived of the rule of the schools and of
under going imprisonment at the will of the chancellor. Neither
in the schools nor anywhere in the university shall they give
such courses of lectures as these, nor allow them to be given,
but shall diligently attend to the positive instruction of their
pupils. . . .

The bachelors about to take their degrees in a certain year
must appear before certain masters, with the good testimony
of some other masters and bachelors. They shall then swear,
touching the sacred objects, that they have heard all the books
of the old logic [99] at least twice, except the books of Boethius,[100]
which it is enough to have read once, and the fourth book of
the *Topics* of Boethius, which they are not required to read. Of
the new logic [99] they shall swear that they have read the books
of *First Topics* and *Outlines* twice, the book of *Later Topics*
at least once. Of grammar they must swear that they have
heard Priscian [101] *On Constructions* twice, the *Barbarism* of Donatus [102] once, or three books of physical matters; that is *Physics*,[103]
Of the Soul, Of Generation and Corruption.[104]

[100] Cf. *ante*, p. 66.   [101] Cf. *ante*, p. 67.   [102] Cf. *ante*, p. 67.
[103] The three titles are of works of Aristotle.

[104] This last paragraph is a statement of the Oxford curriculum in 1267. Cf.
what is said of Cambridge in 1109 in the *Continuation* of Ingulph's *Chronicle of the
Abbey of Croyland* (*tr. cit.*, p. 237): "He (a certain Abbot Joffrid) also sent to his
manor of Cottenham, near Cambridge, the lord Gislebert, his fellow-monk, and
professor of Sacred Theology, together with three other monks who had accompanied him into England; who, being very well instructed in philosophical theo-

In 1296 a patriotic English bishop wrote to the pope, asking for Oxford the same privileges as those already granted to Paris. His letter is as follows:

To the most holy father in Christ, Lord Boniface (VIII), by divine providence of the very holy Roman and universal church highest pontiff, John, by the mercy of the same, humble minister of the church at Carlisle, with reverential obedience sends kisses for his blessed feet.

Great fertility gladdens a mother, and the more virtuous the offspring the greater is the occasion for joy. The inexhaustible fertility of the University of Oxford does not cease to produce

rems and other primitive sciences, went every day to Cambridge, and, having hired a public barn there, openly taught their respective sciences and in a short space of time collected a great concourse of scholars. For in the second year after their arrival, the number of their scholars from both the country as well as the town, had increased to such a degree, that not even the largest house or barn, nor any church even, was able to contain them. For this reason, they separated into different places, and, imitating the plan of study adopted at Orleans, brother Odo, who was eminent in these days as a grammarian and a satirist, early in the morning, read grammar according to the doctrine of Priscian, and the comments of Remigius thereon, to the boys and younger students assigned to him. At the first hour, brother Terricus, a most acute sophist, read the *Logic* of Aristotle, according to the *Introductions* of Porphyry and Averroes, to those who were somewhat older. Then at the third hour, brother William read lectures on the *Rhetoric* of Tully and the *Institutes* of Quintilian. Master Gislebert, being unacquainted with the English language, but very expert in the Latin and French, the latter being his native tongue, on every Lord's day and on the festivals of the Saints, preached to the people the Word of God in the various churches. On feast days before the sixth hour, he expounded to the literates and the priests, who in especial resorted to hear him, a text from the pages of Holy Scripture." The mention of the Spanish-Arabian physician, jurist and philosopher Averroes (*circa* 1126–1178) in this passage destroys its historical reliability, but even if Ingulph and his continuators are the authors of a fourteenth-century historical novel, their statement here may tell us what went on at Cambridge later than the date assigned to these lectures. The earliest reliable mention of Cambridge according to Leach (*op. cit.*, p. 149) is 1231. The Remigius spoken of in the passage is Remigius of Auxerre (born in Burgundy before 850, died about 908), a Benedictine teacher and commentator who wrote on the liberal arts, Priscian and Donatus, the Bible and the mass. The commentaries of Averroes on Aristotle were widely used in the Middle Ages. Porphyry (233–*circa* 304 A.D.) was a Syrian by birth and education and a lecturer on grammar, history and philosophy. Priscian, Tully and Quintilian have been noticed before (pp. 67, 66 and 388 respectively).

many great and useful sons for the ranks of the Lord, so that
it is truly rated as the mother and nurse of English learning, and
is deserving of being held in honor with the affection due to a
mother. Therefore, since a wise son is the gladness of a father,
she ought to be held in favor who increases the house of God
with the wisdom and devotion of such sons.

As I have learned, the apostolic foresight has considered it
best to distinguish the university of the kingdom of France by
such a privilege that all who have attained in any faculty the
rank of the honor of master shall be permitted to deliver lectures in the same faculty anywhere, and to continue these as
long as they please, without a new examination or approbation,
without the duty of going back to the beginning, or of seeking
the favor of any one. I therefore affectionately and devotedly
beg your pious fatherly care that, for increasing the peace and
uniformity among scholastics, it may be pleasing to your apostolic kindness to extend the common privilege of this dispensation to the said University of Oxford. There is truly a fear felt
by many of the great men of the kingdom of England, that
peace cannot long be preserved inviolate by the students, —
a thing which is especially necessary among universities, — unless the English university is acknowledged to be deserving of
being ranked with the rest in liberties and scholastic powers.
May the Lord preserve your Holiness to rule the universal
church through all time ! Dated at Berwick, on the third day
of September, 1296.

"At Merton College, Oxford, the warden and fellows were
bound to meet three times a year at a 'scrutiny,' wherein
each gave his opinion of the condition of the college. Of
three of these meetings some rough notes taken by one
who was present have been preserved." [105] One set of these
notes dated 1339 gives us the following notion of a medieval faculty meeting:

Middleton. William the chaplain has often insulted the fellows.

Handel. It would be well if the senior fellows were summoned
to make peace between Wylie and Finmer.

[105] See Ashley, *Edward III and His Wars*, p. 65.

Westcombe. The noise the fellows make in their rooms.

Humberstone. The quarrel between Wylie and Finmer. The fellows keep dogs, and progress in their studies is prevented by idleness. The statute is not observed, for we have no bursars. Also it would be well if the land in Little Wolford were let to a farmer.

Finmer. Wylie, although appointed under the statute to audit accounts, will not audit them, and though thrice summoned and again called upon by the fellows, has rebelliously refused, and so falls under the statute; and he unjustly receives better commons, and they who ought to proceed against him are too remiss.

Wanting. The warden should not go on insulting the senior fellows in the way he has begun.

Wylie. Somebody should be sent to Stratton to enquire about the college estates and other business.

Lynham. As to allaying the quarrels among the fellows.

Sutton. They ought to have a keeper of pledges,[106] but have not, and there is a deficit; and it is said that some books are sold, without the college or the fellows benefiting by it. The warden does not enforce process against the debtors of the college and especially against the bailiff of Elham; and Wanting owes the bailiff of Elham seven pounds and sixteen pence which belong to the college, and as he excuses himself from all other business, he ought not to take part in these college meetings. . . .

Handel. Would be glad if a volume of decrees and of decretals were placed in the library and if the books of the college were arranged.

Buckingham. Wanting has sold the college horses at Elham, and has kept the money in his hands, and has rendered no account nor has the bailiff. . . . There should not be a number of people taking notes in the meeting.

Dumbleton. Nothing.

Monby. Wylie has publicly, in the presence of all the fellows, insulted Finmer.

[106] Professor Ashley (*Ibid.*, p. 66) suggests that these "pledges" were objects left by students in pawn with the college for loans from college funds; they may also have been deposits for loans from the college library; cf. *ante,* p. 409.

Leverington. The seneschal is not present in chapel on saints' days, but is absent for the most part. . . .

Wylie. Begs that what has been said by Elyndon and Wanting be corrected and recommends charity. The warden should correct it, especially what had been said to the warden in the meeting, and above all what Elyndon said, that the reputations of some of the fellows were tarnished; and how that Durant accused Wylie of planning with the other seniors to prevent the election of a fellow, and that he had this from those who were recently in London.

Middleton. Elham is in fault as to the breaking of the hall door. We ought to have a mill at Seaton.

Handel. This opportunity should be taken of restoring peace. The juniors should show reverence to the seniors, and everyone should be enjoined publicly to observe charity, and each should try to bring this about as far as he can.

Humberstone. The warden ought by statute to get the help of some of the fellows who are impartial to put an end to the quarrel between Wylie and Finmer. Wanting has behaved disrespectfully towards the warden by publicly addressing him as Robert.

The early careers of the medieval universities were troublous, full of struggles for recognition with the civil and ecclesiastical authorities. Especially hard was their conflict with the former, for the university students all wished to be ranked as clerics and enjoy all the privileges of their order, particularly the right of immunity from the ordinary civil courts. The constituted powers in cities and towns, in the interest of law and quiet, naturally wished all the inhabitants to be subject to the same law. This difference of opinion or jurisdiction was the cause of many a "town and gown" riot in university towns. A famous brawl occurred at Oxford in 1209 and is thus described by Roger of Wendover:

About (this) time a clerk, who was studying the liberal arts at Oxford, by accident killed a woman, and when he found she was dead, sought safety in flight. But the bailiff of the town and others who came up and found the woman dead, began to try and find the murderer in his hostel, which he had hired with three other clerks, and not finding the criminal, took his three friends, who knew almost nothing about the murder, and threw them into prison. A few days afterwards, on the orders of the king of the English, in contempt of the liberty of the church, they were taken outside the town and hanged. On this nearly three thousand clerks, masters and scholars alike, left Oxford, not a single one of the whole University remaining. Some of them went to study the liberal arts at Cambridge, some to Reading, but the town of Oxford was left empty.

This attempt to get desired privileges by secession reminds one of the conduct of the plebeians in their contests with the patricians at Rome, and these exoduses, which were numerous, became quite serious in the eyes of the town authorities, for they realized that, notwithstanding the added difficulties and responsibilities that a university community brought to a city, it was an advantage for a municipality to have a university within its borders, because of the additional business brought them thereby. Hence, when in 1334 a secession to Stamford from Oxford had taken place, pressure was brought to bear on King Edward III himself to issue a decree forbidding the erection of a university at Stamford. This incident has added interest because "so late as the first quarter of the nineteenth century every candidate for an Oxford degree was required to take an oath not to lecture at Stamford." [107] The King expressed himself thus:

The king, to the sheriff of Lincoln, greeting. Whereas we are given to understand that many masters and scholars of our

---

[107] *Cambridge History of English Literature*, II, p. 392, note. Chapter xv, from which this note is taken, with its bibliography, is the most convenient reference on the subject we have just been treating. See the reference to the method of disputing in schools in Fitzstephen's *Description of London*, *ante*, p. 311; and to school games in the same document, *ante*, p. 316.

university of Oxford under color of certain dissensions lately, as it is said, arisen in that university, and with other idle pretexts, withdrawing themselves from that university, presume to betake themselves to the town of Stamford, and there carry on their studies and perform scholastic exercises, having by no means sought our assent or license; which, if it were tolerated, would manifestly turn not only to our contempt and disgrace but also to the dispersion of our said university;

We, unwilling that schools or studies should in any wise be carried on elsewhere within our realm than in places where there are now universities, order and firmly enjoin you to go in person to the said town of Stamford, and there and elsewhere within your bailiwick where it is expedient, cause it to be publicly proclaimed with our authority, and prohibition made that any should carry on study or perform scholastic exercises elsewhere than in our said universities, under penalty of forfeiting to us all they can forfeit; and cause us, without delay, to be informed distinctly and openly, in our chancery, and under your seal, of the names of those whom you find disobeying, after this proclamation and prohibition;

For we will that speedy justice be done as is fitting to all and everyone ready to bring their complaints of any violence or injury done to them at the said city of Oxford, before our justices there, specially deputed for this purpose.

Witness the king at Windsor, the second day of August.

By the king and council.[108]

4. *Books and Their Place in Culture.* — Richard d'Aungerville (1281–1345), better known as Richard of Bury, has made himself famous as the greatest private book collector of the age and, by writing a volume on the love of books, has enabled posterity to get his ideas and ideals as a collector. He was left an orphan at an early age and brought up under the care of an uncle who sent him to

---

[108] "This vigorous measure was successful but not until a writ had been issued next year ordering the seizure of the books of the disobedient." Ashley's note, *op. cit.*, p. 35.

Oxford. Of his pursuits at the University, Richard writes, "From an early age, led by we know not what happy accident, we attached ourselves with present solicitude to the society of masters, scholars and professors of various arts, whom perspicacity of wit and celebrity of learning had rendered most conspicuous; encouraged by whose consolatory conversation we were most deliciously nourished, sometimes with explanatory investigation of arguments, at others with recitations of treatises on the progress of physics, and of the Catholic doctors, as it were multiplied and successive dishes of learning. Such were the comrades we chose in our boyhood; such we entertained as the inmates of our chambers, such were the companions of our journies, the messmates of our board and our associates in all our fortunes." His brilliance as a student recommended him as a tutor for the future Edward III, and by that means he was introduced to the public life of his day, becoming a diplomat and statesman. But he never lost his interest in book collecting and used his position to further his favorite avocation. On one diplomatic mission he visited Paris, and of his impression of the city says, "O blessed God of Gods in Sion! what a rush of the flood of pleasure rejoiced our heart as often as we visited Paris the Paradise of the world! There we longed to remain, where on account of the greatness of our love the days ever appeared to us to be few. There are delightful libraries, in cells redolent of aromatics; there, flourishing greenhouses of all sorts of volumes; there academic meads trembling with the earthquake of Athenian Peripatetics, pacing up and down; there, the promontories of Parnassus, and the porticoes of the Stoics. . . . There, in very deed, with an open treasury and untied purse strings we scattered money with a light heart, and redeemed inestimable books with dirt and dust. Every buyer is apt to boast of his bargains; but . . . we will

add a most compendious way by which a great multitude of books, as well old as new, came into our hands.
Never, indeed, having disdained the poverty of religious
devotees, assumed for Christ, we never held them in ab-
horrence, but admitted them from all parts of the world
into the kind embraces of our compassion; . . . to these,
under all circumstances, we became a refuge; to these we
never closed the bosom of our favor. Wherefore, we deserved to have . . . as well their personal as their mental
labors, who going about by sea and land, surveying the
whole compass of the earth, and also inquiring into the
general studies of the universities of the various provinces,
were anxious to administer to our wants, under a most
certain hope of reward. . . . Besides all the opportunities
already touched upon, we easily acquired the notice of
the stationers and booksellers, not only within the provinces
of our native soil, but of those dispersed over the kingdoms of France, Germany and Italy, by the prevailing
power of money; no distance whatever impeded, no fury
of the sea deterred them; nor was cash wanting for their
expenses when they sent or brought us the wished for
books; for they knew to a certainty that their hopes . . .
were secure with us. . . . Moreover, there was always
about us in our halls, no small assemblage of antiquaries,
scribes, bookbinders, correctors, illuminators, and generally of all such persons as were qualified to labor advantageously in the service of books." He would not have
been content with the modest twenty books of Chaucer's
clerk and yet we learn that Richard's collections, called
"an infinite number of books" by Adam of Murimuth,
totaled somewhat more than five cartloads.[109] He made
noble use of his treasures, for in chapters 18 and 19 of
his *Philobiblon* (*Love of Books*) we have the following words:
"We have for a long time, held a rooted purpose . . . to

[109] Cf. Baldwin, *op. cit.*, p. 192.

found in perpetual alms, and enrich with the necessary
gifts, a certain Hall in the revered University of Oxford,
the first nurse of all the liberal arts; and further to enrich
the same . . . with deposits of our books, so that they may
be made common as to use and study, not only to scholars
of the said Hall, but through them to all the students of
the aforesaid University forever. . . . Five of the scholars
dwelling in the aforesaid Hall are to be appointed by the
Master, . . . to whom the custody of the books is to be
deputed. Of which five, three shall be competent to lend
any books for inspection and use only; but for copying
and transcribing we will not allow any book to pass without the walls of the house. Therefore, when any scholar,
whether secular or religious, whom we have deemed qualified for the present favor, shall demand the loan of a book,
the keepers must carefully consider whether they have a
duplicate of that book; and if so, they may lend it to him,
taking a security which in their opinion shall exceed in
value the book delivered; and they shall immediately make
a written memorandum both of the security and of the
book lent. . . . But if the keepers shall find that there
is no duplicate of the book demanded, they shall not lend
such book to any one whomsoever, unless he be of the
company of scholars of the said Hall, except . . . for
inspection within the walls of the foresaid Hall, but not
to be carried beyond them. But to every scholar whatever
of the aforesaid Hall, any book may be available by loan.
. . . And the aforesaid keepers must render an account
every year to the master of the house, and two of his
scholars to be selected by him; . . . and every person to
whom any book has been lent shall exhibit the book once
in the year to the keepers, and if he wishes it he shall
see his security." It is a pity that Richard's collections
were entirely dispersed or destroyed by the time of Edward
VI. After these personal references to Richard we are

ready for some further passages [110] from his book; namely chapters 3, 5, 6 and 12, which are entitled *What are we to think of the price.in the buying of books*, *The complaint of books against the possessioners*, *The complaint of books against the mendicants*, and *Why we have caused books of grammar to be so diligently prepared*.

From what has been said we draw this corollary welcome to us, but, as we believe, acceptable to few: namely, that no dearness of price ought to hinder a man from the buying of books, if he has the money that is demanded for them, unless it be to withstand the malice of the seller or to await a more favorable opportunity of buying. For if it is wisdom only that makes the price of books, which is an infinite treasure to mankind, and if the value of the books is unspeakable, as the premises show, how shall the bargain be shown to be dear where an infinite good is being bought? Wherefore, that books are to be gladly bought and unwillingly sold, Solomon, the sun of men, exhorts us in the Proverbs: Buy the truth, he says, and sell not wisdom.[111] But what we are trying to show by rhetoric or logic, let us prove by examples from history. The arch-philosopher Aristotle,[112] whom Averroes [113] regards as the law of Nature, bought a few books from Speusippus [114] straightway after his death for 72,000 sesterces. Plato,[115] before him in time, but after him in learning, bought the book of Philolaus [116] the Pythagorean, from which he is said to have taken the *Timæus*,[117] for 10,000 denaries, as Aulus Gellius [118] relates in the *Noctes Atticæ*.

[110] The passages so far quoted are from the *Philobiblon*, chaps. 8, 19 and 20 in the translation of Inglis included in Edwards, *Memoirs of Libraries* (2 vols., London, Trübner and Co., 1859), I, pp. 377–383.

[111] Cf. Proverbs 23: 23.   [112] Cf. *ante*, p. 66.   [113] Cf. *ante*, p. 412.

[114] Nephew of Plato and his successor in the school of the Academy.

[115] B.C. 429 or 428–347, cf. *ante*, p. 388.

[116] A contemporary of Socrates, the master of Plato and the chief character in all his *Dialogs*, died B.C. 399.

[117] The *Timæus* of Plato, one of the most obscure of his *Dialogs*, deals with theories of creation and was one of the three Platonic dialogs known in the Middle Ages, the other two being the *Phædo* and the *Meno*.

[118] Aulus Gellius was a Roman grammarian who lived about A.D. 117–180. His *Noctes Atticæ* (*Athenian Nights*) contains many extracts from classical writers and

Now Aulus Gellius relates this that the foolish may consider how wise men despise money in comparison with books. And on the other hand, that we may know that folly and pride go together, let us here relate the folly of Tarquin the Proud in despising books, as also related by Aulus Gellius. An old woman, utterly unknown, is said to have come to Tarquin the Proud, the seventh king of Rome, offering to sell nine books, in which, as she declared, sacred oracles were contained, but she asked an immense sum for them, insomuch that the king said she was mad. In anger she flung three books into the fire, and still asked the same sum for the rest. When the king refused it, again she flung three others into the fire and still asked the same price for the three that were left. At last, astonished beyond measure, Tarquin was glad to pay for three books the same price for which he might have bought nine. The old woman straightway disappeared, and was never seen before or after. These were the Sibylline books, which the Romans consulted as a divine oracle by some one of the Quindecemvirs, and this is believed to have been the origin of the Quindecemvirate.[119] What did this Sibyl teach the proud king by this bold deed, except that the vessels of wisdom, holy books, exceed all human estimation; and as Gregory [120] says of the kingdom of heaven: They are worth all that thou hast?*

. . . .

The venerable devotion of the religious orders is wont to be solicitous in the care of books and to delight in their society, as

thus served as a kind of dictionary of favorite quotations in the Middle Ages. Some of the writers quoted by Aulus are not extant in any other form. The outlines of the reign of Tarquin the Proud are given in Livy (B.C. 59–A.D. 17), *History of Rome*, book i, chapter 49, but Livy does not tell the story of these books. The authorities for that story are Dionysius of Halicarnassus (died A.D. 7), *History of Rome*, book iv, chapter 62, Varro, a Roman writer of the first century B.C., as quoted by Lactantius (see *ante*, p. 67) in his *Institutes of Divinity*, book i, chapter 6, Aulus Gellius, *op. cit.*, book i, chapter 19 and Isidore. of Seville (see *post*, p. 434), *Origins*, book viii, chapter 815.

[119] According to modern authorities, Tarquin assigned two men of equestrian rank to the care of these books; the number was after 367 B.C. increased to ten and the college was not made to consist of fifteen until the first century B.C.

[120] Probably Gregory the Great; cf. *ante*, p. 64.

* By permission of Messrs. Chatto and Windus from their Edition in the *King's Classics Series*.

if they were their only riches. For some used to write them with their own hands between the hours of prayer, and gave to the making of books such intervals as they could secure and the times appointed for the recreation of the body. By those labors there are resplendent to-day in most monasteries these sacred treasures full of cherubic letters, for giving the knowledge of salvation to the student and a delectable light to the path of the laity. O manual toil, happier than any agricultural task! O devout solicitude, where neither Martha nor Mary [121] deserves to be rebuked! O joyful house, in which the fruitful Leah [121] does not envy the beauteous Rachel [121] but action [121] and contemplation [121] share each other's joys! O happy charge, destined to benefit endless generations of posterity, with which no planting of trees, no sowing of seeds, no pastoral delight in herbs, no building of fortified camps can be compared! Wherefore the memory of those fathers should be immortal, who delighted only in the treasures of wisdom, who most laboriously provided shining lamps against future darkness, and against hunger of hearing the Word of God, most carefully prepared, not bread baked in ashes, nor of barley, nor musty, but unleavened loaves made of the finest wheat of divine wisdom, with which hungry souls might be joyfully fed. These men were the stoutest champions of the Christian army, who defended our weakness by their most valiant arms; they were in their time the most cunning takers of foxes, who have left us their nets, that we might catch the young foxes, who cease not to devour the growing vines. Of a truth, noble fathers, worthy of perpetual benedic-

---

[121] Martha (cf. Luke 10: 38–42) and Leah (cf. Genesis 29 and 30) were taken in the Middle Ages as types of the active life; and Mary and Rachel, of the contemplative life. The former was the life of the person out in the world and the latter that of the cloistered monk. Toynbee in his *Dante Dictionary* adduces quotations from Gregory the Great, Hugh of St. Victor and Aquinas to show how Leah was used in this symbolism; Toynbee is annotating Dante, *Purgatory*, xxvii, ll. 100–108. Since Rachel was by Jacob preferred to Leah, and Mary to Martha, by Jesus, medieval philosophers and theologians took the contemplative life to be superior to the active. Dinsmore in his *Aids to the Study of Dante*, pp. 319–322, quotes in translation the teaching of Aquinas as to the relative merits of the two ideals of life, the active and the contemplative. Cf. *post*, pp. 451–455 for Wyclif's protest against the orthodox assumption.

tion, ye would have been deservedly happy, if ye had been allowed to beget offspring like yourselves, and to leave no degenerate or doubtful progeny for the benefit of future times.

But, painful to relate, now slothful Thersites [122] handles the arms of Achilles [123] and the choice trappings of war-horses are spread upon lazy asses, winking owls lord it in the eagle's nest, and the cowardly kite sits upon the perch of the hawk.

> Liber Bacchus [124] is ever loved,
> And is into their bellies shoved,
>   By day and by night;
> Liber Codex [125] is neglected,
> And with scornful hand rejected,
>   Far out of their sight.

And as if the simple monastic folk of modern times were deceived by a confusion of names, while Liber Pater [124] is preferred to *Liber Patrum*,[126] the study of monks nowadays is in the emptying of cups and not the mending of books; to which they do not hesitate to add the wanton music of Timotheus,[127] jealous of chastity, and thus the song of the merrymaker and not the chant of the mourner is become the office of the monks. Flocks and fleeces, crops and granaries, leeks and potherbs, drink and goblets, are nowadays the reading and study of the monks, except a few elect ones, in whom lingers not the image but some slight vestige of the fathers that preceded them. And again, no materials at all are furnished us to commend the canons regular for their care or study of us, who though they bear their name of honor from their twofold rule, yet have neglected the notable clause of Augustine's *Rule*,[128] in which we are commended to his clergy in these words: Let books be asked for each day at a given hour; he who asks for them after the hour is not to receive them. Scarcely any one observes this devout

---

[122] The buffoon in the *Iliad*.   [123] The hero of the *Iliad*.

[124] Names of the classic god of wine.

[125] I.e. the MS. of a book, i.e. bookmaking.

[126] I.e. the *Book of the Fathers*, the writings of the great Christian scholars.

[127] A celebrated Greek musician and poet, a musical innovator, born B.C. 428, died 357.   [128] Cf. *ante*, p. 64.

rule of study after saying the prayers of the Church, but to
care for the things of this world and to look at the plow that
has been left is reckoned the highest wisdom. They take up
bow and quiver, embrace arms and shield, devote the tribute of
alms to dogs [129] and not to the poor, become the slaves of dice
and draughts, and of all such things as we are wont to forbid
even to the secular clergy, so that we need not marvel if they
disdain to look upon us,[130] whom they see so much opposed to
their mode of life.

Come then, reverend fathers, deign to recall your fathers and
devote yourselves more faithfully to the study of holy books,
without which all religion will stagger, without which the virtue
of devotion will dry up like a shred, and without which ye can
afford no light to the world.*

. . . .

Poor in spirit, but most rich in faith, off-scourings of the
world and salt of the earth, despisers of the world and fishers
of men, how happy are ye, if suffering penury for Christ ye know
how to possess your souls in patience![131] For it is not want, the
avenger of iniquity, nor the adverse fortune of your parents,
nor violent necessity that has thus oppressed you with beggary,
but a devout will and Christ-like election, by which ye have
chosen that life as the best, which God Almighty Made Man as
well by word as by example declared to be the best. In truth,
ye are the latest offspring of the ever-fruitful Church, of late
divinely substituted for the Fathers and the Prophets, that your
sound may go forth into all the earth, and that instructed by
our [131] healthful doctrines ye may preach before all kings and
nations the invincible faith of Christ. Moreover, that the faith
of the Fathers is chiefly enshrined in books the second chapter
has sufficiently shown, from which it is clearer than light that
ye ought to be zealous lovers of books above all Christians. Ye
are commanded to sow upon all waters, because the Most High

[129] Cf. Chaucer's description of the prioress and monk, *ante*, pp. 287, 288.
[130] The books are addressing the monks.
[131] The books are addressing the friars.

* By permission of Messrs. Chatto and Windus from their Edition in the *King's Classics
Series.*

is no respecter of persons, nor does the Most Holy desire the death of sinners, Who offered Himself to die for them, but desires to heal the contrite in heart, to raise the fallen and to correct the perverse in the spirit of lenity. For which most salutary purpose our kindly Mother Church has planted you freely, and having planted has watered you with favors, and having watered has established you with privileges, that ye may be co-workers with pastors and curates in procuring the salvation of faithful souls. Wherefore, that the order of Preachers was principally instituted for the study of the Holy Scriptures and the salvation of their neighbors, is declared by their constitutions, so that not only from the *Rule* of Bishop Augustine,[132] which directs books to be asked for every day, but as soon as they have read the prolog of the said constitutions they may know from the very title of the same that they are pledged to the love of books.

But alas a threefold care of superfluities, viz., of the stomach, of dress and of houses, has seduced these men and others following their example, from the paternal care of books and from their study. For, forgetting the providence of the Savior, who is declared by the Psalmist [133] to think upon the poor and needy, they are occupied with the wants of the perishing body, that their feasts may be splendid and their garments luxurious, against the Rule, and the fabrics of their buildings, like the battlements of castles, carried to a height incompatible with poverty. Because of these three things, we books, who have procured their advancement and have granted them to sit among the powerful and noble, are put far from their hearts' affection and are reckoned as superfluities; except that they rely upon some treatises of small value, from which they derive strange heresies and apocryphal imbecilities, not for the refreshment of souls, but rather for tickling the ears of the listeners. The Holy Scripture is not expounded, but is neglected and treated as though it were commonplace and known to all, though very few have touched its hem, and though its depth is such, as holy Augustine [132] declares, that it cannot be understood by the human intellect, however long it may toil with the utmost intensity of

[132] Cf. *ante*, p. 64.   [133] Cf. Psalms 9: 12 and 18.

study. From this he who devoted himself to it assiduously, if only He will vouchsafe to open the door who has established the spirit of piety, may unfold a thousand lessons of moral teaching, which will flourish with the freshest novelty and will cherish the intelligence of the listeners with the most delightful savors. Wherefore the first professors of evangelical poverty, after some slight homage paid to secular science, collecting all their force of intellect, devoted themselves to labors upon the sacred scriptures, meditating day and night on the Law of the Lord. And whatever they could steal from their famishing belly, or intercept from their half-covered body, they thought it the highest gain, to spend in buying or correcting books. Whose worldly contemporaries observing their devotion and study bestowed upon them for the edification of the whole Church the books which they had collected at great expense in the various parts of the world.

In truth, in these days as ye are engaged with all diligence in pursuit of gain, it may be reasonably believed, if we speak according to human notions, that God thinks less upon those whom He perceives to distrust His promises, putting their hope in human providence, not considering the raven, nor the lilies, whom the Most High feeds and arrays.[134] Ye do not think upon Daniel[135] and the bearer of the mess of boiled pottage,[136] nor recollect Elijah[137] who was delivered from hunger once in the desert by angels, again in the torrent by ravens, and again in Sarepta by the widow, through the divine bounty, which gives to all flesh their meat in due season. Ye descend, as we fear, by a wretched anticlimax, distrust of the divine providence producing reliance upon your own prudence, and reliance upon your own prudence begetting anxiety about worldly things, and excessive anxiety about worldly things taking away the love as well as the study of books; and thus poverty in these days is abused to the injury of the Word of God, which ye have chosen only for profit's sake.

With summer fruit, as the people gossip, ye attract boys[138]

---

[134] Cf. Matt. 6: 26–28. [135] Cf. Daniel 6. [136] Cf. Gen. 25: 28–34.
[137] Cf. 1 Kings 19: 5; 17: 6; 10–16.
[138] Cf. the words of Bacon, *ante*, pp. 399–401.

to religion, whom when they have taken the vows ye do not instruct by fear and force as their age requires, but allow them to devote themselves to begging expeditions, and suffer them to spend the time in which they might be learning, in procuring the favor of friends, to the annoyance of their parents, the danger of the boys and the detriment of the order. And thus no doubt it happens that those who were not compelled to learn as unwilling boys, when they grow up, presume to teach though utterly unworthy and unlearned, and a small error in the beginning becomes a very great one in the end. For there grows up among your promiscuous flock of laity a pestilent multitude of creatures, who nevertheless the more shamelessly force themselves into the edifice of preaching, the less they understand what they are saying, to the contempt of the Divine Word and the injury of souls. In truth, against the Law, ye plow with an ox and an ass together,[139] in committing the cultivation of the Lord's field to the unlearned. Side by side, it is written, the oxen were plowing and the asses feeding beside them: since it is the duty of the discreet to preach, but of the simple to feed themselves in silence by the hearing of sacred eloquence. How many stones ye fling upon the heap of Mercury [140] nowadays! How many marriages ye procure for the eunuchs of wisdom! How many blind watchmen [141] ye bid go round about the walls of the Church!

O idle fishermen, using only the nets of others, which when torn it is all ye can do to clumsily repair, but can net no new ones of your own! ye enter on the labors of others, ye repeat the lessons of others, ye mouth with theatric effect the superficially repeated wisdom of others. As the silly parrot imitates the words that he has heard, so such men are mere reciters of all, but authors of nothing, imitating Balaam's ass,[142] which,

---

[139] Cf. Deut. 22: 10.

[140] Mercury, the classical messenger of the gods, was the god of travelers and in his honor heaps of stones were to be found at the cross-roads, each wayfarer being supposed to add one to the heap. Mercury was also the inventor of wise and clever discourse. The allusion is an apt one, for the friars were supposed to be the wandering messengers of a new gospel and were to be pre-eminently preachers of the Word. The irony of Bury's remark is very pointed.

[141] Cf. Isaiah 56: 10 and Song of Solomon 3: 3.   [142] Cf. Numbers 22: 21-30.

though senseless itself, yet became eloquent of speech and the teacher of its master though a prophet. Recover yourselves, O poor in Christ, and studiously regard us books, without which ye can never be properly shod in the preparation of the Gospel of Peace.[143]

Paul the Apostle, preacher of the truth and excellent teacher of nations, for all his gear bade three things be brought to him by Timothy, his cloak, books and parchments,[144] affording an example to ecclesiastics that they should wear dress in moderation, and should have books for aid in study, and parchments, which the Apostle especially esteems, for writing: and especially, he says, the parchments. And truly that clerk is crippled and maimed to his disablement in many ways, who is entirely ignorant of the art of writing. He beats the air with words and edifies only those who are present, but does nothing for the absent and for posterity. The man bore a writer's ink-horn upon his loins, who set a mark Tau upon the foreheads of the men that sigh and cry (Ezekiel ix.); teaching in a figure that if any lack skill in writing, he shall not undertake the task of preaching repentance.

Finally, in conclusion of the present chapter, books implore you: make your young men who though ignorant are apt of intellect apply themselves to study, furnishing them with necessaries, that ye may teach them not only goodness but discipline and science, may terrify them by blows, charm them by blandishments, mollify them by gifts and urge them on by painful rigor, so that they may become at once Socratics in morals and Peripatetics in learning. Yesterday, as it were at the eleventh hour,[145] the prudent Householder introduced you into his vineyard. Repent of idleness before it is too late: would that with the cunning Steward ye might be ashamed of begging so hopelessly; for then no doubt ye would devote yourselves more assiduously to us books and to study.*

. . . .

[143] Cf. Ephesians 6: 11.   [144] Cf. 2 Tim. 4: 13.

[145] An allusion to the comparative youth of the orders of friars; the scriptural allusion is Matt. 20: 1–16.

* By permission of Messrs. Chatto and Windus from their Edition in the *King's Classics Series.*

While we were constantly delighting ourselves with the reading of books, which it was our custom to read or to have read to us every day, we noticed plainly how much the defective knowledge even of a single word hinders the understanding, as the meaning of no sentence can be apprehended, if any part of it be not understood. Wherefore we ordered the meanings of foreign words to be noted with particular care, and studied the orthography, prosody, etymology and syntax in ancient grammarians with unrelaxing carefulness, and took pains to elucidate terms that had grown too obscure by age with suitable explanations, in order to make a smooth path for our students. This is the whole reason why we care to replace the antiquated volumes of the grammarians by improved codices, that we might make royal roads, by which our scholars in time to come might attain without stumbling to any science.*

The number and range of volumes in a medieval monastic library are indicated in the following catalog of the Library at the Monastery of Rievaux. The catalog was written in the fourteenth century and is extant in a MS. in the Library of Jesus College, Cambridge, and first printed in 1843.[146]

(A) *The Codex of Justinian.*[147] *The Decrees of Gratian.*[148] *John* [149] *on the Decrees.* Haymo,[150] *On the Epistles of St. Paul.*

[146] Each item followed by a period in the catalog represents a volume unless otherwise specified. Dashes before an item indicate that the books mentioned were written by the same author as those preceding.

[147] Justinian was Roman Emperor at Constantinople 527–565 A.D., and under his orders the law of the Empire was codified. This involved three tasks, the collection of all that was valuable in the writings of earlier jurists (called the *Digest* or *Pandects*), the collection of the imperial laws proper (called the *Justinian Codex* or *Code*) and the preparation of an elementary treatise on law (called the *Institutes*) for the use of law students. Sometimes the term *Code* is applied to all three of these works together, sometimes to the second work only; it is impossible to tell which is meant here.

[148] Gratian, a Benedictine monk, in 1144 put out his *Decretum* (*Decrees*), a code of canon, that is church, law founded on the *Justinian Code* and the decisions of ecclesiastical officials. Gratian probably taught canon law at Bologna, but the study long faced the opposition of the Church. [149] ? [150] Cf. *ante,* p. 133.

* By permission of Messrs. Chatto and Windus from their Edition to the *King's Classics Series.*

(B) Augustine,[151] *On the City of God.* —, *On John.* —, *On the Psalter,* in five volumes. —, *On the Ten Commandments, On Grace and Free Will, the Epistle of Prosper* [152] *to Augustine,* the *Epistle of Hilary* [153] *to Augustine.* Augustine, *On the Predestination of the Saints, On the Virtue of Perseverance, On Genesis against the Manichœans.*[154] —, *On the Sermon on the Mount, On Nature and Grace* and *Letter to Valentine.*[155] —, *On the Size of the Soul.* Ambrose,[156] *On the Good of Death, On Justice* and *On Widows.* Augustine, *On the Perfection of Justice, On Reproof and Grace* and *God with Us.* —, *On Charity* and his *Retractions.* —, *On Dualism, On the Discipline of Christians, On the Ten Strings,*[157] the *Rule for the Life of Clerics, On Marriage and Concupiscence, Against Julian,*[158] *Against Two Epistles of the Pelagians,*[159] *On Hóly Virginity.* —, *To Simplicianus* [160] *against Pelagius* [159] and others.

(C) *Against Faustus.*[161] —, *On the Trinity.* —, *On Confessions.* —, *On the Words of the Lord.* —, *On the Literal Interpretation of Genesis, Against Damasippus.*[162] *The Letters of Augustine* and —, *In Reply to Pelagius the Heretic.* —, *On Penitence, Whence Evil, Of Free Will, Against Five Heresies, Of Proper Marriage,* a certain part of *On the Perfection of Justice* and Hugo,[163] *On Noah's Ark.* Augustine, *On the Baptism of Infants, To Marcellinus,*[164] *On One Baptism, On the Letter and the Spirit, To Paulinus,*[165] *Yponosticon, Against the Pelagians, On Deaths in the Church,*

[151] Cf. *ante,* p. 64; consult also *Encyclopædia Britannica,* ed. 11, article *Augustine.* [152] A disciple of Augustine. [153] Cf. *ante,* p. 64.

[154] An oriental sect, dualistic in its doctrine, teaching that the universe is the home of two warring powers of about equal might. Augustine was a Manichæan before his conversion to Christianity.

[155] Possibly Bishop Valentine, who labored in Rhætia in the first half of the fifth century. [156] Cf. *ante,* p. 64. [157] Probably a musical work.

[158] Of Eclanum, the most gifted and consistent champion of Pelagianism.

[159] The Pelagians were followers of Pelagius (mentioned later), a British monk of the fifth century who denied human need of divine grace and the doctrine of original sin. [160] ? [161] A Manichæan.

[162] The word *Versus,* which I have rendered *Against,* may also mean *Verses;* since Damasippus seems unknown, it is impossible to tell which rendering is correct.

[163] Hugh of St. Victor (*circa* 1078–1141), mystic philosopher much read in the Middle Ages; the *Enclyclopædia Britannica* article says there is a copy of his works in nearly every monastic library of which we have record. [164] ?

[165] Probably Paulinus of Nola (353–431), who, we know, corresponded with

Against the Letter of a Manichœan and *On the Care to Be shown about Death.* —, *Concerning Christian Doctrine.* —, *Against Lying, To Renatus* [166] *on the Origin of the Soul against the Books of Vincentius,*[167] *To Peter* [168] *against the Books of Vincentius,*[167] *To Vincentius Victor,*[167] *Against the Perfidy of the Arians,*[169] *Against the Adversaries of the Law and the Prophets,* a *Book of Bestiaries* [170] and *The Epistles of Anselm.*[171] Augustine, *On the Harmony of the Evangelists* and two sermons *On Swearing.* The *Soliloquies of Augustine.* —, *Against the Academics* and *On the Order of Monks.*

(D) Bernard,[172] *On the Song of Songs.* Books of Bernard; that is, *The Exposition of the Gospel, The Angel Gabriel Was Sent, On the Degrees of Humility and Pride, On the Varieties of Monastic Discipline, On Grace and Free Will and Love of the Lord,* the *Exhortation to the Templars,*[173] and his *Book to Pope Eugenius* (III). The Sermons of Bernard for the course of the year. The same, —, *On Grace and Free Will,* his *Book to Cardinal Ascelinus* [174] *on Loving God* and the *Verses of Hildebert* [175] *on the Mass.* The same, Bernard, *On Loving God,* his *Sentences on the Trinity, On Foreknowledge, On the Sacrament of the Altar, On Certain Sacraments of Faith, The Epistles of Bernard.* Anselm, *Why God Man, On the Virgin Birth, On the Mount of Humiliation, On Reparation for Human Redemption, Exposition of the Gospel, Jesus En-*

Augustine. Paulinus wrote an *Opus Sacramentorum et Hymnorum* (*Book of the Sacraments and Hymns*) and a *Liber de Laude Generali Omnium Martyrum* (*Book in General Praise of All the Martyrs*). Or the Paulinus mentioned in the text may be Paulinus of Pella (*circa* 376–459), author of a long autobiographic poem, *Eucharisticos* or *Eucharisticon Deo sub Ephemeridis Meœ Textu* (*The Sacrament to God under the Form of My Ephemeral Life*).   166 ?   167 ?   168 ?

169 Followers of Arius, fourth-century Unitarian theologian.

170 Cf. *ante*, p. 192.

171 *Circa* 1033–1109, Archbishop of Canterbury, Italian by birth and education. Attracted by the fame of Lanfranc, Prior of Bec in Normandy, later Archbishop of Canterbury, Anselm came to Bec and, when Lanfranc was made archbishop by William the Conqueror, Anselm succeeded him as prior. Anselm did his literary work at Bec. Appointed Archbishop of Canterbury by William II Rufus, Anselm spent the greater part of his tenure of office in controversy with the King over the civil position of clerics, anticipating the struggle of Becket with Henry II.

172 St. Bernard of Clairvaux (1090–1153), one of the most famous of medieval monks and preachers.   173 Cf. *ante*, p. 299.   174 ?

175 *Circa* 1055–1133, French writer and ecclesiastic, known as *egregius versificator* (*famous verse writer*).

tered into a Certain City, His Life (i.e. Anselm's) and Wimundus,[176] *On the Body of the Lord against Berengarius.*[177] *The Books of Anselm on the Incarnation of the Word, Monologion, Prosologion, the Attack of a Certain Man on the Second, Third and Fourth Chapters of a Work of His* (i.e. Anselm's) *and the Latter's Reply,* the *Letter to Bishop Walerranus.*[178] Anselm, *Tractate on Truth, Tractate on Free Will, On the Fall of the Devil, On the Agreement of Foreknowledge and Predestination and Grace with Free Will, On Similitudes, On Grammar.* Ailred,[179] *On Spiritual Friendship* and *On the Origins of Cloisters. A Book of Sermons* which begins thus, *You Seek from Me,* etc. Ailred,[179] *On the Burdens of Isaiah.* —, *On the Life of St. Edward,*[180] *On the Generosity and Habits and Death of King David, On the Life of St. Bishop Minian,*[181] *On the Miracles of the Church at Hexham. The Epistles of Ailred.*[179] —, *On the Soul. The Mirror of Charity. The Letters of the Roman Pontiffs. The Letters of Cyprian.*[182] Ailred,[179] *On a Bundle of Leaves.*

(E) Origen,[183] *On the Old Testament,* in two volumes. Rabanus,[184] *On Matthew.* Haimo,[185] *On the Epistles of Paul.* Josephus,[186] *The Antiquities.* — —, *On the Jewish War* and Ailred,[179] *On the Generosity of King David. The Sentences of Peter Lombard.*[187]

[176] ?

[177] Died 1088, a heretic on the subject of transubstantiation, which he held to be unreasonable.   [178] ?

[179] An English ecclesiastic and historian (1109–1166), monk and abbot at Rievaux.   [180] I.e. Edward the Confessor.

[181] 360–432, Apostle of the Southern Picts, Bishop of Whitehorn or Whithern.

[182] Saint (*circa* 200–258), Bishop of Carthage, one of the most notable of the early martyrs.   [183] Cf. *ante,* p. 396.

[184] Rabanus or Hrabanus Maurus (*circa* 776–856 A.D.), German Benedictine, ecclesiastic and teacher. He was a pupil of Alcuin at Tours and in 822 became Abbot of Fulda.   [185] Cf. *ante,* pp. 133 and 430.

[186] *Ibid.,* p. 395.

[187] An Italian, as his name indicates. He lived from about 1100 to 1164. He studied at Bologna, Rheims and Paris, where he was a pupil of Abelard. He became a teacher of theology in the Cathedral School of Notre Dame and in 1159 Bishop of Paris, but resigned the next year. His death occurred in 1164. His *Four Books of Sentences* was a collection of observations from Augustine and other fathers on points of Christian doctrine, with objections and replies from authors of repute. It was intended as a manual for scholastic disputants and as such was used for five hundred years as the basis of many lectures and treatises. (Cf. *ante,* p. 399.) It was one of the first books printed and many editions have been published.

434 ENGLISH LITERATURE

(F) *The Morals of St. Gregory Pope*,[188] in five volumes. —, *On Ezechiel.* —, *The Pastoral Care*, the *Book on the Three Kinds of Homicide* and the *Book on the Conflict of Vices and Virtues.* *The Book of Gregory's Dialogs.* *A Book of Fifty Homilies.* *The First Part of the Register.*[189] Augustine, *On True Religion* and *Marsias.*[190] *The Second Part of the Register*[189] and *A Book on the Science of Speaking.* *On the Highest Trinity and the Catholic Faith.* Robert,[191] *On the Apocalypse.* *A Book of Sermons*, certain excerpts from the books of Justinian and passages of the *Bestiaries.*[192]

(G) Ambrose, *On Luke.* —, *On the Blessed Immaculates.* *— On Duties and Sacraments.* *The Letters of Ambrose.* —, *On Virgins*, *On Naboth*, his *Sermon on Fasting*, a book of Prior Richard[193] on *Benjamin and his Brethren, On Certain Parts of the World, On the Seven Wonders of Rome, On the Five Parts of England.* Ambrose, *On the Good of Death, On Fleeing the World, On Widows*, his *Hexameron, On Penitence* and Cassiodorus,[194] *On the Virtues of the Soul.* *The First Part of the Etymologies of Isidore*,[195] the *Exposition of the Grammar of Donatus*,[196] *Certain Derivations Arranged in Alphabetical Order*, and the *Rules of Versification.* *The Second Part of the Etymologies of Isidore, On Certain Proper Names of the Old and New Testaments and Their Meanings*, and a book of Isidore called *Synonyms.* John Chrysostom,[197] *On the Fiftieth Psalm, On the Canaanitish Woman, On Reparation for Backsliding.* Augustine, *On a Brave Woman, The Life of Two Priests, On Ten Abusive Things, The Miracle of the Body and Blood of Our Lord*, Bede,[198] *On Tobias*, Isidore, *On the Highest Good and Divers Virtues.* *A Book of St. Gregory Nazianzen.*[199] An interlinear copy of the Book of Chronicles, certain *Little Expositions of the Epistles of St. Paul* and the *Sermons* of Babio.[200] Laurentius,[201] *On the*

[188] Cf. *ante*, p. 64.
[189] Evidently the books in which daily records of matters important to the monastery were kept.
[190] ?   [191] Perhaps Robert Pulleyn, mentioned later; cf. p. 435.
[192] Cf. *ante*, p. 192.
[193] Richard of St. Victor (?1173), theological writer of allegorical and mystical tendencies.   [194] Cf. *ante*, p. 65.
[195] Archbishop of Seville (flourished ?636): his *Etymologies* in 20 books was a favorite medieval encyclopedia.   [196] Cf. *ante*, p. 67.   [197] *Ibid.*, p. 65.
[198] *Ibid.*, p. 65.   [199] *Ibid.*, p. 396.   [200] ?   [201] ?

Consolation of Friendship, certain decrees of the fathers, and
Ysagoge (Introduction) of Johannicius.[202] *The Letters of Seneca.*[203]
The sermons of Mauricius [204] which begin thus, *Festus upon Festus.* Twenty-eight sermons of St. Bernard, *On the Song of Songs.*
(H) Hugo,[205] *On the Sacraments* in two volumes. —, *On the Contempt of the World*, his *Soliloquy* on the *Pledge of the Soul*, the same, *On the Virginity of St. Mary*, his solution of the question *Why Can There not Be Marriage with One Sex* and his *Didascalion. A Treatise* by Hugh and *The Miracles of the Body and Blood of the Lord.* Hugo, *On Ecclesiastes*, and a book of *Ecclesiastical Dogmas* by Gennadius [206] and a *Eulogy of Master John of Cornwall.*[207] Ivo of Chartres,[208] *Pannormia.* The same, the *Letters of Dindimus* [209] and *Alexander*, the *Letter of Lord Baldwin*,[210] *Abbot of Forda*, a *Sermon concerning St. Thomas* [211] and *St. William* [212] and a salutary piece of advice by a certain wise man *How Rude and Unskilled Persons Should Speak Cautiously of God and the Soul. The Sentences of Hugo.*[213] *The Letters of Ivo* [208] and the *Letters of Hildebert* [214] *Bishop of Le Mans.* Hugo,[213] *On the Hierarchy.* Robert,[215] *On Matthew.* —, *On Leviticus*, a sermon of master Robert Pulleyn,[215] *On All the Necessary Virtues of the Christian Life*, a book of Prior Richard,[216] *On Benja-*

202 ?   203 Cf. *ante*, p. 394.
204 Possibly one of the martyrs under Maximian 286–305 A.D.
205 I.e. Hugh of St. Victor; *ante*, p. 431.
206 Of Massilia (Marseilles), flourished 492–496 A.D. His best known work is a continuation of St. Jerome, *De Viris Illustribus (On famous Men)* by the same title. This work of Gennadius is an important source of knowledge of the 93 writers mentioned in it.   207 Flourished 1176.
208 *Circa* 1040–1116, Bishop of Chartres, a pupil of Lanfranc at Bec.
209 A fictitious King of the Brahmins, who debated inconclusively with King Alexander the Great the merits of the active and the contemplative life. Cf. Schofield, *op. cit.*, p. 302.
210 This is Archbishop Baldwin of Canterbury, who died at Acre on crusade with Richard the Lion-Hearted in 1190.   211 I.e. Thomas a Becket.
212 I.e. William, Archbishop of York, 1140–1154.
213 I.e. Hugh of St. Victor; *ante*, p. 431.
214 *Ibid.*, p. 432.
215 Probably Robert Pulleyn (Pullein), an Englishman (*circa* 1080–1150), who studied in Paris under Abelard, lectured at Oxford on the Scriptures in 1133, became a cardinal under Celestine II and papal chancellor under Lucius II.
216 Cf. *ante*, p. 434.

min and His Brethren, the *Rule of St. Basil.*[217]   *The Letters of Mauricius.*[218]   Books of Mauricius,[218] namely, *The Mirror of Monastic Religion*, his *Apology*, *The Itinerary of Peace*, his book *On Rythm* and *On the Translation of the Body of St. Cuthbert.*[219] *A Lapidary* [220] and certain sermons, sentences and compilations.

(I) Bede,[221] *On Luke.* —, *On Mark.* —, *On the Tabernacle.* —, *On the History of the English.* —, *On Seasons* and certain chronicles of his. —, *On Thirty Questions* and *On Esdras.* —, *On Samuel.* —, *On the Canonical Epistles* and *On the Song of Songs.* —, *On the Life of St. Cuthbert* [219] and Cuthbert,[222] *On the Death of St. Bede.* Two English books.

(K) *The Ecclesiastical History.*[223]   *The History of (H)Egesippus.*[224]   *The History of Henry.*[225]   *The History of Jerusalem.*[226] *The History of the Britons.*[227]   *The Itinerary of Clement.*[228]   *The Sermons* of master Geoffrey Babio [229] and an *Exposition of the Prophets Joel and Nahum.* Orosius,[230] *On the History of the World,* — the *History of the Trojan War* by Dares,[231] the *Verses of Peter Abelard* [232] *to His Son,* and *The English Chronicle.*[233]   Books of Aldhelm,[234] certain names and words from a book of capitularies, Hugo of Folieto,[235] *On the Material Cloister*, the same, *On the Spiritual Cloister*, an *Attack on Solomon. An Exposition of the Gospel, Simon Peter Said to Jesus*, a sermon *On the Labor and Reward of the Saints*, a sermon *On the Nine Months of the Conception and the Eight Days of the Circumcision of Christ*, a sermon *On Holy Easter*, collections of extracts and meditations, a *Treatise on Certain Chapters of the Song of Songs* and a *Handbook of Matters and Words. An Exposition of the Song of Songs*, Ambrose, *On the Song of Songs*, an *Exposition of the Eight Construc-*

[217] Cf. *ante*, p. 64.   [218] *Ibid.*, p. 435.   [219] *Ibid.*, p. 102.
[220] I.e. a book on the mystical virtues of stones; cf. passages translated from the *Lapidary* in Shackford, *op. cit.*, pp. 111–116 and notes.
[221] Cf. *ante*, p. 65.   [222] *Ibid.*, pp. 114–117.
[223] Perhaps that of Hugo of Fleury, who died about 1118.
[224] An ecclesiastical writer of the second century.   [225] ?   [226] ?
[227] Of Geoffrey of Monmouth? cf. *ante*, p. 248.   [228] ?   [229] ?
[230] Cf. *ante*, p. 64. The word *Ormesta* in the Latin title of Orosius' book I have rendered *History* on the authority of Ducange.   [231] Cf. *ante*, p. 404.
[232] *Ibid.*, p. 386.   [233] *The Anglo-Saxon Chronicle?*   [234] Cf. *ante*, p. 65.
[235] ?

tions of Priscian, an *Exposition of the Apocalypse,* the same, an *Exposition of the Song of Songs,* glosses of Boethius,[236] and a *Brief Exposition of Certain Psalms.* John [237] *on the Decrees of Gratian, The Body of the Canon Law.* An interlinear Matthew. An interlinear Acts of the Apostles. Boethius,[236] *On the Trinity,* the *Book of Cato,*[238] the *Passion of St. Laurence,*[239] *Proverbs from the Books of the Poets,* the *Life of St. Mary of Egypt,*[240] Hildebert,[241] *On the Edification of the Soul,* likewise some *Verses* of his, certain hymns, Odo,[242] *On the Powers of Herbs,* Marbodeus,[243] *On the Kinds of Stones,* the *Passion of St. Mauricius,*[244] the *Life of Thais* [245] and other verses, the *Cosmography* of Bernard Sylvester,*[246] the *Passion of St. Thomas* [247] and other verses and remarks. *An Anthology of Pagan Poetry,* the *Passion of St. Laurence* [239] and an *Art of Calculating with Arabic Figures.*

(L) *The Lives of the Fathers,* a *Life of St. Guthlac,*[248] a book

[236] Cf. *ante,* p. 66.   [237] ? cf. *ante,* p. 430.

[238] I.e. Dionysius Cato, the title given to a small collection of moral precepts in verse, which was very popular in the Middle Ages. It is very doubtful if such a person as Dionysius Cato ever existed. The date of the original compilation is the third century B.C. The best known title of the work is *Dionysii Catonis Disticha de Moribus ad Filium* (*Couplets of Dionysius Cato on Morals for His Son*). The book has a *Preface* and 56 injunctions of a simple character, such as *Love your parents,* and 144 moral precepts, each of which is couched in two dactyllic hexameters. The book was much used as a text-book in Latin for young pupils. Thirty editions of it were put out in the fifteenth century. An early English translation was published by Caxton, the first English printer.

[239] A Christian martyr in the Valerian persecution August 10, 258.

[240] A more or less mythical third-century Christian ascetic.

[241] Cf. *ante,* p. 432.   [242] ?

[243] *Circa* 1035–1123, Bishop of Rennes; his book *On Gems* is the source of much material in the medieval *Lapidary.* Cf. Shackford, *op. cit.,* pp. 170, 171.

[244] Cf. *ante,* p. 435.

[245] A Christian saint and penitent in Egypt in the fourth century; a *Life* by Marbodeus is extant.

[246] Of Chartres or more properly of Tours, a twelfth-century philosophical writer of whom little is known. His favorite philosopher was Plato, though he probably knew nothing of Plato's except the *Timæus;* in his Platonic tendency Bernard was unlike most medieval philosophers.

[247] This may be either Thomas a Becket or Thomas the Apostle.

[248] An Anglo-Saxon hermit and saint who lived *circa* 673–714. Probably the *Life* mentioned is that by the monk Felix, which is our authority for the life of Guthlac.

which is called *The Formula for an Honorable Life.*   *A Life of
St. Godric* [249] *the Hermit.   John the Hermit* [250] *on Ten Conferences.
A Book of Fourteen Conferences.* [250]   Prosper,[251] *On the Active and
the Contemplative Life* and *Diadem of Monks.   The Book of Odo.* [252]
*Little Expositions of the Old and New Testaments, Certain Acts
in the Church before the Passion of the Lord,* Augustine, *On the
Psalms,* other compilations and *The Rule Shines Forth.   The Book
of Bishop Heraclis* [253] which is called *Paradise* and The *Persecu-
tion of the Province of Affrica.   The Sentences of Master Walter* [254]
which begin, *Salvation Has Made a Litter for Itself.   The Sentences* which begin thus, *While Silence Is in Our Midst.   The
Rule of John Cassian.* [250]   An interlinear *Psalter* of Abbot Ajlred.[255]
An interlinear *Psalter* of Lord Abbot Ernald.[256]   An interlinear
Psalter of Master Walter.[254] An interlinear *Psalter* of Hurold.
An interlinear *Psalter* of Ralph Barum.   An interlinear *Psalter*
of Simon of Sigillum.   A small interlinear *Psalter* for those on
probation.   A *Psalter* of Geoffry Dinant.   A *Psalter* of Fulco.   A
Psalter of William of Rutland.   A *Psalter of Jerome* [257] which
belonged to William of Barking.

(M) *The Book of Justinian on the Laws.*   A medical book
which is called *A Collection of Antidotes.   The Introduction* [258]
of Johannicius.   *A Large Priscian.*   Priscian, *On Constructions.*
Bernard,[259] *On the Twelve Degrees of Humility, Sermons and Useful
Observations,* the *Apologetics of St. Bernard* and *Interpretations of
Hebrew Names.   Sermons* of St. Bernard which begin *Holy through
Faith* and certain observations.   *An Exposition of the Prophet*

[249] Possibly Godric I, Abbot of Croyland 870–941.

[250] John Cassian (*circa* 360–435), who introduced into Western Europe the rules
of Eastern monasticism.   His two principal works are the *Institutes* and the *Twenty-
four Conferences.*   Ten of these seem to be bound in this volume and the remaining
fourteen in the next.

[251] I.e. Prosper of Aquitaine, a disciple of Augustine, cf. *ante,* p. 431.

[252] Possibly some work of Odo of Cheriton, died 1247, known as a preacher and
fabulist.

[253] Possibly Heraclas, Bishop of Alexandria from 231–247, pupil and opponent
of Origen.

[254] Probably Walter of St. Victor, twelfth-century mystic philosopher and theologian, opponent of Abelard and Peter Lombard.

[255] Cf. *ante,* p. 433.   [256] ? not mentioned in the *Catholic Encyclopedia.*
[257] Cf. *ante,* p. 64.   [258] *Ibid.,* p. 435.   [259] *Ibid.,* p. 432.

Nahum and *On Joel,* observations and sermons and profitable letters of several persons, Laurentius,[260] *On the Creation and Works of the Lord.* *A Collection of Divers Observations Applied to Divers Situations in the Catholic Church* and *Excerpts, Ornately Put, from the Register of Gregory.* Cicero's *Synonyms,* certain matters *About the Calculation of Time* and the *Rules of Versification.* *Rhetoric.* Boethius,[261] *On the Consolation of Philosophy.* Porphyry's [262] *Introduction to the Categories of Aristotle* and other books of dialectic. A book *Of the Miracles of St. Mary.*[263]

(N) *A Book of Homilies for Winter.* *A Book of Homilies for Summer.* *A Passional* [234] *for the Month of October.* *A Passional for the Months of November and December.* *A Passional for the Month of January.* *The Life of St. Sylvester* [235] and lives of other saints. *A Life of St. Ambrose* and of other saints. *Homilies for Quadragesima.* A tripartite *Psalter.*

(O) Jerome,[256] *On the Twelve Prophets* in two volumes. —, *On Jeremiah* and *On Daniel.* —, *On Hebrew Questions, On the Dwellings of the Children of Israel, On the Distances of Places, On the Interpretation of Hebrew Names, On Questions of the Book of Kings, On Chronicles, On the Ten Temptations, On the Six States of Fugitives, On the Song of Deborah,*[267] *On the Lamentations of Jeremiah,* Prudentius,[268] *On Building,* Hugo of Folieto,[269] *On the Cloister of the Soul,* Jer' Gennad',[270] Isidore,[271] *On Illustrious Men,* Cassiodorus,[272] *On the Institutions of Divine Letters,* Ailred,[273] *On a Standard of Weights and Measures, Of the Map.* Bernard, *On the Song of Songs,* an interlinear Jeremiah, the *Minor Works of Bernard,* the letters and observations of several persons, an interlinear list of *Barbarisms, the Letters of Seneca and St. Paul.*[274]

---

[260] ? [261] Cf. *ante,* p. 66. [262] *Ibid.,* p. 412.

[263] I.e. the mother of Jesus. [264] I.e. a list of the saints' days for the month.

[255] Pope from 314–335, to whom Constantine is supposed to have made the famous *Donation;* cf. *ante,* p. 319. The *Life* is legendary.

[266] Cf. *ante,* p. 64. [267] Cf. Judges 5.

[268] A Christian Roman poet born 343 A.D. He was the first really great Christian poet. His *Cathemerinon (Daily Round)* has been translated into modern English verse and is accessible in the *Temple Classics* ed. (E. P. Dutton and Co.).

[269] Cf. *ante,* p. 436. [270] ? [271] *Ibid.,* p. 434.

[272] *Ibid.,* p. 65. [273] *Ibid.,* p. 433.

[274] Generally regarded to-day as spurious.

The Sermons of Peter Manducator,[275] *On the Birth of St. Cuthbert,* the *Passion of St. Thomas Archbishop of Canterbury,*[276] the *Miracle of the Image of St. Mary,* the *Life of St. Olaf.*[277] Certain acts of the Savior, a sermon of Robert Pulleyn [278] the *Rule of Certain Adverbs and the Question of a Certain Construction,* Jerome, *Against Jovinian* [279] *on Mystical Places,* Bede, *On the Metrical Art* and *On Figures of Speech,* Hugo,[280] *On the Training of Novices,* the *Letter of Abbot Patellicus* [231] *to His Bishop* and the *Bishop's Reply.* *The Life of St. Jerome* and his *Letters.* *The Sentences* of Master Robert Melun.[232] *The Sermons* of Abbot Werrus.[233] *The Letters of Sidonius.*[234]

(P) Interlinear Books.

Genesis. Exodus. Isaiah. The same. Job. The same. The Twelve Prophets. The same. The same. Six Prophets. Tobias, Judith, Esther and the Apocalypse. The Song of Songs and the Canonical Epistles. Matthew. Mark. The same. Luke The same. The same. John. The same. The same. The Canonical Epistles. The Epistles of Paul. The same. The Apocalypse. The same and the Song of Songs.

(Q) *A Book of Usages* in two volumes. *A Brief Gloss of the Psalter. Certain Passages from the Gospels briefly Explained,* the *Exhortation of St. Bernard to Pope Eugenius* (III), *Observations of the Father concerning Vices and Virtues* and a *Physics. A Prayer-Book* which begins *Lord Jesus Christ Son of the Living*

[275] Thirteenth-century French theologian.
[276] I.e. Thomas a Becket.
[277] Patron saint of Norway (*circa* 995–1030).
[278] Cf. *ante*, p. 435.
[279] An Italian heretic of the fourth century who opposed asceticism, celibacy, and monachism, held that Mary after the birth of Jesus was no longer a virgin, that the blessedness of heaven does not depend on the merit of good works, and that a Christian cannot sin wilfully.
[280] Possibly Hugh of St. Victor; cf. *ante*, p. 431. [281] ?
[282] An English philosopher and theologian (*circa* 1100–1167). He studied with Hugh of St. Victor and probably with Abelard and was the master of John of Salisbury (cf. *post*, p. 559) and Thomas a Becket. Through the influence of the latter he became Bishop of Hereford in 1163. His *Sentences* have never been published in full but are still in MSS. [283] ?
[284] A Christian author, born at Lyons about 430 and died at Clermont about 480. He became Bishop of Clermont, wrote poems and letters, and is the last representative of the ancient culture in Gaul. His *Letters,* though somewhat rhetorical and ornate, give a unique picture of the life of the times.

THE CULTURAL BACKGROUND 441

God, Bernard, *On Propriety in Poetry*, the *Hours of St. Mary*, the *Institution* of a *Chapter* and *Exposition of Certain Prayers*. The same, a *Prayer-Book* which begins *Lord Jesus Christ Who into This World*. *Sentences* which begin *Do not Desire for Yourself* and Prudentius.[285] An *Explanation of Certain Names and Words in the Epistles of St. Paul, Verses concerning Christ*, sermons of certain fathers on the sacraments of the faith. *A Hand-book, Verses of a Certain Man On the Death of Robert Bloet*,[236] Bishop of Lincoln and the more difficult parts of the Old and New Testaments. Certain comments on philosophy, certain observations of Paul and Isaiah, glossed, an *Anthology of the Gospels*, the *Golden Gem*, a letter of the Bishop of Chartres,[287] wonderfully useful, a book on St. Patrick, a *Conference of the Trinity*, *St. Augustine Himself to Himself*, excerpts from the *Pannormie* of Ivo of Chartres,[287] the *Soliloquy* of Mauricius [288] and interpretations of certain words. A *Psalter* half in verse and certain prayers in rhythm. A little book which is called *An Image of the World* and other observations. A medical book which belonged to Hugh of Beverly.[289]

As contrast and supplement to the foregoing, we include the following list of books, showing the tendencies of lay and courtly taste, bequeathed to Bordesley Abbey, Wor-

[285] Cf. *ante*, p. 439.
[286] Died 1123, chancellor of England under William the Conqueror and William Rufus. He was an indifferent ecclesiastic but a good administrator. Henry of Huntingdon (cf. *ante*, p. 87 and *post*, pp. 553–555) addresses him as patron.
[287] Probably Ivo (cf. *ante*, p. 435), though John of Salisbury (cf. *post*, p. 559) was also Bishop of Chartres and wrote "wonderfully useful Letters."
[288] Cf. *ante*, p. 435.
[289] So far as I know, this is the first time this catalog has been translated or annotated. Edwards, *op. cit.*, I, pp. 333–341, prints it without translation or comment. He also (*ibid.*, pp. 122–235) prints for the first time the catalog of the Library of the Benedictine Monastery of Christ Church, Canterbury. This document, though much longer than the Rievaux catalog, has no greater range of books than the latter. Coulton, *op. cit.*, pp. 529, 530 quotes a standard clerical reference library "of minimum size"; it is especially rich in works on canon law. That ecclesiastics were not always so devotional in their reading as they should have been is suggested in the list of a friar's favorite books which Chaucer recites in the *Canterbury Tales*, D ll. 669–691; cf. Skeat's notes. For a general reference on libraries of this period see Savage, *Old English Libraries* (Chicago, A. C. McClurg and Co., 1912).

cestershire, by Guy Beauchamp Earl of Warwick in 1315.
The list is found in one of the MSS. at Lambeth Palace.

To all those who will see or hear this letter, Guy Beauchamp
Earl of Warwick, Greeting in God: We have given into the
power and keeping of the Abbot and Convent of Bordesley, the
gift to be perpetual, all the romances named below, that is to
say:

A volume which is called the *Thesaurus*.[290] A volume in
which is the first book of *Lancelot* [291] and that of the *Romance
of Ainé*.[292] A *Psalter* in French. A volume of the Gospels and
of *Lives of Saints*. A volume which contains the four principal
Gests of Charles and *of Doon of Mayence* . . . and *of Girard of
Viana* and *of Aimeri of Narbonne*.[293] A volume of the *Romance
of Edward of England* [294] and of *King Charles Doon of Nanteuil*.[295]
And the Romance of Guy of Nanteuil.[296] And a volume of the
Romance of Joseph of Arimathea and of the Holy Grail.[297] And
a volume which tells how Adam was expelled from Paradise and
Genesis.[298] And a volume in which are all the following ro-

[290] I.e. the *Tresor* of the Italian Brunetto Latini (*circa* 1230–1294) to whom
Dante (1260–1320) pays tribute in such a way (cf. *Inferno*, XV, ll. 30, 31) that it
was for long thought that Brunetto was Dante's master. This is probably not the
case. Brunetto wrote his *Tresor* in French "because that language 'is more delightful and more widely known.'" Cf. Johnson, *Selections from the Prose Works of
Matthew Arnold* (Houghton Mifflin Co., 1913), pp. 68, 321.

[291] Cf. Schofield, *op. cit.*, Index and Bibliography.

[292] A conjectural rendering of the Old French *Aygnes;* Aine was an Irish love-
goddess, patroness of Munster and beloved of a Fitzgerald, to whom she bore the
semi-divine wizard Earl Gerald, fourth Earl of Desmond. (Cf. Spence, *Dictionary
of Romance and Romance Writers*, E. P. Dutton and Co., 1913.)

[293] Parts of the Old French epic stories dealing with the exploits of Charlemagne and his peers. It is curious, however, that the list speaks of four principal
gests of Charles; ordinarily but three are mentioned. These romances first appear
in the twelfth and thirteenth centuries.

[294] Possibly an account of the adventures of Edward the Confessor of England;
cf. Schofield, *op. cit.*, p. 281.

[295] Fragments of this twelfth-century French romance are extant.

[296] A romance of the end of the twelfth century.

[297] A popular member of the cycle of grail stories which ultimately was joined
to the Arthurian cycle; cf. Schofield, *op. cit.*, Index and Bibliography.

[298] Two miracle plays, of which the former, the *Adam*, is the oldest French
play. It sprang from the liturgical Christmas play and was written in England in

mances, that is to say, *The Lives of the Fathers* at the beginning and then a *Count of Auteypt*,[299] the *Vision of St. Paul* and then *The Lives of Twelve Saints.* And the *Romance of William Longsword*.[300] And *The Authority of Holy Men* and the *Mirror of the Soul.* A volume in which are contained the *Life of St. Peter and St. Paul.* and other books. And a volume which is called the Apocalypse. And a book of medicine and surgery. And a volume of the *Romance of Guy and the Quæen*[301] entire. A volume of the *Romance of Troy*.[302] A volume of the *Romance of William of Orange and of Tibaut of Araby*.[303] A volume of the *Romance of Amadas and Ydoine*.[304] A volume of the *Romance of Girard of Viana*.[305] A volume of the *Romance of the Brut*[306] and of *King Constantine.* A volume of the *Instruction Aristotle Gave King Alexander.* A volume of the *Death of King Arthur and of Modred*.[307] A volume in which is contained *The Infancy of Our*

the twelfth century, to be played, not inside the church, as were the Latin liturgical plays, but in the church porch. It has three parts, the fall of Adam and Eve, the death of Abel, and a prefiguration of the death of the Messiah with the procession of the prophets who announce the coming of the Redeemer.   [299] ?

[300] Died 1226. Earl of Salisbury, natural brother of Richard the Lion-Hearted, great crusader and founder of Salisbury Cathedral. Many wonders are told in his interesting life. See the article in *The Dictionary of National Biography.*

[301] Perhaps a story of an adventure of Guy, father of Bevis of Hampton, who married a daughter of the King of Scotland. Or perhaps the reference is to Guy of Burgundy, who married Floripas, daughter of Laban, sovereign of Babylon. See Spence, *op. cit.* No romance of the title *Guy and the Queen* is cataloged in the authorities.   [302] See Schofield, *op. cit.*, Index and Bibliography.

[303] A subcycle of the Charlemagne epic with many stories. It belongs to the eleventh century. William was at first a historical person contemporary with Charlemagne and his son Louis, but was later confused with other Williams. See Spence, *op. cit.*

[304] Cf. Schofield, *op. cit.*, Index and Bibliography.   [305] Cf. *ante*, p. 442.

[306] By Wace (flourished 1170), chronicler, born in Jersey and educated at Caen; adapted and translated from Latin into French the *Historia Britonum* (*History of the Britons*) of Geoffrey of Monmouth (cf. *ante*, p. 248). Wace also later, at the request of Henry II, made a general history of the Normans in Normandy and England by rewriting an earlier chronicle of William the Conqueror and making additions to it. This work was named *Roman de Rou* (*Romance of Rollo*) from Rollo, the leader of the Northmen (Normans) in their descent upon Northern France in the tenth century. Wace also wrote other works, e.g. *The Life of St. Nicolas* mentioned below. Cf. Wace's autobiography, *post*, p. 559.

[307] Cf. Schofield, *op. cit.*, Index and Bibliography.

Savior, How He Was Taken into Egypt. And *The Life of St. Edward.*[308] And *The Vision of St. Paul. The Vengeance which the Lord Wreaked by means of Vespasian and Titus* and *The Life of St. Nicolas who Was Born in Patras.*[309] And *The Life of St. Eustace.*[310] And *The Life of St. Guthlac.*[311] And the *Passion of the Savior.* And the *Meditation of St. Bernard*[312] *on Our Lady St. Mary and on the Passion of Her Son Jesus Christ Our Lord.* And *The Life of St. Euphrasia.*[313] And *The Life of St. Radegund.*[314] And *The Life of St. Juliana.*[315] A volume in which is *Instruction for Children* and *A Light for Them.* A volume of the *Romance of Alexander*[316] with pictures. A small red book in which are contained many things. A volume of the *Romance of the Marshals*[317] and *of Fierebras*[318] and *of Alexander.*[316] These books we grant for our heirs and assigns that they stay in the said Abbey.[319]

[308] Cf. *ante,* p. 433.

[309] By Wace; see above. This is Nicolas of Myra or of Bari who died Dec. 6, 345 or 352. He was born at Parara, not Patras, a city of Lycia in Asia Minor and is the saint who presides over giving at Christmas.

[310] Died 29 March, 625. The second abbot of the Irish monastery of Luxeuil in France, which under his care attained renown as a seat of learning and sanctity.

[311] Cf. *ante,* p. 437.   [312] *Ibid.,* p. 432.

[313] Or Euphraxia, virgin saint, born about 380 and died after 410.

[314] Abbess at Poitiers in 567, died 587. She was the unwilling wife of Clotaire, son of Clovis I, King of the Franks. She became a great friend of the Christian poet Fortunatus, for whom see *ante,* p. 67.

[315] Suffered martyrdom in 303 under Diocletian. There is extant an Old English poem on her life.

[316] Cf. Schofield, *op. cit.,* Index and Bibliography.

[317] The word *Marshals* here is a conjectural rendering for the Old French *Mareschans.* William Marshal Earl of Pemboke died in 1219. He was regent of England during the repeated absences of Richard the Lion-Hearted and was a pattern of chivalry in his uncompromising fidelity to his chief. The principal source of our knowledge of his life is a long French poem, *Histoire de Guillaume le Maréchal (History of William the Marshal),* which was discovered about 1890. It was written at the request of Marshal's family about 1225, is based on excellent information and generally regarded as highly valuable by modern scholars. See the article on Marshal in the *Dictionary of National Biography.* The last days of Marshal are summarized in Gautier, *La Chevalerie (Chivalry),* pp. 773–777.

[318] Or Ferumbras cf. Schofield, *op. cit.,* Index and Bibliography.

[319] See the article on Guy Beauchamp in the *Dictionary of National Biography.*

The circulation of books in the Middle Ages was largely determined, as it is to-day, by their price, and, therefore, if we wish to estimate the place of books in medieval culture, it is important to know something of medieval book prices. But notices of these are scattered, and besides, price lists of single commodities without reference to those of other articles are meaningless. Hence, we preface our citation of items from two fourteenth-century account-books, where book prices are listed, by quoting the royal proclamation of 1315, which sets prices for several food-stuffs.

Edward (II), by the grace of God, King of England, Lord of Ireland and Duke of Aquitaine, to the mayor and sheriffs of London, Greeting. We have received a complaint of the archbishop, bishops, earls, barons and others of the commonalty of our kingdom, presented before us and our council, that there is now a great and intolerable dearth of oxen, cows, sheep, hogs geese, hens, capons, chickens, pigeons and eggs, to the no small damage and grievance of them and all others living within the said kingdom. Wherefore, they have pressingly besought us, that we should take care to provide a fit remedy thereof. We, therefore, for the common benefit of the people of the said kingdom, assenting to the aforesaid supplication, as seemed meet, have ordained, by the advice and assent of the prelates, earls, barons and others, being of our council, in our last parliament held at Westminster, that a good saleable fat live ox, not fed with grain, be henceforth sold for 16s. and no more; and if he have been fed with corn, and be fat, then he may be sold for 24s. at the most; and a good fat live cow for 12s. A fat hog of two years of age for 40d. A fat sheep with the wool for 20d. A fat sheep shorn for 14d. A fat goose in our city aforesaid for 3d. A good and fat capon for 2½d. . . . and three pigeons for 1d., and twenty eggs for 1d. And that if it happen that any person or persons be found that will not sell the said saleable goods at the settled price aforesaid, then let the foresaid saleable goods be forfeited to us. And forasmuch as we will that the foresaid ordinance be henceforth firmly and inviolably kept in our said city and the suburbs thereof, we strictly order and command you, that you cause the foresaid ordinance to be proclaimed publicly and distinctly in our foresaid city and the suburbs thereof, where you shall think meet, and to be henceforth inviolably kept, in all and singular its articles, throughout your whole liberty, under the foresaid forfeiture; and by no means fail herein, as you are minded to avoid our indignation, and to save yourselves harmless. Witness ourself at Westminster, the fourteenth day of March, in the eighth year of our reign.

The account-books of Merton College Grammar School for the fourteenth century are extant, and from entries in them we can gather some idea of the prices of books and scholastic expenses and services as follows:

Account. 1308–9.
The boys' expenses.[320]

	£	s.	d.
To John of Mere, their master, when he began	£	2	0
For schoolage of 9 boys in the winter term with the usher's fee		3	4½
For schoolage of 8 boys in Lent		3	4
For a brass pot hired for a year			12
For a Cato [321]			2
For ivory tablets			1½
In shoes and stockings, straw and candles		30	1¾
In schoolage of 10 boys in the summer		3	4
Total	2	3	5¾

1347–8

		s.	d.
Also in parchment bought at different times for artists and grammarians		3	2
Also in a tattered book of Horace [322] bought for the boys			½

[320] Prices of foodstuffs fell at the time of the Black Death; cf. *ante*, pp. 324, 325.
[321] I.e. *The Distichs of Cato*; cf. *ante*, p. 437.
[322] I.e. the works of Horace, the contemporary of Ovid and Virgil. We may

Also in several pairs of white tablets for grammarians for reporting arguments		$2\frac{1}{2}$
Also to Master John Cornwall [323] in the winter term for rent of the house		12
And to his usher		3
Also to the same John for Lent term		10
To the usher for the same time		$2\frac{1}{2}$
Also to the same John for the summer term		12
Total	6	$8\frac{1}{2}$

5. *The Position of the Poet and Literary Man.* — In general, the status of the poet 1066–1400 was somewhat lower than in the previous period; he was regarded more as a mere entertainer and not so much as "guide, philosopher, and friend." One's attitude toward poets and poetry, however, was likely to be determined largely by the general trend of one's sympathies and training, whether clerical or courtly. If the former, one would officially condemn the poet as an agent of the devil, though one might wink

assume that in this period books were made in the same way as in the previous age, cf. *ante*, p. 69. As for the publication and selling of books, see the article by Dr. R. K. Root, *Publication before Printing*, in the *Publications* of the *Modern Language Association of America*, xxviii, 3 (September, 1913), pp. 417–431. The gist of Dr. Root's conclusion is as follows: "It seems plain that . . . the author was in the first instance his own publisher. It was his task to secure the labor of copyists (cf. the remarks of Richard of Bury, *ante*, p. 419) and to oversee and revise their work. How large his first edition may have been we have no means of telling; but it is clear that at the time of publication copies of the work were sent to several patrons or friends. Save accidentally through the indiscretion of a friend, a work was not allowed to circulate until it had received its final revision and had been formally presented and 'released'; though before this it might have become known to a good many people privately. After the formal publication, each copy which had been presented could be freely copied under the direction of its recipient; so that the recipients might become secondary publishers, as it were. To them the author communicated any alterations he might wish to make in the work. From time to time, at the request of friends, he would have made under his supervision new exemplars; and these would naturally incorporate any alterations he might have made in the meanwhile. I have found no evidence to show that the professional booksellers, the *stationarii* and *librarii*, played any direct part in the process of publication." p. 426.   [323] The same master is mentioned, *post*, p. 485.

in secret at the poet's activity; if the latter, one would welcome him with open arms, as an agency of relief from the too tiring monotony of life in a feudal castle or as a pleasant inspirer to chivalric deeds. In the passage to be quoted from Robert Mannyng's (*circa* 1288–1338) *Handlyng Synne* (*Manual of the Sins*), these two attitudes toward poetry and entertainment are seen in somewhat of a contest. Mannyng is also known as Robert of Brunne, and about 1300 he adapted his *Handlyng Synne*, an account of the familiar seven deadly sins, illustrated by tales from the French *Manuel des Péchés* (*Manual of the Sins*) of William of Waddington. Robert also translated into English verse the French *Chronicle* of Peter Langtoft.

If a clerk in orders joust, he is blameworthy; it were better that he break his arm or leg than that he succeed; in truth, if he engage in such activity, it is against the state of holy church.

He (the clerk in orders) may not, according to the decree, act nor see miracles (i.e. miracle plays); for if you take up miracles, they are sinful gatherings and sights.

In the church, however, he may reasonably play the resurrection — that is to say, how God rose, how the human and the divine struggled powerfully in that incident — in order to make men truly believe that He rose with flesh and blood. And he may play without jeopardy how God was born on Christmas night, in order to give men a firm belief that He was born of the virgin Mary.[324]

But if he does it (acts) on the streets or in the woods, it truly seems a sinful spectacle. St. Isidore,[325] I take him to witness — for he says it and it is true, he says it in his book — remarks that they who make such plays as miracles, games or elaborate tournaments before any man, forsake what they adopted at their christening. These are worldly shows which

---

[324] A writer to be quoted later does not agree with this; cf. *post*, pp. 525–543.
[325] Cf. *ante*, p. 434.

you agreed to give up when you became a Christian. At the font the untaught man says, "I forsake you, Satan, with all your vain show and all your works" — that is what you are taught according to clerks. Are you keeping your word — certainly you are not — when you make such a show of yourself (as you do in plays)? You are breaking your covenant with God and serving your sire, the devil. St. Isidore [325] says in his writings, "All those who delight in seeing such things, or lend horses or harness for those purposes, are in danger of being found guilty."

If a priest or clerk lends vestments which have been hallowed by a sacrament, he is more blameable than others; he is guilty of a sacrilege. . . . If he falls into this danger, he should be properly punished for it.

Dances, carols and summer games are the source of much shame. When you consent to take part in these, you are slothful [326] in God's service. And those that sin in this way by means of you shall be required at your hands. What are you going to say about all the minstrels who delight themselves in such things? Their conduct is very risky, it does not show a proper love for God's house. They had rather hear of a dance, of boasting and of pride than of the grace of God or any other sort of wisdom that could be named. Their whole livelihood — clothing, meat and drink — comes from folly. And, to illustrate this, I shall recount what happened once to a minstrel. St. Gregory [327] tells the tale in one of his books.

A minstrel, a goliardeis,[328] came once upon a time to the house of a bishop and asked alms. The porter gave him entrance, at meal time the table was laid and grace was about to be said, when the minstrel started to play with a great noise, loud and high. The bishop had the reputation of being a holy man, (but) he gave the minstrel a place at table and should have said grace. Yet he was so disturbed by the minstrel that he had no grace to say his gracious words with proper devotion because of the noise of the minstrelsy.

[326] All the stories in this section are told to illustrate the sin of sloth.

[327] Probably in his *Dialogs;* cf. *ante*, p. 64.

[328] I.e. a follower of the fabled Bishop Golias, patron of minstrels and wandering students; cf. Symonds, *op. cit.*, pp. 24–27.

The bishop made a solemn complaint and said to all who were there that he would not be a stickler for formality in the presence of the grace of charity. He saw right well, through the Spirit, that vengeance would come quickly (upon the minstrel for his impiety). "Give him the alms and let him go; his death that shall slay him is near." And as the minstrel passed out of the gate, a stone fell down from the wall and killed him on the spot.

This showed that God was not pleased with what the minstrel had done in disturbing the blessing and the good bishop's devotions.

This is told for the gleeman's sake (to warn) him to be careful when he sings his song; and also for the sake of those who hear, that they may not love it so dearly nor have so much pleasure in it as through it to pay less worship to God.

Now, I am going to tell you a story which I have heard of the Bishop St. Robert Grosseteste of Lincoln.[329] He was very fond of hearing the harp because it sharpens men's wit, and so he had his harper's chamber right next to his study. Many times, during the day or at night, he had the comfort of songs and lays. Somebody asked him once why he was so delighted with minstrelsy and why he regarded his harper with so much affection. He replied, "The power of the harp, through skill and proper playing, will destroy the power of the fiend, and the harp is very properly likened to the cross. Another thing gives me comfort here — if God gives us so much solace here through the music which comes from a piece of wood, there must be much more pleasure there with God himself where He dwells. The harp often reminds me of the joy and bliss of heaven. Therefore, good sir, you must learn, when you hear a gleeman, to worship God with all your might, as David says in the Psalter, 'With harp, tabor and glee of symphony, worship God; with trumpets and the psaltery, with stringed instruments, organs and the ringing of bells; with all these worship the Heavenly King.'[330] If you do this, I say without fear that you may listen to minstrelsy."[331]

[329] Cf. *ante*, p. 393.   [330] Cf. Psalms 33, 81, 92, 108, 150.
[331] For the best general and comprehensive treatment of medieval minstrelsy, see E. K. Chambers, *The Mediæval Stage*, I, book 1 (Oxford, Clarendon Press, 1903).

6. *Wiclif's Protests against the Medieval System.* — Roger Bacon[332] and Richard of Bury[333] protested, as we have seen, against various abuses in the medieval way of doing things, but their protests were not thoroughgoing. There was, however, in the fourteenth century, one Englishman of great ability who found that the whole official philosophy of the Middle Ages was wrong. This was John Wiclif, "the morning-star of the Reformation," who used his powerful pen to publish abroad his indictment of the medieval system. In the passages quoted below, Wiclif protests against the clerical decision to keep the Bible from the masses, against the thesis that the contemplative life is superior to the active, against the theory of the confessional and its abuses, against ecclesiastical encroachments on the jurisdiction of the civil power on the ground that the former is superior to the latter, and against the theory of ecclesiastical property.

(*A*) And they (the prelates) are always loath to have men know the life of Christ, for when His life and teachings are known, men will rise in His behalf and priests will be despised for their lives, for they dishonor Christ, both in word and in deed. Accordingly one great bishop of England is ill-pleased at the translation of God's law into English for unlearned men. And he is in the habit of annoying, summoning and prosecuting a certain priest, because he has written (thus in) English (for ordinary) men. And thus (the bishop) is hurting another priest with the help of the Pharisees because he has preached the gospel of Christ in plain terms. O ye men who are on Christ's side, lend us your aid against Antichrist! for the perilous times of which Christ and Paul told long ago are here. But one source of comfort to me is the knights who are fond of the gospel and desire to read the evangel of Christ's life in English. Later, if God will, priests shall be deprived of their prerogatives and shall lose the support which makes them bold against Christ and His law. There are three groups fighting against the sect

---

[332] Cf. *ante*, pp. 391–401.   [333] *Ibid.*, pp. 417–430.

of (real) Christian men. The first is the pope and the cardinals through the false law which they have made; the second is the emperor's bishops who despise the law of Christ; the third is these Pharisees — possessioners and beggars (friars). All these three, enemies of God, are living in hypocrisy, in worldly covetousness, and idleness in God's law. Christ save His church from these enemies for they fight perilously.

(B) When true men teach that according to God's law, common sense and reason, every priest ought to put the force of his mind and will into preaching the gospel, the devil blinds hypocrites to excuse themselves (on the plea of a) feigned contemplative life, and to say that since the contemplative life is the best (life) and priests cannot live in both action (i.e. preaching) and contemplation, they should for the love of God cease preaching and live in contemplation. Observe the hypocrisy of this conclusion. Christ taught and exhibited the best life for priests, as our faith declares, since He was God and could not err. But Christ preached and charged all His apostles and disciples to go and preach the gospel to all men. Hence, the proper office of a priest in this world is to preach and teach the gospel.

.   .   .   .

In this world the best life for priests is a holy life in keeping God's commands and in true preaching of the gospel, as Christ did and charged all His priests to do. But these hypocrites imagine that their selfish indulgence in dreaming and fantasy is contemplation, and that preaching is a (kind of) active life. So they imply that Christ adopted the worse type of life for this world and forced priests to renounce the better and take the worse life. Thus these fond hypocrites accuse Christ of error.

(C) The pope might arrogate to himself the right to name as proper priests whomever he would. He might make a bargain with this priest that he should absolve no one unless he would give him money, or become a partisan of his, and thus Antichrist might easily conquer lordships and even kingdoms for himself. Thus, curates and parish priests might spoil the people as friars have done; and it would be the regular thing to bargain with the pope for the office of priest.

.   .   .   .

So men of conscience will not confess their sins to a priest; for they say that only Christ is able to hear confession properly. And if any slander them or sue them at law, they ask for a priest (really) capable of shriving them, and (say that) they will gladly confess themselves.

(*D*) When Christ was in the hands of His enemies, where ordinarily men forget themselves and their duty, he bethought Himself of this sword (the sword of civil or criminal punishment), and said to Peter, "Put up again thy sword into its place." [334] And there is need that Christ's church pay heed to this word betimes; for this sword and what it stands for may be drawn so far out of its place that it will not be possible to put it back. For this is the status of the sword in many lands where the clergy have secular dominion fully in their power; and it will very likely be in the same condition within a four years in England, unless the knighthood are quick to put their hands on the sword and restore it to its proper place. For we might as well recognize the lethargy that has fallen upon us and allowed the clergy more and more grip on this sword and its perquisites. And they are likely during this sleep of the secular party to pull the sword out of the secular hand suddenly, and thus to get complete control of it, as clerks in divers other lands have. And men ought to realize that if the clergy once gets this sword fully into their power, the secular party may go whistle on an ivy leaf for any property that they will ever return. It would be against the law that they have made as touching such things; for they are bound to get into clerical hands as much property as they can, and in no case to turn anything back into secular hands.[335]

(*E*) The clergy say that they hold their property not privately but in common, as the apostles and perfect people did at the beginning of Christ's church, who had all things in common [336] as clerks and ecclesiastics say they have now. . . . But if we take heed we shall see at a glance how the clergy speak falsely here. . . . For in exactly the same spirit as the baron or the knight possesses and governs his barony or property does the

---

[334] Cf. John 18: 11.   [335] Wiclif was a priest and a lecturer at Oxford.
[336] Cf. Acts 2: 44, 45.

clerk, monk, canon, college or convent manage its property, execute judgment and mete out penalties, such as imprisonment and hanging, with other secular torments, which formerly belonged to the secular arm of the church only.

The Wiclifite conclusions in theology, formulated in twenty-four theses, were, by the ecclesiastical authorities, declared to be, ten of them heretical, and fourteen, erronous. The theses are as follows:

I. — That the material substance of bread and of wine remains, after the consecration, in the sacrament of the altar.

II. — That the accidents do not remain without the subject, after the consecration, in the same sacrament.

III. — That Christ is not in the sacrament of the altar identically, truly and really in his proper corporal presence.

IV. — That if a bishop or priest lives in mortal sin he does not ordain, or consecrate, or baptize.

V. — That if a man has been truly repentant, all external confession is superfluous to him, or useless.

VI. — Continually to assert that it is not founded in the gospel that Christ instituted the mass.

VII. — That God ought to be obedient to the devil.

VIII. — That if the pope is foreordained to destruction and a wicked man, and therefore a member of the devil, no power has been given to him over the faithful of Christ by any one, unless perhaps by the Emperor.

IX. — That since Urban the Sixth, no one is to be acknowledged as pope; but all are to live, in the way of the Greeks, under their own laws.

X. — To assert that it is against sacred scripture that men of the church should have temporal possessions.

XI. — That no prelate ought to excommunicate any one unless he first knows that the man is excommunicated by God.

XII. — That a person thus excommunicating is thereby a heretic or excommunicate.

XIII. — That a prelate excommunicating a clerk who has appealed to the king, or to a council of the kingdom, on that very account is a traitor to God, the king and the kingdom.

XIV. — That those who neglect to preach, or to hear the word of God, or the gospel that is preached, because of the excommunication of men, are excommunicate, and in the day of judgment will be considered as traitors to God.

XV. — To assert that it is allowed to any one, whether a deacon or a priest, to preach the word of God, without the authority of the apostolic see, or of a catholic bishop, or some other which is sufficiently acknowledged.

XVI. — To assert that no one is a civil lord, no one is a bishop, no one is a prelate, so long as he is in mortal sin.

XVII. — That temporal lords may, at their own judgment, take away temporal goods from churchmen who are habitually delinquent; or that the people may, at their own judgment, correct delinquent lords.

XVIII. — That tithes are purely charity, and that parishioners may, on account of the sins of their curates, detain these and confer them on others at their will.

XIX. — That special prayers applied to one person by prelates or religious persons, are of no more value to the same person than general prayers for others in a like position are to him.

XX. — That the very fact that any one enters upon any private religion whatever, renders him more unfitted and more incapable of observing the commandments of God.

XXI. — That saints who have instituted any private religions whatever, as well of those having possessions as of mendicants, have sinned in thus instituting them.

XXII. — That religious persons living in private religions are not of the Christian religion.

XXIII. — That friars should be required to gain their living by the labor of their hands and not by mendicancy.

XXIV. — That a person giving alms to friars, or to a preaching friar, is excommunicate; also the one receiving.[337]

7. *The Growth of a Feeling of Nationality.* — The growth of a feeling of nationality is a marked feature of the cul-

[337] For more material on Wiclif cf. *post*, pp. 588–595. For a general reference to Wiclif and his work, see *The Cambridge History of English Literature*, ii, chapter ii and *Bibliography*.

ture of this epoch and doubtless was a stimulus for the
outburst of literature in the vernacular which marked its
close. The development of this feeling is especially notice-
able among the upper classes, who largely represent impor-
tations from Normandy, Anjou, and other parts of France.
At the beginning of the period their estimate of England
was low. For example, the regard of William the Conqueror for his English kingdom as compared with his
Norman duchy is expressed in his will as thus recorded
by Henry of Huntingdon: [338]

William, King of England, bequeathed Normandy to his
eldest son, Robert; the kingdom of England to William, his
second son; and the treasure he had amassed to his third son,
Henry, by means of which he succeeded in depriving him of his
dominions; [339] a thing displeasing to God, but the punishment
was deferred for a time.

Yet in 1106, forty years after the battle of Hastings,
Angevins, English and Normans, with the flower of Brittany, followed Henry, now King of England, to Normandy in his contest with his elder brother, Robert.
Henry and Robert met at Tenchebrai and Henry was
victorious, thus making Normandy an appanage of the
English crown,[340] as Huntingdon again records.

Upon his laying siege to the castle of Tenerchebrai, the Duke
of Normandy (Robert), having with him Robert de Belesme
and the Earl of Morton with all their adherents advanced
against him (King Henry). The King on his side was not un-
prepared; for there were with him almost all the chief men of
Normandy and the flower of the forces of England, Anjou and
Brittany. The shrill trumpets sounded and the Duke, with his
few followers, boldly charged the King's numerous troops, and,

[338] Cf. *ante*, p. 87.
[339] Huntingdon, being a decided partisan of Henry I as against Robert, means
that Henry should have been given the sovereignty of either England or Normandy.
[340] Normandy had already been mortgaged to William II; cf. *ante*, p. 378.

well trained in the wars of Jerusalem,[341] with his terrible onset repulsed the royal army. William Earl of Morton, also attacking it from point to point, threw it into confusion. The King and the Duke with a great part of their troops fought on foot, that they might make a determined stand; but the Breton knights bore down the flank of the Duke's force, which, unable to sustain the shock, was presently routed. Robert de Belesme, perceiving this, saved himself by flight; but Robert Duke of Normandy and William Earl of Morton were made prisoners. Thus the Lord took vengeance on Duke Robert; because when He had exalted him to great glory in the holy wars, he rejected the offer of the kingdom of Jerusalem, preferring a service of ease and sloth in Normandy to serving the Lord zealously in the defence of the Holy City. The Lord, therefore, condemned him to lasting inactivity and perpetual imprisonment.

Toward the close of the twelfth century there is evidence that English and Normans had become pretty well fused and the basis for national feeling established. This evidence is found in the *Dialogus de Scaccario* (*Dialog on the Exchequer*) of Richard Fitzneale or Fitznigel, otherwise known as Richard of Ely, who died in 1198. He was the son of Nigel Bishop of Ely and became treasurer of England in 1169. He held this office for twenty-nine years, and his experience fully qualified him to write his book on the principles and administration of the English exchequer; a book invaluable to modern scholars because of its definitions of medieval financial and political terms and its description of fiscal procedure. Richard wrote his dialog "by request," as he tells us in the following words: "In the twenty-third year of the reign of King Henry II (1177), while I was sitting at the window of a tower next to the River Thames, a man spoke to me impetuously, saying, 'Master, hast thou not read that there is no use in science or in treasure that is hidden?' When I replied

[341] I.e. the Crusades.

to him, 'I have read so,' straightway he said, 'Why,
therefore, dost thou not teach others the knowledge concerning the exchequer which is said to be thine to such an
extent, and commit it to writing lest it die with thee?'
I answered, 'Lo, brother, thou hast now for a long time
sat at the exchequer, and nothing is hidden from thee,
for thou art painstaking. And the same is probably the
case with the others who have seats there.' But he, 'Just
as those who walk in darkness and grope with their hands
frequently stumble, — so many sit there who seeing do
not perceive, and hearing do not understand.' Then I,
'Thou speakest irreverently, for neither is the knowledge
so great nor does it concern such great things; but perchance those who are occupied with important matters
have hearts like the claws of an eagle, which do not retain
small things, but which great ones do not escape.' And
he, 'So be it; but although eagles fly very high, nevertheless they rest and refresh themselves in humble places;
and, therefore, we beg thee to explain humble things which
will be of profit to the eagles themselves.' Then I, 'I
have feared to put together a work concerning these things
because they lie open to the bodily senses and grow common
by daily use; nor is there, nor can there be in them a
description of subtle things, or a pleasing invention of the
imagination.' And he, 'Those who rejoice in imaginings,
who seek the flight of subtle things, have Aristotle and
the books of Plato; to them let them listen. Do thou
write not subtle but useful things.' Then I, 'Of those
things which thou demandest it is impossible to speak
except in common discourse and in ordinary words.' 'But,'
said he, as if roused to ire, for to a mind filled with desire
nothing goes quickly enough, 'writers on arts, lest they
seem to know too little about many things, and in order
that art might less easily become known, have sought to
appropriate many things, and have concealed them under

unknown words: but thou dost not undertake to write about an art, but about certain customs and laws of the exchequer; and since these ought to be common, common words must necessarily be employed, so that the style may have relation to the things of which we are speaking. Moreover, although it is very often allowable to invent new words, I beg, nevertheless, if it please thee, that thou may'st not be ashamed to use the customary names of the things themselves which readily occur to the mind, so that no new difficulty from using unfamiliar words may arise to disturb us.' Then I, 'I see that thou art angry; but be calmer; I will do what thou dost urge. Rise, therefore, and sit opposite to me; and ask me concerning those things that occur to thee. But if thou shalt propound something unheard of, I shall not blush to say, "I do not know." But let us both, like discreet beings, come to an agreement.' And he, 'Thou respondest to my wish. Moreover, although an elementary old man is a disgraceful and ridiculous thing, I will nevertheless begin with the very elements.'" [342]

He, therefore, asks first the meaning of the word *exchequer* itself and the explanation of this leads to further queries, in the course of which they come upon the word *murder*. In explaining this Fitzneale says:

Murder (Murdrum), indeed, is properly called the secret death of somebody, whose slayer is not known. For "murdrum" means the same as "hidden" or "occult." Now in the primitive state of the kingdom after the Conquest those who were left of the Anglo-Saxon subjects secretly laid ambushes for the suspected and hated race of the Normans, and, here and there, when opportunity offered, killed them secretly in the woods and in remote places: as vengeance for whom — when the kings and their ministers had for some years, with exquisite kinds of tortures, raged against the Anglo-Saxons; and they, neverthe-

[342] Cf. Henderson, *Select Historical Documents of the Middle Ages*, pp. 22, 23.

less, had not, in consequence of these measures, altogether
desisted, — the following plan was hit upon, that the so-called
"hundred" in which a Norman was found killed in this way —
when he who had caused his death was not to be found, and it
did not appear from his flight who he was — should be condemned to a large sum of tested silver for the fisc; some, indeed, to 36, some to 44£, according to the different localities
and the frequency of the slaying. And they say that this is
done with the following end in view, namely, that a general
penalty of this kind might make it safe for the passers by, —
and that each person might hasten to punish so great a crime and
to give up to justice him through whom so enormous a loss fell
upon the neighborhood. . . .

Disciple. Ought not the occult death of an Anglo-Saxon, like
that of a Norman, to be reputed murder?

Master. By the original institution it ought not to, as thou
hast heard: but during the time that the English and Normans
have now dwelt together, and mutually married and given in
marriage, the nations have become so intermingled that one
can hardly tell to-day — I speak of freemen — who is of English
and who of Norman race; excepting, however, the bondsmen
who are called "villani" (villeins), to whom it is not free, if
their lords object, to depart from the condition of their station.
On this account, almost always when any one is found thus
slain to-day, it is punished as murder; except in the case of
those who show certain proofs, as we have said, of a servile
condition.

Disciple. I wonder that this prince of singular excellence
(William the Conqueror), and this man of most distinguished
virtue, should have shown such mercy towards the race of the
English, subjugated and suspected by him, that not only did he
keep the serfs by whom agriculture could be exercised, from
harm, but left even the nobles of the kingdom their estates and
ample possessions.

Master. Although these things do not pertain to the matters
undertaken and concerning which I have bound myself, I will
nevertheless freely expound what I have heard on these matters
from the natives themselves. After the conquest of the king-

dom, after the just overthrow of the rebels, when the king himself and the king's nobles went over the new places, a diligent inquiry was made as to who there were who, contending in war against the king, had saved themselves through flight. To all of these, and even to the heirs of those who had fallen in battle, all hope of the lands and estates and revenues which they had before possessed was precluded: for it was thought much for them even to enjoy the privilege of being alive under their enemies. But those who, having been called to the war, had not yet come together, or, occupied with family or any kind of necessary affairs, had not been present, — when, in course of time, by their devoted service they had gained the favor of their lords, they began to have possessions for themselves alone; without hope of hereditary possession, but according to the pleasure of their lords. But as time went on, when, becoming hateful to their masters, they were here and there driven from their possessions, and there was no one to restore what had been taken away, — a common complaint of the natives came to the king to the effect that, thus hateful to all and despoiled of their property, they would be compelled to cross to foreign lands. Counsel at length having been taken on these matters, it was decided that what, their merits demanding, a legal pact having been entered into, they had been able to obtain from their masters, should be conceded to them by inviolable right: but that, however, they should claim nothing for themselves by right of heredity from the time of the conquest of the race. And it is manifest with what discreet consideration this provision was made, especially since they would thus be bound to consult their own advantage in every way, and to strive henceforth by devoted service to gain the favor of their lords. So, therefore, whoever belonging to the conquered race, possesses estates or any thing of the kind, — he has acquired them, not because they seemed to be due to him by reason of heredity, but because his merits alone demanding, or some pact intervening, he has obtained them.[343]

[343] Chaucer's Man of Law has at his tongue's end the laws of England *since the time of William the Conqueror;* cf. *Prolog to the Canterbury Tales,* ll. 323–324 and Skeat's notes.

Against the Jews, national feeling, combined to be sure
with religious antipathy, often expressed itself in deeds
of violence and murder. Of what happened to the Jews,
for example, at the coronation of Richard the Lion-
Hearted, William of Newburgh [344] speaks as follows:

Richard, the only monarch of the age who bore that name,
was consecrated king at London and solemnly crowned by Baldwin Archbishop of Canterbury on the third day of . . . September (1189), a day which, from the ancient superstition of
the Gentiles, is called evil or Egyptian, as if it had been a kind
of presage of the event which occurred to the Jews. For that
day is considered to have been fatal to Jews, and to be Egyptian rather than English; since England, in which their fathers
had been happy and respected under the preceding king (Henry
II), was suddenly changed against them, by the judgment of
God, into a kind of Egypt where their fathers had suffered hard
things. Though this is an event that is fresh in our memory
and known to all who are now living, yet it is worth the trouble
to transmit to posterity a full narration of it, as proof of an
evident judgment from on high upon that perfidious and blas-
phemous race.

Not only Christian nobles, but also the leading men among
the Jews, had come together from all parts of England to witness the solemn anointing of the Christian sovereign. For those
enemies of the truth were on the watch lest, perchance, the
prosperity which they had enjoyed under the preceeding monarch should smile upon them less favorably under the new king;
and they wished that his first acts should be honored by them
in the most becoming manner, thinking that undiminished favor
would be secured by ample gifts. But whether it was that they
were less acceptable to him than to his father (Henry II), or
whether he was on his guard against them, from some cause,
(of which I am ignorant,) through a superstitious caution, advised by certain persons, he forbade them (by a proclamation,
it is said) to enter the church while he was being crowned, or
to enter the palace while the banquet was being held after the

[344] Cf. *ante*, p. 209.

solemnity of the coronation. After the celebration of the mass was finished, the King, glorious in his diadem, and with a magnificent procession, went to the banquet; but it happened that, when he was sitting down with all the assembly of the nobility, the people who were watching about the palace began to crowd in. The Jews who had mingled with the crowd were thus driven within the doors of the palace. At this, a certain Christian was indignant, and, remembering the royal proclamation against them, endeavored, as it is said, to drive away a Jew from the door, and struck him with his hand. Aroused at this example, many more began to beat the Jews back with contempt, and a tumult arose. The lawless and furious mob, thinking that the King had commanded it and supported them, as they thought, by his royal authority, rushed like the rest upon the multitude of Jews who stood watching at the door of the palace. At first they beat them unmercifully with their fists, but soon, becoming more enraged, they took sticks and stones. The Jews then fled away; and, in their flight, many were beaten so that they died, and others were trampled under foot and perished. Along with the rest, two noble Jews of York had come thither, one named Joceus, and the other Benedict. Of these, the first escaped, but the other, following him, could not run so fast, so that he was caught and, to avoid death, was compelled to confess himself a Christian, and, being conducted to a church, was there baptized.

In the meantime, an agreeable rumor that the King had ordered all the Jews to be exterminated pervaded the whole of London with incredible celerity. An innumerable mob of lawless people, belonging to that city and also from other places in the provinces, whom the solemnity of the coronation had attracted thither, soon assembled in arms, eager for plunder and for the blood of a people hateful to all men by the judgment of God. Then the Jewish citizens, of whom a multitude reside in London, together with those who had come thither from all parts, retired to their own houses. From three o'clock in the afternoon till sunset, their dwellings were surrounded by the raging people and vigorously attacked. By reason of their strong construction, however, they could not be broken into

and the furious assailants had no engines. The roofs, therefore, were set on fire, and a horrible conflagration, destructive to
the besieged Jews, afforded light to the Christians who were
raging in their nocturnal work. Nor was the fire destructive to
the Jews alone, though kindled against them; for, knowing no
distinction, it caught some of the nearest houses of the Christians also. Then you might have seen the most beautiful parts
of the city miserably blazing in flames, caused by her own
citizens, as if they had been enemies. The Jews, however, were
either burnt in their own houses or, if they came out, were received on the point of the sword. . . .

Similar occurrences took place in other parts of England,
as we learn from William and other authorities. Roger of
Hoveden (died 1201?), for example, who, on account of the
part he played in contemporary affairs, is well informed on
late twelfth-century matters, gives the following story of
what happened to the Jews at York:

In the . . . month of March (1190) . . . the sixth day before
Palm Sunday, the Jews of the city of York, in number five
hundred men, besides women and children, shut themselves up
in the tower of York, with the consent and sanction of the keeper
of the tower and of the sheriff, in consequence of their dread of
the Christians; but when the sheriff and the constable sought
to regain possession of it, the Jews refused to deliver it up. In
consequence of this, the people of the city and the strangers
who had come within the jurisdiction thereof, at the exhortation
of the sheriff and the constable, with one consent made an attack
upon the Jews.

After they had made assaults upon the tower, day and night,
the Jews offered the people a large sum of money to depart with
their lives; but this the others refused to receive. Upon this,
one skilled in their laws arose and said, "Men of Israel, listen
to my advice, It is better that we should kill one another, than
fall into the hands of the enemies of our law." Accordingly,
all the Jews, both men as well as women, gave their assent to
his advice, and each master of a family, beginning with the chief

persons of his household, with a sharp knife first cut the throats
of his wife and sons and daughters, and then of all his servants,
and lastly his own. Some of them also threw their slain over
the walls among the people; while others shut up their slain
in the King's house and burned them, as well as the . . . house.
In the meantime, some of the Christians set fire to the Jews'
houses and plundered them, and thus all the Jews in the city
of York were destroyed and all acknowledgments of debts due
to them were burnt.[345]

Indignation at King John for his loss of lands, entailing
loss of prestige upon the nation, is expressed in the following translation of a contemporary Provençal poem:

When I see the fair weather return and leaf and flower appear,
love gives me boldness and heart and skill to sing. Then, since
I do not want matter, I will make a stinging sirvente which I
will send yonder for a present to King John, to make him
ashamed.

And well he ought to be ashamed, if he remember his ancestors, how he has left here Poitou and Touraine, given them to
King Philip without his asking for them. Wherefore all Guienne
laments King Richard who in its defence would have laid out
much gold and much silver. But this man does not appear to
me to care much for it.

He loves better fishing and hunting, pointers, greyhounds and
hawks, and repose; wherefore he loses his property and his
fief escapes out of his hand. Galvaing seems ill-furnished with
courage, so that we beat him here most frequently. And, since
he takes no other counsel, let him leave his land to the lord of
the Groing.

Louis knew better how to deliver William and gave him rich
succor at Orange, when the Almassor had caused Tibaud to
besiege him.[346] Glory and honor he had with profit. I say this
for a lesson to King John who loses his people, because he suc-
cors them not near or far off.

[345] On the medieval attitude towards the Jews, see *ante*, pp. 277; 407. They were
expelled from England in 1290 under Edward I.
[346] A reference to the romance of William of Orange; cf. *ante*, p. 443.

Barons, on this side my lesson of correction aims at you, whose delinquencies it blames. What I have seen you do . . . I am grieved at, for it falls to me to speak of you, who have let your credit fall into the mud. And afterwards you have a foolish sentiment that you do not fear correction. But he who told you ill, it is he who disgraces you.

Lady whom I desire and hold dear, and fear and flatter above the rest, so true is your praise that I know not how to say it or to relate it. . . . As gold is more worth than tin, you are worth more than the best hundred and you are better worth to a young man than are the monks of Caen to God.

Savary,[347] a king without a heart will hardly make a successful invasion. And, since he has a heart soft and cowardly, let no man put his trust in him.

 But the long reign of Henry III (1216–1272) is the time when the national spirit developed most rapidly. This was due to causes partly interior and partly exterior to England. Of the latter, one was the action of the King of France, who in 1244 gave all Norman barons who held lands both in England and on the Continent their choice of which they would relinquish, as Matthew Paris tells below. Another was the fact that King John had declared himself the liege of the Pope, had turned his kingdom over to him and agreed to pay homage and tribute. This gave Innocent III, the most able of the medieval popes, just the opportunity he desired to fill English benefices, as they fell vacant, with his own nominees, and thus to build up what would to-day be called a very efficient political machine. Henry III, coming to the throne a minor, a person of refined tastes and thoroughly submissive to the plans of the Pope, readily acquiesced and brought upon himself the troubles of his reign. It should be remembered that a clerical training was the surest entrance to administrative or fiscal preferment in medieval Europe and

[347] The brother poet to whom the lines were sent.

that, hence, the filling of English church offices with papal foreign appointees inevitably meant that these appointees would have a disproportionate influence in English state affairs.

Of the internal causes, the most potent was the quality of the English baronage of the day, stimulated by their long struggle against the tyranny of King John. William Marshal Earl of Pembroke, Archbishop Stephen Langton of Canterbury, Hubert de Burgh Earl of Kent, Bishop Robert Grossesteste of Lincoln and Simon de Montfort Earl of Leicester are famous names in the history of English leadership and statesmanship. The barons determined that they would not be dominated by foreigners, and their decision came to the test in the Barons' War in which, though defeated by the rising genius of Prince Edward, later Edward I, they made lasting contributions to the cause of English liberty.

"Matthew Paris has justly been considered the best Latin chronicler of the 13th century; and his work contrasts sharply with previous works of the kind. In place of an almost colourless narrative, we have a series of brilliant historical criticisms, a change which is mainly due to the altered policy of the clergy who were compelled to abandon their position of political neutrality for one of active partisanship. His style is constantly vivid and lively, and often marked by considerable humour. . . .

"Matthew, like the majority of the clergy in his day, was a warm supporter of the popular cause. He fiercely denounces alike the encroachments and oppression of the Roman court and the extravagance and tyranny of the king and his foreign kinsfolk. In his pages, indeed, the national sentiment may be said first to receive adequate expression. The wide range of his history should be noticed, for not only is it the best source of information with respect to events in England, but it is also an au-

thority of value for the history of France, of Spain, and
of the struggle between the Papacy and the Empire." [348]

Paris (*circa* 1195–1259) thus records how the King of
France treated the Norman nobles in 1244:

> In the course of those days, the King of France, having con-
> voked at Paris all the people across the water who had posses-
> sions in England, thus addressed them, "As it is impossible that
> any man living in my kingdom and having possessions in Eng-
> land can competently serve two masters, he must inseparably
> attach himself either to me or to the King of England." Where-
> fore, those who had possessions and revenues in England were
> to relinquish them and keep those which they had in France, or
> *vice versa*. And when this came to the knowledge of the King
> of England, he ordered that all people of the French nation
> and especially Normans, who had possessions in England, should
> be disseized of them. Whence it appeared to the King of France
> that the King of England had broken the treaties between them,
> because he had not, as the King of France had done, given the
> option to those who were to lose their lands in one or other of
> the two kingdoms, so that they might themselves choose which
> kingdom they might remain in. . . .

In 1245 the English commons protested to the Pope
against the extortions of Italian prelates in England. A
portion of their letter, as recorded by Paris, reads as
follows:

> . . . It is not without great annoyance and intolerable injury
> to us that . . . religious men should be in any way defrauded
> of their rights of patronage or appointments to churches. But
> now, by you and your predecessors (the popes) . . . Italians,
> of whom there is now an almost endless number, are enriched
> from the churches belonging to the patronage of those very . . .
> men who are called the rectors of the churches, thus leaving
> those whom they ought to defend entirely unprotected, giving
> no care to the souls of the people, but allowing these most

[348] Cf. Hutton, *The Misrule of Henry III*, pp. 150–151 (*English History by Com-
temporary Writers*, G. P. Putnam's Sons, 1887).

rapacious wolves to disperse the flock and carry off the sheep. Hence, they can say with truth that these persons are not good shepherds,[349] as they do not know their sheep, neither have the sheep any knowledge of ·the shepherd. They do not practise hospitality or the bestowal of alms enjoined on the church, but they only receive the fruits to carry them out of the kingdom, impoverishing it in no slight degree, by possessing themselves of its revenues, by which our brothers, nephews and other relations, well-deserving men of the said kingdom, ought to be benefited; and the latter both could and would compassionately and piously put in practice the said works of charity and several others, and would in person serve the said churches, that, according to the words of Paul, those who serve the altar may live by the altar; but they, urged by necessity, are now become laymen and exiles. But in order that the truth may be known to you, these Italians, receiving sixty thousand marks and more each year in England, besides divers other receipts, carry off more clear gain in revenues from the kingdom than the King himself, who is the protector of the church and holds the reins of government in the kingdom. . . .

In 1236 Henry III married Eleanor of Provence, and when she came to England, she brought with her a number of her relatives whom Henry undertook to provide for in England. Hence, the literature of the time is full of complaints of the extravagance of the court. Thus Matthew Paris, again, speaks of conditions in 1252 as follows:

During all this time, through the many-shaped cunning of Satan, the people of England in general, barons, knights, citizens, merchants and laborers and especially religious men, were laboring under a most pestilential infliction; for the higher ranks of the foreigners imposed on the lower classes so many laborious services, and harassed them by so many robberies and injuries, that of all nations existing, England appeared to be in the lowest condition. In one place the houses of merchants, in another their carts and their small possessions were forcibly

[349] Cf. John 10: 11–16.

seized on, and nothing was left as an indemnity for them, save tallages and ridicule. On seeing these proceedings, some even of the more noble of the English, whom I am ashamed to mention by name, said in their pride and with accompanying oaths, "There are now many kings and tyrants in England, and we ought to be kings and tyrannize the same as others;" and so they became worse than the rest. If any one who had been grievously injured laid his complaint before the Poitevins (i.e. Henry's foreign agents), whose heads were turned by their vast riches and possessions, and asked for justice to be done him according to the law of the land, they replied, "We care nothing for the law of the land, what are the customs or ordinances to us?" Thus the natives of the country, especially the religious men, were as dirt in the sight of the foreigners, in whose steps some of the English were not ashamed to follow. On one occasion, Brother Matthew Paris, the writer of this book, and Roger de Thurkeby, a knight and man of letters, were taking their meal together at one table, when Brother Matthew mentioned the aforesaid oppressions, and the above named knight said seriously in reply, "The time is coming, O religious men ! and indeed, now is, when every one who oppresses you thinks he is doing God a service; indeed, I think that these injurious oppressions and troubles are not far short of utter ruin." When the said Matthew heard this speech, it brought to his mind the saying, that "in the last days of the world, there will be men, loving themselves, who have no regard to the advantage of their neighbors."

Matthew further comments on Henry's practice of turning over English revenue and property to foreigners, as follows:

The King . . . persisted in his usual extravagances and . . . continued to distribute the vacant escheats and revenues amongst unknown, scurrilous and undeserving foreigners, in order to inflict an irreparable wound upon the heads of his natural subjects. Not to mention others, we think it right to speak in this volume of the following case, as one out of many. In the service of Geoffrey de Lusignan, the King's brother, was a certain

chaplain who served as a fool and buffoon to the King, the said
Geoffrey his master and all the court, and whose sayings, like
those of a silly jester and cup-bearer, contributed to their amusement and excited their laughter; and on this man the King
bestowed the rich church of Preston, which had formerly belonged to William Haverhull, the lately-deceased treasurer of
the King, the yearly proceeds of which church amounted to more
than a hundred pounds. This same chaplain, a Poitevin by
birth, utterly ignorant alike in manners and learning, we have
seen pelting the King, his brother Geoffrey and other nobles,
whilst walking in the orchard of St. Alban's, with turf, stones
and green apples, and pressing the juice of unripe grapes in
their eyes, like one devoid of sense. Despicable alike in his
gesture, mode of speech and habits, as well as in size and personal appearance, this man might be considered as a stage actor
rather than a priest as he was, to the great disgrace of the
priestly order. Such are the persons to whom the King of England intrusts the care and guardianship of many thousands of
souls, rejecting such a vast number of learned, prudent and
proper men as England has given birth to, who know the language of the natives, and how to instruct the ignorant. In like
manner, also, to provoke the anger and hatred of worthy men,
the King ill-advisedly gave away the other church benefices
which had belonged to the aforesaid William, to unworthy men
and foreigners, whose incapacity and uselessness was shown by
their extraordinary conduct, and who were plainly proved to
be reprobates by their conversation, which was not only scurrilous, but also foolish and obscene. This digression from our
narrative is elicited by our sorrow for the causes of it.

The nationalist movement of the reign culminated in
the Barons' War, in the course of which two important
battles were fought, Lewes, May 14, 1264 and Evesham,
August 4, 1265. The leader of the popular party in both
was Simon de Montfort, who was victorious in the first
but met defeat and death in the second at the hands of
Prince Edward, later Edward I, the general of the court
party. Just after the battle of Lewes, a long Latin poem,

giving a full account of the principles of both factions, appeared, from which we quote in translation the following:-

The English were despised like dogs; but now they have raised their head over their vanquished enemies.

In the year of grace one thousand two hundred and sixty-four, and on the Wednesday after the festival of St. Pancras, the army of the English bore the brunt of a great battle at the castle of Lewes: for reasoning yielded to rage, and life to the sword. They met on the fourteenth of May and began the battle of this terrible strife, which was fought in the county of Sussex and in the bishopric of Chichester. The sword was powerful, many fell, truth prevailed and the false men fled. For the Lord of valor resisted the perjured men and defended those who were pure with the shield of truth. The sword without and fear within routed the former, the favor of heaven comforted very fully the latter. The solemnities of the victor and the sacred crowns give testimony on this contest, since the church honored the said persons as saints and victory crowned the true soldiers. The wisdom of God, which rules the whole world, performed miracles and made a joyful war, caused the strong to fly and the valorous men to shut themselves up in a cloister and in places of safety. Not in arms, but in the grace of Christianity, that is in the church, remained the only refuge for those who were excommunicated; after deserting their horses this counsel alone occurred to the vanquished. And her whom previously they had not hesitated to profane, her whom they ought to have honored in the place of a mother, in her they seek refuge, though little worthy of it, and seek their defence in embracing the wood of salvation. Those whom prosperity caused to despise their mother, their wounds compelled to know their mother. When at Northampton, they succeeded by treachery, the faithless children despised the church; with the sword they disturbed the bowels of the holy mother, and in their prosperity did not merit a successful war. The mother then bore the injury patiently, as though heedless of it, but not letting it pass unmarked: she punishes this and other injuries which were afterwards added, for the madmen ravaged many churches; and the band of enraged men, which has now been thrown into confusion, mercilessly spoiled the monastery which is called Battle, of its goods, and thus they prepared a battle for themselves. The Cistercian monks of Robertsbridge would not have been safe from the fury of the sword, unless they had given five hundred marks to the prince, which Edward ordered to be received, or they had perished. By these and similar deeds they merited to give way and succumb before their enemies. May the Lord bless Simon de Montfort! and also his sons and his army! who exposing themselves magnanimously to death, fought valiantly, condoling the lamentable lot of the English who, trodden under foot in a manner scarcely to be described, and almost deprived of all their liberties, had languished under hard rulers, like the people of Israel under Pharaoh, groaning under a tyrannical devastation. But God, seeing this suffering of the people, gives at last a new Matathias,[350] and he with his sons, zealous after the zeal of the law, yields neither to the insults nor to the fury of the king.

They call Simon a seducer and a traitor; but his deeds lay him open and prove him to be a true man. Traitors fall off in time of need; they who do not fly death, are those who stand for the truth. But says this insidious enemy now, whose evil eye is the disturber of peace, "If you praise the constancy and fidelity, which does not fly the approach of death or punishment, they shall equally be called constant, who in the same manner, go to the combat fighting on the opposite side, in the same manner exposing themselves to the chance of war and subjecting themselves to a hard appelation." But in our war in which we are engaged, let us see what is the state of the case.

The earl had few men used to arms, the royal party was numerous, having assembled the disciplined and greatest warriors in England, such as were called the flower of the army of the kingdom; those who were prepared with arms from among the Londoners, were three hundred set before several thousands; whence they were contemptible to those and were detested by

[350] An aged priest, father of Judas Maccabæus, who, when Antiochus IV Epiphanes in 175–164 B.C. tried to crush out the national Jewish religion, came forward with his five sons, opposed the royal policy, and re-established the Hebrew kingdom.

those who were experienced. Much of the earl's army was raw, fresh in arms they knew little of war. The tender youth, only now girt with a sword, stands on the morning in battle accustoming himself to arms, what wonder if such an unpractised tyro fear, and if the powerless lamb dread the wolf? Thus those who fight for England are inferior in military discipline and they are much fewer than the strong men who boasted in their own valor, because they thought safely and without danger to swallow up, as it were, all whom the earl had to help him. Moreover, of those whom the earl had brought to the battle and from whom he hoped for no little help, many soon withdrew from fear and took to flight as though they were amazed, and of three parts one deserted. The earl with a few faithful men never yielded. We may compare our battle with that of Gideon; [351] in both we see a few of the faithful conquer a great number who have no faith and who trust in themselves as Lucifer did. God said, "If I should give the victory to the many, the fools will not give the glory to me, but to fools." So if God had made the strong to conquer, the common people would have given the credit of it to the men and not to God.

From these considerations it may be concluded that the warlike men did not fear God, wherefore they did nothing to prove their constancy or fidelity, but they showed on the contrary their pride and cruelty; and wishing to confound those whom they despised, issuing forth boldly, they perished quickly. Exaltation of the heart brings on ruin and humility merits to receive the divine grace, for he who does not trust in God, God overthrows his pride. We may bring forward Hamaan and Mordecai; [352] we read that the former was arrogant, the latter a true Israelite; the gallows which Hamaan had prepared for Mordecai, in the morning the wretch bore it himself in order to be hanged upon it. The queen's banquet blinded Hamaan, which he reputed as an extraordinary privilege, but his vain expectation is turned into confusion, when after the feast he is dragged to the gallows. Thus sorrow followed close upon joy when it coupled death with the end of the feast. Very differently it happens to the Israelite whom by God's will the king honors. Goliath is

[351] Cf. Judges 6–9.   [352] Cf. Esther 3–10.

overthrown by the stroke of a little stone,[353] nothing profits him whom God pursues. . . .

Listen to the equity of Earl Simon: when the royal party would be satisfied only with his head and his life, nor would allow his head to be redeemed, but would have it cut off, by whose confusion they hoped the body of the people should be confounded and the greatest part of the state brought into danger, so that the most grievous ruin would immediately follow — may it be long before this happen! — Stephen, by divine grace Bishop of Chichester, groaning deeply for the immense evils which were then impending . . ., the two parties being persuaded to treat of a peace, received this answer from the Earl, "Choose the best men, who have a lively faith, who have read the decretals, or who have taught in a becoming manner theology and sacred wisdom, and who know how to rule the Christian faith, or whatever they may have the courage to decree, they shall find us ready to agree to what they shall dictate, in such a manner that we may escape the stigma of perjury and keep the league as children of God." Hence, it may easily be understood by those who swear, and show little reluctance to despise what they swear receding quickly from it although they swear to what is right, and not rendering whole what they promised to God, with how much care they ought to keep their oath, when they see a man avoiding neither torment nor death on account of his oath, which was made not inconsiderately, but for the reformation of the fallen state of the English nation, which the fraud of an inveterate enemy had violated. Behold Simon, obedient, despises the loss of property, submitting himself to punishment rather than desert the truth, proclaiming to all men openly by his deeds more than by his words that truth has nothing in common with falsehood. Woe to the perjured wretches who fear not God! denying Him for the prospect of an earthly reward or for fear of imprisonment or light punishment; the new leader of the journey teaches to bear all that the world may inflict on account of truth, for it is this which can give perfect liberty.[354] For the Earl had first pledged his oath that whatever the zeal of the wise had provided for the

[353] Cf. 1 Samuel 17: 41–49. [354] Cf. John 8: 32.

reformation of the King's honor and for the repression of wandering error, at Oxford,[355] he would steadfastly keep it and would not change the law then ordained, knowing that such canonical constitutions and such catholic ordinances for the pacific conservation of the kingdom, on account of which he had before sustained no slight persecution, were not to be despised; and because he had sworn to hold them firmly unless the most perfect doctors of the faith should say that the jurators might be absolved, who had before taken such oath, and that no further account was to be made of what they had sworn. Which, when the said bishop recited to the King, and perhaps the artificer of fraud was standing by, the voice of the crowd of arrogant courtiers was raised high, "See now the soldier is to give way to the sayings of clerks! The military order subjected to clerks is debased!" Thus the wisdom of the Earl was despised, and Edward is said to have answered thus, "They shall have no peace unless they put halters about their necks and deliver themselves up to us to be hanged or to be drawn." What wonder if the Earl's heart was then moved, when nothing but the pain of the stake was prepared for him? He offered what he ought to do, but was not listened to; the King rejected measure, forgetting what was good for him. But, as the event of the matter next day taught him, the moderation which he then refused, was afterwards not to be had. In the evening was derided the Earl's devotion, the shock of which was found, next day, to be victorious. This stone, long rejected from the doorway, was afterwards fitted to the two walls.[356] The division of England was on the verge of desolation but the corner-stone [356] was there as a help to the division, the truly singular religion of Simon. The faith and fidelity of Simon alone becomes the security of the peace of all England; he humbles the rebellious, raises those who were in despair, reconciling the kingdom, repressing the proud. And how does he repress them? certainly not by praising them; but he presses out the red juice in the hard conflict; for truth obliges him to fight or to desert the truth, and prudently he chooses rather to devote his right hand to the truth, and by the rough way, which is joined to probity, by the harder

[355] A reference to the *Provisions of Oxford*, 1258.   [356] Cf. 1 Peter 2: 1–8.

and shorter way which is unpleasant to the proud, to obtain
the reward which is given to those who use force, than to displease God by shrinking, and to promote the designs of bad
men by flight. For some men had studied to erase the name of
the English, whom they had already begun to regard with
hatred, against whom God opposed a medicine, since He did
not desire their sudden ruin.

Hence, let the English learn to call in strangers, if they wish
to be exiled by strangers. For these when they desire to en-
large their own glory, and are eager that their own memory stand
always, study to associate with themselves very many of their
own nation and by degrees to make them the principal nobles;
and thus grows the confusion of the natives, with indignation
and bitterness of heart, when the chief men of the kingdom feel
themselves to be beaten down by those who make themselves
their equals, taking from them the things which ought to appertain to them, growing by the things by which they used to grow.
The King ought to honor with escheats and wards his own
people, who can help him in various ways, who, by as much as
they are more powerful by their own strength, are so much the
more secure in all cases. But those who have brought nothing,
if they are enriched by his goods, if they are made great who
were of no account, such men, when they begin to grow, always
go on climbing till they have supplanted the natives; they study
to avert the prince's heart from his own people, that they may
strip of glory those whose ruin they are seeking. And who
could bear such things patiently? Therefore, let England learn
prudently to have a care, lest such perplexity should happen any
more, lest such an adversity fall upon the English. The Earl
studied to obviate this, because it had gained too much head,
like a great sea, that could not be dried by a small effort, but
must be forded by a great assistance from God. Let strangers
come to return quickly, like men of a moment, but not to remain. One of the two hands aids the other, neither of them
bearing more really the grace which belongs to both; let it help,
and not injure, by retaining its place.[357] Each thing would avail
its own possessor if they came so; the Frenchman by doing good

[357] Cf. Romans 12: 4; 1 Corinthians 12: 12–31; Ephesians 4: 25.

to the Englishman, and not seducing by a flattering face, nor
the one withdrawing the goods of the other, but rather by sus-
taining his own portion of the burden. If his own interest had
moved the Earl, he would neither have had any other zeal, nor
would he have sought with all his power the reformation of the
kingdom, but he would have aimed at power, he would have
sought his own promotion only, and made his first object the
promotion of his friends, and would have aimed at enriching his
children, and would have neglected the weal of the community,
and would have covered the poison of falsehood with the cloak
of duplicity, and would thus have deserted the faith of Christianity, and would have subjected himself to the retribution of
dreadful punishment, nor would he have escaped the weight of
the tempest. And who can believe that he would give himself
to death, that he would sacrifice his friends, in order that he
might thus raise himself high? If those who hunt after honor
cover their object cunningly, always meditating at the same
time how they may avoid death, none love more the present
life, none choose more eagerly a position devoid of danger. They
who thirst after honors dissimulate their aim, they make themselves cautiously the reputation which they seek. Not so the
venerable Simon de Montfort, who, like Christ offers himself a
sacrifice for many; Isaac does not die, although he is ready for
death; it is the ram which is given to death, and Isaac receives
honor.[358] Neither fraud nor falsehood promoted the Earl, but
the divine grace which knew those whom it would help. If
you consider the time and the place of the conflict, you will find
that they promised him a defeat rather than victory, but God
provided that he should not succumb. He does not take them
on a sudden by creeping stealthily by night, but he fights openly
when day is come. So also the place was favorable to his enemies, that thus it might appear plainly to all to be the gift of
God, that victory departed from him who put his trust in himself. Hence, let the military order, which praises the practice
of the tournament that so it may be made expert at fighting,
learn how the party of the strong and skilful was here bruised
by the arms of those who were feeble and unpractised: that

[358] Cf. Genesis 22: 1–19.

He may confound the strong, God promotes the weak, comforts the feeble, lays prostrate the firm. Thus let no one now presume to trust in himself, but if he know how to place his hope in God, he may take up arms with constancy, nothing doubting, since God is a help for those who are on the side of justice. Thus it was right that God should help the Earl, for without God he could not overcome the enemy. Of whom should I call him the enemy? — of the Earl alone? or should I recognize him as the enemy of the English and of the whole kingdom? perhaps also of the church and therefore of God? And if so, how much grace ought he to have? He failed to deserve grace who trusted in himself, and he did not merit to be helped who did not fear God. Thus falls the boast of personal valor and so for evermore be praised the Lord of vengeance who gives aid to those who are destitute of force, to a few against many, crushing fools by the valor of the faithful; who sits upon a throne above, and by His own strength treads upon the necks of the proud, bowing the great under the feet of the less. He has subdued two kings and the heirs of kings, whom he has made captives, because they were transgressors of the laws; and he has turned to shame the pomp of knighthood with its numerous retinue; for the barons employed on the sons of pride the arms which, in their zeal for justice, they had taken up in the cause of the kingdom, until victory was given them from heaven, with a great glory that was not expected. For the bow of the strong was then overcome, and the troop of the weak was established with strength; and we have said it was done by heaven, lest any one should boast of it; let all the honor, on the contrary, be given to Christ, in whom we believe! For Christ at once commands, conquers, reigns! Christ delivers His own to whom He has given His promise. We pray God to grant that the minds of the conquerors may not attribute their success to themselves, and let what Paul says be observed by them, "He who would be joyful, let him be joyful in God." [359] If any one of us indulge in vain glory, may God be indulgent to him, and not angry! and may he make our party cautious in future; lest deeds be wanting, may they make themselves a wall! May the power of the Almighty per-

[359] 2 Cor. 10: 17.

fect what it has begun and restore to its vigor the kingdom of the English people ! that glory may be to Himself, and peace to His elect, until they be in the country where He shall lead them. O Englishmen ! read this concerning the battle of Lewes by the influence of which you are saved from destruction; for if victory had gone over to those who are now vanquished, the memory of the English would have lain in disgrace.[360]

During the first half of the fourteenth century the best expression of the national movement is the commercial policy of Edward III, who sought to develop the woolen industry in England. For this purpose he imported Flemish weavers [361] to teach Englishmen their skill. Popular indignation was roused at this, so that to his Flemish protegés the King was forced to give bills of protection like the following:

The King to all bailiffs, etc., to whom these letters may come, Greeting. Know that, whereas John Kempe, of Flanders, weaver of woolen cloths, has come to dwell within our realm of England for the sake of exercising his craft therein and of instructing and informing those who wish to learn the same, and has brought with him certain men and servants and apprentices of that craft:

We take this John, his men, servants and apprentices aforesaid, together with all their goods and chattels, into our protection, and we promise to other men of that craft, as well as to dyers and fullers, wishing to come from across the sea to dwell within our kingdom for the same cause, that similar letters shall be granted. Witness the King, at Lincoln, the 28th day of July (1331?).

Pursuing the same policy, Edward sought to prohibit the exportation of wool, as Adam of Murimuth informs us in the following:

[360] The best reference for the national movement in the reign of Henry III is O. H. Richardson, *The National Movement in the Reign of Henry III* (The Macmillan Co., 1897).

[361] The skill in weaving of Chaucer's Wife of Bath is compared to that of Flemish weavers; cf. Chaucer, *op. cit.*, ll. 459–460.

The King summoned his Parliament for the Monday after the feast of St. Matthew the apostle,[362] and in this he made his eldest son, Duke of Cornwall, the Lord Henry, son of the Earl of Lancaster, Earl of Derby, the Lord William of Bohun, Earl of Northampton, the Lord William of Montagu, Earl of Sarum, the Lord Hugh of Audley, Earl of Gloucester, the Lord William of Clinton, Earl of Huntingdon, the Lord Robert of Ufford, Earl of Suffolk. These creations were made in the second Sunday in Lent, at Westminster; where also he made twenty-four knights. Also in the same parliament it was enacted that no wool growing in England should leave the realm, but that cloth should be made with it in England, and that all weavers of cloth should be welcomed in England wherever they might come from, and that fit places should be assigned to them and that they should have wages from the King until they could make fitting gain by their craft. Also it was enacted that no one should use cloth made outside England and afterwards imported, except the King and Queen and their children. From which statutes no results followed, nor did any one take the trouble to observe them.[363]

Edward's success against the Scotch and his early victories in the Hundred Years' War, coming after the progress of the thirteenth century, help to account for the events of the later fourteenth century, when the English language came into its own and English literature proved an adequate medium of expression for national feeling.[364]

IV. THE LINGUISTIC BACKGROUND

The Norman Conquest of England and its sequence is important in the history of the English language for three reasons: first, it reduced the status of English and made it the speech of a conquered race; second, it accelerated

[362] Sept. 21.
[363] For a modern writer on the woolen industry at this time, see Ashley, *The Early History of the Woolen Industry, Publications of the American Economic Association,* ii (1887), pp. 47–50.   [364] Cf. *post,* pp. 482–486.

the inflectional decay already apparent in late Old English; third, it brought many romance words into the English vocabulary. To the first of these facts we have testimony from contemporary writers; the other two come to light only after study of the language itself, first in its pre-conquest state, and then in its condition after the Conquest.

1. *The Status of English.* — In a previous reference to Henry of Huntington we have already seen that an understanding of Old English was not a part of the equipment of a cultivated man in the early twelfth century.[1] That English had a distinctly lower position than French in the early fourteenth century is indicated in the following passage from the *Chronicle* of Robert of Gloucester. Robert has just been describing the Norman Conquest and at the conclusion of his narrative says:

Thus came England into the hands of Normandy, and the Normans at that time could speak nothing but their own language. And they (still) speak French as they did at home and have their children taught so. Therefore, the upper classes of this land (England) who came of their (Norman) blood, (now) employ the same speech which was received from them; for unless a man knows French, he is little regarded. But men of lower rank hold to English, and to their own speech yet. I imagine that in all the world there are no countries that do not employ (one single, national) speech, except England alone. But people agree that it is best to know both (English and French), for the more a man knows, the more highly is he esteemed.

The nearly contemporary *Cursor Mundi* furnishes evidence to the same effect, as follows:

French rimes I hear commonly recited everywhere. A great many books have been written for Frenchmen. But what has been done for the one who knows no French? Nearly all the

---

[1] Cf. *ante,* p. 87.

inhabitants of England are Englishmen (i.e. they are of Saxon, not Norman lineage); and so it seems most necessary to speak (write) in the language that one will use most there. It seldom happened that the English tongue was praised in France, and we English will be doing French no harm if we do not praise it here. I am writing for ignorant Englishmen who will understand what I say.

But, because of the rising tide of national feeling already discussed, English began to gain a higher position, which fact is expressed in the statute of 1362, as follows:

Because it is often showed to the King by the prelates, dukes and earls, barons and all the commonalty, of the great mischiefs which have happened to divers of the realm, because the laws, customs and statutes of this realm be not commonly known in the same realm, for that they be pleaded, showed and judged in the French tongue, which is much unknown in the said realm; so that the people which do implead, or be impleaded, in the King's court, and in the courts of others have no knowledge nor understanding of that which is said for them or against them by their sergeants and other pleaders; and that reasonably the said laws and customs shall be the more soon learned and known, and better understood in the tongue used in the said realm, and by so much every man of the said realm may the better govern himself without offending of the law, and the better keep, save and defend his heritage and possessions; and in divers regions and countries where the King, the nobles and others of the said realm have been, good governance and full right is done to every person, because that their laws and customs be learned and used in the tongue of the country: the King, desiring the good governance and tranquillity of his people, and to put out and eschew the harms and mischiefs which do or may happen in this behalf by the occasions aforesaid, hath ordained and established by the assent aforesaid, that all pleas which shall be pleaded in his court whatsoever, before any of his justices whatsoever, or in his other places, or before any of his other ministers whatsoever, or in the courts and places of any other lords whatsoever within the realm, shall be pleaded, showed, defended, answered, debated and judged in the English tongue, and that they be entered and enrolled in Latin; and that the laws and customs of the same realm, terms and processes, be holden and kept as they be and have been before this time; and that by the ancient terms and forms of pleaders no man be prejudiced, so that the matter of the action be fully showed in the declaration and in the writ: and it is accorded by the assent aforesaid, that this ordinance and statute of pleading begin and hold place at the fifteenth of St. Hilary [2] next coming.[3]

John of Trevisa, translating the *Polychronicon* of Ralph Higden, comments thus on linguistic conditions in 1385:

There are just as many languages and tongues in this island as there are varieties of people. Yet Welshmen and Scots, who have not mingled with other nations, retain almost their primitive speech, unless it be that the Scots who were for a while in alliance with the Picts have been somewhat affected by the language of the latter. But the Flemings who dwell in Western Wales have abandoned their strange speech and use English. The English, though they had from the beginning three dialects, southern, northern and midland, as they came from three tribes of Germany, by mingling and fusion first with Danes and later with Normans, have spoiled their native language in many cases; and some employ strange stammering, chattering, snarling tones.

This degeneration of the vernacular is because of two things. One is that children in school, contrary to the usage and practice of other nations, are compelled to abandon their native tongue and to construe their lessons and exercises in French, and have done so since the Normans first arrived in England. Furthermore gentlemen's children are taught to speak French from the time that they are rocked in their cradles and play

---

[2] Jan. 14.

[3] But this law did not completely remedy the abuse aimed at. Archbishop Cranmer, in his *Answer to the Fifteen Articles* (1549), says, "I have heard suitors murmur at the bar, because their attornies have pleaded their cases in the French tongue which they understood not." — Cranmer, *Remains and Letters*, p. 170 (*Publications of the Parker Society*).

with children's toys; and country gentlemen imitate these others and try hard to speak French in order to get more fame.[4]

This was commonly the practice before the first plague,[5] but has since been somewhat changed. For John Cornwall,[6] a schoolmaster, changed the method in the Latin school and the translating of French into English; and Richard Pencrych learned that sort of teaching from him and others imitated Pencrych; so that now, in the year of our Lord 1385 . . . in all the grammar schools of England children are giving up French and learning and translating in English. The advantage is that they learn their Latin in less time than was wont to be true; but the loss is that at present children in grammar schools know no more French than do their left heels. This is too bad, especially if they are going abroad for travel. Besides, gentlemen have commonly ceased teaching their children French.

It seems a great wonder that English, which is the native language of Englishmen and their vernacular, has so many varieties (i.e. dialects) in this island; but that the language of Normandy, a strange tongue, has but one dialect among all the men who speak it properly in England. Nevertheless, there are as many sorts of French in the realm of France as there are of English in the kingdom of England. Further, as regards this English language, which is divided into three dialects and is spoken (pure) by very few people in the country, a remarkable thing has taken place; for the men of the East agree better with the men of the West in their speech sounds than do the men of the North with those of the South (i.e. Midland was taking the lead among the dialects). And that's the reason why the Mercians, who are Midlanders, as it were partners of the extremes, understand the neighboring dialects better than Northern and Southern comprehend each other. All language of the Northumbrians, and especially that at York, is so sharp, piercing, harsh and unpleasant, that we Southerners can hardly understand it. I believe that the reason for this difficulty is that the Northerners are near

---

[4] So far Higden, who died about 1364; the remainder of the passage is an addition by Trevisa.

[5] I.e. the first visitation of the Black Death; cf. *ante*, pp. 324–327.

[6] The same master is mentioned *ante*, p. 447.

to strangers and aliens who speak foreign languages; and also because the Kings of England live always at a distance from that country (the North); because they are more inclined to the South and if they travel northward do so with large numbers of followers. The reason for their being more in the South than in the North may be that (the South has) better agricultural land, more people, more noble cities and more useful harbors.

Thomas Usk, secretary to John of Northampton the Wiclifite Lord Mayor of London, wrote, during his imprisonment prior to his execution in 1388, *The Testament of Love*, long ascribed to Chaucer. In one of the opening paragraphs of this work, Usk states his opinion of the position of Latin, French and English in England as follows:

In Latin and French many sovereign wits have been greatly pleased to write and have perfected many noble things; but certainly there are some (in England) who write (a sort of) French poetry in which (real) Frenchmen would take as much delight as we do in hearing Frenchmen's English. And there are many words in English of which we Englishmen scarcely know the meaning. How then should a Frenchman born understand such words any better than a jay chatters English? It is equally true that the minds of Englishmen will not take in the sense of French idioms however much we boast of (our knowledge of) foreign language. Therefore, let clerks write in Latin, for they have an interest in science and are skilled therein; and let Frenchmen also in their French use their queer expressions for it is natural to them; and let us show our quality in such words as we learned in our mother-tongue.

2. *Specimens of the Middle English Dialects with Translations.* — We see that at least one Englishman of the period noticed the varieties of English spoken in the island of Britain. Modern scholars, however, differ from John of Trevisa in finding that the four dialects of the Old English

period persisted into the Middle English period. To these four must be added that of London, a sort of mixture of all, which was coming into prominence. We, therefore, include here five sets of specimens and translations. For the Northern dialect, the successor of the Old English Northumbrian, we have selected a passage from the *Bruce* of John Barbour, Archdeacon of Aberdeen in 1357. This long poem treats, in the manner of a romance, of the deeds and vicissitudes of Robert Bruce, a national hero from Scotch history of a time not long previous to the time of Barbour. In the passage selected, Bruce is reading to his men the *Romance of Ferambrace,* as they cross Loch Lomond.

> The King, the quhilis, meryly
> Meanwhile the monarch, in a merry mood
>
> Red to thaim, that war him by,
> Read to the faithful who with him stayed
>
> Romanys off worthi Ferambrace;
> The romance of the worthy Ferambrace;
>
> That worthily our-cummyn was,
> Of how that hero of the iron arms
>
> Throw the rycht douchty Olyver;
> By doughty Oliver was overcome;
>
> And how the Duk-Peris wer
> And how Duke Paris and ten other men
>
> Assegyt intill Egrymor,
> And one fair woman (there were twelve in all)
>
> Quhar King Lavyne lat thaim befor,
> Were in the mighty castle Egrimor
>
> With may thowsands then I can say.
> By King Lavyne and thousands of his men

And bot eleven within war thai,
Fiercely beseiged, and those few knights within,

And a woman: and war sa stad,
And that brave woman, were so sore beset,

That thai na mete thar-within had,
That they could taste no food but what they seized

Bot as thai fra thar fayis wan.
From their foul foes, yet never did they shrink:

Yheyte sua contenyt thai thaim than,
But the strong tower full manfully they held,

Thai thai the tour held manlily
Till that bold knight, Richard of Normandy,

Magre his fayis, warnyt the King,
Braving the foe, took warning to the King,

That wes joyfull off this tithing:
Who joyful was thereat, for he had feared

For he wend thai had all bene slayne.
That Paris had been slain with all the rest.

Tharfor he turnyt in hy agayne,
Full soon his gallant army in its march

And wan Mantrybill and passit Flagot;
Won Mantrybel, and crossing the Flagot

And syne Lavyne and all his flot,
Fell fiercely on Lavnye and all his fleet,

Dispitusly discumfit he:
And drove them from the place dispiteously,

And deliveryt his men all fre,
Freeing the gallant men within

And wan the naylis and the sper,
The castle.   And he won the nails and spear

And the croune that Jesu couth ber;
That pierced the Savior, and the crown of thorns

And off the croice a gret party
He wore upon the cross, and of the cross

He wan throw his chevalry.
A part he won, all through his chivalry.

The gud King, apon this maner,
With tales like these the good and kindly King

Comfortyt thaim that war him ner;
Gave comfort to his men and made them gay

Till that his folk all passyt was.
And brave at heart, till all had crossed the Lake.[7]

As a specimen of the Midland dialect, the successor of
the Old English Mercian, the *Dedication* to the *Ormulum*
has been selected.

Nu, brotherr Wallterr, brotherr min affterr the flaeshes kinde,
Now   Walter, my brother   in the   flesh,

Annd brotherr min i Crisstenndom thurrh fulluhht annd thurrh
    trowwthe,
And my brother in Christianity through baptism and through
    truth,

Annd brotherr min i Godess hus yet o the thridde wise,
And my brother in God's house still in a third fashion,

thurrh thatt witt hafenn takenn ba an regellboc to follyhenn,
Because we two   have taken   one rule of life to follow,

[7] This passage may be used to supplement those on the popularity of romance,
post, pp. 516–519. Throughout these passages *th* has been used in place of the character þ.

Unnderr kanunnkess had annd lif swa summ Sannt Awwstin sette;
In a   canon's station and life just as St. Augustine ordained;

Icc hafe don swa summ thu badd annd forthedd te thin wille,
I   have done   as   you desired and have executed your will,

Icc hafe wennd inntill Ennglissh goddspelles hallghe lare,
By translating into English the gospel's   holy   lore,

Affterr thatt little witt thatt me min. Drihhtin hafethth lened.
According to the (measure of) the little wit which my Lord has
     lent me.

Thu thohhtesst tatt itt mihhte wel till mikell frame turrnenn,
You thought   that it might indeed to great good   turn,

Yiff Ennglissh follc, forr lufe off Crist, itt wollde yerne lernenn
If   English   folk, for love of Christ, would learn it gladly

Annd follyhenn itt annd fillenn itt withth thohht, withth word,
     withth dede;
And follow   it and   fulfil it in thought, in word, in deed;

Annd forrthi yerrndesst tu thatt icc thiss werrc the shollde wirr-
     kenn,
And, therefore, you desired that I   this work for you should do,

Annd icc hafe forthedd te, acc all thurrh Cristess hellpe,
And I have done it for you, but all through the help of Christ,

Annd unnc birrth bathe thannkenn Crist thatt itt iss brohht till
     ende.
And it behoves both of us thank Christ that it is finished.

     Icc hafe sammnedd o thiss boc tha goddspelles neh alle
     I have gathered   in this book nearly the whole gospel

Thatt sinndenn o the messeboc inn all the yer att messe;
That is   in the massbook for a whole year;

Annd ayy affterr the goddspell stannt thatt tatt the goddspell
     menethth,
And always after the gospel   stands an interpretation,

Thatt mann birrth spellenn to the follc off theyyre sawle nede.
Which one should say   to the people for their souls' good. . .

Icc hafe sett her o thiss boc amang goddspelles worrdess,
I   have set here in this book among the gospel's words,

All thurrh mesellfenn, maniy word the rime swa to fillenn;
Quite on my own responsibility, words to make out the rime;

Acc thu shallt findenn thatt min word, eyywhaer thaer itt iss ekedd, ·
But you will find   that my words, wherever they are inserted,

Mayy hellpenn tha thatt redenn itt to sen annd t'unnderrstandenn
May help   those that read   it to see and to understand

All thess te bettre, hu theyym birrth the goddspell unnderrstann-
    denn.
All   the better, how it behoves them to understand the gospel.

Annd forrthi trowwe icc thatt te birrth wel tholenn mine wordess,
And therefore I trust that it will behove you to suffer my words,

Eyywhaer thaer thu shallt findenn hemm amang goddspelless
    wordess;
Wherever   you   find them among the gospel's words;

For whase mot to laewedd follc larspell off goddspell tellen,
For if one is   to tell the story of the gospel to ignorant people,

He mot wel ekenn maniy word amang goddspelless wordess.
He must add   many a word among the gospel's words. ·

Annd icc ne mihhte nohht min ferrs ayy withth goddspelless
    wordess
And I could   not always my verses with the gospel words

Wel fillenn all, annd all forrthi shollde icc wel offte nede
Fill out   , and for that reason alone I often was forced

Amang goddspelless wordess don min word, min ferrs to fillenn.
Among the gospel words to put my own, my verse to complete.

Annd te bitaeche icc off thiss boc, heh wikenn alls itt
    semethth,
And I beseech you with regard to this book, high duty as it
    seems,

All to thurrhsekenn illc an ferrs, annd to thurrhlokenn offte,
Completely to examine every verse, and to look through it often,

Thatt upponn all thiss boc ne be nan word yaen Cristes lare,
(To see) that in all this book there be no word against Christ's
   lore,

Nan word tatt swithe wel ne be to trowwenn and to follyhenn.
No word that it would not be very safe to trust and to follow. . . .

   Annd whase willenn shall thiss boc efft otherr sithe writenn
   And if any one wishes to transcribe this book,

Himm bidde icc thatt he't write rihht, swa summ thiss boc himm
   taechethth
Him   bid   I   that   he   write it right, just as this book directs
   him,

All thwerrtut affterr thatt itt iss uppo thiss firrste bisne,
Throughout according as   it   is in this first exemplar,

Withth all swillc rime alls her iss sett, withth all se fele wordess;
With just such rimes as here are used, with just as many words;

Annd tatt he loke wel thatt he an bocstaff write' twiyyess
And that he see to it well that he write a letter twice

Eyywhaer thaer itt uppo thiss boc iss writtenn o thatt wise.
Everywhere where it is written in that way in this copy.

Loke he wel thatt he't write swa, forr he ne mayy nohht elles
Let him look well to this, for otherwise he can not

Onn Ennglissh writenn rihht te word, thatt wite he wel to sothe.
Write the words correctly in English, let him be sure of that.

   Annd yiff mann wile witenn whi icc hafe don thiss dede,
   And if one wishes to know why I have done this,

Whi icc till Ennglissh hafe wennd goddspelless hallghe lare,
(Namely,) why into English I have turned the gospel's holy lore,

Icc hafe itt don forrthi thatt all Crisstene follkess berrhless
(Let him know that) I have done it because the salvation of all
   Christians

Iss lang uppo thatt an, thatt teyy goddspelles hallyhe lare
Depends upon this alone, that they the gospel's holy lore

Withth fulle mahhte follyhe rihht thurrh thohht, thurrh word, thurrh dede.
With   full   might   follow   right through thought, word and deed. . . .

Icc thatt tiss Ennglissh hafe sett, Ennglisshe menn to lare,
I who this English have written, to teach Englishmen,

Icc wass thaer thaer I crisstnedd wass Orrmin bi name nemm-nedd;
Was, when I was christened, named Ormin;

Annd icc, Orrminn full innwarrdliy withth muth and ec withth herrte
And I, Ormin, very sincerely, with mouth and also with heart

Her bidde tha Crisstenne menn thatt herenn otherr redenn
Here pray the Christians who hear or read

This boc, hemm bidde icc her thatt they forr me thiss bede bid-denn,
This book   that they for me offer this prayer,

Thatt brotherr thatt tiss Ennglissh writt allre aeresst wrat annd wrohhte,
That the brother who wrote the first copy of this English book,

Thatt brotherr forr hiss swinnc to laen soth blisse mote findenn.
For his labor as reward true blessedness may find.[8]

To represent the Southern dialect, Layamon's account from his *Brut* of the founding of King Arthur's Round Table has been chosen.

Hit wes in ane yeol-daeie that Arthur in Lundene lai;
It was on   a   holy day   that Arthur was in London;

[8] This passage may be used to supplement those already quoted to show the relatively low position of English about 1200. This is all that we know about Ormin, save that on the MS, which is one of the few Middle English autograph MSS. that are extant, is written, "This book is called Ormulum because Orm made it." It is easy to see that the *Dedication* to the *Ormulum* is an important document in the history of English spelling. Just how much weight, however, is to be given to Ormin's spelling is a matter of dispute. On the side of Ormin is Professor Emer-

tha weoren him to i-cumen of all his kineriche,
then were come to him   from all his kingdom (vassals),

of Brutlonde, of Scotlonde, of Irlonde, of Islonde,
from Britain, from Scotland, from Ireland, from Iceland,

and of al than londe the Arthur haefede an honde.
and from all the lands that Arthur had in hand.

alle the haexte theines mid horsen and mid sweines.
All the highest thanes with horses and with swains.

Ther weoren seoven kingene sunes mid feove hundred cnihten
    icumen,
There were seven kings' sons with five hundred knights,

with uten than hired the herede Arthure.
not counting the throng that Arthur commanded.

Aelc hafede an heorte leches heye,
Each had a heart looking high,

and lette   that he weore betere than his ivere.
and thought that he was better than his fellows.

That folc wes of feole londe, ther wes muchel onde,
The people came from many lands and there was much envy,

for the an hine talde haeh, the other muche herre.
because the one rated himself high, the next himself much higher.

Tha bleou mon tha bemen and tha bordes bradden;
Then they blew the trumpets and   spread the tables;

water me brohte an vloren mid guldene laeflen,
water men brought on floor in golden bowls,

seoththen clathes soften al of white seolke.
then soft clothes all of white silk.

Tha sat Arthur adun and bi him Wenhaver tha quene.
Then Arthur sat down and by him Guinevere the Queen.

son; see his *Middle English Reader, Grammatical Introduction, passim.* On the opposite side is the late Professor James Morgan Hart; see his *Development of Standard English Speech* (Henry Holt and Co., 1907).

seoththen sete tha eorles and ther after tha beornes,
Next sat the earls and thereafter the barons,

seoththen tha cnihtes al swa mon heom dihte.
then   the knights just as they were directed.

Tha heye iborne thene mete beoren
The high-born men then bore in the meat

aefne forth rihten tha to than cnihten,
even straight on then to the knights,

tha touward than theinen, tha touward than sweinen,
then to   the thanes,   then to   the swains,

tha touward than bermonnen forth at than borden.
then to   the porters   forth at the board.

Tha duguthe waerth iwraththed; duntes weoren rive:
Then the warriors grew angry; blows were rife:

aerest tha laves hoe weorpen tha while heo ilaesten,
first they threw the loaves while they lasted,

and tha bollen seolverne mid wine ivulled,
and the silver bowls filled with wine,

and seoththen tha vustes vusden to sweoren.
and then   the fists approached necks.

Tha leop ther forth a yung mon the ut of Winet-londe com;
Then jumped up a young man who had come from Winetland;

he wes iyefen Arthur to halden to yifle;
he had been given to Arthur to hold as a hostage;

he was Rumarettes sune, thas kinges of Winette.
he was a son of Rumarette, King of Winet.

Thus seide the cniht there to Arthur kinge,
Thus said the knight there to Arthur the King,

Laverd Arthur buh rathe into thine bure,
"Lord Arthur go quickly into thy chamber,

and thi quene mid the and thene maeies cuthe,
and thy Queen with thee and thy known relatives,

and we this comp scullen to-delen with thas uncuthe kempen.
and we shall settle this contest against these strange warriors."

Aefne than worde he leop to than borde,
Even at the word he leapt on the table,

ther leien tha cnives beforen than leod-kinge;
where lay the knives before the King;

threo cnifes he igrap and mid than anae he smat
three knives he seized and with one   he smote

i there swere the cniht the aerest bigon that ilke fiht,
in the neck the knight who first began that brawl,

that his hefved i thene flor haelde to grunde.
so that his head on the floor fell to the ground.

Sone he floh aenne other thes ilke theines brother;
Soon he slew another,   this same thane's brother;

aer tha sweordes comen seovene he afaelde.
before the swords came seven he had slain.

Ther wes faeht swithe graet; aelc mon other smat;
There was a great fight;   each man smote another;

ther wes muchel blod gute, balu wes an hirede.
there was much blood spilled, bale was in the crowd.

Tha com the king buyen ut of his buren
Then the King came out of his chamber

mid him an hundred beornen mid helmen and mid burnen;
with him a hundred nobles with helmets and with shields;

aelc bar an his riht hond whit stelene brond.
each bore in his right hand a white steel brand.

The cleopede Arthur athelest kingen,
Then cried Arthur,   noblest of kings,

Sitteth sitteth swithe elc   mon bi his live,
"Sit, sit quickly   each man by his life,

and wa swa that nulle don, he scal for-demed beon;
and woe to him that will not, he shall be fordoomed;

Nimeth me thene ilke mon tha this feht aerst bigon,
Bring   me the   man who this fight first began,

and doth withthe an his sweore and drayeth hine to an more,
and put a withy about his neck and drag him to a moor,

and doth hine in an ley ven ther he scal liggen.
and put   him in a   low fen where he shal lie.

And nimeth al his nexte cun tha ye mayen ivinden
And take   all his nearest kin that you can find

and swengeth of tha hafden mid breoden eouwer sweorden;
and cut   off their heads with your broad swords;

tha wifmen tha ye mayen ifinden of his nexten cunden
the women whom you can find of his nearest kin

kerveth of hire neose and heore wlite ga to lose;
cut off their noses and let their beauty go to ruin;

and swa ich wulle al fordon that cun that he of com.
and thus I will quite destroy the family from which he came.

And yif ich avere mare seoththen ihere
And if I ever more afterwards hear

that aei of mine hirede of heye na of loge
that any of my company, be he high or low,

of thissen ilke slehte aeft sake arere,
on account of this same strife ever raise a brawl,

ne sculde him neother gon fore gold ne na gaersume,
there shall go for him as ransome neither gold nor any treasure,

haeh hors no haere scrud, that he ne sculde beon ded,
fine horse nor finer garment, that he should not die,

other mid horsen to-dragen — that is elches swiken lagen.
or be drawn in pieces by horses — that is the law for every traitor.

Bringeth thene halidom and ich wulle swerien ther on,
Bring   the sacred relics and I will swear thereon,

swa ye scullen cnihtes the weoren at thissen fihte,
and so shall ye, knights who were present at this fight,

eorles and beornes, that ye hit breken nulleth.
Ye earls and barons, that ye shall not break this troth."

Aerst sweor Arthur athelest kingen,
First swore Arthur, noblest of kings,

seoththen sworen eorles, seoththen sweoren beornes,
then swore the earls and then the barons,

seoththen sweoren theines, seoththen sweoren sweines,
next swore thanes and next swains,

that heo navere mare the sake nulde arere.
that they never more would raise trouble (on account of this
    fight).

Me nom alle tha dede and to leirstowe heom ladden.
Men took all the dead and laid them in the burial place.

Seoththen me bleou bemen mid swithe murie dremen,
Then they blew the trumpets with very merry sound,

weoren him leof weoren him laed, elc ther feng water and claed,
were they lief, were they loath, each there took water and cloth,

and seoththen adun sete saehte to borden.
and then sat down reconciled at the tables.

al for Arthure aeige athelest kingen.
All this was for fear of Arthur, noblest of kings.

Birles ther thrungen, gleome ther sungen:
Cupbearers there thronged, gleemen there sang:

harpen gunnen dremen, duguthe wes on selen.
harps began to sound, the people were rejoiced.

Thus fulle seoveniht wes than hirede idiht.
Thus for a full week were the people treated.

Seoththen hit seith in there tale, the king ferde to Cornwale,
Then   it   says in the story, the King fared to Cornwall,

ther him com to anan that waes a crafti weorc-man,
where came to him one who was a skilled workman,

and thene king imette and feiere hine graette,
and he met the King and greeted him fair, saying,

Hail seo thu Arthur, athelest kinge,
"Hail, Arthur, noblest of kings,

Ich aem thin age mon, moni lond ich habbe thurh-gan;
I   am thine own liege, many lands have I travelled through;

ich con of treo-werkes wunder feole craftes.
I   know in carpentry many shifts.

Ich iherde suggen bi-yeonde sae neowe tidende,
I have heard over the sea   new tidings,

that thine cnihtes at thine borden gunnen fihte
that thy knights at thy table began a fight

a midewinteres daei; moni ther feollen;
on midwinter's day; that many fell there;

for heore muchele mode morth-gomenn wrohten,
that because of their great pride they wrought murder,

and for heore hehye cunne aelc wolde beon with inne.
and on account of their high lineage each would be nearest you.

Ah ich the wulle wurche a bord swithe hende
But I will make for thee a table very fine

that ther mayen setten to sixtene hundred and ma,
that will seat sixteen hundred and more,

al turn abute, that nan ne beon with ute,
Quite round, so that no one will be further away than another,

with uten and with inne, mon to-gaines monne.
without and within, man opposite man.

Whenne thu wult riden, with the thu miht hit leden,
When thou desirest to travel thou canst carry it with thee,

and setten hit whar thu wulle after thine iwille.
and put it where thou pleasest according to thy will.

and ne dert thu navere adrede to there worlde longen
And then thou wilt never need to fear to the end of the world

that aevere aeine modi cniht at thine borde makie fiht;
that ever any proud knight at thy table make a fight;

for ther scal the hehye beon aefne than loge.
for there shall the high be on a level with the low."

Timber me lete biwinnen and that bord begin;
Lumber they had brought and the table begun;

to feouwer wikene virste that werc wes ivorthed.
in four   weeks' time   the work was finished.

To ane heye daeie that hired wes isomned,
On a festive day the company was gathered,

and Arthur him seolf beh sone to than borde,
and Arthur himself came immediately to the table,

and hehte alle his cnihtes to than borde forth rihtes.
and invited all his knights to come at once.

Tho alle weoren iseten cnihtes to heore mete;
Then all the knights were seated at their meat;

tha spaec aelc with other alse hit weore his brother;
then each spoke with the other as if they had been brothers;

alle heo seten abuten, nes ther nan with uten.
they all sat in a circle, there was no one far away.

Aeveraelches cunnes cniht there wes swithe wel idiht;
Every sort of knight there was well cared for;

alle heo weoren bi ane, the hehye and tha laye;
all were on one level, both the high and the low;

ne mihten ther nan yelpe for othere kunnes scenchen,
no one could boast there of other kinds of drinks,

other his iveren the at than beorde weoren.
different from what his companions had, who were at the same
      table.

This wes that ilke bord that Bruttes of yelpeth,
This was that same table that the Britons boasted of,

and sugeth feole cunne lesinge bi Arthure than kinge.
and tell many sorts of lying tales about Arthur the King.

Swa deth aver alc mon the other luvien ne con;
So does every one who can not love another;

yif he is to him to leof, thenne wule he liyen,
(Or) if he is too dear to him, then he will lie,

and suggen on him wurth-scipe mare thenne he beon wurthe;
and give him a higher rating than he is worth;

ne beo he no swa luther mon that his freond him wel ne on.
there is no man so worthless that his friend will not do well by
     him.

Aeft yif on volke feondscipe arereth
Again, if among the people enmity ever arises

an aever aei time betweone twon monnen,
anywhere between two men,

me con bi than laethe lasinge suggen,
people can always say hateful things about the hateful person,

theh he weore the bezste mon the aevere aet at borde;
though he were the best man who ever ate at table;

the mon the him weore lath, him cuthe last finden.
the man who is hostile to him knows how to find him at last.

Ne al soth ne al les that leod-scopes singeth;
That which popular minstrels sing is not all false nor all true;

ah this is that soththe bi Arthure than kinge:
but this is the truth about Arthur the King:

Nes naever ar swulc king swa duhti thurh alle thing;
there was never before so doughty a king in every way;

for that sothe stond a than writen, hu hit is iwurthen,
for the truth stands in the writings how it happened,

ord from than aenden of Arthur than kinge,
from the beginning to the end of Arthur the King,

no mare no lasse, buten alse his lagen weoren.
no more, no less but just as his laws were.

Ah Bruttes hine luveden swithe and ofte on him liyeth,
But the Britons loved him well and often lie about him,

and suggeth feole thinges bi Arthur than kinge
and say many things about Arthur the King

that naevere nes iwurthen a thissere weorlde-richen.
that never happened in the kingdoms of this world.

inoh he mai suggen the soth wule vremmen
He who would tell the truth can tell enough

seolcuthe thinges bi Arthure kinge.[9]
strange things about King Arthur.

To represent the dialect of Kent the *Postscript* of Dan Michel's *Ayenbite of Inwyt* has been selected.

Nou ich wille thet ye wyte hou hit is y-went
Now I desire that you know how it came about

Thet this boc is y-write mid Engliss of Kent.
That this book is written in the English of Kent.

This boc is y-mad vor lewede men,
This book has been written for ignorant people,

Vor vader and vor modor and vor other ken,
For fathers and mothers and other kin,

Ham vor to berge vram alle manyere zen,
Them to protect from all sorts of sin,

That ine hare inwytte ne bleve no voul wen,
That in their consciences remain no foul stain.

"Huo ase God" is his name yzed
"Who as God" is his name interpreted (literally said)

That this boc made; God him give thet bread
That this book made; may God give him the bread

[9] This incident of the founding of the Round Table is an original addition to the Arthurian story on Layamon's part; his *Brut* is nearly twice as long as that of Wace, whose work he took as the basis of his own; Wace in turn had greatly enlarged the story of Geoffrey of Monmouth, his predecessor. (For biographical material about the three, cf. *post*, pp. 557–559; 579.) Layamon's *Brut* appeared about 1205; it runs to 16,120 lines and yet there are only 90 French words in it, a fact which shows how slow romance words were in coming into the English vocabulary.

Of angles of hevene and therto his red
Of the angels of heaven and in addition His counsel

And onderfonge his zaule huanne thet he is dyad.
And receive   his soul   when he is dead.

Ymende.   Thet this boc is volveld ine the eve of the holy apostles
Add: That this book was finished on the Eve of the holy apostles

Symon an Judas [10] of ane brother of the cloystre of sanyt austin of
Simon and Judas by a brother of the cloister of Saint Augustine of

Canterberi ine the yeare of oure lhordes beringe 1340.
Canterbury in the year   of our   Lord's   birth   1340.

To represent the dialect of London the *English Proclamation of Henry III* (1258) has been chosen.

Henri, thurg Godes fultume King on Engleneloande, Lhoaverd
Henry, through God's help   King in   England,   Lord

on Yrlonade, Duk on Normandi, on   Aquitaine, and Eorl on
in   Ireland,   Duke in Normandy and Aquitaine, and Earl of

Anjow, send igretinge to alle hise holde, ilaerde and ileawede, on
Anjou, sends greeting to all his faithful, learned and ignorant, in

Huntendoneschure: thaet witen ye wel alle thaet we willen and
Huntingdonshire: that   you may know well that we will and

unnen thaet thaet ure raedesmen alle, other the moare dael of
grant that which our councillors, or   the majority   of

heom thaet beoth ichosen thurg us and thurg thaet loandes folk
them who   are chosen   through us and through the   people

on ure kuneriche, habbeth idon and shullen don in the worthnesse
of the country in our kingdom, have done and shall do to the honor

of Gode and on ure treowthe, for the freme of the loande thurg
of God and our   truth,   for the benefit of the land through

the besigte of than toforeniseide redesmen, beo stedefaest and
the care of the aforementioned councillors, may it be steadfast and

---

[10] October 27.

ilestinde in alle thinge abuten aende.   And we hoaten alle ure
lasting   in all   things without end.   And we bid   all our

treowe in the treowthe thaet heo us oyen, thaet heo stedefaestliche
faithful by the troth   they owe us, that they steadfastly

healden and swerien to healden and werien tho isetnesses thaet
hold   and swear to hold   and safeguard the ordinances that

beon imakede and beon to makien, thurg than toforeniseide raedes-
have been made and are to be made, through the aforesaid coun-

men, other thurg the moare dael of heom alswo alse hit is
cillors, or through the majority of them just   as   it has

biforen iseid; and thaet aech other helpe thaet for to done bi
been ordered before; and that each help the other to do according

than ilche othe ayenes alle men riht for to done and to foangen.
to that same oath to do   right and act properly toward all.

And noan ne nime of loande ne of egte wherthurg this besigte
And let no one take any land or other property by which this

muge beon ilet other iwersed on onie wise.   And yif oni other
object may be hindered or jeopardized in any way.   And if any

onie cumen her onyenes, we willen and hoaten thaet alle ure
oppose this injunction,   we wish   and command that all our

treowe heom healden deadliche ifoan.   And for thaet we willen
faithful hold them as mortal enemies.   And since we will

thaet this beo stedefaest and lestinde, we senden yew this writ
that   this be   permanent and lasting, we send   you this open

open, iseined with ure seel, to halden amanges yew ine hord.
writ, sealed with our seal, to keep among you in your archives.

Witnesse us selven aet Lundene thane eytetenthe day on the
Witness ourselves   at London, the   eighteenth day in the

monthe of Octobre in the two and fowertiythe yeare of ure
month of October in the forth-second   year   of our

cruninge.   And this wes idon aetforen ure isworene redesmen,
crowning.   And this was done before   our sworn   councillors,

Boneface Archebischop on Kanteburi, Walter of Cantelow, Bischop
Boniface Archbishop of Canterbury, Walter of Cantelow, Bishop

on Wirechestre, Simon of Muntfort, Eorl on Leirchestre, Richard
of Worcester, Simon of Montfort, Earl of Leicester, Richard

of Clare, Eorl on Glowchestre and on Hurtford, Roger le Bigod,
of Clare, Earl of Gloucester and Hereford, Roger Bigod,

Eorl on Northfolk and Marescallon Engleneloande, Perres of
Earl of Norfolk and Marshall of England, Pierre of

Savveye, Willelm of Fort, Eorl on Aubemarle, Johan of Plesseiz,
Savoy, William of Fort, Earl of Albemarle, John of Plesseiz,

Eorl on Warewik, Johan Geffrees sune, Perres of Muntfort,
Earl of Warwick, John son of Geoffrey, Pierre of Montfort,

Richard of Grey, Roger of Mortemer, James of Aldithele, and
Richard of Grey, Roger of Mortimer, James of Aldithele, and

aetforen othre inoge. And al on tho ilche worden is isend into
before several others. And in just these same terms proclamation

aevriche othre schire over al thaere kuneriche on Engleneloande,
is made in every other shire in the kingdom of England,

and ek intel Irelonde.[11]
and also in Ireland.

3. *The Written Language.* — As regards this topic, all
we can do is to recall the anxious words of Ormin already
quoted [12] as to the copying of his text, and to cite the following passages from Chaucer. The first is his address to his
Troilus and Criseyde near the end of that poem; and the
second, his lines to Adam, his copyist.

Go, my little book, my little tragedy, to the place whence God
may yet send thy maker the power to write something comic!
But, little book, envy thou no poet, but be subject to all song;

---

[11] This *Procamation* refers to the *Oxford Provisions* of 1258; for a translation of
the text of the *Provisions*, see Adams and Stephens, *Select Documents of English
Constitutional History*, pp. 56–63. [12] Cf. *ante*, p. 492.

and kiss the steps when thou seest Virgil, Ovid, Homer, Lucan and Statius pass by.

And because there is so great diversity in English and the writing thereof, I pray God that no one miswrite thee nor "mismeter" thee for lack of proper words. And wherever thou art read, I pray God thou mayst be understood. . . .

Adam Scrivener, if it ever happen that you make another copy of *Boethius* or *Troilus*, may you have scab under your locks, if you do not copy my exemplar correctly. I have to go over your work so many times every day to correct and erase and scratch it out; and all my trouble is because of your negligence and haste.[13]

V. Literary Characteristics

1. *The Spirit of Literature 1066–1400.* — The two sorts of literature which bulk largest in the writings of the period 1066–1400 are the didactic and the romantic; and, if we are adequately to reflect the spirit of the times, these two must be reckoned with. As representative of the first tendency the proem to *Ancren Riwle* (*A Rule for Anchoresses*) has been selected.

"The upright love thee," [1] saith the bride to the bridegroom. There is a Law or Rule of Grammar, of Geometry and of Theology; and of each of these sciences there are special rules. We are to treat of the Theological Law, the rules of which are two: the one relates to the right conduct of the heart; the other, to the regulation of the outward life.

"The upright love thee,[2] O Lord," saith God's bride to her beloved bridegroom, those who love thee rightly, those are upright; those who live by a rule. And ye, my dear sisters, have oftentimes importuned me for a rule. There are many kinds of rules; but, among them all, there are two of which, with God's help, I will speak, by your request. The one rules the heart, and

---

[13] The best reference for the history of the English Language in the period is *The Cambridge History of English Literature*, I, chapter xix, and Bibliography.

[1] Cf. Song of Solomon 1: 4.   [2] Cf. 1 Timothy 1: 5.

makes it even and smooth, without knot or wound-mark of evil or accusing conscience, that saith, "In this thou doest wickedly," or, "This is not amended yet as well as it ought to be." This rule is always within you, and directs the heart. And this is that charity which the Apostle describes . . . "Out of a pure heart and of a good conscience and of faith unfeigned." [3] "Continue," saith the Psalmist, "thy mercy to them that know thee," by faith unfeigned, "and thy righteousness," that is, rectitude of life, "to those who are upright in heart," [3] in other words, who regulate all their wishes by the rule of the divine will; such persons are rightly called good. The Psalmist says, "Do good, O Lord, to those that be good, and to them that are upright in their hearts." [4] To them it is said that they may delight, namely, in the witness of a good conscience. "Be glad in the Lord and rejoice, all ye that are upright in heart," [5] that is, all whom that supreme law hath directed aright which directs all things rightly. Concerning which Augustine saith, "Nothing must be sought contrary to the rule of the supreme authority"; and the Apostle, "Let us all abide by the same rule." [6] The other rule is all outward, and ruleth the body and the deeds of the body. It teaches how men should, in all respects, bear themselves outwardly; how they should eat and drink, dress, take rest, sleep and walk. And this is bodily exercise, which, according to the Apostle, profiteth little,[7] and is, as it were, a rule of the science of mechanics, which is a branch of geometry; and this rule is only to serve the other. The other is as a lady; this is as her handmaid; for, whatever men do of the other outwardly, is only to direct the heart within.

Do you now ask what rule you anchoresses should observe? Ye should by all means, with all your might and all your strength, keep well the inward rule, and for its sake the outward. The inward rule is always alike. The outward is various, because every one ought so to observe the outward rule as that the body may therewith best serve the inward. Now then, is it so that all anchoresses may well observe one rule? . . . All may and ought to observe one rule concerning purity of heart, that is, a

---

[3] Cf. Psalm 36: 10. [4] Cf. Psalm 125: 4. [5] Cf. Psalm 32: 11.
[6] Cf. Philippians 3: 16. [7] Cf. 1 Timothy 4: 8.

clean unstained conscience, without any reproach of sin that is not remedied by confession. This the lady rule effects, which governs and corrects and smoothes the heart and the conscience of sin, for nothing maketh it rugged but sin only. To correct it and smooth it is the good office and the excellent effect of all religion and of every religious order. This rule is framed not by man's contrivance, but by the command of God. Wherefore, it ever is and shall be the same, without mixture and without change; and all men ought ever invariably to observe it. But all men cannot, nor need they, nor ought they to keep the outward rule in the same unvaried manner, . . . that is to say, in regard to observances that relate to the body. The external rule, which I called the handmaid, is of man's contrivance; nor is it instituted for anything else but to serve the internal law. It ordains fasting, watching, enduring cold, wearing haircloth and such other hardships as the flesh of many can bear and many cannot. Wherefore, this rule may be changed and varied according to one's state and circumstances. For some are strong, some are weak and may very well be excused and please God with less; some are learned and some are not, and must work the more and say their prayers at the stated hours in a different manner; some are old and ill favored, of whom there is less fear; some are young and lively, and have need to be more on their guard. Every anchoress must, therefore, observe the outward rule according to the advice of her confessor, and do obediently whatever he enjoins and commands her, who knows her state and her strength. He may modify the outward rule, as prudence may direct, and as he sees that the inward rule may thus be best kept.

No anchorite, by my advice shall make profession, that is, vow to keep anything as commanded, except three things, that is, obedience, chastity and constancy to her abode; that she shall never more change her convent, except only by necessity, as compulsion and fear of death, obedience to her bishop or superior; for, whoso undertaketh anything, and promises to God to do it as His command, binds herself thereto, and sinneth mortally in breaking it, if she break it wilfully and intentionally. If, however, she does not vow it, she may, nevertheless,

do it, and leave it off when she will, as of meat and drink,
abstaining from flesh or fish, and all other such things relating
to dress and rest and hours and prayers. Let her say as many,
and in such a way, as she pleases. These and such other things
are all in our free choice, to do or to let alone whenever we choose,
unless they are vowed. But charity or love and meekness and
patience and truthfulness and keeping the ten old commandments,
confession and penitence, these and such others, some of which
are of the old law, some of the new, are not of man's invention,
nor a rule established by man, but they are the commandments
of God, and, therefore, every man is bound and obliged to keep
them, and you most of all; for they govern the heart, and its
government is the main point concerning which I have to give
directions in this book, except in the beginning and in the concluding part of it. As to the things which I write here concerning the external rule, ye, as my dear sisters, observe them, our
Lord be thanked, and through His grace ye shall do so, the
longer the better; and yet I would not have you to make a vow
to observe them as a divine command; for, as often thereafter
as ye might break any of them it would too much grieve your
heart and frighten you, so that you might soon fall, which God
forbid, into despair, that is, into hopelessness and distrust of
your salvation. Therefore, my dear sisters, that which I shall
write to you in the first, and especially in the last part of your
book, concerning your service, you should not vow it, but keep
it in your heart, and perform it as though you had vowed it.

If any ignorant person ask you of what order you are, as
you tell me some do, who strain at a gnat and swallow the fly,
answer and say that ye are of the order of St. James, who was
God's Apostle, and for his great holiness was called God's brother.
If such answer seems to him strange and singular, ask him,
"What is order, and where he may find in holy writ religion
more plainly described and manifested than in the canonical
epistle of St. James?" He saith what religion is, and what right
order, . . ."Pure religion and without stain is to visit and
assist widows and fatherless children, and to keep himself pure
and unstained from the world." [8] Thus does St. James describe

[8] Cf. James 1: 27.

religion and order. The latter part of his saying relates to anchorites: for there are two parts of this description, which relates to two kinds of religious men; to each of them his own part applies, as you may hear. There are in the world good religious men, especially some prelates and faithful preachers, to whom belongs the former part of that which St. James said; who are, as he said, those who go to assist widows and orphans. The soul is a widow who has lost her husband, that is, Jesus Christ, by any grievous sin. He is likewise an orphan who, through his sin, hath lost the Father in Heaven. To go and visit such, and to comfort and assist them with food of sacred instruction, this, saith St. James, is true religion. The latter part of his saying relates to anchorites, to your religious order, as I said before, who keep yourselves pure and unspotted from the world, more than any other religious persons. Thus the Apostle St. James describes religion and order; neither black nor white does he speak of in his order, as many do, who strain at the gnat and swallow the fly, that is exert much strength where little is required. Paul,[9] the first anchorite, Antony [10] and Arsenius,[11] Macharius [12] and the rest, were they not religious persons and of St. James' order? And St. Sara,[13] Sincletica [13] and many other such men and women with their coarse mat-

---

[9] A more or less mythical Christian hermit, of whom we have a *Life* by St. Jerome.

[10] Founder of Christian monasticism. He was born about 250, retired from the world into the Egyptian desert about 270, and lived alone for about 35 years, at one time going for twenty years without once seeing the face of a human being. In 305, after repeated importunity, he became the leader of a body of monks and devoted himself to the instruction of them for five or six years. Then he withdrew to solitude again and died about 356 or 357. Most of our knowledge of him comes from St. Jerome.

[11] Saint and hermit, born about 354 at Rome, died about 450 at Troe in Egypt. He was the tutor of Arcadius, the son of Theodosius the Great, was well educated and lived in luxury until he was visited by a vision which directed him to leave the world. He obeyed and, withdrawing to the desert, lived, meanly clad, there for 55 years.

[12] Or Macarius, the Egyptian, one of the most famous of the early Christian solitaries. He was born about 300 and died about 390. He was a disciple of St. Anthony and founder of a monastic community in the Scetic desert.

[13] Not in the *Catholic Encyclopædia*.

tresses and their hard hair-cloths, were not they of a good order? And whether white or black,[14] as foolish people ask you, who think that order consists in the kirtle or the cowl, God knoweth; nevertheless, they may well wear both, not, however, as to clothes, but as God's bride singeth of herself, . . . "I am black and yet white," [15] she saith, "dark outwardly and bright within." In this manner answer ye any one who asks you concerning your order, and, whether white or black, say that ye are both through the grace of God, and of the order of St. James, which he wrote, the latter part, . . . that is, what I said before, to keep himself pure and unstained from the world; herein is religion and not in the wide hood, nor in the black, nor in the white, nor in the gray cowl. There, however, where many are gathered together, they should, for the sake of unity, make a point of sameness of clothes, and of other outward things, that the outward sameness may denote the sameness of one love and of one will, every one the same as another. Let them look well that they do not lie. Thus it is in a convent; but, wherever a woman liveth, or a man liveth by himself alone, be he hermit or anchorite, of outward things whereof scandal cometh not, it is not necessary to take so much care. Hearken now to Micah, God's prophet, . . . "I will show thee, O man," saith the holy Micah, God's prophet, "I will show thee truly what is good and what religion is and what order and what holiness God requires of thee. Mark this, understand it, do good, and deem thyself ever weak, and with fear and love walk with the Lord thy God." [16] Wherever these things are, there is true religion, and there is right order; and to do all the other things and leave this undone is mere trickery and deceit. All that a good recluse does or thinks, according to the external rule, is altogether for this end; it is only as an instrument to promote this true religion; it is only a slave to help the lady rule the heart.

Now, my dear sisters, this book I divide into eight distinctions, which ye call parts, and each part treats separately, without confusion, of distinct matters, and yet each one falleth in properly after another, and the latter is always connected with the former.

[14] Referring to the jealousy between the different orders of friars.
[15] Cf. Song of Solomon 1: 5.   [16] Cf. Micah 6: 8.

The first part treats entirely of your religious service.

The next is, how you ought, through your five senses, to keep your heart, wherein is order, religion, and the life of the soul. In this part there are five chapters or sections concerning the five senses, which guard the heart as watchmen when they are faithful, and which speak concerning each sense separately in order.

The third part is of a certain kind of bird, to which David, in the Psalter, compares himself, as if he were an anchorite, and how the nature of those birds resembles that of anchorites.

The fourth part is of fleshly, and also of spiritual temptations, and of comfort against them, and of their remedies.

The fifth part is of confession.

The sixth part is of penitence.

The seventh part is of a pure heart, why men ought and should love Jesus Christ, and what deprives us of His love and hinders us from loving Him.

The eighth part is entirely of the external rule; first, of meat and drink and of other things relating thereto; thereafter, of the things that ye may receive, and what things ye may keep and possess; then, of your clothes and of such things as relate thereto; next, of your tonsure, and of your works, and of your blood-letting; lastly, the rule concerning your maids, and how you ought kindly to instruct them.

In the course of Chaucer's Canterbury pilgrimage, the Monk described in the *Prolog* tells, of certain unfortunate historical characters, a series of stories highly edifying but increasingly tiresome to the Knight, who finally breaks out in protest. He had already told his splendidly romantic tale of Palamon and Arcite and from his criticism of his companion's effort, we can infer what the knightly standards of literary value were.

"Stop," said the Knight, "good sir, no more of this; what you have said is quite enough, indeed; aye, more than enough; for a little gloom goes a good ways with most people, I guess. Speaking for myself, I can say to me it is a great cause of uneasiness to hear of the sudden fall of men who have had great wealth and comfort. In fact, the opposite kind of story, namely that of a man who has been poor, has climbed up, become prosperous and staid so, is a great joy and solace to me. Such a thing is gladsome in my judgment and would be very goodly to tell." "Yes," added the Host, "by St. Paul's bell, you speak quite truly; this monk, he talked loud and told how 'fortune was covered with a cloud,' and of some sort of tragedy — I don't know just what — and, forsooth, of what use is it to bewail and complain of what's done; of course it's painful to hear of misfortune. So, sir Monk, no more of this, God bless you! your story bothers all this company; such talk is not worth a butterfly; for there is no joy nor pleasure in it. Wherefore, sir Monk, or Dan Piers, to call you by your name, I pray you tell us something else, for truly, were it not for the jingling of the bells that hang everywhere on your bridle, by the King of Heaven, I should have fallen asleep, however deep the ruts were. And, if I had, your story would have been in vain, for certainly, as old clerks say, 'If a man lacks an audience, he gains nothing by giving out his wisdom.' And I am sure that the responsibility is on me to take good account of all the tales. Therefore, sir, I pray you tell us a hunting yarn." "No," replied the Monk, "I have no inclination to merriment; let somebody else perform as I have."

Alongside of both the didactic and romantic literature of the epoch, there is a vein of thought that rebels against the higher ideals expressed therein, scoffs at them and turns them to ridicule. This thought finds voice in fabliau and satire, which often become coarse and risqué. Some of this is seen in *The Canterbury Tales* and Chaucer tries to anticipate censure by the following apology for this kind of realism:

But first, I pray you in your courtesy that you will not think I am a villein, if I speak plainly in this matter by reporting the words and expression of the pilgrims, even if I put them down just as they were. For you know this as well as I, that if you are going to repeat his story after a person, you must reiterate as closely as you can every word, if it is in your power, however rough and rude his speech may be. Or else your version will be untrue, or you will have to improvise or make a different story. You may not spare him though he were your brother; you may as well use one word as another, (for you are not ultimately responsible for the tale). Christ Himself spoke plainly in holy writ, and you know well, He was no villein. And further, Plato says — to any one who can read him — the words must be cousin to the deed. Also, I pray you, forgive me if I have in this work portrayed people just as they are — my wit is small, as you will understand.

Edifying literature, directly didactic or allegorical, romance and satire do not exhaust the medieval spirit. The lyric feeling for poetry persisted, often coming to merely incidental expression to be sure, but leaving its record in a small body of poems, religious and secular, which must be reckoned with in any adequate treatment of the period. In the following translation of a students' song, the persistence of the feeling for poetry is registered.

> Sweet in goodly fellowship
>   Tastes red wine and rare O !
> But to kiss a girl's ripe lip
>   Is a gift more fair O !
> Yet a gift more sweet, more fine,
>   Is the lyre of Maro (Virgil) !
> While these three good gifts were mine,
>   I'd not change with Pharaoh.
>
> Bacchus wakes within my breast
>   Love and love's desire,
> Venus comes and stirs the blessed
>   Rage of Phœbus' fire;
> Deathless honor is our due
>   From the laurelled sire:
> Woe should I turn traitor to
>   Wine and love and lyre !

Should a tyrant rise and say,
"Give up wine!" I'd do it;
"Love no girls!" I would obey,
Though my heart should rue it.
"Dash thy lyre!" suppose he saith,
Naught should bring me to it;
"Yield thy lyre or die," my breath,
Dying, should thrill through it! *

2. *The Technique of Vernacular Literature.* — The first discussions of the technique of vernacular literature are found in this period, crude, it is true, but indicative of awakening thought on the subject. We quote first Robert Mannyng's lines on the difficulties of rimed verse. It will be recalled that alliteration, not rime, was the technical feature of Old English verse.

Whatever they (i.e. the writers from whom I draw my stories) have declared in writing and speech, I have set forth in English, the simplest I could find and easiest to pronounce. I have not written for orators, reciters or harpers, but for the love of plain men who do not know difficult English. For there are many who do not understand hard English when they see it in rime; and if they do not know what a thing means, it seems to me its value would be lost. I did not compose my work to be praised, but that ignorant men might be helped. If it were written in tail, foreign, or interlaced (i.e. leonine) rime, there are enough English who could not get the clue to the meaning. Hence, . . . something would have been lost, so that many men who heard it could not follow the story. I hear works of Erceldoun [17] or Kendal sung or recited, but not in their original forms, so that the meaning is lost. You may hear the same in *Sir Tristram.* It is more popular than (any other) stories are or ever were, provided it is repeated as Thomas made it. But I hear no man render it without leaving out some of the rimes. So the labor and fair stories of former generations are well nigh lost.

[17] I.e. Thomas of Erceldoun or "Thomas the Rimer" (flourished 1220–1297), supposed minstrel author of *Sir Tristram* mentioned below.

* By permission of Messrs. Chatto and Windus, from their edition in the *King's Classics Series.*

They (i.e. men of former generations) said in their pride that none were such as they, and all their productions will now disappear. They wrote in such peculiar English that many a one does not understand it. And so I refused to work hard over strange rimes; especially, since my wit was too thin to travail in queer speech, and since I did not know such unusual English as they produced. And men begged me many a time to put (my stories) in easy rimes; they said that if I made them difficult many a one would refuse to listen; for there are extraordinary words that are not in use now. And, therefore, for the common people who would listen to me gladly, I began in easy language for love of the ignorant man, to tell the bold adventures which had been done and described here (in England). For this book I desire no other reward than good prayers when you read it. Hence, all you unlearned lords, for whom I have used this English, pray to God that He give me grace; I travailled for your comfort.[18]

Chaucer's Monk in the following gives us his idea of tragedy:

Tragedy is . . . a . . . story, as old books make us remember, of him who lived in great prosperity and has fallen from his high degree into misery and ends wretchedly. It is commonly written in six-foot verse called hexameter. But it is also written in prose and also in various meters in many different ways. . . . This account ought to suffice.[19]

3. *The Popular Literary Types.* — Professor Schofield's description of the contents of the "Auchinleck" MS., written between 1330 and 1340 will illustrate the state of

[18] The most convenient account of Old and Middle English meters and prosody in general is in *The Cambridge History of English Literature*, i, chapter 18 and Bibliography.

[19] My colleague, Dr. Robert M. Garrett, called my attention to the following in *Das Leidener Glossar* (*The Leyden Glossary*), p. 67 (ed. Glogger, Augsburg, 1901):

Tragoedia bellica cantica DE EUSEBIO
vel fabulatio vel hircania trago *enim* hircus.

Tragedy is a warlike song (FROM EUSEBIUS)
or a goatlike *story* — trago means goat.

literary taste in England 1066–1400. "This beautifully written and illuminated parchment," he says, "now in the Advocates' Library at Edinburgh, contains over forty distinct pieces, many short or fragmentary, others of great length. In disordered juxtaposition may there be found a number of legends of the virgin and various saints, a vision of purgatory, bits of Bible history, and paraphrases of Scripture texts, a didactic treatise on the Seven Deadly Sins, a Debate between the Body and the Soul, a Dispute between a Thrush and a Nightingale respecting women, and a fragment in their praise, a lone fabliau 'How a Merchant did his Wife Betray,' a chronicle of the kings of England, a list of names of Norman barons, and two satires on political conditions in the reign of Edward II. But the bulk is romance, and this of every provenience. The Carlovingian cycle is represented by the poems of *Roland and Vernagu* and *Otuel;* the Arthurian by the Breton lays of *Le Freine, Sir Orfeo, Sir Degare,* and the romances of *Sir Tristram* and *Arthur and Merlin;* English traditions by those of *Guy of Warwick* and his son *Reinbrun,* by *Beves of Hampton* and *Horn Child;* the matter of the East by an account of Alexander, and the originally Greek story of *Flores and Blancheflour;* together with the legendary romance of *Amis and Amiloun* and the Oriental collection of tales known as the *Seven Wise Masters.* Surely such a manuscript could afford pleasure to men in any mood, whatever their literary predilection." [20]

Following this clue, we shall first quote two passages to show the popularity of romance. The first is from *Cursor Mundi,* already [21] cited, and a highly significant testimony, because the writer argues from the popularity of secular romance that people would be equally eager to hear Bible and saintly stories, if they were put in equally interesting

[20] Schofield, *op. cit.,* pp. 14, 15. [21] Cf. *ante,* p. 482.

form. He proposes to try the experiment of giving religious material a romantic flavor.

People are eager to hear rimes and read romances of various sorts. (Thus, they delight in stories) of Alexander the conqueror, of Julius Cæsar the emperor, of the strange strife of Greece and Troy when many thousands lost their lives, of Brutus, that baron bold of hand, who first conquered England, of King Arthur who was so noble that he had no peer in his day. Of the wonders and adventures that befel his knights I know several stories; for example, those of Gawain, Kay and other braves and their defence of the Round Table. (I have heard) how King Charles (Charlemagne) and Roland fought — they would not make peace with the Saracens; of Tristram and his dear Iseult, how he became a fool for her; of Joneck and of Isambrase, of Ydoine and of Amadas. (There are) also several (other) kinds of stories of princes, prelates and kings; songs with strange rimes (in) English, French and Latin. Every one is intent on hearing the tales that please him best.[22]

To supplement this, the following more general passage from *Ywain and Gawain* may be quoted:

Sir Ywain went at full speed through the hall into an orchard, taking his maiden with him. There he found a knight lying under a tree on a cloth of gold. Before him sat a beautiful maiden. Another lady was with them and the maiden in that place read for them to hear a royal romance, but I do not know

[22] On the authority of Jean Bodel, a French poet who, toward the close of the twelfth century, wrote of the wars of Charlemagne against the Saxons, modern scholars have divided the romances into groups or cycles. Bodel, speaking of romance, says, "There are only three 'matters' to an intelligent man, those of France, of Britain and of Rome the great." The "matter" of France includes the romances of Charlemagne and his peers; that of Britain, the Arthurian stories; and that of Rome the great, all the romances of antiquity. It will be noticed that all three of these groups are represented in the names mentioned in this extract from *Cursor Mundi*. There are, however, other romances that will not fall into these groups. Hence, writers like Schofield (*op. cit.*, chapter v) make other groups, such as the matter of England and the matter of the Orient. There are still other isolated stories that come into no group.

what particular story it was. The girl was but fifteen years
old, the knight was lord of all that estate and she was his heir.[23]

The character of a tenth-century religious play, the connection of gilds with dramatic representations, Fitzstephen's
description of London amusements including religious plays,
and the attitude of some clerics toward miracle plays have
already been treated in these pages.[24] Here will be intro-

[23] Passages similar to this are to be found in Chaucer, *Troilus and Criseyde*, ii, ll.
82–84; *Sir Thopas*, ll. 186–189; *Nun's Priest's Tale*, ll. 391–393; *Havelok*, ll. 2320–
2335; *Squire of Low Degree*, ll. 75–82. A passage from Barbour, *Bruce*, iii, ll.
435–466, has already been quoted in another connection; cf. *ante*, pp. 487–489.
For an outline of the story of *Ywain* and *Gawain* see Billings, *A Guide to the
Middle English Metrical Romances* (*Yale Studies in English*, ix, 1901), pp. 154–
156. Baldwin, *op. cit.*, pp. 100–102, reprints Miss Billings' summary. For references for the study of the entire subject of medieval romance, see *The Cambridge
History of English Literature*, i, chapters 12, 13 and 14; Schofield, *op. cit.*, chapter
v; and Baldwin, *op. cit.*, chapters 2, 3 and 4. Mr. Baldwin's treatment gives one
some rather new points of view.

[24] Cf. *ante*, pp. 102, 103; 233–241; 316; 448 respectively. We shall here give
some references to show the persistence and development of drama from the tenth
to the fourteenth century. There was at Beverly in 1220 a play of the Resurrection. This play was outside the church. (Professor Gayley in *Plays of Our Forefathers*, p. 21, quotes the account of an incident which happened during the
production of the play. See his discussion.) Matthew Paris about 1240 refers to
religious plays, adding, "Miracula vulgariter appellamus." ("We commonly call
them miracles." See Morley, *English Writers*, iii, p. 116.) Bishop Grosseteste of
Lincoln wrote in 1244 a circular letter to his archdeacons on the conduct of the
clergy. Among the faults of the latter is the playing of miracles, Mayday plays
and harvest-home plays. (See Grosseteste, *Epistolæ*, Rolls Series, xxv, p. 317.)
This reference indicates that, to the Bishop at least, religious plays were not so
much marked as they once had been by that devotional character which Fitzstephen had assigned to them. The clerk Absolom in Chaucer's *Miller's Tale*
played Herod on a high scaffold. (*Canterbury Tales*, A ll. 3383, 3384.) There is a
reference in the same tale to Noah's difficulty in persuading his wife to enter the
ark. (*Ibid.*, ll. 3539, 3540. Cf. the Noah play in Manly, *Specimens of Pre-Shakespearean Drama*, i, pp. 13–30.) Among the pleasures of the Wife of Bath is going
"to plays of miracles." (*Canterbury Tales*, D l. 558.) The peculiarity of Pilate's
voice in the play became a byword. (*Ibid.*, A l. 3124. Miss Lucy Toulmin Smith,
in her edition of the *York Mystery Plays*, p. lvii, cites a passage from the *Apothegms*
of Erasmus on this same voice; it was "out of measure loude and high.") Wiclif, *De
Officio Pastorali* (*On the Pastoral Office*), chapter 15 (*English Works*, E. E. T. S. ed.,
p. 429) argues for the Bible in English and says that The Lord's Prayer in English

duced five further documents to illustrate the history of
the drama 1066–1400. The first is the proclamation of the
town clerk at York in 1394 of the annual Corpus Christi
festival. This document shows the conditions under which
such plays were given.

Proclamation of the play of Corpus Christi [25] to be made on
the vigil of Corpus Christi. Hear ye, etc. We command on
the King's behalf and that of the mayor and sheriffs of this
city that no man go armed in this city with sword or Carlisle
axe, nor with any other weapon in disturbance of the King's
peace and of the play, nor hinder the procession of Corpus
Christi. And that you leave your harness in your inns, save
knights and squires of worship who have their swords borne
after them, on pain of forfeiture of your weapons and of the
imprisonment of your bodies. And that the men who produce
the pageants play at the places that have been assigned for
that purpose and nowhere else, on pain of the fine heretofore
provided for that offence, namely forty shillings. And that the
men of the gilds and all other men who provide torches come
forth in such array and fashion as has been the custom and
wont before this time, not having weapons but carrying tapers
for the pageants. And officers that are keepers of the peace
(should do their duty) on pain of forfeiture of their franchise
and of bodily imprisonment. And all manner of craftsmen who
bring forth their pageants in order and course by good players,
well arrayed and openly speaking, on pain of losing a hundred
shillings, to be paid to the chamberlain, without appeal. And
that every player that shall play is to be ready in his pageant
at the mid-hour between the fourth and fifth of the morning
(i.e. 10:30 A.M.), and all the other pageants rapidly following,
each after the other, as their course is, without tarrying. Under
the penalty to be paid to the chamberlain of eight pence.

is given in the play of York. (Cf. *ante*, pp. 233–237.) In another place (*ibid.*, p. 206)
Wiclif speaks of playing "a pagyn (pageant) of the devil at Christmas." A passage
in *Piers the Plowman's Creed* puts haunting taverns and mixing in miracles in the
same category. (Ed. Skeat, ll. 106, 107.)
   [25] Corpus Christi Day is May 29.

The next document, an account of the cost [26] of the Corpus Christi pageant at York in 1397, when Richard II came to see it, will further illustrate the preceding topic, and will also indicate some of the properties used in giving the play.

Item: For coloring four robes for the work of the pageant	4s.
And for painting the pageant	2s.
And for a new banner with apparatus	12s. 2d
And for carrying material out to the gate to greet the King and bringing it back	2s. 1d.
And for 20 fir spars at said gate at meeting the King	5s. 10d.
And for 19 saplings bought of John de Craven for aforesaid gate	6s. 8d.
And to 8 porters bringing and moving the pageant	5s. 4d.
And to the janitor of Holy Trinity for looking after the pageant	4d.
To actors	4d.
To minstrels at the Feast of Corpus Christi	13s. 4d.
And for bread, venison pasties, wine and meat, and for neckcloths for the mayor and leading citizens on the day of the play	18s. 8d.
And to the minstrels of the Lord King and other lords who came in	7£ 8s. 4d.
And to the chamberlain for a red and white robe to receive the King in	58s. 10d.

That the status of actors at the beginning of the fourteenth century was somewhat dubious at least, is indicated in the following passage from the *Penitential* of Thomas de Cabham Bishop of Salisbury, who died in 1313:

There are three kinds of actors. Some (i.e. the first kind) transform and transfigure their bodies by base leapings and gestures, or by stripping themselves disgracefully, or by putting on horrible masks; and all such are damnable, unless they give up

---

[26] Chambers, *op. cit.*, ii, appendix w, prints many lists of accounts, but very few in the period 1066-1400 are itemized so that one can get from them any definite ideas as to the various items of expense.

their work. There are others who do nothing at all but act criminously, having no fixed abode, but they follow in the trains of magnates and tell indecent tales about absentees in order to please those present. Such also are damnable, because the Apostle forbids eating with such, and they are called scurrilous vagabonds, because they are good for nothing but stuffing themselves and telling evil tales. And then there is a third sort of actors who have musical instruments to delight mankind; and of such there are two varieties. Some frequent public drinking festivals and lascivious gatherings and sing there divers songs to move men to lust; and these are as bad as the others (described above). There are others called clowns who sing of the deeds of great men and the lives of saints, and comfort men in sickness or distress and perform innumerable tricks, as do the leapers and performers, male and female, and others who play in base costumes and make ghosts appear by incantation or other means. If, however, they do not do this, but, accompanied on their instruments, sing of the deeds of great men and of other edifying things that may comfort men, as has been said before, they may be supported, as Pope Alexander says. For when a certain clown asked him whether the soul of one engaged in such business could be saved; the Pope asked him in turn whether there was no other occupation by which he could make a living. The clown replied that there was not. Wherefore, the Pope granted that he might live by his trade (and be saved); provided he would abstain from the above mentioned lascivity and baseness. It should be noted that all sin mortally who give of their substance to scurrilous persons or lechers or the aforesaid actors. To give to actors is nothing but perdition.

In the passage regarding minstrels and plays already [27] quoted from *Handlyng Synne*, it is stated that the clergyman may reasonably take part in the play of the resurrection in order to impress the fact of Christ's rising upon the minds of the people. What this play was is seen in the following passage from an account of the ritual and ceremonies of Durham Abbey. The account should be

[27] Cf. *ante*, pp. 448–450.

compared with the Winchester trope translated and quoted above.[28]

Within the Abbeye Church of Durham, uppon Good Friday theire was marvelous solemne service, in the which service time, after the Passion was sung, two of the eldest Monkes did take a goodly large Crucifix, all of gold, of the picture of our Saviour Christ nailed uppon the crosse, lyinge uppon a velvett cushion, havinge St. Cuthbert's armes uppon it all imbroydered with gold, bringinge that betwixt them uppon the said cushion to the lowest greeces (steps) in the Quire; and there betwixt them did hold the said picture of our Saviour, sittinge of every side, on ther knees, of that, and then one of the said Monkes did rise and went a pretty way from it, sittinge downe uppon his knees, with his shoes put of, and verye reverently did creepe away uppon his knees unto the said Crosse, and most reverently did kisse it. And after him the other Monke did so likewise, and then they did sitt them downe on every side of the Crosse, and holdinge it betwixt them, and after that the Prior came forth of his stall, and did sitt him downe of his knees, with his shoes off, and in like sort did creepe also unto the said Crosse, and all the Monkes after him one after another, in the same order and in the mean time all the whole quire singinge an himne. The service beinge ended, the two Monkes did carry it (the crucifix) to the Sepulchre with great reverence, which Sepulchre was sett upp in the morninge, on the north side of the Quire, nigh to the High Altar, before the service time; and there lay it within the said Sepulchre with great devotion, with another picture of our Saviour Christ, in whose breast they did enclose, with great reverence, the most holy and blessed Sacrament of the Altar (the communion bread), senceinge (perfuming with incense) it and prayinge unto it upon their knees, a great space, settinge two tapers before it, which tapers did burne unto Easter day in the morninge, that it was taken forth.

There was in the Abbey Church of Duresme (Durham) verye solemne service uppon Easter Day, betweene three and four of the clock in the morninge, in honour of the Resurrection, where

[28] Cf. *ante*, pp. 102, 103.

two of the oldest Monkes of the Quire came to the Sepulchre, being sett upp upon Good Friday, after the Passion, all covered with red velvett and embrodered with gold, and then did sence (burn incense before it) it, either Monke with a pair of silver sencers sittinge on theire knees before the Sepulchre.   Then they both rising came to the Sepulchre, out of the which, with great devotion and reverence, they tooke a marvelous beauti-full IMAGE OF OUR SAVIOUR, representing the resurrection, with a crosse in his hand, in the breast whereof was enclosed in bright christall the holy Sacrament of the Altar, throughe the which christall the Blessed Host (the communion bread) was conspicuous to the behoulders.   Then, after the elevation of the said picture, carryed by the said two Monkes upon a faire velvett cushion, all embrodered, singinge the anthem of *Christus resurgens* (*Christ rising*), they brought it to the High Altar, settinge that on the midst thereof, whereon it stood, the two Monkes kneelinge on theire knees before the Altar, and senceing it all the time that the rest of the whole quire was in singinge the aforesaid anthem of *Christus resurgens*.   The which anthem beinge ended, the two Monkes tooke up the cushions and the picture from the Altar, supportinge it betwixt them, proceeding, in procession, from the High Altar to the south Quire dore, where there was four antient Gentlemen, belonginge to the Prior, appointed to attend theire cominge, holdinge upp a most rich CANNOPYE of purple velvett, tached round with redd silke and gold fringe; and at every corner did stand one of theise ancient Gentlemen, to beare it over the said image, with the Holy Sacrament, carried by two Monkes round about the church, the whole quire waitinge uppon it with goodly torches and great store of other lights, all singinge, rejoyceinge, and praising God most devoutly, till they came to the High Altar againe, whereon they did place the said image there to remaine untill the Ascension day. . . .

Over the (second of the iii Alters in that place) was a merveylous lyvelye (lifelike) and bewtiful Immage of the picture of our Ladie, so called the LADY OF BOULTONE, which picture was maide to open with gymmers (hinges) from her breaste downdward.   And within the said immage was wrowghte and pictured the immage of our Saviour, merveylouse fynlie gilted, houldinge uppe his handes, and houldinge betwixt his handes a fair large CRUCIFIX OF CHRIST, all of gold, the which crucifix was to be taiken fourthe every Good Fridaie, and every man did crepe unto it that was in that church at that daye. And ther after yt was houng upe againe within the said immage.

The grounds of clerical opposition to miracle plays are exhaustively and effectively stated in the following late fourteenth-century homily.

Here begins a treatise of miracle playing.

Know ye, Christian men, that as Christ is God and man and the way, the truth and the life, as says the Gospel of John [29] — the way to the erring, the truth to the ignorant and doubting, life to those who are weary from their struggle to reach heaven — , so Christ did nothing that was not effective in the way of mercy, in truth of righteousness, and in life by yielding everlasting joy for our continual mourning and sorrowing in the vale of tears. In the case of the miracles, therefore, that Christ did here on earth, either of Himself or through His saints, they were so effective and so earnestly done, that to sinful men that err they brought forgiveness of sin, setting them in the way of right belief; to doubtful men, they brought wisdom better to please God and a lively hope in God to be steadfast in Him; and to the way-weary, for the great penance and suffering of tribulation that men must have therein, they brought the love of doing charitable deeds, in comparison with which everything else is of little weight, and the willingness to suffer death, which most men fear, on account of the everlasting life and joy that men most love and desire, and the hope of which puts away all weariness here of the way of God. Therefore, since the miracles of Christ and His saints were so effective, as in our own creed we certainly state, no man should use in jest and play the miracles and works that Christ so earnestly wrought to our healing; for whosoever does so, errs in faith, rejects Christ and

[29] Cf. John 14: 6.

scorns God. He errs in the faith, because he takes the most precious works of God in play and jest, and so takes His name in vain and misuses our faith. Ah! Lord! since an earthly servant dare not make sport of what his earthly lord takes seriously, much more should we not make our fun of those wonderful things that God so seriously wrought for us; for truly, when we do so, fear of sin is taken away, as a servant when he fools with his master loses his fear of offending him, especially when he jokes about what his master takes seriously. And just as a nail driven in holds two things together, so fear driven toward God holds and sustains our faith in Him. Therefore, as playing and joking about the most serious works of God takes away that fear of God that men should have, so it also takes away our faith and the greatest aid to our salvation. And, since robbing us of our faith is more like taking vengeance than sudden death; and when we make light of the most serious works of God, such as His miracles, God takes away from us His graces of meekness, fear and reverence, and our own faith; when we play His miracles, as men do now-a-days, God takes more vengeance on us than does a lord who suddenly slays his· servant, because he was too familiar with him. And, just as such a lord then indeed says to his servant, "Play not with me but with your equals," so, when we make game of the miracles of God, He, taking from us His grace, says to us more earnestly than the aforesaid lord, "Play not with Me but with your equals." Therefore, playing such miracles is rejecting Christ; first, by giving way in the plays to our flesh, to our lusts and to our five senses; whereas God wrought wonders to the bringing on of His bitter death, and to the teaching of penance, and to the avoidance of cultivating the senses, and to the mortifying of them. And this is the reason why the saints notice that we never read much in holy writ about Christ's shrinking from anything, but only of His long penance, many tears and shedding of blood, in order to teach us that all our acts here should discipline the flesh and teach us to bear adversity. Hence, all that we do and are that is different from these three (i.e. penance, tears and shedding of blood) utterly reverses Christ's works, so that St. Paul says, "If ye be out of the discipline of

which all good men have been made perceivers, then are ye
adulterers and not sons of God." [30] And since miracle playing
is the opposite of doing penance, since plays are performed and
cast with great joy, miracle playing reverses discipline, for in discipline (or perhaps discipleship) the very voice of our Master Christ
is heard, as a pupil hears the voice of his master; and the word
of God in the hand of Christ is seen, at which vision all our
other senses tremble for fear and quake, as does a child at seeing his master's ferule; and the third in very discipline is the
turning away from and forgetting all the things that Christ
hates and turned away from here, as a child under discipline of
his master turns away from all the things that his master has
forbidden him, and forgets them, for the great mind he has to
do his master's will. And for these three writes St. Peter, "Be
ye humbled under the mighty hand of God that he may en-
hance you in the time of visitation, casting all your cares upon
Him." [31] That is, *be ye humbled*, that is to Christ, hearing His
voice, by very obeisance to His behests; and *under the mighty
hand of God* seeing evermore His staff in His hand to chastize
us if we wax wanton or idle, bethinking us, as St. Peter says,
that "hideous and fearful it is to fall into the hands of God on
high"; [32] for, just as it is the highest joy to remain in the hand
of the mercy of God, so it is most hideous and fearful to fall
into the hands of the wrath of God. Therefore, let us meekly
fear Him here, always seeing and picturing His staff over our
heads, and then shall He raise us up elsewhere in the time of
His gracious visitation. So that we do cast our cares upon Him,
that is, we do all our other earthly works — we are not bidden
do His spiritual works — trusting more freely and speedily and
pleasantly in Him who careth for us.[32] That is, if we do for
Him what it is in our power to do, He shall marvellously do for
us what it is in His power to do, both in delivering us from all
perils and in graciously giving us all that we need or will ask of
Him. And, since no man can serve two masters, as Christ says
in the gospel,[33] no man may hear at once equally effectively the
voice of the Master Christ and of his own lusts. And since

[30] Cf. Hebrews 12: 8.   [31] Cf. 1 Peter 5: 6, 7.
[32] Cf. Hebrews 10: 31.   [33] Cf. Matthew 6: 24.

miracle playing is of the lust of the flesh and mirth of the body, no man may effectively hear them and the voice of Christ at once, as the voice of Christ and the voice of the flesh are the calls of two contrary lords; and so miracle playing nullifies discipline, for as St. Paul said, "Every real discipline in the time that now is, is not a joy but a mourning." [34] Also, since it makes us see vain sights of disguise, array of men and women by evil continence, each urging the other to lechery and contention, as after most bodily mirth comes the greatest contention, as such mirth unfits a man for patience and inclines him to gluttony and other vices, . . . it does not allow a man to concentrate his entire attention on the staff of God over his head, but makes him keen for all such things as Christ by the deeds of His passion bade us forget. Hence, such miracle-playing, in its effects on penance, on discipline and on patience, nullifies the behests of Christ and His deeds. Also, such miracle-playing is scorning of God, for, just as intentional omission of what He bids is despising God, as did Pharaoh, so jestingly taking God's bidding or words or works is scorning Him, as did the Jews that mocked Christ. Therefore, since these miracle plays take in mockery the serious works of God, no doubt they scorn God, as did the Jews that mocked Christ, for they laughed at His passion as these latter laugh and mock at the miracles of God. Hence, as the former scorned Christ, so these latter scorn God, and, just as Pharaoh, wroth to do what God commanded him, despised God, so these miracle players and maintainers, pleasantly omitting to do what God bids them, scorn Him. He, forsooth, has bidden us all hallow His name, rendering fear and dread with our whole mind for His works, without any jesting or mockery, as all holiness is in men thoroughly in earnest; hence, in playing the name of God's miracles, as the actors pleasantly omit to do what God bids them, they scorn His name and so Himself.

But, in opposition to these considerations, men say that they play these miracles for the worship of God, and thus are different from the Jews who mocked Christ. Also, they say, men are frequently by such plays converted to good living, since men and women see in these spectacles that the devil, by their array

[34] Cf. Hebrews 12: 11.

through which they entice each other to lechery and pride, makes them his servants in bringing themselves and many others to hell, whence they will have a far worse time hereafter by their proud array here than they have honor here. And then they also reflect that all this worldly life here is but vanity for a while, like the plays, and come to leave their pride and take upon themselves the meek conversation of Christ and His saints. For this reason, they say, miracle plays turn men to faith and do not pervert them. Also, they continue, frequently through such plays men and women, seeing the passion of Christ and of His saints, are moved to compassion and devotion, weeping bitter tears, so that they do not scorn God but worship Him. And then (they add that it is) profitable to men and to the worship of God to exhibit and set forth all the means by which men may see sin and be drawn to virtue; and that, as there are men who will be converted to God by means of serious deeds only, so there are others that prefer to be converted in jest and sport; so that it is a convenient time to try to convert the people by games and plays, such as miracle plays and other sorts of mirth. Also, they say, men must have some recreation, and it is better, or at least, less bad for them to have their recreation in playing miracles than in playing other sorts of things. Also, (they argue) since it is permissible to have the miracles of God painted, why is it not equally proper to have them played, since men may better read the will of God and His marvellous works in the representation of them on the stage than in paintings, and better that they be held in men's mind and often repeated in plays rather than in paintings, for painting is a dead book whereas acting is a lively one?

To the first argument we reply that such miracles are not played to the worship of God, for they are performed more to be seen of the world and to please the world than to be seen of God or to please Him; as Christ never gave us example of them, but they are a heathen institution, the work of men who ever dishonored God, saying that to the worship of God which ever vilifies Him; therefore, as the wickedness of heathen disbelief lies to itself when they say that their idolatry is to the worship of God, so men's desire now-a-days to follow their own lusts lies to itself when they say that such miracle plays are for the worship of God. For Christ says that adulterers seek such signs, as a rake seeks signs of love, but no deeds of love; so, since these plays are only empty signs of love with no deeds, they are not only contrary to the worship of God, in both sign and deed, but they are traps of the devil to catch men to believe in anti-Christ, as words of love without the reality are tricks of a rake to secure a partner in fulfilling his evil desire. Both because these miracles are mere lies, since they are signs without deeds, and because they are pure vanity since they take the miracles of God in vain according to their own lust — and certainly lying and vanity are the most effective schemes of the devil to draw men to believe in anti-Christ — . . . it is forbidden to priests not only to take part in miracle plays, but even to see or hear them, lest they who should be the tackle of God to catch men for and hold them in the faith of Christ, should be made, on the contrary, through hypocrisy the tools of the devil to secure men for belief in anti-Christ. Therefore, just as a man, swearing in vain by the names of God, and saying that he worships God and despises the devil whereas he lyingly does the reverse, so players of miracles, as they are idle workers though they say that they do it to the worship of God, vainly lie; for, as says the gospel, "Not he that says Lord! Lord! shall come to the bliss of heaven, but he that doeth the will of the Father of Heaven shall come to His kingdom." [35] So much more, not he that plays the will of God worships Him, but only he that does His will in deed. As, therefore, men by feigned tokens beguile and really despise their neighbors, so by such feigned miracles men beguile themselves and despise God, like the tormentors who mocked Christ.

And as anent the second argument, we say that just as a virtuous deed is sometimes the occasion of evil, like the passion of Christ to the Jews, an occasion not given them but taken by them, so evil deeds once in a while are the occasion of good, as for example, the sin of Adam was the occasion of the coming of Christ, not given by sin but offered by the great mercy of God. Likewise, miracle playing, though it be a sin, may happen to

[35] Cf. Matthew 7: 17.

be the opportunity of converting men, but, as it is a sin, it is far more often the occasion for perverting them, not only in the case of individuals but in that of whole communities, as it causes a whole people to be occupied in vanity contrary to the behest of the Psalter, which says to all men and especially to priests who read it every day in their service, "Turn away thine eyes that they see not vanities," [36] and again, "Lord, thou hast hated all waiting vanities." [37]   How, then, may a priest play in interludes, or give himself to the sight of them? since it is so expressly forbidden him by the foresaid command of God; namely since he curses every day in his service all those that turn away from the commands of God; but alas a greater shame is it that priests now-a-days must curse themselves all day — at least as many as cry, "Watt, shrew," [38] cursing themselves. Thus, miracle playing, since it is against the command of God that directs us not to take God's name in vain, is against our faith, and, hence, cannot give occasion for turning men to faith but must turn them away; and for this reason many men imagine that there is no hell of everlasting pain, but that God merely threatens us and will not punish us indeed, as miracle plays are only shows and not realities.   Therefore, these plays pervert not only our faith but also our hope in God, by which saints trusted that the more they abstained from such plays, the greater reward they should have from God; and, therefore, holy Sara, the daughter of Raguel, hoping for high meed from God, said, "Lord, thou knowest that I never coveted man and have kept myself clean from all lusts and have never mingled with players," [39] and by this true confession to God, as she hoped, had her prayers heard and obtained great reward from God; and, since a young woman of the Old Testament, to keep her bodily virtue of chastity and worthily to enter into the sacrament of matrimony when her time should come, abstained from all manner of idle playing and from all company of idle players, much more a priest of the New Testament, who has

[36] Cf. Psalm 119: 37.   [37] Cf. Psalm 31: 6.

[38] This must have been a remark in one of the miracle plays.

[39] Sara, daughter of Raguel, a character in the apocryphal book of Tobit; cf. chapter 3: 14, 15.

passed the time of his youth and should keep not only his chastity but all other virtues, and minister not only the sacrament of matrimony but all the others, and especially is bound to minister to all the people the precious body of Christ, ought to abstain from all idle playing both of miracles and of everything else. For surely, since the Queen of Sheba, as says Christ in the gospel, shall condemn the Jews who would not receive the wisdom of Christ,[40] much more this holy woman Sara, at the day of doom, shall condemn those priests of the New Testament who give themselves to plays, falsifying the holy manners approved by God and Holy Church; therefore, priests ought to be very much ashamed who turn to shame this good holy woman and the holy body of Christ which they take in their hands, the which body never gave itself to play but only to such things as are contrary to play, such as penance and the suffering of persecution. And so this miracle playing not only reverses faith and hope, but very charity, by which a man should wail for his own sins and those of his neighbors, and especially those of priests; for miracle playing withdraws not only one person but all the community from deeds of charity and penance unto deeds of lust and such things and feeding our wits. So then, these men who say, "Let us play a play of anti-Christ and of the day of doom that some men be converted thereby," fall into the heresy of those that reverse the apostle and say, "Let us do evil that good may come," [41] to condemn whom, as the apostle says, is righteous.

We answer the third argument as follows, saying that such miracle playing gives no occasion for genuine and necessary weeping, but that the weeping that befals men and women at plays is not principally because of true inward sorrow for their sins, nor in good faith, but comes from what they see outside them (i.e. the play). Sorrow before God is not allowable but rather to be reproved; for, since God Himself reproved the women that wept over Him in His passion,[42] much more are they to be reproved who weep over the mere play of Christ's passion, ceasing to weep for the sins of themselves and their children, as Christ bade the women who wept over Him.

[40] Cf. Matthew 12: 42.   [41] Cf. Romans 3: 8.   [42] Cf. John 20: 11–18.

And by this we answer the fourth argument, saying that no man can be converted except by the earnest effort of God and not by vain playing; for what the Word of God or His sacraments cannot bring about, can hardly be effected by playing which has no virtue but is full of error. Therefore, just as the tears that men often shed at such plays are commonly feigned, witnessing that they love the pleasure of their bodies and their worldly prosperity more than God and the prosperity of their souls, and, therefore, have more compassion for pain than for sin, they falsely weep for lack of worldly prosperity rather than for lack of spiritual well-fare, as do those who are damned in hell; just so oftentimes the conversion that men seem to experience after such exhibitions is but feigned holiness, worse than is other earlier sin. For if he were truly converted, he would hate to see all such vanity as the commands of God forbid, even if through such a play he take occasion by the grace of God to flee sin and follow virtue. And if any man say here, "If this playing of miracles were sin, why does God convert men thereby," we should answer that He does so to commend His mercy to us, that we may think how utterly good to us He is. Because, while we are thinking against Him, doing idly and withstanding Him, He thinks of mercies for us and sends us His grace to flee from all such vanity. And because there should be nothing sweeter to us than that sort of divine mercy, the Psalter calls this mercy the blessing of sweetness, where it says, "Thou camest before him in the blessing of sweetness," [43] which sweetness, although very pleasant to the spirit, is very troublesome to the body, if it is genuine; as flesh and spirit are rivals, this sweetness in God cannot be experienced while a man is occupied with seeing a play. Therefore, the priests that call themselves holy and busy themselves with such play are very hypocrites and liars.

And we answer the fifth argument in this way, saying that real recreation is faithful occupation in false works in order the more ardently to do greater, and, therefore, such miracle playing or the seeing of plays is not real recreation but a false and worldly sort, as the deeds of the patrons of such plays

[43] ?

prove. For they have never tasted divine sweetness, travailing so much therein that their body would not suffice to bear such a travail of the spirit. But as one goes from virtue to virtue, they go from lust to lust, so that they dwell the more steadfastly in them, and, therefore, as this feigned recreation of playing miracles is a false conceit, so it is double villainy, worse than though they played pure vanity. For now the people give credence to many mingled falsehoods, for other mingled truths, and make out that to be good which is evil; and so oft times it would be less ill if they played ribaldry than if they played miracles. And if men ask what recreation men should have on the holiday after their holy contemplation in the church, we say to them two things; one, that if they had really occupied themselves in contemplation before, they would neither ask this question, nor desire to see vanity; the second, that his recreation should be in works of mercy to his neighbor and in delighting himself in all good conversation with his neighbor, as before he delighted himself in God, and in all necessary works that reason and nature demand.

And to the last argument, we say that painting, if it be truthful and not mixed with falsehood, and not too anxious to feed men's senses, and not an occasion of idolatry to the people, is but as plain letters to a clerk in reading the truth. But such is not the case with miracle plays which are made rather to delight people physically than as books for the ignorant; and, therefore, if they are lively books, they are rather books that teach wickedness than books that teach goodness. Hence, good men, seeing that their time is too short for even their serious activity, and feeling that the day of reckoning is coming on fast, and not knowing when they shall go hence, flee all such idleness, yearning to be with their spouse Christ in the bliss of heaven.

Some half-friendly delayer of his soul's health, ready to excuse the evil and, like Thomas of India,[44] hard to convince, says that he will not accept the foregoing condemnation of miracle

[44] I.e. Thomas the Apostle, who, according to some non-canonical gospels and legendary lives, was the apostle of India. For Thomas' skeptical spirit see John 14: 5; 20: 25, 27, 28.

plays unless men show him plainly that according to holy writ
they are contrary to our faith. Wherefore, in order that his
half friendship may become complete, we beg him to consider
first . . . the second commandment, where God says, "Thou
shalt not take the name of the Lord thy God in vain." [45] And,
since the marvellous works of God are His name as the good
works of a craftsman make his reputation, . . . it is in this
commandment forbidden to take the wonders of God in vain.
And how may they be more taken in vain than where they are
made the instruments of men's jests, as when they are played
by mummers? And since God wrought His works in earnest,
we should take them earnestly; otherwise, forsooth, we take
them in vain. Reflect then, friend, and determine whether
your faith declares that God performed His miracles in order
that we might play them. No, it says to you, "He wrought
them in order that you might fear and love Him." And certainly great fear and fervent love do not allow playing or joking with Him. Thus, since plays reverse the will of God and
the end for which He wrought His wonders for us, there is no
doubt but that miracle playing is really taking God's name in
vain. And if this isn't enough for you, though it would satisfy
a heathen who, therefore, will not represent his idolatry on the
stage, I beg you to read in the Book of Life, that is Christ
Jesus, and see if you can see in Him that He gave us example
of taking part in plays. No, He was just the opposite and our
faith curses whatever leads us to exceed or fail to reach what
Christ gave us the pattern for doing. How, then, dare you say
yourself that you will believe nothing but what can be shown
to be a part of our faith? And, since in matters that please the
natural man, such as plays, you will not try to repress them
unless it can be proved by the faith to be necessary, much more
in things of the spirit — always exemplified in the life of Christ
and so fully written in the Book of Life, such as ceasing to play
miracles and putting away all jesting — you should not hold
against it, unless it can be shown to be contrary to the faith,
in as much as in all doubtful matters one should stand with the
party that is more favorable to the Spirit and comes closer to

[45] Cf. Exodus 20: 7.

the example of Christ. And just as every falsehood and every sin destroys itself, so your answer refutes itself, and, hence, you may well know that it is not true but thoroughly unnatural. For, if you had a father who had suffered a degrading death in order to secure your heritage for you, and you, afterward, should unthinkingly burn up the documentary evidence of your owner-ship in order to make a spectacle for your self, there is no doubt but that all good men would deem you unnatural. Much more, God and all His saints deem all those Christians unnatural who play or applaud the play of the death or miracles of the most kind father Christ who died in order to bring men to the ever-lasting heritage of heaven.

But, peradventure, you will say here that even if producing plays is a sin, . . . it is a small one. But be sure, dear friend, that every sin, be it never so small, if it is maintained and preached as good and profitable, is deadly; and, therefore, the prophet says, "Woe to them that call good evil and evil, good!" [46] and, therefore, the wise man condemns those who rejoice when they do evil; and, therefore, all saints say that it is human to fall, but diabolical to remain fallen. Hence, since this falling is sin, as you acknowledge, and is firmly maintained and people delight in it, there is no doubt that it is deadly sin, worthy of condemnation, diabolical, not human. Lord, since Adam and Eve and all mankind were driven out of Paradise, not only for eating the apple but also for trying to conceal their sin, much more miracle playing, not only defended but steadfastly main-tained, is damnable and mortal, since it perverts not only one man but a whole people, who call good evil and evil, good. And, if this will not satisfy you, although it should be enough for every Christian that nothing should be done beyond the doctrine that Christ taught, consider what God did in the case where we read that at the command of God, because Ishmael played with his brother Isaac,[47] both Ishmael and his mother were cast out of the house of Abraham. The reason for this was that by such playing Ishmael, who was the son of a servant, might have beguiled Isaac out of his heritage; and Isaac was the son of the free wife of Abraham. Another reason was that, since

[46] Cf. Isaiah 5: 20.   [47] Cf. Genesis 21: 9–14.

Ishmael was born after the flesh and Isaac after the spirit, as the apostle says,[48] it was an example that the play of the flesh is not agreeable nor helpful to the spirit, but conduces to the taking away of the spirit's heritage. And a third reason was to prefigure that the Old Testament, which is the covenant of the flesh, may not be ranked with the New Testament, which is the covenant of the spirit; and if the former be kept equally with the latter, real freedom is abrogated and the heritage of heaven nullified. Hence, since the play of Ishmael with Isaac was not lawful, much more carnal jesting with the spiritual works of Christ and His saints is not lawful, for His miracles were intended to convert men to faith, since there is far more contradiction between carnal play and the serious deeds of Christ than between the estate of Ishmael and that of Isaac, and also since the play of Ishmael and Isaac was a symbol of the war between flesh and spirit. Therefore, as two things of entirely opposite nature cannot come together without harm to each, as experience teaches, and that party will do harm that has the stoutest attack, and that will be most hurt that is weakest, so playing, which is carnal, with the works of the spirit is to the detriment of both body and soul, and the body will do most harm to the soul, since in such plays the body is most prominent. . . . And, as in good things the thing symbolized is always better than the symbol, so in evil things the thing symbolized is always worse than the symbol, since the jesting of Ishmael with Isaac is the symbol of the dance the body leads the spirit, and the symbol is evil, the thing symbolized is far worse. Consequently, playing with the miracles of God deserves heavier vengeance — and is a greater sin — than the jesting of Ishmael with Isaac deserved — which was a smaller sin; and, as the companionship of a thrall with his lord makes the master despised, so much more fooling with the miracles of God makes them despised, for play-acting in comparison with the miracles of God is far more churlish than can be the relation of any servant to his lord; and, hence, the playing of Ishmael, who was the son of a menial, with Isaac, who was the son of a free woman, was justly reproved and both the mother and the son

[48] Cf. Galatians 4: 21–31.

removed from his company; much more men's joking with the wonders of God should be reproved and put out of human company. And thus, as the apostle says, [49] as there is no benefit to be derived from intercourse between the devil's instrument to pervert men, such as the devices of the flesh, and God's means of converting them, such as His miracles, . . . as it is a downright lie to say that for the love of God he will be a good friend of the devil, so it is a downright lie to say that for the love of God he will play His miracles; for in neither is the love of God shown but His commandments are broken. And since the ceremonies of the old law were carnal though God-given, they should not be classed with the new covenant which is spiritual; for as the game of Ishmael with Isaac intended to deprive the latter of his heritage, so the observance of the old law in the new regime would take away men's belief in Christ and make them go backward; that is, from the spiritual living of the new covenant to the carnal living of the old. Much more play-acting deprives men of their faith in Christ and is a veritable backward step from the deeds of the spirit to mere lip-service done after the lusts of the flesh, which are quite contrary to the acts of Christ, and, therefore, we shall find that it was never practised among real Christians. But lately so-called religious people have manifested their faith in tokens only and not in deeds, and priests have performed their office in signs only and for money and not in acts, and, hence, the apostasy of these latter draws many people after them, as the apostasy of Lucifer the archangel drew many from heaven after him.

And if this, friend, will not satisfy you, which even the eyes of the piteously blind might see, take heed how the coming of contraries together (has ill results), as in the case of the contact of the children of Abner and the children of Joab.[50] In their conflict three hundred and sixty men and doubtless more were slain, whereas the representation of spiritual works according to the lusts of the flesh does still more harm, as flesh and spirit are more determined enemies (than were Abner and Joab). For it is with plays as it is with apostates who preach for what there is in it; for, just as the latter hold worldly gain of more

[49] ?   [50] Cf. 2 Samuel 3.

value than the word of God, since they make the word of God
but a means to their own aggrandizement, so these miracle
players and their patrons are simple apostates, both because they
subordinate God and exalt themselves — for they have God in
mind only for the sake of their plays — and also because they
delight more in the play than in the miracle itself — as an
apostate delights more in his actual gains than in the truth of
God and praises more highly things of outward comeliness than
matters that are inwardly fair and Godward. And it is for this
reason that miracle playing is a real danger to the house of God;
for, just as a jealous man, seeing his wife trifling with his kind-
nesses and using them as means to love another man than himself, doesn't wait very long before chastising her, so, since God
is more jealous of His people — as He loves them more than
any man loves his wife — He, seeing His grace in His miracles
subordinated, men's lusts exalted and men's wills preferred to
His own, it is no wonder though He send vengeance soon thereafter; as must needs be for His great righteousness and mercy;
and, therefore, it is that the wise man says, "The end of mirth
is sorrow and often your laughter shall be mingled with sadness."
And for this reason, as experience proves, ever since this kind
of apostacy reigned among the people, the vengeance of God
never ceased to visit us, either in the form of pestilence or war
or floods or dearth or some other ill, and usually when men are
most untimely merry sadness follows soon. Therefore these
plays now-a-days bear witness to three things; first, great sin
beforehand; second, great folly in the act; and third, great
vengeance afterwards. For, just as the children of Israel, when
Moses was up on the mountain busily praying for them, mis-
trusted him and worshipped a golden calf [51] and then ate and
drank and rose to play and then lost 22,000 men by death; so,
as this incident registered first their idolatry and then their
mistrust of Moses when they should have believed him most and
their folly in the deed and the vengeance that followed, miracle
playing is a good testimony to men's avarice and covetousness
in the first place — and this is idolatry, as the apostle says, for
what they should spend upon the needs of their neighbors, they

[51] Cf. Exodus 32.

lay out on plays and then are grouchy about paying their debts
and their rent, though they don't grudge paying out twice as
much on plays. Further, in order to assemble men to raise the
price of food (i.e. they persuade people to come to town to see
the plays and then raise prices) and to stir them to pride, gluttony and boasting, they give these plays. And also in order to
have the wherewithal themselves to see the plays and to hold
fellowship with gluttony and lechery while the plays are going
on, they busy themselves the more greedily beforehand to beguile their neighbors in buying and selling; and so this playing
of miracles now-a-days is a convincing proof of covetousness,
that is idolatry. And, just as Moses at that time was on the
mountain in greatest travail for the people, so now Christ is
in heaven with His Father praying most devotedly for the
people; and, nevertheless, as the children of Israel in their folly
did at that time their utmost to annul the great labor of Moses,
so men now-a-days, according to the hideous idolatry of covetousness in the producing of plays, do their utmost to nullify the
attentive prayer of Christ in heaven for them, and so their
plays bear witness to the extent of their foolish acts. And hence,
as the children unnaturally said to Aaron when Moses was on
the mountain, "We know not how it is with Moses, make us,
therefore, gods to go before us," so men now-a-days, equally
unnaturally, say, "Christ no longer performs miracles, let us,
therefore, play His old ones," adding many reasons so plausibly
that the people give as much credence to them as to the truth,
and so they forget to be instant in prayer like Christ, for the
idolatry in which men indulge at such plays. Idolatry, I say,
for men honor these plays as much as or more than the word
of God when it is preached, and, therefore, they speak blasphemy when they say that acting does more good to the people
than the word of God when it is preached. Ah Lord ! what is
a greater blasphemy against Thee than to promise to do Thy
bidding (and then only play at doing it), as do those who preach
that the word of God does far less good than that which is ordained by man only and not by God, namely, miracle plays. Just
as we call the representation of miracles miracles, so the children
of Israel called the golden calf god; in which they had in mind

the ancient miracles of God, and before that image they worshipped and sang praise, as they worshipped and sang praise to God because of His wondrous works for them, and, therefore, they did idolatrously. So now-a-days, since many people worship and praise only the semblance of the miracles of God as much as the word of God in the preacher's mouth by which all miracles are done, there is no doubt but that the people are more idolatrous now in such miracle playing than were the people of Israel at the time of their worship of the calf, in as much as the lies and lusts of miracle plays are more contrary to God and more accordant with the devil than was the golden calf that the people worshipped. And, therefore, the idolatry then was but a prophecy of men's idolatry now, and, therefore, the apostle says these things happened to them in a figure,[52] and the devil is delighted with the plays, as he gets most gain by deceiving men by semblances of the means by which men were formerly converted to God, but by which the devil formerly was pained. Therefore, without question, such performances deserve much more vengeance than did the rejoicing of the children of Israel after they had worshipped the golden calf, as miracle plays make sport of greater and more abundant favors from God.

Ah Lord! since the games of the children bear witness of the sins of their fathers before them, and their own original sin and their own lack of wisdom, and hence their later punishment shall hurt them more, so much more this playing of miracles bears witness of men's hideous sins and their forgetting of their Master Christ and their own folly and the folly of malice passing that of children and that there is great vengeance to come upon them — more than they may be able patiently to bear because of the great delight that they have in their play. But, friend, peradventure you say that no man shall make you believe that it is not good to play the passion of Christ and other events in His life. But, as opposed to this, hear how, when Elisha went up to Bethel, children playfully came up to him and said, "Go up, bald head, go up, bald head," [53] and how he therefore cursed them and how two wild bears came out of the wild wood

[52] Cf. Hebrews 9: 9; 11: 19.   [53] Cf. 2 Kings 2: 23, 24.

and tore them all to pieces, two and forty of them; and as all
saints say that the baldness of Elisha betokens the passion of
Christ, then, since by this story it is clearly shown that men
should not make a jest of a symbol of the passion of Christ,
nor with a holy prophet of Christ, much more in the New Testament when men should be wiser, kept farther from joking and
more closely directed to serious action and Christ more feared
than was Elisha in his day, men should not play the passion of
Christ upon pain of greater vengeance than was wreaked upon
the children who mocked Elisha. For surely, the playing of His
passion is but mockery of Christ, as has been said before, and,
therefore, dear friend, behold how nature tells that the older
a man grows the more unnatural it is for him to play, and therefore the book says, "Cursed be the children a hundred years of
age!" And certainly the world, as the apostle says, is now at
its ending . . .; therefore, because of the approach of the day
of doom, all God's creatures are vexed and angry at men's playing, especially miracle playing, as will be shown in earnest and
with vengeance at the last day; and miracle playing is now
unnatural for all creatures, and, hence, God is sending now-a-days
more wisdom to men than He did before, because they ought
now to leave off playing and give themselves up to more serious
business, more pleasing to God. Also, friend, take heed to what
Christ says in the gospel, namely, "As it was in the days of
Noah when the great flood was approaching, men were eating and
drinking and giving way to their passions, and fearfully came
God's vengeance in the flood upon them, so shall it be with the
coming of Christ at the last day," [54] so that when men give
themselves up most to their playing and mirth, fearfully shall
the day of doom come upon them with great vengeance. Therefore, beyond doubt, friend, this miracle playing that is now in
vogue is but a true threat of sudden vengeance upon us; and,
therefore, dear friend, let us spend neither our wits nor our
money upon plays but let us exert ourselves to do good in great
fear and penance, for truly the weeping and physical devotion
in plays are but as the strokes of a hammer on every side, to
drive out the nail of our fear of God and the day of doom and

[54] Cf. Matthew 24: 37–39.

to make the way of Christ slippery and hard for us, like rain on paths of clay. Then, friend, if we are bound always to play, let us play as did David before the ark of God [55] and as he spoke before Michal his wife who despised his dancing, wherefore he spoke to her in this manner, "The Lord liveth, so I shall dance before the Lord who hath chosen me rather than your father and all his house, and He hath decreed that I shall be leader of the people of Israel, and I shall dance for I am to be made greater than I am, and I shall be meek in my own eyes and to the handmaidens of whom you speak I shall appear more glorious." So this playing has three phases; the first is that we see in how many ways God has given us His grace, passing our neighbors; and we should be that much more grateful, fulfilling His will and more confident in Him in the face of all manner of reproach from our enemies. The second phase consists in continual devotion to God Almighty and in being foul and reprovable in the world's eyes, as Christ and His apostles showed themselves and as David said. The third phase consists in being as lowly in our own eyes or more humble than we appear to others, setting least store by ourselves, as we know more of our own sins than of those of any one else, and then before all the saints of heaven and before Christ at the last day, and in the bliss of heaven we shall be more glorious, in as much as the better we exhibit the three aforesaid phases here. The which three phases well to play here and then to come to heaven, grant us the Holy Trinity! Amen.[56]

Passages already quoted have shown the interest and variety of medieval writers of history on English soil. The prefatory material to the work of William of Newburgh,[57] now to be quoted, will show that one of these writers had critical method as well.

[55] Cf. 2 Samuel 6: 14–22.

[56] All the references needed for the study of the medieval drama will be found in the *Cambridge History of English Literature*, v, chapters 1, 2 and 3 and Bibliography. The most satisfactory collection of texts is Manly, *Specimens of Pre-Shakespearean Drama*, i (Ginn and Co., 1897).

[57] Newburgh has already been quoted; cf. *ante*, pp. 209–211; 462–464.

The Prefatory Epistle

*A prefatory and apologetic Epistle to the ensuing Work, addressed
to the abbot of Rievaux, by William, canon of Newborough.*

To his reverend father and lord, Ernald, abbot of Rievaux,
William, the least of the servants of Christ, prayeth,
that when the Prince of Shepherds shall appear, there
may be given to him an unfading crown of glory.

I HAVE received the letters of your holiness, wherein you
deign to assign to me the care and labor of writing (for the
knowledge and instruction of posterity) a history of the memorable events which have so abundantly occurred in our own times;
although there be so many of your own venerable fraternity
better qualified to accomplish such a work, and that more ele-
gantly; but this, I perceive, arises from your kind desire to
spare, in this respect, the members of your own society, who
are so fully occupied in the duties of monastic service, as well
as to prevent the leisure hours kindly granted to my infirmity
from being unemployed. Indeed, I am so devotedly bound by
your kind regard to me, that, even were your commands more
difficult, I should not venture to gainsay them; but since your
discrimination does not impose upon me any research into profound matters or mystical exposition, but merely to expatiate,
for a time, on historic narrative, as it were for mental recreation only (so easy is the work), I have, consequently, no sufficient ground of refusal remaining. Wherefore, by the assistance
of God and our Lord, in whose hands both of us and our words
are, and relying on the prayers of yourself and your holy brotherhood, who have condescended to unite their repeated entreaties
to the command of your holiness, I will attempt the labor you
recommend; premising, however, some few necessary matters
before I commence my history.

HERE ENDS THE EPISTLE

The history of our English nation has been written by the
venerable Beda, a priest and monk, who, the more readily to
gain the object he had in view, commenced his narrative at a
very remote period, though he only glanced, with cautious brev-

ity, at the more prominent actions of the Britons, who are known
to have been the aborigines of our island. The Britons, however, had before him a historian [58] of their own, from whose
work Beda has inserted an extract; this fact I observed some
years since, when I accidentally discovered a copy of the work of
Gildas. His history, however, is rarely to be found, for few
persons care either to transcribe or possess it — his style being
so coarse and unpolished: his impartiality, however, is strong
in developing truth, for he never spares even his own countrymen; he touches lightly upon their good qualities, and laments
their numerous bad ones: there can be no suspicion that the
truth is disguised, when a Briton, speaking of Britons, declares, that they were neither courageous in war, nor faithful
in peace.

For the purpose of washing out those stains from the character of the Britons, a writer in our times has started up and
invented the most ridiculous fictions concerning them, and with
unblushing effrontery, extols them far above the Macedonians
and Romans. He is called Geoffrey,[59] surnamed Arthur, from
having given, in a Latin version, the fabulous exploits of Arthur
(drawn from the traditional fictions of the Britons, with additions of his own), and endeavored to dignify them with the name
of authentic history; moreover, he has unscrupulously promulgated the mendacious predictions of one Merlin, as if they were
genuine prophecies, corroborated by indubitable truth, to which
also he has himself considerably added during the process of
translating them into Latin. He further declares, that this Merlin was the issue of a demon and woman, and, as participating
in his father's nature, attributes to him the most exact and
extensive knowledge of futurity; whereas, we are rightly taught,
by reason and the holy scriptures, that devils, being excluded
from the light of God, can never by meditation arrive at the
cognizance of future events; though by the means of some types,
more evident to them than to us, they may predict events to

---

[58] Reference is here made to Gildas, an extract from whose *History* occurs in
the *Ecclesiastical History* of Beda, I, xxii, 50.

[59] The celebrated Geoffrey of Monmouth; cf. *ante*, pp. 248; 404 and *post*,
557–558.

come rather by conjecture than by certain knowledge. Moreover, even in their conjectures, subtle though they be, they often deceive themselves as well as others: nevertheless, they impose on the ignorant by their feigned divinations, and arrogate to themselves a prescience which, in truth, they do not possess. The fallacies of Merlin's prophecies are, indeed, evident in circumstances which are known to have transpired in the kingdom of England after the death of Geoffrey himself, who translated these follies from the British language; to which, as is truly believed, he added much from his own invention. Besides, he so accommodated his prophetic fancies (as he easily might do) to circumstances occurring previous to, or during his own times, that they might obtain a suitable interpretation. Moreover, no one but a person ignorant of ancient history, when he meets with that book which he calls the *History of the Britons,* can for a moment doubt how impertinently and impudently he falsifies in every respect. For he only who has not learnt the truth of history indiscreetly believes the absurdity of fable. I omit this man's inventions concerning the exploits of the Britons previous to the government of Julius Cæsar, as well as the fictions of others which he has recorded, as if they were authentic. I make no mention of his fulsome praise of the Britons, in defiance of the truth of history, from the time of Julius Cæsar, when they came under the dominion of the Romans, to that of Honorius, when the Romans voluntarily retired from Britain, on account of the more urgent necessities of their own state.

Indeed, the Britons, by the retreat of the Romans, becoming once more at their own disposal — nay, left to themselves for their own destruction, and exposed to the depredation of the Picts and Scots — are said to have had Vortigern for king, by whom the Saxons, or Angles, were invited over for the defence of the kingdom: they arrived in Britain under the conduct of Hengist, and repelled the irruptions of the barbarians for a time; but afterward, having discovered the fertility of the island, and the supineness of its inhabitants, they broke their treaty, and turned their arms against those by whom they had been invited over, and confined the miserable remains of the people, now called the Welsh — who had not been dispersed — within inaccessible woods and mountains. The Saxons, moreover had, in the course of succession, most valiant and powerful kings; among whom was Ethelberht, great grandson of Hengist, who, having extended his empire from the Gallic ocean to the Humber, embraced the easy yoke of Christ at the preaching of Augustine. Ailfred, too, king of Northumberland, subdued both the Britons and the Scots with excessive slaughter. Edwin, who succeeded Ailfred, reigned at the same time over the Angles and Britons; Oswald, his successor, governed all the nations of Britain. Now, since it is evident that these facts are established with historical authenticity by the venerable Beda, it appears that whatever Geoffrey has written, subsequent to Vortigern, either of Arthur, or his successors, or predecessors, is a fiction, invented either by himself or by others, and promulgated either through an unchecked propensity to falsehood, or a desire to please the Britons, of whom vast numbers are said to be so stupid as to assert that Arthur is yet to come, and who cannot bear to hear of his death. Lastly, he makes Aurelius Ambrosius succeed to Vortigern (the Saxons whom he had sent for being conquered and expelled), and pretends that he governed all England superexcellently; he also mentions Utherpendragon, his brother, as his successor, whom, he pretends, reigned with equal power and glory, adding a vast deal from Merlin, out of his profuse addiction to lying. On the decease of Utherpendragon, he makes his son Arthur succeed to the kingdom of Britain — the fourth in succession from Vortigern, in like manner as our Beda places Ethelberht, the patron of Augustine, fourth from Hengist in the government of the Angles. Therefore, the reign of Arthur, and the arrival of Augustine in England, ought to coincide. But how much plain historical truth outweighs concerted fiction may, in this particular, be perceived, even by a purblind man through his mind's eye. Moreover, he depicts Arthur himself as great and powerful beyond all men, and as celebrated in his exploits as he chose to feign him. First, he makes him triumph, at pleasure, over Angles, Picts, and Scots; then, he subdues Ireland, the Orkneys, Gothland, Norway, Denmark, partly by war, partly by the single terror of his name. To these he adds

Iceland, which, by some, is called the remotest Thule, in order that what a noble poet flatteringly said to the Roman Augustus

"The distant Thule shall confess thy sway," [60]

might apply to the British Arthur. Next, he makes him attack, and speedily triumph over, Gaul — a nation which Julius Cæsar, with infinite peril and labor, was scarcely able to subjugate in ten years — as though the little finger of the British was more powerful than the loins of the mighty Cæsar. After this, with numberless triumphs, he brings him back to England, where he celebrates his conquests with a splendid banquet with his subject-kings and princes, in the presence of the three archbishops of the Britons, that is London, Carleon, and York — whereas, the Britons at that time never had an archbishop. Augustine, having received the pall from the Roman pontiff, was made the first archbishop in Britain; for the barbarous nations of Europe, though long since converted to the Christian faith, were content with bishops, and did not regard the prerogative of the pall. Lastly, the Irish, Norwegians, Danes, and Goths, though confessedly Christians, for a long while possessed only bishops, and had no archbishops until our own time. Next this fabler, to carry his Arthur to the highest summit, makes him declare war against the Romans, having, however, first vanquished a giant of surprising magnitude in single combat, though since the times of David we never read of giants. Then, with a wider licence of fabrication, he brings all the kings of the world in league with the Romans against him; that is to say, the kings of Greece, Africa, Spain, Parthia, Media, Iturea, Libya, Egypt, Babylon, Bithynia, Phrygia, Syria, Bœotia, and Crete, and he relates that all of them were conquered by him in a single battle; whereas, even Alexander the Great, renowned throughout all ages, was engaged for twelve years in vanquishing only a few of the potentates of these mighty kingdoms. Indeed, he makes the little finger of his Arthur more powerful than the loins of Alexander the Great; more especially when, previous to the victory over so many kings, he introduces him relating to his comrades the subjugation of thirty kingdoms by his and their

[60] Cf. Virgil, *Georgics*, 1, l. 30.

united efforts; whereas, in fact, this romancer will not find in the world so many kingdoms, in addition to those mentioned, which he had not yet subdued. Does he dream of another world possessing countless kingdoms, in which the circumstances he has related took place? Certainly, in our own orb no such events have happened. For how would the elder historians, who were ever anxious to omit nothing remarkable, and even recorded trivial circumstances, pass by unnoticed so incomparable a man, and such surpassing deeds? How could they, I repeat, by their silence, suppress Arthur, the British monarch (superior to Alexander the Great), and his deeds, or Merlin, the British prophet (the rival of Isaiah), and his prophecies? For what less in the knowledge of future events does he attribute to this Merlin than we do to Isaiah, except, indeed, that he durst not prefix to his productions, "Thus saith the Lord"; and was ashamed to say, "Thus saith the Devil," though this had been best suited to a prophet the offspring of a demon.

Since, therefore, the ancient historians make not the slightest mention of these matters, it is plain that whatever this man published of Arthur and of Merlin are mendacious fictions, invented to gratify the curiosity of the undiscerning. Moreover, it is to be noted that he subsequently relates that the same Arthur was mortally wounded in battle, and that, after having disposed of his kingdom, he retired into the island of Avallon, according to the British fables, to be cured of his wounds; not daring, through fear of the Britons, to assert that he was dead — he whom these truly silly Britons declare is still to come. Of the successors of Arthur he feigns, with similar effrontery, giving them the monarchy of Britain, even to the seventh generation, making those noble kings of the Angles (whom the venerable Beda declares to have been monarchs of Britain) their slaves and vassals.

Therefore, let Beda, of whose wisdom and integrity none can doubt, possess our unbounded confidence, and let this fabler, with his fictions, be instantly rejected by all.

There were not wanting, indeed, some writers after Beda, but none at all to be compared with him, who detailed from his days the series of times and events of our island until our own recollection; men deserving of praise for their zealous and faithful labors, though their narrative be homely. In our times, indeed, events so great and memorable have occurred, that, if they be not transmitted to lasting memory by written documents, the negligence of the moderns must be deservedly blamed. Perhaps a work of this kind is already begun, or even finished, by one or more persons, but, nevertheless, some venerable characters, to whom I owe obedience, have deigned to enjoin such a labor, even to so insignificant a person as myself, in order that I, who am unable to make my offerings with the rich, may yet be permitted, with the poor widow, to cast somewhat of my poverty into the treasury of the Lord: [61] and, since we are aware that the series of English history has been brought down by some to the decease of King Henry the First, beginning at the arrival of the Normans in England, I shall succinctly describe the intermediate time, that, by the permission of God, I may give a more copious narrative from Stephen, Henry's successor, in whose first year I, William, the least of the servants of Christ, was born unto death in the first Adam, and born again unto life in the Second.[62]

[61] Cf. Mark 12: 41–44.

[62] On historical composition in the period see *The Cambridge History of English Literature*, i, chapter 9 and Bibliography. Also Buckle, *History of Civilization in England*, chapter 6. (The Origin of History and the State of Historical Literature in the Middle Ages.) On Arthurian material in the chronicles, see R. H. Fletcher in *Harvard Studies and Notes in Philology and Literature*, x, 1906. With William of Newburgh's opinion of the Arthurian stories, cf. the following paragraph from William of Malmesbury (*op. et. tr. cit.*, p. 315): "At that time (*circa* 1087), in a province of Wales called Ros, was found the sepulcher of Walwin (Gawain), the noble nephew of Arthur; he reigned, a most renowned knight, in that part of Britain which is still named Walwerth; but was driven from his kingdom by the brother and nephew of Hengist, . . . though not without first making them pay dearly for his expulsion. He deservedly shared with his uncle the praise of retarding for many years the calamity of his falling country. The sepulcher of Arthur is nowhere to be seen, whence ancient ballads fable that he is still to come. But the tomb of the other . . . was found in the time of King William, on the sea-coast fourteen feet long: there, as some relate, he was wounded by his enemies, and suffered shipwreck; others say, he was killed by his subjects at a public entertainment. The truth consequently is doubtful; though neither of these men was inferior to the reputation they have acquired."

Other literary types of the period, such as vision, debate, allegory, lyric, sermon,

VI. REPRESENTATIVE AUTHORS

Literature continues [1] to be prevailingly anonymous, though, happily, during the period 1066–1400 a larger share can be assigned to definite authors than in the preceding period. Literary biography, however, still is practically non-existent, and modern knowledge of the lives of authors remains dependent on scant and scattering notices in chronicles and legal documents and the modest remarks of writers themselves, notices which the historical critic must reconcile and piece together if he is to have a running account. The following is a list of writers representative of the various languages written in England, of the different interests of the age, and of the several types of literature.

Of Marie de France, a French woman living in England, the author of a charming collection of lays and of a series of Æsopic fables, we know only what is said in the following *Prolog*.

Those to whom God has given the gift of comely speech, should not hide their light beneath a bushel,[2] but should willingly show it abroad. If a great truth is proclaimed in the ears of men, it brings forth fruit a hundred-fold; but when the sweetness of telling is praised of many, flowers mingle with the fruit upon the branch.

According to the witness of Priscian,[3] it was the custom of ancient writers to express obscurely some portions of their books, so that those who came after might study with greater diligence to find the thought within their words. The philosophers knew

letter and satire, have already been illustrated in these pages. Legal documents have also been quoted. The best written romance of the age and the best fitted to illustrate the qualities of the type is Chaucer's *Knight's Tale*. That Chaucer could see the absurd side of romantic literature is shown in his parody *Sir Thopas*. For the identification of proper names in the romances and much of the other literature of the Middle Ages, see Lewis Spence, *A Dictionary of Medieval Romance and Romance Writers* (E. P. Dutton and Co., 1913).

[1] Cf. *ante*, p. 103.   [2] Cf. Matthew 5: 15.   [3] Cf. *ante*, p. 67.

this well, and were the more unwearied in labor, the more subtle in distinctions, so that the truth might make them free.[4] They were persuaded that he who would keep himself unspotted from the world[5] should search for knowledge, that he might understand. To set evil from me, and to put away my grief, I purposed to commence a book. I considered within myself what fair story in the Latin or Romance I could turn into the common tongue. But I found that all the stories had been written and scarcely it seemed the worth my doing, what so many had done. Then I called to mind those Lays I had so often heard. I doubted nothing — for well I knew — that our fathers fashioned them, that men should bear in remembrance the deeds of those who have gone before. Many a one, on many a day, the minstrel has chanted to my ear. I would not that they should perish, forgotten by the roadside. In my turn, therefore, I have made of them a song, rimed as I am able, and often has their shaping kept me sleepless in my bed.

In your honor, most noble and courteous King, to whom joy is a handmaid, and in whose heart all gracious things are rooted, I have brought together these lays and told my tales in seemly rime. Ere they speak for me let me speak with my own mouth and say, "Sire, I offer you these verses. If you are pleased to receive them, the fairer happiness will be mine, and the more lightly I shall go all the days of my life. Do not deem that I think more highly of myself than I ought to think,[6] since I presume to proffer this, my gift." Hearken now to the commencement of the matter.[7]

---

[4] Cf. John 8: 32.   [5] Cf. James 1: 27.   [6] Cf. Romans 12: 3.

[7] It is generally assumed that the author of the *Lays* is the same as the author of the *Fables*, who signs herself in an *Epilog* as follows, "Marie ai num, si suis de France" (My name is Marie and I am of France"). Marie writes in French but not, as might be expected, in the Anglo-Norman dialect; her language is Île de France. All the extant MSS. are of the thirteenth or fourteenth centuries, but the language of the poems dates them in the second half of the twelfth century. It is usually assumed, though there is no statement to that effect in the work, that the *Lays* were dedicated to Henry II of England. The *Fables* were written for a Count William, usually thought to be William Longsword, Earl of Salisbury. Denis Pyramus, a contemporary French author, testifies to the popularity of Marie's *Lays* in the following terms, "And Dame Marie also, who in rime wrought and built

Henry of Huntingdon (1084?–1155), already quoted,[8] in the Dedicatory Epistle to his History gives us a view of the value of history which throws light on the sort of man he was.

To Alexander Bishop of Lincoln.

As the pursuit of learning in all its branches affords, according to my way of thinking, the sweetest mitigation of trouble and consolation in grief, so I consider that precedence must be assigned to history, as both the most delightful of studies and the one which is invested with the noblest and brightest prerogatives. Indeed, there is nothing in the world more excellent than accurately to investigate and trace out the course of worldly affairs. For where is exhibited in a more lively manner the grandeur of heroic men, the wisdom of the prudent, the uprightness of the just and the moderation of the temperate than in the series of actions which history records? We find Horace [9] suggesting this, when in speaking of Homer's story, he says,

> "His works the beautiful and base contain, —
> Of vice and virtue more instructive rules
> Than all the sober sages of the schools."

Crantor,[9] indeed, and Chrysippus [9] composed labored treatises on moral philosophy, while Homer unfolds, as it were in a play, the character of Agamemnon for magnanimity, of Nestor for prudence, of Menelaus for uprightness, and on the other hand portrays the size of Ajax, the feebleness of Priam, the wrath of Achilles and the fraud of Paris; setting forth in his narrative

and thought out the verses of her *Lays*, which are not at all true. And she is much praised for them and the rimes loved everywhere, . . . by count, baron and chevalier and . . . (people) have them read and take delight (in hearing them) and they have them repeated oft. The *Lays* are a solace to ladies who listen and ease their hearts." *La Vie Seint Edmund le Rey* (*The Life of St. King Edmund*), ll. 35–46, ed. Arnold, *Memorials of St. Edmund's Abbey* (*Rolls Series*, xcvi, 1892, pp. 138, 139). Denis is trying to secure an audience for his true historical poem by pointing to the popularity of a merely fictitious one; his words may be taken as a supplement to those of the *Cursor Mundi* on the popularity of romance; cf. *ante.*, p. 518. This St. Edmund King was the patron saint of St. Edmundsbury Abbey, of which Jocelin of Brakelond wrote his *Chronicle;* cf. *ante*, pp. 268–287.

[8] Cf. *ante*, pp. 87, 456.   [9] Cf. *Epistles*, Book I, 2, ll. 1–5.

what is virtuous and what is profitable, better than is done in the disquisitions of philosophers.

But why should I dwell on profane literature? See how sacred history teaches morals; while it attributes faithfulness to Abraham, fortitude to Moses, forbearance to Jacob, wisdom to Joseph: and while, on the contrary, it sets forth the injustice of Ahab, the weakness of Oziah, the recklessness of Manasseh and the folly of Rehoboam. O God of mercy, what an effulgence was shed on humility, when Moses, after joining with his brother in an offering of sweet-smelling incense to God, his protector and avenger, threw himself into the midst of a terrible danger,[10] and when he shed tears for Miriam, who spoke scornfully of him, and was ever intercedinng for those who were malignant against him ! How brightly shone the light of humanity when David,[11] assailed and grievously tried by the curses, the insults and the foul reproaches of Shimei, would not allow him to be injured, though he himself was armed, and surrounded by his followers in arms, while Shimei was alone and defenceless; and afterward when David was triumphantly restored to his throne, he would not suffer punishment to be inflicted on his reviler. So, also, in the annals of all people, which indeed display the providence of God, clemency, munificence, honesty, circumspection and the like, with their opposites, not only provoke believers to what is good and deter them from evil, but even attract worldly men to goodness and arm them against wickedness.

History brings the past to the view as if it were present and enables us to judge of the future by picturing to ourselves the past. Besides, the knowledge of former events has this further pre-eminence, that it forms a main distinction between brutes and rational creatures. For brutes, whether they be men or beasts, neither know nor wish to know whence they come nor their own origin nor the annals and revolutions of the country they inhabit. Of the two, I consider men in this brutal state to be the worse, because what is natural in the case of beasts, is the lot of men from their own want of sense; and what beasts could not acquire if they would, such men will not though they

[10] Cf. Exodus 4: 27, 31; 5: 1.   [11] Cf. 2 Samuel 16: 5–14; 19: 23.

can. But enough of these, whose life and death are alike consigned to everlasting oblivion.

With such reflections, and in obedience to your commands, most excellent prelate, I have undertaken to arrange in order the antiquities and history of this kingdom and nation, of which you are a most distinguished ornament. At your suggestion, also, I have followed, as far as possible, the *Ecclesiastical History* of the Venerable Bede, making extracts, as well, from other authors, with compilations from the chronicles preserved in ancient libraries. Thus, I have brought down the course of past events to times within our own knowledge and observation. The attentive reader will learn in this work both what he ought to imitate, and what he ought to eschew; and if he becomes the better for this imitation and this avoidance, that is the fruit of my labors which I most desire; and, in truth, the direct path of history frequently leads to moral improvement.

William [12] of Malmesbury (1090?–1143), Henry's contemporary, thus records his zeal for study in general, for that of history in particular, and his view of the historian's function.

A long period has elapsed since, as well through the care of my parents as my own industry I became familiar with books. This pleasure possessed me from my childhood: this source of delight has grown with my years. Indeed, I was so instructed by my father that, had I turned aside to other pursuits, I should have considered it as jeopardy to my soul and discredit to my character. Wherefore, mindful of the adage, "Covet what is necessary," I constrained my early age to desire eagerly that which it was disgraceful not to possess. I gave, indeed, my attention to various branches of literature, but in different degrees. Logic, for instance, which gives arms to eloquence, I contented myself with barely hearing. Medicine, which ministers to the health of the body, I studied with somewhat more attention. But now, having scrupulously examined the several branches of ethics, I bow down to its majesty, because it spontaneously unveils itself

[12] Cf. *ante*, pp. 144–157; 375–377.

to those who study it, and directs their minds to moral practice; history more especially; which, by an agreeable recapitulation of past events, excites its readers, by example, to frame their lives to the pursuit of good or to aversion from evil. When, therefore, at my own expense, I had procured some historians of foreign nations, I proceeded during my leisure at home, to enquire if any thing concerning our own country could be found worthy of handing down to posterity. Hence it arose that, not content with the writings of ancient times, I began myself to compose; not indeed, to display my learning which is comparatively nothing, but to bring to light events lying concealed in the confused mass of antiquity. In consequence, rejecting vague opinions, I have studiously sought for chronicles far and near, though I confess I have scarcely profited any thing by this industry. For perusing them all, I still remained poor in information; though I ceased not my researches as long as I could find any thing to read. What I have clearly ascertained concerning the four (Anglo-Saxon) kingdoms, however, I have inserted in my first book, in which I hope Truth will find no cause to blush, though perhaps a degree of doubt may sometimes arise. I shall now trace the monarchy of the West Saxon kingdom through the line of successive princes, down to the coming of the Normans: which if any person will condescend to regard with complacency, let him in brotherly love observe the following rule, "If before he knew only these things (i.e. if he already knew all that he finds in the book), let him not be disgusted because I have inserted them; if he knows more, let him not be angry that I have not spoken of them"; but rather let him communicate his knowledge to me, while I am still alive, that, at least, those events may be noted on the margin of my history, though they are not mentioned in the text. . . . It is by no means the part of an historian to give entire credence to flattering reports, or to deceive the credulity of his readers. . . . There will perhaps be many in different parts of England, who may say that they have heard and read some things differently related from the mode in which I have recorded them: but if they judge candidly, they will not, on this account, brand me with censure; since, following the strict laws of history, I have asserted nothing but what I have learned either from relators, or from writers, of veracity. But, be these matters as they may, I especially congratulate myself on being, through Christ's assistance, the only person, or at least the first, who, since Bede, has arranged a continued history of the English. Should any one, therefore, as I already hear it intimated, undertake, after me, a work of a similar nature, he may be indebted to me for having collected materials, though the selection from them must depend upon himself.

Geoffrey of Monmouth [13] (1100?–1154), maligned yet popular, or perhaps maligned because popular, deliberately set himself the task of writing the history of the Kings of Britain, that is, the Kings of the Welsh. He claims this particular province as his own by reason of having in his possession an ancient book in the British language which he undertakes to render into Latin, as he tells us in his *Preface*.

Oftentimes in turning over in mine own mind the many themes that might be subject-matter of a book, my thoughts would fall upon the plan of writing a history of the Kings of Britain, and in my musings thereupon meseemed it a marvel that, beyond such mention as Gildas and Bede have made of them in their luminous tractate, naught could I find as concerning the kings that had dwelt in Britain before the Incarnation of Christ nor even as concerning Arthur and the many others that did succeed him after the Incarnation, albeit that their deeds be worthy of praise everlasting and be as pleasantly rehearsed from memory by word of mouth in the traditions of many peoples as though they had been written down. Now whilst I was thus thinking upon such matters, Walter, Archdeacon of Oxford, a man learned not only in the art of eloquence, but in the histories of foreign lands, offered me a certain most ancient book in the British language that did set forth the doings of them all in due succession and order from Brute, the first King of the Britons, onward to Cadwallader, the son of Cadwallo, all told in stories

[13] Cf. *ante*, pp. 248; 404; 544–550.

of exceeding beauty. At his request, therefore, albeit that never
have I gathered gay flowers of speech in other men's little gardens, and am content with mine own rustic manner of speech
and mine own writing-reeds, have I been at the pains to translate this volume into the Latin tongue. For had I besprinkled
my page with high-flown phrases, I should only have engendered
a weariness in my readers by compelling them to spend more
time over the meaning of the words than upon understanding
the drift of my story.

Unto this my little work, therefore, do thou Robert, Earl of
Gloucester,[14] show favor in such wise that it may be so corrected by thy guidance and counsel as that it may be held to
have sprung, not from the little fountain of Geoffrey of Monmouth, but rather from thine own deep sea of knowledge, and
to savor of thy salt. Let it be held to be thine own offspring,
as thou art the offspring of the illustrious Henry, King of the
English. Let it be thine, as one that hath been nurtured in the
liberal arts by philosophy, and called unto the command of
armies by thine own inborn prowess of knighthood; thine, whom
in these our days Britain haileth with heart-felt affection as
though in thee she had been vouchsafed a second Henry. . . .

Howbeit their kings (i.e. of the British) who from that time
have succeeded in Wales I hand over in the matter of writing
unto Karadoc [15] of Lancarvan, my contemporary, as I do those
of the Saxons unto William of Malmesbury and Henry of Huntingdon, whom I bid be silent as to the Kings of the Britons,
seeing that they have not that book in the British speech which
Walter, Archdeacon of Oxford, did convey hither out of Brittany, the which being truly issued in honor of the aforesaid
princes, I have on this wise been at the pains of translating into
the Latin speech.

Geoffrey's Latin history soon attracted translators to
render it into French. By one of these, Geoffrey Gaimar,

---

[14] An illegitimate son of Henry I.

[15] Or Caradoc or Caradog (died 1147), a Welsh ecclesiastic and chronicler, one
of the group of writers patronized by Robert, Earl of Gloucester. He wrote
a continuation of Geoffrey of Monmouth, which in its original form is no longer
extant.

it was translated into French verse before 1150; but Gaimar's version was early eclipsed by that of Wace, whose brief autobiography reads as follows:

If anybody asks who said this, who put this history into the romance language, I say and I will say to him that I am Wace of the Isle of Jersey, which lies in the sea, toward the west, and is a part of the fief of Normandy. In the Isle of Jersey I was born, and to Caen I was taken as a little lad; there I was put at the study of letters; afterwards I studied long in France. When I came back from France, I dwelt long at Caen. I busied myself with making books in romance; many of them I wrote and many of them I made.

John of Salisbury (circa 1120–1180) was a partisan of Thomas à Becket, an important person at the literary court of Henry II and Bishop of Chartres in 1176. He is the author of the *Polycraticus*, of the *Metalogicus* and of about three hundred extant letters. The *Polycraticus*, "The Statesman's Book," "contrasts the vain pursuits of men of his day with the best precepts of the philosophers, pointing out the frivolous or vicious pleasures that are opposed to reason and right." [16] The *Metalogicus* is invaluable as a storehouse of information regarding the matter and form of scholastic education and remarkable, like the *Polycraticus*, for its cultivated style and its humanistic tendency.[17] His *Letters*, written to the leading men of the time, throw much light on the literary, political and scientific position of the twelfth century. From the *Metalogicus* we quote John's account of his own education, and from one of his letters, his statement of his sentiments on mountaineering in the Alps.

When I was a very young man, I went to study in France, the year after the death of that lion in the cause of justice,

[16] Schofield, *op. cit.*, p. 51.
[17] See the article on John of Salisbury in the *Enclycopædia Britannica*, ed. 11.

Henry King of England.[18]   There I sought out that famous
teacher and peripatetic philosopher of the Palatine,[19] who at
that time presided at Mont St. Geneviève and was the subject
of admiration to all men.   At his feet I received the first rudiments of this art, and showed the utmost avidity in picking up
and storing away in my mind all that fell from his lips.   When,
however, much to my regret, Abelard left us, I attended
Master Alberic,[20] a most obstinate dialectician and unflinching
assailant of the nominalist sect.   Two years I stayed at Mont
St. Geneviève, under the instruction of Alberic and Master
Robert de Melun,[21] if I may so term him, not from the place
of his birth, for he was an Englishman, but by the surname
which he gained by his successful governance of his schools.
One of these teachers was scrupulous even to minutiæ, and everywhere found some subject to raise a question; for the smoothest
surface presented inequalities to him, and there was no rod so
smooth that he could not find a knot in it, and show how it
could be gotten rid of.   The other of the two was prompt in
reply, and never for the sake of subterfuge avoided a question
that was proposed; but he would choose the contradictory side,
or by a multiplicity of words show that simple answer could not
be given.   In all questions, therefore, he was subtle and profuse,
whilst the other in his answers was perspicuous, brief and to the
point.   If two such characters could ever have been united in the
same person, he would be the best hand at disputation that our
times have produced.   Both of them possessed acute wit and an
indomitable perseverance; I believe they would have turned out
great and distinguished men in physical studies, if they had supported themselves on the great base of literature and more
closely followed the tracks of the ancients, instead of taking
such pride in their own discoveries.   All this is said with reference to the time during which I attended them.   For one of
them afterwards went to Bologna and there unlearnt what he
had taught; on his return he also untaught it: whether the
change was for the better or the worse, I leave to the judgment
of those who heard him before and after.   The other of the two

---

[18] I.e. Henry I.   [19] Cf. *ante*, pp. 387–389.   [21] Cf. *ante*, p. 440.
[20] *Circa* 1080–*post* 1154; author of several philosophical works.

was also a proficient in the more exalted philosophy of divinity wherein he gained a distinguished name. With these teachers I remained two years and became versed in commonplaces, rules and elements in general, which boys study and in which my teachers were most weighty, so that I seemed to know them as well as I knew my own nails and fingers. There was one thing which I had certainly attained to, namely, to estimate my own knowledge higher than it deserved. I fancied myself a sciolist because I was ready in what I had been taught. I then, beginning to reflect and to measure my strength, attended on the grammarian William de Conches [22] during the space of three years; I read much at intervals: nor shall I ever regret the way in which my time was then spent. After this I became a follower of Richard l'Evêque, [22] a man who was master of every kind of learning, and whose breast contained much more than his tongue dared give utterance to; for he had learning rather than eloquence, truthfulness rather than vanity, virtue rather than ostentation. With him I reviewed all that I had learnt from the others, besides certain things, which I now learnt for the first time relating to the quadrivium, in which I had already acquired some information from German Hardewin. [22] I also again studied rhetoric, which I had before learnt very superficially with some other studies from Master Theodoric, [22] but without understanding what I read. Afterwards I learnt it more fully from Peter Hely. [22] My maintenance, by God's blessing on me, — for I was very poor and distant from friends and relatives, — was supplied me by the sons of noblemen whom I instructed: this made me of necessity, and at their request, frequently recall to memory what I had heard before. I then formed a close intimacy with Master Adam, [22] a man of most acute understanding, and — whatever others may think — of much learning, who gave his particular attention to Aristotle. Though he was my tutor, he communicated to me what he knew, and laid himself open to me in a manner which he had never used before except to a very few; for he was thought to be a very envious man. Meanwhile I taught the first elements of logic to William [22] of Soissons who afterwards invented some-

[22] Known only as masters in the schools.

thing to assail the antiquity of logic, to draw unexpected consequences, and to destroy the opinions of the ancients; and at last I handed him over to the aforementioned preceptor. There he perhaps learnt that the same thing is not the same, *etc.*, but I could never be brought to believe that from one impossibility, all impossibilities could arise. I was at last rescued from all this by the poverty of my condition, the request of companions and the advice of my friends that I should undertake the office of a tutor. I obeyed their wishes; and on my return after three years, finding Master Gilbert,[23] I studied logic and divinity with him: but he was very speedily removed from us, and in his place we had Robert de Poule,[23] a man amiable alike for his rectitude and his attainments. Then came Simon de Poissy[23] who was a faithful reader but an obtuse disputator. These two were my teachers in theology only. In this manner twelve years having passed away whilst I was engaged in these various occupations, I determined to revisit my old companions whom I found still engaged with logic at Mont St. Geneviève.[24]

In his later life, John was "engaged in many kinds of official business, some of which required great tact. Be-

[23] Known only as masters in the schools.

[24] As comment on this long stay of John's in France, cf. the following lines of Chrestien de Troyes, a French poet of the twelfth century:

> Or vous ert par ce livre apris,
> Que Gresse ot de chevalerie
> Le premier los et de clergie;
> Puis vint chevalerie à Rome,
> Et de la clergie la some,
> Qui ore est en France venue.
> Diex doinst qu'ele i soit retenue
> Et que li lius li abelisse
> Tant que de France n'isse
> L'onor qui s'i est arestee!

("Now by this book you will learn that first Greece had the renown for chivalry and letters: then chivalry and the primacy in letters passed to Rome, and now is it come to France. God grant it may be kept there; and that the place may please it so well, that the honor which has come to make stay in France may never depart thence!" — Tr. Matthew Arnold in *The Study of Poetry*, ed. Johnson, *Riverside Literature Series*, p. 69. *Cligés*, ll. 30–39, Johnson's note.)

fore 1169 he had crossed the Alps ten times on missions
to Rome" [25] and on one of these trips, he writes as follows:

Pardon me for not writing. I have been on the Mount of
Jove; on the one hand looking up to the heavens of the mountains, on the other shuddering at the hell of the valleys; feeling myself so much nearer to heaven that I was more sure that
my prayer would be heard. "Lord," I said, "restore me to my
brethren, that I may tell them, that they come not into this
place of torment." Place of torment, indeed, where the marble
pavement of the stony ground is ice alone, and you cannot set
down a foot safely; where, strange to say, although it is so slippery that you cannot stand, the death, into which there is every
facility for a fall, is a certain death. I put my hand in my scrip,
that I might scratch out a syllable or two to your sincerity; lo,
I found my ink-bottle filled with a dry mass of ice: my fingers,
too, refused to write: my beard was stiff with frost, and my
breath congealed into a long icicle. I could not write the news
I wished.[26]

[25] Cf. Schofield, *op. cit.*, p. 51.
[26] The letter is dated from the Great St. Bernard Pass. Coulton, *op. cit.*, pp. 14–
18, quotes three other medieval accounts of mountain climbing. On medieval taste
in landscape, cf. the following, "Mediæval landscape we can easily . . . reproduce
for ourselves. We know what men loved; we know what they habitually saw about
them. The country was still in large tracts wild and savage, overgrown with vast
forests like those through which the knights in mediæval romance perpetually
wander. Even so late as the time of Elizabeth, we know that one-third of England
was unreclaimed waste land. Here and there the grim castle of a feudal lord, its
thick walls and frowning turrets witnessing to the military character of the age,
would break the monotony, but hardly relieve the terror of the woods. Or, again,
the sweet sound of unseen bells would draw the traveller to some spot where 'a
little lowly hermitage' or a stately abbey spoke of the mighty power of the Church.
Of course, wide regions even apart from the towns were by this time subdued to
human use and smiling fertility; yet the general character of scenery during the
middle ages must have been wild and fierce. Men are governed by desire for contrast. We in our peaceful days crave precipice and savage height and raging torrent, and take our holiday pleasure in the wildest regions we can discover. It is,
then, no wonder that people in the middle ages loved and sought in landscape all
which was gently ordered, even, and serene. The mediæval idea of beauty is a
garden-close. Flowering trees bend above its symmetrical walks, roses bloom there
forever, and clear fountains softly splashing join in the melody of birds. In this
garden pace fair damsels, a faint perpetual smile in their gray eyes. Young squires

Giraldus Cambrensis, whose account of his French education has already been quoted,[27] was the most voluble autobiographic writer of his age. He not only wrote a lengthy book on his own life, but he indulged himself, like Mr. Bernard Shaw of our time, in the composition of numerous prefaces which exhibit his fondness for "showing off" his learning and connections with the great. In the following passage from his *Autobiography* (*De Rebus a se Gestis, On Matters Accomplished by Himself*), Giraldus relates how he recited his *Topography of Ireland* at Oxford.

Giraldus . . . crossed from Ireland into Wales, where also his *Topography*, which he had begun, he applied his studious mind wholly to complete. In the process of time, the book having been finished, desiring not to hide his light under a bushel but to set it on a candlestick that it might give light,[28] he arranged to recite his book at Oxford, where clergy and learning were most vigorous and eminent in England, before a great audience. And since there were in his book three distinctions (sections), the recitation lasted for three days; on the first of which he entertained all the poor of the whole town whom he sum-

and pretty pages move in attendance, and all take their joy together in the fresh sweet morning air of an undying May. Rocks and mountains cause abhorrent shudder to the mediæval mind. Dante's spirits in purgatory climb for their penance a lofty height; but because they are blessed, though once sinful, the mountain is laid out for them in neat terraces, and when they reach the top they will find that the peak has been smoothed away, and a delightful level garden planted for their refreshment. The wild primeval sense of fellowship with the stormy sea, which marked in so striking a way the rude literature of our Saxon forefathers, has also vanished. Nature is loved in the middle ages, but loved not for her spiritual power, but for her fertility and peace. The treatment of landscape in mediæval art and literature is conventional and formal; it has no range of observation or depth of insight, though it almost always possesses a charm of its own." Vida D. Scudder, *Introduction to the Study of English Literature*, pp. 60–62 (Globe School Book Co., 1901). For further references on John of Salisbury, see Sandys, *History of Classical Scholarship*, I; Stubbs, *Seventeen Lectures on Medieval and Modern History;* and Poole, *Illustrations of the History of Mediæval Thought.* See also A. C. Krey, *John of Salisbury's Attitude towards the Classics*, XVI, Part II, *Transactions of the Wisconsin Academy of Sciences, Arts and Letters,* Dec. 1909.

[27] Cf. *ante*, pp. 383–385. [28] Cf. Matthew 5: 15.

moned to his hospitality. The next day, all the doctors of the
various faculties and their disciples of greater fame and reputation. On the third, the remaining students together with the
local military and many burgers. This was a sumptuous and
noble affair, indeed, because the authentic and ancient days of
the poets were therein in some measure restored; nor does the
present age nor any record of antiquity register its like had in
England.

In the following words Giraldus tells us his aim in the
History of the Conquest of Ireland and defends the *Topography of Ireland* from the charge of including fabulous
stories.

Forasmuch as in my *Topography of Ireland* I have described
at large the site of the island, its singularities, and those of
sundry things contained in it, the marvels in which nature has
there indulged out of her ordinary course, and the origin of the
various races settled in it from the earliest ages until these our
own days, I have now undertaken, at the earnest request of
many persons of high rank, to set forth in a separate volume the
annals of events which have occurred in our own days relating
to the last and recent conquest of Ireland.[29] For if I have been
able to give a tolerably clear account of times long past, and of
things which happened in ages so far preceding our own, how
much more exact will be my narrative of transactions which
have taken place under my own observation, of the greatest
part of which I have been eyewitness, and which are so fresh
in my memory that I cannot have any doubt about them. The
Topography treats of localities and events connected with ancient times, the History deals with the present.

But methinks I see some one turn up his nose, and, disgusted
with my book, hand it to another, or throw it aside, because the
reader will find all things in it plain, clear and easy of appre-
hension. But let him know that I have written chiefly for the
use of the laity and of princes who have but little learning, and
desire things to be related in so simple and easy a style, that

[29] The Pope in 1154 had granted Ireland to Henry II.

all may understand them. For we may be permitted to use popular language when the acts of the people, as well as of their superiors, are to be reduced to writing. Besides, it has been my endeavor to compose all my works in a popular style, easy to understand, however I may have added to it some ornament from my own stores; and I have therefore entirely rejected the old and dry method of writing used by some authors. And, inasmuch as new times require new fashions, and the philosopher bids us follow the examples of the old men in our lives, and of the younger men in our words, I have earnestly aimed to adopt the mode of speech which is now in use and the modern style of eloquence. For since words only give expression to what is in the mind, and man is endowed with the gift of speech for the purpose of uttering his thoughts, what can be greater folly than to lock up and conceal things which we wish to be clearly understood, in a tissue of unintelligible phrases and intricate sentences? To show ourselves sciolists in a knowledge of our own, shall we take pains so to write, that others may see without comprehending and hear without understanding? Is it not better, as Seneca says, to be dumb than to speak so as not to be understood? The more, then, language is suited to the understanding, though framed with a certain elegance of style, the more useful it will be, as well as suited to the tastes of men of letters. . . .

Inasmuch also as some malevolent person has made slanderous attacks on my *Topography*, a work not to be despised, I have thought it worth my while to introduce here a few words in its defence. The elegance of its scholastic style has obtained uniform praise from all quarters; and though it is contrary to my detractor's nature to commend anything, he is ashamed and afraid to cavil at my First and Third Distinctions. But it is no easy matter to act a counterfeit part, and my critic, not being able quite to change his natural disposition, that he might at least do some mischief, and vent the malignity with which he was bursting, he boldly cavils at the Second Distinction, hoping that by convicting me of falsehood in that he shall discredit the whole. His objections are of this sort: the author, he says, "introduces a wolf talking with a priest; he draws a picture of a creature with the body of a man, and the extremities of an ox; he tells us of a bearded woman. . . ." Let him, however, if he is so shocked at these stories, read in the Book of Numbers how Baalam's ass spoke, and the prophet chid the ass. Let him read the lives of the Fathers, and he will find Anthony conversing with a satyr; and that Paul the hermit was fed in the desert by a raven. Let him also read the voluminous works of Jerome,[30] the *Hexameron* of Ambrose [30] and the *Dialogs* of Gregory.[30] He will find Augustine's [31] volume *De Civitate Dei* (*On the City of God*), and especially Books 16 and 21, full of prodigies. Let him read also the eleventh Book of Isidore's *Etymologies*,[31] concerning marvels; his twelfth Book, respecting beasts; and his sixteenth, respecting precious stones and their virtues. Let him also examine the works of Valerius Maximus,[32] Trogus Pompeius,[33] Pliny [34] and Solinus; [35] and in all these he will find many things at which he may cavil in the same manner. After reading these, I say, will he condemn the whole works of these great writers on account of some extraordinary accounts which they have inserted in them? But let him be better advised, and consider well the remark of St. Jerome,[30] that there are many things contained in the Scriptures which,

[30] Cf. *ante*, p. 64.   [31] *Ibid.*, p. 431.

[32] Known to us as the compiler of a large collection of historical anecdotes, entitled *De Factis Dictisque Memorabilibus Libri ix* (*Nine Books on Memorable Deeds and Words*). He lived in the reign of the emperor Tiberius, to whom he dedicated his book. "In an historical point of view the work, though turgid in style, and uninspired with any originality of thought, is by no means without value, since it preserves a record of many curious events not to be found elsewhere; but its statements do not always deserve implicit confidence." *Smith's Smaller Classical Dictionary.*

[33] Lived in the first centuries B.C. and A.D., author of a universal history in 44 books, called *Historiæ Philippicæ*, because the history of the various peoples was grouped around the Macedonian Empire founded by Philip, father of Alexander the Great.

[34] Pliny the Elder (23 A.D.–79 A.D.), author of the *Natural History* in 37 books, the source of much material in Isidore of Seville and other medieval encyclopedias.

[35] *Circa* 238 A.D. "Author of a geographical compendium, divided into 57 chapters, containing a brief sketch of the world as known to the ancients, diversified by historical notices, remarks on the origin, habits, religious rites and social condition of the various nations enumerated. It displays but little knowledge or judgment." Smith, *op. cit.*

though they seem to be incredible, are nevertheless true. For nature cannot prevail against the God of nature; and every creature ought not to abhor, but to admire and hold in reverence, the works of the Creator. To adopt also the words of Augustine [31] on this subject, "How can anything be against nature which exists by the will of the great Creator?" A prodigy, therefore, is not contrary to nature, but contrary to the common course of nature; and, therefore, as it is not impossible for God to ordain and create whatsoever things He listeth, no more is it impossible for Him to alter and change into what forms He listeth the things He has already created.

In the final *Preface* to the *History of the Conquest of Ireland*, addressed to King John, Giraldus gives John advice regarding the government of Ireland in a way that shows his interest in the country.

> *To his most revered lord, and beloved in Christ, John, the noble and illustrious King of England, Lord of Ireland, Duke of Normandy and Aquitaine and Count of Anjou: Giraldus dedicates his work, wishing him all health in body and soul and the prosperous issue of all his worldly affairs.*

It pleased your excellent and noble father, King Henry, some time ago, when I was in attendance on himself, to send me over to Ireland in your company.[36] Having noted while I was there sundry notable things which were strange and unknown in other countries, I made a collection of materials with great industry, from which, on my return to England, after three years' labor, I published a *Topography of Ireland*, describing the country and the wonders of it; not forgetting the honor your father had gained from that beforehand. The work so pleased him — for, a rare thing in our times, he was a prince of great literary attainments — that at his instance, I afterwards renewed or rather continued my labors, and composed the present work on the recent conquest of that kingdom, made by him and those under him. But, as worth is more commended than rewarded, I received no remuneration for either of these books.

[36] John went to Ireland in 1185.

But since, through neglect or rather your many occupations, the recollection of that land, not the least among the islands of the West, which you visited long since,[36] seems to have faded from your mind, I have undertaken to refresh it, by dedicating to your highness a corrected and fuller edition of my work. The history commences with the time when Prince Dermitius, driven into exile by his subjects, took refuge with your father in Normandy,[37] and obtained aid from him, and is continued until your first arrival in the island, when I attended you; and I have honestly related all that was done, whether for good or evil, by the several leaders of expeditions and nobles who went over to Ireland, in regular order from the first to the last.

Here, then, as in a bright mirror, and far more clearly, and certainly by the light of historical truth, it may be ascertained, seen and reflected to whom the greatest share of the glory of this conquest ought justly to be attributed; whether to the men of the diocese of St. David's my own kinsmen, who were the first adventurers, or to those of Llandaff,[38] men, truly, of better descent than enterprise, for they went over on the invitation of the first conquerors, and tempted by the example of their success to embark in a similar adventure — or lastly, whether it be due to the third expedition,[39] which consisted of a large force, amply supplied with arms, provisions and everything necessary.

Much was assuredly done by him who made the beginning, much by him who went over with additional forces and added strength to the first enterprise; but far more by him who gave his whole authority to the two former expeditions, and sanctioned them by his license, and at last, by going over himself, reduced the whole country to submission, and resolutely completed the whole undertaking, though his too hasty return from the island, caused by the unnatural conspiracy of his sons,[40] prevented order being fully settled on a firm foundation.

[37] Dermitius or Diarmait appealed to Henry II in 1166.
[38] The leader of the men of Llandaff was Richard de Clare, Earl of Pembroke.
[39] Henry himself was in Ireland from October, 1171 to April, 1172.
[40] Young Henry, Richard and Geoffrey rebelled against their father, Henry II, in 1173.

Do not undervalue, then, noble King, what cost your father and yourself so much toil, and do not part with so much glory and honor to strangers who are both unworthy and ungrateful; nor for the sake of an island of silver hazard the loss of one of gold; for the one does not exclude the other, but both together become doubly valuable. The gold of Arabia and the silver of Achaia enrich the same treasury, though in different heaps. Besides, other considerations may induce you not to be unmindful of your dominion of Ireland. It has pleased God and your good fortune to send you several sons . . . and you may have more hereafter. Two of these you may raise to the thrones of two kingdoms, and under them you amply provide for numbers of your followers by new grants of lands, especially in Ireland, a country which is still in a wild and unsettled state, a very small part of it being yet occupied and inhabited by our people.

But if neither the desire of augmenting your own glory, nor of royally endowing and elevating one of your sons, will induce you to extend your fostering care to your dominions of Ireland, you ought at least to protect and reinstate in their rights those veteran warriors who have served your father and yourself with so much devoted fidelity, by whose enterprise that land was first taken possession of, and by whose valor it is still retained, but who are constantly supplanted by new-comers, reaping the fruits of other men's labors, and advanced more by their good luck than by their valor. It should be your care to abate the pride and humble the insolence of such men as these; for, if report speaks true, their folly is risen to such a pitch of arrogance and presumption, that they even aspire to usurp in their own name all the rights of dominion belonging to the princes of that kingdom.

Wherefore, you should take the greatest care that when you have any designs of extending your conquests in the interior of the country, you should keep a close watch on what is passing in the Eastern districts, and use your utmost efforts to recover, by God's grace, what has been unjustly alienated there; for you have nothing to fear in the West if you leave no danger in the rear. It would doubtless be a sign not only of great negligence, but of idle folly, and a great reproach, were you to harbor

in your own towns and castles, and on your own lands, which
although they may be in the West, would lie closer on your rear,
domestic enemies, who are ever plotting treason, and only wait
for time and opportunity to break into open revolt. It would
be like wrapping snakes in the folds of your robe, or nourishing
fire in your bosom which was ready to burst into flame. It is
unsafe for princes to foster any hydra-heads in their dominions.
It is especially unsafe for island princes to have in their terri-
tories any other frontier marches than the sea itself.

Moreover, if for these reasons, or any of them, you should
be induced to pity and relieve your land so often mentioned,
which is now desolate and in a manner deserted, and to reduce
it to a state of order, not unprofitable to you and yours, permit
me to offer your royal majesty some advice, though it may
savor of the freedom of speech which is natural to Welshmen
like myself, and which we can neither alter nor get rid of. I
refer to the two pledges which your father gave to Pope Adrian,
when he obtained his permission to invade and conquer Ireland,
and acted most prudently and discreetly for his own interest,
and those of his family and people, when he secured the sanction of the highest earthly authority to an enterprise of so much
magnitude, which involved the shedding of Christian blood.
One was, that he would raise up the church of God in that
country, and cause a penny to be paid to St. Peter for every
house in Ireland, as it is done in England; according to the
tenor of the bull of privilege granted by the said Pope, and
obtained from him by your father's prudence and policy, and
now laid up in the archives at Winchester, as is hereafter set
forth in the present History. But Solomon says in the Proverbs,
"Nothing less becomes a prince than lying lips," [41] and it is
especially dangerous to lie to God, and for a creature to take
upon himself to set at naught his Creator. In order, therefore,
to deliver the soul of your father who made these promises, and
your own soul and those of your children, it is highly fitting
that you, having no other shield of defence against the anger of
the Righteous Judge for so much Christian blood already shed,
and perhaps still to be shed, should be very careful to fulfil

[41] Cf. Proverbs 17: 7.

your father's vows. And if by so doing God may be honored in this conquest, as is becoming and right, you may expect that the earthly prosperity of you and yours will be augmented, and above all, that eternal happiness will be your portion at last.

These promises not having hitherto been performed, the divine justice has therefore, we may well believe, suffered calamities of two kinds to happen by way of judgment. The one is that the completion of this conquest, and the profit to be drawn from it, have been deferred; the other, that the first and principal invaders of Ireland, namely, Robert Fitzstephen, who was the first of our countrymen who landed there, and as it were opened and showed the way to others, as also Hervey de Mont-Maurise, Raymonde, John de Courcy and Meyler never had any lawful issue of their bodies begotten. Nor is it any marvel. The poor clergy in the island are reduced to beggary. The cathedral churches, which were richly endowed with broad lands, by the piety of the faithful in old times, now echo with lamentations for the loss of their possessions, of which they have been robbed by these men and others who came over with them, or after them, so that to uphold the church is turned into soiling and robbing it.

It is the part of a good prince to redress these evils; for it concerns his honor, to say nothing of his duty to God, that the clergy throughout his dominions, whose place it is to assist him faithfully in his councils, and in all the more weighty affairs and principal acts of his government, should be relieved of their grievances, and enjoy the honors and privileges which are their due. Moreover, in order that some acknowledgment and propitiation may be made to God for this bloody conquest and the profits of it, the promised tax of the Peter's Pence should be paid in future. It is but small, and this moderate payment frees all, while it is not a burthen to any.

I would further add, with your permission, that in memory of this conquest of Ireland, made by the English, and because, in the course of years, there are great changes in the succession of lords, so that in process of time the right of inheritance often devolves on heirs by descent in remote degrees, and even utter strangers in blood, a fixed annual tribute in gold or birds, or perhaps in timber, should be reserved by some written instrument, in order to show to all future times that the realm of Ireland is subject to the crown of England by an indissoluble bond.

Considering also that annals of events, heard through an interpreter, are not so well understood, and do not fix themselves in the mind so firmly as when they are published in the vernacular tongue, it would be well, if such be your pleasure, that some man of learning, who is also skilled in the French language, be employed to translate this work of mine, which has cost much labor, into French; and then, as it would be better understood, I might reap the fruits of my toil, which hitherto, under illiterate princes, have been lost because there were few who could understand my works. Hence a man of great eloquence, Walter Mapes, Archdeacon of Oxford, has often said to me in conversation, with his usual facetiousness and that urbanity for which he is remarkable, "You have written a great deal, Master Giraldus, and you will write much more; and I have discoursed much: you have employed writing; I, speech. But though your writings are much better and much more likely to be handed down to future ages than my discourses, yet, as all the world could understand what I said, speaking as I did in the vulgar tongue, while your works, being written in Latin, are understood by only a very few persons, I have reaped some advantage from my sermons; but you, addressing yourself to princes, who were, doubtless, both learned and liberal, but are now out of date, and have passed from the world, have not been able to secure any sort of reward for your excellent works, which so richly merited it." It is true, indeed, that my best years, and the prime of my life, have been spent without any remuneration or advancement arising out of my literary labors, and I am now growing old, and standing, as it were, on the threshold of death; but I neither ask, nor expect, worldly recompense from any one. My only desire is, and it is all I ought to desire, that, first and above all, I may partake of the divine mercy vouchsafed me by Him who giveth all things freely, through good works; His grace cooperating, nay, being the sole efficient cause; and next, that through my poor literary works I may obtain favor with the world, if ever the pursuits of learning should again be held in esteem, and recover their former eminence; although my reward may be deferred till further times, when posterity is sure to award honor to every man according to his just deserts.

The Walter Mapes or Map referred to by Giraldus contrived, in the midst of his busy life of preaching, politics, and diplomacy, to compose one book on which most of our knowledge [42] of his career depends. This is the book *De Nugis Curialium* (*Courtiers' Trifles*), which impresses a modern reader rather as a note-book of interesting stories and experiences than as a finished work. We quote four passages. Map begins thus:

"I am in time and I speak of time," says Augustine,[43] and adds, "I know not what time is." I likewise can say that I am in the court and speak of the court, and know not, God knows, what the court is. I know, however, that the court is not time; it is temporal, to be sure, changeable, varying, local and wandering, never remaining in the same place; in my retreat I lose sight of it altogether; on my return, I find little or nothing of what I left; become a stranger I see it outside me. The court is the same but its members change. If I shall have described the court, as Porphyry defines genus,[44] perhaps I shall not lie in saying that this multitude in some way relates itself to a

[42] The writings of Giraldus Cambrensis have many references to the career of Map.

[43] Wright quotes a passage from Augustine, *Confessions*, Book xi, chapter 25, which I translate thus, "And I confess to thee, Lord, that I am so far ignorant of the nature of time; and again I confess to thee, Lord, that I know that I am saying this in time, and that I have been talking of time for some time, and that the passage of time is nothing else than a delay in time. How do I know this, when I am ignorant of the nature of time?"

[44] Cf. *ante*, p. 412. Wright quotes from Porphyry, *Isagogus*, chapter 2, a passage, which I translate thus, "For genus is called a collection of individuals relating themselves in some way to a single chief and in turn to each other." This, says Wright, is Boethius' literal rendering of the Greek of the original. Wright adds that Map was probably quoting from memory and confused his quotation with what follows in Boethius; this I render as follows: "And indeed the principle of each generation is first called genus, then the multitude of those which are under one head."

single chief. We (i.e. the courtiers) at least are an infinite multitude, striving to please one alone; and to-day we are one multitude; to-morrow we shall be another.

Later on Map has the following record of reading and conversation at the table of Thomas a Becket:

I was present at the table of the good Thomas then Archbishop of Canterbury; there sat there two white [45] abbots talking of many miracles of . . . Bernard,[46] taking their beginning from what the letter of Bernard says in condemnation of Master Peter,[47] chief of the nominalists, who sinned more in his reasoning than in his knowledge of divinity; for in the latter he communed with his own heart; in the former he labored against his heart and undertook many tasks in opposition to it. *The Letter of Lord Bernard Abbot of Clairvaux to Pope Eugenius*, who had been one of his monks and whom no one of his own order has succeeded (as pope), was being read. In that letter is contained the statement that Master Peter was the proud image of Golias [48] and that Arnold of Brescia [49] was his standard-bearer, and, taking an excellent opportunity against this worst of methods (nominalism), the abbots praised Bernard and extolled him to the stars. And so, John Planeta, because he was unwilling to hear this of the good master (Abelard), said, "I saw one miracle on Mount Pessulanus which many wondered at;" and when asked to relate it, said, "To him whom you have properly called a famous man, was brought bound a certain maniac to be cured; and, sitting on a large mule, Bernard addressed the unclean spirit, with the people who had gathered all silent, and at length said, 'Loose his chains and set him free.' The spirit, however, when it felt itself going, threw stones at the Abbot himself as

[45] I.e. Carmelites.   [46] Cf. *ante*, p. 432.

[47] I.e. Abelard; cf. *ante*, pp. 387–389.

[48] Mythical bishop of the wandering students, whence their songs are called Goliardic. To Map himself has long been ascribed the authorship of many of these poems which ridicule monasticism and monks. The ascription of the authorship to Map is now regarded as without foundation in fact.

[49] *Circa* 1100–1155, an Italian cleric connected with the twelfth-century movement for ecclesiastical reform. He studied under Abelard and tried to apply his doctrines to political conditions.

long as he could, and, instantly following Bernard as he fled
through the villages, even when caught by the people, always
had his eyes on him, because his hands were held." The story
didn't please the presiding officer of the meal and he said to
John in a threatening tone, "Do you call this a miracle?" John
replied, "Those who were present called this a miracle worthy
to be remembered, because the maniac was mild and kind to all
and vexed the hypocrite alone, and this to me has so far been
(an example of) the punishment of presumption." Likewise two
white abbots were talking of the aforementioned man (Bernard)
in the presence of Gilbert Foliot Bishop of London, commending
his miracles; and, after many points had been brought out, one
said, "Although these things which are reported of St. Bernard,
may be true, yet I saw him once when his miraculous power
failed him. A certain man from the borders of Burgundy asked
him to come and cure his son. We went and found the son dead.
Lord Bernard bade that the body be brought into a secluded
room, and, after he had sent everybody else away, lay down
upon (super) the body, and after offering a prayer, got up; but
the boy did not get up, for he lay there dead." Then I said,
"He (Bernard) was the most unhappy of monks; for I never
heard of a monk who sat down on a boy but that the boy at
once got up after him." The abbot blushed and several went
out to laugh. It was stated, however, of this same Bernard,
after this defection of his power, that a second incident happened
to him, not at all favorable to his fame. Walter Count of
Namour died in a Carthusian convent and was buried there.
Therefore, Lord Bernard flew (convolavit) down to his grave and
when he had fallen on his face and prayed a long time, the
Prior begged him to come to breakfast, as it was time. But
Bernard said to him, "I shall not leave here until brother Walter
speaks to me;" and he cried with a loud voice saying, "Walter,
come forth." But Walter, because he did not hear the voice of
Jesus and did not have the ears of Lazarus, did not obey.[50]

Because . . . Arnold of Brescia was mentioned in our talk,
a statement may be made, if you please, about his identity, as
we have heard from a man of that time, a great man indeed

[50] Cf. John 11.

and of much literature, Robert de Burneham. This Arnold was summoned after Abelard by Pope Eugenius, was allowed no defence and condemned in his absence, not because of his writing but because of his preaching. Measured by blood Arnold was noble and great, by learning very great, by devotion in the first rank, indulging himself in the matter of food and raiment only when direst necessity compelled. He went about preaching, seeking not his own but the Lord's and was loved and admired by all. When he reached Rome, the Romans were devoted to his doctrine. He came finally to the papal court and saw the tables of the cardinals laden and delicate in golden and silver dishes; in his letters he took them gently to task for this (luxury) in the presence of the pope, but they bore it ill, and cast him out. But he returning to the city, began tirelessly to teach. The citizens thronged to him and heard him gladly. It happened, moreover, that they learned that Arnold had preached in the presence of the pope on the contempt of wealth and mammon and had been cast out. They gathered round the papal court, cursed the pope and the cardinals, called Arnold a good and just man and the others avaricious, unjust and evil, said that they were not the light of the world but its dregs and . . . scarcely kept themselves from violence. After this brawl had been with difficulty quieted and legates had been sent to the emperor, the pope denounced Arnold as a heretic and excommunicate, and the messengers did not come back until they had seen to it that Arnold was hanged.

In 1179 Map attended the Lateran Council in Rome and was deputed to examine and cross-question the deputies of the Waldenses, a rising sect of heretics. Of this incident he says:

- I saw at the council in Rome under the celebrated Pope Alexander III the Waldensees, rabble, unlearned, named from their founder Waldo who was a citizen of Lyons. They presented to the pope a book in the vernacular of Gaul, in which a text of the Psalter and several other books of both the Old and the New Testaments together with a gloss were contained. They sought with much fervor that the right of preaching be confirmed to them, because they seemed to themselves to be prepared, though they were scarce tyros. For it is a matter of tradition that birds, when they see that they are not subject to snare nor net, think that all ways are open to them. . . . I, the least of many thousands who were called (delegates to the council), derided them, when a discussion or debate arose over their petition, and, charged by a certain great prelate to whom that greatest pope had joined the care of confessions, sat to hear the case. After many skilled and prudent lawyers had been called in, two Waldensees who seemed to be leaders of the sect were brought to me, to dispute with me of the faith, not for the sake of finding out the truth, but that, after I had been convinced, my mouth, like the mouth of one speaking evil, might be closed. I confess I sat down in trepidation, lest, my sins pressing on me, the power of speech in so great a council should be denied me. The prelate bade me, who was ready to answer, proceed against them. At first, therefore, I proposed some very easy questions which no one should be ignorant of, knowing that to a rude ass drivers offer lettuce unworthy of their own lips, "Do you believe in God the Father?" They answered, "We do." "And in the Son?" "Yes." "And in the Holy Spirit?" "We believe." And they were made fun of by manifold clamor of all and went out in confusion, and properly so, because they were governed by no one and sought to be governors, like Phaethon, who didn't know the names of his horses. The Waldensees nowhere had a home . . . but went about barefoot, clad in sheepskins, having no private property, but all things in common, like the apostles, naked following a naked Christ.

In view of the fact that to Map has been ascribed the authorship of several Arthurian romances, it is important and interesting to see what his opinion of the romances was.

The industry of the ancients outstrips us; they render deeds which were past to them present to us, and we are dumb, wherefore their memory lives among us and we are unmindful of our own time. Remarkable miracle! the dead live and the living are buried in their place. And our times also have something

perhaps of Sophocles not lacking the buskin. Yet famous deeds
of modern great men lie hid, and insignificant shreds of antiquity
are exalted. This is doubtless the reason why we know how
to find fault, but not to write; we seek to criticize and deserve
to be criticized. So the double tongues of detractors make poets
rare. Thus minds are torpid and geniuses perish; thus the
innocent serenity of our time is disturbed, and its light is
dimmed though from no lack of material; but craftsmen are
lacking and we are not esteemed. Cæsar in Lucan, Æneas in
Virgil live in many praises; the vigilance of the poets is
the greatest, not the least, thing in their favor. To us only
the folly of minstrels celebrates the divine nobility of the
Charleses [51] and the Pepins; [51] no one speaks of the present
Cæsars, yet their characters are ready to the pen with their
bravery, temperance and universal admiration.

Layamon (flourished 1200) merits notice as the first
important writer of the English vernacular after the Norman Conquest. So much of his life and work as he thought
should be known we have in his own words — and this is
all we know of him.

There was a priest in the land who was named Layamon; he
was the son of Leovenath — may the Lord be gracious to him !
— he dwelt at Ernley, at a noble church upon Severn's bank.
Pleasant there it seemed to him, near Radestone where he read
books. It came into his mind and chief thought that he would
tell the noble deeds of the English; what they were named and
whence they came, who had first possessed the English land,
after the flood that came from God; that destroyed here all
that it found alive, except Noah and Shem, Ham and Japhet
and their four wives, who were with them in the ark. Layamon
began to journey wide over this land and procured the good
books which he took for authority. He took the English book
that Saint Bede made; another he took in Latin that Saint
Albin made and the fair Augustine who brought baptism in
hither; the third book he took and laid it there in the midst,

[51] I.e. Charlemagne and his father, celebrated in romance.

that a French clerk made, who was named Wace, who could write well, and he gave it to the noble Eleanor who was the high King Henry's queen. Layamon laid before him these books and turned over the leaves; lovingly he beheld them — may the Lord be merciful to him! He took pen in his fingers and wrote on book-skin and set the words together and the three books compressed into one. Now prayeth Layamon, for love of Almighty God, that each good man that shall read this book and learn this counsel, say together these true words, for his father's soul who begat him, and for his mother's soul who bore him to be man, and for his own soul, that better befall it. Amen!

The life of Robert Mannyng of Brunne must be imagined from the following passages in *Handlyng Synne* (1303) and *The Story of England* (1338):

Of Brunne I am, if any blame me; Robert Mannyng is my name; blessed be he by the God of heaven who will graciously remember me; in the third Edward's time was I when I wrote this history; I was in the house of Sixille; Dan Robert of Malton whom you know wrote it for his companions' delight when they desired pleasure. . . .

To all Christian men under the sun, and to the good men of Brunne, and especially all by name of the fellowship of Sempringham, Robert of Brunne gives greeting — in all the goodness that may be had — of Brunne Wake in Kesteven, six miles beyond Sempringham.

I dwelt in the Priory fifteen years in the company, in the time of good Dan John of Camelton, now departed; in his time was I there ten years and knew and heard of his manners; then with Dan John of Clinton five winters I lived; Dan Philip was master at the time I began this English rime; the year of grace then happened to be a thousand three hundred and three. . . .

Now of King Robert Bruce shall I tell still more and of his brothers Thomas and . . . sir Alexander for whom I am sorry — they both got into trouble for deeds they did. Alexander was a masterful artist and made a carven king in Cambridge for the clergy before his brother was king. There has been no one since who was so successful as he in art and but one before him who read in Cambridge. Robert (i.e. King Robert Bruce) made a celebration for him, for he was there then, and he who wrote and made this rime saw the whole thing. . . .

Now have we told of the Britons, of kings and some barons, how they maintained this land, from the time of Brutus who first discovered it up to the time of Cadwallader. Now we are going to leave off riming about the Britons and shall tell of the English who began to live here after the Britons. The English took the land at God's command and their period we call the English period. Everything is called English that is spoken in this language; Frankish speech is called romance — clerks and men of France say so. Peter Langtoft, a canon tonsured in the house of Bridlington, wrote all this history of the English kings in romance. . . . He wrote down all the deeds they did and I translated after him. I can follow and get his meaning but cannot imitate his fine diction; I am not worthy to open his book. . . . When Peter began his book he besought a holy clerk to give him grace to succeed — namely that holy man called St. Bede — for he found much in his books; Bede made five books of English history. And I shall pray him likewise to give me grace to write well and put this into rime. . . .

For ignorant men I undertook in the English tongue to make this book. For many are of such a character that they will gladly listen to tales and rimes: in games and feasts and at the ale-house men like to listen to idle tales which may often lead to villainy; for such men I have made this rime as a better way to spend their time. . . .

Lords, who are now here, listen and hearken to the *Story of England* as Robert Mannyng found it written and has put it into English, not for the learned but for the ignorant, for those who live in this country and know no Latin nor French, to give them solace and joy when they sit together.

And it's a good thing to know the state of the land, . . . what sort of people first settled it, . . . and it is good for many reasons to hear of the deeds of the kings, to know which were fools and which wise, which of them knew most, and which did wrong and which right, and which maintained peace, and which made war. . . .

One master Wace in French told all the *Brut* which he translated from Latin, from Æneas to Cadwallader. Then master Wace leaves off; and just as far as Wace goes I follow with my English in the same way; for Wace rimes all the Latin while Peter Langtoft sometimes skips. Master Wace told all the *Brut* and Peter Langtoft the deeds of the English. Where Wace stopped Langtoft began and told the story of England; as he says, so say I.

Richard Rolle of Hampole (*circa* 1290–*circa* 1349) is noteworthy as one of the first writers of original English prose after the Conquest. Our knowledge of his life is derived from a *Legenda et Officium etc.* (*Legend and Office, etc.*) prepared shortly after his death by the nuns of Hampole in anticipation of his canonization, which, however, did not occur. A translation of the relevant parts of the *Legend and Office* reads as follows:

The saint of God Richard the Hermit was born on a farm at Thornton in the diocese of York. At the proper time, moreover, by the industry of his parents he was apprenticed to learning. And when he was of more mature years, Master Thomas de Neville, formerly Archdeacon of Durham, honorably placed him at the University of Oxford where he was deemed very proficient in study. He desired to be imbued with the theological doctrines of sacred scripture more fully and completely than with physic and the discipline of secular science. At length, in the nineteenth year of his life, considering the duration of mortal life uncertain and its end fearful, especially to those who either give way to the indulgence of the flesh or labor only to heap up riches and for this strive with schemes and tricks — though they mostly trick themselves —, he concluded, through the inspiration of God, thinking betimes of his latest plans, not to be taken in the snares of sin but to return from Oxford to his father's house. One day he said to his sister who loved him with a tender affection, "Sister beloved, you have two tunics, one white and the other gray, which I should very much like to have. I beg you, as far as you can, to grant my request and bring the garments along with a rain hood belonging to my father to the wood nearby." She was glad to comply and, as she had agreed, brought the articles to the grove the next day, though she had no idea of what her brother intended to do. But when he had received the clothes, he at once cut off the sleeves of the gray tunic and the trimmings off the white one, and in some way contrived to sew sleeves on his own under garment that the whole outfit might serve his purpose. He then took off his own outer garments and put on his sister's white robe, over which he put the gray one and struck his arms through the sleeve holes. He then put the rain hood on his head in such a way that after some fashion at that time he might get for himself a rough likeness to a hermit. But when his sister had seen what was going on, she cried in her amazement, "My brother is crazy, my brother is crazy." When he heard this he drove her from him with threats and immediately fled far away, lest he should be seized by his friends and acquaintances.

> The saint flees to solitude,
> He enters then a celestial order,
> Seeking the sweetness of a holy life.
> The abbot love there maintains a perfect rule,
> Soon gives the formula for a holy life.

After putting on the garments of a hermit and leaving his parents, he went to a certain church on the Eve of the Assumption of the Blessed Virgin, Mother of God, in which he knelt to pray in a place where the wife of a faithful knight, Sir John de Dalton, was wont to worship. When she entered the church to hear vespers, the servants of the knight tried to crowd Richard out, but Lady de Dalton in humility would not allow it. When Richard rose from his devotions at the conclusion of vespers, the sons of the knight, who had been students at Oxford, said that they knew that (the stranger) was the son of William Rolle and that they had known him at Oxford. On the day of the Assumption Richard again entered the church and, without any suggestion from any one, put on the dress of an assistant and chanted matins and the office of the mass with the rest (of the clergy). When, further, the gospel had been read in the mass, after seeking the blessing of the priest, he entered the pulpit and preached a wonderfully edifying sermon to the people so that so great a multitude of people were touched with compunction at his words that they could scarce keep from tears, and testified that they had never before heard a discourse of such power and force. Nor was it remarkable since he was the special vessel of the Holy Spirit, sounding from His influence, whose province it is, as the apostle says in Romans, to scatter His grace as He pleases and to cause groanings unutterable.[52]

.   .   .   .[53]

After mass, therefore, the aforementioned knight (Sir John de Dalton) invited him to dine, (and), when he had entered his manor, Richard stayed in an old tumbled down hut, being unwilling to enter the hall but rather sought to fulfil the gospel injunction which says that when you have been invited to a wedding-feast you should sit in the lowest seat, until he who has invited you, says to you, "Friend go up higher,"[54] which was fulfilled in his case. For when they had looked diligently for him and had found him in the abovementioned hut, the knight seated him at table above his own sons. Richard himself, moreover, was such a perfect guardian of his silence that not a single word came from his mouth. And when he had satisfied himself, he rose before they took out the table and was going out. The knight who had called him said that this was not usual, and after repeating the statement got him to stay. When the meal was over he again wished to leave but the knight, who desired to have a private conference with him, kept him until, when all the rest who had been there had gone, he asked him whether he was the son of William Rolle. (And Richard said he was.) . . .[53]

After Sir John had examined him in secret and on perfect evidence had determined he was sane, he clothed him in proper garments according to Richard's wish and kept him a long time on his estate, giving him lodging in a solitary place and providing him with all the necessaries of life. And he accordingly began with all diligence day and night to strive for a more perfect life,

[52] Cf. Romans 8.
[53] The omitted portion involves verses commenting on the situation.
[54] Cf. Luke 14: 10.

and in every way he could to excell in the contemplative life
and flame with divine love. . . .[55]

Most admirable and especially useful were the occupations of
this saint in holy exhortations by which he converted many to
God, and also in his sweet writings, treatises and books, written
to edify his neighbors, which all reproduced in the hearts of worshippers a most grateful harmony; and among other remarkable
things, it was noticed that, when he was once seated in his cell
after dinner, the lady of the manor and many with her came to
him and found him writing very rapidly. They asked him to
stop and speak some word of edification to them. And at once
he exhorted them to follow the best virtues, leave the vanities
of the world and confirm their hearts in the love of God. But
he did not at all on that account stop writing for two hours.
. . . This could not have been, had not the Spirit at that time
directed his hand and tongue especially when distractions were
continually breaking in and his talk was altogether different
from what he was writing. So much was he in the Spirit at
times when he prayed, that others took off the tattered garment
with which he was covered, nor did he know nor notice that it
was patched, mended and put back on him. . . .[56]

A curious collection of travelers' tales dating from about
1350 was for a long time ascribed to Sir John Mandeville.
Modern criticism has concluded that there was no such
person. But we have the book, and its prolog is an interesting document, as a reading of it will prove.

Forasmuch as the land beyond the sea, that is to say, the
Holy Land, which men call the Land of Promise or Behest, surpassing all other lands, is the most worthy land, most excellent,
and lady and sovereign of all other lands, and has been blessed

[55] The omitted portion describes the various models Richard set himself, his
mystic experiences, mortified life, fasts and vigils.

[56] The omitted portion describes Richard's temptations and miracles and re-
counts his longing for death. The document concludes with the statement that,
when a woman whom he had cured needed his aid again, she sent a messenger for
him, who found him dead. On Richard, see *The Cambridge History of English
Literature*, ii, chapter 2 and *Bibliography*.

and hallowed by the precious body and blood of our Lord Jesus
Christ; in the which land it pleased Him to take flesh and blood
of the Virgin Mary, to compass that holy land with His blessed
feet; and there He would in His blessedness be born of the said
blessed and glorious Virgin Mary, and become a man, and work
many miracles, and preach and teach the faith and law of Christian men unto His children; and there it pleased Him to suffer
much reproof and scorn for us; and He that was King of Heaven,
of Air, of Earth, of Sea and of All Things Therein Contained,
would only be called King of the Jews; and that land He chose
before all other lands, as the best and most worthy land, and
the most virtuous land in all the world; for it is the heart and
center of all the world; witness the philosophers who say, "The
virtue of things is in their midst"; and that in that land He
would lead His life and suffer passion and death at the hands of
the Jews for us; to buy and deliver us from the pains of hell
and death without end; which had been ordained for us because
of the sin of our first father Adam and because of our own sins
also; for, as for Himself, He had deserved no evil; for He never
thought nor did evil: and He that was King of Glory and of
Joy might best in that place suffer death; because He chose
that land rather than any other to suffer His passion and death
in; for he that will publish anything in order to make it known,
will have it cried and proclaimed in the central square of a
town; so that the thing which is proclaimed and announced may
reach all parts equally soon: just so, He who was the Former
of all the world, would suffer for us at Jerusalem; that is, the
center of the world; to the end and intent, that His passion
and His death, that was published there, might be known equally
early in all parts of the world. See how dear He bought man,
whom He made in His own image, and how dear He redeemed
us, for the great love He bore us, and we never deserved it of
Him. For no more precious chattels nor a greater ransom could
be offered for us than His blessed body, His precious blood and
His holy life that He enslaved for us. Ah dear God! what love
He had for us His subjects when He that never trespassed would
for us trespassers suffer death! Right well ought we to love and
worship, to fear and serve such a Lord; and to honor and praise

such a holy land that brought forth such Fruit through which
every man is saved, unless from his own fault. Well may that
land be called a delightful and fruitful land that was wet and
moistened with the precious blood of our Lord Jesus Christ;
the which is the same land that our Lord promised us as an
inheritance. And in that land He would die, as if He had seized
it to leave it to us His children. Wherefore, every good Christian man that has the power and the wherewithal, should take
pains with all his might to conquer our rightful heritage and
drive out all unbelievers. For we are called Christian men after
Christ our Father. And if we are true children of Christ, we
ought to claim the heritage that our Father left us and take it
out of heathen men's hands. But now, pride, covetousness and
envy have so inflamed the hearts of the lords of the world, that
they are more busy in disinheriting their neighbors than in claiming and conquering their rightful heritage just mentioned. And
the common people, who would lay out their bodies and property
to conquer our heritage, cannot do it without the lords. For a
throng of people without a leader or a chief lord is like a flock of
sheep without a shepherd; they scatter and disperse and know
not whither to go. But would God that the temporal lords and
all secular lords were in harmony and with the common people
would take this holy voyage over the sea. Then I trow well
that within a short time our rightful heritage aforementioned
would be reconciled and put in the hands of the proper heirs
of Jesus Christ.

And inasmuch as a long time has passed since there was a
general expedition or voyage over the sea; and many men desire
to hear of the Holy Land and get solace and comfort thereby;
I, John Mandeville, although I am not worthy, who was born
in England, in the town of St. Albans, passed the sea in the year
of our Lord 1322, on St. Michael's Day, and have been a long
time oversea, and have seen and gone through many divers
lands and many provinces and kingdoms and isles, and have
passed through Tartary, Persia, Armenia, the little and the great;
through Libya, Chaldea, and a great part of Ethiopia; through
the land of the Amazons, the greater part of India, the less and
the greater; and throughout many other islands that are about

India; where dwell many divers peoples, and of varied manners and laws and of strange shapes of men. Of which lands and isles I shall speak more plainly hereafter. And I shall describe to you some part of the things that are there, at the proper time when they occur to me; and especially for them who desire and intend to visit the Holy City of Jerusalem and the holy places that are around it. And I shall tell them the way to take thither. For I have many times passed and ridden that way in the goodly company of many lords: thank God.

And you are to understand that I have translated this book out of Latin into French and rendered it in turn out of French into English that every man of my nation may understand it. But lords and knights and other nobles and worthy men who know but little Latin and have been beyond sea will know and understand whether I err in describing or setting forth or otherwise; that they may correct and amend it. For things passed out of one's mind or not seen for a space are soon forgotten; because the mind of man cannot be stimulated nor restrained, because of human frailty.

John Wiclif (1320?–1384), because of his prominence in the church and theology, came to be unusually well known in the world and "got his name into" the chronicles. An anonymous writer in the Harleian MSS. number 2261 thus describes Wiclif in 1377:

Master John Wiclif, doctor of divinity in the University of Oxford, began to sustain openly in the said University erroneous conclusions contrary to the state of the universal Church and conclusions of heresy, and especially against canons, monks and religious men possessionate, which drew to him in this time divers fellows of the same sect dwelling in Oxford, going barefoot with long gowns of russet, that they might publish and fortify their errors against men contrarious to them, preaching openly the said errors. Among whom they said that the sacrament in the altar after the sacrament or consecration is not the very body of Christ. Also he said that temporal lords and men might take away meritoriously the goods (of) men of the Church sinning or trespassing. Nevertheless the Pope with his council damned xxiii conclusions as vain, erroneous and full of heresy, and sent bulls direct to the Metropolitan of England and the Bishop of London that they should cause the said Master John to be arrested and to examine him of the said conclusions. That inquisition done, and a declaration made, the Archbishop of Canterbury commanded and prohibited the said Master John and his codisciples to use the said conclusions, and so they were still for a season. But soon after, by supportation of lords and other noblemen, they took to them more wicked opinions, and had great continuation in their malice.[57]

Adam of Usk in his Chronicle has the following to say of Wiclif and his followers in 1382:

According to the saying of Solomon, "Woe to thee, O land, when thy king is a child," [58] in the time of the youth of the same Richard (II) many misfortunes, both caused thereby and happening therefrom, ceased not to harass the kingdom of England . . . even to the great disorder of the State, and to the last undoing of King Richard himself and of those who too fondly clung to him. Amongst all other misfortunes, nay, amongst the most wicked of all wicked things, even errors and heresies in the catholic faith, England, and above all, London and Bristol, stood corrupted, being infected by the seeds which one master John Wycliffe sowed, polluting, as it were, the faith with the tares of his baleful teaching. And the followers of this master John, like Mahomet, by preaching things pleasing to the powerful and rich, namely, that of withholding of tithes and even of offerings and the plundering of temporal goods from the clergy were praiseworthy, and, to the young, that self-indulgence was a virtue, most wickedly did sow the seed of murder, snares, strife, variance and discords, which last unto this day, and which, I fear, will last even to the undoing of the kingdom. . . . The people of England, wrangling about the old faith and the new, are every day, as it were, on the very point of bringing down

[57] Cf. *ante*, pp. 451–455.
[58] Cf. Ecclesiastes 10: 16. It is rather suggestive that the same quotation is applied to the condition of England in the *Vision of William concerning Piers the Plowman;* cf. B text, *Prolog*, l. 193; C text, I, l. 206.

upon their own heads rebellion and ruin. And I fear that in the end it will happen as once it did, when many citizens of London, true to the faith, rose against the Duke of Lancaster to slay him, because he favored the said master John, so that hurrying from his table into a boat hastily provided, he fled across the Thames, and hardly escaped with his life.

The Bull of Pope Gregory XI. to the University of Oxford against Wiclif reads in translation as follows:

Gregory, bishop, servant of the servants of God, to his beloved sons the chancellor and University of Oxford, in the diocese of Lincoln, grace and apostolic benediction.

We are compelled to wonder and grieve that you, who, in consideration of the favors and privileges conceded to your university of Oxford by the apostolic see, and on account of your familiarity with the Scriptures, in whose sea you navigate, by the gift of God, with auspicious oar, you, who ought to be, as it were, warriors and champions of the orthodox faith, without which there is no salvation of souls, — that you through a certain sloth and neglect allow tares to spring up amidst the pure wheat in the fields of your glorious university aforesaid; and what is still more pernicious, even continue to grow to maturity. And you are quite careless, as has been lately reported to us, as to the extirpation of these tares; with no little clouding of a bright name, danger to your souls, contempt of the Roman church, and injury to the faith above mentioned. And what pains us the more is that this increase of the tares aforesaid is known in Rome before the remedy of extirpation has been applied in England where they sprang up. By the insinuation of many, if they are indeed worthy of belief, deploring it deeply, it has come to our ears that John de Wycliffe, rector of the church of Lutterworth, in the diocese of Lincoln, Professor of the Sacred Scriptures, (would that he were not also Master of Errors,) has fallen into such a detestable madness that he does not hesitate to dogmatize and publicly preach, or rather vomit forth from the recesses of his breast certain propositions and conclusions which are erroneous and false. He has cast himself also into the depravity of preaching heretical dogmas which strive to subvert and weaken the state of the whole church and even secular polity, some of which doctrines, in changed terms, it is true, seem to express the perverse opinions and unlearned learning of Marsilio of Padua[59] of cursed memory, and of John of Jandun, whose book is extant, rejected and cursed by our predecessor, Pope John XXII, of happy memory. This he has done in the kingdom of England, lately glorious in its power and in the abundance of its resources, but more glorious still in the glistening piety of its faith, and in the distinction of its sacred learning; producing also many men illustrious for their exact knowledge of the holy Scriptures, mature in the gravity of their character, conspicuous in devotion, defenders of the catholic church. He has polluted certain of the faithful of Christ by besprinkling them with these doctrines, and led them away from the right paths of the aforesaid faith to the brink of perdition.

Wherefore, since we are not willing, nay, indeed, ought not to be willing, that so deadly a pestilence should continue to exist with our connivance, a pestilence which, if it is not opposed in its beginnings, and torn out by the roots in its entirety, will be reached too late by medicines when it has infected very many with its contagion; we command your university with strict admonition, by the apostolic authority, in virtue of your sacred obedience, and under penalty of the deprivation of all the favors, indulgences, and privileges granted to you and your university by the said see, for the future not to permit to be asserted or set forth to any extent whatever, the opinions, conclusions, and propositions which are in variance with good morals and faith, even when those setting them forth strive to defend them under a certain fanciful wresting of words or of terms. Moreover, you are on our authority to arrest the said John, or cause him to be arrested and to send him under a trustworthy guard to our venerable brother, the Archbishop of Canterbury, and the Bishop of London, or to one of them.

[59] Or Marsiglio (*circa* 1280–*circa* 1343) with John of Jandun between 1324 and 1326 wrote *Defensor Pacis* (*Defender of the Peace*). The thesis of the book is that the way to peace in the world is for the Church to give up any claim to temporal power. Marsilio argues for the separation of Church and State, pleads for religious liberty, and denies the right of the Church to punish heresy.

Besides, if there should be, which God forbid, in your university, subject to your jurisdiction, opponents stained with these errors, and if they should obstinately persist in them, proceed vigorously and earnestly to a similar arrest and removal of them, and otherwise as shall seem good to you. Be vigilant to repair your negligence which you have hitherto shown in the premises, and so obtain our gratitude and favor, and that of the said see, besides the honor and reward of the divine recompense.

Given at Rome, at Santa Maria Maggiore, on the 31st of May, the sixth year of our pontificate.

Wiclif's reply to the papal summons to come to Rome in 1384 is written, as we should expect of the reformer, in English. In modernized spelling it reads thus:

I have joy fully to tell what I hold, to all true men that believe and especially to the Pope; for I suppose that if my faith be rightful and given of God, the Pope will gladly confirm it; and if my faith be error, the Pope will wisely amend it.

I suppose over this that the gospel of Christ be heart of the corps of God's law; for I believe that Jesus Christ, that gave in his own person this gospel, is very God and very man, and by this heart passes all other laws.

I suppose over this that the Pope be most obliged to the keeping of the gospel among all men that live here; for the Pope is highest vicar that Christ has here in earth. For moreness of Christ's vicar is not measured by worldly moreness, but by this, that this vicar follows more Christ by virtuous living; for thus teacheth the gospel, that this is the sentence of Christ.

And of this gospel I take as belief, that Christ for time that he walked here, was most poor man of all, both in spirit and in having; for Christ says that he had naught for to rest his head on. And Paul says that he was made needy for our love. And more poor might no man be, neither bodily nor in spirit. And thus Christ put from him all manner of worldly lordship. For the gospel of John telleth that when they would have made Christ king, he fled and hid him from them, for he would none such worldly highness.

And over this I take it as belief, that no man should follow the Pope, nor no saint that now is in heaven, but in as much as he follows Christ. For John and James erred when they coveted worldly highness; and Peter and Paul sinned also when they denied and blasphemed in Christ; but men should not follow them in this, for then they went from Jesus Christ. And this I take as wholesome counsel, that the Pope leave his worldly lordship to worldly lords, as Christ gave them, — and move speedily all his clerks to do so. For thus did Christ, and taught thus his disciples, till the fiend had blinded this world. And it seems to some men that clerks that dwell lastingly in this error against God's law, and flee to follow Christ in this, been open heretics, and their fautors been partners.

And if I err in this sentence, I will meekly be amended, yea, by the death, if it be skilful, for that I hope were good to me. And if I might travel in mine own person, I would with good will go to the Pope. But God has needed me to the contrary, and taught me more obedience to God than to men. And I suppose of our Pope that he will not be Antichrist, and reverse Christ in this working, to the contrary of Christ's will; for if he summon against reason, by him or by any of his, and pursue this unskilful summoning, he is an open Antichrist. And merciful intent excused not Peter, that Christ should not clepe him Satan; so blind intent and wicked counsel excuses not the Pope here; but if he ask of true priests that they travel more than they may, he is not excused by reason of God, that he should not be Antichrist. For our belief teaches us that our blessed God suffers us not to be tempted more than we may; how should a man ask such service? And therefore pray we to God for our pope Urban the sixth, that his old holy intent be not quenched by his enemies. And Christ, that may not lie, says that the enemies of a man been especially his home family; and this is sooth of men and fiends.

But here we are especially interested in Wiclif as a literary man, because to him belongs the honor of first translating into the English speech the entire Bible, a work that has had a remarkable influence on English literary style, as well as upon English thought. What a contemporary thought of Wiclif's work in this field is indicated in the following remarks of Henry Knighton:

At this time flourished Master John Wycliffe, rector of the church of Lutterworth in the county of Leicester, the most eminent doctor of theology of those days. In philosophy he was second to none, in scholastic learning incomparable. This man strove especially to eclipse the thoughts of others by the depth of his knowledge and the subtlety of his reasoning, and to differ from them in opinion. He is reported to have introduced into the church many opinions which were condemned by the learned men of the universal church. These will, in part, be described in the proper place. He had as a forerunner John Ball,[60] just as Christ had John Baptist, who prepared His way before Him in such opinions and disturbed many by his teachings, at least so it is said. I have made mention of him before. This Master John Wycliffe translated from the Latin into the tongue of the Angles (though not of the angels) the gospel which Christ intrusted to the clergy and learned men of the church, in order that they might gently minister it to the laity and to the weak according to the exigency of the times and the need and mental hunger of each one. Thus to the laity and even to such women as can read, this was made more open than formerly it had been even to such of the clergy as were well educated and of great understanding. Thus the evangelical pearls have been scattered abroad and trampled by the swine,[61] and that which used to be dear to clergy and laity is now a common jest in the mouth of both. The gem of the clergy has become the toy of the laity.

John Capgrave, an English chronicler of the next century, thus records the death of Wiclif:

In the 9th year of this king (Richard II), John Wiclif, the organ of the devil, the enemy of the Church, the mirror of hypocrisy, the nourisher of schism, by the rightful doom of God, was smitten with a horrible palsy throughout his body. And this

---

[60] Cf. *ante*, pp. 330–350.   [61] Cf. Matthew 7: 6.

vengeance fell upon him on St. Thomas' [62] Day in Christmas, but he died not till St. Silvester's [63] Day. And worthily was he smitten on St. Thomas' Day, against whom he had greatly offended, letting (hindering) men of that pilgrimage; [62] and conveniently died he in Silvester's feast, against whom he had venomously barked for dotation (endowment) of the Church.

The present controversy over the authorship of the poem or poems called collectively *The Vision of William concerning Piers the Plowman* has already [64] been referred to. The traditional autobiography of William Langland, long called the author, we have in his own words in the latest or C version of the text, as the late Professor Skeat named it. Mr. Burrell has rendered it into modern English as follows:

Thus I woke, God wot, where I dwelt in Cornhill.
Kit [65] my wife and I, dressed like a loller (vagabond or beggar),
And among the London lollers little was I set by,
And among the hermits (trust me for that),
For I made verses on them as my wit taught me.

Once when I had my health, in hot harvest time,
And my limbs to labor with, and loved good fare,
And nothing in life to do, but drink and sleep,
In health of body and mind,
I came on Conscience, and Reason met me,
He met and questioned me, and my memory roamed back,
And Reason reproved me.

"Canst thou serve as a priest or sing in church?
Make a haycock in the field or pitch the hay?

[62] I.e. Thomas a Becket; the reference to the pilgrimage means that Wiclif advised people not to do penance by making the pilgrimage to Canterbury and leaving an offering there.

[63] I.e. Pope Silvester I; on the dotation or endowment referred to below, cf. *ante*, p. 319. St. Thomas' Day is Dec. 29; St. Silvester's, Dec. 31.

[64] Cf. *ante*, pp. 242-247; 255-257; 330.

[65] She is referred to again C text, XXI, l. 473, where a daughter, Kalote, is also mentioned.

Canst mow or stock or bind the sheaves?
Canst reap or guide the reapers? Canst rise early?
Canst blow the horn, and keep the kine together,
Lie out o'nights, and save my corn from thieves?

"Make shoes or clothes, or herd the sheep?
Trim hedge, use harrow, or drive the swine and geese,
Or do any other work that the people need
To win some living for them that be bedridden?"
"Nay," said I, "God help me,
I am too weak to work with sickle or with scythe.
I am too long,[66] believe me, to stoop low down,
Or to last for any time as a true working man."

"Then hast thou lands to live by or rich lineage
That findeth thee thy food? An idle man thou seemest;
Thou art a spender and canst spend; thou art a spill-time,
Or thou beggest thy living at men's buttery hatches;
Thou art a Friday-beggar, a feast-day beggar in the churches;
A loller's life is thine, little to be praised.
Righteousness rewardeth men as they deserve.
THOU SHALT YIELD TO EACH MAN AFTER HIS WORKS.[67]
Thou art maybe broken in body or limb,
Maimed maybe through mishap, therefore art thou excused?"

"When I was young," quoth I, "many a year ago,
My father and my friends set me to school
Til I knew thoroughly what Holy Scripture said,
What is best for the body, what is safest for the soul.
Yet never did I find since my friends died
A life that pleased me save in these long clothes,
If I must live by labor and earn my living
I must needs labor at the work I learned.
EACH MAN IN WHAT CALLING HE IS CALLED THERE DWELL HE.[68]

[66] The author calls himself *Long Will*, B text, XV, l. 148. He is called *Will*, C
text, II, l. 5; XI, l. 71; A text, XII, ll. 99, 103.
[67] Cf. Matthew 16: 27; Revelation 2: 23.
[68] Cf. 1 Corinthians 7: 20, 24.

"I live *in* London and I live *on* London,
The tools I labor with, to get my living by,
Are the Lord's Prayer, my Primer, my Dirges and my Vespers,
And sometimes my Psalter and the Seven Psalms;
I sing masses for the souls of those that give me help,
And they that find me food welcome me when I come,
Man or woman, once a month, into their houses;
No bag have I nor bottle, only my belly.

"Moreover, my lord Reason, men should, methinks,
Constrain no cleric to do common work,
The tonsured clerk, a man of understanding,
Should neither sweat nor toil, nor swear at inquests,
Nor fight in the van of battle, nor hurt his foe.
RENDER NOT EVIL FOR EVIL.[69]
They be the heirs of heaven, all that are ordained,
And in choir and church, Christ's own ministers.
THE LORD IS THE PORTION OF MINE INHERITANCE.[70]
Clerks it becometh for to serve Christ,
And for folk unordained to cart and work,
And no clerk should be tonsured save he be the son
Of frankleyns and free men and of wedded folk;
Bondmen and bastards and beggars' children,
These are the sons of labor, *these* are to serve lords,
To serve God and the good as their station asketh.

"But since bondmen's sons are made into bishops,
And bastards' bairns are made archdeacons,
And soap-makers and their sons are knights for silver's sake,
And lords' sons be their laborers and have mortgaged their rents
And to support this realm have ridden against our foes
To comfort the Commons and honor the king,
And monks and nuns that should support the poor
Have made their own kin knights and paid the fees for it,
Popes and patrons refuse poor gentle blood,
And take the sons of Mammon to keep the Sanctuary;
Holiness of life and Love have long to us been strangers,

[69] Cf. 1 Thessalonians 5: 15.   [70] Cf. Psalms 16: 5.

And will be till these things wear out, or they be somehow
  changed.
"Therefore, rebuke me not, Reason, I pray thee,
For in my conscience I know what Christ would have me do.
Prayers of a perfect man and his discreet penance,
These be the dearest work that our Lord loveth."

Quoth Conscience, "By Christ, I see not where this tendeth,
But to beg your life in cities is not the perfect life,
Save you be in obedience to Prior or to Minster."
"That's truth," said I, "I do acknowledge it,
That I have lost my time, mis-spent my time,
And yet I hope that even as one who oft hath bought and sold
And always lost and lost and at the last hath happened
To buy him such a bargain that he is better for ever
And all his loss is at the last only as a leaf,
Such winning is his, under God's grace,
THE KINGDOM OF HEAVEN IS LIKE THE TREASURE ETCETERA,[71]
A WOMAN WHO FOUND A PIECE OF SILVER . . . ETCETERA,[72]
Even so hope I to have of Him that is Almighty
A gobbet of His grace; and then begin a time
That I shall turn to profit all the days of my life."

"I counsel thee," quoth Reason, "hurry to begin
The life that is commendable and dear to the soul;"
"Aye, and continue in it," quoth Conscience.

So to the kirk I went to honor my Lord;
Before the Cross upon my knees I knocked my breast,
Sighing for my sins, saying my prayer,
Weeping and wailing till again I was asleep.

"To write anything like a biography of Gower, with the
materials that exist, is an impossibility. Almost the only
authentic records of him, apart from his writings, are his
marriage-license, his will, and his tomb in St. Saviour's
Church; and it was this last which furnished most of the

---

[71] Cf. Matthew 13: 44.   [72] Cf. Luke 15: 9.

material out of which the early accounts of the poet were composed." [73] We shall quote here Mr. Macaulay's paraphrase of the marriage-license, his version of the will, various pertinent passages from the works of the poet and the description of the tomb by the Elizabethan antiquary John Stow. The contents of the marriage-license are as follows:

"25 Jan. 1397–8. A license from the bishop of Winchester for solemnizing the marriage between John Gower and Agnes Groundolf, both parishioners of St. Mary Magdalene, Southwark, without further publication of banns and in a place outside their parish church, that is to say, in the oratory of the said John Gower, within his lodging in the Priory of Saint Mary Overey in Southwark. Dated at Highclere."

At the beginning of a verse epistle dedicating his *Vox Clamantis* (*Voice of One Crying*) to Archbishop Arundell of Canterbury (1396–1414), Gower writes:

This epistle, written in his heart's devotion, John Gower old and blind has sent to the Most Reverend Father in Christ and his own special lord, Thomas of Arundell, Archbishop of Canterbury, Primate of all England and Legate of the Apostolic See. Whose state to the rule of His church may the Son of the Virgin, our Lord Jesus Christ, direct and happily preserve, who with God the Father and Spirit lives and rules as God for ever. Amen.

Of the origin of his English poem *Confessio Amantis* (*Confession of One Loving*) Gower writes in his *Prolog:*

The books of those who wrote before us remain and we are thereby instructed of what was written then: hence, it is proper that we also in our time among us here write of modern events, as we have example of the ancients that it can be so. That when we are dead and elsewhere, there may be a remainder for the ear of the world in times coming after this.

But, because people say, and it is true, that one who writes entirely to instruct often dulls a man's wit if he is going to read

[73] Cf. Macaulay, *The Works of John Gower*, IV, p. vii.

all day, . . . I would take a middle course and write a book between the two, somewhat of learning and somewhat of pleasure, so that some one may like more or less what I write. And because few men are writing in our English, I intend to make a book for England's sake, the sixteenth year of King Richard.

This *Prolog* is extant in two forms, an earlier and a later. The two agree thus far with the exception that in the earlier *King Richard's sake* is the expression used instead of *England's sake*, and the dating year is not mentioned. The earlier form then continues:

A book for King Richards's sake to whom belongs my allegiance with all my heart's obedience in everything that a liege man can or ought to do for his king. So far forth I recommend myself to him who may entirely command me, and pray to the High King who causes every king to reign, that his crown may long be his. I recall and wish it understood, as it once happened, in the town of New Troy (London) which took its first joy from Brutus, that as I once came rowing along the River Thames, as fortune would chance, I met my liege lord. And so it befell, as I came nigh and he saw me, that he bade me come into his barge. And when I was in company with him, amongst other said, he laid this charge on me, and bade me do my utmost to write something new for him, that he might see it after the form of my writing.

And thus at his command my heart is the more glad to do his behest; and also my fear is the less that envy will not bring it about to censure and blame unreasonably what I shall write. A gentle heart stills his tongue so that it will distill no malice, but praises what is praiseworthy. But from him who cares not for his words and does everything wrong I pray the Heavenly King to shield me.

And though the world is wild and full of such jangling, whatever may befall, the king's command shall not be neglected. I, hoping to deserve his thanks, shall follow his will — otherwise I were inexcusable, for that which a king asks may not be denied.

Perhaps a reason for the substitution of *England* for *Richard* in the *Prolog* to the *Confessio Amantis*, and the omission of the following lines, may be that Gower gradually drew away from Richard to Henry IV, for whom the poet declares himself thus in the *Dedication* to his *Ballades:*

Your suitor [74] and humble vassal, your Gower [75] who is wholly your subject, since you have received the crown, will do you service other than I did before, now in ballade, which is the flower of song, now in virtue where the soul has its heart: he who trusts in God has the better part.

In another French poem Gower has an apology for writing in French:

To the university of all the world John Gower sends this envoy; and if I have not the fashion of a Frenchman, pardon me that I lead you astray from it (pure French): I am English, so I seek in this way to be excused. . . .

Gower has left the following survey of his literary career:

Because each one is bound to impart to others what he has received from God, John Gower, wishing, while yet there is time, to render somewhat of an account of his stewardship [76] of the things which God has given him in the flesh, composed in the midst of his labor and leisure three books for the notice of others for the sake of doctrine in the following order:

[74] The French word that I here translate *suitor* is *oratour;* Macaulay suggests another rendering, namely, "The poet means no doubt to speak of himself as one who is bound to pray for the king."

[75] The meter here shows that the name *Gower* was pronounced a dissyllable (Macaulay's note). The poet writes his full name into the verse of the *Confessio Amantis* twice, viz., viii, ll. 2321, 2908. In the *Prolog* to the first book of the *Vox Clamantis*, ll. 19–24, Gower works out his name thus, "If you ask the name of the writer, lo that word lurks implicit in the three following verses. Take the first two letters of *Godfrey* and put *John* before them, and let *Wales* add its first letter; then let *ter*, losing its first letter, contribute its other members and the order of the name composed in such a form is clear."

[76] The Latin word here is *villicacionis* (*vilicationis*), which some of Gower's biographers have rendered *management of a country estate*, and have thence inferred that the poet was a country gentleman.

The first book, given out in the Gallic tongue, is divided into ten books, and, treating of the vices and virtues, as well as of the various classes in this world, tries to show by a straight path the way by which a transgressing sinner ought to return to the knowledge of his Creator. And the title of this same book is announced as *Speculum Meditantis* (*Mirror of One Meditating*).[77]

The second book, composed in Latin verse, treats of the various misfortunes that happened in the time of Richard II in England. Wherefore, not only the chiefs of the kingdom, but the commons suffered torment and the most cruel king himself because of his faults, falling from his high position, was thrown at last into the pit which he had digged. And the name of this volume is called *Vox Clamantis*.

That third book which on account of reverence for his most vigorous lord Henry of Lancaster, then Earl of Derby, is finished in the English tongue, according to the prophecy of Daniel, discourses on the changes in the kingdoms of this world from the time of King Nebuchadnezzar to our own. It treats, likewise, according to Aristotle, of the things in which King Alexander was taught as well in course of life as in doctrine. Yet the principal matter of this book puts the emphasis on love and the infatuated passions of lovers. And appropriately the name *Confessio Amantis* was specially chosen for this.

Mr. Macaulay's version of Gower's will is as follows:

"The testator bequeathes his soul to the Creator, and his body to be buried in the church of the Canons of St. Mary Overes, in the place specially appointed for this purpose. To the Prior of the said church he bequeathes 40*s.*, to the subprior 20*s.*, to each Canon who is a priest 13*s.* 4*d.*, and to each of the other Canons 6*s.* 8*d.*, that they may all severally pray for him the more devoutly at his funeral. To the servants of the Priory 2*s.* or 1*s.* each according to their position; to the church of St. Mary Magdalene 40*s.* for lights and ornaments, to the parish priest of that church 10*s.*, 'that he may pray and cause prayers to be offered for me'; to the chief clerk of the same church 3*s.*

---

[77] Long thought lost but discovered by Mr. Macaulay in 1895 (cf. his ed., i, p. lxviii) and published under the caption *Mirrour de l'omme* (*Mirror of Man*).

and to the sub-clerk 2s. To the following four parish churches
of Southwark, viz.: St. Margaret's, St. George's, St. Olave's,
and St. Mary Magdalene's near Bermondsey, 13s. 4d. each for
ornaments and lights, and to each parish priest or rector in
charge of those churches 6s. 8d., 'that they may pray and cause
and procure prayers to be offered for me in their parishes.' To
the master of the hospital of St. Thomas in Southwark 40s., to
each priest serving there 6s. 8d. for their prayers; to each sister
professed in the said hospital 3s. 4d., to each attendant on the
sick 20d., and to each sick person in the hospital 12d., and the
same to the sisters (where there are sisters), nurses and patients
in the hospitals of St. Anthony, Elsingspitell, Bedlem without
Bishopsgate, and St. Maryspitell near Westminster; to every
house for lepers in the suburbs of London 10s., to be distributed
among the lepers, for their prayers: to the Prior of Elsingspitell
40s., and to each Canon priest there 6s. 8d,

"For the service of the altar in the chapel of St. John the
Baptist, 'in which my body shall be buried,' two vestments of
silk, one of blue and white baudkin and the other of white silk,
also a large new missal and a new chalice, all which are to be
kept for ever for the service of the said altar. Moreover to the
Prior and Convent the testator leaves a large book, 'recently
composed at my expense,' called *Martilogium*, on the understanding that the testator shall have a special mention of himself
recorded in it every day.

"He leaves to his wife Agnes £100 of lawful money, also
three cups . . ., two salt-cellars and twelve spoons of silver,
all the testator's beds and chests, with the furniture of hall,
pantry and kitchen and all their vessels and utensils. One
chalice and one vestment are left to the altar of the oratory
belonging to his apartments. He desires also that his wife
Agnes, if she survive him, shall have all rents due for his manors
of Southwell in the county of Northampton (?) and of Mul-
toun in the county of Suffolk, as he has more fully determined in
certain other writings given under his seal.

"The executors of this will are to be as follows: Agnes his
wife, Arnold Savage, knight, Roger, esquire, William Denne,
Canon of the king's chapel, and John Burton, clerk. Dated in

the Priory of St. Mary Overes in Southwark, on the feast of the Assumption of the Virgin, MCCCCVIII." [78]

John Stow, the Elizabethan antiquary, in his *Survey of London*, thus describes the tomb of Gower, the earliest extant obituary monument to an English man of letters:

John Gower, esquire, a famous poet, was then an especial benefactor to that work, and was there buried on the north side of the said church, in the chapel of St. John, where he founded a chantry: he lieth under a tomb of stone, with his image, also of stone, over him: the hair of his head, auburn, long to his shoulders, but curling up, and a small forked beard; on his head a chaplet, like a coronet of four roses; a habit of purple, damasked down to his feet; a collar of esses gold about his neck; under his head the likeness of three books, which he compiled. The first, named *Speculum Meditantis*, written in French; the second, *Vox Clamantis*, penned in Latin; the third, *Confessio Amantis*, written in English, and this last is printed. *Vox Clamantis*, with his *Cronica Tripartita* (*Tripartite Chronicle*), and other, both in Latin and French, never printed, I have and do possess, but *Speculum Meditantis* I never saw, though heard thereof to be in Kent. [79]

The earliest lives of Chaucer belong to the sixteenth century and are mostly legendary. Nineteenth-century research has composed the present standard biography from references in legal documents and public records, passages in his writings, and references to him in those of his contemporaries. We shall quote here passages from his own works, a royal letter regarding him, a reference by Gower, and a poem by Eustache Deschamps, a contemporary French writer.

[78] "The will was proved, Oct. 24, 1408, at Lambeth before the Archbishop of Canterbury (because the testator had property in more than one diocese of the province of Canterbury), by Agnes the testator's wife, and administration of the property was granted to her on Nov. 7 of the same year" (Macaulay).

[79] The standard works on Gower are Macaulay's ed., Oxford, Clarendon Press, 4 vols., 1902; and Macaulay's article in *The Cambridge History of English Literature*, ii, chapter 6 and *Bibliography*.

A description of Chaucer in the *Canterbury Tales* agrees pretty well with extant portraits generally regarded as authentic.

When all this miracle (the story of Hugh of Lincoln by the Prioress) had been told, every man was so sober that it was wonderful to see, until our Host began to jest, and then at first he looked at me, saying, "What sort of man are you; you look as if you were searching for a hare, for I notice that you are always staring at the ground.

"Come here and look up merrily. Now cheer up, sirs, and let this man have a chance; he is shaped in the waist about like me; for any woman, small and fair of face, he would be a doll to embrace. He seems elvish by his behavior, for he talks with no one.

"Now do you tell us a story as others have; let it be one of mirth and begin at once." "Host," said I, "Do not be displeased for I know no other story except one in rime that I learned long ago." "Well, that'll be all right," said he, "now shall we hear something unusual,[80] I think, from his look."

Chaucer in these words records his delight in books and nature:

Habitually, both for pleasure and profit, I often read books, as I told you. But wherefore do I say all this? Not long ago, it happened that I was looking at a book which was written in ancient letters; and in it I read the whole day fast and eagerly to learn a certain matter. For out of old fields, as men say, comes all this new science that we learn. But now to the purpose of this matter, I was so delighted in reading on that the whole day seemed very short to me. . . .

And if old books were gone the key to remembrance would be lost. We ought, therefore, to honor and believe these books when we have no other proof. And for my part, though I know but little, I delight in reading books and to them I give faith and credence, and in my heart have them in reverence so thor-

---

[80] Chaucer then proceeds to tell the *Rime of Sir Thopas*, which the company can't stomach; he then perpetrates the *Tale of Melibeus* on them.

oughly that there is no game will take me from them unless
it be seldom on a holiday, except when May is come and I hear
the birds sing and the flowers are coming up. Then, farewell
my book and my devotion.

Chaucer had a son Louis ten years old who was anxious
to learn something about astronomy. So the poet compiled
for the little boy a manuscript book on the subject and
wrote a *Prolog* to it, which reads in part as follows:

Little Louis, my son, I perceive well by certain evidences
your ability to learn sciences touching numbers and proportion;
and as well I regard your constant desire in special to study a
treatise on the astrolabe. Therefore, since a philosopher says,
'he wraps himself in his friend, who gives heed to the rightful
prayers of his friend,' I have given you a sufficient *Astrolabie*
for our location, made according to the latitude of Oxford. And
by means of this little treatise I purpose to teach you a certain
number of conclusions pertaining to this instrument. I say
certain conclusions for three reasons. The first is this: trust
well that all the conclusions that have been found, or else possibly might be found in so noble an instrument as the astrolabe,
are not known perfectly to any mortal man in this region, I
suppose. Another cause is this: that, truly, in any treatise on
the astrolabe that I have seen, there are some conclusions that
will not work in every case; and some are too hard for your
tender ten years to conceive. This treatise, divided into five
parts, will I show you in easy rules and simple words in English;
for of Latin you as yet know but little, my little son. But
nevertheless, these true conclusions in English will be as sufficient for you as for those noble Greek clerks in Greek, for
Arabians in Arabic, for Jews in Hebrew and for Romans in
Latin. For the Romans translated them first out of other
languages into their own; that is, Latin. And God knows that
in all these languages and in many more these conclusions have
been satisfactorily learned and taught, and by different rules,
just as various routes lead divers people the right way to Rome.
Now will I meekly pray every discreet person who reads or

hears this little treatise to excuse my rude writing and my super-
fluity of words, for two reasons. The first is, that difficult style
and hard subject-matter together make a heavy task for such
a child to learn. And the second reason is this, that truly it
seems wiser to me to repeat an important matter (often) than
that he forget it (by hearing it) once. And, Louis, if so be that
I show you in my easy English as true conclusions, touching
this matter, and not only as true but as many and as subtle,
as are shown in any common Latin treatise on the subject, show
me the more gratitude; and pray God save the King, who is
lord of this language, and all who owe him faith and loyalty,
each in his degree, the greater and the less. But consider well
that I do not assume that I have searched out this matter by
my own original labor and wit. I am but an ignorant compiler
of the labors of the old astrologers and have translated it into
my English solely to teach you. And with this sword shall I
slay envy.

Chaucer is the first English poet to show the influence
of Italian literature, of which there were three great masters, Dante (1265–1321), Petrarch (1304–1374), and Boccaccio (1315–1375) in the fourteenth century. He made
use of Dante in the *Hous(e) of Fame*, the *Monk's Tale*,
the invocation to the Virgin in the *Prioress' Tale*, and many
scattered lines and phrases. Chaucer refers to Dante by
name five times,[81] but the following passage is the only
reference involving more than two lines. Near the conclusion of his story of Ugolino [82] the Monk in Chaucer's
tale says:

Of this tragedy you should have had enough. If any one
wishes to follow it further, let him read [82] the great poet of
Italy who is called Dante, for he can tell the whole from point
to point, not one word will he omit.

[81] These references are: *Hous(e) of Fame*, l. 450, *Legend of Good Women, Prolog*,
l. 336, *Monk's Tale*, l. 471, *Wife of Bath's Tale*, ll. 270, 271 (here Dante is styled
"the wise poet of Florence"), and *Friar's Tale*, l. 222.
[82] The story of Ugolino Dante tells in *Inferno*, XXXIII.

Chaucer used for his *Clerk's Tale* Petrarch's Latin version of Boccaccio's Italian story cf Griselda, shows Petrarch's influence in a certain passage in *Troilus and Criseyde*,[83] and refers to Petrarch by name three times.[84] The following from the *Prolog* to the *Clerk's Tale* is the most extended reference:

I'll tell you a story which I learned at Padua [85] from a worthy clerk, as is shown by his words and work. He is now dead and nailed in his chest, I pray God rest his soul. The name of this laureate poet and clerk was Francis Petrarch whose sweet rhetoric illumined all Italian poetry.

Chaucer drew more from Boccaccio than from both the other two together, yet he never mentions him by name.

Of Chaucer's contemporary reputation in England we have a testimony from Gower. At the conclusion of the *Confessio Amantis*, Venus says to the Lover of the poem:

And greet well Chaucer when you meet, as my disciple and my poet; for in the flower of his youth in sundry wise, as he knew how, he made for my sake songs and ditties glad of which the land is full; wherefore, I am most beholden to him in particular above all others. And so in his old days you may give him this message, that he in his later age, to furnish a conclusion for all his work, as he is my servant, make his testament of love.[86] Do this errand as you have your shrift above, that my court may record it.[87]

Chaucer's reputation had gone abroad also, as we see in this poem of a contemporary French writer, Eustache Deschamps:

[83] Cf. Book I, ll. 400 *seq.*

[84] These references are: *Monk's Tale*, l. 335 (here Petrarch is called my " Maister Petrark"), *Prolog* to *Clerk's Tale*, ll. 26–33 and *Clerk's Tale*, l. 1091.

[85] We know that Chaucer made two trips to Italy and might have met Petrarch personally; the question raised by this reference is, did he, is the clerk here Chaucer, or is this a mere literary reference?

[86] This is a reference to no particular extant work.

[87] Chaucer in turn refers to Gower as "the moral Gower"; cf. *Troilus and Criseyde*, Book v, l. 1866.

O Socrates, full of philosophy, Seneca in morals and angelic in works, great as Ovid in poetry,[88] to the point in speech, wise in rhetoric, lofty eagle, who by your vision, illumine the kingdom of Æneas (i.e. England), the isle of giants found by Brutus, and who have sown flowers and planted a rose-garden for those ignorant of the language of France; great translator, noble Geoffrey Chaucer.

You are the god of worldly love, in England, and of the rose,[89] in the angelic land where Anglo-Saxons flourish; England is the name given to it, according to the latest etymology. Into good English you translate books: and long since have you set up an orchard, for which you did demand plants from poets in order to give them a reputation, great translator, noble Geoffrey Chaucer.

To you for this reason, from the springs of Helicon, whose source is wholly in your charge, I beg an authentic work to quench my philosophic thirst: my Gallic throat will be quite dry until you give me to drink. I am Eustace who (write to you) and shall have plants of my own; but take in good part the works of a tyro, so that you will have something of mine, great translator, noble Geoffrey Chaucer.

THE ENVOI

Lofty poet, . . . in your garden I should but meddle: (but) consider what I mentioned first, your noble planting, your sweet melody. And to satisfy me (i.e. that I may know that I am eligible to enter the garden), write back, I pray you, great translator, noble Geoffrey Chaucer.

Late in life, apparently, Chaucer fell into money difficulties and wrote a poem *To His Empty Purse* which he sent to Henry IV in hopes of getting help. This is the poem in a modern English version:

[88] On these comparisons of Chaucer to the great of the past, see Lounsbury, *Studies in Chaucer* (Harper and Brothers, 1892), Chapter 5 (The Learning of Chaucer).

[89] Doubtless a reference to Chaucer's translation of the *Romance of the Rose*.

To you, my purse, and to no other wight
Complain I, for you are my lady dear!
I am so sorry, now that you are light;
For, sure, unless you make me heavy cheer,
I were as lief be laid upon my bier;
And so unto your mercy thus I cry,
Be heavy again, or else I'll surely die!

Now vouche me safe this day ere it be night,
That I of you the blissful sound may hear,
Or see your color like the sunshine bright,
For yellowness, that never had a peer.
You are my life, my pilot me to steer,
Queen of my comfort and good company:
Be heavy again, or else I'll surely die!

Now, purse, who are to me my life's clear light,
And savior, in this human world down here,
Out of this town now help me through your might,
Since treas'rer mine to be you seem to fear;
For "friarlike" I'm shorn so very near.
But yet I pray unto your courtesy:
Be heavy again, or else I'll surely die!

    Chaucer's Envoi
O conqueror of Brutus' Albion,
Who both by line and free election,
Are our true King, this song to you I send;
And you, who all our harm can quite amend,
Have mind upon my supplication!

The desired help came in the following letter:

The King, to all to whom these presents may come: Greeting. It appeareth to us, by inspection of the Rolls of Chancery of Richard, late King of England, the Second after the Conquest, that the same late King caused his letters patent to be made to this effect:

"Richard, by the Grace of God, etc.: Greeting. Know ye,

that we of our especial favor, and in return for the service which
our beloved esquire, Geoffrey Chaucer, hath bestowed, and will
bestow on us in time to come, have granted to the same Geoffrey twenty pounds, to be received each year at our Exchequer,
at the terms of Easter and St. Michael, by equal portions, for
his whole life.   In witness whereof we have caused to be made
these our letters patent.   Ourself witness at Westminster, 28th
of February, in the seventeenth year of our reign."

It appeareth also to us, by inspection of the Rolls of the
Chancery-court of the same late King, that he caused his other
letters patent to be made to this effect:

"Richard, by the Grace of God, etc.: Greeting.   Know ye that,
of our especial grace, we have granted to our beloved esquire,
Geoffrey Chaucer, one cask of wine, to be received every year
during his life, in the port of our city of London, by the hands
of our chief butler for the time being.   In witness whereof, etc.

"Witness ourselves at Westminster, on the 13th day of
October, the twenty-second year of our reign."

We in consideration that the same Geoffrey hath appeared
before us in our Chancery-court personally, and hath made
corporal oath, that the aforesaid letters have been casually lost,
have thought proper that the tenor of the record of the same
letters be transcribed by these present.   In witness, etc.

The King being witness, at Westminster, the 18th day of
October, 1399.*

At the conclusion of the *Parson's Tale* in the Canterbury series, Chaucer, speaking in his own person, prays
his readers that he may be forgiven for having written
a number of his works, most of them in fact.   This section
of the *Parson's Tale* had been declared spurious by some
critics, but the present tendency is to regard it as genuine,
and, since it gives in the author's own words the complet-
est list of his works, we quote it here.

Now I pray all those who may read or listen to this little
treatise, that if there is anything in it that pleases them, they

* Quoted by permission of Messrs. Chatto and Windus, from their edition in the *King's Classics
Series.*

thank our Lord Jesus Christ for it, from whom all wit and all goodness come; and that if there is anything that displeases them, they put it to the account of my lack of skill, and not to that of my will, that would fain have done better if I had had the ability. For our Book says, "All that is written, is written for our instruction," [90] and that is my intent.

Wherefore, I meekly beseech you, for the mercy of God, that you pray for me that Christ have mercy on me and forgive me my sins, and especially for having translated and written worldly vanities, which I repudiate in (these) my *Retractions;* namely, the *Book of Troilus,* the book also *Of Fame,* the *Book of the Twenty-five Ladies,* the *Book of the Duchess,* the book of St. Valentine's Day of the *Parliament of Birds,* the *Tales of Canterbury* — at least, such as tend to sin; the *Book of the Lion* and many another book, if I could remember them; and many a song and many a lecherous lay, of which may Christ forgive me the sin.

But for the translation of Boethius, *On the Consolation of Philosophy* and other books of *Legends of the Saints,* and homilies and books of morality and devotion, for these I thank our Lord Jesus Christ and His blissful Mother and all the saints of heaven, beseeching them that they from henceforth to the end of my life may send me grace to bewail my guilt and strive for the salvation of my soul; and grant me the grace of real penitence, confession and satisfaction, that I live well in this present life, through the benign grace of Him who is King of Kings and Priest over all Priests, who bought us with the precious blood of His heart, so that I may be one of those to be saved at the day of doom. Who with the Father and the Holy Spirit lives and rules as God for ever and ever. Amen.[91]

[90] Cf. 2 Timothy 3: 16.

[91] The indispensable book for Chaucer bibliography is E. P. Hammond, *Chaucer: a Bibliographical Manual* (The Macmillan Co., 1908). The texts of the earliest lives of Chaucer are given there, pp. 1–35. Lounsbury, *op. cit.,* i, pp. 133–142, gives a translation of the *Life* by Leland, Chaucer's first biographer. The chapter on Chaucer in the *Cambridge History of English Literature,* ii, is by Professor Saintsbury. Dr. Hammond, in her *Chaucer: a Bibliographical Manual,* devotes pp. 51–69 to a discussion of the Chaucer canon; she cites two other lists of his works by Chaucer, viz., *Legend of Good Women, Prolog,* ll. 405 *seq.* and head-link to the *Man of*

Law's Tale, Canterbury Tales, B, ll. 39 *seq.* Professor Tatlock, in an article, *Chaucer's Retractions*, in the *Publications of the Modern Language Association in America*, xxviii, 4 (December, 1913), pp. 521–529, shows that in his *Retractions* Chaucer was following in the tradition of St. Augustine, Bede, Giraldus Cambrensis, and others. For articles on all the writers included in this section of Representative Authors, pp. 551 *seq.*, see the *Dictionary of National Biography*. William of Malmesbury, Geoffrey of Monmouth, Henry of Huntingdon, Wace, John of Salisbury, Walter Mapes, Giraldus Cambrensis, and Layamon, with extracts designed to exhibit their several styles, are all treated in Wright, *Biographia Britannica Literaria*, ii, the *Anglo-Norman Period* (London, John W. Parker, 1846). The matter quoted above in these pages from Orm, Dan Michel of Norgate, Roger Bacon, Richard of Bury, and William of Newburgh, may be used to supplement the matter given in this section.

INDEX

[*Numbers refer to pages. Titles of books and articles are italicized.*]

INDEX

617

Bartholomæus Anglicus, 383, 401; *De Proprietalibus Rerum, ibid.*
Basil, St., 64, 396 (his *Rule* for Monks), 436.
Bassas, 4.
Bateson, Mary, *Mediæval England,* 201, 211.
Battle of Brunanburh, 82–87.
Battle of Maldon, 13.
Bayeux Tapestry, 157.
Beadohild, 72.
Beauchamp, Guy, Earl of Warwick, books bequeathed by, to Bordesley Abbey, 441–444.
Beaw, ancestor of Alfred the Great, 119.
Becket, Thomas à, archbishop of Canterbury and martyr, 161, 162–166, 231, 309, 310, 320, 385, 432, 435 (?), 437, 440, 575, 595.
Bedwig, ancestor of Alfred the Great, 119.
Bede, English historian and scholar, 1, 3, 4, 42, 43, 44, 47, 56, 62, 65, 74, 96, 98, 99, 101, 102, 104, 107–117, 118, 133, 139, 190, 436, 440, 544, 545, 547, 549, 555, 557, 579, 581, 613.
Beldeg, ancestor of Alfred the Great, 119.
Bell's English History Source Books, 186, 262.
Benedict Biscop, abbot of Jarrow, 56, 57, 58, 59, 111, 113.
Benedict of Nursia, St., *The Rule of,* 19, 46, 164, 262, 288, 292.
Benedict of Peterborough, 162.
Beowulf, 13, 19, 34, 35, 71, 72, 88, 153.
Berkhampstead, 143.
Bernard of Clairvaux, St., 258, 432, 435, 438, 439, 440, 441, 575, 576.
Bertha, queen of Ethelbert of Kent, 44.
Bestiary, 192, 432, 434.
Bible and people, 135–139, 451, 594.
Billings, A. H., *Guide to the Middle English Metrical Romances,* 519.
Biographia Britannica Literaria, by Thomas Wright, 65, 108, 613.
Birinus, bishop, 98.
Birmingham, 231, 232.
Bishop, political functions of, 22, 23, 61, 173.
Black Death, 324, 446.

Black Prince, 181, 184, 185.
Bland, A. E., Brown, P. A., and Tawney, R. H., *English Economic History: Select Documents,* 228.
Boccaccio, 608.
Bodel, Jean, on the "matters" of romance, 518.
Boethius, Roman philosopher, 66, 131, 132, 258, 393, 411, 437, 439, 574; Alfred the Great's tr. of *On the Consolation of Philosophy,* 131, 132; Chaucer's, 506, 612.
Bohn Antiquarian Library, 1, 69, 87, 157, 248, 364.
Boniface, St., English missionary to Germany, 38, 107.
Bonner Beiträge zur Anglistik, 70.
Book, 69, 78, 246, 414, 417–430.
Book of Epigrams, by Bede, 114.
Book of Hymns, by Bede, 114.
Book of Orthography, by Bede, 114.
Book of the Art of Poetry, by Bede, 114.
Book of the Life and Passion of St. Anastasius, by Bede, 113.
Book of the Life and Passion of St. Felix Confessor, by Bede, 113.
Book of the Lion (?) by Chaucer, 612.
Book of the Twenty-five Ladies (Legend of Good Women?) by Chaucer, 612.
Book of Tropes and Figures, by Bede, 114.
Bordesley Abbey, books bequeathed to, 441–444.
Boycott, 262.
Bradwardine, Thomas, archbishop of Canterbury, 325.
Bravery among the Germans, 9, 12.
Breguoin, 4.
Brembre, Nicholas, 320–324, 349.
Bretwalda (Chief Teutonic ruler of Britain), 5.
Britain, Briton, 1, 2, 3, 4, 5, 19, 38, 39, 42, 43, 44, 52, 56, 57, 58, 59, 60, 68, 69, 74, 87, 96, 98, 119, 122, 124, 125, 151, 248, 545, 546–550, 557, 558, 581.
Brittany, 146, 160, 456.
Brond, ancestor of Alfred the Great, 119.
Brown, C. F., *Irish-Latin Influence in Cynewulfian Texts,* 82.
Bruce, by John Barbour, 487–489, 519.
Brut, by Layamon, 493–502.